Disability Histories

DISABILITY HISTORIES

Series editors: Kim E. Nielsen and Michael Rembis

Disability Histories explores the lived experiences of individuals and groups from a broad range of societies, cultures, time periods, and geographic locations who either identified as disabled or were considered by the dominant culture to be disabled. Conceiving of disability and disabled experiences broadly, and spanning a range of embodiments, the series highlights innovative approaches to disability history that deepen our understanding of the past.

Disability Histories

Edited by
**SUSAN BURCH AND
MICHAEL REMBIS**

UNIVERSITY OF ILLINOIS PRESS

Urbana, Chicago, and Springfield

Publication of this book was supported by a grant from Middlebury
College.
Library of Congress Control Number: 2014951006
ISBN 978-0-252-03874-7 (hardcover)
ISBN 978-0-252-08031-9 (pbk.)
ISBN 978-0-252-09669-3 (e-book)

Contents

List of Keywords

Centuries

Eighteenth century
Nineteenth century
Twentieth century
Twenty-first century

Geographical Areas

Africa
Europe
North America
South America
South Asia

Sources

Art
Artifacts
Government documents
Interviews
Labor

Legal documents
Literature
Manuscripts and archival materials
Medical documents
Memoirs
Organizational reports
Plays
Serials
Speeches
Visual materials

Themes

Activism
Bodies, medicine, and contested knowledge
Citizenship and belonging
Culture
Family, daily life, and community
Labor
Law and policy
Media
Slavery
Technology
Theory
War

Acknowledgments

From original concept to publication, this anthology benefited from a wide community of collaborators. Thanks first go to our authors. We are fortunate to have such talented, engaged, and patient colleagues. In addition to their individual chapters, authors on this project workshopped the introduction, spent hours talking over research issues, and contributed to the broader guiding concepts of this work. Numerous outside readers provided valuable feedback on drafts as well, including students and colleagues at our home institutions. Reading through individual chapters, they affirmed what we saw as some of the signature qualities of the collection: a commitment to accessibility, original approaches to disability history, and attention to the complexity of human experiences and identities. We especially want to thank Lauri Umansky, Bobby Buchanan, and Steven Noll for careful and constructive reviews of the manuscript.

We are grateful to the community of scholars, activists, and artists who in their own ways have influenced the content of this collection. The Disability History Association and the Society for Disability Studies—leading international professional organizations—have worked to foster socially and culturally integrated spaces where participants engage in deeply nuanced and intellectually rich conversations. These exchanges have sparked innovative research in many disciplines, including disability history.

Thanks also go to our intrepid editor at the University of Illinois Press, Laurie Matheson, for her enthusiastic interest in *Disability Histories*. Other UIP colleagues who helped produce this anthology deserve recognition, too. Every historian should be so lucky to work with a press that values historical work so deeply. We would like to thank Middlebury College for its generous subvention support, which has helped produce this collection.

Finally, we wish to express our gratitude to friends and family who saw us through this project. Susan considers herself fortunate to be surrounded by the wonderful community at and near Middlebury College. The center of Susan's world, Ian M. Sutherland, deserves adoration, thanks, and more. Other stars in her universe extend far beyond the Green Mountains, and she is grateful for all of them. Mike would like to thank his family in Toronto and Chicago, always in his heart and never far from his thoughts. This work especially honors Carlos and the memory of his grandfather Alex Rembis (1937–2012) and his great-uncle Christ Rembis (1931–2012). Mike would also like to thank his many friends, colleagues, and students at the University at Buffalo and in the broader Buffalo community. Their collaborations, conversations, much-needed diversions, love, and support have sustained him through this project.

Disability Histories

Re-Membering the Past

Reflections on Disability Histories

SUSAN BURCH AND MICHAEL REMBIS

Disability is central to understanding history. It exists on a fluid and dynamic continuum, and, as disability studies scholars and disability historians have revealed, disability in all of its complex and contradictory brilliance is a common experience. Its vast constellation of meanings and lived realities expressed through equally diverse concepts and interpretive lenses are intricately tied to the past and to the study of the past.

Disability is ubiquitous, yet it is also irreducible. Lived experiences of disability defy universalized or essentialized interpretations. They do not conform to common historical narratives of unilinear progress. Over the past three decades, scholars engaging in historical research in various fields and different parts of the world have increasingly explored and analyzed what many disabled people have long known: that there are many different ways to think about disability and disabled people.[1] Although historians find commonalities among individuals and groups and trace continuities over time, it would be unfair and inaccurate to say that there has been a singular "disabled experience."[2]

Because disability is often experienced in conflicting and contradictory ways, critical disability scholars who have sought to illuminate its many historical manifestations and meanings have come to different and in some cases competing conclusions.[3] Stories from polio communities, for example, reveal a spectrum of human emotions and common experiences, such as isolation and longing, as well as very real struggles—with separations from family and friends, grueling and occasionally cruel medical treatment, disabling attitudes, and inaccessible environments. They also reveal colorful recollections of rivalries and friendships, lovers and losses, and sustaining and nurturing communities. The richness of disability history complicates the common, narrow depictions of polio survivors as victims, as passive recipients of care, or as heroic overcomers. As historian Dan Wilson and others have shown, people's experiences with disability were consistently and continuously marked by many forces, including—but not limited to—class, race, gender, age, and place, all of which affected the options available to them.[4] Interpreting disability in its many manifestations and sociocultural locations has encouraged historians to (re)consider the importance of religious, political, and economic systems and major events such as epidemics and wars that have shaped (and often constrained) daily lives and given them meaning.

By studying disability in the context of shifting beliefs, attitudes, technologies, and practices at various times and in numerous social and geographical locations, disability historians have shaped our understanding of disability as a lived experience. As Julie Livingston explained in her essay, "Insights from an African Disability History," ideas about "normality" and "ability" varied widely. "In Botswana," she argues, "reduced mobility and physical strength, as well as blindness and a range of other infirmities, have long marked understanding of senescence. These were not regarded as disabilities: indeed, they were 'normal' and in some cases even expected impairments. Historically, they also were recognized to accompany increased spiritual insight and other abilities."[5] Embedded socially, culturally, and materially in the lives of a diverse array of historical actors, disability reflects complex processes of creation and re-creation in both local and global contexts. Disability is not static or ahistorical. On the contrary, decades of scholarship have shown a range of disabled experiences.[6]

Since its beginning, the field of disability history has provided a rich space for scholars interested in thinking more expansively about disability to push at the boundaries of what has been considered "impairment." Sarah Rose, for instance, has illustrated how the pervasive presence of (previously overlooked) disabled American laborers, whose bodies sustained considerable damage from work, invites greater scrutiny of the relationship between "impairment" and "productivity."[7] Susan Cahn's work in this volume in a similar way reveals the instability of the historical category "Borderline Personality Disorder," complicating not only standard medical categories but also who qualifies as disabled and what qualifies as a disability.[8] These and other works reveal that socially and historically situated understandings of disability may—and often do—change over time and that disabled people themselves play an active role in both creating and re-creating the various meanings that get attached to experiences with impairment, experiences and meanings that ultimately have very real material effects.

As disabled people also have long understood, disability in its many manifestations has never been a discrete identity category. It, like other socially created identity categories, occupies intricately interconnected yet unstable cultural locations. Historical work on disability and disabled people has simultaneously reflected and shaped the concept that disability is intimately connected with race, gender, sexuality, age, ethnicity, and socioeconomic status, among other formative aspects of peoples' lives. Often work emanating from this "intersectional" or "interdependent" approach has relied heavily upon the theories of feminist, Chicano/a, postcolonial, and critical race and ethnic scholarship.[9] Recent work on the history of deaf American Jews, for example, reveals how complex negotiations tempered by gendered expectations and immigrant experiences constructed and fortified interlocking Jewish, deaf, and Jewish deaf cultures in the early twentieth century.[10] Perspectives on disabled veterans in Russia during the same time period shatter the typically gendered binary upon which Western scholars have based their definition of disability. According to historian Laura Phillips, specific (local) social behaviors and environmental circumstances dictated whether men and women were viewed as disabled or nondisabled.[11] Disability, like other identity categories, is not static or natural, nor is it consistently and readily self-evident. Its boundaries must be continually policed and maintained through various discursive practices and material structures that often are intimately and inextricably rooted in other ways of being in the world. Denaturalizing and historicizing disability in ways similar (although not identical) to sex, gender, and race has enabled disability studies scholars to forge more powerful critiques of heteronormative, ableist ideas of everything from work and productivity to ability, beauty, desire, and eroticism.

By recognizing the potentially disruptive and destabilizing forces bound up in a critical understanding of disability, historians have, in turn, provided a powerful interpretive lens through which scholars can re-member (or reconstitute) the past. Many works in disability history, for example, have questioned the interpretation of disability that has increasingly dominated most Western cultures since the 1700s, often referred to as the "medical model" of disability. Various historical actors operating under this framework, including disabled people themselves, understood disability as a loss or deficit that was fixed, natural, timeless, and rooted in individual bodies. Naming and critiquing this medical interpretation of disability has enabled disability historians to develop and apply a social and sociopolitical analysis of disability without completely abandoning the history of medicine or the body. This particular critical lens, which grew out of numerous individual and collective struggles for dignity, identity, and rights, has encouraged greater analysis not only of the corporeality of disability (or its embodiment) but also the social and relational aspects that characterize a disabled existence.[12]

Such lines of inquiry have invited provocative reinterpretations of what "disability" in all its manifestations—conceptual, lived, and interpretive—has meant. For example, forays into the experiences of physical pain and other kinds of embodied suffering that the sociopolitical model of disability has not yet accounted for challenge disability scholars to assess the limits of this critical framework.[13] Explorations of disability and social-medical histories as dynamic and mutually constitutive similarly invites critical self-reflection within the field. As historian Catherine Kudlick has provocatively proposed in her essay in this volume, in order "to gain a more nuanced understanding of the past, scholars need to refine our definition of disability so that it can hold a number of counterintuitive notions simultaneously." What if, Kudlick asks, historians equated "symptoms of disability not automatically with disaster and failure but possibly as omens of survival and good fortune?" In answering her own question, Kudlick proposes that "if disability had a different sociocultural valence, the equation with survival would introduce new avenues for exploring. . . . the human condition." Ways of knowing that were once confined to a narrow set of "acceptable" tropes expand into a variegated array of complex representations and interpretations that in turn open new space for understanding history itself.

Scholars engaging in disability history, librarians, and archivists have challenged historians to transform their research practices. Historically, archives, special collections, and other troves of valuable sources located around the world did not include disabled people or disability-related terms in their indexes. Efforts to preserve materials often overlooked institutions and communities associated with disabled people and minimized or excluded references to disability when it was present in the records. The persistence of social stigma and the "medical model" of disability compelled individuals and groups who collected and organized historical sources to see disability as something that lay outside the purview of historians. Bureaucratic policies that restricted access to the sources most readily associated with disability further hampered efforts to study disability and disabled people in history. Many libraries, archives, and special collections were physically and financially inaccessible to disabled and nondisabled researchers—and many remain so. Things are changing but much work remains. The presence of disability history and disabled researchers has encouraged—to varying degrees—more inclusive designs and policies in traditional places of historical study. Collaborative efforts by scholars, librarians, and archivists have resulted in the creation of rich disability history repositories that include virtual (online) archives, material archives, and oral history collections.[14] Some, such as the Regional Disability History Archive in Toledo, Ohio, have focused specifically on local disability communities, while others, such as Gallaudet University's Library Deaf Collections and Archive, have collected material from across the globe and foster geographically and temporally expansive research in deaf histories.[15] These and other archives are working to gather regional, national, and transnational sources and to educate the public about disability history. This valuable work in creating or making disability history is crucial, not only for studying the past but also for changing the present and building a better future.

Expanding the archive also has done the important work of compelling researchers to engage with the stories of people whose bodies and minds may not have conformed to norms historians are typically trained to examine and value. Examples from disability oral history illustrate this; oral histories have been particularly useful sources for many works in disability history. Everyone has a story, but not all stories have been captured and conveyed in ways that easily transmit across generations. For instance, deaf oral history interviews conducted in sign languages model additional options for sharing knowledge through visual means. Integrating facilitated communication in the process of oral history research that involves individuals or groups that a dominant culture may consider "nonverbal," including individuals living with what is currently labeled "cognitive impairment" or "developmental disabilities," will close some of the gaps among the many means of expression available to humans.[16] Including disabled people as valued research subjects will enrich all fields of history and expand ways of gathering and interpreting historical data.

Similarly, disability history research increasingly reflects an interest in material culture. As Katherine Ott writes in her essay, "Both the artifacts owned and used by people with disabilities and those that are used upon them or that are encountered in life create possibilities, impose limits, assert political and ideological positions, and shape identity." This is illustrated in emerging online museums and material exhibits that showcase disability histories. *Out from Under: Disability History and Things to Remember*, an exhibit mounted at the Royal Ontario Museum in 2008 by members of the Ryerson University community, drew attention to the important role disabled Canadians have played in the nation's cultural and civic life. The Smithsonian National Museum of American History and the United States Holocaust Museum, too, have included disability histories and artifacts as part of their national and international missions to distribute knowledge.[17] Universally designed exhibit spaces, signature features of these and other exhibits, reinforced and reflected the belief that every body should have access to this work.

In part, disability history seeks to re-member the past, to repopulate it and recover sources about and by individuals and groups who in many cases have been overlooked or actively ignored or silenced. Yet scholars engaging in disability history seek to do more than simply include disabled people as an additive component in an already well-formed historical narrative-analysis. Taking their cue from women's historians and scholars who study other marginalized populations, disability historians have taught us that recovering and re–membering the past are not enough. Recognizing disability as an analytic or interpretive frame, as a category or label, and as a lived experience forces us not only to re-member the past but also to rethink it. As the essays in this collection will show, disability history engenders myriad transformative possibilities that point to exciting new pathways for understanding the past.

A Road Map for This Collection

The evolution of the field of disability history is reflected in the structure of this collection. Readers will find essays that explore a wide geographical and temporal space and that examine new populations and communities. The chapters in this anthology intentionally transcend a singular focus on disability in history, grappling instead with a constellation of factors that shape historical identities, communities, and moments. Expanding these boundaries invites us to revisit fundamental questions: What sources "count" in historical work? Whose stories have not yet been included in our narratives? Why? To what extent has there been change and continuity over time and across places? Placing essays in dialogue with one another around significant themes encourages additional reflection.

Part One—Family, Community, and Daily Life—recognizes that relationships and lived experiences shape our understandings of disability. In Chapter 1, Daniel Blackie presents a comparative examination of the family lives of disabled and nondisabled Revolutionary War veterans in the early United States (1776–1840). The central argument of "Disability, Dependency, and the Family in the Early United States" is that contrary to the hypotheses advanced by some scholars, disabled veterans were contributing, integrated members of their families and communities. Penny Richards explores the possibilities of building a biography about a man with developmental disabilities in the nineteenth-century U.S. South in her essay "Thomas Cameron's 'Pure and Guileless Life,' 1806–1870: Affection and Developmental Disability in a North Carolina Family." As Richards notes, Thomas Cameron himself wrote very little, but his family's letters are rich and frequently include news or opinions about his activities, covering a period from his childhood through his sixties. The collected correspondence also records the family dynamics that supported Cameron, emotionally and practically, through his education and adulthood. Allison Carey draws upon the earliest U.S. and Canadian memoirs written by parents of children with intellectual disability, covering the period 1950 to 1989, in her chapter, "Parents and Professionals: Parent Reflections on Professionals, the Support System, and the Family in the Twentieth-Century United States." This project examines parents' perceptions of and expressions of "intimate citizenship," how public practice shaped intimate family lives, and how parents of disabled children sought to alter public practice to better meet their own intimate needs. The chapter "Historical Perceptions of Autism in Brazil: Professional Treatment, Family Advocacy, and Autistic Pride, 1943–2010," co-authored by Pamela Block and Fatima Gonçalves Cavalcante focuses on the role of families, education and medical professionals, and autistics in shaping the meaning, representation, and responses to neurodiverse children and adults in Brazil from 1943 to 2010. In the section's last essay, Herbert Muyinda draws on life stories of landmine survivors. "Negotiating Disability: Mobilization and Organization among Landmine Survivors in Late Twentieth-Century Northern Uganda" examines the importance of political organizing in shaping the experiences of people with disabilities.

Part Two spotlights cultural histories, drawing attention to the ways that disability as a concept, lived experience, and analytical framework reflects and contributes to societal traditions and beliefs. Katherine Ott's "Disability Things: Material Culture and American Disability History, 1700–2010" considers artifacts as primary evidence and offers examples of how the history of disability shifts into new registers when it is studied through its material culture. In "The Contergan Scandal: Media, Medicine, and Thalidomide in 1960s West Germany," Elsbeth Bösl draws attention to the intersection of pharmaceuticals, disability, media, and the welfare state in the Federal Republic of Germany. According to Bösl, the public outrage over the disabling impact of thalidomide prompted German society to struggle with normative questions about human difference, technical risks, and disability in light of the nation's complicated history. An interest in remembrance also guides John Kinder's essay, "'Lest We Forget': Disabled Veterans and the Politics of War Remembrance in the United States, 1780–2010." Kinder offers an overview of the politics of disabled veterans' remembrance in the United States. Treating remembrance as both a collective process and political practice, the essay highlights attempts of disabled veterans—and those claiming to speak on their behalf—to mobilize public displays of memory to articulate a privileged social identity in modern American society, separate from civilians and other disabled people.

As many scholars around the world have shown, medical approaches to disability and disabled people have played a fundamental role in the past. Part Three—Bodies, Medicine, and Contested Knowledge—encourages innovative engagements with the complex relationship between disabled people and medicine or medical power-knowledge. In the opening essay of this section, "Smallpox, Disability, and Survival in Nineteenth-Century France: Rewriting Paradigms from a New Epidemic Script," Catherine Kudlick argues that disability history and the history of medicine would each benefit from exploring the role of disability and survival in past epidemics. Using the example of smallpox in early nineteenth-century France, Kudlick reveals how public health measures helped define modern understandings of disability. Dea Boster's "'Unfit for Ordinary Purposes': Disability, Slaves, and Decision Making in the Antebellum American South" uses antebellum state appellate court decisions, primarily from breach-of-warranty litigation suits in the lower South, to identify how the terms "sound" and "unsound" were used to describe African American slaves. Slaves with disabilities, who existed in a nebulous space between "human" and "chattel," often confronted double standards that influenced the legal and medical cultures of the South and social dialogue on able-bodiedness and disability. Frances Bernstein considers the connections among popular culture, the medical profession, and the Soviet state in her essay, "Rehabilitation Staged: How Soviet Doctors 'Cured' Disability in the Second World War." Bernstein uses critiques of theatrical plays to examine the impact of the mass disabling of Red Army soldiers during and after World War II, addressing how the state and the medical profession responded to the challenges posed by the "invalids of the patriotic war." In "The Curious Case of the 'Professional Hemophiliac': Medicine, Disability, and the Contested Value of Normality in the United States, 1940–2010," Stephen Pemberton responds to scholars interested in the relationship between disability and medicine by considering the paradox of the "professional hemophiliac" in the United States in the era of HIV-AIDS. Susan K. Cahn also explores the late twentieth century but travels along different boundaries in her chapter, "Border Disorders: Mental Illness, Feminist Metaphor, and the Disordered Female Psyche in the Twentieth-Century United States." Cahn builds on insights from disability studies about the social construction of illness and feminist critiques of borderline personality disorder to explore questions of mental illness, the self, and suffering.

Citizenship and belonging are themes that unite the essays in Part Four. Anne Quartararo's "The Paradox of Social Progress: The French Deaf Cultural Community and the Ideals of the Third Republic at the Turn of the Twentieth Century" explores the intersections of politics, language, education, and citizenship. Quartararo demonstrates that even though leading French politicians and deaf cultural elites shared social and economic concerns, different understandings of the role of education, language, and cultural identities complicated political reform efforts and alliances in nineteenth-century France. In "Incompetency: Property, Disability, and the Making of the Unfit Citizen in the United States, 1860s-1940s," using evidence from competency hearings in Wisconsin, Kim Nielsen examines changing historical standards of civic fitness. By determining whether or not adults were unable to manage property and thus required adult guardians, competency hearings reinforced the linkage between citizenship rights and competence by quite literally taking away the right to own and manage property from citizens deemed unsatisfactory. In his essay, "'Salvaging the Negro': Race, Rehabilitation, and the Body Politic in World War I America, 1917–1924," Paul Lawrie examines how federal efforts to rehabilitate disabled African American veterans produced new forms of racial knowledge and labor control in interwar America. Lawrie argues that officials of the Federal Board of Vocational Education (the agency charged with veterans' rehabilitation) fused scientific management with a eugenic mindset to develop a catalog of racial taxonomies in which labor fitness was directly linked to color and the body. Positing war as work, this chapter presents an alternative corporeal map of African American proletarianization that was actively mediated through the postwar state. Audra Jennings's chapter, "Engendering and Regendering Disability: Gender and Disability Activism in Postwar America," explores the work of the American Federation of the Physically Handicapped (AFPH). She examines how gendered ideals stigmatized disabled Americans and, conversely, how disability activists—both men and women—marshaled gendered language and ideals to normalize disability in the United States in the 1940s and 1950s. Finally, Jagdish Chander considers self-advocacy in twentieth-century India in his chapter, "Self-Advocacy and Blind Activists: The Origins of the Disability Rights Movement in Twentieth-Century India."

The histories included in the four sections in this volume are representative of four critically important areas of study within disability history. They, in turn, seek to place disabled people and their families, allies, and friends at the center of historical analysis and create a more complex understanding of the lives of disabled people. As you read the essays, we encourage you to ask yourself whether or not the historians have been successful in recovering the voices and experiences of disabled people. We also encourage you to find connections and continuities among the essays in the various sections. Although each of the four fields represented here have emerged as their own discrete subdisciplines in disability history, there is considerable methodological, theoretical, and analytical overlap among the essays. Our hope is that you will put them in conversation with one another and use them as a means of drawing out additional rich and nuanced renderings of disability history.

One Way to Use This Book

Readers can draw important lessons from each chapter in this collection, but various combinations of readings may especially complement diverse interests. To encourage greater dialogue and discovery, guiding questions and introduction open each section. Keywords also accompany each chapter and appear in a comprehensive list following the table of contents. Providing these cross-references highlights the relationships among all the essays. We hope this will draw attention to the historian's craft, making more transparent methodological approaches, sources, geographical and temporal boundaries, and topics. For example, while Daniel Blackie's essay appears in the "Family, Community, and Daily Life" section, it focuses on late colonial and revolutionary-era America. Readers particularly drawn to court cases as primary sources may pair Kim Nielsen's essay from the

"Citizenship and Belonging" section with Dea Boster's chapter in the "Bodies, Medicine, and Contested Knowledge" section. Encouraging new frameworks for the essays invites readers to engage rigorously with the works, which we hope will spark interest in new work in the field.

The essays gathered here reflect an intentional commitment to studying a wider spectrum of historical subjects, contexts, and understandings of the past. Works included in this collection consider, for example, earlier and later time periods than many disability historians have considered; most historical works in the field have tended to focus on the global North and West and the early nineteenth century through the mid-twentieth century. By including works beyond these commonly studied geographical and temporal sites, our project also seeks to foster the important—but as yet incomplete—process of decentering the United States and Western Europe as the primary locations of study in disability history. Some works in this collection extend beyond one nation or region; we deeply value opportunities for greater study outside constructed national boundaries and the importance of engaging with a rich historical context.

Admittedly, this anthology cannot claim to be comprehensive, nor can it claim to be definitive in providing answers to the many interesting and difficult questions raised by disability histories. Rather, this project reflects and ultimately is a product of the time and context in which it has been created. Despite the strong analytical and intellectual rigor of the scholarship included herein, this collection has its limits. There remains much room to interrogate sources and stories, especially those outside North America and Western Europe, those that occurred at earlier moments in human history, and those that involve historically marginalized groups *within* disabled communities. In many ways, this anthology represents a finite but valuable new chapter in a long history of disability. It intentionally offers many new places to look, more options for "doing" critical disability history, and new methods for expanding who and what is considered to have historical value.

Notes

1. This collection builds on a strong foundation in disability history and studies, yet it diverges from past scholarship in significant and important ways. For the past decade, Paul K. Longmore and Lauri Umansky, eds., *The New Disability History: American Perspectives* (New York: New York University Press, 2001) has served as a primary text in disability history. Since its publication, scholars have significantly advanced the theoretical, methodological, topical, and geographical boundaries of this field. Yet most existing anthologies focus only marginally on history/historical studies, and virtually all history anthologies fail to include disability and people with disabilities. Previous historical collections in disability studies, such as William O. McCagg and Lewis H. Siegelbaum, eds., *The Disabled in the Soviet Union:*

Past and Present, Theory and Practice (Pittsburgh: University of Pittsburgh Press, 1989); David A. Gerber, ed., *Disabled Veterans in History* (Ann Arbor: University of Michigan Press, 2000); Katherine Ott, David H. Serlin, and Stephen Mihm, eds., *Artificial Parts, Practical Lives: Modern Histories of Prosthetics* (New York: New York University Press, 2002); Stephen Noll and James Trent, eds., *Mental Retardation in America: A Historical Reader* (New York: New York University Press, 2004); and John Vickrey Van Cleve, ed., *The Deaf History Reader* (Washington, D.C.: Gallaudet University Press, 2007) offer important insights into disability history but focus exclusively on specific populations. Interdisciplinary anthologies, such as Rosemarie Garland Thomson, *Freakery: Cultural Spectacles of the Extraordinary Body* (New York: New York University Press, 1996); Gary L. Albrecht, Katherine Delores Seelman, and Michael Bury, eds., *Handbook of Disability Studies* (Thousand Oaks, Calif.: Sage Publications, 2001); Bonnie G. Smith and Beth Hutchison, eds., *Gendering Disability* (New Brunswick, N.J.: Rutgers University Press, 2004); Susan Burch and Alison Kafer, eds., *Deaf and Disability Studies: Interdisciplinary Perspectives* (Washington, D.C.: Gallaudet University Press, 2010); and Lennard J. Davis, ed., *Disability Studies Reader* (New York: Routledge, 2010) pay comparatively limited attention to history as a field of study.

2. See, for example, Umansky and Longmore, *The New Disability History*. Often-cited works include Douglas Baynton's insightful chapter "Disability and the Justification of Inequality in American History," in *The New Disability History*, edited by Lauri Umansky and Paul Longmore (New York: New York University Press, 2001); and Catherine Kudlick's compelling essay "Why We Need Another 'Other,'" *American Historical Review* 108, no. 3 (2003): 763–93. See also Teresa Meade and David Serlin, eds., *Radical History Review* 94 (Winter 2006) for a discussion of disability history in varying contexts told largely through the lens of a Western and, more specifically, a U.S.-based conceptualization of disability rights movements.

3. See, for example, Richard K. Scotch, *From Good Will to Civil Rights: Transforming Federal Disability Policy* (Philadelphia: Temple University Press, 1984); Philip M. Ferguson, *Abandoned to Their Fate: Social Policy and Practice toward Severely Retarded People in America, 1820–1920* (Philadelphia: Temple University Press, 1994); Rosemarie Garland-Thomson, ed., *Freakery: Cultural Spectacles of the Extraordinary Body* (New York: New York University Press, 1996); Robert M. Buchanan, *Illusions of Equality: Deaf Americans in School and Factory, 1850–1950* (Washington, D.C.: Gallaudet University Press, 1999); Kim E. Nielsen, *The Radical Lives of Helen Keller* (New York: New York University Press, 2004).

4. See, for example, Daniel J. Wilson, *Living with Polio: The Epidemic and Its Survivors* (Chicago: University of Chicago Press, 2005); *Whatever Happened to Polio* (http://americanhistory.si.edu/polio/index.htm), exhibit at the Smithsonian National Museum of American History; Carol Poore, *Disability in Twentieth-Century German Culture* (Ann Arbor: University of Michigan Press, 2007).

5. Julie Livingston, "Insights from and African History of Disability," *Radical History Review* 94 (Winter 2006): 120. See also Julie Livingston, *Improvised Medicine: An African Oncology Ward in an Emerging Cancer Epidemic* (Durham, N.C.: Duke University Press, 2012).

6. For excellent examples of works that center on disability as a concept, see Paul K. Longmore, "Uncovering the Hidden History of People with Disabilities," *Reviews in American*

History 15 (1988): 355–364; Lennard Davis, *Enforcing Normalcy: Disability, Deafness, and the Body* (London: Verso, 1995); and Douglas Baynton, *Forbidden Signs: American Culture and the Campaign against Sign Language* (Chicago: University of Chicago Press, 1996). Other works that emphasize constructions of disability and deafness in the popular media include John S. Schuchman, *Hollywood Speaks: Deafness and the Film Entertainment Industry* (Urbana: University of Illinois Press, 1988); and Martin F. Norden, *The Cinema of Isolation: A History of Physical Disability in the Movies* (New Brunswick, N.J.: Rutgers University Press, 1994).

7. Sarah Rose, "'Crippled' Hands: Disability in Labor and Working-Class History," *Labor: Studies in the Working-Class History of the Americas* 2, no. 1 (Spring 2005): 27–54.

8. For other examples, see Steven Noll and James W. Trent, eds., *Mental Retardation in America: A Historical Reader* (New York: New York University Press, 2004); Mary Felstiner, *Out of Joint: A Private and Public Story of Arthritis* (Lincoln: University of Nebraska Press, 2005); Sara Scalenghe, "The Deaf in Ottoman Syria, 16th–18th Centuries," *The Arab Studies Journal* 12/13 (Fall 2004/Spring 2005): 10–25; Geoffrey Reaume, "Mad People's History," *Radical History Review* 94 (Winter 2006): 170–182; Alison Carey, *On the Margins of Citizenship: Intellectual Disability and Civil Rights in Twentieth-Century America* (Philadelphia: Temple University Press, 2009).

9. See, for example, Anne Borsay, *Disability and Social Policy in Britain since 1750: A History of Exclusion* (Basingstoke: Palgrave, 2005); Natalia Molina, "Medicalizing the Mexican: Immigration, Race, and Disability in the Early-Twentieth-Century United States," *Radical History Review* 94 (Winter 2006): 22–37; Julie Livingston, "Insights from an African History of Disability," *Radical History Review* 94 (Winter 2006): 111–126; Susan Burch and Hannah Joyner, *Unspeakable: The Story of Junius Wilson* (Chapel Hill: University of North Carolina Press, 2007); Anna Stubblefield, "'Beyond the Pale': Tainted Whiteness, Cognitive Disability, and Eugenic Sterilization," *Hypatia* 22, no. 2 (2007): 162–181; Poore, *Disability in Twentieth-Century German Culture*; Dea Boster, "An 'epeleptick' Bondswoman: Fits, Slavery, and Power in the Antebellum South," *Bulletin of the History of Medicine* 83, no. 2 (2009): 271–301; Michael A. Rembis, *Defining Deviance: Sex, Science, and Delinquent Girls, 1890–1960* (Urbana: University of Illinois Press, 2011); Ellen Samuels, "Examining Millie and Christine McKoy: Where Enslavement and Enfreakment Meet," *Signs* 37, no. 1 (2011): 53–81; Kim E. Nielsen, *A Disability History of the United States* (Boston: Beacon Press, 2012).

10. Sarah Abrevaya Stein, "Deaf American Jewish Culture in Historical Perspective," *American Jewish History* 95, no. 3 (2009): 277–305.

11. Laura L. Phillips, "Gendered Dis/ability: Perspectives from the Treatment of Psychiatric Casualties in Russia's Early Twentieth-Century Wars," *Social History of Medicine* 20, no 2 (2007): 333–350.

12. Classic examples of this kind of work include Henri-Jacques Stiker, *A History of Disability*, translated by W. Sayers (1983; repr., Ann Arbor, Mich.: University of Michigan Press, 1999); Nora Groce, *Everyone Here Spoke Sign Language* (Cambridge: Harvard University Press, 1985); Ferguson, *Abandoned to Their Fate*; Garland-Thomson, *Freakery*; Martin S. Pernick, *The Black Stork: Eugenics and the Death of "Defective" Babies in American Medicine and Motion Pictures since 1915* (New York : Oxford University Press, 1996); Buchanan, *Illusions of Equality*; David Gerber, ed., *Disabled Veterans In History* (Ann Arbor: University of Michigan Press, 2000); Nielsen, *The Radical Lives of Helen Keller*.

13. See, for example, Diane Driedger and Michelle Owen, eds., *Dissonant Disabilities: Women with Chronic Illnesses Explore Their Lives* (Toronto: Canadian Scholars' Press/Women's Press, 2008); Anna Mollow, "Identity Politics and Disability Studies: A Critique of Recent Theory," *Michigan Quarterly Review* 43, no. 2 (2004): 269–296.

14. See, for example, the University of California, Berkeley's Bancroft oral history collection on disability rights and independent living (http://bancroft.berkeley.edu/collections/drilm/) and the Disability Archive UK (http://www.disability-archive.leeds.ac.uk/).

15. For more on the Toledo Regional Disability History Archive, see http://www.utoledo.edu/llss/disability/historyarchive/index.html. See also Gallaudet University's Library Deaf Collections and Archive (http://www.gallaudet.edu/library_deaf_collections_and_archives.html). Another excellent example is the Museum of disABILITY History; see http://museumofdisability.org/.

16. For thoughtful critiques of oral history and its intersections with deaf and disability communities, see John S. Schuchman, "Oral History and Deaf Heritage: Theory and Case Studies," in *Looking Back*, edited by Harlan Lane and Renate Fischer (Hamburg: Signum, 1993), 515–532; Karen Hirsch, "Culture and Disability: The Role of Oral History," *The Oral History Review* 22, no. 1 (1995): 1–27; Martin Atherton, Dave Russell, and Graham Turner, "Looking to the Past: The Role of Oral History Research in Recording the Visual History of Britain's Deaf Community," *Oral History* 29, no. 2 (2001): 35–47; Donna F. Ryan, "Deaf People in Hitler's Europe: Conducting Oral History Interviews with Deaf Holocaust Survivors," *The Public Historian* 27, no. 2 (2005): 43–52.

17. In addition to its general collections, the Smithsonian National Museum of American History has mounted disability-specific exhibits, including *The Disability Rights Movement* (http://americanhistory.si.edu/disabilityrights/) and *Whatever Happened to Polio* (http://americanhistory.si.edu/polio/index.htm). Both exhibits were curated by historian Katherine Ott. The United States Holocaust Museum exhibit *Nazi Persecution of the Disabled: Murder of the "Unfit"* is also online at http://www.ushmm.org/museum/exhibit/focus/disabilities/. The exhibit *The Lives They Left Behind: Suitcases from a State Hospital Attic* offers a particularly compelling example: see http://www.suitcaseexhibit.org/indexhasflash.html.

PART ONE

Family, Community, and Daily Life

As many historians have demonstrated, disability embodies multiple dimensions: as a category or label, as a lived experience, and as an interpretive framework. The authors in this section share an interest in writing social histories of disability and highlighting the important role of different types of relationships. Focusing on disability "at the ground level" draws attention to historically marginalized groups and topics. Although they recognize the importance of studying nondisabled and other elite historical actors, social historians of disability seek to move away from these top-down approaches and toward a study of disabled people in their everyday lives. Focusing on family, community, and daily life is one way social historians of disability recover and recount disabled lives in all their complexity. As you read this section, consider the following questions:

1. Historically, who and what defined community and family? How have decisions been made about who belongs and who is excluded?
2. How does studying daily life change your understanding of disability in history?
3. Compare the ways each author explores power and privilege.
4. Consider the different analytical tools employed in these essays. How do they shape the essays?
5. How do the scholars' choices about time period, geographic location, and subject matter influence the histories of disability included in this section?

CHAPTER 1

Disability, Dependency, and the Family in the Early United States

DANIEL BLACKIE

KEYWORDS: *Centuries:* eighteenth; nineteenth; *Geographical Areas:* North America; *Sources:* manuscripts and archival materials, government documents; *Themes:* family, daily life, and community; citizenship and belonging; culture; war

In October 2011, the *New York Times* reported the effective demise of the Community Living Assistance Services and Supports (CLASS) Act following an announcement by the U.S. government that it would not implement the law. This was disappointing news for many disabled people and their families, as the act would have helped defray some of the costs of disability-related care. Seeking to put a human face on the story, the authors of the article drew readers' attention to a woman whose family was apparently "staggering under the burdens of caring for her bedridden parents," one of whom was an amputee. Families like these, the report implied, would have benefited greatly from the CLASS Act. Now, however, they faced continued hardship and possible financial ruin. Disabled people in the article are portrayed as fundamentally passive and dependent, "burdens" who require a lot from their families but contribute little.[1]

Disability is commonly associated with dependency in American culture. The *New York Times'* coverage of the CLASS Act reflects this. As the paper's story indicates, such associations tend to promote the idea that disabled people are only ever the recipients of care. This chapter challenges such a view by examining the family lives of disabled veterans in the early United States, from 1776 to roughly

1830. The evidence presented suggests that most disabled veterans did not merely receive care but were also significant caregivers. By foregrounding disability, the chapter sheds fresh light on the history of the new nation and the family and shows that experiences of disability are always profoundly shaped by social and cultural factors.

Revolutionary War Pension Files and the Study of Disability

The Revolutionary War, in which the United States gained independence from Great Britain, was fought between 1775 and 1783. In terms of human lives, it was an incredibly costly conflict. An estimated 25,000 American service personnel, or roughly 12.5 percent of General Washington's forces, died during the war and perhaps as many as another 25,000 were wounded and survived.[2] In recognition of the hardships endured by Revolutionary soldiers, Congress enacted a series of national pension laws for veterans after the war. These laws concerned two types of pensions: invalid pensions and service pensions. Invalid pensions were granted to veterans who had been injured in the war; service pensions were awarded primarily on the basis of length and type of military service.[3]

By the early 1820s, around 20,000 Revolutionary War veterans had received pensions from the United States, either as invalids or service pensioners.[4] The application papers these men submitted to get a pension are a treasure trove of information.[5] Few historians, however, have examined this rich source with questions of disability in mind.[6] As this chapter demonstrates, used carefully, pension documents have much to tell us about the position of disabled people in early America.

In the pages that follow, special attention is given to the files of 153 disabled Revolutionary War veterans. These veterans can be classified as "disabled" because they received invalid pensions from the federal government and were therefore categorized as such by the authorities. According to invalid pension legislation, a veteran was considered disabled if he was either fully or partially incapable of laboring for a living. Given that labor was generally regarded as men's work in the early Republic, this definition of disability was a highly gendered one.[7]

Later on in their lives, starting around 1818, the disabled veterans at the center of this project also applied for and received service pensions. The pension papers of these men are especially rich historical sources, as their files generally contain more information about their lives than those of veterans who were pensioned as invalids only. Focusing on these men has the added advantage of allowing us to compare the situation of disabled veterans with nondisabled veterans. Irrespective of whether they were "disabled" or not, *all* veterans who applied for service pensions had to submit evidence according to the same rules and regulations. Thus, the applications for service pensions submitted by nondisabled veterans contain the same kinds of information about the lives of applicants as those made by disabled veterans.

A comparative approach to the pension files is particularly helpful when thinking about the significance of disability in the lives of ex-servicemen, as it allows us to filter out the general conditions of veterans' lives from those pertaining to disabled veterans specifically. The observations regarding disability and the family presented in this chapter are based on a comparison of the pension papers of the targeted 153 disabled veterans with those of an equivalent number of nondisabled veterans. The difference between the two groups is that the former received invalid pensions before taking up service pensions while the latter did not. The only other major criterion used to select the two groups was that all the veterans studied submitted applications under the service pension act of May 1820. The reason for targeting these men is that the documentation produced as a result of this law is arguably the most informative found in the Revolutionary War pension files, especially in relation to the study of the family.[8]

The general profile of the two groups is remarkably similar. Both disabled and nondisabled veterans tended to come from New England and were overwhelmingly white.[9] They were also of a similar age; when they made their pension declarations in the 1820s, applicants were, on average, in their mid-sixties. They were also fairly poor compared to the standards of the time; over half of both groups had estates valued at less than $50. In terms of their collective characteristics, disabled and nondisabled veterans were virtually identical.[10] The evidence presented in this chapter indicates that the family lives of disabled and nondisabled veterans were also quite similar.

The Family in Early America

Nowadays, the difference Americans draw between family and household seems quite clear. Family usually refers to a group of people related by blood or marriage, while household is used to designate a group of people who live together in the same dwelling. In early America, this distinction was less clear cut. Consider the following statement given by 70-year-old disabled veteran Elijah Estes in August 1820: "My family consists of myself my wife aged 70 years One free person named William Ham aged 10 years & a whiteman named Robert Thompson aged 20 years."[11]

Estes's declaration was part of his application for a service pension under the act of May 1820. As neither Ham nor Thompson was apparently related to the old veteran, Estes's inclusion of them as members of his "family" is telling. Like other early Americans, family for Estes seems to have been based as much on co-residence as on kinship. The "family" details submitted by ex-servicemen in response to the 1820 act need to be seen in this light. When applicants listed the family members living with them, they were not necessarily referring to relatives. To a large extent, the family information given by veterans in the 1820s is probably a better reflection of the composition of their households than of the composition their families—at least in the way we understand these terms today. My comments in this chapter relate primarily to the family as a unit of co-residence rather than one of kinship, even though early Americans did sometimes understand family in kinship terms.[12]

Families were the fundamental social unit of early American society. Economic production, political representation, and the transfer of property between generations were all based on the family. From a disability history perspective, however, perhaps the most significant family function at this time was the provision of care. In an era that predated the widespread existence of special care facilities for sick and injured people, early Americans usually turned to their families for help in times of illness or incapacity. Families were expected to provide care and were under a legal obligation to do so. To borrow the words of one historian, the family was quite simply early America's "premier welfare institution."[13]

Most families at this time were organized along patriarchal lines. Family and household heads were nearly always white males. Although not impossible, it was fairly unusual for women or blacks to assume household headship. In 1790, for instance, less than one-thirteenth of the households detailed in the U.S. census were headed by women and a staggering 92 percent of black Americans were enslaved and therefore subordinate members of their masters' households.[14] Such figures plainly attest to the formidable influence of gender and race on the structure of the early American family.

As heads of families, white men were very powerful. They controlled all the major resources of their households, including the labor of their children and the property of their wives. They were also permitted to inflict corporal punishment on family members should they see fit. In the eyes of the law, husbands, fathers, and masters ruled supreme within their households. Wives and co-resident children, along with slaves and servants, were regarded as dependents.

Family heads were responsible for the support of their dependents and were expected to use their considerable powers to that end.[15] Male heads were arguably the least dependent members of a household, at least in theory. This point needs to be borne in mind when considering the issue of disabled veterans and dependency in the early United States. If a veteran became the recognized head of a family and maintained that position, he could never, in principle, become a dependent in the same way as women, children, and most black Americans. In making this point, however, it is also important to recognize that few Americans were ever truly independent in the early United States.

Despite the ideology of racialized patriarchy that underpinned early American families, relationships within those families, even between fathers and children, were usually characterized by interdependence. Without the productive contributions of their wives, children, or other "dependents," most family heads would have found it incredibly difficult to produce enough to subsist comfortably. Given the rural and preindustrial character of the early American economy, family labor was crucial to a household's well-being.[16] All family members, including heads, were enmeshed in webs of reciprocity that were difficult to break. An examination of the family lives of disabled veterans highlights this point.

Family Care in the Revolutionary Period

During the Revolutionary War, America's military Medical Department was frequently unable to meet all the care needs of sick or wounded troops. Military hospitals were often poorly staffed and supplied and eyewitness accounts of the conflict abound with reports of patients going without adequate food or bedding. In one way, those who got into a hospital were actually quite lucky: at least they had a roof over their heads. Sometimes sick and wounded men did not even get this most basic of amenities but were left outside without shelter, exposed to the elements.[17]

To make up the shortfall in medical care provided by the army, many soldiers turned to their families for assistance. That they did so underscores the key role the family played in the early American system of care. Even at times of severe social dislocation, such as during the Revolutionary War, families remained central to the economies of care that sustained early Americans through periods of illness or injury.

Family care seems to have been particularly easy to access in the early years of the war, when most of the fighting took place around Boston. Given that almost a quarter of American troops came from Massachusetts, many of the men injured during the Siege of Boston (1775–76) were close to their homes at the time of their injuries. Consider, for example, the case of disabled veteran Benjamin Farnum, who was wounded in his leg at the Battle of Bunker Hill in 1775. As Farnum was from the nearby town of Andover, news of his wounding quickly reached his home. Obviously concerned about his condition, family members speedily arranged for him to be brought back to Andover where they could oversee his care. Other soldiers who were injured close to their homes also appear to have benefited from swift family assistance.[18]

Not all soldiers were as fortunate as Farnum. Many fell ill or were wounded a long way from home. Even in these cases, some men were able to call on family for help. It was not uncommon, for instance, for family members to travel great distances to aid sick or wounded soldiers in far-off places. When this was impossible, soldiers who were fit enough sometimes made the long journey home without family company. Numerous ill or injured soldiers did their utmost to get back to their families for care whenever they could and by whatever means necessary. Family care, however it was delivered, undoubtedly played a crucial role in the survival of many Americans during the war. Without it, the death toll of America's fight for independence would probably have been much greater.[19]

Solomon Parsons was one of the men injured in the war who survived the conflict to be pensioned as an invalid. Wounded in the thigh at Monmouth in June 1778, Parsons returned home to his father's place a few months later to recuperate. His recovery was long. According to a letter found in his pension file, the veteran was unable to work for seven years because of his wounds. During that time, Parsons's father supported him.[20] As a significant majority of disabled veterans were young and unmarried when they joined the army, other invalid pensioners probably had similar experiences. With no homes of their own, many sick and wounded soldiers had little choice but to return to the homes of their parents following their discharge from the army.[21]

Like Parsons, some returning veterans were so incapacitated by their wounds that they could do little for their own support. It was during the earliest phases of their convalescence that disabled veterans were probably most dependent on help from their families, especially their parents. It was very rare, though, that disabled veterans were totally incapacitated for the rest of their lives. Most injured ex-servicemen eventually recovered their health enough to make some kind of economic contribution to the households in which they resided.[22] Moreover, although injured ex-servicemen may have lived in their fathers' homes for a time while they recuperated, most did not remain there long. Instead, they fairly quickly went on to establish their own families and create new households of which they were the heads.

Key to success in the enterprise of family formation was finding a wife with whom to have children. Information found in the pension files of disabled veterans reveals that four out of five of them were married at least once in their lives. This is almost exactly the same proportion as nondisabled veterans who married. A significant majority of disabled veterans, moreover, appear to have married after they were injured but before they were pensioned as invalids. The impairments of disabled ex-servicemen seem to have had no measurable impact, either positively or negatively, on their ability to find wives. In other words, while disability was not a significant barrier to marriage, the women who married disabled veterans during the war and early postwar years were not drawn to their husbands by the lure of an invalid pension.[23]

The pension files also reveal that most disabled veterans, like their nondisabled peers, had children. Indeed, judging from the descriptions given by pension applicants in the 1820s, disabled veterans and their wives were very successful at establishing enduring family units together.

Veteran Households in the 1820s

The first fact to emerge from an examination of the papers submitted in response to the 1820 pension act is that veterans overwhelmingly lived in families. Hardly any lived alone. At the time of their depositions, disabled veterans outlined families that contained, on average, three to four persons. These families were generally nuclear in structure and consisted of a veteran, his wife, and his child(ren). Quite typical in terms of family size and structure were the households described by disabled veterans such as Levi Farnsworth and Hezekiah Sawtell. In June 1820, 62-year-old Farnsworth stated that he lived with his 59-year-old wife, Abigail, and his teenage daughter, Lovina. 59-year-old Sawtell's "family" consisted of his 48-year-old wife and his two children, Josiah, aged eighteen, and Monica, fifteen.[24] The examples of Sawtell and Farnsworth are also quite representative in that both men had younger wives. The pension depositions made in the 1820s reveal that the spouses of disabled veterans were, on average, five to six years younger than their husbands.

Averages, however, flatten out diversity. In calling attention to the family circumstances of statistically typical applicants such as Sawtell and Farnsworth, it is important to recognize that not all disabled veterans lived like them. Significant numbers also lived in simple conjugal families, consisting solely of a veteran and his wife.[25] Others lived in much larger and complex families. In his pension declaration of July 1820, for example, Humphrey Hunt gave details of a family totaling thirteen persons: himself, his wife, nine children, and two grandchildren.[26] Although the families of few disabled veterans in the 1820s were this large, like Hunt's, many contained nonnuclear family members such as grandchildren or other persons.[27] In most cases, these nonnuclear households tended to consist primarily of the veteran's relatives. Despite the broad definition of family in the early United States, kinship was the central foundation upon which most veteran households were built.

Some historians such as Margaret Pelling, who specialize in other countries and periods, have posited that disability may have affected the compositional structure of households in the past. The thinking behind this view is that some disabled people have particularly demanding needs. In an effort to meet these needs, families have historically modified their makeup in some way. For example, in her study of disability in sixteenth-century Norwich, England, Pelling has argued that some families may have retained children longer to help care for disabled parents or other adults.[28] Alternatively, because of the traditionally gendered character of caregiving, the households of disabled people may have been deliberately populated with more women than they might otherwise have been. This would allow families to care more effectively for disabled members according to the cultural ideals of the time. While such hypotheses may hold for other times and places, they do not seem valid for the early United States, at least in the case of Revolutionary War veterans.

A comparison of the family data submitted by ex-servicemen in the 1820s reveals that there was no measurable difference between the families of disabled veterans and nondisabled veterans. Nondisabled veterans lived in families of similar size, type, composition, and diversity as those described by disabled veterans. There is no evidence that the families of disabled veterans were more likely to contain greater numbers of children or women to provide disability-related care. Collectively, the families of nondisabled veterans in the 1820s were virtually identical to those in which disabled veterans lived. It seems, then, that disability generally had very little impact on the outward appearance of the early American family.[29]

In the 1820s, an average American household contained around five persons.[30] Seen in this light, the families described by veterans in the 1820s, seem relatively small. Despite this, it would be wrong to conclude that the families of veterans were peculiar in terms of their size. While they may have been smaller than other American families in the 1820s, this was more a reflection of the age of veterans than a significant divergence from demographic norms. As veterans were typically in their mid-sixties when they submitted their applications in the 1820s, they were well past their prime fathering years and were old men by the standards of the time.[31] It is thus not surprising that the households of veterans were generally smaller than those of other (younger) men. As their children grew up and left home, the households of ex-servicemen, like those of other men, naturally decreased in size.[32]

Genealogical research for a smaller sample of pension applicants suggests that disabled veterans fathered an average of nine children during their lives. Generally speaking, the first of these children were born soon after marriage, when veterans were in their mid- to late twenties. After that, disabled veterans typically had a child about every two years until they were in their late forties, when their last child was born. Often, the youngest child had a different mother than the eldest, as it was fairly common for disabled ex-servicemen to outlive their first wives and remarry.[33] In terms of births and marriages, disabled veterans seem to have broadly conformed to the general demographic patterns of the time, as discerned by other historians.[34] Again, disability does not appear to have radically affected the development and growth of these men's families. Disabled veterans married and had children just as other early American men did.

Headship

Headship of a family in the early United States rested in large part on a (white) man having a wife and children. As soon as he married and established a household of his own, he tended to assume the status of head, along with all the legal powers that entailed.[35] Given that nearly all disabled veterans were also husbands and fathers, then, most seem to have fulfilled one of the main criteria for family headship. Data from the pension files and the U.S. censuses of 1790–1840 certainly support this conclusion. Both of these sources indicate that a significant majority of disabled veterans attained the status of head of family and maintained this well into old age. The equivalent figures for nondisabled veterans are virtually identical. It would appear, therefore, that disabled veterans were just as likely to attain and retain headship as nondisabled veterans. For ex-servicemen at least, disability was plainly no barrier to the attainment of the socially desirable position of family head.[36] The power most heads held over their dependents was largely rooted in gender and race, not physical ability or strength. Recognizing this fact complicates any discussion of disability, dependency, and the family in the new nation.[37]

While census and other demographic data from the early United States may show that the gender and racial barriers to headship confronting women and blacks were great, they also indicate that such obstacles were not insurmountable. Although relatively few in number, some white women and black men did become household heads.[38] A similar, if more tentative, impression emerges from the pension declarations of veterans in the 1820s. Whereas a significant majority of white applicants were almost certainly heads around the time of their submissions, the position of black applicants is less clear. This is partly because there are so few blacks in the two groups of veterans studied and partly because the family details found in their pension files are often too sketchy to advance general conclusions about their households. The limited evidence that exists suggests that while most black applicants appear to have had wives or children, by the 1820s they were less likely to be recognized household heads than white applicants. Just as it did for all early Americans, race shaped the family lives of veterans, including disabled veterans. For black pension applicants, such as disabled veteran Prince Vaughan, who reported in 1820 that he had no family or children "residing with him," race may have made the attainment or retention of headship more difficult. The fact that some black veterans were heads in the 1820s demonstrates, however, that race was not always an absolute barrier to headship.[39]

Heads had a duty of care and support toward their families. They were supposed to exercise their powers benevolently with this goal in mind. Like other early American men, disabled veterans were keenly aware of these cultural expectations.

In his pension application of July 1820, Joel Porter mentioned that he had three adult daughters living with him. Although the women were in "usual health" and could presumably contribute something to their own upkeep, Porter declared that they were "dependent on me in case of accident or sickness."[40] In saying this, Porter was acknowledging that as head of his household, it was he who was ultimately responsible for supporting his family in times of injury or illness.

There may, of course, be a degree of posturing in the pension declarations of men such as Porter. Perhaps applicants sought to persuade pension officials that they conformed to early American standards of manliness. Given the gender ideology of the time, they would certainly have been under strong cultural pressure to do so.[41] While we should recognize this and approach the pension files critically, it seems that many applicants took their responsibilities as heads seriously. Historical sources abound with evidence of the ways disabled veterans used their control of household resources to maintain their families. In the late 1820s, for example, Clement Sewall reported that he had "exhausted" his property supporting and educating his large family.[42] Many ex-servicemen were also prepared to go into debt to provide for their families. Edward Warren certainly did. In 1822, he declared that he had run up debts of almost $260, a large part of which was for the medical care of his recently deceased wife.[43]

The Flow of Care in Early American Households

In thinking about disability and dependency, Peregrine Horden's observations regarding the nature of care are particularly insightful. As Horden points out, the concept of care is broad. It entails much more than hands-on nursing or medical services. It also includes emotional and financial support. In short, care can be anything that helps a person meet their medical, emotional, psychological, or practical needs.[44] If we keep this broad definition in mind, it seems clear that through their actions as family heads, disabled veterans were significant caregivers within their households. In a sense, then, their position as head of household insulated them from the kind of full dependency experienced by women and children.

In drawing attention to the fact that headship stopped disabled veterans from acquiring the same dependent status as their wives and children, I do not mean to imply that these men were only ever caregivers. They were not. For example, although Clement Sewall used his position as head to actively support his family (by "exhausting" his property), by the late 1820s, he admitted that his wound, along with other "infirmities," meant he required the "services of others" in his daily life.[45]

The disability-related care needs of men such as Sewall could prove challenging for their families, especially their wives. In his pension deposition of May 1820,

73-year-old James Trowbridge claimed that he had been "laid up" for most of the postwar period because of his wounds. During that time, Trowbridge was cared for by his wife. This role appears to have been an arduous one for Mrs. Trowbridge, even though she was nearly twenty years younger than her husband. According to the veteran's testimony, his wife had "ruined her health in taking care of me."[46] Clearly, caring for disabled people could be difficult, physically demanding work.

The example of Mrs. Trowbridge indicates the gendered nature of caregiving in the early United States. Though not always related to disability, hands-on care tasks in early American families were generally regarded as the province of women.[47] To a large extent, the pension files confirm this generalization. Even a cursory glance at their contents reveals the significance of women to the networks of care that sustained veterans and their families. William De Witt, for instance, acknowledged the importance of his daughter to his household's welfare in 1828 when he stated that she did "the principal part of the housework and the taking care of the family."[48]

Despite the undeniable importance of women as caregivers in early America, it would be wrong to assume that men never performed nursing or similar practical care tasks. While the constraints of gender were powerful, they were not absolute, at least when it came to care. As other historians have pointed out, it was not uncommon for early American men to sometimes assume the role of primary carer in their households, especially in times of family sickness or injury.[49] Evidence from the pension files suggests that this may also be true for disabled veterans.

The depositions made by pension applicants in the 1820s contain a wealth of information about the health of the new nation. This information sheds light on the early American healthscape and further complicates our understanding of the flow of care within households.[50] More precisely, it forces us to question popular assumptions about disabled people and their relationship to care. These often equate disability with passivity and dependency and are connected with the idea that disabled people are more likely to be the recipients of care than caregivers.

As an examination of the pension files indicates, illness and impairment were ubiquitous in the early United States. It was not only pensioners that the U.S. government had categorized as "disabled" or "invalids" that experienced physical impairment. Many "nondisabled" veterans were also severely limited in their bodily abilities. Truman Mead, for example, never received an invalid pension. In his application of August 1820, however, the 60-year-old Mead reported that he was "totally unable to labour or even walk without assistance."[51] Mead seems to have been as incapacitated as the most "disabled" invalid pensioners. Many other nondisabled veterans were too.[52] This is hardly surprising when we recall that nondisabled applicants under the 1820 act, who had an average age of 66, were also old men by the standards of the time.

Age took its toll on the bodies of all Americans, including those, of course, who had never served in the Revolutionary War. In their pension applications of the 1820s, 54 percent of disabled veterans reported the ill health or incapacity of other family members. Many of these people were the elderly wives of applicants. 73-year-old Hannah Burgess, for instance, was described by her disabled husband in 1820 as a "cripple" who was unable "to do any kind of work."[53]

Younger family members also experienced ill health and impairment. Like Hannah Burgess, Moses S. George's 20-year-old son, Daniel, was also labeled a "cripple," as was John Newman's unnamed 19-year-old stepson.[54] Other children of disabled veterans were variously described as "insane," "weakly," "debilitated," or "sickly" by their fathers.[55] The picture that emerges from the pension files, then, is clear: ill health, impairment, and incapacity were major features of the early American healthscape. That this is the case helps explain why the "disabilities" of disabled veterans did not radically affect the family lives of these men or the overall composition, structure, and size of their households vis-à-vis nondisabled veterans. "Disabling" bodily or mental conditions were such prosaic features of life at this time that families developed the capacity to accommodate disability organically. In other words, because they had to deal with ill health and impairment on a regular basis, families did not have to readjust radically to manage disability. The structures, composition, or mechanisms to do that were a natural part of the fabric of early American families.[56]

An appreciation of the healthscape of the early United States does more than help explain the comparative similarities between disabled and nondisabled veteran households. It also throws into question the relative place of disabled people in early American networks of care. The example of the Delano family is particularly instructive in this respect.

Disabled veteran Seth Delano had been wounded in the head at Tarrytown in 1779. In June 1820, while a resident of Maine, he applied for a service pension. The declaration he submitted described a family of three beset by ill health and incapacity: the 68-year-old disabled veteran himself, his wife Rebecca, aged 67, and his 30-year-old daughter, also named Rebecca. Both women appear to have been even more incapacitated than Delano. The younger Rebecca was "blind and able to do nothing towards her support," while her mother was "so feeble as to be confined to her bed" most of the time. As nobody else was apparently living with the Delanos at this time, the health information disclosed by Seth raises the question of who really cared for whom. While Seth may have indeed received disability-related care from his family, it seems equally likely that the disabled veteran may have performed care tasks for his wife and daughter. Just because Delano had been officially classified as disabled by the government, there is no reason to assume that he was less capable of caring for his family than they were for him.[57] Recognizing the internal healthscape of the Delano household compels us to realize this.

This observation is based on the assumption that the care needs of Delano's family were largely met from within his household. Admittedly, such an assumption is not unproblematic. In the early United States, Americans who required welfare assistance were rarely institutionalized. Instead, they were often provided for by the authorities or other concerned persons within their own homes. Given this, it is possible that the Delanos obtained essential nursing or care services from their local community. They may even have had a son or other close relatives living nearby who helped them, as the federal census of 1820 suggests.[58]

Despite these caveats, however, the fact that Delano's declaration does not specifically detail the flow of care to his family is significant. Although the 1820 act granted pensions to veterans on the basis of military service, these benefits were only intended for the most impoverished. To get on the pension roll, applicants not only had to fulfill the law's service requirements, they also had to convince officials that they were poor.[59] Consequently, veterans such as Delano who applied under the 1820 act had a strong incentive to mention any external assistance, including care, they, or their families, received. Because of this, the pension files are filled with references to the medical or care services provided by people from outside the households of veterans.[60] That Delano's file makes no mention of external aid, then, suggests that most of the everyday care needs of his family were probably met from within his household.

The idea that Delano was a significant provider of hands-on care for his wife and daughter despite his "disability" is echoed in the declarations of other ex-servicemen. Like Delano, many disabled veterans also detailed families in which nobody appears to have been completely free of serious ill health or impairment. These cases similarly complicate any conclusions about the position of disabled people in the household economy of care. Like Delano, the pension files of these men may not provide definitive proof that disabled veterans were hands-on carers, but they certainly offer plenty of suggestive evidence. By allowing us to sketch the general healthscapes in which ex-servicemen lived, the pension files force us, at the very least, to rethink popular ideas about disability and dependency.

Conclusion

Disabled Revolutionary War veterans lived fairly ordinary family lives—ordinary, that is, in relation to nondisabled veterans and probably in relation to the early American population more generally. Disabled ex-servicemen married, had children, acted as family heads, and lived in similar households as their nondisabled peers. In short, disability seems to have had no major impact on the structure of the families of disabled veterans or the position of ex-servicemen within them. Due to the ubiquity of ill health and impairment, early American families were quite adept at managing disability. That is not to say that this was always done with ease or that impairment was of no consequence to the households of veterans. As the example of James Trowbridge and his wife illustrates, sometimes the care needs of disabled veterans could prove very challenging for their families.

While we must acknowledge the difficulties caused by impairment and ill health, however, it is inaccurate to equate disability with dependency. As this chapter has shown, disabled veterans were hardly ever totally dependent on the help of others. On the contrary, their families were often more dependent on them, both in principle and in practice. As family heads, disabled veterans were responsible for the welfare of their wives, their children, and any other dependent members of their households. They were expected to use their extensive powers to that end, and many did. To a large extent, disabled veterans were insulated from full dependency by their position as heads. In the culture of early America, of course, that position was highly gendered and racialized. Recognizing this highlights how disability is inflected by gender and race, as other disability scholars have long insisted.[61]

Despite the powerful influence of gender, disabled veterans may have done more than simply use their control of household resources to support their families. Some may also have ventured into the culturally prescribed province of women by performing practical care tasks for family members. Whether as hands-on carers or overseers of care, disabled veterans undoubtedly occupied central positions in their families and in the networks of care that sustained them. This discovery further illuminates the historical agency of disabled people. But an examination of the family lives of disabled Revolutionary veterans does much more than that. By foregrounding disability as an analytic category, it not only opens up new vistas in the history of disability and the early United States; it also invites more complex understandings of care, dependency, and the family.

Notes

I would like to thank Susan Burch, Michael Rembis, and Katja Huumo for their helpful comments and suggestions.

1. Gardiner Harris and Robert Pear, "Still No Relief in Sight for Long-Term Needs," *New York Times*, October 24, 2011, http://www.nytimes.com/2011/10/25/health/25seniors .html?pagewanted=all (accessed July 13, 2012).

2. Casualty estimates from Howard H. Peckham, ed., *The Toll of Independence: Engagements and Battle Casualties of the American Revolution* (Chicago: University of Chicago, 1974), 130–134; John Shy, *A People Numerous and Armed: Reflections on the Military Struggle for American Independence*, rev. ed. (Ann Arbor: University of Michigan Press, 1990), 250.

3. William H. Glasson, *History of Military Pension Legislation in the United States* (New York: Columbia University Press, 1900), 10, 25–52; John P. Resch, *Suffering Soldiers: Revolutionary War Veterans, Moral Sentiment, and Political Culture in the Early Republic* (Amherst: University of Massachusetts Press, 1999).

4. The vast majority of these pensioners received pensions for military service, not wartime injury. Glasson estimates that only 2,000–3,000 Revolutionary war veterans ever received pensions as invalids. Glasson, *History of Military Pension Legislation*, 39, 51.

5. For examples of historical studies that draw extensively on the pension files, see Emily J. Teipe, *America's First Veterans and the Revolutionary War Pensions* (Lewiston: Edwin Mellen Press, 2002); Paula A. Scott, *Growing Old in the Early Republic: Spiritual, Social, and Economic Issues, 1790–1830* (New York: Garland Publishing, 1997); Resch, *Suffering Soldiers*.

6. To my knowledge, the only full-length study of disability to use the pension files currently available is Daniel Blackie, "Disabled Revolutionary War Veterans and the Construction of Disability in the Early United States, c. 1776–1840," PhD diss. (University of Helsinki, 2010), http://urn.fi/URN:ISBN:978–952–10–6343–5 (accessed December 1, 2011).

7. Ibid., 113–114; Jeanne Boydston, *Home and Work: Housework, Wages, and the Ideology of Labor in the Early Republic* (New York: Oxford University Press, 1994).

8. Blackie, "Disabled Revolutionary War Veterans," 5–16.

9. Only four disabled veterans (2.6 percent) and two nondisabled veterans (1.3 percent) were certainly black. These figures may underrepresent the true number of black veterans, though, as the pension files rarely record the racial backgrounds of applicants explicitly. I have assumed veterans were white unless a file categorically states otherwise.

10. Blackie, "Disabled Revolutionary War Veterans," 14–15.

11. Military pension file of Elijah Estes, "Revolutionary War Pension and Bounty-Land Warrant Application Files," microfilm M804, Records of the Department of Veterans Affairs, Record Group 15, National Archives and Records Administration, Washington, D.C. Elijah Estes, file number S39499. Subsequent references to pension files found on microfilm M804 are cited as PF. References also include "Dis" (for disabled) or "Nondis" (for nondisabled). These designations are my own and are not part of the official file numbers used by the National Archives. To locate a cited pension file in the archive, simply search for the file by the veteran's name and file number. File numbers usually start with "S" or "W."

12. Jack Larkin, *The Reshaping of Everyday Life, 1790–1840* (New York: HarperPerennial, 1989), 9–10; John R. Gillis, "Home," in *Encyclopedia of the New American Nation*, edited by Paul Finkelman (Detroit: Charles Scribner's Sons, 2005); Ruth Wallis Herndon, *Unwelcome Americans: Living on the Margins in Early New England* (Philadelphia: University of Pennsylvania Press, 2001), 49; Blackie, "Disabled Revolutionary War Veterans," 143–146.

13. Robert V. Wells, "Population and Family in Early America," in *The Blackwell Encyclopedia of the American Revolution*, edited by Jack P. Greene and J. R. Pole (Oxford: Blackwell, 1994); Joan M. Jensen, *Loosening the Bonds: Mid-Atlantic Farm Women, 1750–1850* (New Haven, Conn.: Yale University Press, 1986), 22; Scott, *Growing Old in the Early Republic*, 129; Herndon, *Unwelcome Americans*, 156; David B. Danbom, *Born in the Country: A History of Rural America*, 2nd ed. (Baltimore, Md.: Johns Hopkins University Press, 2006), quote from 87.

14. Daniel Scott Smith, "Female Householding in Late Eighteenth-Century America and the Problem of Poverty," *Journal of Social History* 28, no. 1 (1994): 83; United States Bureau of the Census, *Historical Statistics of the United States, 1789–1945* (Washington: U.S. Government Printing Office, 1949), 25.

15. Kathleen Fawver, "Gender and the Structure of Planter Households in the Eigh-teenth-Century Chesapeake: Harford County, Maryland, in 1776," *Early American Studies* 4, no. 2 (2006): 442–470; Toby L. Ditz, "Afterword: Contending Masculinities in Early America" in *New Men: Manliness in Early America*, edited by Thomas A. Foster (New York: New York University Press, 2011), 265–266; Christopher Clark, *Social Change in America: From the Revolution through the Civil War* (Chicago: Ivan R. Dee, 2006), 71–72; Jensen, *Loosening the Bonds*, 18.

16. Daniel Vickers, *Farmers & Fishermen: Two Centuries of Work in Essex County, Massachusetts, 1630–1850* (Chapel Hill: University of North Carolina Press, 1994), 293–294; Larkin, *The Reshaping of Everyday Life*, 11.

17. Blackie, "Disabled Revolutionary War Veterans," 58–63.

18. Sarah Loring Bailey, *Historical Sketches of Andover* (Boston: Houghton, Mifflin & Co., 1880), 323–327; Benjamin Farnum (Dis), PF S5375; Blackie, "Disabled Revolutionary War Veterans," 70–72.

19. Caroline Cox, *A Proper Sense of Honor: Service and Sacrifice in George Washington's Army* (Chapel Hill: University of North Carolina Press, 2004), 149–150; Blackie, "Disabled Revolutionary War Veterans," 72–75.

20. Solomon Parsons (Dis), PF S5883.

21. Blackie, "Disabled Revolutionary War Veterans," 161.

22. Ibid., 117–125.

23. Ibid., 146–148.

24. Levi Farnsworth (Dis), PF S34823; Hezekiah Sawtell (Dis), PF W24907.

25. See, for example, Amasa Grover (Dis), PF S38751.

26. Humphrey Hunt (Dis), PF W23375.

27. Twenty percent of the disabled veterans who gave detailed information about the composition of their families in the 1820s indicated that their households contained nonnuclear family members.

28. Margaret Pelling, "Old Age, Poverty and Disability in Early Modern Norwich: Work, Remarriage and Other Expedients" in Margaret Pelling, *The Common Lot: Sickness, Medical Occupations and the Urban Poor in Early Modern England* (London: Longman, 1998), 134–154.

29. Blackie, "Disabled Revolutionary War Veterans," 150, 162–163.

30. Resch, *Suffering Soldiers*, 225.

31. The mean average age of disabled and nondisabled veterans at the time of their submissions was 65 and 66, respectively. Paula Scott argues that early Americans generally considered 60 to mark the start of old age; Scott, *Growing Old in the Early Republic*, 8–12.

32. Census data suggest that the households in which disabled veterans lived during the first decade of the nineteenth century were, on average, almost twice the size of those recorded in the pension applications of the 1820s. Blackie, "Disabled Revolutionary War Veterans," 160 (Figure 4).

33. My generalizations here are based on research into the lives of thirty-nine disabled veterans for whom I have been able to find particularly rich genealogical material in their pension files and other sources.

34. See, for example, David Hackett Fischer, *Growing Old in America* (New York: Oxford University Press, 1977), 56, 228; Gloria L. Main, "Rocking the Cradle: Downsizing the

New England Family," *Journal of Interdisciplinary History* 37, no. 1 (2006): 41–42; Michael R. Haines, "Long-Term Marriage Patterns in the United States from Colonial Times to the Present," *The History of the Family* 1, no. 1 (1996): 20–21.

35. Fawver, "Gender and the Structure of Planter Households," 447.

36. Blackie, "Disabled Revolutionary War Veterans," 151–158.

37. For more on race in the United States, particularly the construction and significance of whiteness as a racial category, see David R. Roediger, *The Wages of Whiteness: Race and the Making of the American Working Class*, rev. ed. (New York: Verso, 2002), 19–64; and Matthew Frye Jacobson, *Whiteness of a Different Color: European Immigrants and the Alchemy of Race* (Cambridge, Mass.: Harvard University Press, 1999), 15–38. For important work that explores the intersection of disability and race in the nineteenth century, see Dea Hadley Boster, "Unfit for Bondage: Disability and African American Slavery in the United States, 1800–1860" (PhD diss., University of Michigan, 2010); Jenifer L. Barclay, "'Cripples All! Or, The Mark of Slavery': Disability and Race in Antebellum America, 1820–1860" (PhD diss., Michigan State University, 2011).

38. Smith, "Female Householding," 83–107; Fawver, "Gender and the Structure of Planter Households"; Shane White, "'We Dwell in Safety and Pursue Our Honest Callings': Free Blacks in New York City, 1783–1810," *Journal of American History* 75, no. 2 (1988): 445–470.

39. Prince Vaughan (Dis), PF S42603. The other five black veterans' files examined in preparing this study, on which my comments here are based, are Guy Watson (Dis), PF S39874; Ambrose Lewis (Dis), PF S36041; Levi Caesar (Dis), PF S39269; Jack Green (Nondis), PF S43631; Henry Tabor (Nondis), PF W1331.

40. Joel Porter (Dis), PF S20144.

41. For more on masculinity in early America, see Thomas A. Foster, *Sex and the Eighteenth-Century Man: Massachusetts and the History of Sexuality in America* (Boston: Beacon Press, 2006); Thomas A. Foster, ed., *New Men: Manliness in Early America* (New York: New York University Press, 2011); and Anne S. Lombard, *Making Manhood: Growing up Male in Colonial New England* (Cambridge, Mass.: Harvard University Press, 2003).

42. Clement Sewall (Dis), PF S20192.

43. Edward Warren (Dis), PF S10264.

44. Peregrine Horden, "Household Care and Informal Networks: Comparisons and Continuities from Antiquity to the Present," in *The Locus of Care: Families, Communities, Institutions and the Provision of Welfare Since Antiquity*, edited by Peregrine Horden and Richard Smith (London: Routledge, 1998), 24.

45. Clement Sewall (Dis), PF S20192.

46. James Trowbridge (Dis), PF S43205.

47. For women as carers in early America, see Laurel Thatcher Ulrich, *A Midwife's Tale: The Life of Martha Ballard, Based on Her Diary, 1785–1812* (New York: Vintage Books, 1990); and Rebecca J. Tannenbaum, *The Healer's Calling: Women and Medicine in Early New England* (Ithaca: Cornell University Press, 2009).

48. William De Witt (Dis), PF S43476.

49. Shawn Johansen, *Family Men: Middle-Class Fatherhood in Early Industrializing America* (New York: Routledge, 2001), 73; Lombard, *Making Manhood*, 24–27.

50. My use of the term healthscape differs from the way place and health researchers, or geographers of health, use it. Geographers of health use the term to call attention to the way context affects people's health. I also use healthscape to highlight the importance of context, but unlike geographers of health, I do not use the term to stress a causal link between context and people's *actual* health. Rather, I emphasize the connection between the collective state of health of a community and the way that this shapes perceptions of and responses to ill health and disability. For more on the way place and health researchers understand the term healthscape, see Daniel Rainham, I. McDowell, D. Krewski, and M. Sawada, "Conceptualizing the Healthscape: Contributions of Time Geography, Location Technologies and Spatial Ecology to Place and Health Research," *Social Science & Medicine* 70, no. 5 (2010): 668–676.

51. Truman Mead (Nondis), PF S42968.

52. See, for example, Abijah Lewis (Nondis), PF S37161; Jesse Sabin (Nondis), PF S33369; Jesse Robertson (Nondis), PF S39049.

53. James Burgess (Dis), PF S44718.

54. Moses S. George (Dis), PF S39569; John Newman (Dis), PF S25329.

55. Amos Camp (Dis), PF S45322; Levi Chubbuck (Dis), PF S45632; Andrew Griswold (Dis), PF W17963; Joel Phelps (Dis), PF S35028.

56. My comments here echo those of Anne Borsay. In her study of disability in Britain, Borsay notes that "for most of the modern era . . . family structures were predisposed towards supporting disabled people in the community." Anne Borsay, *Disability and Social Policy in Britain since 1750* (Basingstoke: Palgrave Macmillan, 2005), 178.

57. Murtie June Clark, comp., *The Pension Lists of 1792–1795 with Other Revolutionary War Pension Records* (Baltimore, Md.: Genealogical Publishing Co., 1991), 16; Seth Delano (Dis), PF S15802; Entry for Seth "Dillano," Plantation 6, Oxford Co., Maine, Ancestry. com, *1820 United States Federal Census* (Provo, UT: Ancestry.com Operations, Inc., 2010), http://www.ancestry.com (accessed December 1, 2011).

58. Raymond A. Mohl, *Poverty in New York, 1783–1825* (New York: Oxford University Press, 1971); David J. Rothman, *The Discovery of the Asylum: Social Order and Disorder in the New Republic* (Boston: Little, Brown & Co., 1990); Plantation 6, Oxford Co., Maine, *1820 U.S. Federal Census*.

59. Blackie, "Disabled Revolutionary War Veterans," 3.

60. Tables 28 and 29 in Resch, *Suffering Soldiers*, 222–223. For examples of disabled veterans who drew pension officials' attention to the importance of external medical services to their families, see Jerathmeel Doty (Dis), PF S39450; Edward Warren (Dis), PF S10264; Moses Cass (Dis), PF W22733; and Amaziah Chappell (Dis), PF S44749.

61. See, for example, Carol Thomas, *Female Forms: Experiencing and Understanding Disability* (Buckingham: Open University Press, 1999); and Susan Burch and Hannah Joyner, *Unspeakable: The Story of Junius Wilson* (Chapel Hill: University of North Carolina, 2007).

CHAPTER 2

Thomas Cameron's "Pure and Guileless Life," 1806–1870

Affection and Developmental Disability in a North Carolina Family

PENNY L. RICHARDS

> . . . Did her anguished mind
> In love bestowed no consolation find?
> Oh yes! She found it, for Affection gives,
> alike to who bestows and who receives,
> She soothed the sinless idiot's helpless lot
> And in her task her greater woes forgot.
>
> —Anonymous, "Affection's Triumphs, Pt. 1,"
> *Southern Literary Messenger*, May 1837

KEYWORDS: *Centuries*: nineteenth; *Geographical Areas*: North America; *Sources*: manuscripts and archival materials; *Themes*: family, community, and daily life

In nineteenth-century sentimental literature, the "poor hard-working widow and her idiot son" were picturesque stock figures, meant to inspire readers to consider their own burdens lighter by comparison, to dramatize the rewards of maternal devotion, and to justify the sacrifices required of families in a world without many alternative supports for people with what are now called "developmental disabilities." To maximize the pathos, the mother and son live on the margins, perhaps selling fruit; they have no other family and quietly forestall outside intrusions. As a self-contained pair, they fulfill each other's emotional and material needs completely.[1]

Nineteenth-century American families knew disability in a more crowded, interdependent world—among extended kin, in workplaces, in schools, on plantations and at churches. Recently, historians have begun to study these family and community stories.[2] Two contexts provide the settings for much of the current historical work on lay experiences with mental disability: inheritance and institutionalization. In the first, historians draw on wills and court testimony to determine the lay and legal understandings of mental incapacity. What behaviors, appearances, and mistakes would have signaled developmental disability or madness in the past? In the second context, families and communities are examined at the point of choosing (or resisting) institutional placement—again, focusing on the behaviors and appearances that warranted institutionalization.[3] These are promising directions for research in a subject that often resists standard approaches. Both contexts, however, rely on snapshots of families at the zenith of dysfunction: when death has prompted a legal dispute over inheritance or when resources have been exhausted and institutional placement is the last recourse.[4]

In this project, another kind of evidence is engaged, collected family correspondence spanning over sixty years, to reconstruct the life circumstances of one southern man.[5] The dramatic events that punctuated Thomas Cameron's life did not center on his disability or continued dependence or conflict among kin. In his mostly happy life story, we have a chance to glimpse how developmental disability was experienced not only beyond the asylum but also beyond the courtroom, the poorhouse, and the doctor's office. As a case study in southern history, it highlights the functional aspects of extended regional networks based on kinship, profession, and religious affiliation and of the sentimental emphasis on "affection" in antebellum white family relationships. The accommodations that were necessary for Thomas Cameron's lifelong comfort, dignity, and contentment fit easily within the structures of planter-class life.

Thomas Amis Dudley Cameron was the second child and first son of Duncan and Rebecca Bennehan Cameron. He was born in Hillsborough, North Carolina, in the summer of 1806. Duncan was a white Virginia-born lawyer, and Rebecca was the only daughter of a prosperous local white merchant and landowner. Apparently a healthy baby, Thomas walked at about fourteen months and was described as "highly diverted" by his baptismal splash in 1809.[6] A tutor was hired when Thomas was five. Two years later, a grandfather described Thomas and his cousin as "slow and fonder of play than of books," but his indulgent tone raised little alarm. By 1814, however, Thomas's progress was lagging; tutor Willie Mangum wrote to Duncan Cameron that "it is probably that his improvement is not commensurate with your expectation, the obvious reason of which is indolence." He elaborated: "When there are immediate objects of incitement, his attention becomes fixed, and he improves very well; but when they are removed, or become stale by frequency of recurrence, he relapses into inattention."[7]

Thomas Cameron's "indolence" became more worrisome the next year, when his brother Paul, who was two years younger, began to surpass him in basic skills such as letter writing. Other children were noticing Thomas's shortcomings. His Older sister Mary Ann, while reporting her own academic frustrations, expressed dismay at Thomas's inability to correspond with her. "I am very sorry that Brother Thomas does not improve so much," she scrawled.[8]

Definitive diagnosis of any specific disorder is probably impossible after two centuries. Thomas Cameron appears to have experienced mild-to-moderate developmental disability by today's definitions. Admittedly, historians have been cavalier with such labels or have used euphemisms. For example, biographies of Thomas Jefferson have been reluctant to use specific language to describe his sister Elizabeth, preferring vaguer terms for the child who was not educated with the other Jefferson girls and who was mentally disabled enough to need constant supervision into adulthood.[9] By contrast, Jefferson's brother Randolph has been labeled "retarded," although he inherited property, lived on his own, married, raised children, and corresponded with his illustrious brother.[10] Instead of following such precedents, this project understands Thomas Cameron as having a developmental disability, based on several factors evident in the family correspondence.[11]

First, *his legal status in adulthood remained that of a dependent*. Before developmental disabilities were seen mainly as educational or medical issues, mental incompetence was a legal judgment: courts determined if an individual was competent to stand trial, make valid contracts, marry, or manage funds.[12] Duncan Cameron was a judge, so his legal treatment of his elder son bears particular significance. Thomas inherited money and extensive property from Duncan, but only through trustees (his brother, his sister, and his sister-in-law). As the elder son, Thomas would ordinarily have controlled his family's vast plantations; instead, first-son duties and privileges were reassigned to his only brother. Paul wrote home from college, "I see too well the duties that must devolve upon me when I arrive at the age of manhood, and enter on the active scene of life, the only son to be the pillar and support of the family on account of my most unfortunate brother." Thomas worked, traveled, and voted as an adult white man, but he never lived away from his siblings' supervision and his accounts were managed entirely by Paul. Though he retained most privileges of his race and gender, Thomas Cameron was still treated as less than fully responsible.

Second, *he had generalized, significant learning difficulties since childhood*. Thomas was by all accounts a well-mannered, pleasant, curious boy. He was never troublesome at school, in an era when southern students were notoriously rowdy.[13] Nonetheless, although he was eager to please, Thomas was challenged by the most basic academic expectations. Penmanship and the composition of sentences were difficult. Arithmetic and abstract concepts completely escaped his grasp, said one teacher: "He commits to memory with considerable ease but does not seem capable of comparing ideas or in a word reasoning with much force or accuracy."[14] Thomas Cameron's formal education had ended by age 20. At that time he was able to compose simple sentences, copy, and spell phonetically. He attended to his personal care, rode horses unassisted, and spoke clearly enough to be understood. He was welcomed at social gatherings and as a house guest, indicating that his interpersonal skills were acceptable, though the subtleties of conversation remained a challenge.

The third basis for assuming developmental disability in Thomas Cameron's case is that *he had some accompanying physical issues*, significantly motor problems. Thomas was described as having a "muscular debility," as lacking "vigour of body," and as needing to improve his posture, gait, and general bearing. The prevailing belief of the day, which the Camerons shared, was that climate was involved; that the heat, humidity, and "sickliness" of the South made some European Americans delicate and that a bracing northern winter might improve his constitution.[15] He was not sickly like his sisters, who spent years seeking restorative cures at spas and clinics, but he was considered awkward and prone to lassitude. While at military school in Vermont, he was not at first included in some exercises expected of the other cadets.[16] There was always concern that his physical movements were markedly weaker, slower, or less fluid and that he would not protect himself from extreme temperature or exertion. Such physical differences are consistent with some forms of developmental disability as it is understood today.

Finally, *his family and others recorded their special efforts to accommodate his needs throughout his life*. Thomas Cameron was born to advantage, in many senses. His family commanded vast resources, so in the most obvious sense, he was fortunate. More subtly, Thomas was born into a cultural context that accommodated the effects of developmental disability. Planter society admired individual achievement and intelligence but also upheld such interpersonal, communal ideals as honor, duty, usefulness, and affection.[17] Through an elaborate system of networks based on extended kinship, professional relationships, and religious affiliation, planter-class families could claim support from a wide range of connections without ever seeking more formal assistance.[18] The preference for affection and duty over individualism, for informal arrangements over formalized systems of support, had many consequences for southern society, but these cultural preferences generally served Thomas Cameron well throughout his life.

Thomas Cameron was educated in the 1810s and 1820s, years before North Carolina provided public education and well before any southern state offered specialized schooling for students with disabilities. This period may be characterized as "chaotic" and "disorganized" by educational historians, but from the family's perspective, it might have offered great flexibility and parental control.[19] Individual families shouldered the costs of educating their children, evaluated teachers, arranged transportation and sometimes even classroom space, and to some extent dictated the pace and content of the curriculum offered to their children. School proprietors had the discretion to admit or deny admission to any student, to teach according to parents' expectations, and to compose classes as need dictated. Age-grading was generations away: it was unremarkable to find young children and teenagers studying the same lesson, side by side.[20] The "disorganized" schooling scene of the early republic was full of potential for the very fortunate parents who were able to navigate and afford its various offerings, especially for a child with unusual educational needs.

Thomas's father, Duncan Cameron, took the lead in finding home tutors, locating schools, and weighing various plans. At first, Duncan's closest kin and professional contacts sufficed to meet the child's needs in the South. As a judge, he traveled about North Carolina and knew educated people, including aspiring lawyers who were willing to exchange their tutoring services for access to Duncan's legal mentorship. Among the tutors who worked with young Thomas Cameron was Willie Person Mangum (1792–1861), later a longtime senator for North Carolina.[21] Between tutors, Thomas and his cousin William Anderson were sent to study with their grandfather, Rev. John Cameron of Lunenberg, Virginia. Rev. Cameron adored his grandsons,[22] but Thomas's aunt Mary Anderson named the real goal of the arrangement, the hope that Thomas and her son "will always be affectionate to each other."[23] William's presence was further seen as a spur to Thomas's education, "as I make them spell some lessons together, in order to put Tom in the way of getting, or preparing his lesson by himself,"[24] explained their grandfather. Many planter families made similar arrangements in order to solidify bonds with extended family members.[25]

When Thomas's intellectual shortcomings became more apparent, Duncan Cameron sought alternatives that would preserve his son's good nature while offering him a decent education. His brother John in Fayetteville offered to find a school in that city in a frankly worded letter that shows how Thomas, then age 9, was seen by this uncle:

> I need not, I hope, assure you, with what affectionate care I would watch over him. . . . As to the propriety of sending him from home, I can have no doubt; the truth is obvious, and I know it has not escaped your observation, that he is so aware of Paul's superiority over him, that it discourages him. The remark is so often made, without his ability to do better, that from being at first mortified, he becomes callous. In a public seminary he will have more to excite him.[26]

John A. Cameron went on to suggest that Thomas might benefit from alternative approaches. In 1816 he suggested entering Thomas in a Lancasterian school, a factory-like setting that was usually considered as a cost-efficient method of educating the urban poor. While Duncan did not follow the suggestion, this was one of several times that a nontraditional program was proposed for Thomas. Thomas later, very briefly, attended a Fellenberg-based school in Connecticut in 1825, where the curriculum probably included gardening and carpentry.[27] His parents' openness to such diverse ideas is testimony to their efforts to find a suitable education for their son regardless of ideology or custom. John's advice, though blunt, also demonstrates the family's sensitivity to Thomas's feelings about his more talented younger brother. He was not to be sent away from home to relieve his mother's burdens or to receive a better education but to avoid confronting a painful situation that obstructed his best efforts—and only if he could be sure to receive "affectionate care," whatever his schooling was.

Eventually, when he was a teenager, Thomas Cameron was sent to northern schools to improve his physical condition. Now more distant reaches of Duncan's extensive network of contacts became instrumental. One of Duncan's cousins had married a Kollock from New Jersey. Shepard Kollock (1750–1839) was a prominent printer during the American Revolution who was based in Elizabethtown, New Jersey. His son, also called Shepard (1795–1865), was a clergyman. Both Shepard Kollocks knew Rev. John Churchill Rudd (1779–1848), rector of St. John's Church in Elizabethtown. Rudd advertised that he would host a small number of male students in his home, starting in 1817, promising "a situation favorable to the attainment of a good education, and the preservation of their morals."[28] In 1820, the fourteen-year-old Thomas Cameron was accepted into Rudd's school.

Rev. and Mrs. Rudd nurtured a homey atmosphere for their charges. The Camerons supplemented the familiarity by dispatching friends and relatives to monitor Thomas's well-being. One visitor reported, in a typical summary, "I was happy on visiting Mr. Rudd to find your son in the enjoyment of good health & spirits, very comfortably situated, and making progress in his studies."[29] Friends and relatives accompanied Thomas while he traveled and hosted him during his journey. His uncle Thomas Bennehan escorted Thomas to Vermont in 1824, to judge whether the school there was appropriate for his nephew. Along the way, the pair stayed with relatives in Virginia, James Hamilton in New York, and Bishop T. C. Brownell of Hartford. Their hosts were cordial and welcomed Thomas Cameron specifically: "I was sorry your son could not . . . have stayed some days longer with us," wrote Hamilton in 1823.[30] In no sense could Thomas be said to have been hidden from view or neglected during his schooling in the North; on the contrary, he was placed in the care and company of prominent individuals while traveling and learning and he was surrounded by close acquaintances of his family much of the time.

At the Rudd school, Thomas Cameron garnered special attention from the minister and his wife. Rudd was confident in Thomas's potential:

The points on which I think he has improved very perceptibly are in his activity and vigour of body and general comprehension & notice of things. His advances in learning will I believe be very slow, but under the blessing of God, I trust his improvement will be considerable.[31]

His activities on Thomas's behalf included close observation, adaptations to pedagogy, and including the boy in social life. "I have very minutely observed the mind of Thomas," he declared, and he identified patterns in young Cameron's mental processes.[32] He described times when Thomas's "mind has not seemed composed" and when he displayed "a certain heedless manner."[33] His attention, Rudd noted, seemed to fluctuate:

> It seems much easier to comprehend sometimes than at others & he apparently takes interest in his studies one day, which a few days after it is found difficult to excite him. I remark the same inequality in his disposition to play. At times he is a very attentive observer, of all that passes, at others he appears listless.[34]

"He wants a certain balance of thought," Rudd concluded. "As he is much in the house, and from his quiet disposition an object of attention to us all, we endeavour to quicken him with conversation." Rudd tried other pedagogical strategies. He tried to rouse Thomas's interest in writing by assigning personalized phrases for exercise, "My father lives in North Carolina," for example.[35]

Physical stimulation was also part of the program. The first winter Thomas spent in Elizabethtown, Rudd wrote, "He grows, and is more like our northern lads than when you left him. I am inclined to think, judging from present appearances, that our winter will be of essential service to him." Beyond the invigorating change of climate, Thomas played actively with the other boys, and there was talk of sending him for dancing lessons. Other students offered social encouragement to the shy young Cameron, who in turn elicited protective feelings in his peers: "I think he has reason to be fond of them as I observe, in some especially, a desire to aid him & see that he has kind treatment," Rudd assured the Camerons.[36]

Thomas did not acquire many hoped-for skills in his time with Rudd: at age 17, he still could not write a letter on his own. He warmed to geography, perhaps because maps provided a visual aid, and lessons were learned by rote, which suited his retentive memory. Rudd acknowledged the modest academic progress, saying that "tho' it is not in my power to be of the extensive service to him that I could wish, I still flatter myself that he is doing as well as can be reasonably expected." After Thomas returned to North Carolina, Rudd wrote to Duncan and remembered the boy fondly, asking after his happiness.[37] Whatever skills Thomas attained, he was welcomed into Rudd's surrogate family, which took pleasure in his company and was anxious for his well-being. He stayed healthy those three years and returned home glad to meet his new sister, Mildred.

Duncan Cameron, who maintained hope that Thomas could improve further, contacted Alden Partridge (1785–1854). Partridge was a colorful character who could only have successfully operated a school in the looser climate of the 1820s. One biographer calls him an "undeniably contentious and combative individual";[38] he was a stubborn, self-promoting entrepreneur. Thomas Bennehan described him as "a man I have no doubt of strong nervous mind but with little polish of manners."[39] Partridge, fresh from a superintendency at West Point, founded the American Literary, Scientific, & Military Academy (ALS&MA) in Vermont to promote the idea central to his work—that a nation dependent on citizen-soldiers needed to train young men for command. His school, the first "military academy" for adolescent American boys, drew students from all regions, especially from elite families of the South.

It may seem strange that the Camerons would place Thomas with Captain Partridge. The quiet teen was not suited for military command and Partridge was not a kindly man like Rudd. But Partridge had an excellent reputation for teaching mathematics, which Duncan Cameron thought Thomas could grasp with good instruction, and Partridge's methods included strenuous physical training. These features, combined with the school's New England location, promised the desired improvements. Duncan Cameron wrote a letter of inquiry to Partridge that is the most specific and detailed testimony we have about Thomas's personality, limitations, and strengths as a young man, as assessed by his father:

> Sir, my eldest son a youth in his 18th year has laboured under a species of muscular debility from his infancy which in this climate and under the influence of the warm weather in summer continued to increase on him until the spring of 1820, when I placed him in a private seminary at Elizabeth Town N. Jersey. . . . The weakness of which I have spoken, appears in some degree to have reached his mental powers—for although his understanding in general is good & his memory acute and retentive, his mind appears on some points to be feeble, particularly in its efforts to combine numbers. . . . I am desirous of placing him for a few years still further to the North, and in a seminary where regular bodily exercise is a part of academic discipline. . . . He is amiable in his disposition, mild of temper, docile & obedient, affectionate, and of morals most pure—in short I know of no defect in his character, which is susceptible to self-remedy.[40]

Partridge, surely perceiving a chance to impress an influential southerner and gain further recruits, accepted the challenge.

Duncan was still not certain that the military academy would suit his son; he instructed Thomas Bennehan (who was escorting young Thomas to Vermont) that he should linger: "Try to stay a week or so, that you form some opinion as to his capacity for adapting himself to his new condition, and the duties growing out of it. Have his uniform dress prepared, see how it becomes him, how he suits it; that he is pleased with it."[41] Despite Duncan's concerns, Thomas quickly took to the routines of the ALS&MA. He was assigned a North Carolinian roommate who promised to be Thomas's protector. He was eager to be fitted for a uniform. While he was not immediately included in the rigorous military drills, he would eventually participate in Partridge's famous marches through New England. Partridge led his cadets on foot to distant destinations, testing their endurance while advertising his unique school and entertaining townspeople with a military spectacle. Students recorded their route in maps and journals. Thomas's "constant & unwearied exertions to acquire his lessons & to make improvement" surprised the academy's acting headmaster in 1824.[42]

Visitors to the ALS&MA found Thomas more robust in physique after all this hiking and drilling. When Paul Cameron joined his brother at Middletown, Connecticut (the school had relocated during Thomas's stay), in 1825, he wrote to their sister, "In point of strength, he walks much straighter than he did and pays some more respect to his person than he formerly did."[43] The Camerons were roommates at the Partridge school, and several of their cousins attended at the same time.[44] There were other improvements. Cousin W. E. Anderson believed "Tom much improved . . . owing it is probable to his free intercourse with his fellow students, and the friendly care which they all take in not provoking or plaguing him."[45] Although ALS&MA was a military school that enrolled many rowdy southern teens, headmaster Williston insisted that Thomas would never be mistreated on account of his disability: "The cadets are always ready to laugh at affected peculiarities &c but are too generous & manly to make *natural* weaknesses a theme of ridicule."[46] Thomas probably gained confidence from the responsibilities assigned to him (marching a class, calling roll) and from successfully negotiating a raucous dormitory life. Paul noted his brother's newfound pride of appearance, saying "he takes more pains with his clothes and so have I learned to be more careful."[47]

Thomas made some academic progress at ALS&MA but still not as much as his father dared to hope. Letter writing, for example, remained a challenge. Thomas developed a secretiveness about his letters, insisting on privacy in his correspondence. Perhaps this emerged from his greater personal assertiveness, or perhaps he was more self-conscious about the comparative quality of his writing. He refused to allow roommates or even his brother to read or correct his writing, with the unfortunate effect that his letters did not reach their addressees. The teen did improve his performance in other subjects. "Cadet Cameron is reciting regularly in Eng. Grammar & in reading; he appears to be improving in both; he reads more distinctly & correctly," summarized his instructor. Paul also noticed his clearer speech, saying "he converses a great deal better than he did."[48]

Perhaps the most impressive evidence of Thomas's progress is the last letter
he wrote before returning to North Carolina in 1826. Alone among the very few
surviving letters by Thomas, it is clearly not dictated by a teacher—it is longer,
its spelling is mostly phonetic, the handwriting is more fluid, and its colloquial
expressions must be Thomas's own:

> I reciv you leter 25 of this month i am very glad to reciv you leter it pleas me very
> much, to go home. Captin reciv you leter the same time. i almost forgoten home
> almost. i hope this be the last letter i yankeyland. ill write you in phildelphay. i hop
> to seyu in god heth. hi midred of mey how is the military cademey go one i hope
> cuin war for hilth can. teney te new in orang couty how they come think about a
> godel howdos the cro in orange couty. i have sean captin spencer he ttalk bout hav-
> ing tomove i th carolinay. Give my lov but my fiends. i hope to s th versone i remane
> yu fationate sone T CAmron.[49]

In this letter, Thomas shows improvement in language and penmanship. Grammar, punctuation, and capitalization are nonstandard, but the sentences are mostly
complete and the letter contains the usual niceties of the day, showing an awareness of social conventions. Beyond the skills and knowledge displayed, the letter's
contents reveal an individual expressing his own preferences, plans, and affections
and indicating the past, the present, and the future from his perspective. Life at
military academy strengthened Thomas in many ways. Now, at 20, he could return to his family, where he was indeed a "fationate sone," and enjoy the home he
"almost forgoten."

Thomas Cameron made the transition at leaving school with impressive ease.
As a young adult, he had a home life, a work life, and a social life, in each case bal-
ancing his desire for independence with his need for assistance. Thomas's success
in each of these spheres benefited from his family's affection and resources and
from the informal support networks that embraced him as a useful and beloved
member. The Cameron family lived in several locations in North Carolina. Homes
in Hillsborough and Raleigh and plantations at Stagville, Fairntosh, and Person
County together formed their physical "home." This distribution across counties
might seem to work against a supportive home life. But Thomas loved to ride his
horse and he rode between these locations alone at his own discretion. Thomas's
regular rides became a crucial means of communication among family members:
Thomas carried written messages and gave oral reports of the conditions elsewhere—the health of siblings, slaves, and crops; the travel plans of his brother and
father; even the menus of memorable meals were material for Thomas's eagerly
awaited messages. "The Capt [his nickname] is with us now, his visits are perfect
treats, he has so much 'home news' to tell us," his sister-in-law wrote.[50]

The distances between various linked households gave Thomas an important
role as message carrier. Those distances also allowed him to serve as male escort

to women, especially to his sister-in-law Anne. In Thomas's company, Anne could journey to see her parents in Alamance without taking Paul Cameron away from his business concerns. Thomas was the only male to escort his sisters to a cousin's deathbed across county lines. Thomas's status as an adult white male mattered more than his cognitive abilities for this purpose, and his availability made him a great help to his family.[51]

Thomas's leisure was spent in the family circle, engaging in typical male activities such as smoking and perusing the newspapers. He sat before the fire with his brother, father, or uncle, though he conversed little: Paul called him "so much of a quaker" and joked that every night was a "silent meeting" with Thomas. A sister wrote that Thomas had once not spoken for a week. He enjoyed listening to letters read aloud, a regular occurrence. And he loved to "romp" with his nieces and nephews: "Thomas has given a good deal of his time to the children, they seem very much attached to him, as he unquestionably is to them," Paul commented in 1844.[52]

The Camerons expressed familial bonds in small gestures, especially while apart. When the rest of the white household was away, Thomas awaited their return "on the piazza, looking anxiously out for us." (Thomas was never truly alone on a plantation; enslaved and hired helpers were always present.) When Thomas was away, his nieces missed him at the dinner table. The mutual affection between Thomas and his sister-in-law shines in her letters: "Dear good brother Tom has been a *brother* indeed, it has only been necessary for me to express a wish before him to have it performed," Anne marveled to Paul. Paul wrote earnestly from a visit to Alabama, "I think of him often and love him much more than I was fully aware of until I got into so much trouble and so far away from him." And Thomas asked Anne to write that "he is doing all he can to keep things straight" in Paul's absence.[53]

Some of what Thomas was doing to "keep things straight" involved working on the family plantations. He was busy all day when health and weather permitted, appearing among the family only for meals. His visits to his sisters in Raleigh would end abruptly when he became restless without employment. Reports from Fairntosh and Stagville frequently mention Thomas Cameron and Thomas Bennehan working late nights in the lumber house or the pork house or getting flour ready or supervising the cotton harvest. "Poor fellows, they have gone through their harvest and now will be much refreshed by a few days of *rest*, and will much enjoy your society," commented Paul to his mother in 1840. Thomas might work too much, to the detriment of his health: "Thomas is well, and as much devoted to his cotton pickers as ever," Paul assured their father, "under this injunction, however, that he stoops not himself to the work." Thomas was also warned against too much sun or overexertion and not to stay out in the "night air" at the lumber house. These warnings reflected a concern for his well-being but also implied that he had limited judgment, limited consideration of the racial divisions of labor on a plantation, and a focused enthusiasm for work.[54]

Another job was tended less consistently. In 1831, Thomas Cameron was officially appointed postmaster for Stagville. The previous postmaster, Wilkins, had been dismissed for neglecting his duties. There are forms in the family papers, signed by Thomas, that probably should have been returned to Washington. Thomas was forced to give up this post in 1838, and Paul Cameron took over. He too would eventually be dismissed for negligence. This chronic failure to make returns to Washington or otherwise comply with regulations was not a function of Thomas's disability but a general problem in southern rural post offices. He did the job no worse than his able-bodied predecessor and successor.[55]

Thomas had a social life as a member of the Cameron family. With his siblings and other relatives, he attended weddings and deathbeds. One family friend commented after an 1848 party, "I was glad to see your brother Tom taking a little recreation; he seemed to enjoy himself, tho, silently, as usual." He requested his Sunday suit be sent to him for a wedding, showing an awareness of social norms and a concern for his personal appearance. Letters indicate that Thomas attended church services as well. When he fell ill on a short trip, neighboring relatives took Thomas under their care, sending word to the Camerons explaining his whereabouts. As a Cameron, Thomas gained social access to a wide network and was included in celebrations and rituals by kin and friends.[56]

Thomas also had friends of his own. A neighbor, Mumford Boylan, was his traveling companion at times, and they stayed in each other's homes. Another friend and neighbor, Mr. Cain, took Thomas to a mass meeting in a nearby county in 1844. When there was an illness at Cain's house in 1848, Thomas visited the sickbed on his own. In 1836, nearby Hillsborough, North Carolina, was in controversy: the commissioners wanted to tax bowling alleys and billiard tables in order to discourage any associated drinking and prostitution. Were these among the entertainments that attracted Thomas and his friends? If so, his family, though aware of Hillsborough's dubious diversions, did not interfere with Thomas's independent social life. He is described, instead, as going into town "to pick up the news."[57]

Perhaps Thomas Cameron's most significant social activities, with and without his family, were political. Thomas Cameron was, in his brother's description, a "very ardent Whig" who "would be glad to attend a Whig club every night." He regularly accompanied his father or brother to the polls to cast his vote. He attended an election rally in Lipscomb to hear the candidates' addresses in 1848, a year in which Paul noted, "he seems determined to do his own voting." He also attended a Whig meeting with a family friend that year.[58] The 1830s and 1840s were a volatile period in North Carolina politics, so Thomas Cameron's vote would not have been seen as trivial; and his strong attraction to voting and party functions may be related to the rowdy hoopla surrounding political events in that tumultuous era.[59] No other feature of Thomas Cameron's middle years indicates so definitively how he was accepted by the wider society as an adult white male.

Minimal adjustment was needed in the life of a plantation bachelor to make it Thomas's. Except for the fact that he did not write letters, his life would have been quite similar to that of his uncle Thomas Bennehan, with whom he worked, traveled, and sometimes lived. Neither man was ever left alone at Fairntosh without caretakers in the form of enslaved cooks, housekeepers, and other supports. Both men were considered suitable escorts for Paul's wife and children and trustworthy supervisors of plantation routines. Their unattached status allowed more flexibility to travel in support of Paul's work, without competing demands.[60] This role made Thomas Cameron's move into adulthood easy for him to accomplish and easy for the wider social circle to recognize and accept.

One event shattered, temporarily, Thomas Cameron's home, work, and social lives, while demonstrating their strength and importance. In September 1837, while riding alone between the family home in Raleigh and plantations in Orange County, "he was *shot*," in his brother's shocked words, "by an *unseen* and as yet *unknown hand*!" "This dark deed" was considered an attempted robbery. After shots were fired, Thomas held on to his horse and bolted away from the area. His injuries were serious: one eye was badly damaged; his shoulder, neck, hand, and nose were wounded; and lockjaw appeared imminent.[61] His visibility and independence left him vulnerable to this crime. According to Paul, Tom's riding habits were "well known to almost any man upon the road, he ordinarily leaves Orange on Friday and returns on Monday."[62] The attacker—who was never identified—was waiting for Thomas to ride by, according to those who inspected the site.[63] Thomas could speak within a week of the incident, but he had not seen or heard anyone, only the trees and the gun's discharge. He rarely carried much money, but he was carrying a letter from Duncan to Paul, fulfilling his usual role as family messenger.[64]

The Camerons mobilized their social network. Paul kept his father-in-law, Thomas Ruffin, apprised of news in more painful detail than he shared with closer kin. Ruffin's son Sterling, who had earlier lost his sight from an eye disease, had been treated in Philadelphia by Isaac Hays, a noted oculist.[65] Thomas was sent north for the same expertise. Hays wrote a detailed evaluation of Thomas Cameron's injury and prospects; he diagnosed nerve damage and muscular paralysis and recommended "galvanism" as one possible treatment. Thomas was also dosed with opium preparations for his "high nervous excitement" and pain.[66] It is unclear whether Thomas ever recovered sight in that eye or whether there were lasting facial scars; if partial blindness or scarring remained, Thomas may have been presented with new disabilities beyond those that he had successfully managed in his first 30 years.

Thomas left his responsibilities untended in the aftermath of the shooting, most significantly his postmaster job. While he was never diligent in that position, he was officially dismissed during his recovery, and the post was reassigned to Paul. By the spring following his September attack, however, Thomas seems to have returned to visiting between family homes, complaining about his tailor, and riding his horse.

One might imagine Thomas Cameron's adult life as carefree (with the exception of that incident in 1837). It was not. He loved his sisters, nieces, and nephews, and a year seldom passed without a death in this dear circle.[67] Four of his sisters died from tuberculosis between 1837 and 1840. Another, Mildred, was chronically ill and partially paralyzed. In 1843, when his mother lay dying, Thomas was taken on tours of the state, first with his father and then with his uncle, perhaps to shield him from his mother's decline or to keep him out of the way during her time of intense need. Thomas Bennehan died in 1847, and in 1853, the death of Duncan Cameron followed several years of poststroke impairment.[68] At Duncan's passing, Thomas became a property holder, and Paul and Margaret Cameron took more active roles as his trustees.

The timing of these new responsibilities was difficult for both siblings. Paul's wife Anne was, by 1853, a longtime opium addict because of the pain of losing four children (another, Thomas's favorite niece Molly, would die in 1855), and her repeated confinements. Anne's struggles with addiction rendered her attachment to Thomas poignant—neither was fully capable alone, but together they could travel safely and look to each other's needs. Paul was responsible for managing his own lands, slaves, and finances plus those of his sisters and Thomas, while seeing that his children were being educated with various tutors and at school. In 1856, he began a two-year term in the state senate. Paul became frustrated with Thomas during these busy years: he fumed when Thomas forgot to say goodbye before leaving home; he warned the tailor to make plain black suits for Thomas rather than the "stage driver coats" and expensive fabrics Thomas would choose; he complained that Thomas spent too much time "out in too hard weather against my wishes & entreaty." Months after Duncan's passing, Paul sounded completely overwhelmed by his new status as the Cameron patriarch: "I have felt that it would be a *relief* if I could go away from & forget home & its cares."[69]

Margaret was also busy with other things besides her middle-aged brother's care. At age 40, she agreed to marry George Washington Mordecai, her father's successor as bank president in Raleigh. The wedding happened less than five months after Duncan Cameron's death. Mildred Cameron joined the newlyweds on honeymoon, and the sisters spent much time in the North seeking cures for Millie's various complaints. While in the north, Margaret felt she was neglecting Thomas's care, especially when he fell ill in 1856: "It has grieved me to think of his being ill and *I* not near to perform the acts of tenderness and love which he so justly deserves at my hands," she fretted. "Whenever anything is the matter with this dear afflicted one I always feel as if I must take the place of my sainted mother."[70] Thomas was never in danger of feeling neglected: Paul canceled meetings to stay by Thomas's side during the worst spells, niece Rebecca read the newspaper to him, and the younger nieces and nephews were "taken up for his entertainment."[71] His appetites for food and tobacco revived, and he recovered before summer.

In the turmoil immediately preceding the Civil War, Thomas Cameron remained a source of joy for his siblings, his cousins, and their children and even grandchildren. Cousin William Anderson was amused to report that when he spent a weekend with Thomas alone at the Raleigh house, they ate like princes because he ordered "hot rolls & oysters, buckwheat cakes & molasses." Thomas's love of rich food was catered to by the family's slaves and employees when no other authorities were around to moderate his wishes, and William was delighted to be the beneficiary of this arrangement.[72] After sixty years together, Thomas was still sometimes unsure when Paul was joking, prompting many anecdotes in his nieces' letters. By the end of his life, he was affectionately known to five generations of his family, from his grandparents to the children of his nieces. Remembering her uncle Thomas, Annie Collins recalled that "he bestowed a large share of his love on my children . . . he tickled Rebecca a great deal & we laughed at him for nursing her up and getting her to sleep in church when she sat next to him."[73]

Many of Paul Cameron's papers from the Civil War era were destroyed to obscure his activities during the Confederacy.[74] Little can be known about Thomas's understanding of the war or its aftermath. Thomas stayed at the Fairntosh plantation through the war, while Paul's family lived in Hillsborough and their sisters lived in Raleigh. Maybe the farm was safer, preserving Thomas's most comfortable routines and roles; he was reluctant to leave except for holidays.[75] Paul continued to order his brother's clothing during the war, explaining that "Thomas keeps his clothes at so many places that I can never know what he has."[76] Niece Rebecca commented in spring of 1865 that "he must have had a lonely winter; so much of the time he has been kept indoors . . . & at night he does not read at all." Paul may have shuffled some funds to load Thomas's accounts with Confederate notes toward the end of the war, in case "the worst should ever befall us."[77] Paul had long found Thomas's separate accounts useful, but in this instance he might have taken advantage of Thomas's disability, assuming that Confederate investments would be less burdensome to his brother when the South fell.

After the war, Thomas lived quietly in Raleigh with Margaret, George, Mildred, and George's sister Ellen.[78] This arrangement allowed frequent visits to and from his brother's family and other kin. He continued to escort his nieces on the road, and he continued to be stubborn about his plans. Paul wrote, "It is of no avail to say a sound, but just to let him do as he wishes without telling him so."[79] In the first week of 1870, he attended a dinner party with his brother-in-law George. Two weeks later, Thomas Cameron died from typhoid pneumonia at age 63. His death was sudden. His final week involved desperate medical treatments (quinine, "turpentine emulsion," sugar, chicken soup, wine, and blistering). At the end, he was "using laudanum, very freely," looking "restless . . . haggard and worn out."[80] Margaret and Paul and niece Maggie attended Thomas in his last hours.

The condolences sent to Margaret recall a dearly loved friend and a solid member of his family, his neighborhood, and larger social circles. Many emphasize his "life of piety & purity,"[81] which letter-writers were sure would gain his eternal reward and his reunion with loved ones gone before. George's sister Emma wrote a typical passage:

> With how much tender pity you will miss one to whom for so many years you have been as much a mother as a sister; who was as docile to you as a child, and with whom your word was a law of love. He lived a harmless and pure life, and performed all the duties he recognised, with a devotion well deserving our imitation.[82]

He was remembered as loving, kind, obedient, "ripe for the kingdom."[83] His faults were acknowledged, but only in the gentlest terms, and his good points were highlighted as worthy of imitation.

Thomas Cameron was buried in Raleigh among family members. His gravesite is marked with a handsome obelisk, similar to those nearby. The inscription quotes the beatitude, "Blessed are the pure in heart, for they shall see God." This Gospel reference is a common sight on gravestones of children and young women, but on the monument to a man who died in his sixties, it is unusual. Thomas's "pure and guileless" nature remained his most valued quality to those who loved him, even in death.[84]

Thomas Cameron's biography highlights the functional role of affection in a white southern family's life. The Camerons responded to Thomas's disability with resources that extended beyond their material wealth. With affection as the basis for their expectations, Thomas participated fully in family life, in all the ways they valued most: playing with his cousins, worrying over a sick nephew, escorting women on the road, carrying news between distant relations. Thomas Cameron received care, but he also returned care in sincere acts of service to his family. With affection as the primary criterion, any difficulties posed by Thomas's limits were minimized and his real strengths shone.

Knit from both power and affection were the support networks that proved crucial to Thomas Cameron's successful inclusion. In childhood, he benefited from the claims his father could make in the name of kinship. His brother Paul and sister

Margaret accepted their responsibilities for Thomas early in life and never seriously wavered in their commitment to his happiness. His neighborhood offered independence in the form of friendly companions, hospitable homes, and reasonably safe travel. In death, he prompted an outpouring of loving remembrances from widely dispersed acquaintances who were connected through a web of relationships to his mourning survivors.

With the depth and flexibility of these networks, the Camerons were equipped to accommodate Thomas's needs. As a child, he received the best education available in his era, through connections with kind educators who ensured loving treatment and stimulating, healthful environments. As an adult, his preferred routines and social behaviors were accepted, included in the plans of others, made useful rather than grinding in their predictability. When he was injured in 1837, the network yielded referrals to an oculist in Philadelphia; when he sought new clothing, the tailor in his circle could be trusted to offer him suits that met both his eccentric tastes and his more sober needs. He was not treated as a child but filled the valued role of "bachelor uncle," like his uncle Thomas Bennehan had before him: he was a handy extra man, someone who was trustworthy. He did not have the obligations of a household head, but he carried all the authority of his family's name and position.

Thomas Cameron's case is not a representative one. His story defines the upper reaches of what was possible, given all available resources (which, for the Camerons, rested upon and included the command of enslaved laborers), for a person with developmental disabilities within antebellum southern planter culture. It suggests that cognitive disability was not universally perceived as a terrible burden, not always hidden as shameful or embarrassing, in the early nineteenth century. Even later in the 1800s, when medical and reform literature began to portray people with disabilities as a threat to society, old ways remained in effect for Thomas Cameron. This study should encourage other research using family correspondence as a rich record of domestic lives around disability in the past.

Notes

1. Penny L. Richards, "'Beside Her Sat Her Idiot Child': Families and Developmental Disability in Mid-Nineteenth-Century America," in *Mental Retardation in America: A Historical Reader*, edited by Steven Noll and James Trent (New York: New York University Press, 2004).

2. Cherry Bamberg Fletcher, "Peleg Gifford's Tale," *Rhode Island History* 63 (Fall 2005): 51–68; Gudrun Hopf, "'Cretins' and 'Idiots' in an Austrian Alpine Valley in the Late 19th and Early 20th Centuries: Interests, Social Norms, and Institutions Involved in the Attribution of 'Imbecility,'" *Crime, History, and Societies* 3, no. 1 (1999): 5–27; Mark Jackson, "'It Begins with a Goose and Ends with a Goose': Medical, Legal, and Lay Understandings of Imbecility in *Ingram v. Wyatt*, 1824–1832," *Social History of Medicine* 11, no. 3 (1998): 361–380;

David Wright, "Getting Out of the Asylum: Understanding the Confinement of the Insane in the Nineteenth Century," *Social History of Medicine* 10, no. 1 (1997): 137–155; and Steven Noll, "Patient Records as Historical Stories: The Case of Caswell Training School," *Bulletin of the History of Medicine* 68, no. 3 (1994): 411–428.

3. Emily K. Abel, *Hearts of Wisdom: American Women Caring for Kin, 1850–1940* (Cambridge: Harvard University Press, 2000), 201–238.

4. A third context that highlights the social experience of disability is when a crime has been committed (and a trial record produced); see Douglas V. Shaw, "Infanticide in New Jersey: A Nineteenth-Century Case Study," *New Jersey History* 115 (Spring/Summer 1997): 3–31. Susan Burch and Hannah Joyner, *Unspeakable: The Story of Junius Wilson* (Chapel Hill: University of North Carolina Press, 2007) is a fine twentieth-century example, except that in Wilson's case the subject was never afforded a trial to record.

5. Laurel Thatcher Ulrich, "Derangement in the Family: The Story of Mary Sewall, 1824–25," in *Medicine and Healing: The Dublin Seminar for New England Folklife Annual Proceedings: 1990*, edited by Peter Benes (Boston: Boston University Press, 1992), 168–184; S. B. Thielman, "Community Management of Mental Disorders in Antebellum America," *Journal of the History of Medicine and Allied Sciences* 44, no. 3 (1989): 351–374. On "vernacular" sources, see Elizabeth Bredberg, "The History of Disability: Perspectives and Sources," *Disability Studies Quarterly* 17 (Spring 1997): 108–116.

6. Details are derived from family correspondence in the Cameron Family Papers, Southern Historical Collection, University of North Carolina at Chapel Hill, henceforth CFP, SHC-UNC and from additional information from the collection's unpublished guide (Marion Hirsch and Lisa Tolbert, compilers, "Cameron Family Papers: Inventory," June 1989, SHC-UNC) and from Jean Bradley Anderson, *Piedmont Plantation: The Bennehan-Cameron Family and Lands in North Carolina* (Durham, N.C.: Historical Preservation Society of Durham, 1985).

7. Willie Mangum to Duncan Cameron, October 5, 1814, CFP, SHC-UNC.

8. Mary Ann Cameron to Rebecca Cameron, May 5, 1815, CFP, SHC-UNC. Mary Ann was attending school in Warrenton, N.C.; Penny L. Richards, "'A Thousand Images, Painfully Pleasing': Complicating Histories of the Mordecai School, Warrenton, North Carolina, 1809–1818" (PhD diss., UNC-Chapel Hill, 1996), 84–94.

9. In *Jefferson, the Virginian* (Boston: Little Brown & Co. 1948), 38, 116–117, 165, Dumas Malone calls Elizabeth "unfortunate," "sad," and "subnormal" and says she "wandered in both body and mind." Fawn M. Brodie calls Elizabeth "retarded," and "rather deficient in intellect"; see *Thomas Jefferson: An Intimate History* (New York: W. W. Norton & Co., 1974), 70–71. See also Page Smith, *Jefferson: A Revealing Biography* (New York: American Heritage Publishing Co., 1976), 12.

10. Norman K. Risjord, *Thomas Jefferson* (Madison, Wisc.: Madison House, 1994), 4. The best source on Randolph Jefferson is Bernard Mayo, ed., *Thomas Jefferson and His Unknown Brother* (Charlottesville: University Press of Virginia, 1981). See also Dumas Malone, *The Sage of Monticello* (Boston: Little Brown & Co., 1981), 153–156.

11. These criteria were first applied in Penny L. Richards and George H. S. Singer, "'To Draw out the Effort of His Mind': Educating a Child with Mental Retardation in Early-Nineteenth-Century America," *Journal of Special Education* 31, no. 4 (1998): 443–466.

12. I. Hecht and F. Hecht, "Mara and Benomi Buck: Familial Mental Retardation in Colonial Jamestown," *Journal of the History of Medicine and Allied Sciences* 28, no. 2 (1973): 171–176.

13. Anya Jabour, "Masculinity and Adolescence in Antebellum America: Robert Wirt at West Point, 1820–1821," *Journal of Family History* 23, no. 4 (1998): 393–416; Jan Price Greenough, "'Forgive Us Our Sins': Rule and Misrule in Antebellum Southern Schools," *Southern Historian* 21 (Spring 2000): 5–24; Robert F. Pace and Christopher A. Bjornsen, "Adolescent Honor and College Student Behavior in the Old South," *Southern Culture* 6 (Fall 2000): 9–28.

14. E. B. Williston to Duncan Cameron, June 19, 1824, CFP, SHC-UNC.

15. Duncan Cameron to Thomas Ruffin, April 24, 1820, Thomas Ruffin Papers, SHC-UNC, reproduced in J. G. deRoulhac Hamilton, ed., *The Papers of Thomas Ruffin*, vol. 1 (Raleigh: North Carolina Historical Commission, 1918), 234–235: "I . . . place my son Thomas at a school in a colder climate, than that in which we live, in the fond hope that his muscular strength will be increased, and his mental faculties invigorated." See also David N. Livingstone, "The Moral Discourse of Climate: Historical Considerations on Race, Place, and Virtue," *Journal of Historical Geography* 17, no. 4 (1991): 413–434; M. A. Stewart, "'Let us begin with the weather': Climate, Race, and Cultural Distinctiveness in the American South," in *Nature and Society in Historical Context*, edited by Mikulas Teich, Roy Porter, and Bo Gustafsson (Cambridge: Cambridge University Press, 1997), 240–256.

16. E. B. Williston to Duncan Cameron, June 19, 1824, CFP, SHC-UNC.

17. The poem quoted in the epigraph, "Affection's Triumphs," depicts the triumph of Affection over Ambition; see also Anya Jabour, "Albums of Affection: Female Friendship and Coming to Age in Antebellum Virginia," *Virginia Magazine of History and Biography* 107, no. 2 (1999): 125–158.

18. Robert C. Kenzer, *Kinship and Neighborhood in a Southern Community: Orange County, North Carolina, 1849–1881* (Knoxville: University of Tennessee Press, 1987); also Joan Cashin, "The Structure of Antebellum Planter Families: 'The Ties That Bound Us Was Strong,'" *Journal of Southern History* 56 (February 1990): 55–70; Jane Turner Censer, *North Carolina Planters and Their Children, 1800–1860* (Baton Rouge: Louisiana State University Press, 1984); Lorri Glover, *All Our Relations: Blood Ties and Emotional Bonds among the Early South Carolina Gentry* (Baltimore, Md.: Johns Hopkins University Press 2000); and Anya Jabour, "Male Friendship and Masculinity in the Early National South: William Wirt and His Friends," *Journal of the Early Republic* 20, no. 1 (2000): 83–111.

19. F. Rudolph, *Curriculum: A History of the American Undergraduate Course of Study since 1636* (New York: Jossey-Bass, 1977).

20. David L. Angus, Jeffrey L. Mirel, and Maris A. Vinovskis, "Historical Development of Age Stratification in Schooling," *Teachers College Record* 90 (Winter 1988): 211–236.

21. Joseph Conan Thompson, "Willie Person Mangum: Politics and Pragmatism in the Age of Jackson" (PhD diss., University of Florida, 1995).

22. Rev. John Cameron to Rebecca Bennehan Cameron, December 16, 1813, CFP; Rebecca Bennehan Cameron to Duncan Cameron, November 8, 1813, CFP.

23. Mary Read Anderson to Duncan Cameron, February 21, 1814, CFP.

24. Rev. John Cameron to Duncan Cameron, December 31, 1813, CFP.

25. Cashin, "The Structure of Antebellum Planter Families."

26. John A. Cameron to Duncan Cameron, February 1, 1816, CFP.

27. Dell Upton, "Lancasterian Schools, Republican Citizenship, and the Spatial Imagination in Early Nineteenth-Century America," *Journal of the Society of Architectural Historians* 55, no. 3 (1996): 238–257; David Hogan, "Modes of Discipline: Affective Individualism and Pedagogical Reform in New England, 1820–1850," *American Journal of Education* 99, no. 1 (1990): 1–56; James McLachlan, *American Boarding Schools: A Historical Study* (New York: Charles Scribner's Sons, 1970); and Carl F. Kaestle, ed., *Joseph Lancaster and the Monitorial School Movement: A Documentary History* (New York, 1973). See also Thomas Church Brownell to Duncan Cameron, April 11, 1825, CFP, SHC-UNC: "In a day or two I shall take him to Windsor . . . for the purpose of placing him in a school conducted by two very judicious instructors on the Fillemberg [*sic*] plan."

28. Quoted in *St. John's Church, Elizabeth, New Jersey Two Hundred and Fiftieth Anniversary: Historical Brochure, 1706–1956* (Elizabeth, N.J.: s.n., 1956), 16.

29. James D. Johnson to Duncan Cameron, January 23, 1823, CFP.

30. James Hamilton to DC, October 18, 1823, CFP.

31. John C. Rudd to Duncan Cameron, December 21, 1820, CFP.

32. John C. Rudd to Duncan Cameron, May 24, 1822, CFP.

33. John C. Rudd to Duncan Cameron, May 29, 1822; John C. Rudd to Duncan Cameron, June 8, 1821, both CFP.

34. John C. Rudd to Duncan Cameron, March 15, 1822, CFP.

35. John C. Rudd to Duncan Cameron, June 13, 1822; John C. Rudd to Duncan Cameron, March 15, 1822, both CFP.

36. John C. Rudd to Duncan Cameron, December 21, 1820; John C. Rudd to Duncan Cameron, August 12, 1820, both CFP.

37. John C. Rudd to Duncan Cameron, July 9, 1823; John C. Rudd to Duncan Cameron, November 20, 1823, both CFP.

38. Dean Paul Baker, "The Partridge Connection: Alden Partridge and Southern Military Education" (PhD diss., University of North Carolina at Chapel Hill, 1996); Gary Thomas Lord, "Alden Partridge's Proposal for a National System of Education: A Model for the Morrill Land-Grant Act," *History of Higher Education Annual* 18 (1998).

39. Thomas Dudley Bennehan to Duncan Cameron, May 10, 1824, CFP.

40. Duncan Cameron to Capt. Alden Partridge, January 20, 1824, CFP.

41. Duncan Cameron to Thomas Bennehan, April 23, 1824, CFP.

42. E. B. Williston to Duncan Cameron, May 16, 1824, CFP.

43. Paul C. Cameron to Mary Ann Cameron, July 1825, CFP.

44. Censer, *North Carolina Planters and Their Children*, 58; Richards, "'A Thousand Images, Painfully Pleasing,'" 56–58.

45. W. E. Anderson to Duncan Cameron, December 1825, CFP.

46. E. B. Williston to Duncan Cameron, May 16, 1824, CFP. See also Lorri Glover, "An Education in Southern Masculinity: The Ball Family of South Carolina in the New Republic," *Journal of Southern History* 69, no. 1 (2003): 39–70.

47. Paul C. Cameron to Duncan Cameron, February 16, 1826, CFP.

48. J. Holbrook to Duncan Cameron, January 6, 1825; Paul C. Cameron to Duncan Cameron, February 16, 1826, both CFP.

49. Thomas A. Cameron to Duncan Cameron, September 25, 1826, CFP.

50. Anne Ruffin Cameron to Paul C. Cameron, January 20, 1850, CFP. On honorific titles held by lesser sons in plantation society, see Bertram Wyatt-Brown, *Southern Honor: Ethics and Behavior in the Old South* (Oxford: Oxford University Press, 1983), 354–355.

51. Anne Ruffin Cameron to Paul C. Cameron, December 26, 1845; Paul Cameron to Duncan Cameron, May 17, 1845, both CFP.

52. Mildred Cameron to Paul C. Cameron, January 18, 1845; Paul C. Cameron to his sisters, November 15, 1849; Paul C. Cameron to his sisters, February 8, 1844, all CFP.

53. Paul C. Cameron to Duncan Cameron, August 26, 1842; Anne Ruffin Cameron to Paul C. Cameron, December 26, 1845; Paul C. Cameron to Duncan Cameron, December 30, 1845; Anne Ruffin Cameron to Paul C. Cameron, January 10, 1845 (but may be 1846), all CFP.

54. Paul C. Cameron to Rebecca Bennehan Cameron, June 29, 1840; Paul C. Cameron to Duncan Cameron, November 6, 1839, both CFP.

55. Hirsch and Tolbert, "Cameron Family Papers: Inventory." Subseries 5.5 of the Cameron Family Papers concerns the Stagville Post Office.

56. M. McL. Bryant to Mildred Cameron, October 21, 1848; Paul C. Cameron to Duncan Cameron, October 12, 1848; Paul C. Cameron to Duncan Cameron, November 30, 1847, all CFP.

57. Mary Ann Cameron to Paul C. Cameron, June 26, 1836; Thomas Dudley Bennehan to Duncan Cameron, October 10, 1844; Paul C. Cameron to Duncan Cameron, November 30, 1848; Paul C. Cameron to Rebecca Bennehan Cameron, September 16, 1836; Paul C. Cameron to Margaret B. Cameron, July 7, 1848; R. Hooker to Paul C. Cameron, December 10, 1836, all CFP.

58. Paul C. Cameron to Duncan Cameron, July 12, 1848; and Paul C. Cameron to Duncan Cameron, July 31, 1848, both CFP. Duncan Cameron was "an unswerving Federalist," a mentor to Willie P. Mangum, and a longtime Whig member of Congress; see Jean Bradley Anderson, *Durham County* (Durham, N.C.: Duke University Press, 1990), 77. Paul Cameron is listed among the "prominent Whigs who bolted to the Democrats" in 1855; see Thomas E. Jeffrey, *State Parties and National Politics: North Carolina, 1815–1861* (Athens: University of Georgia Press, 1989), 249. Kenzer discusses Whig/Democratic politics in an antebellum Orange County in *Kinship and Neighborhood in a Southern Community*, 52–70. In the 1840s, the Whig Party in North Carolina was accused of being controlled by a "Hillsboro-Raleigh clique"; see Michael F. Holt, *The Rise and Fall of the American Whig Party: Jacksonian Politics and the Onset of the Civil War* (New York: Oxford University Press, 1999): 391–392; and Hugh Talmadge Lefler and Albert Ray Newsome, *North Carolina: The History of a Southern State* (Chapel Hill: University of North Carolina Press, 1963): 357. Drew Gilpin Faust, analyzes such political "cliques" in *A Sacred Circle: The Dilemma of the Intellectual in the Old South, 1840–1860* (Baltimore, Md.: Johns Hopkins University Press, 1977).

59. Ballots in antebellum North Carolina were frequently cast in the midst of drinking, dancing, sports, speeches, and feasts that were sponsored by candidates to woo voters.

See Kenzer, *Kinship and Neighborhood in a Southern Community*, 58–62, on electoral "treating"; Guion Griffis Johnson, *Antebellum North Carolina: A Social History* (Chapel Hill: University of North Carolina Press, 1937), 104–105; and Lefler and Newsome, *North Carolina*, 344.

60. Work on bachelorhood in the early republic and antebellum periods has begun to emerge. See especially John Gilbert McCurdy, "'Your Affectionate Brother': Complementary Manhoods in the Letters of John and Timothy Pickering," *Early American Studies* 4, no. 2 (2006): 512–545. John Pickering had epilepsy and remained a bachelor at home in Massachusetts, looking after his parents and widowed sisters. Timothy married, went to war, and had an illustrious career in Washington, D.C. See also Vincent J. Bertolini, "Fireside Chastity: The Erotics of Sentimental Bachelorhood in the 1850s," *American Literature* 68, no. 4 (1996): 707–737; and Howard P. Chudacoff, *The Age of the Bachelor: Creating an American Subculture* (Princeton, N.J.: Princeton University Press, 1999).

61. Paul C. Cameron to Thomas Ruffin, September 6[?], 1837, Thomas Ruffin Papers, SHC-UNC.

62. Paul C. Cameron to Thomas Ruffin, September 13, 1837, Thomas Ruffin Papers, SHC-UNC.

63. While there is no mention of such issues in relation to this event in the family papers, the Camerons were heavily and visibly involved in the railroads, which received a new commitment of state aid in 1837. Thomas could have been attacked because of resentment of the tax increases required for such support. See Lefler and Newsome, *North Carolina*, 347, 355.

64. Duncan Cameron to Paul C. Cameron, September 5, 1837, CFP.

65. Thomas Ruffin to Anne M. Ruffin, September 9, 1835, Thomas Ruffin Papers, SHC-UNC (text also available in Hamilton, *The Papers of Thomas Ruffin*, 2:145–147.

66. Report written by Dr. Isaac Hays, November 1, 1837, CFP; Anne Ruffin Cameron to Mrs. Thomas Ruffin, September 9, 1837, Thomas Ruffin Papers, SHC-UNC.

67. Hirsch and Tolbert, "Cameron Family Papers: Inventory."

68. Paul C. Cameron to Thomas Ruffin, August 17, 1851, Thomas Ruffin Papers, SHC-UNC, text reprinted in Hamilton, *The Papers of Thomas Ruffin*, 2:312–313: "He makes some improvement in his powers of locomotion, but as yet he is not willing, I fear hardly able, to walk by himself. No improvement as yet in the left arm. I think the *hand* exhibits a more *life*like appearance."

69. Paul C. Cameron to Margaret Cameron Mordecai, May 16 and 21, 1853; Paul C. Cameron to Col. Roulhac, November 15, 1854; Paul C. Cameron to Margaret Cameron Mordecai and Mildred C. Cameron, February 1, 1855; Paul C. Cameron to Margaret B. Cameron, April 21, 1853, all CFP.

70. Margaret Cameron Mordecai to Paul C. Cameron, February 25, 1856, CFP.

71. Paul C. Cameron to Margaret Cameron Mordecai and Mildred Cameron, February 27, 1856, CFP.

72. William E. Anderson to Margaret Cameron Mordecai, December 6, 1855, CFP.

73. Rebecca Cameron to George W. Mordecai, March 2, 1863; Anne Cameron Collins to Anne Ruffin Cameron, February 6, 1870, both CFP.

74. Paul Cameron, George Mordecai, and Thomas Ruffin had to appeal individually for reinstatement of their citizenship because their positions during the Confederacy

left them out of the general amnesty. See Paul C. Cameron to Thomas Ruffin, September 15 and October 4, 1865, Thomas Ruffin Papers, SHC-UNC, reprinted in J. G. deRoulhac Hamilton, ed., *The Papers of Thomas Ruffin*, vol. 4 (Raleigh: North Carolina Historical Commission, 1920), 26, 35.

75. Rebecca Cameron to George W. and Margaret Cameron Mordecai, March 2 and 27 and April 13, 1863, CFP, SHC-UNC.

76. Paul C. Cameron to Margaret Cameron Mordecai, June 25, 1862, CFP, SHC-UNC.

77. Rebecca Cameron Anderson to Margaret Cameron Mordecai, March 24, 1865; Paul C. Cameron to George W. Mordecai, June 25, 1864, both CFP, SHC-UNC.

78. Cameron family holdings were not destroyed by Union troops, although there was some looting and the horses at Stagville were appropriated for the use of northern soldiers, according to Abner Jordan, a slave at the plantation in 1865. See George P. Rawick, ed., *Born into Slavery: Slave Narratives from the Federal Writers' Project, 1936–38: North Carolina Narratives*, vol. XI, part 2 (Washington, D.C.: Library of Congress, 2000), 36, http://memory .loc.gov/cgi-bin/ampage?collId=mesn&fileName=112/mesn112.db&recNum=0. Fairntosh remained in the hands of Cameron descendants until the 1970s. Stagville is now a historical site with archaeological and educational programs, including displays on the Cameron family and plantation life. See Kenzer, *Kinship and Neighborhood in a Southern Community*, 94.

79. Paul C. Cameron to Margaret Cameron Mordecai, July 30, 1869, CFP, SHC-UNC.

80. George W. Mordecai to Paul C. Cameron, January 19, 1870, and Maggie Cameron to Anne Ruffin Cameron, January 20, 1870, both CFP, SHC-UNC.

81. Rebecca Cameron Graham to Margaret Cameron Mordecai, January 22, 1870, CFP.

82. Emma Mordecai to Margaret Cameron Mordecai, January 23, 1870, CFP.

83. Mary J. Lucas to Margaret Cameron Mordecai, January 26, 1870, CFP.

84. Margaret Cameron Mordecai to Paul C. Cameron, April 11, 1870, CFP.

CHAPTER 3

Parents and Professionals

Parents' Reflections on Professionals,
the Support System, and the Family
in the Twentieth-Century United States

ALLISON C. CAREY

KEYWORDS: *Centuries*: twentieth; twenty-first; *Geographical Areas*: North America; *Sources*: memoirs; *Themes*: citizenship and belonging; bodies, medicine, contested knowledge; family, daily life, and community; activism

Since the 1950s, parents of children with disabilities have fought to increase access to quality professional services to support their children and families and help them attain a high quality of life. In scholarship focusing on parent involvement, we often see polarized depictions of parents as either vigilantes who challenge the system or collaborators who are complicit in a medical ableist system of normalization. Increasingly though, scholars are recognizing that parents do not fit such simple categories.[1] Parents negotiate with experts to access the benefits of professional expertise while trying to avoid potential negative outcomes such as usurpation of parental authority or the imposition of demands they consider unreasonable.[2] Drawing upon fourteen memoirs published by parents of children with intellectual disability from 1950 to 1989 primarily in the United States (one author resides in Canada and another in Britain), this chapter examines parents' expressions of how their intimate family lives are shaped by interaction with professionals and how they seek to access, challenge, and reform professional attitudes, practices, and systems to better meet their families' needs.[3]

Memoirs offer an exciting opportunity to examine parents' voices in disability history. These voices are often overlooked because many histories rely extensively on sources produced by professionals. The memoirs I analyze are not necessarily accurate depictions of the events they describe, nor are they representative of the experiences of parents of children with intellectual disabilities.[4] Rather, they represent the attempts of a small set of parents to shape the public discourse related to disability, the family, and the community. When taken in this light, these memoirs offer insight into a significant modern form of activism among parents with children with intellectual disabilities. In the analysis of any data source, we must give particular attention to the workings of privilege.[5] These memoirs were written by parents who were financially secure, well educated, white, living in nuclear families (at least when the children were born, although some later divorced), and living in wealthy, democratic nations. Thus, these parents had the resources that allowed them to access, assess, and criticize the systems with which they interacted and to use memoir as a form of activism. As will be seen, although they at times recognized their own privileged position, more often than not they failed to consider how race, class, education, and their position as nondisabled parents affected their experiences and perspectives.

While these memoirs provide a rich source of data on numerous topics, this chapter focuses on the perceived relationship between parents and the world of professionals. These stories reveal the tension parents experienced as they sought helpful professional expertise yet also had to contend with professional neglect, prejudice, and claims to authority that dismissed parents' basis of authority. As the service system developed through the 1970s and 80s, this tension heightened as the opportunities to benefit from professional intervention expanded but so did the invasiveness and reach of professional systems in shaping the private lives of families. Parents found themselves struggling against the intrusion into the family by increasingly inflexible and often ineffective professionalized, medicalized, and bureaucratized systems. By revealing and exploring this tension over time, this analysis moves beyond depictions of parents simply as compliant with or resistant to medical/professional regimes and adds necessary historical nuance to understandings of the relationship between family, professionals, and service systems over time.

Acceptance of and Resistance
to Medical Expertise and Institutionalization

In the late nineteenth and early twentieth centuries, mothers were increasingly expected to follow the direction of physicians and professional childcare experts in order to harness the power of science and technology in raising their children, a trend referred to as scientific motherhood. Scientific motherhood elevated motherhood to the status of a profession in an era when industrialization and emerging technology threatened to devalue the importance of nurture. Simultaneously, for some women it threatened to reduce their own symbolic status as childcare experts and to place blame upon them for the failures of their children.[6] Unlike most parents, parents of children with intellectual disabilities found themselves in a particular quandary: professionals labeled their children as deficient, yet largely dismissed the ability of parents to help them. Leading experts of the day, influenced by eugenic thinking, depicted intellectual disability as a genetic deficiency that caused deviance and degeneracy.[7] Because professionals assumed that feeblemindedness was inherited, parents were directly implicated in any deficiencies and the social problems associated with them. Even after the popularity of eugenics dissipated, through the 1950s and 60s many physicians continued to stigmatize children with intellectual disabilities and their families, offering a bleak prognosis, providing little guidance or support for families rearing their child at home, and recommending institutionalization, especially for children with Down syndrome, even though long wait lists precluded many parents from following this advice.[8] Thus, whereas scholars note how the new regimes of expert advice constrained mothers by demanding that they parent in particular ways, parents of children with intellectual disabilities faced a different kind of constraint: the lack of useful professional guidance to help them raise their child at home and thereby attain the valued position of a mother who was adeptly raising and nurturing her child. Instead, many parents were presented with the "choice" of relinquishing their parental roles to institutional staff who provided little actual nurture or medical treatment or raising their child at home with little or no public or professional support. It may not be surprising that by the 1950s, when both the medical profession and the ideology of scientific motherhood were at the height of their prestige, parents of children with intellectual disabilities longed for effective professional support and offered sharp resistance to much of the medical expertise they actually encountered.

The memoirists who placed their children in institutions by no means offered total compliance with medical professionals. Historian Janice Brockley argues that institutions represented both a resource and a restriction to parents.[9] Some of the earliest authors in this set of memoirs accepted the medical opinion given to them, including the need for institutionalization, yet still criticized the general state of medical care for people with intellectual disabilities. For example, Pearl Buck (1950) deeply appreciated receiving medical confirmation that her daughter Carol would "never be normal," and she sought out a high-quality residential facility to provide care to Carol.[10] Buck explicitly acknowledged that her financial stability allowed her to identify highly qualified doctors, secure a placement for Carol at a prestigious private institution, and continue to actively engage in her maternal role through frequent visits. Instead of recommending compliance, she urged parents to be critical consumers of medical advice and warned them against the ignorance and bad advice many doctors offered. She explicitly condemned the state of most institutions, referring to one that she visited as "an abode of horror" where the patients were "herded together like dogs."[11]

John Frank (1952) also trusted his doctors when they told him that his son Peter had "no future."[12] Frank and his family doctor worked together to locate an institution and convince Frank's wife that she should accept the need for Peter's institutionalization despite her fervent desire to keep her son at home. In his memoir, Frank advised parents to find the best medical advice they could; however, like Buck, he acknowledged that high-quality medical care was more than most people could afford, complained that most affordable placements were completely unacceptable, and cautioned parents to beware of charlatans "who will promise miracles at high prices."[13] Frank counted himself among the few lucky parents who managed to secure a decent and affordable placement. He ended his book with a plea for reform to increase both the number of affordable institutions that supported the development of disabled children and the ability of parents to help their children. Both Frank and Buck knew that their access to high-quality residential care was rare and that most individuals with intellectual disabilities went without trustworthy medical care, whether they lived in an institution or at home.

Some parents challenged the medical profession after the promises of institutionalization were not realized. When Lucille Stout (1959) gave birth to a child with Down syndrome, she was told that her daughter Carol was "an institutional case and should be placed as soon as possible" and forgotten.[14] No information was available to support the concept of raising a child with Down syndrome at home, and Lucille and her husband saw no alternative to institutionalization. Instead of making family life normal, as promised, though, institutionalization devastated her family. Stout was wracked by guilt, her marriage became unhappy, and her eldest child was plagued with anxiety that he might also be abandoned should he disappoint his parents. Stout recalled, "Carol's existence was like a living death . . . a shadowy figure hovering on the outskirts of various family activities."[15] After taking a college course that explained positive strategies to support and educate "exceptional" children and attending meetings of the local parents' organization, Stout and her husband visited Carol and eventually reintegrated her into their home (after ten years of institutionalization), a decision that, according to Stout, enabled their family to finally recover from the "wounds of deceit" inflicted upon them by medical professionals. Stout expressed bitterness about the context of their decision to institutionalize. If they had had suitable counseling from the start, she believed, "Carol could have remained in the home without causing any more psychological harm to the family than had been done."[16] For Stout, it took ten years of heartache and access to an emerging community of parent activists and professionals who supported at-home care before she felt able to challenge professional advice.

In the 1960s and 1970s, horrific stories of abuse and neglect in institutions increasingly were published in the news, and authors publishing in the 1970s and 1980s no longer imagined that institutions would provide an ideal community, peer friendships, and lifelong happiness.[17] Despite this ideological shift, the paucity of community services still led some parents to reluctantly rely on the institutions. Josh Greenfeld had repeated nightmares in which he imagined his son, Noah, in an institution. He came to dread Noah's growth as they moved closer to a time when he would no longer be able to prevent Noah from engaging in self-destructive behavior or withstand Noah's physical abuse. Despite his fear and loathing of institutions and his recognition that institutionalization was not in Noah's best interest, Greenfeld eventually felt he had no other option and placed Noah in an institution, only to bring him home again after Noah experienced excessive aversive "therapy."

Similarly, Nicola Schaefer ([1978] 1999) dreaded the growth of her significantly disabled daughter, Catherine, as each pound seemed to make the provision of care more difficult.[18] Although Schaefer likened institutions to imprisonment and although she admitted that Catherine seemed to shut down whenever she stayed at the nearby institution, Schaefer relied on a local institution for temporary respite on several occasions. In the 1970s and early 1980s the Schaefers were not aware of any community-based residential services that served individuals with multiple significant disabilities, and long-term institutional placement loomed as a daunting threat to their family and their daughter. Professionals still classified individuals with multiple significant disabilities such as Noah and Catherine as appropriate clients for institutionalization.

Fern Kupfer's (1988) son, Zachariah, required 24-hour care, was frequently unhappy and unresponsive, had severe intellectual disabilities, and experienced serious medical complications that led to his death at the age of 16.[19] Whereas most authors faced a system that recommended institutionalization, Kupfer experienced the opposite. By the late 1970s, public policy had begun emphasizing community and home-based care, especially for children. Despite this philosophical commitment, the professional system failed to offer sufficient support for Zachariah's intensive needs. Unable to handle the care demands, Kupfer sought institutional placement but was repeatedly denied. To Kupfer, the state enforced what she perceived as imprisonment by enforcing family care without providing adequate support services. Kupfer saw the trend away from residential placement as something that narrowed an already impossibly slim range of options for mothers who had tremendous caregiving responsibilities while making them feel more guilt about seeking placement. While she expressed more optimism than Greenfeld or Schaefer about the care Zachariah would receive in an institution, she also acknowledged the potential conflict of interests between her interests and Zach's. Like the other authors, Kupfer criticized the dilapidated conditions of many institutions. She eventually secured a placement for Zachariah at a private facility.

Kupfer's memoir was highly controversial due to its advocacy of institutional placement for young children, especially because it was published in 1982, when the dominant philosophy rejected institutionalization. Although six of these authors placed their children for some time in institutions, Kupfer is the only author after the 1950s who actively defended institutional care. In this respect her memoir is quite different from the other memoirs written in the 1970s and 80s. However, in other ways, her memoir is very similar to the others. It speaks of the failure of community services to provide adequately for children such as Zach who have significant and life-threatening medical complications and the devastating impact on families who face intense pressures to provide care and to strive toward the goals of normalization and self-determination in the absence of basic, appropriate services and support.

Considered collectively, these parents did not simply comply with or reject medical expertise or institutional care. Rather, they tried their best to negotiate the medical, institutional, and community service systems to meet the needs of their disabled offspring in a context of limited options. They accepted some forms of assistance and rejected and/or criticized other forms. They all wrote in part to call public attention to the fact that the choices offered by professionals and the service system failed to meet their needs and at times even pitted the needs of parents against those of their children. They also acknowledged that they were privileged in comparison to most parents. If they found it challenging to find resources and useful support, then those dilemmas were likely magnified for the vast majority of other parents.

Acceptance and Resistance: Advocating for Community, Home-Based Care

For many parents, the primary problem of institutionalization was not the lack of placements or the quality of care but the fact that the dominance of institutionalization enforced the devaluation of their children and led to limited services in the community. Those who sought to keep their disabled child at home tended to be more critical of medical professionals than those who chose to use institutional care. Parents in the former group felt that the majority of medical professionals were at best useless and at worst an obstacle to their family's efforts to find a fulfilling life with a disabled child at home. For these parents, acceptance of their child and the establishment of a happy family too often required them to dismiss the expertise of medical professionals and discover for themselves the attributes of their child and how best to integrate their child into the family.

Parents of children with Down syndrome were some of the first parents of children with intellectual disabilities to offer a strong and direct challenge to the medical community's role in childrearing, most likely because they were confronted with medical prejudice almost immediately at the birth of their child and still in the 1960s were most often advised to institutionalize their child early in his or her life.[20] For example, when Nigel Hunt was born in 1947, his parents were told soon thereafter that regardless of how much effort they exerted, their son would always be an "idiot."[21] Despite this prognosis, Nigel grew up able to read, write, travel, and make friends, serving as living proof of the error of medical prognosis. His father, Douglas Hunt (1967), assured parents "that the 'experts' are often wrong and that almost all defective children are capable of being taught a great deal more than people care to admit."[22] Similarly, in the 1940s doctors told Sophia Grant (1957) that her son would never learn or go to school.[23] However, Grant demonstrated that through a rigorous routine of home education he could learn basic math and reading, some French, and to play the piano. Like Hunt's statement, Grant's condemnation of the medical profession was explicit and harsh: "People do not know what to do, and yet they have the audacity to give such authoritative and final advice to the distracted mothers who come to them. . . . A word of comfort here, mothers. Don't let them get you down, for they have not the slightest idea what to do with these mentally retarded children. In fact, it is a waste of time to consult them."[24] Even as late as 1970, when Claire Canning (1975) gave birth to a baby with Down syndrome, doctors told her that there was no hope of incorporating her daughter Martha into her family and that she should immediately place her in an institution.[25] Canning defied this advice and wrote her story in part to publicize a successful story of a family who kept their disabled child at home.

Even parents who praised their own doctors for offering useful advice about raising their children at home warned parents, as Buck and Frank had, of the preponderance of medical professionals who were ignorant, prejudiced, and/or charlatans. For example, Dale Evans Rogers (1953), who relied heavily on a skilled medical team to treat her daughter's medical concerns and employed a live-in nurse, sharply criticized the medical community for their devaluation of the lives of children with disabilities.[26] Nancy Roberts (1968) praised her own doctor's honest and helpful approach but cautioned that "the scientific approach unaccompanied by appreciation of spiritual values inherently contains the seeds of the violation of human dignity."[27] Summarizing the situation in 1982, Martha Jablow stated, "The medical profession still has a long way to go in accepting a retarded child as a full human being with the same rights as everyone else."[28] Like parents who chose institutionalization, these parents cautiously used medical advice when it was helpful and dismissed advice that was not helpful.

More than simply using or not using the advice offered, parents sought to re-form the medical profession and the service system for families of children with intellectual disabilities. Most important, all of these parents challenged the notion that their child had no value and deserved no assistance. To showcase the worth of their children and dispel negative stereotypes, parents proudly described them as beautiful, happy, and loving; able to adapt to family life; independent and able to learn; capable of employment; as spiritual people; and as capable of function-ing in the community. Parents also commonly argued that their children had the capacity to teach others valuable lessons. Roberts stated, "I am not always sure who is educating whom! While we are trying to train and teach David, I have the strange feeling that we are receiving instruction from him."[29] These lessons or gifts included patience, gratitude, the joy of living, respect for humanity and diversity, and acceptance of God's plan.

According to these authors, these children were not that different from other children, nor were they inevitably "tragedies." Claire Canning, who explicitly set out to write "a hopeful story of mental retardation" to help families understand and appreciate children with Down syndrome, opened her book by describing Martha as a gift.[30] Jane Bernstein (1988) ended her memoir with the affirming sentiment, "I can no longer imagine my life without you."[31] By accepting a disabled child, these families had grown richer and more vibrant. They hoped that the public and professionals would not only see this point but also extend it: a community that accepts disabled children and their families would be enriched, not burdened, by their presence.

Parents resisted stereotypes regarding their families by showcasing the role of a disabled child at home in *creating* a happy family. After integrating her daughter back into their family after ten years of institutionalization, Stout proclaimed, "I feel sure she is making their [Carol's siblings] lives richer, and they will be better adults for having had a sister like Carol."[32] Hunt described the "untold joy" of par-enting Nigel and how they probably faced fewer problems than parents of most "modern teenagers."[33] Canning glowingly stated that Martha played the "special role" in her family of always offering love, and Schaefer described their family life as "richer" because of the presence of Catherine.[34]

In addition to highlighting their positive experiences, parents wrote about the challenges their families faced. Mothers in particular felt a heavy responsibility day after day, hour after hour. After her husband left for work one day, Bernstein poi-gnantly cried, "She is mine alone, my sightless child, my problem."[35] Male authors, including Frank and Greenfeld, noted the particular strains on women because of the gendered expectations about childcare, but they also described stressors on their own health, relationships, and careers. Greenfeld even began to document the frequency that fathers with disabled children developed debilitating diseases. Kupfer and Greenfeld, who had children with particularly challenging disabilities, often spoke of the severe physical and mental strain they experienced and of the loss of their ambitions. Several memoirists spoke of marital tensions and of the strains on siblings.[36]

While these discussions might be interpreted as contributing to a discourse on the "burden" of disability, they do not typically blame the child with the disability for these problems. Rather, the overriding view is that people with disabilities are essential members of our families, communities, and nations who are worthy of care, love, respect, and support. To the extent there is tragedy or burden, it arises largely from an unsupportive society that stigmatizes and abandons individuals and families in need. This common storyline raises awareness of the problems families face in raising children with disabilities in order to secure greater social support.

The Emergence of Therapies

In the 1970s, the feminist movement and popular criticisms of the medical profession encouraged mothers to question medical intervention and reclaim their own expertise. Ironically, mothers of children with intellectual disabilities were finally gaining systematic access to public education, community-based services, and more effective medical therapies such as speech and physical therapy, giving them more reason to comply with the advice of professionals. Parents had dreamed of medical professionals who would provide useful therapy and guidance to support them in fulfilling their parental role, and the emergence of the expanded array of health professionals and therapies in the 1970s and 1980s seemed a step toward the realization of this dream. The new therapies were based on the philosophy that children with disabilities could learn, they offered far more tangible benefits than prior medical interventions had, and they could be implemented both in residential facilities and at home. Many parents were eager to work with experts toward the goal of improving the well-being and "normalization" of their children.

Despite the newfound benefits of medical partnership, memoirists felt the contradictions of engaging with professionals. First, allying with professionals created significant concerns for parents because professionals expected them to serve as extensions of the medical/therapeutic professions and to transform their homes into sites of therapeutic practice. As new community-based interventions developed, the concept of "intensive mothering" of parents of children with intellectual disabilities was born, in which parents, especially mothers, were expected to ensure the success of their children.[37] Professionals typically defined success for children with disabilities as the achievement of "normalized" and "well-adapted" behaviors. Kupfer complained that programs put "virtually all the responsibility for physical therapy on the parents—really the mother."[38] Bernstein found herself responsible for administering daily injections to her daughter and performing a litany of "infant stimulation" exercises at home, and Greenfeld discussed the tremendous pressures to "work" with his son, Noah. These responsibilities transformed parental roles, leading Bernstein to note sadly that she spent her time "working," rather than playing, with her daughter.

Parents were also given tremendous responsibility for identifying, coordinating, and carrying out therapeutic regimens. For example, although Schaefer was overjoyed to get hydrotherapy for her daughter, she received it only after she had identified and requested it and provided transportation to it. Parents also had to train therapists with limited exposure to children with particular disabilities. Schaefer summarized the overall situation: "The prevailing attitude towards parents who chose to care for seriously handicapped children at home was that they were expected to bear the full responsibility of management."[39]

Not only were parents expected to take on the roles of doctor, therapist, and care manager, they were expected to do so selflessly and endlessly. The new hope for development imposed expectations on parents to achieve the successful integration and normalization of their children, often still with very limited support. Scholars such as Amy Sousa and Linda Blum examine narratives in which mothers of children with disabilities portray themselves as "warrior-heroes" or "vigilantes" selflessly battling for their child's welfare against the system.[40] Interestingly, while the authors in the set of memoirs I analyze recognized this growing expectation, they advised parents to resist taking on that identity. For example, Kupfer reminded mothers that they too had lives worthy of living, and Jablow advised parents to "drop the martyr role" and take time for themselves.[41] Greenfeld stopped working with his son for long periods of time, admitting that at times he found the exercises too frustrating or fruitless. For parents, finding a balance between focusing on the child and focusing on their own needs was difficult and the expectation of selfless devotion was not easily dismissed; many of these memoirists devoted a tremendous amount of time and resources to their children yet expressed considerable guilt for not working more hours with them. Although these parents were often unable to take their own advice, they warned other parents about the path of selfless devotion and recognized the burden it placed on them.

These dilemmas must be situated in the context of privilege. The expectation that parents would identify, manage, and enact complex therapeutic regimes in their homes presupposed a level of education, financial security, and time flexibility that was unavailable to many parents. Thus, these dilemmas and the advice about finding balance were largely rooted in a middle-class perspective. Parents with low incomes, parents in racially segregated areas, or parents with little education would likely have been less able to meet these expectations. Moreover, they would have been more likely to face exclusion from therapeutic regimens because they lacked the resources to identify and take advantage of opportunities and because of physicians' beliefs about the inability of low-income and minority populations to comply with complex regimens of care.[42] Parents who did not have access to such care may have found themselves having to choose between public institutions and largely unsupported in-home care. Also, minority communities may have felt less desire or community pressure to interact with "experts."

Hence, from the 1950s through the 1980s the relationship between parents of children with disabilities and medical professionals was clouded by parents' uncertainty about the value of medical advice. Often right from their child's birth, parents' interactions with professionals were on troubled ground as they felt compelled to assess the validity of the advice of physicians and the values that guided it. In the 1970s, though, as potentially beneficial therapies became available in the community, parents were less ready to dismiss medical professionals as biased and ineffective. Through their engagement with the health care professions, families faced increasing pressure to become an extension of the public sphere, a place where professionals guided parent behavior and beliefs. In response, these memoirists expressed a need to resist such medicalization and retain the intimate and private aspects of family life at the same time that many of them sought the benefits of medical intervention. Public pressure on the family mounted with the concomitant expansion of "the system" through special education and other community services, to which we will now turn.

The Expanding Professional Service System

In addition to wanting the new therapies offered by health professionals, parents desired a holistic set of services and supports. Advocacy for more education for their children took center stage in the activism of parents, who had long been demanding a shift from a medical to an educational and developmental paradigm for their children. Parents hoped that access to quality education would usher in dramatic changes in the opportunities available to their children.[43] In the 1970s and 1980s, the community-based disability service system grew significantly as a result of activism and new laws. This growth corresponded with the growth of social services more broadly in the United States that was facilitated by social initiatives that included the War on Poverty, the Civil Rights Movement, and the broader application of civil rights frameworks by a variety of marginalized communities demanding equal rights to education, job opportunities, and community resources. The memoirs reflect this growth; later memoirists discuss a broader range of services and professionals who entered their lives that included social workers, counselors, special educators, and policy makers.

Memoirs written before the 1970s describe very meager community support systems that typically had no appropriate educational or community programs. In comparing her child's experience with that of a blind child, Stout (1959) complained, "There were schools for the blind. They could be trained to fill useful, productive places in life. There was public understanding and acceptance for the blind. But for my child there was nothing. *Nothing!!*"[44] Some parents even found it difficult to find books in the library on the subjects of retardation or Down syndrome. Parents particularly desired educational opportunities for their children, but they were rare and often disappointing before 1975, when legislation was passed that mandated the provision of public education for children with disabilities. For example, although Grant demanded that her son be allowed to attend public school, his teacher ignored him and the principal notified her that teachers "could not be bothered with children of Peter's caliber."[45] Grant withdrew him, and she became his full-time, at-home teacher. When her son learned material in many subjects, she realized that he had been excluded primarily because of his diagnosis of Down syndrome, not because of his actual limitations. Hunt described similar problems gaining access to a quality education for his son, Nigel. Hunt remembered that the school personnel at his son's "special" school took the "worst possible attitude" toward children with disabilities, assuming that they lacked skills, enforcing deficiencies, and allowing interaction only with other disabled children. Hunt moved his son to a private school where Nigel was accepted, challenged, and integrated with nondisabled children. Hunt noted that this was a rare opportunity since most schools would not accept a child with Down syndrome; it was offered to Nigel only because Hunt began working at the school.[46]

By the 1970s, education and community support for intellectually disabled children and their families were clearly expanding. Jablow's daughter, Cara, benefited from an experimental intensive early intervention program that began at the age of one month; later, she attended an integrated preschool. Cara went on to "shatter" the myth that children with Down syndrome could not learn.[47] Canning's daughter, who also had access to an innovative and rare program specifically for children with Down syndrome, also made substantial progress. Parents offered these stories as models of success and noted that access to appropriate education was still rare.

For many parents, education was hit or miss. Schaefer's daughter, Catherine, had multiple significant disabilities, and when she turned five in 1966 the Schaefers could not find schools or programs that would accept her. Through local organizing and political pressure on local officials, Schaefer succeeded in the early 1970s in forcing the school district to create a program to serve children with multiple handicaps. Schaefer frequently denounced the lack of educational services and wondered what Catherine might have accomplished if she had had access to effective early educational opportunities. Although Greenfeld's son, Noah, became school age after 1975, he still had difficulty finding an appropriate placement for him. At the opening of his memoir, Greenfeld complained that he had become completely disenchanted with both orthodox medicine and public education because the experts "neither really know nor genuinely begin to care."[48] The lack of quality public education heavily affected families: parents of children with disabilities had less time for themselves, they felt more pressure to take on the roles of educator and therapist, and they felt more guilt if they did not do so.

Social workers and counselors became common figures in the newly emerging community-based system of services. Parents told some positive stories of inter-actions with these professionals, such as when a social worker directed Bernstein to several useful programs, but they also told many negative ones. Social work-ers and counselors often were seen as offering little meaningful assistance and merely reinforcing the opinion of the establishment by burdening families with responsibility for the progress of disabled children. For example, when Greenfeld placed his son in a school for children with disabilities, he discovered that school policies actually mandated counseling for all parents. He and his wife were furious: "The assumption that any family who has a child like Noah must need counseling is abhorrent to us. It places the burden of responsibility—read, the assignation of guilt—back upon the parents."[49]

The problem was not just one of individual professionals; as the systems grew, the problems became institutionalized. In contrast to the problems created by the lack of services in the 1950s, memoirs from the 1970s and 1980s offer many examples of an increasingly inflexible, incomplete, and incomprehensible system. For example, although children with a single diagnosis may have had programs and services at their disposal, children with multiple disabilities were often excluded because they did not fit neatly into traditional categories. Programs for children who were blind or had cerebral palsy were considered inappropriate for children with intellectual disabilities, and programs for children with intellectual disabilities were unavailable to children with physical and sensory disabilities. Jablow described another policy catch-22: her daughter Cara was able to stay in her age-appropriate grade level with the support of intensive services but was then denied services when she tested on grade level.[50] Thus, the system guaranteed her failure because she lost her services every time she achieved grade level. Therapies and services, such as speech therapy, were often funded through the school district and therefore were only available to school-aged children, even though the need began earlier and extended after school age. Parents found that they had to spend time fighting for reimbursement, nego-tiating costs and benefits, and making educational decisions with teams who had decision-making authority regarding services. Even though families were formally asked to join in these decisions, there seemed little room for negotiation given the paucity of potential services and the authority of the professionals.[51] Whereas in the 1950s and 1960s family had been largely ignored and excluded, now professionals determined programs, peers, level of inclusion, and likely destinies.

Moreover, parents were still left with tremendous gaps in care and with the sig-nificant costs associated with the care and accommodations their children needed. Schaefer's family spent thousands of dollars for wheelchairs and accessibility features for their home and automobile, and Greenfeld noted the great expense of therapies and in-home care. Greenfeld also noted the frequent exclusion of children with severe disabilities from a variety of programs, a practice that disadvantaged the children with the greatest need. Greenfeld's and Kupfer's memoirs are notable for their focus on children with significant disabilities for whom the system offered very little. In a time when inclusion was being advocated, it went out of fashion, so to speak, to admit that some children were unlikely to become productive in typical ways; that some children were violent, poorly adjusted, or experienced mental health or medical problems along with intellectual disability; or that some families were breaking apart under the pressure. Kupfer called the constant talk among professionals of her son's "progress" nothing more than nonsense, and described him instead as experiencing an "eternity of babydom."[52] In sharp contrast to the other memoirists, Kupfer referred to herself as an "emotional amputee" and coined the term the "handicapped family" to describe families whose intense caregiving demands impeded their "normal" functioning.[53] Greenfeld too was at times shockingly honest about his negative feelings toward his son and his own despair: "I despair when I am with him. I want to get away from him, to get him out of my life."[54] Regarding his son's lack of progress, he said "for every step forward Noah takes, there is another one backward—and two to the side."[55]

Both Kupfer and Greenfeld expressed love for and devotion toward their children. Their negativity is not a condemnation of their children. It is a demand that society and professionals recognize that their children were unlikely to become productive members of society, their children were challenging, and their families were breaking apart. They deserved and needed support. These memoirs complicate the progress narrative typically used by professionals and the expectation that parents will cooperate in the use of this narrative. Kupfer and Greenfeld argued that professionals and providers of disability services needed to recognize and respect the range of individuals and families, not just the happy, productive, ideal ones.

Even problems in the system were supposed to be resolved through the "active" parent. Bernstein noted that while new mothers were dealing with issues of rage and denial, the "old hands were busy learning to operate within the system."[56] First, the public realm had invaded their households by demanding that parents serve as therapists and educators, and now they were being told that "good parents" advocated for their child and challenged the system. Ironically, the "good" parent had to simultaneously find services and partner with professionals *and* constantly challenge the system.

The expansion of services was supposed to be guided by respect for the family and offer them more options, but it brought the bureaucratization of the "system," a process that included institutionalized values and goals, bureaucratic policies and procedures, categorical eligibility, and funding streams. The system provided only piecemeal services, failed to meet the holistic needs of real families, often hindered the well-being of families, and invaded families' private lives and pushed responsibilities, expectations, values, and expenses on them.

Conclusion

In many ways, these memoirs represent and respond to the tension between public and private. Parents sought to benefit from access to professional systems as they simultaneously sought to defend their family from the invasiveness of these systems. This is a tension modern American families experience: parents are expected to raise their children to be productive and to harness the advice of childcare experts and a range of professionals to ensure this outcome. For parents of children with disabilities this pressure is particularly great and particularly problematic. In the era of institutionalization, parents faced the dilemmas of whether to comply with medical professionals who advised placing the child in an institutional setting or raise their child essentially without support. Parents in the 1970s and 1980s faced the more subtle but still challenging dilemma that arose when they sought out professionals who offered a more inclusive, supportive model of services yet needed to resist the increasing intrusion of professionals in their home life. In response to these issues, parents often treated professionals and the services they offered as a potential resource to be used or rejected as they strove for the well-being of their disabled child and their family. At times the interests of the disabled child and the parents aligned and at other times they did not. In either case, professionals became both a tool and point of resistance for parents.

This small set of memoirs reveals the variability and complexity of parent narratives regarding their relationships with professionals. As a set, these memoirists sought support from experts but insisted on the freedom to resist professional invasion in their intimate family lives and intrusion on their parental authority. They sought the creation of a comprehensive affordable accessible system of services yet wanted personalized, flexible care that was free from the rigidity of bureaucracy. They sought professionals who valued their children yet also recognized their feelings of loss and despair as legitimate. These tensions represent the dramatic manifestations of the modern family's dilemmas as it seeks to provide the highly idealized love, warmth, and privacy of family life for children yet must negotiate with the public sphere as represented by experts and bureaucracies.[57] This dilemma is heightened for families with disabled children because of the greater levels of professional intervention that often occur in the home and the historical and contemporary mistreatment of people with disabilities by the very systems and experts that are supposedly there to serve them.

In many ways, these memoirs demand that professionals be attentive to diversity, including (a) the diversity of children with intellectual disabilities, some of whom can perform on grade level and others of whom have skills so minimal that academic tests are meaningless, some of whom are relatively easy to raise and some of whom present significant challenges; (b) the diversity of disabilities, some of which manifest as a single disability and others that manifest in complex combinations or with unknown etiologies; and (c) the diversity of families, some of whom have seemingly boundless energy, joy, and resources and others of whom are depleted emotionally, physically, and/or financially, some of whom share values with the service system and some of whom do not. Yet these narratives fall far short of representing the broad range of diversity that exists. These middle-class, white, nuclear families benefited from their social and economic capital. The abilities of these families to identify services, critique those services, articulate their experiences, and create social change may be far greater than they are for many other families, whose interactions with professionals and social systems are more fraught with injustice, discrimination, and neglect yet whose need for support and services may be even greater. These authors also rarely attend to their privilege as parents without disabilities and the ways their voices, instead of the voices of their disabled family member, comes to shape public policy. We see parents' call for reform, but we do not see how disabled family members perceive their own relationships with professionals and their families. This is likely a very different story, one that has begun to emerge in memoir with the rise of the self-advocacy movement.[58]

Notes

I thank Richard Scotch, Susan Burch, and Michael Rembis for their helpful feedback.

1. Dan Goodley, "Becoming Rhizomatic Parents: Deluze, Guattari, and Disabled Babies," *Disability and Society* 22, no. 2 (2007): 145–160; Colin Ong-Dean, "Reconsidering the Social Location of the Medical Model: An Examination of Disability in Parenting Literature," *Journal of Medical Humanities* 26, nos. 2–3 (2005): 141–158; Sara Ryan and Katherine Runswick-Cole, "Repositioning Mothers: Mothers, Disabled Children, and Disability Studies," *Disability and Society* 23 no. 3 (2008): 199–210.

2. See Gail Landsman, "Mothers and Models of Disability," *Journal of Medical Humanities* 26, nos. 2–3 (2005): 121–139; Ong-Dean, "Reconsidering the Social Location of the Medical Model"; Erica Prussing, Elisa Sobo, Elizabeth Walker, and Paul S. Kurtin, "Between 'Desperation' and Disability Rights: A Narrative Analysis of Complimentary/Alternative Medicine Use by Parents for Children with Down Syndrome," *Social Science and Medicine* 60, no. 3 (2005): 587–598.

3. In the memoirs I analyze, which date from 1950 to 1989, just before the passage of the Americans with Disabilities Act, parents identified their child with a label associated with intellectual disability. In some memoirs the intellectual disability constituted the primary diagnosis (e.g., Down syndrome, mental retardation) and in others the child had

multiple diagnoses such as cerebral palsy, brain damage, epilepsy, and/or autism with an intellectual disability. Because no systematic listing of these books exists, this sample may not represent the entire population of such books.

4. For scholarship on the use of memoir in historical analysis, see Susan Kucler and Walter Welion, eds., *Images of Memory: On Remembering and Representation* (Washington, D.C.: Smithsonian Institution Press, 1991); Mary Jo Maynes, Jennifer L. Pierce, and Barbara Laslett, *Telling Stories: The Use of Personal Narratives in the Social Sciences and History* (Ithaca, N.Y.: Cornell University Press, 2008).

5. Cindee Carlton, "The Obscuring of Class in Memoirs of Parents of Children with Disabilities," *Disability & Society* 25 no. 7 (2010): 849–860.

6. For scholarship on scientific motherhood, see Rima D. Apple, *Perfect Motherhood: Science and Childbearing in America* (New Brunswick, N.J.: Rutgers University Press, 2006); Kathleen Jones, "'Mother Made Me Do It': Mother-Blaming and the Women of the Child Guidance Movement," in *Bad Mothers: The Politics of Blame in Twentieth-Century America*, edited by Molly Ladd-Taylor and Lauri Umansky (New York: New York University Press, 1998), 99–126; Jennifer Burek Pierce, "Science, Advocacy, and 'The Sacred and Intimate Things of Life': Republican Motherhood as a Progressive Era Cause in Women's Magazines," *American Periodicals* 18 no. 1 (2008): 69–95.

7. For works that focus on the constructed threat of the "feebleminded," see Allison C. Carey, *On the Margins of Citizenship: Intellectual Disability and Civil Rights in Twentieth-Century America* (Philadelphia: Temple University Press, 2009); Nicole H. Rafter, "The Criminalization of Mental Retardation," in *Mental Retardation in America*, edited by Steven Noll and James W. Trent Jr. (New York: New York University Press, 2004), 232–257; James W. Trent Jr., *Inventing the Feeble Mind: A History of Mental Retardation in the United States* (Berkeley: University of California, 1994).

8. The rate of institutionalization in America for people with intellectual disabilities climbed through the 1950s and 60s, reaching a peak in 1969, when almost 200,000 individuals diagnosed as "mentally retarded" were housed in institutions. Charlie K. Lakin, Sheryl Larson, Patricia Salmi, and Amanda Webster, *Residential Services for Persons with Developmental Disabilities: Status and Trends through 2009* (Minneapolis: University of Minnesota, Research and Training Center on Community Living, Institute on Community Integration, 2010), 13.

9. For scholarship on parents and institutionalization, see Janice Brockley, "Rearing the Child Who Never Grew: Ideologies of Parenting and Intellectual Disability in American History," in *Mental Retardation in America*, edited by Steven Noll and James W. Trent Jr. (New York: New York University, 1994), 130–164; Katherine Castles, "'Nice, Average Americans': Postwar Parents, Groups, and the Defense of the Normal Family," in *Mental Retardation in America*, edited by Steven Noll and James W. Trent Jr. (New York: New York University, 1994), 350–371.

10. Pearl S. Buck, *The Child Who Never Grew* (1950; repr., Bethesda, MD: Woodbine House, 1992).

11. Ibid., 69.

12. John P. Frank, *My Son's Story* (New York: Alfred A. Knopf, 1952), 57.

13. Ibid., 58.

14. Lucille Stout, *I Reclaimed My Child: The Story of a Family into Which a Retarded Child Was Born* (Philadelphia: Chilton Company, 1959), 10.

15. Ibid., 24.

16. Ibid., 78.

17. Examples of press exposés include Bill Baldini, "Suffer the Little Children," NBC10 report, 1968, http://www.preservepennhurst.org/default.aspx?pg=26, accessed October 2012; Burton Blatt and Fred Kaplan, *Christmas in Purgatory: A Photographic Essay on Mental Retardation* (Boston: Allyn and Bacon, 1966); Geraldo Rivera, *Willowbrook: A Report on How It Is and Why It Doesn't Have to Be That Way* (New York: Random House, 1972).

18. Nicola Schaefer, *Does She Know She's There?* (1978; Markham, Ontario: Fitzhenry and Whiteside, 1999).

19. Fern Kupfer, *Before and After Zachariah* (Chicago: Academy Chicago, 1988).

20. Simon Olshansky, Gertrude C. Johnson, and Leon Sternfeld, "Attitudes of Some GP's Towards Institutionalizing Mentally Retarded Children," *Mental Retardation* 1 no. 1 (1963): 18–20, 57–59.

21. Douglas Hunt, preface, in Nigel Hunt, *The World of Nigel Hunt: The Diary of a Mongoloid Youth* (New York: Garrett, 1967), 15–41, 22. Douglas Hunt writes only the preface, and the book itself is written by his son Nigel. "Idiocy" was a common legal and medical term in America through the early twentieth century.

22. Ibid., 22.

23. Sophia Grant, *"One of Those": The Progress of a Mongoloid Child* (New York: Pageant, 1957).

24. Ibid., 11.

25. Claire D. Canning and Joseph P. Canning Jr., *The Gift of Martha* (Boston: Children's Hospital Medical Center, 1975), 12.

26. Dale Evans Rogers, *Angel Unaware* (Westwood, N.J.: Fleming H. Revel, 1953), 29, 39–40.

27. Nancy Roberts and Bruce Roberts, *David* (Richmond: John Knox, 1968), 51.

28. Martha Moraghan Jablow, *Cara: Growing with a Retarded Child* (Philadelphia: Temple University, 1982), 183.

29. Roberts and Roberts, *David*, 63.

30. Canning and Canning, *The Gift of Martha*, 9.

31. Jane Bernstein, *Loving Rachel: A Family's Journey from Grief* (Urbana: University of Illinois, 1988), 279.

32. Stout, *I Reclaimed My Child*, 87.

33. Hunt, *The World of Nigel Hunt*, 30–31.

34. Canning and Canning, *The Gift of Martha*, 17.

35. Bernstein, *Loving Rachel*, 45.

36. For a discussion of tensions between spouses and between siblings, see for example Bernstein, *Loving Rachel*, 63, 130; Josh Greenfeld, *A Client Called Noah* (New York: Henry Holt and Company, 1986), 74–103; Fern Kupfer, *Before and After Zachariah*, 63–72; and Nicola Schaefer, *Does She Know She's There?*, 14–21, 257.

37. The term "intensive motherhood" is associated with Charon Hays, *The Cultural Contradictions of Motherhood* (New Haven, Conn.: Yale University Press, 1996).

38. Fern Kupfer, *Before and After Zachariah*, 82.

39. Nicola Schaefer, *Does She Know She's There?*, 122. Also see Jablow, *Cara*, 124.

40. Linda M. Blum, "Mother-Blame in the Prozac Nation: Raising Kids with Invisible Disabilities," *Gender and Society* 21 no. 2 (2007): 2020–2026; Amy Sousa, "From Refrigerator Mothers to Warrior-Heroes: The Cultural Identity Transformation of Mothers Raising Children with Intellectual Disabilities," *Symbolic Interaction* 34, no. 2 (2011): 220–243.

41. Jablow, *Cara*, 180.

42. Gregory L. Weiss and Lynne E. Lonnguist, *The Sociology of Health, Healing and Illness*, 6th ed. (Upper Saddle River, N.J.: Pearson Education, 2009).

43. For a discussion of parent activism and education, see Kathleen W. Jones, "Education for Children with Mental Retardation: Parent Activism, Public Policy, and Family Ideology in the 1950s," in *Mental Retardation in America*, edited by Steven Noll and James W. Trent Jr. (New York: New York University, 2004), 351–370; Larry A. Jones, *Doing Disability Justice: 75 Years of Family Advocacy* ([Olympia?]: Larry A. Jones, 2010); Margaret A. Winzer, *A History of Special Education: From Isolation to Integration* (Washington, D.C: Gallaudet University, 1993).

44. Stout, *I Reclaimed My Child*, 33.

45. Grant, *"One of Those,"* 44.

46. Hunt, *The World of Nigel Hunt*, 29–30.

47. Jablow, *Cara*, xii.

48. Greenfeld, *A Place for Noah*, 3. See also Greenfeld, *A Client Called Noah*, 207.

49. Greenfeld, *A Place for Noah*, 173.

50. Jablow, *Cara*, 118, 152.

51. For a discussion of parents' perceptions of the team approach as actually a conflict-laden process, see Chrissie Rogers, "Motherhood and Intellectual Disability: Partnership Rhetoric?," *British Journal of Sociology of Education* 32, no. 4 (2011): 563–581.

52. Kupfer, *Before and After Zachariah*, 164.

53. Ibid., 191, 77.

54. Greenfeld, *A Place for Noah*, 15.

55. Ibid., 20.

56. Bernstein, *Loving Rachel*, 258. Greenfeld and his wife dealt with the system in part by creating their own programs that they could control. Schaefer organized with other parents to exert political pressure for appropriate educational programming.

57. For a discussion of the tension between private sphere of family and public sphere, see Elaine Tyler May, *Homeward Bound* (New York: Basic Books, 1988); Judith Stacey, *Brave New Families* (Berkeley: University of California, 1988).

58. For examples of memoirs by self-advocates and people with intellectual disabilities, see Nick Cobos, *Dreamers Don't Quit* (Amigo Press, 2003); Mary F. Hayden, ed., *Living in the Freedom World* (Minneapolis, Minnesota: University of Minnesota, 1997); Roland Johnson, *Lost in a Desert World* (Plymouth Meeting, Pa.: Speaking for Ourselves, 1999).

CHAPTER 4

Historical Perceptions
of Autism in Brazil

Professional Treatment, Family Advocacy,
and Autistic Pride, 1943–2010

PAMELA BLOCK AND FÁTIMA GONÇALVES CAVALCANTE

KEYWORDS: *Centuries*: twentieth; *Geographical Areas*: South America; *Sources*: interviews; organizational reports; government documents; *Themes*: activism; bodies, medicine, contested knowledge; citizenship and belonging; culture; family, daily life, and community; law and policy

Exploring the history of autism in Brazil presents numerous challenges.[1] Historically and internationally there has always been variety in the way autistic people, their capacities, and their perceived "limitations" have been represented in biomedical, psychosocial, and cultural frameworks.[2] Professionals, family members, and autistics themselves theorize, understand, and represent autism in different ways. The variety of perspectives is visible in the continuing depictions of autistic people as "suffering" from psychiatric illness, cognitive or behavioral disability, deafness, or "mental retardation." In this chapter, we explore how historical, political, social, and cultural factors such as ethnicity, gender, age, socioeconomic status, and national origin have shaped conceptualizations of autism in Brazil. We focus on four key periods of organizational and political change for autistic Brazilians: (1) the early to mid-twentieth century, when psychiatrists controlled treatment modalities for certain types of minds and bodies, which often included institutionalization; (2) a period of mental health reform that began in the 1970s, during the years after the most recent (mid-1960s) Brazilian dictatorship, and expanded in the 1980s, when minority groups increasingly fought for political and social "re-democratization"; (3) the growth of parent advocacy movements, also during the 1980s, that featured mother-driven advocacy efforts to move from psychiatric care to community-based education for autistic children; and (4) the emergence of autistic citizenship movements centered on the concept of neurodiversity and on Orgulho Autista (Autistic Pride) in the early years of the twenty-first century. Using archival and ethnographic research, we consider the entangled experiences of autistics and family members who have navigated often-contradictory medical and educational discourses, practices, and systems, highlighting the diverse experiences of autism and authority. Throughout this chapter, we consider how Brazilian cultural tendencies toward hierarchy, political action, and collective action have shaped autistic identity over time.

Medical and Educational Experts as Authorities, 1900–1980s

In the late nineteenth and early twentieth centuries, psychiatric and other medical and educational professionals became increasingly interested in people who would most likely be considered "autistic" today. When autism emerged as a diagnosis in the 1940s, it was seen as a psychiatric category. In 1943, U.S. child psychiatrist and physician Leo Kanner introduced the concept of "autistic disturbances of affective contact," which he considered a syndrome.[3] In the following year, Austrian pediatrician and medical professor Hans Asperger identified autism as a disability characterized by "disturbed social interaction."[4] These and subsequent diagnoses framed autism as a psychiatric condition. Psychiatrists and other medical professionals in Brazil generally adopted these categories and accepted the notion that doctors had a primary role in "managing" the "condition." Mainstream Brazilian society also adopted this understanding of autism and autistics.[5]

Since its origin, Brazilian psychiatry has imported theoretical models, institutions, and therapies from Europe and the United States.[6] Yet it was also significantly influenced by local histories and cultures, such as the regionally specific experiences of Brazilians with European colonization and the institution of slavery: approaches to medically identified "pathological" behavior were shaped by both global scientific discourses and local beliefs about race, social status, and gender.[7] For most of its history, Brazil was involved in the institution of slavery. When Portugal colonized Brazil in the late fifteenth century, the nation became deeply invested in the African slave trade. The process of colonization included the exploitation and genocide of indigenous populations, the importation and forced labor of African slaves, and the dynamic interplay of Catholic, African, and Indian spiritual and cultural beliefs and practices. In 1822, King Pedro I of Portugal established the Empire of Brazil. When King Pedro returned to Portugal in 1831, he left his son to rule the Brazilian monarchy. King Pedro II ruled Brazil from 1831 to 1889. Although slavery ended in 1888 by official decree of King Pedro II, it left in its wake complex intersecting conceptualizations of gender, race, and ethnicity that played out very differently in Brazil than they did in North America or Europe.[8]

A distinguishing feature of early Brazilian doctors is that some of them came from families of mixed racial heritage. One of the founders of Brazilian psychiatry, eugenics, and mental hygiene, Dr. Juliano Moreira, for example, descended from African slaves.[9] Clearly, the racialized aspects of eugenics were very different in Brazil than in northern countries. Moreira and those who followed him contested European-influenced discourses of the late nineteenth century that warned of the physical and moral dangers of miscegenation."[10] The alternative formulations Moreira and other Brazilian intellectuals advocated, including Alberto Guerreiro Ramos and Gilberto Freyre, presented mixed racial heritage as a positive strength.[11] They also adopted Lamarckian theories of genetics, believing that sociocultural and public health changes would strengthen Brazil's national gene pool.[12] Early twentieth-century psychiatric case studies clearly highlight stereotypes about the roles of women, working-class men, people of color, residents of psychiatric institutions, and, implicitly, elite, highly educated, and usually light-skinned doctors.[13]

Psychiatric approaches dominated autism treatment in Brazil for most of the twentieth century. Brazilian psychiatric and mental health professionals led movements that advocated a variety of treatment strategies for autism, in contrast to professionals who still believed in psychiatric treatments based on institutionalization. Psychiatrists claimed this authority on the basis of their professional understanding of what autism was and what it meant. Yet theories and practices differed widely and featured several schools of thought, competing systems of classification, and heated debates about the use of medication versus psychoanalysis.[14] No consensus was reached in the period 1900 to 1950, and the treatment tendencies fluctuated between medical-pedagogical care and neurological or biological interventions. In the 1960s, demedicalized sociological, psychosocial, psychodynamic, and psychoanalytic approaches became more popular in child and adolescent psychiatry in Brazil.[15] These changes were partly based on an assumption that the causes of psychiatric disability, including autism, were psychosocial in nature and could be treated through psychoanalysis. There was no expectation of cure, just a search for inner social-behavioral organization.

Until the 1960s, psychiatric units were asylums based on theories of moral correction. They were isolated from society; most of them were located in rural areas or at the edge of cities. As the visionary Machado de Assis (1839–1908) says in his classic chronicle *O Alienista*,[16] "inconvenient" family or community members could be depicted as "dangerous," put in an asylum, and isolated from society. The main character of his book, Dr. Simão Bacamarte, who saw his job as caring for "the soul's health," said: "Madness, the object of my studies, was once known as an island lost in the ocean of reason; I am beginning to suspect that it is a continent."[17] Machado's use of irony here illustrates how vague diagnoses were in the late nineteenth to early twentieth centuries. The treatment environment was also problematic. In the early decades of the twentieth century, several "children's pavilions" were built as annexes to psychiatric hospitals located on the fringes of some of Brazil's larger cities.[18] These were meant to be models of cleanliness, respectful treatment, and education. However, as the residential population increased, living conditions deteriorated. In addition, many residents lived their entire lives in institutions.

During the 1960s, some medical experts continued to claim the authority to diagnose and define "treatment" using institutional models, but others began to recognize the significance of family and sociocultural factors in treatment outcomes. Although diagnoses had changed since the 1940s, many psychiatrists and other medical specialists remained committed to a narrow medical interpretation of autism. They maintained that certain behavioral qualities were pathological, and they recommended specific kinds of psychiatric "treatments" to remedy what they viewed as a medical "problem." However, other clinicians in the 1960s began using psychoanalysis and rejected traditional psychiatric approaches, preferring a sociological approach that favored demedicalized treatments. At the end of the 1960s and beginning of the 1970s, critics of the traditional psychiatric model denounced the harmful asylum model and reinforced the emergence of social psychiatric approaches. In the 1970s, there was an explosion of psychosocial, psychodynamic, and psychoanalytic approaches to autism. By the 1980s, the deinstitutionalization movement was fully formed, based on the idea of the dismantling of the asylum system. This reform of psychiatry took place in the context of broader social change: Brazil ratified a new constitution in 1988.[19]

Education experts also played an authoritative role in defining autism and autistics in Brazil. In the 1930s, educational and developmental psychologist Helen Antipoff (1892–1974) worked with multidisciplinary groups of professionals across Brazil to begin a movement that advocated for community-based education for "exceptional" children. This was the first large-scale effort to educate disabled children in Brazil. Numerous children who were served by this movement may have been autistic but were not diagnosed as such because systematic diagnosis of autistic children did not begin until the 1980s in Brazil. Children who today would be labeled autistic were mixed with other groups of children, either those who were considered intellectually disabled or those who had been diagnosed as psychotic. A diagnosis that led to placement in one of these groups determined what type of treatment they would receive; those who were diagnosed as intellectually disabled received education and those who were diagnosed as psychotic were treated psychiatrically. Because this process of categorization was replicated throughout Brazil, it had a direct and significant impact on the experiences of autistic Brazilians in the mid-twentieth century.[20] However, from the 1930s until the 1970s, Antipoff developed an alternative to existing medical and psychoanalytic treatment, focusing instead on community-based educational and therapeutic rehabilitation interventions.[21] She is considered a pioneer in Brazil. She mentored generations of psychologists, educators, and rehabilitation professionals and established the field of special education in Brazil. She focused on education, therapeutic intervention, and vocational training rather than biomedical treatment, and she worked on integrating individuals into educational systems and developing strategies for helping individuals develop social skills in order to promote participation in community life.

Antipoff was based in the rural state of Minas Gerais, far from the centers of power, for the duration of the Vargas dictatorship (1937–1945). Since the end of the monarchy in 1889, Brazil has shifted between the two political extremes of democracy and military dictatorship.[22] Progressive groups that organized to change gender or economic inequalities flourished in periods of democracy, only to be brutally crushed in periods of political repression. Many people were jailed or killed in the 1930s, during the Vargas dictatorship. Professionals, especially women who were identified with radical groups, were jailed, banished, or were blocked from working in their areas of expertise for more than a decade. Psychiatrist Nise da Silveira, a socialist and feminist who strongly opposed aggressive forms of treatment for all forms of mental and cognitive disability, was jailed for over a year and then blacklisted for many years. She was an early proponent of demedicalization and deinstitutionalization of adults with psychiatric diagnoses.[23] Antipoff, a Russian immigrant, had lived and worked for years with street children in early communist Russia before moving to Brazil to educate teachers and work with disabled children. Because she had worked in communist Russia, she was careful to distance herself from ideological and political debates that might get her into trouble during the fascist regime. Although initially Antipoff's efforts in the public school system were impeded by the restrictions imposed during the Vargas dictatorship, she circumvented this barrier by founding a series of private schools for "exceptional" students called Pestalozzi societies.[24] In 1945, the Pestalozzi Society of Brazil, a national organization, was formed within the national eugenics movement offices of the Brazilian League of Mental Hygiene. Independent Pestalozzi Society chapters spread throughout the country (there were over 200 by the 1990s). Antipoff's inclusive and cross-disability approach welcomed children (and later adults) with a range of characteristics and diagnoses. Her approach was unique and progressive—quite distinct from the segregation that was common in the United States during the same period. Antipoff even opened her rural schools to local farm children in an early example of "inclusive" education. She chose the term "exceptional" (which is currently criticized in Brazil in the same way that "special" is critiqued in the United States) to contest the negative labels that other professionals were using in this era, such as "abnormal," "subnormal," and "deficient." She considered *excepcional* to be a non-pejorative term for people identified as intellectually disabled, gifted, artistic, or eccentric in some way.[25]

From its inception in 1929, the Pestalozzi Society was a venue where women educators and clinicians could progress professionally.[26] Beginning in the 1950s, supported by Antipoff and her well-educated white female students, new parent-driven advocacy groups were formed, developed primarily by mothers of children identified as intellectually disabled, to promote community-based education for disabled children. The Associações de Pais e Amigos de Pessoas Excepcionais (APAE), which began within the Pestalozzi societies in the 1950s, was influenced by the parent-based advocacy movement in the United States. The APAE grew rapidly and over 1,500 chapters had been established throughout Brazil by the end of the twentieth century.[27] It continued to function and even flourish during periods of dictatorship, because although its members were seen as apolitical, they often had deep roots in local power structures; otherwise they would not survive. During the Pinochet dictatorship (1964–1985), for example, wives of prominent generals (and generals themselves) were involved in the executive leadership of the Rio de Janeiro chapter, which received financial support from military sources.[28] During the last half-century, there has been poor financial support from the government for special education and disabled students have been included in regular schools in only limited ways. The absence of state support for vulnerable disability groups has led to the mobilization of strong family associations such as APAEs in order to provide educational, vocational, therapeutic and social assistance to children and adults with intellectual and developmental disability. At the APAEs, autism was sometimes treated as an intellectual impairment, but sometimes the idea of it as a psychiatric condition was rejected.

By the middle of the twentieth century, the establishment of clear clinical distinctions between intellectual and psychiatric diagnoses led to the systematic segregation of autistics into psychiatric treatment routes rather than the community-based educational ones. Autism was seen as a primary affective disorder that also often included levels of intellectually disability and "psychotic disorganization," a disorder that should be treated by psychoanalytic, psychiatric, or educational approaches. Only after the cognitivists' studies of the 1970s that offered new insights into the functioning of autistic individuals[29] was it possible for professionals to begin to see autism as a "primary cognitive disorder," a "spectrum of developmental disorders" with cognitive and social origins. Even today in Brazil, there is no consensus on whether autism is an "affective disorder with psychotic and

relational problems" or a "cognitive disorder with a triad of impaired social interaction, communication, and imagination, associated with a rigid and repetitive
pattern of behavior."[30]

Families and Other Allies, 1980s–2010

In the late 1970s, Brazil experienced a period of political "re-democratization"
known as the *abertura*, or "opening." This process was evident even within the walls
of the asylum. Academic discourses on psychiatry focused on human rights, and
this passed into the public domain through denunciations in the press against
violence in institutions and segregating autistics from society in psychiatric hospitals. In the 1970s, mental health care workers formed a *movimento antimanico-
mial* (movement for deinstitutionalization). After a decade of advocacy, this led
to structural changes in the 1980s and a new focus on community-based mental
health care. When the dictatorship ended in 1985, a large-scale campaign was
formed called "Direct [Elections] Now!" This popular movement supported the
first direct democratic election for the president of the Brazilian republic since
1961.[31] The election took place in 1989, a year after the adoption of the new constitution, which included numerous social advances and important changes in the
area of health care provision. In 1987, the movement to replace psychiatric institutions with community-based organizations and strategies for providing services
outside the asylum model organized a national congress in Bauru. This meeting
intensified the debate about psychiatric reform within in the field of medicine,
among those who managed institutions, within the judiciary, and within society
and culture more generally. At the same time, a larger health care reform movement that focused on access to general health care services proposed the Unified
Health System (Sistema Único de Saúde; SUS), which sought to provide universal
health care for all Brazilian citizens.

Both movements resulted in changes in the quality of life for residents of institutions and the deinstitutionalization of large numbers of individuals. Large
residential institutions were transformed into facilities that provided outpatient
services and short-term residential treatment for those in crisis. Many institutions
were closed.[32] After a decade of debate within society and among members of the
judiciary, a major reform of psychiatric care was approved in the Brazilian Congress in 2001 (Law 10.216). This law which is still being implemented, has brought
about both advances and hardships. The advances include community-based psychosocial treatment centers for individuals and their families. Unfortunately for
many residents in institutions across Brazil, the process of deinstitutionalization
was unregulated, and too often people were released into the community without
adequate support.

Brazil's new constitution gave those with the highest levels of poverty, inequality, and social exclusion the most political protection. Though the focus was on making the health care system accessible to diverse populations and addressing varying needs with specific treatment programs (e.g., with attention to differences related to gender, race, sex, ethnicity, and regionality), the needs of some groups were not recognized or addressed. Autistics and their families constituted one of these groups. Traditionally, civil society had assumed the major responsibility for creating and maintaining community-based education services, such as personal and therapeutic support, psychosocial assistance, inclusion in education and vocational training, and programs that provided support for daily living for disabled people. State support was limited, and this did not change substantially after constitutional reform. Parents of disabled children from the middle or higher classes created their own private facilities that provided clinical care and education. In addition, nonprofit organizations provided services such as education, vocational training, and therapeutic treatment that should have been the state's responsibility. Without consistent state support, these services were difficult to sustain, but the parents persisted.

Frustrated by the government's lack of support, a group of mothers of autistic children took on the task of providing alternatives to the narrow options medical and educational professionals advocated. Their efforts focused on rejecting the asylum model, publicizing the absence of specialized services, and challenging medical treatment modalities based on biological or pathological patterns and interpretations of autism that they felt were both unhelpful and inaccurate. These middle-class mothers studied the international literature on autism and treatment programs and introduced new evidence-based approaches to supporting their autistic children by stimulating their personal and social skills; integrating them in daily community life; developing sports, artistic, and work activities for them; and using educational tools and supportive behavioral approaches according to individualized levels of development. They mobilized to create, maintain, and improve access to multidisciplinary services for autistics that had never before been available in Brazil. However, this was not just about gender-based social action, it was also a process by which a group of families with a shared middle-class identity and a common cause—autism—collectively fought established hierarchies to address political and social needs.

In 1983, the first Association of Friends of Autistics in São Paulo (Associação de Amigos do Autista; AMA-SP) was formed. It was one of the first parents' associations in Brazil. São Paulo, the most advanced industrial state of Brazil, had the largest number of community-based treatment, education, and work opportunities for different disability groups, except the autistic group, whose specific needs were not visible in the history of Brazilian disability at that moment, since autistics were placed in groups of intellectually or psychiatrically impaired children. The AMA-SP focused on creating community-based education and services for autistic individuals that provided alternatives to the existing treatment approaches by structuring an approach that was grounded in the development of behavioral and social skills. The mothers who led the AMA-SP contradicted unfounded assumptions that mothers of autistics were "refrigerator mothers."[33] They worked with great skill, creativity, and social solidarity to build a complex organization and a strong support network for autistics and their families.[34]

The AMA was influenced by the earlier woman-led Pestalozzi and APAE movements for community-based education for disabled children and by North American models of treatment and education for autism. As in these other cases, this movement presented a challenge to the male-dominated medical establishment that had provided few and ineffective options for autistic children and their families. The AMA-SP created a national network with other associations, branches of the Brazilian Association of Autism (Associação Brasileira de Autismo; ABRA), that provided educational support and training in social skills, community living, and therapeutic services that were previously unavailable to autistic children and, eventually, vocational services for autistic adults. This mother-driven national network came to see autism as a cognitive and developmental disability rather than a psychiatric "dysfunction." In describing the success of the AMA-SP, one of the mothers said, "The success that has been achieved transformed this barrier [autism] into a much greater cause and resulted in the construction of something important."[35]

The AMA promoted itself as an organization that had collected knowledge from the principal centers of autism treatment in the United States and Europe. The models of rehabilitation it offered were based in education and vocational training. Incorporating medical, educational, social, and cultural components, the group sought to structure the environment and the daily tasks of autistic individuals around ordinary routines. It also helped families find strategies to help autistics acquire habitual practices and independence in daily life, learn methods of communicating with autistics, and find strategies for including autistics in sports and other leisure activities. This was not simply a copy of a northern service model transplanted to Brazil without critical reflection. Rather, the Brazilian model of services for autistics was created through a process based in realities in Brazil and in consultation with international specialists. For example, regional music and dance were incorporated into daily routines and sports and activities of cultural significance were adapted to enable autistic students to participate. Educational processes were individualized, for example focusing on daily life activities for some, scholarly pursuits for others, and support for inclusion in mainstream education as much as possible for all.[36]

The empowerment of the families who joined the AMA (and the mothers who led the organization) as they created specialized support for autistics in Brazil reinforced crucial positive qualities. For example, Ana Maria, Marisa, and Marli, three of the mothers who were leaders in the organization, demonstrated the social, intellectual, and emotional ability to cope with multiple forms of social adversity. From a starting place of no services for autism, no understanding of autism in society, no opportunities for autistic children and adults, and a complete lack of funding, these mothers spent twenty years building a sophisticated state-of-the-art approach and specialized services based on international and national best practices. They moved beyond the traditional mothering role to acquire skills and knowledge to manage a pioneer organization with national relevance in Brazil. They believed that with the right kind of support, autistics could progress, increase their awareness of themselves and their families, and achieve a sense of solidarity. The secret to the success they found with autistics was complex, although they used simple strategies: social cooperation and the creation of different types of support systems for autistics. Over three decades they used different strategies to strengthen and grow. They asked for federal support so they could travel abroad to learn about autism and so they could bring international consultants to Brazil to educate them about how they could diversify services and educational approaches. They created television commercials to promote their ideas about autism throughout Brazil. They ran a huge fund-raising auction—with no previous experience—and raised enough money to purchase a small farm, where they created their first community-based program. As they grew, they needed to open other chapters. So they raised additional money to fund a new building in the city of São Paulo. They created a model program for autistics with high support needs that focused on daily life, socialization, personal and social competence, and respite care. Together with other mothers, they developed patience and learned to cope with all kinds of pressure and meet many challenges. In the process of building the AMA, participants learned and grew as individuals. They became part of a greater whole that engaged in innovative social practices that the women would never have imagined being able to develop and implement individually.[37]

Some challenges grew from tensions between professional models and parent-driven models. At times, it was difficult for professionals to cede authority to parents. Some parents were critical of the movement to deinstitutionalize their children when community-based alternatives were not in place. Mothers responded to this challenge by forming their own community-based alternatives. In the historical development of educational alternatives for those with intellectual disability, it was professionals who created the first organizations, the Pestalozzi societies, in the 1930s. In turn, these organizations supported the mothers who started the APAEs in the 1950s. The AMA followed this model in the 1980s, but professionals did not support AMA groups in the way they had supported the APAE. Parents led the way in the AMA's development of community-based autism services, and the professionals followed in their wake.

Motivated by the need for both better services and social support, mothers created new social practices that became vectors of success for themselves and their children. In 1985, they began organizing regular events that focused on national and international scientific research and brought together renowned professionals. In effect, they started their own unofficial "autism school without walls" for parents and professionals. Over a period of almost thirty years, they used these events to disseminate relevant information from the United States, Europe, and Brazil, to increase the organization's sustainability and to become an authoritative voice. This is very different from what happened in the United States, where parents engaged in fund-raising but professionals controlled the institutions and the research. In Brazil, parents directed the flow of information and the development of services. This was more than a philanthropic model and it was more than a professional model. It was a dynamic, diverse, and critically subjective model that incorporated medical, educational, social, and cultural influences. It was also a rights-based approach. Parents felt that their children had a right to education and services that the government and medical professionals were not providing, and they created their own institutions to make up for the lack.[38]

AMA members became authorities about and provided resources on autism across the lifespan that presented an alternative to the treatment modalities medical and psychiatric professionals provided. They facilitated the exchange of knowledge and information among autism organizations in Brazil and those in international organizations in the United States, the United Kingdom, Argentina, Peru, Venezuela, Chile, and Colombia.[39] Not all the programs created by the AMA were community based; projects also included a residential school and a home for autistic adults in the city of São Paulo.[40] In both residential and community-based settings, mothers of autistic children implemented a pedagogical model that provided structured individualized activities for each autistic child. They created a model of educational and therapeutic service provision that met basic needs by addressing activities of daily living such as feeding and teaching strategies for eating independently, taking care of clothes, dressing and undressing, bathing, using the bathroom, learning how to cook, learning how to clean and organize a room, and learning how to read and follow instructions. They also taught parents strategies for best supporting their children and provided supplemental support for families whose children experienced significant impairments. They created teaching strategies associated with different levels of education with the goal of helping autistic children enter regular educational contexts. They developed strategies to make it possible for autistic children and adults to participate in sports and physical activities. All of these strategies for providing educational and social support had the goal of developing the abilities of autistic children so they could participate in daily activities and develop personal and social competence. This was accomplished through structuring the routine and lifestyle of autistics and decreasing the caregiving responsibilities of their families. This approach is significant, because it provided an alternative narrative of autism than had previously been provided by psychiatric models and it restored power to families, especially to mothers.

The mothers of the AMA worked for three decades to develop sustainable alternatives for their children and other Brazilian autistics. They created their own methods and developed technical, strategic, and political skills. By 2000 they had imported expertise from multiple international sources, created an institutional space in São Paulo, and helped form a network of forty-six AMA chapters in fourteen Brazilian states in addition to the Brazilian Association of Autism (Associação Brasileira de Autismo; ABRA).[41] Twenty-three of these chapters participated in a meeting in São Paulo in 2000, half of all the associations in Brazil. The mothers of the AMA and the associations that have spread across Brazil and the world demonstrate the importance of active participation and of engaging parents as partners in the process of including autistic individuals in contemporary society. Currently, AMA-SP has five chapters, four of which belong to the AMA and one of which is run in cooperation with the secretary of health for São Paulo state.

In the 1990s, advocacy movements from increasingly diverse sources resulted in advances in educational, therapeutic, and vocational services for autistic individuals. The heated debates that were taking place in the country pointed to the need for structural changes after deinstitutionalization. It was necessary to deconstruct the asylum models of treatment and their consequence, the exclusion of autistics from society. It took a decade to finally change thinking and practices related to mental health services. A major milestone in this process was the Psychiatric Reform Law (2001). In mental health and in special education, two distinct traditions, Brazilian professionals still had not reached a consensus about how to view autism; some saw it as an affective issue and some saw it as a cognitive issue. At the turn of the twenty-first century, professionals began to address the issue of autism using biological and cognitive theories, following trends in other parts of the world. In clinical practice, however, many psychiatrists, psychologists, and social workers continued to view autism within a psychodynamic and psychoanalytic perspective. Thus, there was a difference of opinion between human development and mental health professionals involved in theoretical study and those engaged in applied research, clinical, institutional, and laboratory practice. This divergence is due to the fact that family associations (such as the AMA and ABRA) support a cognitivist approach that differs from the tradition that continues to predominate in Brazil that is based on more than a century of research and practice in psychiatric and psychoanalytic affective treatments. Training in the area of autism is still scarce in Brazil; specialized courses exist in only a few institutions and universities. Over time, families with autistic children became increasingly frustrated about the fact that the only community-based options available were medication or psychoanalysis—neither of which, according to mothers, seemed to improve the quality of life for their children, especially considering the broad spectrum of autism-related conditions.[42] Eventually, reforms in the field of psychiatry and parent advocacy organizations such as the AMA contributed to the creation of new treatment modalities, including day treatment provided by multidisciplinary teams and psychosocial care centers, some integrating educational and vocational approaches, others offering global assistance (medical, psychological, social, physiotherapy, psychiatry, speech therapy, occupational therapy, musical therapy, family support), and others offering community living programs.[43]

In the early 2000s, a new wave of parent-led movements formed to provide solutions to the problems of the lack of education and treatment for autistic children and adults. They created institutions such as Mão Amiga (Helping Hand) in Rio de Janeiro, the now defunct Associação em Defesa do Autista (ADEFA) in Niterói in Rio de Janeiro State, and the Associação Baiana de Autismo in the state of Bahia. Like the AMA, these organizations were formed because parents who found that the government was not providing services and education for their children were not satisfied. According to one of the parents once affiliated with ADEFA, two of the largest service providers in Rio de Janeiro, APAE and Fundação Municipal Lar Francisco de Paula—Rio de Janeiro, were still refusing to accept autistic children. Public schools accepted autistic children only after parents fought for this legal right. Even when autistic children were accepted into a public school, they often were provided with just a few hours of classes in a segregated setting. Private schools charged high fees and did not offer financial assistance. In 2007, ADEFA created a website in partnership with other organizations to begin a movement to advocate for national policies to promote civil rights for people on the autistic spectrum. In 2009, discussions began among autistic advocacy organizations throughout Brazil about several municipal, state, and national laws to increase the rights of autistic Brazilians to education and inclusion in mainstream society. On December 27, 2012, Congress passed and the president signed one new law (12.764) and altered an existing disability rights law (8.112) to provide autistic citizens with the same rights as other disabled citizens.[44]

The 1980s were an important time of redemocratization in Brazil, when a variety of social movements were searching for better health and education systems and were addressing historical and political disparities related to ethnicity, gender, age, and socioeconomic status. Constitutional reform in Brazil in 1988 included health care reform, mental health care reform, and increased participation in the democratic process. However, political change for disabled people was limited because the new laws did not mandate government funding. Service and educational organizations for the disabled struggled to survive because they received little government funding; financial support came primarily from private sources, often from parents' associations. As in the 1950s, when the APAEs began providing specialized attention to intellectually disabled children, in the 1980s the AMAs created alternatives for autistic individuals and participated in the spirit of progress that reforms in health care and education in Brazil had begun. Today, although mental health care professionals still have the authority to treat autistics using psychiatric and psychoanalytic approaches (in addition to cognitive approaches), the AMA has made significant progress. In the three decades since it was founded, it and other community-based programs have spread across the country, and autistic people in Brazil have gained an interdisciplinary model of treatment and support. These resources include treatment modalities based on cognitive and developmental theories, programs that focus on education and social integration, and significant input from families of autistic people.

The Autistic Citizenship Movement, 1990s–2010

Building in part on the activism of mothers and on broader disability rights work in Brazil, autistic rights and autism self-advocacy movements added new interpretations of what it meant to be an autistic Brazilian. Autistic Brazilians and their family members claimed authority in their own lives and worked through rights-based organizations to get legislation passed that would give autistic people the same rights to employment and social service benefits that other disability groups had. Identifying with a broader transnational autistic community, some Brazilians claimed autism and neurodiversity as cultural identities. They also claimed membership in international autistic advocacy networks that have emerged since the early 2000s. Providing accurate knowledge about autism was a primary goal for this community. Most Brazilians still knew very little about autism, and what they knew mostly came from Hollywood movies or media reports, which often conveyed inaccurate or exaggerated portrayals of autism. As in many Western nations, Brazilian mainstream media typically presented only certain kinds of stories about autistic people, such as those about almost supernatural autistic savants who could memorize a phone book after a quick glance or who could play a piece on the piano after listening to it only one time.[45] These stories may be harmful because they limited the public's perceptions about the capabilities of autistics and offered few alternatives between the two extremes of freakish displays and institutionalization.

Self-advocates offered a different story about what autism means. For example, Claudio Ferreira Costa, a professor of philosophy at the Federal University of Rio Grande do Norte, posted a video on YouTube in 2009 about his experiences as an "Aspie."[46] This video was viewed over 50,000 times between February 2009 and February 2014. In the video, Dr. Costa discusses his feelings of social distance and awkwardness and the difficulties he has with making friends. He says that at first he was afraid that he might have a psychiatric diagnosis or some "grave moral defect." He thought, "If I don't make friends, maybe it is because I don't deserve them or, what I preferred to think, they didn't deserve me." While he was abroad in the 1990s, he saw a film in which a mother described her child who had been diagnosed with Asperger syndrome, and he recognized himself. "It is different from the loss of an arm, which everyone can see, or homosexuality, which society is coming to understand and respect. For this reason it is more stigmatized." This is the main reason he posted this video. "Just like there is gay pride, there ought to be Asperger pride," he says. Costa's depiction of autistic experience provides an alternative to other framings by mothers and by medical professionals. He and other Brazilian autistic self-advocates have claimed the authority to define what autism means to them, as people who experience it directly. For the first time in Brazil, autistic people have begun to define themselves and what they see as the most important issues in their lives. Autistic adults such as Costa have been present in society all along, but many of them did not realize they were autistic or identify as such.

In the early 2000s, a growing number of autistic Brazilians began to seek community, virtually and face to face in order to share their stories with each other and the world. They began to develop collective responses and identify opportunities to assert their role in representing what autism meant and the kinds of responses they desired from society as autistic people. Also during this time, the Brazilian disability rights movement began to document its own history. In 2010, the book *História do Movimento Político das Pessoas com Deficiência no Brasil* (History of the Political Movement of People with Disability in Brazil) was published and a documentary film of the same title was produced.[47] Independent living centers, which were first established in the major cities in the 1990s, have now spread throughout the country. Sophisticated discourses of disability rights and disability studies have begun to emerge across Brazil. Cross-disability perspectives have become more accepted. Those who had in the past been diagnosed as psychiatric patients and excluded from disability activism began to start their own movements, which manifested in events such as the Orgulho Louco (Mad Pride) parades that have taken place each year across Brazil, from Bahia to Rio Grande do Sul, since 2007.

Since 2008, Orgulho Autista (Autistic Pride) demonstrations and events have been held on June 18th in Brasília, Brazil's capital city.[48] One of the organizers of this event, Fernando Cotta, a parent of an autistic child, states: "This day is a celebration of neurodiversity of individuals on the autism spectrum to promote the concept that those identified as autistic do not suffer from a nasty pathology, just like those who have dark skin don't suffer from a skin disease." According to Cotta, Autistic Pride directly confronts biomedical conceptualizations of human "racial purity"—the belief that all human brains should be identical. Cotta is making a clear connection between the fight for autism rights and the fight for rights based on racial characteristics. This is a Brazilian twist on conceptualizations of neurodiversity and autistic pride.

Conclusion

A transformation in the experiences of Brazilian autistics took place between the early 1900s and the early 2000s. Families insist that previous practices of classifying autism as a psychiatric condition and treating it with medication, institutionalization, and psychoanalysis were ineffective. Although it is important to acknowledge that social psychiatry and a variety of psychoanalytical approaches were developed as result of reforms in mental health care, there is still a tension between those who believe that medication is the answer for autistic individuals and those who advocate psychosocial care. The heated debate among mental health care professionals between those who see autism as an affective disorder (a psychosis) and those who see it as a cognitive disorder (attributable to developmental delay) continues today in Brazil. At first, social movements that pushed for the deinstitutionalization of those who had been given psychiatric diagnoses and constitutional protections for vulnerable populations did not change the invisibility of autistics in public policy and health care policy reforms. Mothers of autistic children responded to this social erasure by organizing to address the lack of support among professionals and in government policies. They created a movement that succeeded in rendering autism visible in Brazil and internationally. Since the early twenty-first century, autistic adults have had access to opportunities to develop skills, complete formal educations, build professional careers, and connect to other autistics through virtual networks. These changes have brought about an entirely new paradigm of support and exchange. Given this history, the documentation of the collective experiences of autistic Brazilians is important, as they are related to other social, political and citizenship struggles.

Over the past seventy years, attitudes toward autistic Brazilians have been shaped by a variety of health care practices, psychotherapies, social-educational approaches, community-based programs, and self-advocacy movements. Health care and social work professionals were the sole shapers of such attitudes in the beginning of that period, but over time, parents and autistic self-advocates have

claimed the right to tell their own stories. Brazil is characterized by a tension between a cultural tendency toward hierarchy, as evidenced by cycles of dictatorship,
and affinity-based yet intersectional collective action. Over time, this has resulted
in a profound tangle of political and sociocultural constraints and transformations
in the experiences of autistics. These in turn have shaped changing and competing
attitudes among professionals, family members, and the general public. In future
years, as Brazilian autistic adults increasingly come to articulate their own experiences and desires, we expect that this complex interplay between professionals,
family members, and autistics will continue to shift and move in new directions.

Notes

We would like to thank Gustavo Medeiros and Julceli Antunes, whose contributions to
early drafts were essential in framing this chapter. We also thank Gretchen Specht, a
graduate of Stony Brook University, and Daniela de Carvalho Braga, a recent graduate
of the Bachelors Degree in Psychology Program at Universidade Veiga de Almeida and a
recipient of a grant from the Amparo Foundation for Research in Rio de Janeiro, for their
help with literature searches about autism in Brazil and organizing the bibliography.

1. The terminology we use in this publication is a conscious and careful choice. It represents the preference of the U.S. and international neurodiversity and autistic self-advocacy
movements, including the Brazilian Orgulho Autista (autism pride) movement, that autism
be presented as a pride-based social identity. We recognize that other movements, including key disability rights movements in Brazil, prefer "people-first" language, but we have
chosen to use the language preferred by most autistic self-advocates.

2. See Uta Frith, *Autism and Asperger Syndrome* (Cambridge: Cambridge University Press,
1991); Oliver W. Sacks, *An Anthropologist on Mars: Seven Paradoxical Tales* (New York: Knopf,
1995); Temple Grandin, *Emergence: Labeled Autistic*, edited by Margaret Scariano (Novato,
Calif.: Arena Press, 1986).

3. Leo Kanner, "Autistic Disturbances of Affective Contact," *Nervous Child* 2 (1943):
217–250.

4. Douglas Biklen with Richard Attfield, Larry Bisonnette, Lucy Blackman, Jamie Burke,
Alberto Frugone, Tito Rajarshi Mukhopadhyay, and Sue Rubin, *Autism and the Myth of the
Person Alone* (New York: New York University Press, 2005), 31.

5. Aside from a few isolated exceptions, surviving documentation of the early history
of autism in Brazil comes to us through the archives of medical and educational facilities
and professional organizations, including the Brazilian national eugenics organization,
the Liga Brasileira de Hygiene Mental (Brazilian League of Mental Hygiene). For more
information about the social context in which autistics may have experienced the dawn
of psychiatry in Brazil, see Jurandir Freire Costa, *História da psiquiatria no Brasil: Um corte
ideológico*, 4a ed. rev. e ampliada ed. (Rio de Janeiro: Xenon, 1989). Members included the
leading psychiatrists and neurologists in Brazil; see "List of Members," *Archivos Brasileiros
de Hygiene Mental* 1, no. 1 (1923): 229–230. Another central organization was the Sociedade
Brasileira de Psicanálise (Brazilian Society for Psychoanalysis), founded in 1929. The

development of Brazilian psychoanalysis coincided with the more radical components of Brazilian eugenics and mental hygiene; see Jane Russo, *O mundo psi no Brasil* (Rio de Janeiro: Jorge Zahar Editor, 2002).

6. Francisco B. Assumpção Jr. and Ana Cristina M. Pimentel, "Autismo infantil," *Revista Brasileira de Psiquiatria* 22 (2000): 37–39; Costa, *História da psiquiatria no Brasil*; Russo, *O mundo psi no Brasil*; Ana Maria Galdini Raimundo Oda, "História da psiquiatria Juliano Moreira: clima, raça, civilização e enfermidade mental," *Psychiatry on line Brasil* 18, no. 2 (2012), http://www.polbr.med.br/ano12/wal0212.php.

7. Jose Otavio Pompeu e Silva, ed., *Nise da Silveira—coleção memória do saber* (Rio de Janeiro: Publicação da Fundação Biblioteca Nacional—Fundação Miguel de Cervantes, 2012); Artur Ramos, *Guerra e relação da raça* (Rio [de Janeiro]: Departamento editorial da União nacional dos estudantes, 1943); Nina Rodrigues, *O alienado no direito civil Brasileiro*, 3rd ed. (São Paulo: Companhia Editora Nacional, 1938).

8. Robert M. Levine, *The History of Brazil* (Westport, Conn.: Greenwood Press, 1999).

9. Oda, "História da psiquiatria Juliano Moreira." Moreira received his medical degree in 1891 at the age of 18, just three years after slavery was abolished in Brazil. He traveled and studied psychiatry extensively throughout Europe with some of the noted German and French psychiatrists of the early twentieth century, including Emil Kraepelin, Paul Flechsig, Richard von Krafft-Ebing, Georges Gilles de La Tourette and Valentin Magnan.

10. Nina Rodrigues, *O alienado no direto civil Brasileiro.*

11. Oda, "História da psiquiatria Juliano Moreira"; Ramos, *Guerra e relação da raça* ; Gilberto Freyre, *The Masters and the Slaves: A Study in the Development of Brazilian Civilization* (New York: Knopf, 1956).

12. Pamela Block, "Institutional Utopias, Eugenics, and Intellectual Disability in Brazil," *History and Anthropology* 18, no. 2 (2007): 177–196; Nancy Stepan, *The Hour of Eugenics: Race, Gender, and Nation in Latin America* (Ithaca, N.Y.: Cornell University Press, 1991).

13. Antonio Austregésilo, *Mimetismo nos imbecis e idiotas*, edited by Hospicio Nacional (Rio de Janeiro: Archives-Bibloteca, 1906).

14. Brazilian psychiatrists were in two camps, both of which directly influenced treatment of autistics: the "organicists" who were influenced by Kraepellin and Bleuler and the psychobiologists of the French school, who emphasized a comprehensive view of the child in a developmental perspective; and those who adopted psychoanalysis as a treatment strategy for those labeled with "psychopathologies." Kanner's classification system for child psychiatric diagnoses (including autism), which encompassed environmentalist, functionalist, and mental hygiene approaches, and the French classificatory and nosographical systems that referred to autism as a "psychosis" that was treatable through a combination of psychoanalysis and developmental approaches influenced diagnosis and treatment; Assumpção and Pimentel, "Autismo infantil." In the 1950s neuropsychiatry grew to have increasing influence, and the tension between the psychoanalytic approaches that rejected categorical diagnoses and the nosological classificatory systems persisted into the twenty-first century.

15. Franco Rotelli and Fernanda Nicácio, *Desinstitucionalização* (Sao Paulo: HUCITEC, 1990); Cristiane S. Paula, Sabrina H. Ribeiro, Eric Fombonne, and Marcos T. Mercadante,

"Brief Report: Prevalence of Pervasive Developmental Disorder in Brazil: A Pilot Study," *Journal of Autism and Developmental Disorders* 41, no. 12 (2011): 1738–1742.

16. See Machado de Assis, *O alienista* (São Paulo: editora Ática, 1994).

17. Ibid., 17.

18. Fernandes Figueira, "Educação medico-pedagogica das crianças atrasadas," *Archivos Brasileiros de Psychiatria, Neurologia e Medicina Legal* 6, nos. 1–2 (1910): 320–331.

19. See Francisco B. Assumpção Jr., *Psiquiatria infantil Brasileira: um esboço histórico* (São Paulo: Lemos Editorial, 1995).

20. After fleeing the Russian revolution in 1908, Antipoff trained as a psychologist in Switzerland. He returned to Russia in 1916 to work with Dr. Lev Vygotsky, creator of the cultural-historical school of psychology. She returned to Geneva in 1924 to complete a doctorate in developmental and educational psychology with Edouard Claparède, founder and editor of the *Archives de Psychologie*, at the Institute Jean-Jacques Rousseau. Her doctoral cohort included Jean Piaget. After receiving her doctorate, Antipoff was recruited in 1929 to educate Brazilian teachers. After several extensions of a short-term contract, Antipoff decided to remain in Brazil and become a citizen.

21. Block, "Institutional Utopias."

22. Thomas E. Skidmore, *Black into White: Race and Nationality in Brazilian Thought* (Durham, N.C.: Duke University Press, 1993).

23. Several feminists and radicals who happened to be Jewish immigrants were deported back to Germany and perished in the Holocaust. See Pompeu e Silva and Jose Otavio, ed., *Nise da Silveira—coleção memória do saber* (2012).

24. Block, "Institutional Utopias"; Carmen Nava, "Lessons in Patriotism and Good Citizenship: National Identity and Nationalism in Public Schools during the Vargas Administration, 1937–1945," *Luso-Brazilian Review* 35, no. 1 (1998): 39.

25. Helen Antipoff, "Espirito e atividade da sociedade Pestalozzi do Brasil," *Arquivos Brasileiros de Higiene Mental* 16, no. 17 (1945–1946): 59–69; Daniel I. Antipoff, *Helena Antipoff, sua vida, sua obra* (Rio de Janeiro: J. Olympio, 1975); Block, "Institutional Utopias."

26. Antipoff, *Helena Antipoff, sua vida, sua obra*.

27. Block, "Institutional Utopias."

28. See, for example, Pamela Block, "Biology, Culture and Cognitive Disability: 20th Century Professional Discourse in Brazil and the United States" (PhD diss., Duke University, 1997); Block, "Institutional Utopias"; Gal. Floriano Moura Brasil Mendes, "Vinte e cinco anos da primeira apae do Brasil," *Mensagem da APAE* 6, no. 16 (1977): 12–16.

29. The cognitive theories appeared in the 1970s. Ritvo was the first one to correlate autism as a cognitive deficit, not seeing it as a psychosis anymore but as a "developmental disturbance"; see Edward R. Ritvo and Ed M. Ornitz, *Autism: Diagnosis, Current Research and Management* (New York: Spectrum, 1976). Rutter defined autism as a "behavioral syndrome with an organic etiology"; M. Rutter, "Diagnosis and Definition of Childhood Autism," *Journal of Autism Child Schizophrenia* 8, no. 2 (1978): 139–161. Wing and Gould see autism as a triple impairment: severe social impairment, severe difficulty in verbal and nonverbal communication, and the absence of imaginative activities; see Lorna Wing and Judith Gould, "Severe Impairments of Social Interaction and Associated Abnormalities

in Children: Epidemiology and Classification," *Journal of Autism and Developmental Disorder* 9 (1979): 11–30.

30. For a book that sees autism as a psychotic and cognitive impairment, see C. A. Araujo, *O processo de individuação no autismo* (São Paulo: Memnon, 2000). See also L. Wing and J. Gould, "Severe Impairments of Social Interaction and Associated Abnormalities in Children: Epidemiology and Classification," Journal of Autism and Developmental Disorders 9 (1979): 11–29. In this classic study, Wing and Gould studied 35,000 children and identified three different impairments within the autistic spectrum disorders.

31. Skidmore, *Black into White*.

32. One innovative program in the 1990s and early 2000s was a community center created at the Centro Psiquiátrico Pedro II. Empty wards were opened and renovated into spaces for community groups to use for free. Exercise classes, senior groups, vocational programs, and college courses were among the activities offered on the site. This brought the local community inside the walls of the institution, demystified it, and made it a part of the local community. People still living at the institution or in transitional housing were able to attend the programs as fellow community members. See Assumpção and Pimentel, "Autismo infantil"; Costa, *História da psiquiatria no Brasil*; and Russo, *O mundo psi no Brasil*.

33. In the 1950s and 1960s, psychoanalytic theorist Bruno Bettleheim introduced the medical community to the idea that autism was caused by cold and indifferent mothers, called "refrigerator mothers." This perspective was later refuted. See B. Bettleheim, *The Empty Fortress: Infantile Autism and the Birth of the Self* (New York: Free Press, 1967). Kanner presented the families of autistics as pathological and psychoanalysts promoted this assertion as part of the argument that autism was a psychosis; see Kanner, "Autistic Disturbances of Affective Contact." Later, organic etiologies were developed that characterized autism as cognitive and social impairments; these theories had different implications for treatment and rehabilitation.

34. They did this in times of political turmoil and with little governmental assistance. Set in São Paulo, the Brazilian city with the highest concentration of rehabilitation institutions in the country, Cavalcante's 2003 study provided a history and a genealogy of three families, specifically the families of three mothers, Ana Maria, Marisa, and Marli, who were founders of the first Brazilian Association of Friends of Autists.

35. Quoted in Fátima Gonçalves Cavalcante, *Pessoas muito especiais: a construção social do portador de deficiência e a reinvenção da família* (Rio de Janeiro: Editora Fiocruz, 2003), 398.

36. For a history of the AMA, see "Ética das virturdes: Guilherme, Débora e Renato," in Cavalcante, *Pessoas muito especiais*, 297–403. For the AMA's guide for parents, see Ana Maria S. Mello, *Autismo guia prático*, 2a Edição (São Paulo: AMA, 2001).

37. Cavalcante, *Pessoas muito especiais*.

38. Ibid.

39. Autism Society of America; The National Autistic Society (UK); Asociación Argentina de Padres Autistas; Asociación Chilena de Padres y Amigos de los Autistas, AN-THIROS (Colombia); Sociedad Venezolana Para Niños e Adultos Autistas (Venezuela); Centro de Actividades Especiales (Peru).

40. This was established because the government does not assume responsibility when aging parents die or become unable to care for their children. The AMA built residential options to provide a place for such children after the death of their parents.

41. Mello, *Autismo guia prático*.

42. Cavalcante, *Pessoas muito especiais*.

43. In 1989, the Program of Interdisciplinary Services for Autistic and Psychotic Children (PAICAP) was created. It provides children with focused workshops in areas that include music, body in movement, the visual arts, and psychoeducational stimulation and was one of the first programs in Rio de Janeiro that focused on inclusion in a public school setting; see Cavalcante, *Pessoas muito especiais*. In the same year, the other major psychiatric hospital in Brazil, Instituto Philippe Pinel (then a federal hospital), initiated an intensive day hospital program (NAICAP) for autistic and psychotic children; see Paula et al., "Brief Report: Prevalence of Pervasive Developmental Disorder in Brazil." Also in 1989, the Study Group on Autism and Childhood Psychosis (GEPAPI) was formed, marked by a strong Anglo-American influence. In 1992, the Dr. Ulysses Pernambucano Municipal School for children and adolescents with psychosis and autism was started at the oldest psychiatric hospital in Brazil, the Centro Psiquiátrico Pedro II (CPPII). This school was a collaboration between CPPII, the Helen Antipoff Institute (for special education), and the municipal Department of Education and favored an integrated approach to health and education.

44. Presidência da República, Casa Civil Subchefia para Assuntos Jurídicos, "LEI Nº 12.764, de 27 de Dezembro de 2012," http://media.wix.com/ugd/9ea61f_db236f83acf 486b43bd997394c9eec4c.pdf.

45. Beth A. Haller, *Representing Disability in an Ableist World: Essays on Mass Media* (Louisville, Ky.: Advocado Press, 2010).

46. Claudio Ferrera Costa, "Minha síndrome de Asperger," YouTube video, http://www .youtube.com/watch?v=64mEKoP3dKg.

47. For information about both the book and the documentary film, see História do Movimento Político das Pessoas com Deficiência no Brasil, http://www.pessoa comdeficiencia.gov.br/app/publicacoes/historia-do-movimento-politico-das-pessoas -com-deficiencia-no-brasil.

48. Escola Especial Meu Mundo, "Agenda," http://www.amigosdoautista.com.br/evento1 .htm; Fernando Cotta, "A vida do meu filho: orgulho autista," http://avidadomeufilho.blogspot .ca/2009/06/orgulho-autista.html.

CHAPTER 5

Negotiating Disability

Mobilization and Organization among Landmine Survivors in Late Twentieth-Century Northern Uganda

HERBERT MUYINDA

KEYWORDS: *Centuries*: twentieth; twenty-first; *Geographical Areas*: Africa; *Sources*: interviews; government documents; organizational reports; *Themes*: family, daily life, and community; bodies, medicine, contested knowledge; culture; citizenship and belonging; war; technology; activism

On one of the busiest streets in Gulu town—the regional capital of northern Uganda—there is a blue and white signpost with the words Gulu Landmine Survivors' Association (GULMSA). A group of landmine survivors erected the signpost in November 2004, when Pact Omega,[1] a USAID-funded NGO, gave them funds to rent an office in Gulu town. Just outside the GULMSA office sits a woman, a landmine survivor, tending to whoever comes to buy clay stoves, cooking pots, water pots, flowerpots, baked bricks, and other clay materials—all products of a project run by GULMSA. Inside the office, the secretary of the association attends to visitors and provides information about the association—why it was formed and its activities. Landmine survivors on tricycles and in wheelchairs or on crutches with prostheses on their legs continuously come and go; this is a meeting place for them. It provides an address from where different activities, both individual and collective, can be coordinated. It is the center of their organizing efforts and for many the center of their lives.

This chapter centers on local disability movements in northern Uganda from 1986 to 2006, focusing especially on landmine survivors. It draws primarily on life stories, conducted in 2005 and 2006 with forty-seven landmine survivors (thirty women and seventeen men). All of the survivors contacted in this study had had at least one of their lower limbs amputated. These primary sources are a valuable resource for historians. War and the displacement it often causes can hinder the creation and preservation of the types of sources on which disability historians typically rely. Extant medical documents offer only limited insights into the lived experiences of disabled people. Oral interviews add a more complex and human dimension to the historical record. It is important to note, however, that these sources have limitations. Historians must consider, for example, external and internal factors that may shape what people share and the level of factual accuracy of what people say. By placing these oral interviews in a broader context of Ugandan history and culture, I will analyze a disability community through the lens of its mobilization and organization for much-needed resources and economic empowerment. As this chapter seeks to demonstrate, a historical consideration of emerging disability activist groups offers important stories that challenge commonly held meanings of community and disability in specific regions and transnationally.

This project demonstrates that place matters. As historians endeavor to understand disability in economically marginalized settings and postconflict areas, a focus on local ways of responding to events becomes extremely important. This is particularly true in places such as Uganda and sub-Saharan Africa generally, where formal institutions historically have been weak and the delivery of social services has been limited or completely nonexistent. Local responses to these challenges illustrate the powerful role of community networks, gendered social and economic roles, and culturally contingent ideas about activism and citizenship.

The Violent Past and the Use of Antipersonnel Mines

For over two decades (1986–2006), the people in northern Uganda suffered a protracted war between the government of Uganda and the Lord's Resistance Army (LRA). Local populations regularly experienced violence and brutality, often resulting in countless injuries and various bodily impairments.[2] The war also undermined Uganda's infrastructure, weakening its social and economic fabric.

The violent conflict began when soldiers from the former national army, the Uganda National Liberation Army (UNLA), fled to the north after being ousted from government by the new president, Yoweri Museveni, and his National Resistance Army (NRA). The UNLA forces were defeated in March 1986, but many remnants of the former army joined with Acholi politicians to form the Uganda People's Democratic Army that same month.[3] The Acholi are situated in central northern Uganda, east of the Nile, and have an estimated population of 1.6 million people. They consider themselves a distinct ethnic group; it has been suggested that the ancestors of the Acholi were part of an "original tribe" called Luo in the Sudan that splintered around 1650.[4]

In 1986–1987, Alice Lakwena, an Acholi priestess, formed another rebel group, the cult-like Holy Spirit Movement (HSM; sometimes called the Holy Spirit Mobile Forces), which she led in rebellion against the Ugandan government. She took the name Lakwena (the Acholi word for "messenger"), claiming to be channeling a powerful warrior spirit. She also proclaimed that she could make HSM fighters "immune" to bullets in battle. The HSM offered hope for both worldly and spiritual redemption in a dark hour of despair; the Acholi had been ousted from power and were facing persecution and, many believed, possible extinction.[5] Lakwena managed her army using cleansing rituals and strict moral rules of behavior that made her very popular. The Acholi people believed that the rebel movement was acting on their behalf after the new NRM regime ousted them from power. However, the HSM was overpowered by government forces in November 1987 and fled to Kenya.[6] Lakwena's defeat left a significant power vacuum, and in 1987, many of her followers joined the insurgent LRA under Joseph Kony, which had been active since 1986.[7]

Although the conflict in northern Uganda began in 1986, severe casualties for civilians including those due to anti-personnel (AP) mines were rare until 1996.[8] Until that time, civilians were not targets and they largely supported the rebels against the government. In addition, the LRA-initiated violence concentrated in scattered places of fighting that were usually removed from civilian locations. As the rebel factions resisted government forces, terror spread across the whole of Acholi land. Although the rebels initially targeted armed government forces, they soon turned against civilians.[9] In 1991, the government of Uganda launched Operation North, a brutal campaign aimed at weakening the rebels' political and military strength. The operation created strong animosity between the government and the civilian population and between the local population and LRA rebels. The Lord's Resistance Army consequently increased its direct attacks on civilians, and these attacks included the use of AP landmines.

Foreign support for the LRA worsened the situation.[10] The Sudanese government provided military support to Kony and his LRA when peace talks between the Ugandan government and LRA rebels failed in 1994. It was commonly recognized that the government of Sudan, which is perceived globally as an Arab state, assisted the LRA in retaliation for Uganda's support of the (Southern) Sudanese People's Liberation Army (SPLA). Until it signed a Comprehensive Peace Agreement in 2005, the SPLA, led by John Garang, waged war against the Sudanese government. The military support the Sudanese offered the LRA included anti-personnel landmines, and these became the signature of the northern Ugandan conflict. The LRA began using landmines in northern Uganda in 1994, after the Sudanese assistance began, and most of the casualties were suffered during and after 1996.

AP mines are among the most dangerous weapons in armed conflict. The devices are designed to explode when a person walks on or even near them. Most injuries from landmines are to the limbs and usually lead to surgical amputation. Fragments from the blast can cause damage in other parts of the body, mainly the eyes, ears, and genitalia. Similar to other countries affected by landmines such as Afghanistan, Angola, Mozambique, Cambodia, and Iraq, mines in Northern Uganda were usually placed in strategic locations, such as water points, food sources, pathways, and in the bush and in forests, places that are often frequented by civilians as sources of daily sustenance such as food, water, firewood, and hiding places in times of insecurity.[11] Each of the fighting forces—government of Uganda forces and the LRA—used mines to deny the other side access to these vital resources. There was often little or no information about the location of mines because they were placed and used on an ad hoc basis. Indeed, the ambiguity over exact locations of landmines contributed to the larger goal of terrorizing people and destabilizing communities. Civilians found themselves in an impossible situation. Many generally understood that there were landmines in the places that were once their gardens, for example, but they ventured into these dangerous spaces out of necessity: without food and supplies they would die.

As historian David Gerber has shown, disability is a central feature of war.[12] AP mines were used in World War II; in Africa they were used in Egypt and Libya in 1942. It has been estimated that AP mines caused up to almost one-third of the physical disabilities soldiers sustained during World War II. Although there are no official figures from northern Uganda since systematic studies could hardly be carried out because of insecurity in the area, it is estimated that injuries in that region due to anti-personnel landmine blasts, gunshots, bombs, stampedes, torture, mutilation, and other forms of bodily harm led to increased numbers of people with disabilities and that the proportions may be higher than average for the whole country because of the conflict.[13] For example, a review of hospital records from northern Uganda between July 1998 and February 2006 by the Italian NGO AssociazioneVolontari per il Servizio Internazionale (AVSI) and the Gulu Regional Orthopedic Workshop identified mines as the main cause of injury and disability in northern Uganda.

Although the continued use of AP landmines is justified by the belief that they can be used "correctly," publicly available historical records and evidence of what happened in northern Uganda do not support that perspective. On the contrary, available evidence suggests that landmines were most often used incorrectly, either intentionally or because of the impracticability of observing specific rules in the heat of battle. These sources have not provided any analytical evidence of the military utility of AP mines in actual battle.[14] Mines are easy and cheap to plant but extremely difficult and costly to remove. If not cleared, they can last for decades and continue to kill or mutilate long after a conflict has ended. As late as 1996, clearance of mines used in World War II was still under way in countries such as Vietnam, Holland, and Slovakia.[15]

The longevity of the mines and their random dispersal in rural areas make it difficult to know the true extent of the global landmine hazard. What is known is the human suffering that they cause. An estimated 800 people die monthly from injuries related to landmines and 15,000–25,000 people are maimed or killed by landmines each year.[16] Approximately 80 percent of these casualties are civilian. The actual numbers may be higher, given that many incidents occur in remote areas without medical facilities to document them.[17] In northern Uganda there has been serious concern about landmines despite the relative peace since August 2006, when the LRA and Uganda signed the Agreement on Cessation of Hostilities. People leaving the IDP camps to go back to their original villages were worried since many mine areas had not been mapped out or deactivated. Uganda signed the Convention on the Prohibition of the Use, Stockpiling, Production and Transfer of Anti-Personnel Mines and on their Destruction (the Ottawa Treaty) on December 3, 1997, and ratified it on February 25, 1999. It entered into force in August 1999. The Ottawa Treaty requires the implementation of a Mine Action Programme comprised of humanitarian de-mining, destruction of stockpiles, victim assistance, and mine risk education and advocacy. The Ugandan army removed a large number of mines in 2003–2005. However, progress has been inadequate, despite provisions in the National Policy on Internally Displaced Persons, which states that the government must ensure that areas of return are cleared of mines and unexploded ordnance.[18]

Mine Survivors in Uganda

Cultural expectations have directly influenced landmine survivors' experiences with disability in Uganda. As anthropologists Susan Whyte and Benedicte Ingstad explain, when and how a person becomes disabled matters.[19] In Uganda, gendered expectations, especially for adult women, exacerbate the negative impact of acquiring disabilities. In the Acholi community, married women historically have been expected to look after relatives from both sides of the couple's family. This means that women are primarily responsible for gathering food, water, and firewood. Performing these tasks make women especially vulnerable to landmines. As researchers have documented, most Ugandans who suffer injuries in farms and gardens, on footpaths, around water points, and in forests are women.[20]

Gendered notions of ideal bodies also influence the responses to disability. Acholi ideas of a "normal woman" assume that a woman is ambulatory, for example. This both reflects and reinforces the expectations that women will procure food, cook, rear children, and oversee other domestic tasks. Married women who became disabled lost significant cultural capital. Acholi men expressed embarrassment when their wives could not acquire enough food or host traditional communal gatherings or otherwise perform other gendered tasks. In a strongly traditional culture, many men were reluctant to cross gendered social lines and take on responsibilities previously assumed by their wives. In this context, stigma intensified around disabled women. Husbands also complained that women "looked different" after they became disabled, that they were no longer "beautiful." Men expressed frustration that disabled spouses impeded their own experiences in the public realm; some specifically noted that they could no longer walk and move around "comfortably" with disabled women. When pressed, men focused on moments when women disabled by landmines needed assistance or complained of pain in different parts of their bodies. Spouses cast disabled women as "burdens." Anecdotal evidence suggests that most men in northern Uganda abandon spouses who become disabled. Out of the thirty female landmine survivors interviewed, twenty-nine had been abandoned by their husbands. Men sent their disabled wives back to their parents, usually with their children.

In contrast, most men who acquired disabilities as adults remained in their marriages. This is mainly because traditionally among the Acholi, marriages were built upon the strength of contracts sealed through bridewealth, or *limnyom*. The amount of payment for *limnyom* has changed over time. In the early twentieth century, during the colonial period, it included five to eight cows, six sheep, six spearheads, and any number of goats. By the late twentieth century, when cattle and all other animals were scarce because of insecurity and displacement, families made cash payments. *Limnyom* also sometimes includes gifts for the brother of the bride, a goat for the paternal aunt, a goat for the maternal uncle, a suit for the bride's father, *gomesi* (the traditional dress) for the bride's mother, and other presents from the groom's family. The *limnyom* is usually contributed by the man's family and shared by the woman's family. This transfer of wealth, which ensures that a woman and her offspring belong to a particular man's lineage, is central in maintaining the male-dominated culture of the Acholi. In addition, men have historically controlled land and other resources in the family.[21] This meant that most women were compelled to stay in marriages even if they wanted to leave their disabled spouses; in addition to the stigma of leaving a husband, repaying the bride wealth typically was too costly for wives' relatives.[22]

However, fundamental cultural traditions enable the Acholi community to provide care and support for disabled men and women. Strong intercommunity connections define the Acholi: communal planting, harvesting, and eating are valued. In polygamous families, wives often share domestic work and provide support for one another. Culturally sanctioned attention to and care for community members deemed vulnerable or weak, including orphans, widows, and disabled people, is valued.[23] Indeed, families are presumed to suffer consequences if they abandon or neglect their kin, leaving the vulnerable individual to die with a "bad heart" (that is, in a state of unhappiness). The Acholi believe that relatives will die one by one, be infected by incurable diseases, suffer misfortunes of all kinds, and be ostracized by society if they do not care for their disabled kin. Because most Acholi people fear ostracism and curses, disabled people, whether young or old, are much respected in their families.

Other disadvantaged members of society, such as "barren"[24] women, and survivors of Hansen's disease (leprosy), were also treated with care. The head of household had the responsibility to instruct the people in his compound to provide care and to ensure that the disabled person was given food, was kept clean, and that his or her hut was lit at night. This assistance was usually the responsibility of women in the homestead, although sometimes adults could instruct children to do it.

Historically, particular family members were thought to have powers to curse family members who failed to fulfil their familial obligations or who "misbehaved." The paternal aunt—*waya*—for instance, was known to have powers to curse her nieces in case of any unacceptable behavior such as neglecting or undermining disadvantaged people. To avoid such curses, members of a family, particularly the head of the homestead, ensured that the necessary care and protection was given to a disabled person. Although the war disrupted these practices by separating families and by displacement, many families and communities still provided different forms of support to disabled people. However, such support could be afforded only with difficulty.

Issues at Stake

The violent conflict in northern Uganda was largely characterized by displacement and encampment that posed serious challenges to the families and communities on which most disabled people depended for their protection and livelihood. Since the early 1990s, over 80–90 percent of the population have fled their homes and villages and traveled to camps for internally displaced people (IDP). By 2005, there were over 1.2 million people in IDP camps in northern Uganda.[25] Most social service providers, both NGOs and government departments also closed and left, especially in rural areas, because personnel feared possible death, mutilation, and other forms of injury caused by war.

The IDP locations lacked basic facilities and services that are essential for subsistence.[26] The Ugandan government made no advance arrangements to provide appropriate health services, sanitation, and food in any of the designated locations, resulting in new states of debility created by crowding, entrenched hunger, and poverty, among other things. There was no way to earn a living in these camps, and most people survived on relief. Lethal communicable diseases such as cholera and dysentery often emerged in the camps because of crowding, inadequate water supply, and poor hygiene.[27] These conditions motivated both individuals and groups to organize to meet the needs of landmine survivors.

Although Uganda is one of the few countries in Africa that has developed a national policy on disability, the policy has been implemented only in peaceful and politically stable settings; areas in conflict situations have been neglected. The Ugandan constitution, created in 1995, emphasized political representation for marginalized groups and recognition of the rights and dignity of people with disabilities. The country's affirmative action policy states that people with disabilities will be represented in Parliament and on local councils from the village to the district level; in addition, the cabinet includes a minister of state in charge of disabilities. Article 35 of the Ugandan constitution states that persons with disabilities have a right to respect and human dignity and that the state and society shall take appropriate measures to ensure that they realize their full mental and physical potential.[28] Because of this, many Ugandans, especially in peaceful areas, became increasingly aware of the needs and potentials of disabled people.[29]

However, there was very little government programming regarding disability in northern Uganda, despite the fact that disabilities were some of the main consequences of the war. There were hardly any indications of efforts to improve the conditions of life for people with disabilities, particularly those in rural areas. Although disability has seemed to be a priority area for the Ugandan government since the creation of the constitution, this is true only at a policy level; implementation of and funding for programs has been inadequate. At the district level, for instance, since the mid-1990s, when new disability policies were promulgated, authorities often seemed to be waiting for plans to be handed down from the central government. This inhibits the implementation of even simple local measures that would not necessarily require funding but would make important differences in the lives of disabled people. Examples of the types of initiatives that were not implemented included launching a disability awareness campaign, using district council by-laws to create tax-free stalls or specified areas to encourage people with disabilities to launch small businesses; and ensuring that new structures, at least in urban settings, were disability friendly and included design features such as wide doors, verandas, modified toilet and latrine facilities, and ramps.

Unlike in developed countries, in northern Uganda, the lack of adequate resources to deal with the more persistent and seemingly overwhelming problems of disease, conflict, and entrenched poverty often removed disability from the list of priorities. State policy seemed instead to value protecting the political image of the government—as being seen to be doing something—and had less to do with solving the real problems of people with disabilities. Local governments were supposed to provide financial support for activities for people with disabilities, especially activities that would help them mobilize and organize, but because of the marginalized status of disability and the chronic shortage of government resources, the districts ended up funding only national Disability Day celebrations; all government-owned disability rehabilitation centers were either nonfunctional or completely closed. The disability rehabilitation centers established by the colonial government in the 1950s to care for leprosy and polio survivors closed in the mid-1990s due to war and lack of support by the local governments.[30]

Some funding agencies seemed to feel that disability rehabilitation was not a "good investment." Little real value was attached to the lives of people with disabilities. Some service delivery organizations also perceived people with disabilities as incapable of making their own decisions and incapable of taking control of their lives; they viewed disabled people as always needing to be helped or as objects of pity and charity.[31] Many microfinance organizations in northern Uganda, for instance, did not lend money to people with disabilities because they thought that such people would not repay the loans. One NGO employee stated:

> Giving out loans is based on one's or a group's ability to pay back; and the ability to pay back, is determined by the ability to generate income. The problem is to believe or get convinced that a person who misses a limb and cannot walk normally will be able to work, get enough income and be able to pay back the loan. I do not think money can change their lives. Even giving them money and other assistance because they are disabled, like the NGOs are doing, will never change them from what they are, they are different, and they live a different life from other people.[32]

In some cases certain individuals, groups, and institutions used disability as a political instrument in their struggle to legitimize their presence as players in conflict-related emergencies and/or relief delivery activities. Some organizations, particularly nongovernmental organizations, mobilized people with disabilities into groups and took photographs of them as part of a process of acquiring support to improve the lives of disabled people. But after organizing and acquiring information about war victims, organizers never went back to them. People with disabilities complained that such agencies used information about their conditions to get money that they used for other things. For instance, during the presidential and parliamentary election campaigns in February 2006, many politicians organized disabled people into groups and promised to support them and improve their quality of life through those groups. After the elections, hardly any of these politicians went back to address the problems of disabled people or tried to fulfill the promises they made during their campaign. In 2007, the Acholi Parliamentary Group raised the issue of widespread exploitation of disability and demanded that individuals and organizations who used the suffering of the people of northern Uganda to gain wealth or social position be expelled from the northern Uganda region and that in the case of NGOs involved in this, their licenses to operate in the area be canceled.[33] The parliamentarians agreed that it was unfair for people to reap benefits from biological differences, which they referred to as the "misfortunes" of others. The chairman of Gulu District Council warned that

> politicians and self-seeking NGOs should stop pretending that they are helping disabled persons. They want to use the conditions of these people to fundraise. They know that the term disability sells highly to the international community. I have seen this humanitarian circus here [in] Gulu and the whole region affected by the war. (Leader of the Acholi Parliamentary Group, speaking in Uganda's 7th Parliament)

Another problem mine survivors faced was that when they articulated their issues, they used a language that the larger nondisabled population considered "unfriendly" and "confrontational"; this may have inhibited their ability to affect change, at least initially. They presented their concerns in ways that conflicted with dominant cultural assumptions about the role or place of disabled people in society. Their protests and demands were often made in the form of complaints, quarrels, and hostile demonstrations, methods that were perceived as unaccommodating and intolerant of other people's views. The larger public viewed the "phraseology" of the communication of the mine survivors as negative: "we demand," "we condemn," and "we are appalled" were not phrases that Ugandan people were accustomed to hearing from disabled people. Survivors often blamed the authorities for their fate, which the larger public disparaged as a stance that worked against friendly responses and effective interventions. The general public perceived mine survivors as complainers and not as contributors to solutions to their own problems. From 1986, these obstacles prevented disability issues from reaching the political agendas of government and other authorities, and especially in the mid-1990s, when people suffered the most war-related disabilities.

From the 1990s to 2005, efforts to bring problems of mine survivors to the attention of the public were made through the isolated efforts of churches, NGOs, the media, and sympathetic individuals. The suffering, fears, and challenges landmine survivors faced were often presented using sanitized language that intentionally or inadvertently oversimplified and reduced the magnitude and seriousness of mine survivors' problems. This was partly because mine survivors were perceived as a "small group of people" that had a negligible political impact. This perception translated into neglect by the government and other support agencies and led to ad hoc interventions that were quite inadequate for addressing their real problems.

Mobilization and Organization
from the Bottom Up

As Julie Livingston has observed in her work on debility and the moral imagination in Botswana, disability is about bodies and social relations; it is a biosocial identity that is at once both biologically grounded and socially parsed.[34] Livingston argues that while much of disability activism in the West (Europe and the United States) has promoted "independence," in Africa people have understood themselves to be living in a web of dependencies, and they have striven to manage and foster the nurturing side of these dependencies.

For a long time in Uganda, people with disabilities were perceived as incapable of making their own decisions or taking control of their lives; they were viewed as people who always needed to be helped, as objects of pity and charity.[35] This perception has been challenged for the past two decades through international and national disability activities. For example, the global disability movement, which was the part of the UN's work to equalize opportunities for marginalized people, sought to organize the "weak" into the workforce. The UN's Decade for People with Disabilities (1983 to 1992) accelerated the disability rights movement, a campaign that had always involved people with disabilities themselves. These initiatives were propelled by the slogans "nothing about us without us" and "disability is not inability" that were developed as a protest against marginalization.[36] But in northern Uganda these slogans were not effective because of economic and social insecurity, and people with disabilities there resorted to a bottom-up strategy whereby landmine survivors organized themselves into an association.

Mine survivors in northern Uganda organized the Gulu Landmine Survivors' Association (GULMSA) in April 2005. The process of forming GULMSA started in early 2002 when Akia (not her real name), a landmine survivor, was informed by a neighbor, who had heard a radio announcement, that all people injured during the war between the government of Uganda and the LRA were invited to attend a meeting at the district rehabilitation office. At subsequent meetings, injured people were registered. Akia was a regular at most of the meetings. In November 2004, when the International Campaign to Ban Landmines wanted to identify a mine survivor to represent Uganda at an international landmine conference in Nairobi, Akia was chosen because of her regular attendance at these district-level meetings.

At the conference, participants reported on the activities of mine survivors in their countries, but Uganda did not have anything to present because there were no activities to report. Akia realized that this was because, after decades of war, landmine survivors in Uganda were not organized, while participants from other countries belonged to organizations. When she returned to Uganda, Akia decided to mobilize other mine survivors to form an association. With assistance from the district rehabilitation office, Akia and a few other mine survivors formed the GULMSA and Akia was elected chairperson. It was not common for women to take up leadership roles among the male-dominated Acholi society.[37] However, in this case a woman assumed leadership of the mine survivors' organization partly because a majority of the mine survivors were women and because the social consequences of physical disability, mainly stigmatization, neglect, and loss of marriage, affected mostly women.[38]

GULMSA was registered as a community-based organization with the major goal of advocating for the needs of landmine survivors. In Uganda, like many other African countries and unlike most Western countries, "needs" for disabled persons were emphasized more than rights, partly because authorities had little appreciation of rights-based arguments and the strategies activists typically used, such as critical advocacy, litigation, and demonstrations, to achieve human rights.[39] Instead, authorities typically viewed rights-based approaches as expressions of opposition to government, and they often suppressed them. GULMSA sought to empower mine survivors by getting start-up grants so members could begin activities that could help them earn a living, a critical need in Uganda.

Achievements of GULMSA

When she spoke in public, Akia often outlined the achievements of GULMSA, pointing to how landmine survivors lobbied the government and NGOs for attention through their organization. Mine survivors obtained funding from NGOs to obtain counseling skills and strategies for presenting narrative testimonies. They became skilled at presenting themselves and advocating for their needs in parliament, at conferences, in churches, at schools, and among fellow mine survivors. One of the mine survivors said:

> This togetherness is what makes our life. . . . We decide everything that affects us together, and we share the benefits and the problems. Many of us had so many problems before becoming members of GULMSA but now things are changing for the better for most of the members. This organization has really made us what we are since it helps bring us together and support each other in different ways. Other people and organizations can easily identify and help us through this organization. When we come together we also pool funds, skills, competencies and talents on our own, which gives our organization advantages such as access to credit, discounts, and better interest rates. . . . It also enhances accountability and governance, which are key to the success of activities and survival of our association.[40]

By the end of 2006, with advocacy, mobilization and organizational skills in hand, mine survivors organized support for themselves by initiating peer counseling.

Each landmine survivor learned the most effective ways to give an account of his or her injury and how to make communities aware of how they got injured, the experiences they went through, and what others had to avoid. These outreach efforts to a large extent changed perceptions of and attitudes toward their condition, both among themselves and within the community. They counseled their colleagues, shared experiences, and discussed how to adapt to and live with their conditions. Peer counseling sessions involved both landmine survivors and their families. These interventions helped normalize people with disabilities in the minds of the larger population, an important factor in influencing social perception of their conditions and even the meaning of their conditions.

All forty-seven members of GULMSA have acquired mobility devices. This is one of the group's most important achievements. The equipment they have obtained includes wheelchairs, artificial limbs, calipers, surgical boots, and corsets. GULMSA advocated for locally adapted designs for wheelchairs and other mobility aids that would be appropriate to the local terrain and would therefore be easy to maintain and cheap to replace. Some of the mobility devices, especially those not manufactured locally, were quite unsuitable for local conditions, particularly the crowded conditions in the camps. Some of the donated wheelchairs and tricycles were too big for the space between the huts in the camps and difficult to ride on the narrow, bushy footpaths, especially when going to the gardens; they were also difficult to protect because they were too big to be kept inside the huts. Some disabled people also complained that the tricycles often broke down because of the topography of the camps, which includes deep potholes and uneven ground.

Through GULMSA, a number of NGOs came forward to support the mine survivors. Pact Omega, a USAID-funded NGO that supports disability-related activities in northern Uganda, helped GULMSA acquire an office and provided training in the business skills of small business management and budgeting and accounting. Pact Omega also offered training in tailoring, craft production, hairdressing, carpentry, electronic repair, pottery, and other small business occupations. The training in life skills was appropriate to the physical conditions of most mine survivors as they did not involve a lot of physical movements, and mastering record keeping enabled members to earn some income and get on with their lives.

Once GULMSA had an established office and began offering life skills training, more landmine survivors joined the organization, and by the end of 2005 membership had increased from fifteen to more than fifty. In addition, branches had formed in various areas of northern Uganda affected by the war. Pact Omega also provided training in organization and group dynamics and advocacy and counseling skills and provided mobility devices such as tricycles and artificial limbs for the war survivors. Canadian Physicians for Aid and Relief supported individual members by paying for mobility devices and modified latrines. It also provided rotating credit, medical treatment supported by AVSI, counseling services, and follow-up support for mine survivors in rural IDP locations.

One other important result of GULMSA activities was the shift toward the belief that people with disabilities are not necessarily a liability to the community and can make decisions about their conditions. For instance, Pact Omega and other funding agencies sought ideas from mine survivors and asked them what they needed. Through this approach, mine survivors' participation in activities intended to improve their life conditions increased, their communication and organization skills improved, and they gained ownership of their activities with minimum outside interference. Remarkable improvement was also made among women. Mobilization and organization enabled them to acquire the skills and start-up capital they needed to launch small-scale businesses that support them. In fact some of them, like Akia, were elected as community leaders.

GULMSA also greatly contributed to the reduction of stigma. Stigma was commonly experienced by mine survivors, but those who suffered most from it were former rebel fighters. Beginning in 2002, after a military campaign code-named Operation Iron Fist weakened LRA forces, some rebel fighters, particularly those who had been injured, began to return to civilian life. Although they were able to leave rebel activities behind and become officially accepted by government and rehabilitation institutions, they could not easily go back to their communities. Apart from their immediate families, most people in their villages disliked the former fighters and used abusive language toward them. One former LRA fighter felt that he was being discriminated against because of his combat past:

> People referred to us as killers, looters, people who were possessed with spirits of those we had "killed" and people who pillaged people's property. No body [sic] trusted us to do business with them because they looked at us as potentially "dangerous" people who could do anything. There was perpetual suspicion in whatever we tried to do, and people hardly worked with us unless one was a close relative or did not know that we were former combatants. Someone had given me his motorcycle and I had started a motor-cycle taxi business, but the moment he learnt that I was a former fighter, he removed it from me. (former LRA fighter)[41]

The situation became more complicated when impaired former fighters regularly were questioned about how and where they had acquired their disabilities. Stigmatization extended to the families of the former fighters. For example, people refused to allow their children to interact with the former fighters' children, believing that the children of the rebels were also possessed with dangerous spirits and therefore posed a threat. As one former LRA rebel commander explained:

> I had to remove all my children from the village and had to bring them to Gulu town because when they played with other children, the parents of those children warned

them that they were playing with "rebels"—they called our children "rebels." They told them that our children were dangerous: that they could harm them. . . . They gave their children instructions to abandon our children—it was really bad.

People also feared that government would perceive them as "rebel collaborators" if they associated with the former fighters. Some of the NGOs also found it especially difficult to assist returning fighters who had never gone through the formal systems of rehabilitation because there was fear that the NGOs could be perceived as rebel collaborators by the government or as government agents by the rebels. Many mine survivors in this category lived in anxiety about their future and had low self-esteem, and they seemed to be struggling to adjust from the life of a combatant to life in the new civilian setting. To counter this problem, GULMSA initiated campaigns to change discriminatory attitudes against group members who were former rebels. A number of former fighters stated that peer counseling sessions prepared them psychologically to accept their condition and to relate freely with others.

Conclusion

Although disability may be perceived as a devastating life event, it can be a basis for people to come together to achieve particular objectives. In some situations, disability may provide common ground that individuals can use to organize and mobilize to improve the circumstances of their lives. In developing countries, violent conflicts are often the main cause of disabilities and create the local circumstances in which disabled people live and in which they have to manage their lives. Mine survivors in northern Uganda lacked both substantial traditional kinship support from their families because of displacement and because the means of livelihood of family members was severely compromised. In addition, it was nearly impossible for them to access services from formal institutions since most of these institutions were forced to leave the area or stop their activities because the area was too insecure. This created a need for mine survivors to come together as war victims with sociobiological differences to advocate for and establish a mechanism through which to attract interventions into their lives.

Unlike some disability organizations in Uganda and other parts of Africa that were founded by outsiders, often nondisabled people, GULMSA was formed from the bottom up. Disabled people themselves organized to advocate for what they needed. Because of the group's advocacy campaigns, various agencies that included government departments and NGOs came on board to support mine survivors in different ways. Although GULMSA is supported by international disability organizations such as Pact Omega, it did not take a human rights approach, unlike disability rights organizations in Europe and the United States.[42] Instead, GULMSA pursued a "special needs" approach by identifying those who had been affected by landmines and mobilizing them into a functional organization. This close look at the mobilization, organization, and activism of mine survivors in northern Uganda shows that while broader historical understandings of disability cannot be over-looked, generalizations about how affected people respond to disability-related events may not be accurate in frequently changing, fluid situations in conflict and postconflict settings. Focusing on the varying ways affected people respond to the challenges posed by war-related disability can be useful in increasing our under-standing of the history of disability and disabled people.

Notes

1. Pact Omega supports disability activities that targeted various categories of disabled persons. The organization still exists but is no longer active in Uganda.

2. UNICEF, "Home Based Care for Children in Internally Displaced People's Camps in Uganda," baseline study, Kampala, Uganda, 2004, 9.

3. Robert Gersony, "The Anguish of Northern Uganda: Results of a Field-Based Assess-ment of the Civil Conflicts in Northern Uganda," report submitted to the United States Embassy, Kampala, and USAID Mission, Kampala, July 1997, 20, http://pdf.usaid.gov/pdf _docs/PNACC245.pdf; Refugee Law Project, "Behind the Violence: Causes, Consequences and the Search for Solutions to the War in Northern Uganda," Working Paper no. 11, Refugee Law Project, Kampala, http://reliefweb.int/report/uganda/refugee-law-project -working-paper-no-11-behind-violence-causes-consequences-and-search.

4. Joseph Pasquale Crazzolara, "The Lwoo People," *Uganda Journal* 5 (1937): 1–21.

5. Ruddy Doom and Koen Vlassenroot, "Kony's Message: A New Koine? The Lord's Resistance Army in Northern Uganda," *African Affairs* 98, no. 390 (1999): 5–36.

6. Refugee Law Project, "Behind the Violence," 13.

7. Ibid., 14; Doom and Vlassenroot, "Kony's Message."

8. Medecins Sans Frontieres, "Life in Northern Uganda: All Shades of Grief and Fear," December 2004, 10, http://www.msf.org.au/uploads/media/uganda04.pdf.

9. Refugee Law Project, "Behind the Violence," 6.

10. Support also came indirectly from more powerful countries, such as the United States, which supported the largely Christian SPLA, and China, which supported the Sudanese government in order to obtain oil and other raw materials.

11. Associazione Volontari per il Servizio Internazionale, "Restoring Survivors' Hope: AVSI Survivors' Programme in Northern Uganda," AVSI Regional Office, Kampala, 2004, http://www.avsi.org/wp-content/uploads/2011/09/RestoringHope.pdf; Associazione Volontari per il Servizio Internazionale, "AVSI Uganda Annual Report 2006: The Human Challenge," AVSI, Kampala: AVSI, 2006, 4, http://www.avsi-usa.org/docs/pdf/Uganda Report2006.pdf.

12. See David Gerber, *Disabled Veterans in History* (Ann Arbor: University of Michigan Press, 2000).

13. NUDIPU, editorial in *National Union of Disabled Persons in Uganda Newsletter* 2 (2000): 8.

14. K. Rutherford, "The Evolving Arms Control Agenda: Implications of the Role of NGOs in Banning Antipersonnel Landmines," *World Politics* 53, no. 1 (2000): 74–114.

15. Gino Strada, "The Horror of Land Mines," *Scientific American* 274, no. 5, (May 1996): 40–45.

16. Robin M. Coupland, "Assistance for Victims of Anti-Personnel Mines: Needs, Constraints and Strategy," International Committee of the Red Cross, Geneva, 1997, 1–30, http://www.markusthonius.de/downloads/mcoupland.pdf.

17. Frank Jarle Bruun, "Hero, Beggar, or Sports Star: Negotiating the Identity of the Disabled Person in Nicaragua," in *Disability and Culture*, edited by Benedicte Ingstad and Susan Reynolds Whyte (Berkeley: University of California Press, 1995), 198; Nicholas E. Walsh and Wendy S. Walsh, "Rehabilitation of Landmine Victims—the Ultimate Challenge," *Bulletin of the World Health Organization* 81, no. 9 (2003): 665.

18. Jeffrey V. Rosenfeld, "Landmines: The Human Cost," *ADF Health: Journal of the Australian Defence Force Health Service* 1 (September 2000): 93, http://www.defence.gov.au/health/infocentre/journals/ADFHJ_sep00/ADFHealthSep00_1_3_093–098.pdf.

19. S. R. Whyte and B. Ingstad, "Disability and Culture: An Overview," in *Disability and Culture*, edited by B. Ingstad and S. R. White, 3–32 (London: University of California Press, 1995).

20. Associazione Volontari per il Servizio Internazionale, "Restoring Survivor's Hope"; Associazione Volontari per il Servizio Internazionale, "Uganda Annual Report 2006."

21. Andrev B. C. Ocholla-Ayayo, *Traditional Ideology and Ethics among the Southern Luo* (Uppsala: Scandinavian Institute of African Studies, 1976), 98; F. K. Girling, *The Acholi of Uganda* (London: Her Majesty's Stationery Office, 1960), 46–47.

22. Ocholla-Ayayo, *Traditional Ideology and Ethics among the Southern Luo*.

23. Girling, *The Acholi of Uganda*, 46–47.

24. "Barren" is a somewhat controversial label; it implies an inability to conceive, and the blame often falls on women. See M. Kohrman, *Bodies of Difference: Experiences of Disability and Institutional Advocacy in the Making of Modern China* (Berkeley: University of California Press, 2005).

25. UNICEF, "Home Based Care for Children in Internally Displaced People's Camps in Uganda."

26. Sverker Finnstrom, "For God and My Life: War and Cosmology in Northern Uganda," in *No Peace No War: An Anthropology of Contemporary Armed Conflicts*, edited by Paul Richards (Athens: Ohio University Press, 2005), 110.

27. Herbert Muyinda, "Limbs and Lives: Disability, Violent Conflict and Embodied Sociality in Northern Uganda (PhD thesis, University of Copenhagen, 2008), 38.

28. Constitution of Uganda (1995), http://www.statehouse.go.ug/sites/default/files/attachments/Constitution_1995.pdf.

29. A. Ndeezi, *The Disability Movement in Uganda: Progress and Challenges with Constitutional and Legal Provisions on Disability* (Kampala: Oscar Industries, 2004), 6.

30. Muyinda, "Limbs and Lives," 183.

31. Ibid.; Maria Kengere, "Development in Disability: The Uganda Experience," paper presented at the Expert Meeting for Inclusion of Disability in Dutch Development Co-

operation Policy and Practice, September 16, 2003; Ndeezi, "Disability Movement in Uganda," 4.

32. Martin Okello, Local Micro-Finance Manager, Gulu, interview with Herbert Muyinda, January 2006.

33. Chris Ocowun, "Acholi MPs Probe NGOs," New Vision/Africa News Service, June 12, 2007.

34. Julie Livingston, *Debility and Moral Imagination in Botswana* (Bloomington: University of Indiana Press, 2005), 7.

35. Kengere, "Development in Disability"; Ndeezi, "Disability Movement in Uganda."

36. National Union of Women with Disabilities in Uganda, "A Report on the Needs Assessment of Women with Disabilities in Uganda, 2001"; J. E. Bickenbach, "Disability Human Rights, Law and Policy," in *Handbook of Disability Studies*, edited by G. L. Albrecht, K. D. Seelman, and M. Bury (New York and Thousand Oaks: Sage, 2001), 565–584.

37. Ocholla-Ayayo, *Traditional Ideology and Ethics among the Southern Luo*; Girling, *The Acholi of Uganda*, 46–47; E. E. Evans-Pritchard, *Witchcraft, Oracles, and Magic among the Azande* (Oxford: Clarendon Press, 1976).

38. Muyinda, "Limbs and Lives," 132; P. Spittal and Herbert Muyinda, "Socio-Cultural and Economic Effects of Landmines in Northern Uganda: Implications for Healthcare and Rehabilitation of Landmine Victims," Injury Control Centre, Kampala, Uganda, 2000.

39. Kengere, "Development in Disability"; B. Ingstad, "Seeing Disability and Human Rights in the Local Context: Botswana Revisited," in *Disability in Local and Global Worlds*, edited by Benedicte Ingstad and Susan Reynolds Whyte (Berkeley: University of California Press 2007), 254.

40. Gulu Landmine Survivors Annual Report, Landmine Survivors Association—GULMSA, Gulu, 2008, 3.

41. Muyinda, "Limbs and Lives," 167.

42. H. J. Stiker, *A History of Disability* (Ann Arbor: University of Michigan Press, 1999).

PART TWO

Cultural Histories

The question of what constitutes culture—how it contributes to historical meanings and experiences of disability—is a key area of study in current scholarship. The following essays examine cultural histories of disability from diverse vantage points. They use both discursive analyses and analyses of material culture. The guiding questions below are intended to spark new insights as you engage with this history.

1. According to these essays, how does culture shape the meanings of disability in history?
2. In what ways have people with disabilities and broader understandings of disability shaped cultures?
3. How do interpretations of history shift when disability, race, gender, age, and socioeconomic status are considered simultaneously?
4. How do the sources used in each essay contribute to specific understandings of history and historical experiences?
5. Representation is a key—and contested—term in cultural studies. How do these authors understand and use representation(s) of disability?

CHAPTER 6

Disability Things

Material Culture and American Disability History, 1700–2010

KATHERINE OTT

KEYWORDS: *Centuries*: eighteenth; nineteenth; twentieth; twenty-first; *Sources*: artifacts; *Themes*: culture; family, daily life, and community; citizenship and belonging; bodies, medicine, and contested knowledge; theory

Joystick. Velcro. TV remote. Straitjacket. Communication board. White cane. Sex toy. Thorazine. Wedding ring. Wheelchair. Curb cut. Cochlear implant.[1] The experience of disability, as is all human experience, is grounded in the human body and mediated through the environment. The environment is constituted of the culture-bound material culture of its era and includes architecture, assistive devices, media, clothing, food, technology, and all the other objects that surround us. Human relationships are established and mediated through these objects. Both the artifacts owned and used by people with disabilities and those that are used upon them or that are encountered in life create possibilities, impose limits, assert political and ideological positions, and shape identity. This chapter considers artifacts as primary evidence and offers examples of how the history of disability shifts into new registers when studied through its material culture. It proceeds from the assumption that artifacts actively shape and define disability.[2]

Two broad themes emerge from a material culture approach to the history of disability. First, disability is relational. As an identity, position, category of analysis, affinity, or life experience, disability is created through relationships among people, with things, to power and resources. These relationships are shaped by the senses and are sometimes connected to language. Disability is both a personal, individual experience and a collective one. Disability scholars have established that it is essential to understand disability as a cultural and social phenomenon.[3] Relations between group members and the state, the community, families, and other representatives of authority are mediated by material culture, and social relations are revealed through object relations.[4]

Second, disability is unique in the extent to which it is bonded with technology, tools, and machines as a medium of social interaction. Most struggles for civil rights address issues such as segregation, exclusion, paternalism, and discrimination. Unlike people who are singled out because of racial, gender, and sexuality differences, people with disabilities usually require accommodation to overcome barriers to sensory, physical, or neural processing. This entails material change in addition to legal and legislative action.

On Material Culture

As categories of definition and analysis, race, gender, and sexuality inhabit many of the same material spaces as disability. Their relationships to power, normalcy, and access to rights and civic experiences have physical, three-dimensional manifestations. Objects such as skin lighteners, hair straighteners, cosmetic surgeries, dresses and leather pants, bus lifts, and bar stools are the material props through which cultural identity is interpreted. Identities, dreams, fears, desires, and everyday lives are all grounded in the material world. Nearly thirty years ago, Michel de Certeau described how ordinary people appropriate and manipulate cultural products that do not originate with them. Consumers creatively reshape power and expressive relationships as they traverse the worlds in which they are caught.[5] Yet we seldom think about the interactions and relationships among ourselves, what we know, and the material world. Material culture is the concrete, sensory zone of reality that emerges from the psychic matrix of cultural information. A person who uses a rigid pole to navigate along the sidewalk is immersed in the cultural formations of urban design, visual impairment, materials science, and community.

Objects give a tactile, sensory dimension to the past. They provide access to lived experience and nonverbal aspects of relationships. For historians, one of the most difficult modalities of peoples' lives to retrieve from the past is how bodies move. Documentation of the significant relationship between control or the perceived lack of control and people with disabilities is limited. Bodies that are unmodulated in movement, speech, or thought, those that cause a scene or bring attention to themselves because they do not fulfill standards of etiquette, are hard to recover. Historical documentation of people in motion, especially bodies that move in unconventional ways has existed only since the advent of cinema. Media footage is ideal but rare. Objects can help restore that lost knowledge. The heft of a prosthetic limb, the rigidity of a brace, the absence of padding on wheels, the size and shape of an ear trumpet, a boot with four-inch soles, lenses tinted green or rose—these objects document movement.

The histories of nations, economies, and power are constructed through concepts of race, gender, and sexuality. The interdependence of these elements is well established. We study gender, race, and sexuality not as add-ons but as constituents of what it means to be human. The analytical category of disability is beginning to be understood as constituting gender, race, and sexuality and nations, economies, and power.[6] Physicality and capacity, including disability, configures what we know about the world and our relationship to it. Material culture is the literal, physical constituent of everything, of course. But more important, material culture conveys information. It demonstrates figurations of disability, race, gender, and sexuality.

In addition, disability is no more dichotomous than race, gender, and sexuality are. A person is not either/or. These concepts are flexible and culture-bound, and boundaries shift across eras and locations. Dirt streets, blue jeans, hairstyles, census categories, and barbeques are specific to times and places. The boundaries of disability also shift from person to person, depending on things such as where a person is, what she or he is doing, whether a person is feeling safe or excluded, or what and how many resources are available. Disability is also dynamic and contextual. No one is always disabled for all things; disability depends on the person, the environment, and the activity. Historical context provides crucial information about these issues. Material culture is a fruitful resource for understanding how such abstract configurations are created and for comprehending their flexibility.

Disability artifacts circulate within spheres of exchange. These spheres may be as informal as a parent adapting a toy or one neighbor bartering for the use of a vehicle in exchange for assistance with grocery shopping. In northern California in the 1970s, Ed Roberts gave a respirator that he no longer used to Paul Longmore, constituting both recycling and a form of gift-giving. Formal exchange includes all the ways people with disabilities have become both participants in and targets of a lucrative commercial market through their purchases of consumer products, special-purpose devices, health services, and similar commodities.[7]

Value is fluid: the value of an object and its benefit for the parties involved in the exchange varies with each transaction. All objects possess value that depends upon human emotion, rarity, aesthetic appearance, history, and other ineffable qualities.[8] Some transactions can create parity, such as the procurement of voice-activated software in the workplace or the placement of elevating blocks under a desk. The same blocks have a different meaning when they are used under a conjugal bed or a dining room table. Other transactions amplify possibilities, such as the key that a state hospital inmate fashioned from the found materials of nails wrapped in wire. The key's components, things that were commonly used in construction,

Figure 6.1. The value of discarded materials suddenly increases when someone finds them useful. An unknown inmate at Wisconsin's Winnebago Mental Health Institute wrapped this nail with copper wire to craft this key. Courtesy of Division of Medicine and Science, National Museum of American History, Smithsonian Institution, Washington, D.C.

had been discarded and repurposed. The key itself likely increased the personal worth of the key-maker through its potential for an encounter with a lock that would yield to it.[9]

It is essential to analyze closely the exchange, the artifact, and the desires of all those involved. Because power often is inequitably distributed, the agency of people with disabilities may be thwarted in the transaction and in analysis of the transaction. Objectification, especially through the use of metaphor, impedes and skews understanding of the relationship of material culture to disability. For example, metaphor intervenes when prosthetics become analogs for power, capacity, access, or identity or when the experience of disability becomes a frontier or borderland for traversing social terrain. This is not to condemn the use of metaphor but rather to highlight its pitfalls when working with material culture. People are neither metaphors nor abstractions. Objects provide direct and literal experience. Figurative analysis, because of its reliance upon language, does not work well for many of the core issues in material culture analysis.[10]

Language is limited in its utility for interpreting material culture on several fronts.[11] For one thing, words are general and experience is individual and specific. For example, a curb cut is understood as a ramped area on street corners, but the particular, individual characteristics of every curb cut are different. The angle, the state of repair, the width, and the direction in which it feeds vary widely. The metaphoric spirit of curb cuts is not equivalent to any actual curb cut. Consequently, the words are misleading. They create a unity that does not really exist. Another important difference is that objects are the thing that words are about. The words convey the meaning but do not embody it. Objects provide a direct experience, not a mediated or facilitated one. This is particularly important in relation to communication styles and preferences. Some people primarily rely upon sensory thinking—understanding through tactile or other sensory modes. Sensory thinking does not follow linguistic logic and syntax. Touching a thing communicates different information than spelling and reading the word. In certain kinds of neural difference, the person comprehends everything first as a visual image and then as letters and words.

On Theory

In material culture, as elsewhere, theory is important for what can be accomplished with it. Application of theory to a concrete, practical field that is constituted by hands-on work such as material culture can produce intellectual gymnastics that are interesting to observe but ultimately unfruitful. Objects are the things themselves and have physical presence. Theories recreate aspects of objects in abstract form and rely on words and the willingness of the theorist to create understanding. A cautious examination of several theories of especial relevance to disability and material culture follows.

Disability is relational and an essential convergence is the one that takes place between person and thing. The conceptual difference between a thing and an object merits a closer look. Bill Brown's "thing theory" attempts to make sense of the thing-object intersection. For him, things are what circulate around us, the large and small bits of matter that we encounter in the world. Once we notice them by projecting a thought onto them, whether by chance ideation or the deliberate naming of them, they become objects. Things are abstract, partially comprehended instances of material form. A hollow plastic tube for drinking becomes a straw. The thing is perceived, a use is imagined, and a name is assigned. Brown explains that simply by noticing or interacting with something, we render it an object.[12] This distinction helps explain the flow from unawareness to consciousness and the role of objects in the interaction. It also gives definition to the threshold between thing and object.

Objectification of the world is a constant and unavoidable pitfall. Objectification can happen easily when studying people without things and things without people. It is inherent in our apprehension of the world and is a thorn in all scholarly work. The problem of objectification has no satisfying resolution. We are, ultimately, simply our singular selves and everything beyond us is an object of our consciousness. We humans cannot transcend our objectification of what surrounds us. Pragmatically then, in relation to the study of objects, analysis needs to be capacious, open, and inclusive of numerous possibilities. Theory helps in this, but it can misdirect significance and derail a full discussion of the power and function that objects carry.

Two areas in which objects are intensely attractive but objectification can become a trap are Actor Network Theory and its close relative, Affect Theory. Actor Network Theory has been influential in material culture through its use by historians of science and technology, anthropologists, and archeologists. Affect Theory is the cultural studies, literary criticism, and political science version (vital materiality). Scholars interested in Affect Theory have begun to embrace disability studies.[13] The interdisciplinary nature of the theory makes its application slippery. This theoretical area is fraught with the potential for objectifying of people with disabilities and the associated dangers of that process. Consequently, the relationship of ANT and AT to disability material culture bears examination.

The concept of "affect" as used in Affect Theory is understood as the aptitude for causing an effect, that is, the aptitude for being an actant. Affect refers to the capacity to act and be acted upon. It encompasses gestures, motions and movements, linguistic meanings, and other influences on encounters among beings. Beings may be animate or inanimate; humans are only one contributor to the dynamism of the world.[14] Although people with disabilities are folded into the monolith of humans, human history is not so simple or reductive.

Designating people with disabilities as simply another genre of actants—that is, as equivalent agents with animals, other humans, and inanimate forms—ignores the history of disability and the power wielded by others over "the thing." Humans, animals, and objects are not equivalent; history and experience demonstrate otherwise. It is true that objects have agency and take on a life of their own, but all actants are not equal, and effect is uneven. Creating equivalency among all actants in a network erases the uneven histories of oppression among them. Among human populations, people with disabilities have an enduring history of oppression that has yet to be acknowledged or integrated into scholarship and common comprehension. As a consequence, the embedded necessity of speaking for "others" undermines the applicability of the theory.

Here, objectification has another, more subtle role in the material culture of disability. People with disabilities experience objectification and essentialization on a daily basis, whether through being invisible to others or as a focus for staring or the aversion of a gaze.[15] The very language of Affect Theory requires more inspection and qualification. Terms such as "thing," "it," and "object," which are commonly used in Affect Theory, have been used to refer to people with disabilities in literature, art, and vernacular speech. In encounters that stigmatize, a "thing" is an unknown, incoherent mass, not necessarily human. With recognition and awareness, she or he transitions to object. The move to "human" follows next. Within Affect Theory, the comprehension of nonhuman affect relies upon a metaphorical understanding of actants beyond the observer. Yet people are not metaphors. People with disabilities exist in real time and space. They are not figurative versions of something or somebody else.

The application of theory in any context raises ethical issues related to paternalism and the act of speaking for others. Theory can be the handmaiden of power by creating categories, circumscribing possibilities, and imposing the will of the theorist. Should theories be understood and accessible to those who are theorized about? This is an especially important question for people who have historically been spoken for and about but have seldom had the opportunity to represent themselves. People who communicate with signs and gestures or who do not formulate sentences and concepts in ways that are acceptable or understandable beyond their family or community nonetheless have a claim on the legitimacy of what is said about them and how such statements are used. The history of disability includes numerous struggles by groups and individuals, such as People First, Self Advocates, and Psychiatric Survivors, to make professionals accountable for the theories they have created about them.

And finally, theory can be a method of containment. It can directly or indirectly kill diversity, creativity of expression, and wildness. Its purpose is to explain and make sense of the confusing peculiarities of existence. The history of disability is full of examples of attempts to manage the unmanageable. People make convenient but inadequate metaphors. In short, application of theory requires constant vigilance and sharing of power. The contribution of Exchange Theory, Thing Theory, Actor Network/Affect Theory, and others to our understanding of the material culture of disability is that they draw attention to the politics of how people and things connect in the world. They loosen the constrictions of the modern body that is bounded and defined by medical frameworks and its technological relations.

On Technology

In its relationship to disability, technology leads a symbolically dense existence both because of the place of technology in modern culture and because of the nature of disability. Since at least the mid-twentieth century, the realm of technology has eclipsed human dignity and reputation in significant ways. The efficiency of technologies of war, medicine, and science surpass human capacities. Moreover, those who wield technology, who dispense it, control, invent, and regulate it, usually have a tenuous connection to its recipients. Technology rules our lives. Modern technologies assure that no life is beyond danger from them.

Disability differs markedly from other subjectivities that have been marginalized and disfranchised because of its need for technology. Reliance upon technology to facilitate life's activities or to counter barriers is equally or more important than legislative and legal action. Technology, whether as a tool, a machine, a device, or a simple artifact is inseparable from disability. And in the perception of many typically-abled people, a person with a disability often becomes merged with the technology she or he uses—"the one in the wheelchair," "the artificial voice guy." Consequently, technology inhabits a suspect yet essential space in the material culture of disability.

Basic life activities such as dressing, eating, bathing, and shopping are tied to one's capacity to use objects or actual people as aids. At least since the 1950s in the United States, a formal relationship between people and objects has been used for evaluative purposes. First with the elderly and then adapted for use with people with disabilities, tests that measure a person's capacity to engage in activities of daily living (ADLs) are used by social workers and health care providers to assess a person's functionality and determine the level of government benefits available. Mastery of objects is the conceptual basis for assessment. Does the person do personal laundry, use the telephone, manage his or her own medication, shop independently?[16] A person's access to resources relies upon appropriate use of material culture. Objects are thus symbols of "competency." The linking of competency to facility with tools is a throwback to eighteenth- and nineteenth-century anthropologies of civilization. Scientists ranked a peoples' relationship to savagery by assessing the degree to which they used technologies such as railroads, telegraphs, and weaponry. Eugenics provided the scaffold for this organizing hierarchy from inferior to superior. Technology use continues as an evaluative metric. Although the eugenic underpinnings are hidden, worthiness of assistance and implied civic worth are often symbolized by technology.[17]

The objects disabled people use to perform daily activities also illustrate how technology makes disability situational. Adapted flatware, adult sippy cups, Velcro, hearing aids, TV remotes, and garage door openers serve the same purposes as smoke alarms, electric can openers, and air conditioners in creating personal independence through technological dependency. The absence of or availability of a specific device can radically alter the environment and can consequently create or remove exclusion: a lift on the bus that works, a door handle with a lever arm, a captioning chip. A person in one situation is independent and in a different environment is disabled. In addition, every technology is assistive and objects themselves are neutral. For example, at what point does comfort become categorized as assistive? The stigmatization of the boundaries of use between some bodies and others is largely arbitrary. For example, are the neck pillows and reclining seats for long airplane trips comfort items or are they assistive devices?

Many technologies used for daily life fall under the medical classification. Medical engineering has traditionally played a central role in creating commodities for people with disabilities. The medical model of disability, in turn, influences object design. Medical inventors and designers share the goal of creating devices and objects that make the person as "whole" as possible. They work from the assumption that disability is a deficit that needs to be fixed or ameliorated. This is a core principle of the medical model of disability and continues to dominate rehabilitation and therapeutic practice. This approach entails an aesthetic of discretion. Engineers strive to minimize the visibility of the "fix" and maximize wholeness.[18] As a consequence, function is primary and the beauty of the device is secondary. Engineers tend to be interested primarily in how the device works. Product designers attend to consumer appeal and are not usually part of the development team. The results are functional but usually drab objects.

Equally problematic, development teams usually create prototype equipment and products without the participation of people with a range of bodily differences. People with disabilities often have a more complicated aesthetic when they serve as designers/inventors or consumers. Their relationship with the artifact is more intimate and enduring. Leg braces, helmets, leg bags, and ports are worn on the body and impinge on all the issues related to clothing and fashion. Wearing a technology orients the consumer in a different and more complicated register. For example, a split hook prosthetic hand is visibly different from a human hand and is more functional than an articulated hand for most uses. But wearing a split hook may have limitations for the hand-holding that accompanies courtship and romance. A telescoping white cane instead of a rigid one or a sports wheelchair make political and ideological statements about the users to others. The aesthetics of rehabilitation in hospitals reflect a hierarchy in which the consumer is near the bottom. These are aesthetic considerations that go beyond engineering specifications.

Aesthetics, then, are illustrative of power. The technology associated with polio demonstrates these power dynamics as expressed through objects. Poliomyelitis is an enterovirus that was first described in 1789. It is ingested and from the gut it travels through the blood to the central nervous system and motor neurons. There it produces so much virus that the cell membranes burst open and die. The death of motor neurons causes paralysis in the muscles connected with them. The first reported cases of polio in the United States were in Vermont in 1894. Polio infections peaked in this country in 1952. Today, vaccination is performed on children using either liquid drops of greatly weakened ("live") virus or an injection of inactivated ("dead") virus.

The history of vaccination to prevent the disease is rich in material culture.[19] The use of the polio vaccine illustrates the intimacy of medical artifacts, disability, and authority. Polio is the focus of an international containment effort. In an earlier epidemic of another disease, vaccinators for smallpox used the Ring Method of vaccinating everyone around the person diagnosed with it. In resource-poor

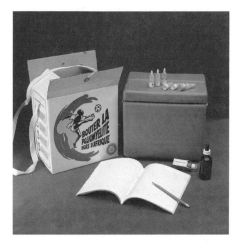

Figure 6.2. Global polio vaccination efforts entail millions of each type of hundreds of artifacts, such as these coolers, vaccine vials, ink bottles, and ledger. The objects create and mediate relationships that are powerful expressions of disability, culture, and authority. Courtesy of Division of Medicine and Science, National Museum of American History, Smithsonian Institution, Washington, D.C.

countries where polio remains active, vaccinators use a method based on National Immunization Days (NID). On National Immunization Day, workers fan out across the country with the goal of vaccinating every child under five years old. In January 2001, vaccinators in India vaccinated 150 million children, or about 6,000 children per second. Such an incredible feat relies upon numerous objects. Before the day, workers use banners, flyers, radio spots and other means to advertise the effort. They wear hats, vests and other NID-specific gear to mark themselves.

The necessary equipment includes vehicles and coolers to transport the frozen drops, vials of vaccine, tally books for writing down who was vaccinated and where, ink bottles for marking pinkie fingers with indelible ink, and candy rewards for the vaccinated children. In many places there are no street names or house numbers, so chalking the door helps others know that the home was visited. Transportation may be by camel, canoe, motorcycle, automobile, or bicycle. These relationships are established and mediated through artifacts: the vaccinators with UNICEF coolers, the vaccine in its vials marked with minute bits of information in several languages, and the recipients. Objects are central to this interaction and are the primary constituent of the relationships among these people. No vials of vaccine, no interaction.

But this is only part of the material record of polio. Traditional medical history presents people with disabilities as patients or cases. The successful search for the polio vaccine followed by its dissemination is the narrative core of these histories. Furthermore, in most historical accounts of polio, the children who got polio only make cameo appearances to create drama and to pull on the reader's heartstrings, heightening the urgency of the quest for a vaccine. Histories typically recount the science, politics, and economics of polio, ignoring its material culture. The narrative deepens and shifts when the material culture that accompanies the people who had the disease is examined. For example, the inclusion of a Milwaukee torso brace or a Drinker iron lung moves the person with polio to the center of analysis by raising compelling questions about who was there. These questions and the people related to the artifacts remain unasked and invisible when historians rely only upon scientific reports, statistics, and policy. The limitation of the prose or print record makes it easy to ignore people other than as invocations of the stereotypical heroic overcomer or tragic victim. Every object is the result of human action and taking objects seriously entails asking questions about all the people related to them. The children who had polio actually get to grow up and have complex lives. Their associated objects have a significant impact over the course of the rest of their lives—from iron lungs and respirators and spinal tap needles in the acute phase to devices and accessories used in the rehabilitation phase, to adaptive objects and architecture for the postdisease phase. The influence of curb cuts, wheelchairs, kitchen equipment, universal design, and the Americans with Disabilities Act (ADA) reverberates throughout society. Material culture both helps transform a "case" into a person and provides deeper understanding of familiar events.

People come back into the story when attention is given to objects. With polio, the people who had it become as equally influential in the historical trajectory as health care providers, caseworkers, and scientists. The invigorated presence of people with disabilities, in turn, raises other issues, such as stereotypes, scapegoating, stigmatizing language, discrimination, patient rights, and state power.

The role of objects in activities of daily living and in the history of polio illustrates how objects have many lives, serve many purposes, and have a multitude of meanings attached to them. As possessions they extend the self out into the world. As things that are supervised, objects extend the authority of the state and usurp an individual's ownership of his or her body. In polio, the vaccine is deployed and performed, with the arm of the state literally depositing it in the mouths of children. The children who had polio and then grew to adulthood use technology and wear objects.

Things Everywhere

Just as disability is relevant to all aspects of history, its material culture is found everywhere. Material culture captures subtle and complicated historical relationships that are not always found in letters, journals, and monographs. Disability material culture is not limited to ADLs, rehabilitation, and medicine. It includes toys, fashion, food, clothing, souvenirs, and more. For example, every small town with a state hospital or asylum produced souvenir postcards of the facility as expressions of civic pride.[20]

Figure 6.3. In this postcard that demonstrates early twentieth-century civic pride, a group of medical staff members gather under the portico of a six-story building at the State Hospital for the Insane in Jacksonville, Illinois. Courtesy of Division of Medicine and Science, National Museum of American History, Smithsonian Institution, Washington, D.C.

From the late nineteenth century until at least the mid-twentieth century, asylums were architectural showpieces and important employers. Thousands of postcards with images of them were printed, purchased, and sent. The postcards themselves had little information printed on them, beyond the name of the facility and the location of the brick or concrete mass. Objects such as souvenir postcards, plates, and spoons visually normalized institutionalization and simultaneously made it invisible. Asylums were tourist attractions, alongside natural stone arches, covered bridges, and the county courthouse. Visual acceptability and familiarity made whatever happened inside equally acceptable.

Different meanings are embedded in a lavender apron created in Santa Fe, New Mexico, by Kitchen Angels, a volunteer nonprofit organization similar to Meals on Wheels.[21] It was founded by a gay man and serves a range of clients, especially those with HIV and AIDS. As a generic kitchen apron, it is a gendered garment, one historically associated with women's work. Its lavender color and the organization it represents give it more overt sexuality than many other work garments. It is a disability garment in three registers. People with AIDS are protected from

Figure 6.4. This lavender apron from the Kitchen Angels in Santa Fe, New Mexico, simultaneously expresses disability, gender, sexuality, domesticity, and medical subjectivity. Courtesy of Division of Medicine and Science, National Museum of American History, Smithsonian Institution, Washington, D.C.

discrimination under the Americans with Disabilities Act. The agency where the apron is used serves the classic charity category of the shut-in, the invalid, the housebound, the handicapped. The apron, in a sense, is one of the instruments used in the treatment of "invalids." Yet none of the historical shame or stigma of the "the invalid" is evident in the lively design of the apron or in the literature of the organization. Lastly, the apron is part of the community of objects related to food for PWA's, people with AIDS, a word form borrowed from the people-first play book via the 1983 Denver Principles, a statement written by people with AIDS that lays out a platform of self-advocacy. This stance is similar to the position of the self-advocacy group People First, founded in 1974, which forcefully argues that its members are people first, not some designated impairment, and should speak for themselves on issues related to them. The apron, then, is a rich object with disability connections that are essential to its comprehension.

Another unlikely place to uncover disability is in the simple child's swivel toy that allows the user to mix and match bodies.[22] The toy has several sides, each with

Figure 6.5. Disability is a useful category for analysis of toys, especially how toys teach children about what is culturally appropriate. Various animal bodies can be created with this swivel toy, which teaches that anomalous bodies are whimsical and perhaps humorous. Courtesy of the author.

the image of an animal in three segments. Picture books for children in which the reader flips the divided pages to make funny faces use the same premise and format. Simple didactic lessons about the natural order of things and normalcy are embedded here. The toy guides what goes with what so that trans-species matches are obviously aberrant and humorous. The toy can be read as reinforcing cultural beliefs about the undesirability of diversity in bodily difference. It also teaches children that crossing boundaries produces anomalies and that it is appropriate to laugh at the result.

Implicit in this toy and in many disability artifacts is the larger issue of eugenics and the pervasiveness of eugenic concepts in contemporary culture. According to the toy, there are correct and incorrect bodies. Parental monitoring of infant development is a similar expression of eugenic framing of bodies. Parents use baby books to plot a child's growth or his or her first words, head size, weight, and various other milestones.[23] Baby books are accepted as repositories of memory and employ the sentimentality of memory for eugenic purposes. Baby books are powerful eugenic records that reinforce an aspiration to "normalcy."

Figurations of correct and incorrect bodies are not just mapped onto actual human bodies; the design aesthetics of products can have eugenic foundations, as well.[24] Prolific and influential twentieth-century industrial designers such as Norman Bel Geddes, Raymond Loewy, and Henry Dreyfus embraced ideal types, efficiency, and concepts of hygienic form grounded in eugenics. Their 1930s streamline style can be understood as a reflection of an evolutionary and eugenic ideology. The hybrid field of Universal Design counters this aesthetic. Since the late 1960s, architects and product designers, primarily in the United States, have been creating designs that center on the concept of accessibility. The resulting barrier-free environments, consumer products, and software are statements of social justice.[25]

In summary, there are many benefits to analyzing disability history through its material culture. Ideas alone are not enough. Ideas are disseminated in concrete form. Said another way, knowledge does not exist outside of the material manifestation of it. Comprehension of a subject is grounded in both language and material literacy. For example, different aspects of illness come to the forefront when the information comes through material culture. With polio, nearly all of the written histories focus on the rivalry between the researchers Jonas Salk and Albert Sabin and the production of a vaccine. The focus is largely on the race for the vaccine and the egos of Salk and Sabin. The material record reveals a different story. It demonstrates that both vaccine methods are necessary. The incremental contributions of the numerous researchers who worked out the physical parts of the process have more significance, too. The Salk-Sabin rivalry becomes secondary, an interesting sideshow. Furthermore, objects demonstrate the significance of the people who contracted the disease and how their lives guided the unfolding of events. Just as a historian of polio would be remiss in not examining the extant letters and papers of all the important scientists and policy makers, the omission of material culture produces an equally inadequate history. Lived inequalities produce unequal historical accounts. Material culture realigns the historical emphasis by restoring the agency and presence of those who did not leave archival evidence.

For most people, the lives of other people inhabit a place in the imagination—a mythic, nostalgic, or anxious place. This place in the imagination is easily accessed through objects. See or touch an iron lung, a hearing aid, or a panel of the AIDS Quilt. The response to the presence of the object propels the observer into the body and life of another person. Lastly, people come back into the narrative when attention is given to objects. Those who left few written records, the anonymous, the marginal, or poor, often left objects behind or used objects similar to ones that still exist. With historical context and the tools of material culture, we can touch those who are long gone and retrieve their histories; the gains for historians who use evidence from objects are unique and wide-ranging. In other words, when we pay attention to material culture in its historical context, we are able to understand people much better.

Notes

1. The full history of most of these objects has yet to be written, and not many attempts have been made to explain the relationship of material culture to disability. For an overview, see Katherine Ott, "Disability and Disability Studies," in *Material Culture in America: Understanding Everyday Life*, edited by Helen Sheumaker and Shirley Wajda (Santa Barbara, Calif.: ABC Clio, 2008), 152–156.

2. As a museum curator, a significant amount of my attention is consumed with objects and their meaning. Over the years, Susan Burch has worked with me continuously in interpreting disability history through its material culture. Much of the analysis in this chapter either originated in or was sparked through conversation with her. The nature of our collaboration makes the pilfering of these ideas both fun and fully ethical.

3. See, for example, Susan Burch and Hanna Joyner, *Unspeakable: The Story of Junius Wilson* (Chapel Hill: University of North Carolina Press, 2007); Leonard J. Davis, *Bending over Backwards: Essays on Disability and the Body* (New York: New York University Press, 2002); Helen Deutsch and Felicity Nussbaum, eds., *"Defects": Engendering the Modern Body* (Ann Arbor: University of Michigan Press, 2000); and Paul K. Longmore and Laurie Umansky, eds., *The New Disability History: American Perspectives* (New York: New York University Press, 2001).

4. Social relations as object relations is the insight of Karl Marx. He explained this in "The Fetishism of Commodities and the Secret Thereof," in Karl Marx, *Capital*, vol. 1 (1865; repr., London: Penguin Classics, 1990).

5. See Michel de Certeau, *The Practice of Everyday Life* (Berkeley: University of California Press, 1984).

6. For conceptualizations of this, see works such as Kim Nielson, *The Radical Lives of Helen Keller* (New York: New York University Press, 2004); Bonnie G. Smith and Beth Hutchison, eds., *Gendering Disability* (New Brunswick: Rutgers University Press, 2004); and James Trent Jr., *Inventing the Feeble Mind: A History of Mental Retardation in the United States* (Berkeley: University of California Press, 1994).

7. Good sources for understanding objects within spheres of exchange include Arjun Appadurai, "Introduction: Commodities and the Politics of Value," in *The Social Life of Things: Commodities in Cultural Perspective*, edited by Arjun Appadurai (Cambridge: Cambridge University Press, 1986), 3–63; Mary Douglas and B. Isherwood, *The World of Goods: Towards an Anthropology of Consumption* (New York: Basic Books, 1979); Igor Kopytoff, "The Cultural Biography of Things" in Appadurai, *The Social Life of Things*, 64–91; Marcel Mauss, *The Gift: Forms and Functions of Exchange in Archaic Society* (London: Routledge and Kegan Paul, 1974).

8. For a good discussion of value, see "Valued Possessions: The Worth of Things," chapter 2 of Prasad Boradkar, *Designing Things: A Critical Introduction to the Culture of Objects* (Oxford, New York: Berg, 2010), 45–74.

9. See homemade key from Winnebago Hospital, Winnebago, Wisconsin, date and maker unknown, Collections of the Division of Medicine and Science, National Museum of American History, Smithsonian Institution.

10. For more on this, see Katherine Ott, "The Sum of Its Parts: An Introduction to the History of Prosthetics," in *Artificial Parts and Practical Lives: Modern Histories of Prosthetics*, edited by Katherine Ott, David Serlin, Stephen Mihm (New York: New York University Press, 2002), 1–42.

11. One of the best discussions of the comparative merits of language in relation to artifacts is John Kouwenhoven, "American Studies: Words or Things?," in *Material Culture Studies in America*, edited by Thomas Schlereth (Nashville, Tenn.: American Association of State and Local History, 1982), 79–92.

12. See Bill Brown, "Thing Theory," *Critical Inquiry* 28, no. 1 (2001): 1–22.

13. Affect theory, actor network theory, and vital materialism are interdisciplinary and have proponents in the fields of political science, cultural studies, philosophy, and queer studies. See, for example, Jane Bennett, *Vibrant Matter: A Political Ecology of Things* (Durham, N.C.: Duke University Press, 2010); Gilles Deleuze and Feliz Guattari, *A Thousand Plateaus*, trans. Brian Massumi (Minneapolis: University of Minnesota Press, 1987); Bruno Latour, *Reassembling the Social: An Introduction to Actor Network Theory* (Oxford: Oxford University Press, 2005); Eve Sedgwick, *Touching Feeling: Affect, Performativity, Pedagogy* (Durham, N.C.: Duke University Press, 2003). Scholars who connect disability and affect theory in their teaching and publications include Robert McRuer, Rachel Gorman, Mel Y. Chen, and Jasbir Puar. See, for example, Mel Y. Chen, *Animacies: Biopolitics, Racial Mattering, and Queer Affect* (Durham, N.C.: Duke University Press, 2012); and Jasbir Puar, "Prognosis Time: Towards a Geopolitics of Debility, Capacity, and Affect," *Women and Performance: A Journal of Feminist Theory* 19, no. 2 (2009):161–172.

14. Assemblage is Jane Bennett's term. See her *Vibrant Matter*.

15. For the dynamics of staring and stigma, see Kenny Fries, *Staring Back: The Disability Experience from the Inside Out* (New York: Plume, 1997); David Hevey, *The Creatures Time*

Forgot: Photography and Disability Imagery (New York: Routledge, 1992); and Susan M. Schweik, *The Ugly Laws: Disability in Public* (New York: New York University Press, 2009).

16. For examples of ADLs, which were originally primarily used for evaluating the elderly, see M. P. Lawton and E. M. Brody, "Assessment of Older People: Self-Maintaining and Instrumental Activities of Daily Living," *Gerontologist* 9 (1969): 179–186.

17. The English, for example, partially justified subjugation of India because they had built the rail lines in that country, which they understood as clear signs of European racial superiority. For more on the connection of technology with superiority, see Michael Adas, *Dominance by Design: Technological Imperatives and America's Civilizing Mission* (Cambridge: The Belknap Press, 2006).

18. For more on design considerations related to disability, see Graham Pullin, *Design Meets Disability* (Cambridge: MIT Press, 2009).

19. For an overview of the history, scientific understanding, and relationship of polio to people with disabilities, see the online exhibit *Whatever Happened to Polio?*, www.american history.si.edu/polio. This exhibit is also a good source for the material culture of disability.

20. For the history of tourism and souvenirs, see Marguerite Shaffer, *See America First: Tourism and National Identity, 1880–1940* (Washington, D.C.: Smithsonian Institution Press, 2001); and Hal Rothman, ed., *The Culture of Tourism, the Tourism of Culture: Selling the Past to the Present in the American Southwest* (Albuquerque: University of New Mexico Press, 2003). See also Christraud Geary and Virginia-Lee Webb, eds., *Delivering Views: Distant Cultures in Early Postcards* (Washington, D.C.: Smithsonian Institution Press, 1998).

21. Lavender fair apron, Kitchen Angels, Santa Fe, New Mexico, 2010, Collections of the Division of Medicine and Science, National Museum of American History, Smithsonian Institution.

22. Child's swivel toy, Sevi Krogufant ars edition, Italy, 1980s, collection of the author.

23. For more on baby images as eugenic instruments, see Shawn Michelle Smith, "Baby's Picture Is Always Perfect: Eugenics and the Reproduction of Whiteness in the Family Photograph Album," in *The Nineteenth-Century Visual Culture Reader*, edited by Vanessa Schwartz and Jeannene Przyblyski (New York: Routledge, 2004), 358–370.

24. For discussion of the streamline style and the role of industrial designers in the popular expression of eugenic aesthetics, see Christina Cogdell, *Eugenic Design: Streamlining America in the 1930s* (Philadelphia: University of Pennsylvania Press, 2004).

25. For more on Universal Design, see Selwyn Goldsmith, *Designing for the Disabled: The New Paradigm* (New York: Architectural Press, 1997); Ronald Mace, Jim Mueller, and Molly Story, *The Universal Design File: Designing for People of All Ages and Abilities* (Raleigh, N.C.: Center for Universal Design, North Carolina State University, 1998).

CHAPTER 7

The Contergan Scandal

Media, Medicine, and Thalidomide in 1960s West Germany

ELSBETH BÖSL

KEYWORDS: *Centuries*: twentieth; twenty-first; *Geographic Areas*: Europe; *Sources*: manuscripts and archival materials; serials; memoirs; *Themes*: culture; bodies, medicine, and contested knowledge; family, daily life, and community; citizenship and belonging; activism; media

Between 1959 and 1962 more than 3,000 babies were born with a specific type of embodied difference in the Federal Republic of Germany. During this time doctors diagnosed an unprecedented combination of deformities of the extremities, inner organs, and ears.[1] By 1961 pediatricians had established that the children in question had been exposed to medications containing thalidomide during pregnancy; most of the mothers had taken the sedative Contergan, which was invented and sold by the pharmaceutical manufacturer Grünenthal AG. The political scandal that evolved around Contergan in the 1960s was the first in West Germany to involve a pharmaceutical product and disability.

The Contergan complex is a highly specific and relatively isolated experience with particular disabilities. Strikingly, pharmaceutical technology *created* the embodied differences highlighted in this study. Subsequently, medical experts generated facts about something they referred to as "thalidomide syndrome," constructing a specific type of disability within an exceptionally short period of time. When the media picked up and began reporting on scientific constructions of "thalidomide syndrome," it created stereotypical images of a "new" disability and a specific group of disabled persons, the "Contergankinder."[2] The ensuing medical and scientific interventions, which were enforced by policy measures, meant that a new disability community and identity came into being. The particular "scandal" that emerged in Germany during the early 1960s, and scandals more generally, are valuable historic sites for understanding disability because they vividly reveal contested social questions and disclose significant cultural expectations. The impact of and public attention to Contergan prompted German society to face fundamental questions about human difference, technical risks, and disability.

The Contergan scandal became a key moment in West German history and a symbol of the decade. It was deeply anchored in the broader collective memory of Germany and became an icon of postwar German history. In many ways, it can be interpreted as a metaphor for German society; it represented both tensions over the Nazi past and ambivalence about modern technology in an increasingly modernized postwar nation. Ultimately, this complex history offers an important means through which scholars can reexamine German society and culture by analyzing the various meanings of Contergan.

As many researchers have shown, disability is a contingent and historical category. It develops from perceptions of embodied difference within changing sociocultural constellations, structures, and discourses.[3] This essay examines the construction of the Contergankind (Contergan child) in the 1960s. West Germany had successfully completed postwar reconstruction and was experiencing enormous economic growth. The modernized welfare state was booming and seemed to have ever-growing resources. During this period, a majority of the population lived in relative prosperity. Under these conditions, sensitivity toward social problems increased, as did public involvement in disability-related issues.[4] The thalidomide incident happened right at the time when attention, interests, and social values noticeably were shifting in a direction that made the scandal all that more visible. Not only doctors and the media but also the emergence of a prosperous postwar welfare state shaped how Germany and the world perceived Contergan and the people affected by it, propelling disability issues and disabled people into the public spotlight.

This project draws on a variety of primary sources. The available scientific and medical sources, which are considerable, reflect the dominant position medicine has inhabited in the histories of disability in the twentieth century in Western Europe and North America. At the same time, various local, regional, and national newspapers and magazines—dominant forms of media in the 1960s—provide valuable information about broader social attitudes and public engagement with Contergan. Letters to the editor in particular offer direct public responses to the thalidomide scandal. As with all sources, these materials have inherent limitations. Medical and scientific documents portray a fairly narrow understanding of disability and disabled people. Records of pharmaceutical companies reveal the extent of the resources the industry invested in shaping what and how information was shared. Newspaper editorial boards chose which letters to publish. Political, cultural, and logistical expectations at least partly influenced which voices and opinions were "heard." Newspaper reporting, especially letters to the editor, encourages simplicity over complexity. It is important to recognize also that only a minor percentage of readers ever write to editors. This means that letters to the editor give only partial information about social attitudes. However, as literary studies scholars such as Andrea Mlitz have suggested, readers usually choose to convey positions they think are acceptable to their social and cultural group.[5] Thus, the letters included in this chapter illustrate to some degree the tensions related to and understandings of disability at the time. They also demonstrate the powerful role of the media in shaping the meanings of disability.

The Creation of the Contergankind

The creation of the Contergankind is rooted in pharmaceutical history. By 1960, the manufacturer Grünenthal AG had introduced seven different drugs to the German market containing thalidomide in prescription and nonprescription hypnotics and sedatives. At least fifteen other compounds were marketed in other countries.[6] Before the first commercial launch in 1957, the company had tested the product using the conventional procedures. However, it did not perform any tests for teratogenicity, the potential to interfere with typical embryonic development. German federal legislation left the developing, testing, and marketing of pharmaceutical items to manufacturers, relying entirely on the diligence and self-regulation of industries, pharmacists, and physicians.[7]

Contergan soon became an enormous commercial success. Consuming sedatives was routine in German society of the 1950s. Drugs that aided sleep were regarded as both a symbol of modernity and as evidence of the advances of pharmaceutical research. Many viewed sedatives as an indispensable remedy for what they regarded as the necessary consequences of modern urban life: stress, nervousness, and restlessness. Approximately 1.2 billion doses of Contergan were sold between 1957 and November 1961. Because it was free of barbiturates, it was considered entirely harmless, and it was explicitly marketed as such by Grünenthal AG. Doctors recommended it as a viable drug to help babies sleep. In colloquial German, Contergan was called the "Kinosaft" ("cinema juice"), indicating it was widely used when parents wanted a night out.[8]

Prior to autumn 1961, Germans generally were unaware that if thalidomide is consumed during the early stages of pregnancy, it can cause a wide range of health problems for fetuses. Earlier that year however, general practitioners had

Figure 7.1. Chemie Grünenthal product advertisements were premised on the notion that Contergan was harmless. This print ad appeared in a Grünenthal corporate magazine sent to doctors in 1959. Compared to other ads published in the magazine at the same time, Contergan advertisements were very costly and elaborately designed. Source: Advertisement, *Die Grünenthal Waage* 2, no. 1 (1959), reproduced in Klaus-Dieter Thomann, "Die Contergan-Epidemie. Ein Beispiel für das Versagen von Staat, Ärzteschaft und Wissenschaft?" *Die Contergankatastrophe—Eine Bilanz nach 40 Jahren*, edited by Ludwig Zichner, Michael A. Rauschmann, and Klaus-Dieter Thomann (Darmstadt: Steinkopff, 2005), 14.

observed and begun discussing the increase in children born with unique combinations of "birth defects." This led Widukind Lenz, a geneticist at the Pediatric Hospital at the University of Hamburg, to interview mothers systematically.[9] His research ruled out genetic causes and environmental toxins.[10] Instead, Lenz believed that pharmaceuticals were at the root of the new pediatric disabilities. In the fall of 1961, he approached Grünenthal AG about Contergan, but the company refused to remove its product from the market. The manufacturer had responded similarly throughout that year when other medical professionals had expressed concerns over unexpected effects on the nervous system of adults who had taken the medication.[11] Undeterred, Lenz sought public support by contacting the national press on November 26th.[12] The media maneuver yielded immediate results. Although it denied responsibility for any wrongdoing, Grünenthal AG removed all of its thalidomide products from the German market the next day. Lenz's action also sparked what would become known as the "Contergan scandal"—a media-political-medical-social watershed moment in German history that transformed the nation's engagement with science and technology industries.

The Contergan scandal brought children into a place of prominence in the German medical and political agenda. Before, children had been largely ignored in disability concepts and rehabilitation programs. The whole system was geared toward the functional normalization of an adult (white, native born, male, and heteronormative) clientele. Following the ideology of the German welfare state and traditional disability policy, doctors, rehabilitation personnel, and political advocates had concentrated their attention on (re-)establishing functionality and creating future employability.[13] Professionals continued this approach when the many individuals and groups involved in the Contergan scandal "discovered" disabled children; they assumed that they could simply adapt established rehabilitation models to their young patients.

In the 1960s, disability was largely understood as a medical concept in Germany. Not surprisingly, in this era medical experts were particularly influential in debates about and management of disability and in rehabilitation practices. Moreover, rehabilitation medicine traditionally had strong connections to orthopedics, and German specialists in this field had the institutional resources, access to scientific fora, and political support to put themselves forward as leading authorities. Medical professionals were only just beginning to categorize non-orthopedic physical conditions and cognitive and psychological differences as disabilities. In this instance, doctors largely ignored the sensory and internal symptoms that many children exposed to Contergan exhibited. This contributed to the distinctly orthopedic concept of the Contergan phenomenon that emerged. Specialists focused on so-called dysmelia: in medical terms from that time, these were congenital disorders of the extremities referring mostly to missing or malformed limbs due to genetic causes or to exposure to damaging substances.

In medical and mainstream publications, doctors primarily defined how Contergankinder would be understood. Importantly, they themselves figured prominently within this representation, typically as "protagonists" who would "fix" damaged children. The "cure" in this instance involved therapy programs, including physiotherapy, operations, and prosthetics.[14] As Oskar Hepp, the director of the University of Münster Orthopedic Hospital, put it in an address to the federal secretary of health in 1963: "If the children are treated with the right operations and technology they will become normal citizens like you and me."[15] Doctors were convinced—and they sought to convince others—that Contergankinder needed to appear normal and perform in typical ways in order to find meaning and joy in life. Indeed, for Hepp and many others, true "citizenship" depended on this.[16]

The Contergan affair might have remained primarily in the realm of medicine had it not been for growing concerns about broader threats to German society's safety and well-being. For example, West German media provided extensive coverage of the flood disaster in Hamburg in February 1962 and its aftermath.[17] Images of stranded citizens and destroyed buildings alongside growing death tolls reminded readers of their human vulnerability. It also fostered a sense of vigilance, a determination to prevent similar catastrophes. In this charged environment, and nearly half a year after the original announcement of thalidomide's side effects, *Bild*, a superregional publication with the largest circulation of daily newspapers in the republic, sounded a new alarm. Headlines ran across *Bild* and other newspapers that exclaimed "3,000 babies ill forever! 3,000 children are cripples!" and "Doctors speak of a catastrophe. Help immediately!"[18] From April to October 1962, local, regional, and national newspapers and magazines continuously drew readers' attention to this current example of human-made "catastrophe." The coverage varied in style but not in topics, argument structure, and general approach.[19]

The decision of the mainstream media to focus on Contergan was remarkable because at this time the press hardly ever featured disability issues. In the 1950s, many nondisabled Germans had been deeply engrossed with their own pressing challenges and had concentrated on their return to "normality" after the war. Few had wanted to be reminded of the Nazi crimes that disability discourse would necessarily have brought up. Reports about disabled veterans were the one exemption to this rule, but these media accounts were regarded primarily as issues of postwar reconstruction rather than as disability matters.[20] The shift to consider Contergan, and specifically children affected by thalidomide, reflected both continuities and changes in societal attitudes. Disability remained a stigmatized identity and rhetoric and representations emphasized that Contergankind were suffering.[21] While this maintained long-standing stereotypes of disability in German culture, it also provided space for a complicated "solution." Government officials praised medical technologies, prostheses, and assistance—key examples of a caring welfare state—as tangible evidence that German people and the nation were not merely healing but thriving.

The twinned images of suffering and overcoming became central and fixed features of the Contergankind figure in mainstream media. In photos and texts, the children were presented as innocent, miserable, and charming victims of a bitter fate.[22] The press emphasized optimistic prognoses for the children. The women's monthly periodical *Constanze*, for example, praised medical aids and showed pictures of loving parents cuddling winsome infants and playing with resourceful toddlers. Captions identified one disabled child as "a splendid chap" ("Prachtkerl"), while others were described as "intelligent," "cute," "at ease," "content," and "plucky" children who only waited for society to accept them "as equal partners."[23] Complementing these representations was the projection of a bright, normalized future. A 1962 *Constanze* article entitled "Contergan Children Have a Future" ["Contergan-Kinder haben eine Zukunft"] was typical in this regard. A picture of a family of six playing a game of ring around the roses in a beautiful garden in full bloom accompanied the story. The smiling parents held hands with three nicely dressed girls and a toddler with an apparent thalidomide-induced lack of upper arms. The caption read "Little Christoph is comfortable in his parents' garden in Opladen. He can grip very well already with his hands."[24] Another photo of a father holding his son and kissing the boy's short arms fills another page. This caption read: "The curly head from Menden in Sauerland with his father. The cheerful boy called Jan delights in his toys when his parents are not there."[25] Such images and words put readers at ease, both affirming their (presumed) status as nondisabled people and encouraging them to support the children as they supported the nation. Charity appeals in this period, such as the *Bild* campaign of August 1962 called the "Baby-Penny" ("Baby-Pfennig") became a popular vehicle for expressing interest in the Contergan community.[26] Aktion Sorgenkind (Mission Problem Child), an enormously successful TV lottery founded in 1964, also regularly conveyed both figures of suffering, dependence, and deficiency and exaggerated stories of heroic overcoming.[27] Because of the popularity of Aktion Sorgenkind and the pervasiveness of its messages, these newspaper and TV charity drives, among other media efforts, reinforced the image of the suffering but eager, promising but needy, brave but forever childlike Contergankind in the minds of many Germans.[28] The images that presented these children as both needy and inspiring sought multiple ends, including funding for medical research and expressions of patriotism and community. They also created profits for the media outlets that featured them.[29]

At the same time, the image of suffering but plucky children intensified public scrutiny of official measures by the federal government. Headlines such as "Just Begging for Money for Victims" ["Nur Bettelgeld für die Opfer"] and "Bonn: Everything Done. Thalidomide Victims Know Differently" ["Bonn: alles getan. Contergan-Opfer wissen es anders"] simultaneously elicited public outrage while reinforcing the image of the children's overall neediness.[30]

Doctors regularly presented themselves as the answer to society's concerns about the well-being of the Contergankinder. Orthopedists especially circulated a logic of compensation and normalization by technical means, and the press cast them as the children's greatest hope.[31] Newspapers consistently invoked medical experts as witnesses and facilitators in articles that assured readers that the children would find their way into society as entirely "normal" persons.[32] In this crafting of the story of the Contergan scandal, prostheses were euphorically declared technical miracles. In the fall of 1962, for example, *Constanze* featured orthopedist Oskar Hepp, who explained that expertly crafted prostheses would completely take over the functions of missing hands or feet.[33] Readers of the highly popular entertainment magazine *Quick* were shown a photo of Hepp fitting a one-year-old child with prostheses in an article entitled "They Learn to Live" ["So lernen sie leben"].[34]

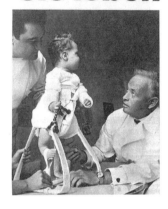

Figure 7.2. Oskar Hepp with a patient. The heading says "German Doctors Help Contergan Children. They Learn to Live." Source: "So lernen sie leben," *Quick*, November 23, 1962.

In the following year the leading news magazine, *Der Spiegel*, praised pneumatic arm prostheses as a "technological marvel."[35] The accompanying image prominently featured orthopedist Ernst Marquardt playing with a young girl who wore prostheses. Affirming both the expertise of medical professionals and the positive power of technology, the caption exclaimed the girl's success: "Eating, playing, drawing in three days."[36]

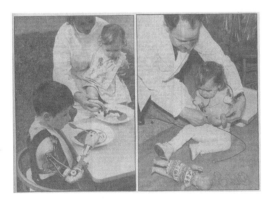

Figure 7.3. Ernst Marquardt. Note that the little girl is eating with her feet in the image on the left. The caption says "Contergan-Kinder with prostheses: Eating, playing, drawing after three days." Source: "Prothesen mit Gas," *Der Spiegel*, May 22, 1963, 81.

Contergan and/as the German Condition

What are we to make of these images, considering the social climate of the 1960s? A critical disability analysis invites new interpretations of this period in German history. As the media and medical discourse about Contergankind demonstrates, the nation was searching for its place in the world. The Contergan narrative of struggle and overcoming obstacles through achievement corresponded to the German postwar narrative of reconstruction and success through collective effort.[37] Citizens of West Germany were just beginning to experience significant prosperity and material security in the 1960s. The nation was even taking major steps toward reintegration into the international community as an equal and trustworthy partner. In the collective memory of the nation, this was seen as a rewarding process of "overcoming."

National reconstruction, however, was not the only broad issue reflected in the Contergan debates. Attempts to shape the thalidomide story also point to other national discourses. For instance, financial interests and strong belief in biomedicine prompted Hans Mau, a leading orthopedist, to advise his colleagues emphatically against calling attention to the technical risks of modern civilization by mentioning the pharmaceutical product.[38] Other doctors sought to downplay the causes of the incident in order avoid blaming and thus alienating mothers; these medical professionals recognized that they needed mothers to cooperate unhesitatingly in their extensive rehabilitation plans.[39] In light of this predicament, many orthopedists obscured the technical character of the phenomenon by using unspecific morphological terms, such as "defects of the extremities" and "dysmelia" instead of speaking or writing about the various disorders in terms such as "thalidomide syndrome."[40] Through their choice of words, orthopedists created the image of a disorder that was very similar to other more "natural" disorders they had previously encountered and competently treated.[41]

Nature played a unique role in the constructed image of Contergan. Medical discourse on thalidomide in this period was rich in metaphors of avalanches, floods, plagues, epidemics, and shipwrecks.[42] Linking the Contergan scandal to natural disasters drew on broader social concerns about environmental disasters that had been heightened by floods and other disasters the nation had experienced in this era. Implying that the problems arising from Contergan consumption was similarly "natural" and thus generally unavoidable (or at least that the causes were somewhat neutral) enabled doctors to avert suspicion from their own profession as culpable agents. Medical and scientific professionals were in fact part of the invention of thalidomide through their participation in the testing process and marketing efforts and through the prescriptions they wrote.[43] Instead, the professional interpretation drew positive attention to their efforts to "cure" what "nature" had produced. By portraying themselves as objective healers, doctors could address the harmful effects of Contergan and distance their medical practices from the root cause of the disabilities they were treating.

Mainstream media coverage also used naturalizing metaphors.[44] In contrast to doctors, however, the popular press linked metaphors of natural disasters specifically to the risks of modern technologies. This resulted in terms such as "drug disaster" and "Contergan catastrophe" or "Contergan epidemic."[45] In addition, authors often criticized the dangers of pharmaceutical technology. This combination of naturalistic and technology-oriented terminology revealed the media's deeply ambivalent relationship to the uncritical acceptance of pharmaceuticals. Although critiques of Contergan regularly acknowledged that risks had been taken recklessly, at the same time, technology was highly valued as a symbol of modernity and progress.[46] Thus, many authors condemned risky drug consumption practices while assuring readers that other "safe" technologies—prosthetics, surgery, and medical aids—would mend the damage that had been done. Coverage of prosthetic rehabilitation in particular allowed a conviction that technology would ultimately compensate for whatever problems it may have caused to shine through.

Inextricably tied to the emerging depiction of the Contergankind was the complex history of Nazism. Poignantly aware of Nazi crimes against disabled people, West Germans struggled to come to terms with their recent past. Portraying Contergankinder as achievers, as integrated, "normal" people, could—on a discursive level—affirm West Germany's transformation into an efficient, reliable economy and democratic state that had left behind its Nazi past. In this context, the typical framing of Contergankinder as innocent victims of a cruel fate[47] may be interpreted as a parallel to the 1960s interpretation of how "quite average" Germans had fallen prey to or been innocently seduced by the Nazi regime.[48] With positive futures awaiting them, Contergankinder echoed the promise of a safe and productive German society. Nazi atrocities, however, continued to haunt the Contergankind story, particularly in bioethical debates over reproductive rights, in which it figured prominently.

International events exacerbated these tensions. Two international media stories made explicit connections between thalidomide, "mercy killing," and abortion. In July 1962, a story broke in Belgium about Suzanne and Jean Vandeput, who were acquitted in court for killing their baby daughter. The child had been born with disabilities attributed to Contergan. As part of their defense, the Vandeputs argued that doctors had told them that there was no hope for the girl. Essentially, they asserted, they had committed a "mercy killing" rather than a murder.[49] Most German newspapers reacted guardedly. Significantly, many authors focused on the parents almost to the exclusion of the central issue—that a child had actually been killed because of her disability. Very few articles referred openly to Nazi crimes, but the reference was implicitly clear.

Readers, however, discussed quite frankly whether the life they thought such children could expect was worth living. Metaphors of pain, sorrow, and helplessness marked their outpourings. Many authors concluded that a bitter fate awaited these children. In a sample of thirty letters from the time period that dealt explicitly with the killing in Belgium or generally with the question of killing a disabled child, nearly half expressed the idea that children with disabilities such as those the Contergankind had were better off dead than alive.[50] Many readers praised the Vandeputs for having the courage to spare their child from an "unbearable life," and many felt that mercy and motherly love were the parents' motivations.[51] In a particularly passionate response to the Vandeput stories, one woman exclaimed:

> Truly outraged, I read that the sorrow stricken parents Suzanne and Jean Vandeputte [sic] from Lüttich were accused of infanticide. What matters here is not the act but the motive. They only wanted to spare the poor human [the German original uses a diminutive form] a terrible fate. The sooner it happened, the less the child became aware of it. How can one now condemn this unhappy mother, who was so much looking forward to her first child and then had to go through the dreadful experience of being condemned so harshly? Do those moralizers, as I will call them, not consider that this little human being [the same diminutive form as above] could never have dried its tears, cleaned its little nose [diminutive form of nose], eaten an apple [diminutive form of apple], played with a doll, or even lovingly have caressed a doggy or a kitten [diminutive form of kitten]. The mother did the right thing and so did the doctor. It would be irresponsible to punish them for this.[52]

Another contributor who wrote to the editor of *Quick* concluded: "It does not only take courage to raise such a child to adulthood; I believe it takes even more courage and even more love to decide to spare him the agonizing life of a cripple."[53] One woman's letter to the same magazine added: "This woman did not part lightly with her child but out of deep heartbreak and only for its own good. She thought only of her child."[54] While this example offered a direct critique of "mercy killing," most letters typically offered ambiguous reactions. Many reflected underlying and sustained support for killing severely disabled children to "spare" them their "ordeal."

A second story that emerged in August that same year involved U.S. TV host Sherri Finkbine, who had used a drug containing thalidomide during her pregnancy. Fearing that her fifth child might be born with thalidomide embryopathy, Finkbine had sought an abortion. When an Arizona hospital cancelled the procedure, she turned to a clinic in Sweden. Her public campaign to "alert other women" about thalidomide and reproductive rights drew international attention. German newspapers picked up the story, focusing in particular on the question of whether Finkbine had a *moral* right to abort a fetus because it was potentially disabled.[55] In 1962, abortions were illegal in West Germany and broad public debates on liberalizing abortion law had not fully entered the public realm.[56] Not surprisingly then, press accounts denounced Finkbine's decision as ethically disputable, but at the same time they offered sympathy for her.[57] As one *Quick* article explained, "Nobody can deny this woman compassion. There are certainly only few people who do not respect her decision—although religious and ethical reasons speak against it."[58]

Letters to the editor offered varying positions on abortion, but a common theme emerged that echoed the response to the Belgian couple: many contributors believed that women should not have to bear the "burden" of a disabled child. Responding to Finkbine's story, newspaper readers criticized as "barbaric" laws that made abortion illegal in cases when disability was suspected. One author called for female solidarity: "It is so inhuman, so barbaric that laws exist which force us women to bear such children that every woman in that [Finkbine's] situation should draw the attention of the stakeholders to her and [to] this madness."[59] Others linked the two international events by projecting the futures of disabled children who were allowed to live. As one letter to the editor expressed, "Maybe later parents will have to expect to be reproached by their child: Why did you not allow me to die at birth? I am a cripple, inept and a burden for my fellow men."[60] Another wrote: "All the pitiable children in your photos indeed look quite cheery and content with their artificial limbs. However, pity and horror take hold of one when one considers that these unsuspecting creatures will have to master life as adults one day."[61] These concerns were amplified in a subsequent letter: "Sure, one 'rescues' these children and cares for them—but what will be when they are adults and become acutely aware of everything?"[62] While many letters voiced similar ableist concerns, only a small proportion of letters expressed openly racist and eugenic notions and demanded that active measures be taken.[63] One reader of *Frankfurter Allgemeine Zeitung*, the leading conservative nationwide newspaper, for example, asked that all Contergankinder be killed at birth or be sterilized in order to avoid public expense.[64] Another declared that a family with healthy children was worth more than "keeping alive a cripple who is a burden to himself and his surroundings."[65]

These kinds of reactions, however, were opposed by other readers. Challenges typically drew attention to the inhumanity of eugenicist ideas. Others mentioned religious beliefs and the unassailable right to life as attested in the German Fundamental Law (Grundgesetz, the equivalent of a constitution). Quite often these readers referred to Nazi crimes and compared their opponents to the Nazis who had murdered disabled people.[66] Some advocates argued that life was always and unconditionally worth both living and protecting.[67] To them, murder was fundamentally wrong whether a child was disabled or not. As one reader succinctly noted, "It was and will remain murder."[68] Others expressed the idea that disability could be—and was to be—redeemed through achievement.[69]

These and other letters to the editor included descriptions of what a disabled child could or could not achieve, suggesting that most authors had little if any knowledge of what it was actually like to live with physical impairments.[70] One reader, for example, thanked *Revue* for its "educational" work;[71] another reported reading the autobiographical account of a deaf and blind man who had "mastered his fate and said "'yes' to life."[72] Another seemed to express a sentimentalized admiration for disabled people, claiming that "it is known that there were armless people who bravely eked out a living."[73] Although statistics suggest that at least 5 to 10 percent of the German population lived with what today would be defined as disabilities, the viewpoints of people who had direct experience and understanding of disability were generally absent from the public dialogue.[74]

A few notable exceptions came from parents. One who had an adult daughter with dysmelia, for instance, asserted that killing a disabled child illustrated a profound misunderstanding of love. This author further suggested that the Vandeputs were merely selfish parents who wanted to be spared the responsibility of rearing a disabled child. Pointedly, the parent asked: "Why did they kill? Allegedly of love! What a misjudgment of love. . . . Was it not actually done out of egoism, out of fear of the enormous obligation, of the doing without that comes with it?[75] The mother continued:

> Maybe I am more entitled to be heard about this report than anyone else because I have a child with two arms without elbows and deformed hands. I will never forget crying all night long out of despair because I, too, thought about how my daughter would never be able to clean her little nose. And again we were desperate when the barely twelve-week-old child did not want to use her arms and hands at all but was using her toes to grip things from the beginning. . . . She was obviously aware of her predisposition. It would lead too far to recount everything that has happened in my daughter's life since these dark days. Just this: She has a career, which allows her to prove herself and feeds her.[76]

Shortly thereafter, two mothers contributing to *Bunte* described their children as "lovingly shepherded by everyone" while they themselves were blamed because they had used Contergan.[77] Drawing attention to the impact on families, and particularly on mothers, these advocates offered an important counternarrative to the stories of Contergankind offered by medical experts and in the mainstream media.

Occasionally, disabled people directly engaged as well. Their opinions varied, reflecting the actual diversity within the community labeled under the monolithic category disabled. One adult woman, for example, wrote to *Revue* that she was deeply shocked by the news from Belgium. She had lost an arm during the war but had learned to manage her own household. She confessed, "But it is still terrible to be crippled, I have not been able to put up with [it even] to the present day." The author worried about the children's future, believing that they would never be fully independent regardless of the technical aids they received. "People (the healthy) forget quickly. Who will remember Contergan in 15 or 20 years when these children are grown up?" she warned. In her opinion, the mother who killed her baby must have loved her because she spared her an ordeal. "Would those who now condemn this Belgian mother be prepared to raise an armless child themselves?"[78] Conspicuously absent from the public debates at the time were contributions by disabled people who actively challenged this position.

Decades later, members of the Contergan community offered their reflections and demanded recognition through public protest. For example, in 1981 some men and women once categorized as Contergankinder participated in the German movement of emancipation for disabled people and took an active part in a "Cripples' Tribunal" ("Krüppeltribunal"). This show trial culminated a series of German disability activists' protestations during the UN International Year of Disabled Persons. The tribunal, modeled on Amnesty International's "Russell Tribunals," protested abuses. Participants in the mock trial impeached the welfare state for its violation of human rights, existing structures of segregation, architectural barriers, and degrading attitudes.[79] This public action was important in part because it compelled mainstream society to contend with adults who had always been known—and remembered—as disabled children, as evidenced by the name ascribed to their community: Contergankinder. Claiming authority as experts of their own lives and challenging this infantilizing representation, these activists contributed to the broader disability rights work that marked the 1980s and early 1990s.

Others since have gone public with their own histories of Contergan.[80] Jurist and disability rights advocate Theresia Degener, for example, contested the dominant, medicalized narrative that valorized prosthetic normalization. Degener was fitted with arm prostheses as a toddler. At four she was filmed for the educational film *Ohne Arme* (Without Arms), one of several documentaries that demonstrated and promoted prosthetics for children. These films, like medical and popular journals of the time, represented prosthetic technology as miraculous, orthopedists as benevolent experts, and "successful" prosthetic users as little heroes. As an adult, Degener offered her recollections of her experiences with prostheses in an essay for a leading feminist magazine:

When I was three years old I was issued the first cosmetic hands. With these prostheses I could not even manage half of what I could do with my feet because they disabled me in all respects. I could not play with them because I did not feel anything.

I crashed into everything because I could not get used to having such funny arms on both sides of the upper part of my body. I could not run with these prostheses because they were too heavy for me and the chafing broke the skin on my shoulders. And finally, I mustn't fall with them in order not to break them. . . . When I was eating I felt like a robot: I would press the wrong button and the food landed on my plate instead of my mouth.[81]

In addition to providing an important critical assessment of prosthetics, Theresia Degener revealed the damaging actions of doctors and journalists during the Contergan scandal. As Degener explained, these adults regularly displayed the children—often undressed—in hundreds of photos and several films in order to prove their points. Theresia Degener's account was by no means exceptional. Many others also reported how they refused to use prostheses when they grew older because of the many inconveniences and shared lived experiences that complicated the carefully crafted image cultivated in the 1960s and 1970s.[82] As Catia Monser, another so-called Contergankind, explained in her 1993 autobiography *Contergan/Thalidomid. Ein Unglück kommt selten allein* (Contergan/Thalidomide: When It Rains It Pours), men and women with thalidomide-induced impairments had diverse experiences and perspectives. Criticizing the demeaning construction of the Contergankind category and its treatment, she wrote:

The image of "the homogenous group" sticks to us like that of the Contergan child. Nondisabled social scientists, psychologists, doctors, pedagogues, politicians, social workers, journalists etc. analyze our interiority, allot us to our places in society or ban us from it, tell us and dictate what we have to do, how we have to feel, and what we have to think.[83]

Responding in many ways to Degener's and Monser's call to reconsider the history and meaning of the Contergan story, in 2007 German film producer and director Niko von Glasow developed a film and photography project entitled *NoBody's Perfect*. Dedicated to the Contergan experience—his own and those of others—the work highlighted photographs by Ania Dabrowska. Her dignified and attractive art nudes of men and women disabled by the effects of Contergan were inspired by Caravaggio's lighting and symbolism: the series showed individual full-length naked models posed in front of a black background. The pictures challenged cultural concepts of physical beauty and disability, compelling viewers to gaze directly at people who typically received stares or averted looks. Von Glasow's accompanying film provided broader context for the art photos, detailing how he found his models and how the photos were produced. Intimate, emotional, and often quite humorous, the documentary modeled an empowered representation of disability by centering on the models' individual journeys and exploring how they understood themselves and how they wanted to be seen and understood by others.

Figure 7.4. Portrait of Doris Pakendorf by Ania Dabrowska and Niko von Glasow, 2007. In Niko von Glasow, *NoBody's Perfect*, edited by Ulrich Kühne (München: Elisabeth Sandmann 2008).

Conclusion

The Contergan scandal offers a rich opportunity to consider the complex intersections of medicine and rehabilitation and popular media in the construction of a specific disability—as a category, as an experience, and as an interpretive framework. A critical disability analysis teaches us to consider the diversity within the category "disability" and demonstrates the limits of claiming a unified, common disability history. Contergan was much more than "a disability experience." The individuals, families, and communities affected by Contergan varied widely, as did their perspectives and approaches to this experience. This becomes very obvious, for instance, when we compare the naturalizing approach of the medical experts who strove to maintain their own authority and portray themselves as the bearers of the technological "fix" to the supposedly natural "problem" with disabled peoples' accounts of how they understood and experienced the appropriation of their lives and bodies. The story of Contergan in Germany also reminds us that context *matters*: in this case, the emerging welfare state, politics, institutions, cultural values, and the environment in Germany profoundly shaped how Contergan was understood in the late twentieth century. Using disability as an analytic tool and framework reveals Germany's struggle to define itself in the 1960s and after, opening new paths for exploring this nation's history.

Notes

My wholehearted thanks go to editors Susan Burch and Michael Rembis for their commitment to this chapter. I am also grateful to Andrea Spiegel and Ludwig Paulsen at Technische Universität München for offering technical support and procuring hard-to-get material.

1. The number of children who died before at or shortly after birth has not been tallied.

2. The argument that follows is based on research conducted for a project on how concepts of disability were constructed in the medical and political discourse of the Federal Republic of Germany between 1949 and the mid-1970s. See Elsbeth Bösl, *Politiken der Normalisierung. Zur Geschichte der Behindertenpolitik in der Bundesrepublik Deutschland* (Bielefeld: Transcript, 2009). Analytically, Contergan stands for a dense complex of discursive statements, attitudes, policies, and actions in the realms of politics, science, and the media. I analyzed scientific magazines and material related to disability from the medical experts' fora to find out how concepts were generated and discussed. Those experts and stakeholders in politics and other realms of authority were not disabled.

3. For a methodological and theoretical overview on disability history, see Paul K. Longmore and Lauri Umansky, "Disability History: From the Margins to the Mainstream," in *The New Disability History: American Perspectives*, edited by Paul K. Longmore and Lauri Umansky (New York: New York University Press 2001), 1–29; Catherine Kudlick, "Disability History: Why We Need Another 'Other,'" *American Historical Review* 108, no. 3 (2003), 3: 763–793; Susan Burch and Ian Sutherland, "Who's Not Yet Here? American Disability History," *Radical History Review* 94 (Winter 2006): 127–147. For an overview of culturalistic approaches to German disability history, see Elsbeth Bösl, Anne Klein, and Anne Waldschmidt, eds., *Disability History: Konstruktionen von Behinderung in der Geschichte. Eine Einführung* (Bielefeld: Transcript, 2010). I use "discourse" in the sense of Michael Foucault's concept but have adapted it according to Reiner Keller's usage in *Wissenssoziologische Diskursanalyse. Grundlegung eines Forschungsprogramms* (Wiesbaden: VS-Verlag, 2008).

4. See Axel Schildt, "Modernisierung im Wiederaufbau. Die westdeutsche Gesellschaft der fünfziger Jahre," in *Die Kultur der fünfziger Jahre*, edited by Werner Faulstich (München: Fink, 2002), 11–20, 14; Wilfried Rudloff, "Rehabilitation und Hilfen für Behinderte," in *Geschichte der Sozialpolitik in Deutschland seit 1945*, vol. 4, *1957–1966 Bundesrepublik Deutschland. Sozialpolitik im Zeichen des erreichten Wohlstandes*, edited by Michael Ruck and Marcel Boldorf (Baden-Baden: Nomos, 2007), 463–502, 466.

5. See Andrea Mlitz, *Dialogorientierter Journalismus. Leserbriefe in der deutschen Tagespresse* (Konstanz: UVK, 2008), 364–369; and Julia Heupel, *Der Leserbrief in der deutschen Presse* (München: Verlag Reinhard Fischer, 2007), 155–178.

6. See Walburga Freitag, *Contergan. Eine genealogische Studie des Zusammenhangs wissenschaftlicher Diskurse und biographischer Erfahrungen* (Münster: Waxmann, 2005), 35.

7. A registration law that was passed in August 1961 prompted the Federal Health Office to check product licensing and register new preparations. Again, testing was left to the manufacturers. For an overview and further reading, see Arthur Daemmrich, "A Tale of Two Experts: Thalidomide and Political Engagement in the United States and West Germany," *Social History of Medicine* 15, no. 1 (2002): 1:137–158, 140–141; Axel Murswieck, *Die staatliche Kontrolle der Arzneimittelsicherheit in der Bundesrepublik und den USA* (Opladen: Westdeutscher Verlag 1983); and Ute Stapel, *Die Arzneimittelgesetze 1961 und 1976* (Stuttgart: Deutscher Apothekerverlag, 1988).

8. For examples of Contergan advertisements, see "Gefahr im Verzuge," *Der Spiegel*, December 5, 1962; Beate Kirk, *Der Contergan-Fall: Eine unvermeidbare Arzneimittelkatastrophe? Zur Geschichte des Arzneistoffes Thalidomid* (Stuttgart: Wissenschaftliche Verlagsgesellschaft, 1999), 266–267. For "Kinosaft," see Wolfgang Cyran, "Die Contergan-Tragödie," *Frankfurter Allgemeine Zeitung*, September 12, 1962; and "Chiffre K 17," *Der Spiegel*, June 3, 1968.

9. German pediatrician and medical geneticist Widukind Lenz (1919–1995) was the son of Fritz Lenz, one of the ideological leaders of the Rassenhygiene movement before and under the National Socialist regime. Widukind Lenz, however, adopted a rather non-eugenicist position in his doctoral thesis. After 1945 he worked in Göttingen, in Kiel, and at the Department of Pediatrics at the University of Hamburg, where he was offered a chair in human genetics in 1959. In 1965, Lenz became director of the Institute of Human Genetics in Münster. He committed himself strongly to the Contergan trial, exposing himself to attacks from the defense attorneys.

10. During the 1950s there was both medical and media interest in teratogenic substances. Drugs such as insulin, barbiturates, and sulfonamides were discussed, as were the potential teratogenic effects of nuclear weapons tests. In 1959, the secretary of the interior published an academic report on the causes and statistics of birth defects titled "Bericht über die Häufigkeit und die Ursachen von Missgeburten in der Bundesrepublik Deutschland seit 1950." However, pharmaceutical law was not changed. See "Antrag der Fraktion der FDP betr. Zunahme von Missgeburten" (FPD Bundestag Fraction: Motion Pertaining to Increase in Birth Deformities), *Bundestagsdrucksache* 3, no. 386 (May 14, 1958); and "Bundesministerium des Innern: Bericht betr. Zunahme von Missgeburten" (Federal Ministry of the Interior: Report Pertaining to Increase in Birth Deformities), *Bundestagsdrucksache* 3, no. 954 (March 18, 1959); Kirk, *Der Contergan-Fall*, 129–135, 140–141; Klaus-Dieter Thomann, "Die Contergan-Epidemie. Ein Beispiel für das Versagen von Staat, Ärzteschaft und Wissenschaft?," in *Die Contergankatastrophe—Eine Bilanz nach 40 Jahren*, edited by Ludwig Zichner, Michael A. Rauschmann, and Klaus Dieter Thomann (Darmstadt: Steinkopf, 2005), 15–17.

11. See, for example, Horst Frenkel, "Contergan-Nebenwirkungen," *Deutsche Medizinische Wochenschrift*, May 6, 1961, 970–975; and "Zuckerplätzchen forte," *Der Spiegel*, August 16, 1961. For later articles on the discovery of teratogenic effects, see Wilhelm Kosenow and Rudolf Arthur Pfeiffer, "Micromelie, Haemangion und Duodenalstenose," *Monatsschrift für Kinderheilkunde* 109 (1961): 227; Hans Rudolf Wiedemann, "Hinweis auf eine derzeitige Häufung hypo- und aplastischer Fehlbildungen der Gliedmaßen," *Medizinische Welt*, September 16, 1961, 1863–1866; August Rütt, "Die Therapie der Dysmelie

(Wiedemann-Syndrom)," *Archiv für orthopädische und Unfall-Chirurgie* 55 (1963): 239; and "Kalte Füße," *Der Spiegel*, December 12, 1961. The earliest case report from the English-speaking world was William Griffith McBride, "Thalidomide and Congenital Abnormalities," *Lancet* 2, no. 1358 (1961): 1358.

12. Christoph Wolff, "Mißbildungen durch Schlaftabletten?," *Die Welt am Sonntag*, November 26, 1961.

13. Bösl, *Politiken der Normalisierung*, 43–44.

14. See, for example, Oskar Hepp, "Die Häufung der angeborenen Defektmissbildungen der oberen Extremitäten in der Bundesrepublik Deutschland," *Medizinische Klinik* 57, no. 11 (1962): 419–420; Hans Mau, "Die Behandlung der angeborenen Gliedmaßenmißbildungen," *Deutsche Medizinische Wochenschrift* 88 (1963): 1064–1065; Rütt, "Die Therapie der Dysmelie (Wiedemann-Syndrom)," 329–341; Kurt Lindemann, "Zur Prognose und Therapie schwerer Gliedmaßenfehlbildungen," *Acta Orthopaedica Scandinavica* 32 (1962): 298–306; and Wolfgang Maier, "Die Frühbehandlung der Extremitäten-Dysmelien," *Deutsche Medizinische Wochenschrift* 88 (1963): 69–74.

15. "Wenn die Kinder richtig operativ und technisch versorgt werden, werden sie zu normalen Bürgern wie Du und ich," October 4, 1963, Bundesarchiv B 142 1825, Federal Ministry of Health, Division I A 5, Record, "Protokoll der Besprechung am 4.10.1963."

16. Bösl, *Politiken der Normalisierung*, 84–86. The way medical experts steered the attention of political and media figures to this newly defined disability had amplified ramifications. For example, the credit system that was originally built to quantify "defects" was later used to calculate compensation payments. Since it omitted thalidomide-induced sensory problems and inner symptoms without accompanying orthopedic disorders, some people affected by thalidomide could not gain access to legal compensation and social security benefits. For an analysis of this, see Walburga Freitag, "Bodycheck—wieviel Körper braucht das Kind? Über wissenschaftliche Diskurse der Habilitation so genannter Contergan-Kinder," in *Kinder—Körper—Identitäten. Theoretische und empirische Annäherungen an kulturelle Praxis und sozialen Wandel*, edited by Heinz Hengst and Helga Kelle (Weinheim/ München: Juventa, 2003), 168.

17. For more on the connections between natural disasters and German politics and culture, see Franz Mauelshagen, "Flood Disasters and Political Culture at the German North Sea Coast: A Long-Term Historical Perspective," *Historical Social Research/Historische Sozialforschung* 32, no. 3 (2007): 133–144. For the Hamburg flood, see Jens Ivo Engels, "Gefährlicher Wasserstand im 'Wirtschaftswunderland'. Die Hamburger Sturmflut vom Februar 1962," in *Katastrophen. Vom Untergang Pompejis bis zum Klimawandel*, edited by Gerrit Jasper Schenk (Ostfildern: Thorbecke, 2009), 171–181. Characteristic examples of press coverage are "Stadt unter," *Der Spiegel*, February 28, 1962; "Als die große Sturmflut kam," *Die Zeit*, February 23, 1962; "Die fliegenden Rettungsboote," *Die Zeit*, March 3, 1962.

18. Dietrich Beyersdorf, "3.000 Babys warten auf unsere Hilfe," *Bild*, April 18, 1962.

19. For example, see "Gefahr im Verzuge"; Beyersdorf, "3.000 Babys warten auf unsere Hilfe"; "So lernen sie leben"; "Contergankinder haben eine Zukunft," *Constanze*, September 1962; Johann Georg Reismüller, "Wer soll diesen Kindern helfen?," *Frankfurter Allgemeine Zeitung*, August 18, 1962.

20. On pensions and postwar reconstruction, see Lutz Wiegand, "Kriegsfolgenbewältigung in der Bundesrepublik Deutschland," *Archiv für Sozialgeschichte* 35 (1995): 71; Kurt-Alphons Jochheim, Ferdinand Schliehe, and Helfried Teichmann, "Rehabilitation und Hilfen für Behinderte," in *Geschichte der Sozialpolitik in Deutschland seit 1945*, vol. 2, *1945–1949: Die Zeit der Besatzungszonen Sozialpolitik zwischen Kriegsende und der Gründung zweier deutscher Staaten*, edited by Udo Wengst (Baden-Baden: Nomos 2001), 568.

21. Beyersdorf, "3.000 Babys warten auf unsere Hilfe"; "Nicht Hüte, sondern Hilfe," *Bild*, August 22, 1962; Dietrich Beyersdorf, "Contergan: Der Staat hat versagt," *Bild*, August 25, 1962; Alfred Weber: "Wir sorgen für ihre Zukunft," *Bild*, September 1, 1962; "So lernen sie leben," *Quick*, November 25, 1962; Reismüller, "Wer soll diesen Kindern helfen?"

22. E.g., "So lernen sie leben"; Weber, "Wir sorgen für ihre Zukunft"; Dietrich Beyersdorf, "Mutterliebe siegte," *Bild*, September 1, 1962, Joachim Neander, "Als der Mann starb, nahm sie Contergan," *Bild*, September 3, 1962.

23. "Contergankinder haben eine Zukunft."

24. "Der kleine Christoph fühlt sich wohl im Garten seiner Eltern in Opladen. Er kann mit seinen Händen schon sehr gut greifen"; "Contergankinder haben eine Zukunft."

25. "*Der Lockenkopf aus Menden im Sauerland mit seinem Vater. Der fröhliche Junge, Jan heißt er, vergnügt sich, wenn die Eltern nicht da sind, mit den Spielsachen*"; ibid.

26. "Der Baby-Pfennig: *Bild*-Aktion: Helft Contergan-Kindern!," *Bild*, August 31, 1962; "Baby-Pfennig rollt schon," *Bild*, September 1, 1962; "Zehn Millionen Pfennige für die Opfer," *Bild*, October 1, 1962.

27. Aktion Sorgenkind was founded by the public law TV station ZDF and private welfare organizations. Historian Gabriele Lingelbach has studied the images of disabled persons created by this charity between 1964 and the present; see Gabriele Lingelbach, "Konstruktionen von 'Behinderung' in der Öffentlichkeitsarbeit und Spendenwerbung der Aktion Sorgenkind seit 1964," in *Disability History. Konstruktionen von Behinderung in der Geschichte. Eine Einführung*, edited by Elsbeth Bösl, Anne Klein, and Anne Waldschmidt (Bielefeld: Transcript, 2010), 129–136; and Gabriele Lingelbach, *Spenden und Sammeln. Der westdeutsche Spendenmarkt bis in die frühen 8oer Jahre* (Göttingen: Wallstein, 2009). The lottery brought in 7.2 million Deutsche Mark within its first six months. By 1970 nearly 35 million Deutsche Mark had been collected and passed out to nurseries, schools, rehabilitation centers, and many other institutions. Beneficiaries were not limited to Contergankinder, although donation publicity was focused on these children in the early years because Contergan provided a competitive advantage in the market for charitable contributions. See the following notes from the Federal Press Office: "Aufzeichnung für das Gespräch des Bundespräsidenten mit Theodor Schober, Präsident der Inneren Mission und Vorsitzender der Bundesarbeitsgemeinschaft der Freien Wohlfahrtsverbände," February 2, 1966, Bundesarchiv B 122 5261; Aktion Sorgenkind e.V., Geschäftsstelle Bonn, regulations: "Richtlinien für die Vergabe von Mitteln aus der Aktion Sorgenkind," no date, Bundesarchiv B 122 5261.

28. Consequentially, members of the emancipation movement of the 1970s and 1980s criticized the charity and countered these images by making their own disability experiences public. See Susanne von Daniels, Theresia Degener, Andreas Jürgens, and Frajo

Krick et al., *Krüppel-Tribunal. Menschenrechtsverletzungen im Sozialstaat* (Köln: Pahl-Rugenstein, 1983), 75; and Carol Poore, *Disability in Twentieth-Century German Culture* (Ann Arbor: University of Michigan Press, 2007), 183.

29. For a study of telethons in the United States that addresses similar issues, see Paul Longmore, "Conspicuous Consumption and American Culture," in Longmore, *Why I Burned My Book and Other Essays on Disability* (Philadelphia: Temple University Press, 2003).

30. For sources, see Beyersdorf, "3.000 Babys warten auf unsere Hilfe"; "Sie müssen helfen—Frau Ministerin," *Bild*, May 22, 1962; "Nur Bettelgeld für die Opfer," *Bild*, June 19, 1962; "Nicht Hüte, sondern Hilfe"; Beyersdorf, "Contergan: Der Staat hat versagt"; "Contergan: Keine Hilfe!," *Bild*, August 30, 1962; "Bonn: alles getan. Contergan-Opfer wissen es anders," *Bild*, September 6, 1962; "Contergan-Babys in der ganzen Welt," *Bild*, September 12, 1962; "Völlig falsch," *Bild*, September 2, 1962; "Gutes Beispiel: Hilfsplan für die Contergan-Babys," *Bild*, September 29, 1962; "Sie wollen nicht betteln," *Bild*, October 1, 1962; "Der Staat zahlt keine Rente für Contergan-Kinder," *Bild*, July 18, 1962; Reismüller, "Wer soll diesen Kindern helfen?"; Jürgen Serke, "Contergan-Eltern sind enttäuscht," *Die Welt*, September 7, 1965.

31. Weber, "Wir sorgen für ihre Zukunft"; "So lernen sie leben"; "Prothesen mit Gas," *Der Spiegel*, May 22, 1963. The hero cult even touched U.S. magazines; see, for example, "Help for Thalidomide Victims," *Time*, April 26, 1963.

32. For a prominent example, see "So lernen sie leben."

33. "Contergankinder haben eine Zukunft."

34. "So lernen sie leben."

35. "Orthopädisches Wunderwerk," quoted in "Prothesen mit Gas." See also Weber, "Wir sorgen für ihre Zukunft"; "So lernen sie leben"; "Chiffre K 17."

36. "Essen, Spielen und Malen nach drei Tagen" quoted from "Prothesen mit Gas." Pictures such as this one play an important part in constructing images of disability from the perspective of the predominantly nondisabled rehabilitation experts and journalists. We must assume that the persons displayed were not consulted to obtain permission. Since they cannot be identified and thus cannot be consulted now, historians of disability need to treat these photos with the utmost respect and care.

37. For example, Edgar Wolfrum, "Die Anfänge der Bundesrepublik, die Aufarbeitung der NS-Vergangenheit und die Fernwirkungen für heute," in *Solidargemeinschaft und Erinnerungskultur im 20. Jahrhundert*, edited by Ursula Bitzegeio, Anja Kruke, and Meik Woyke (Bonn: J. H. W. Dietz Nachf., 2009), 363–377.

38. Mau, "Die Behandlung der angeborenen Gliedmaßenmißbildungen," 1064. Mau's interest was in minimizing demands for financial compensation from the manufacturer.

39. Ernst Marquardt, "Bericht über den Stand der technischen Hilfen für Dysmeliekinder," *Jahrbuch der Deutschen Vereinigung für die Rehabilitation Behinderter* (1965/66): 178; Hepp, "Die Häufung der angeborenen Defektmissbildungen der oberen Extremitäten in der Bundesrepublik Deutschland," 424.

40. For the usage of terms such as "Dysmelien," "Dysmeliekinder," "Extremitätenmißbildungen," "Gliedmaßenmißbildungen," and "Kinder mit (schweren) Mißbildungsformen" see Hepp, "Die Häufung der angeborenen Defektmissbildungen der oberen Extremitäten in der Bundesrepublik Deutschland," 419–420; Lindemann, "Zur Prognose

und Therapie schwerer Gliedmaßenfehlbildungen"; Oskar Hepp, "Zur medizinischen Betreuung und über die soziale Hilfe für Kinder mit Gliedmaßenfehlbildungen," in *Hilfe für das behinderte Kind. Kongreßbericht über Fragen der behinderten Kinder, 8.-12. Juni 1964 in Köln*, edited by Bundesausschuss für gesundheitliche Volksbelehrung e.V. (Stuttgart: Paracelsus, 1966), 27–34; Mau, "Die Behandlung der angeborenen Gliedmaßenmißbildungen," 1064–1065; Rütt, "Die Therapie der Dysmelie (Wiedemann-Syndrom)," 330; W. Buschhaus, "Elternberatung von Kindern mit schweren Gliedmaßenfehlbildungen im Bereich des Gesundheitsamtes Solingen," *Die Rehabilitation* 2, no. 3 (1963): 141.

41. See, for example, Kurt Lindemann, "Begrüßung," in *Monographie über die Rehabilitation der Dysmelie-Kinder*, vol. 2, *Dysmelie-Arbeitstagung am 5. und 6.11.1965 in der Orthopädischen Anstalt der Universität Heidelberg*, edited by Bundesministerium für Gesundheitswesen (Frechen/Köln: Bartmann, 1967), 8; D. Muthmann, "Zehn Jahre Entwicklung und Erprobung von Hilfen für behinderte Kinder. Tagung der Arbeitsgemeinschaft für technische Orthopädie und Rehabilitation e.V. Bonn," *Die Rehabilitation* 12, no. 3 (1973): 187–188.

42. Hepp, "Die Häufung der angeborenen Defektmissbildungen der oberen Extremitäten in der Bundesrepublik Deutschland," 419–420; Oskar Hepp, "Begrüßung," in *Monographie über die Rehabilitation der Dysmelie-Kinder. Dysmelie-Arbeitstagung am 17. und 18.10.1964 in der Orthopädischen Universitätsklinik und Poliklinik Münster*, edited by Bundesministerium für Gesundheitswesen (Frechen: Bartmann, 1965), 5; E. Güntz, "Begrüßung," in *Monographie über die Rehabilitation der Dysmelie-Kinder*, vol. 3, *Dysmelie-Arbeitstagung am 24. und 25.7.1966 in Hannover*, edited by Bundesministerium für Gesundheitswesen (Frechen: Bartmann, 1967), 10.

43. See Freitag, *Contergan*, 49.

44. For examples from the press, see, for example, Beyersdorf, "3.000 Babys warten auf unsere Hilfe"; "Gefahr im Verzuge"; "So lernen sie leben"; and "Contergankinder haben eine Zukunft."

45. For representative examples of the use of the terms "Arzneimittelunglück" ("drug disaster"), "Contergan-Katastrophe" ("Contergan catastrophe"), and "Contergan-Epidemie" ("Contergan epidemic"), see "Gefahr im Verzuge"; "So lernen sie leben"; "Gegen u.a.," *Der Spiegel*, May 27, 1968; "Prothesen mit Gas"; "Chiffre K 17"; and "Konten gesperrt," *Der Spiegel*, April 21, 1969.

46. For a short theoretical look at why modern societies perceive specific incidents as catastrophes, see Greg Bankoff, "No Such Thing as Natural Disasters: Why We Had to Invent Them," *Harvard International Review*, August 24, 2010, hir.harvard.edu/no-such-thing-as-natural-disasters, accessed July 3, 2012. For an introduction to historical disaster research in Europe, see Gerrit Jasper Schenk, "Historical Disaster Research: State of Research, Concepts, Methods and Case Studies," *Historical Social Research* 32, no. 3 (2007): 9–31.

47. See, for example, "Nur Bettelgeld für die Opfer"; Beyersdorf, "Contergan: Der Staat hat versagt"; and "So lernen sie leben." For an example from experts' debates see Güntz, "Begrüßung," 10.

48. See, for example, Norbert Frei, *Vergangenheitspolitik. Die Anfänge der Bundesrepublik und die NS-Vergangenheit* (München: DTV, 1999); Detlef Garbe, "Äußerliche Abkehr, Erinnerungsverweigerung und 'Vergangenheitsbewältigung': Der Umgang mit dem Nationalsozialismus in der frühen Bundesrepublik," in *Modernisierung im Wiederaufbau. Die westdeutsche*

Gesellschaft der 50er Jahre, edited by Axel Schildt and Arnold Sywottek (Bonn: J. H. W. Dietz Nachf., 1998), 693–716; Detlef Siegfried, "Zwischen Aufarbeitung und Schlußstrich. Der Umgang mit der NS-Vergangenheit in den beiden deutschen Staaten 1958 bis 1969," in *Dynamische Zeiten. Die 60er Jahre in den beiden deutschen Gesellschaften*, edited by Axel Schildt, Detlef Siegfried, and Karl Christian Lammers (Hamburg: Hans Christians Verlag, 2000), 77–113.

49. "Ist meine Frau wirklich eine Mörderin?," *Quick*, October 21, 1962; "Kindsmord aus Elternliebe," *Bunte*, July 4, 1962; "The Thalidomide Disaster," *Time*, August 10, 1962.

50. Authors regularly used the word "Qual" ("agony") to describe how they imagined life for the children. See, for example, Elsa L., letter to the editor, referring to the article "Ist meine Frau wirklich eine Mörderin?," *Quick*, November 18; and Helga B., letter to the editor, referring to the article "Ist meine Frau wirklich eine Mörderin?," *Quick*, November 18. See also Erika V., letter to the editor, *Quick*, November 11, 1962, referring to the article "Ist meine Frau wirklich eine Mörderin?"; Margret D., letter to the editor, *Quick*, November 18, 1962, referring to the article "Ist meine Frau wirklich eine Mörderin?"; E. B., letter to the editor, *Bild*, August 27, 1962 referring to the article "Verbrechen oder Mutterliebe?"; H. H., letter to the editor, *Bild*, August 27, 1962, referring to the article "Verbrechen oder Mutterliebe?"; E. S., letter to the editor, *Bunte*, August 8, 1962, referring to the article "Kindsmord aus Elternliebe"; M. Philipp, letter to the editor, *Bild*, August 25, 1962 referring to the article "Nicht Hüte, sondern Hilfe"; E. E., letter to the editor, *Bild*, August 27, 1962, referring to the article "Verbrechen oder Mutterliebe?"; J. F., letter to the editor, *Bild*, August 27, 1962 referring to the article "Verbrechen oder Mutterliebe?"; H. S., letter to the editor, *Bunte*, September 19, 1962, referring to the article "Kindsmord aus Elternliebe"; S. L., letter to the editor, *Bunte*, July 25, 1962, referring to the article "Kindsmord aus Elternliebe."

51. See, for example, S. L., letter to the editor, *Bunte*, July 25, 1962; E. Sch., letter to the editor, *Bunte*, August 8 1962; M. L., letter to the editor, *Revue*, December 7, 1962.

52. "*Mit wahrer Empörung lese ich, daß man die leidgeprüften Eltern Suzanne und Jean Vandeputte aus Lüttich des Kindsmordes bezichtigt. Hier kommt es doch nicht auf die Tat an, sondern auf das Motiv zur Tat. Man wollte dem armen Menschlein doch nur ein furchtbares Schicksal ersparen. Je eher es geschah, desto weniger merkte es das arme Kind. Wie kann man nun diese unglückliche Mutter verurteilen, die sich doch so auf ihr erstes Kind freute und dann die entsetzliche Feststellung machen mute, so hart verurteilt zu werden. Denken diese 'Übermoralischen,' wie ich sie nennen will, nicht darüber nach, daß sich dieses arme Menschlein nie allein die Tränen trocknen, das Näschen putzen, ein Äpfelchen essen, mit einer Puppe spielen, oder gar ein Hündchen oder Kätzchen liebevoll hätte streicheln können? Die Mutter hat recht getan und der Arzt auch. Es wäre unverantwortlich, Mutter und Kind dafür zu bestrafen*"; Erna K., letter to the editor, *Bunte*, July 25, 1962.

53. "*Es gehört nicht nur Mut dazu, ein solches Kind großzuziehen. Ich glaube, mehr Mut und noch mehr Liebe braucht man für den Entschluss, ihm ein qualvolles Leben als Krüppel zu ersparen*"; Erika V., letter to the editor, referring to the article "Ist meine Frau wirklich eine Mörderin?," *Quick*, November 11, 1962.

54. "*Diese Frau hat sich nicht leichtfertig von ihrem Kind getrennt, sondern aus tiefem Herzeleid und nur zum Besten ihres Kindes. Sie hat nur an ihr Kind gedacht*"; Margret D., letter to the edi-

tor, referring to the article "Ist meine Frau wirklich eine Mörderin?," *Quick*, November 18, 1962.

55. "Stockholm ist meine letzte Rettung: *Bild*-Interview mit der Contergan-Mutter," *Bild*, August 6, 1962; "Verbrechen oder Mutterliebe?," *Bild*, August 22, 1962; "Alle Mütter werden mich verstehen," *Bunte*, September 5, 1962; "Der Fall Sherri Finkbine: Hysterische Show oder verzweifelte Angst?," *Bunte*, September 5, 1962.

56. See, for example, Michael Schwartz, "Abtreibung und Wertewandel im doppelten Deutschland: Individualisierung und Strafrechtsreformen in der DDR und in der Bundesrepublik in den sechziger und siebziger Jahren," in *Auf dem Weg in eine neue Moderne? Die Bundesrepublik Deutschland in den siebziger und achtziger Jahren*, edited by Thomas Raithel, Andreas Rödder, and Andreas Wirsching (München: Oldenbourg 2009), 113–130.

57. "Stockholm ist meine letzte Rettung"; "Alle Mütter werden mich verstehen"; "Mit Unglück hausiert man nicht," *Quick*, August 19, 1962; Beyersdorf, "Verbrechen oder Mutterliebe?"

58. "*Niemand wird dieser Frau menschliches Mitgefühl versagen können. Sicher wird es nur wenige geben, die ihre Entscheidung nicht respektieren—obwohl religiöse und ethische Gründe dagegen sprechen*"; "Mit Unglück hausiert man nicht."

59. "*Dass es Gesetze gibt, die uns Frauen zwingen, solche Kinder zur Welt zu bringen, ist so unmenschlich, so barbarisch, dass jede Frau in dieser Situation das Interesse der Verantwortlichen auf sich und diesen Wahnsinn ziehen sollte*"; Margret R., letter to the editor, *Quick*, August 19, 1962, referring to the article "Mit Unglück hausiert man nicht." Also see Hugo W., letter to the editor, *Frankfurter Allgemeine Zeitung*, September 5, 1962, referring to several articles on the abortion of disabled children; H. R., letter to the editor, *Frankfurter Allgemeine Zeitung*, September 13, 1962; Herta St., letter to the editor, *Quick*, November 11, 1962, referring to the article "Ist meine Frau wirklich eine Mörderin?"; J. F., letter to the editor, *Bild*, August 27, 1962, referring to the article "Verbrechen oder Mutterliebe?"; Erna H., letter to the editor, *Bunte*, November 14, 1962.

60. "*Vielleicht später von dem Kind den Vorwurf erwarten: Warum habt ihr mich nicht schon bei der Geburt sterben lassen. Ich bin ein Krüppel, unbeholfen und falle nur meinen Mitmenschen zur Last*"; E. E., letter to the editor, *Bild*, August 27, 1962, referring to the article "Verbrechen oder Mutterliebe?"

61. "*Die bedauernswerten Kinder auf Ihren Photos sehen tatsächlich mit ihren künstlichen Gliedmaßen alle ganz vergnügt und zufrieden aus. Aber Mitleid und Entsetzen packt einen, wenn man daran denkt, dass diese ahnungslosen Geschöpfe eines Tages als Erwachsene das Leben meistern müssen*"; Else H., letter to the editor, *Quick*, December 16, 1962 referring to the article "So lernen sie leben."

62. "*Gewiß, man 'rettet' diese Kinder und bemüht sich um sie—aber was wird sein, wenn sie erwachsen sind und ihnen alles voll zu Bewusstsein kommt?*"; Heinz W., letter to the editor, *Quick*, November 18. 1962, referring to the article "Ist meine Frau wirklich eine Möderin?"

63. For more examples, see Georg E., letter to the editor, *Bunte*, August 22, 1962, referring to the article "Kindsmord aus Elternliebe" and several letters to the editor published in July and August 1962; M. S., letter to the editor, *Bunte*, August 8, 1962, referring to the article "Kindsmord aus Elternliebe" and letters to the editor published

in July 1962; P. L., letter to the editor, *Bunte*, August 8, 1962, referring to the article "Kindsmord aus Elternliebe" and letters to the editor published in July 1962.

64. H. R., letter to the editor, *Frankfurter Allgemeine Zeitung*, September 13, 1962.

65. *"Die Erhaltung eines Krüppels, der sich selbst und seiner Umgebung zur Last wird"*; Hugo W., letter to the editor, *Frankfurter Allgemeine Zeitung*, September 5, 1962, referring to several articles on the abortion of disabled children.

66. Hans-Jürgen F., letter to the editor, *Frankfurter Allgemeine Zeitung*, September 5, 1962; Friedrich v. H., letter to the editor, *Frankfurter Allgemeine Zeitung*, September 21, 1962; I. K., letter to the editor, *Frankfurter Allgemeine Zeitung*, September 21, 1962; Gerhard M., letter to the editor, *Frankfurter Allgemeine Zeitung*, September 13, 1962, referring to the letter to the editor by Karl Th.; Heinz K., letter to the editor, *Frankfurter Allgemeine Zeitung*, September 13, 1962; Friedrich v. H., letter to the editor, *Frankfurter Allgemeine Zeitung*, September 21, 1962, referring to the letter to the editor by H. R.; Gerhard M., letter to the editor, *Frankfurter Allgemeine* Zeitung, September 13, 1962, referring to the letter to the editor by Karl Th.; Hans-Jürgen F., letter to the editor, *Frankfurter Allgemeine Zeitung*, September 13, 1962; P., letter to the editor, *Bunte*, August 8, 1962, referring to the article "Kindsmord aus Elternliebe" and letters to the editor published in July 1962; Georg E., letter to the editor, *Bunte*, August 22, 1962, referring to the article "Kindsmord aus Elternliebe" and several letters to the editor published in July and August 1962.

67. Ruth L., letter to the editor, *Quick*, December 23, 1962, referring to the article "So lernen sie leben"; C. W. R., letter to the editor, *Frankfurter Allgemeine Zeitung*, September 21, 1962, referring to several articles of August and September 1962; Gerhard M., letter to the editor, *Frankfurter Allgemeine Zeitung*, September 13, 1962, referring to the letter to the editor by Karl Th.; Friedrich v. H, letter to the editor, *Frankfurter Allgemeine Zeitung*, September 21, 1962, referring to the letter to the editor by H. R.; Hans-Jürgen F., letter to the editor, *Frankfurter Allgemeine Zeitung*, September 13, 1962; Georg E., letter to the editor, *Bunte*, August 22, 1962, referring to the article "Kindsmord aus Elternliebe" and several letters to the editor published in July and August 1962; M. S., letter to the editor, *Bunte*, August 8, 1962, referring to the article "Kindsmord aus Elternliebe" and letters to the editor published in July 1962; P. L., letter to the editor, *Bunte*, August 8, 1962, referring to the article "Kindsmord aus Elternliebe" and letters to the editor published in July 1962.

68. Quoted from Eva T., letter to the editor, *Revue*, December 12, 1962. For similar remarks see Georg E., letter to the editor, *Bunte*, August 22, 1962, referring to the article "Kindsmord aus Elternliebe" and several letters to the editor published in July and August 1962; P., letter to the editor, *Bunte*, August 8, 1962, referring to the article "Kindsmord aus Elternliebe" and letters to the editor published in July 1962; M. S., letter to the editor, *Bunte*, August 8, 1962, referring to the article "Kindsmord aus Elternliebe" and letters to the editor published in July 1962; Sieglinde W., letter to the editor, *Quick*, November 18, 1962, referring to the article "Ist meine Frau wirklich eine Mörderin?"; Paula W., letter to the editor, *Quick*, November 18, 1962, referring to the article "Ist meine Frau wirklich eine Mörderin?"; Maria M., letter to the editor, *Revue*, December 2, 1962; Susanne R., letter to the editor, *Revue*, December 2, 1962; Egon Sch., letter to the editor, *Revue*, December 9, 1962.

69. Georg E., letter to the editor, *Bunte*, August 22, 1962, referring to the article "Kindsmord aus Elternliebe" and letters to the editor published in July and August 1962; P., letter to the editor, *Bunte*, August 8, 1962, referring to the article "Kindsmord aus Elternliebe" and letters to the editor published in July 1962; name withheld by the editors, letter to the editor, *Bunte*, September 26, 1962, referring to the article "Der Fall Sherri Finkbine."

70. Else H., letter to the editor, *Quick*, December 16, 1962; Elsa L., letter to the editor, *Quick*, November 18, 1962.

71. "Aufklärungsarbeit," Susanne R., letter to the editor, *Revue*, December 7, 1962.

72. *"Hat sein Schicksal gemeistert und sagt 'Ja' zum Leben,"* Georg E., letter to the editor, *Bunte*, August 22, 1962. The autobiography was part of a brochure from Oberlinhaus, a Protestant institution for disabled persons in Potsdam.

73. *"Es soll schon Menschen gegeben haben, die sich ohne Hände wacker durchs Leben schlugen"*; S. L. letter to the editor, *Bunte*, July 25, 1962.

74. Statistics are notoriously unreliable because of variation in methods and parameters for collection, especially with regard to congenital problems, but there were at least 1.5 million disabled veterans in Western Germany in the early 1950s, about 3 percent of the population. For data on 1951, see Norbert Stegmüller, "Die zahlenmäßige Entwicklung der Kriegsopferversorgung nach dem 2. Weltkriege," *Bundesversorgungsblatt* 6 (1955): 81. Additionally, some years earlier, polio epidemics had left some thousands of persons impaired. Since the German polio experience has not yet been worked on, we have to rely on primary sources, such as "Fürsorge bei Kinderlähmung und deren Folgeerscheinungen," *Nachrichtendienst des Deutschen Vereins für öffentliche und private Fürsorge* 33, no. 5 (1953): 147–150; "Die Eingliederung der Kindergelähmten und Querschnittsgelähmten," *Nachrichtendienst des deutschen Vereins für öffentliche und private Fürsorge* 37, no. 11/12 (1957): 343–345.

75. *"Warum töteten sie? Angeblich aus Liebe! Welche Verkennung der Liebe.... Geschah es nicht letzten Endes doch aus Egoismus, aus Angst vor der ungeheuren Verpflichtung, vor dem damit verbundenen Verzicht?"*; Name withheld, letter to the editor, *Bunte*, September 26, 1962, referring to the article "Der Fall Sherri Finkbine."

76. *"Vielleicht habe ich mehr Recht, zu diesem Bericht Stellung zu nehmen als jeder andere. Denn ich habe ein Kind mit zwei Armen ohne Ellenbogen und verbildeten Händen. Ich werde die verzweifelt durchweinten Nächte nie vergessen, Denn auch ich dachte an das Näschen, das mein Töchterchen nie würde putzen können. Und dann verzweifelten wir aufs Neue, als wir merkten das kaum zwölf Wochen alte Kind seine Händchen und Ärmchen gar nicht benutzen wollte, sondern von Anfang an die Zehen zum Greifen nahm. Es wusste also in sich selbst von seiner Veranlagung.... Es würde hier zu weit führen, hier alles zu erzählen, was sich seit jenen dunklen Tagen im Leben meiner Tochter zugetragen hat. Nur so viel: Sie hat einen Beruf, in dem sie sich bewähren kann und der sie zu ernähren vermag"*; name withheld by the editors, letter to the editor, *Bunte*, September 26, 1962 referring to the article "Der Fall Sherri Finkbine."

77. *"Von allen Menschen mit Liebe umsorgt"*; Hanna, letter to the editor, *Bunte*, November 14, 1962; also see Elfriede P., letter to the editor, *Bunte*, November 14, 1962.

78. *"Und es ist dennoch furchtbar ein Krüppel zu sein, ich habe mich bis heute noch nicht damit abfinden können. Die Menschen (die Gesunden) vergessen schnell. Wer weiß in 15 oder 20 Jahren,*

wenn diese Kinder groß sind, noch von Contergan? Was soll dann aus den armen Kindern werden, wenn die Eltern tot sind? Sie werden immer auf fremde Hilfe angewiesen sein, den ohne Prothesen, und seien sie noch so gut, können sie sich nicht selber waschen. Ob die Menschen, die diese belgische Mutter verurteilen, wohl bereit wären, ein armloses Kind aufzuziehen? Ich finde die Mutter liebte ihr Kind sehr, deswegen hat sie ihm ein Leben ohne Freude und ohne Zukunft ersparen wollen"; Name withheld, letter to the editor, *Revue*, December 9, 1962.

79. The tribunal's objectives and impeachments were published under the title "Cripples' Tribunal. Violations of Human Rights in the Welfare State." See von Daniels et al., *Krüppel-Tribunal*.

80. See, for example, Franziska Heller, *Der Kampf mit dem Honigbrot. Lebenserinnerungen einer Contergangeschädigten* (Augsburg: AK-Verlag, 1997). See also the autobiography of tenor Thomas Quasthoff, *Die Stimme. Autobiografie* (Berlin: Ullstein, 2004).

81. *"Mit drei Jahren wurden mir die ersten 'Schmuckhände' verpasst. Prothesen, mit denen ich nicht einmal halb so viel anfangen konnte wie mit meinen Füßen, sie behinderten mich auf allen Ebenen. Mit ihnen konnte ich nicht spielen, weil ich nichts fühlte. Mit ihnen eckte ich überall an, weil ich mich nicht daran gewöhnen konnte, an beiden Seiten meines Oberkörpers noch so komische Arme zu haben. Ich konnte mit diesen Prothesen nicht rennen, weil sie mir zu schwer waren und mir die Schultern wund drückten, schließlich durfte ich mit ihnen auch nicht hinfallen, damit sie nicht kaputtgingen. . . . Beim Essen fühlte ich mich wie ein Roboter, ich drückte den falschen Knopf und das Essen landete auf dem Teller anstatt in meinem Mund"*; Theresia Degener, "Die Emanzipation ist leichter für mich," *Emma* 5, no. 5 (1981): 16.

82. For such accounts and for scientific studies of the phenomenon, see, for example, Astrid Kolter, "Die Behinderung selbst erlebt," in *Contergan—30 Jahre danach*, edited by Fritz Uwe Niedthard, Ernst Marquardt, and Jürgen Eltze (Stuttgart: Thieme, 1994), 7; Brigitte Kober-Nagel, "Contergankinder, ihre Aussichten in Schule und Beruf" (PhD diss., München, 1979), 23, 43–44; Freitag, *Contergan*, 222, 230–232, 319–321, 363–364, 386–389; Wilhelm Bläsig, "Ausbildung dysmeler Jugendlicher," *Die Rehabilitation* 12, no. 2 (1973): S119–121; Muthmann, "Zehn Jahre Entwicklung und Erprobung von Hilfen für behinderte Kinder," 188.

83. *"Die 'homogene Gruppe' haftet uns an wie das Contergan-Kind. Nicht behinderte SozialwissenschaftlerInnen, PsychologInnen, ÄrztInnen, PädagogInnen, PolitikerInnen, SozialarbeiterInnen, JournalistInnen etc. analysieren unser Innenleben, weisen uns den Platz zu in dieser Gesellschaft oder verbannen uns aus ihr, sagen und schreiben uns vor, was wir zu tun hätten, wie wir uns fühlen und was wir zu denken haben"*; Catia Monser, *Contergan/Thalidomid: Ein Unglück kommt selten allein* (Düsseldorf: Eggcup, 1993), 22.

CHAPTER 8

"Lest We Forget"

Disabled Veterans and the Politics
of War Remembrance in the United States

JOHN M. KINDER

> God of our Father, Lord of our far-flung battle line.
> Beneath whose hand we hold dominion over palm and pine.
> Lord of hosts, be with us yet.
> Lest we forget. Lest we forget.
> —American Legion prayer, circa 1920s

> The greatest casualty is being forgotten.
> —Wounded Warrior Project official website, 2011

KEYWORDS: *Centuries*: nineteenth; twentieth; twenty-first; *Geographic Areas*: North America; *Sources*: visual materials; serials; organizational reports; *Themes*: culture; activism; war.

On the morning of Saturday, December 17, 1921, crowds gathered across the United States for one of the largest (and most lucrative) memorial campaigns of the Great War era: Forget-Me-Not Day. The event was the brainchild of the recently formed group Disabled American Veterans of the World War (DAV), the nation's premier service organization for veterans with physical and mental impairments. Standing on street corners, in government buildings, and in hotel lobbies, participants sold millions of handcrafted crêpe-paper "forget-me-nots" to be worn in remembrance of U.S. war casualties. Where the artificial blooms were unavailable, volunteers peddled drawings of the pale blue flowers and cardboard lapel pins with the phrase "I Did Not Forget" printed on the front. Proceeds from the sales drive went toward funding clubhouses, recreational camps, and assorted relief programs for permanently disabled veterans.[1]

Like other veteran-themed flower sales that emerged from World War I, Forget-Me-Not Day was designed with two goals in mind: to honor the "fallen war dead" and to remind the American people of the lingering hardships disabled veterans and their families faced.[2] At the same time, Great War veterans and their political allies used the event and others like it to advance a broader ideological claim: that "remembering" disabled veterans was a vital part of the nation's expanding social compact with the men (and women) who bore the scars of battle. In an official dispatch that was reprinted in newspapers around the United States, DAV founder Robert S. Marx told nonveterans, "Forget-Me-Not day is to remind you of those promises that were made to those who have come back to you, broken, and to enable you, in a very small way, to help these men to help themselves."[3] But Marx and his disabled comrades remained skeptical about whether veterans would be remembered. Barely three years after the Great War's end, many beneficiaries of the DAV believed that they had already been forgotten, casualties of a memorial culture better suited to remembering the dead than to honoring war's disabled survivors (Figure 8.1).[4]

What exactly were the American people expected to remember about disabled veterans? And why did they need to be remembered in the first place? In recent decades there has been an outpouring of scholarship on the relationship between collective trauma and cultural memory, a form of mass remembrance produced through public rituals, mass media representations, and civic engagement. Al-

Figure 8.1. This poster, which features the official slogan of Forget-Me-Not Day, attempts to differentiate between disabled veterans' relief and "charity," a form of public welfare associated with children, the elderly, and dependent women. Typical of Forget-Me-Not Day campaign materials, the poster also relies upon a visual rhetoric of sentimentality to reiterate the American public's profound sense of obligation to disabled veterans. Reprinted in the *Oakland Tribune*, December 2, 1921, B3.

though very little of this work has focused on disabled veterans per se, a growing number of scholars have chronicled the ways similarly marginalized populations have deployed memorial practices—from parades and fund-raising drives to pop culture imagery—to forge collective identities and give meaning to their shared experiences.[5] As an analytical category, memory offers disability scholars an important tool for exploring how disabled people have sought to challenge dominant historical narratives, many of which either erase disabled peoples' presence or relegate them to the fringes of modern society. It also reveals a form of disability activism and civic engagement that long predates the disability rights movements of the post–World War II era.

This essay offers an overview of disabled veterans' memorial culture in the United States, from poetic images of "suffering soldiers" in the post–Revolutionary War era to the disabled veteran–themed recycling bins and websites of the present day. It treats war remembrance as both a collective process and a political practice, one that disabled veterans and other "memory activists" have used to win rights and recognition from the state and from the American people.[6] While broad in scope, much of my discussion focuses on two periods that I consider to be watersheds in the political history of disabled veterans' remembrance. The first encompasses the two decades immediately following World War I, a period when veterans' organizations made widespread efforts to mobilize mass culture and public ritual in remembrance of disabled vets. The second period began in the aftermath of the arrival of Web 2.0 in the late 1990s, was intensified after the September 11, 2001, attacks on the United States, and continues to this day. Against the backdrop of the "Global War on Terror" and what diplomatic historian Andrew Bacevich calls the "New American Militarism," veterans and their corporate allies have turned to both traditional and digital remembrance practices to build community and reaffirm the nation's obligations to its wounded warriors.[7] Throughout U.S. history, disabled veterans—and those who claim to speak on their behalf—have sought to use public displays of remembrance to articulate a privileged political identity separate from that of able-bodied veterans and other disabled people. They have demanded alternative forms of memorialization—artifacts, public rituals, and legislative actions—that not only honored their bodily sacrifices but addressed the long-term physical, economic, and social consequences of war-related impairment.

None of this memory work has come easily. Traditional codes of military masculinity have long required disabled veterans—indeed, all ex-soldiers—to downplay their own hardships and focus their memorial energies on the sacrifices of others, especially the dead. Since World War I, moreover, disabled veterans' remembrance strategies have clashed with normative discourses of rehabilitation, which tend to equate "forgetting" with psychological health and social integration. In addition, many disabled veterans have struggled to come to terms with the memorial function of their own bodies. As permanent (and frequently visible) repositories of war's violence, disabled veterans' bodies "resist the closure of history and provide a perceptible site for a continual remembering of . . . war's effects," in media scholar Marita Sturken's words.[8] Not surprisingly, much of disabled veterans' remembrance work has been aimed at constructing a public memory of war that is decidedly open ended, one that forces nondisabled Americans to "remember" that war's traumas do not disappear at war's end.

Ultimately, this essay argues that public battles for disabled veterans' remembrance reflect deep anxieties about war-produced disability in modern American society. In staging their memorial parades, fund-raising events, commemorative dinners, and Major League Baseball "theme" nights, disabled veterans and their allies have attempted to establish a permanent sense of public obligation toward disabled veterans—an obligation that demands a never-ending recognition of disabled veterans' bodily sacrifices. In the process, disabled veterans' memorial practices have affirmed a deeply problematic model of disability, one that both fetishizes veterans' war injuries as markers of manly courage and identifies them as the primary obstacles to social reintegration. Consequently, although a number of former soldiers have played an active role in disability rights movements, their remembrance work has contributed to a widening rift between disabled veterans and other disability groups by suggesting, either explicitly or implicitly, that disabled veterans' impairments are the only ones worth remembering.

Absent Memories

Whether they know it or not, most Americans live within a short distance of a war memorial. U.S. cityscapes are littered with monuments, civic shrines, and "living memorials" to the nation's military past, from small stone tablets and cemetery cairns to gleaming marble temples and modern sports stadiums. Yet within this martial-memorial tradition, one group is notable for its absence: disabled veterans. While government agencies and private citizens have erected literally thousands of memorials to honor those in "eternal bivouac," war's disabled survivors have been largely erased from the built memory of American warfare. Visitors to the recently constructed World War II national monument in Washington, D.C., for example, could easily leave with the impression that virtually no U.S. combat troops returned home with life-changing physical and mental impairments. Two of the monument's twenty-four bronze bas-relief panels depict what appear to be wounded soldiers, but there is no reference to veterans' experiences after the conflict. The case is much the same at war memorials across the country, which tend to venerate the dead while all but ignoring the ongoing struggles of war's living casualties.

To a casual observer, Americans' failure to memorialize disabled veterans makes little sense. After all, disabled veterans do not have to rely upon others to perform their memory work—if collectively organized, they can serve as agents of their own remembrance, shaping the way their individual and collective experiences are perceived within the broader culture. More to the point, memory is a valuable cultural commodity, one of the few bargaining chips historically marginalized groups such as disabled veterans can use to win tangible benefits from the state. As the founders of Forget-Me-Not Day well understood, carefully targeted remembrance practices can pay substantial dividends, economic and otherwise. No less important, the group identity of disabled veterans is directly tied to their ability to perpetuate the memory of war—or at least their version of it—in the public arena. Put simply, disabled veterans have much to gain when they are remembered and much to lose when they are forgotten.

So why are disabled veterans so underrepresented in the nation's military-memorial culture? Public apathy is partly to blame. Assurances that the public will "never forget," so ubiquitous in wartime, are invariably among the first casualties of postwar demobilization. No less responsible is a tradition of masculine silence that disabled veterans' groups cultivate to this day. Despite the increasing racial and gender diversity of the U.S. military, disabled veteran culture—indeed, veteran culture as a whole—continues to promote a cult of hypermasculinity that equates expressions of vulnerability with weakness and effeminacy. In the eyes of many disabled veterans, it remains something of an unspoken rule that "real men" do not draw attention to their injuries, and they certainly do not complain about them to outsiders. When interviewed, disabled veterans are expected to be optimistic about their recovery and steadfast in their belief that they would "do it all over again" if they had the choice. Moreover, centuries of military culture have taught them to downplay their own remembrance needs in favor of those who made the "ultimate sacrifice."

Beyond disabled veterans' self-imposed silence, their absence from the nation's martial memory is also a problem of cultural idiom—specifically, the failure of traditional memorial conventions to address the ongoing needs and experiences of war's most vulnerable survivors. As military historian Theo Farrell points out, "The struggle for memory is the struggle for political identity." When reflecting upon past conflicts, "political and military elites usually seek to frame collective memories of national glory, determination, and heroism; memories to give purpose to war and the state."[9] To this end, traditional modes of memorialization, such as statuary or monuments, play an important role in helping postwar societies satisfy their "sentimental and nationalist" cravings for heroism and meaning. However, as historian Seth Koven has shown, conventional war memorials—which rely on classical motifs and political allegory—tend to inhibit public recognition of disabled veterans' ongoing experiences of physical and social impairment.[10] While a visit to the Tomb of the Unknown Soldier can leave even the most cynical critics of war teary-eyed, the monument does nothing to improve the lives of disabled veterans, particularly where their physical and economic needs are concerned. As a result, until quite recently, disabled veterans have eschewed brick-and-mortar memorials in favor of veteran-themed fund-raisers, public legislation, and other modes of remembrance more likely to result in concrete benefits for themselves and their families.

More than anything else, though, the absence of built monuments to disabled veterans reflects the complex, even tortured, relationship of disabled veterans to the concept of *historical closure*. Beyond a tendency to idolize former combatants, most war memorials promote a linear or progressive model of history, drawing clear-cut distinctions between past and present. Constructed weeks, months, even years after the end of a war, they are meant to allow visitors a chance to reflect, mourn, heal, and move forward with their lives.[11] For many disabled veterans, however, closure proves impossible. Some injuries never heal, and those that do often leave behind scars, somatic reminders that the past is never fully past. Memorials' inherent promise of closure is especially problematic for men and women in the grips of post-traumatic stress disorder (PTSD), perhaps the most pervasive form of war-produced disability of the modern era. "Helpless victims of their memory," mentally damaged veterans are condemned to relive former traumas; they are, quite literally, possessed—taken over in body and mind—by unassimilated images of the past.[12] Historian Jay Winter has described "shell shock" (the PTSD of the Great War era) as "a kind of syntax about the war, an ordering of stories and events elaborated by men who served. In this narrative, some men never demobilized; they were frozen in time, not out of choice, but out of injury."[13] Veterans with PTSD—and, to some degree, all disabled veterans—pose a fundamental challenge to the linear models of memory, temporality, and history upon which traditional modes of memorialization depend. As one severely disabled veteran recently remarked, wars do not end when "the last bullet is shot. War, for a lot of us, continues for the rest of our lives."[14]

From the Revolutionary Era to the Vietnam War

Given the many obstacles lined up against the nation's first generation of disabled veterans, it should come as no surprise that Americans made little effort to commemorate them. After the Revolution, there were no large-scale veterans' organizations to take up the mantle of disabled veterans' remembrance, and until the mid-nineteenth century, the United States lacked a national network of soldiers' homes, the primary incubator of disabled veterans' collective identity in Europe at that time.[15] War memorials of any kind were few and far between; many observers felt they "smacked too much of the monarchical regimes of Europe."[16] Consequently, the commemorative culture of the Early Republic tended to focus on a "fairly narrow group of martyrs and heroes around whom an American nation might unite in grateful praise."[17] Disabled veterans were not entirely missing from this tradition, as historian Sarah Purcell has shown. Within a decade after the end of the Revolution, social commentators were using "stark images of poor and starving veterans" to bolster "calls to remember the common soldier" and connect "those calls to negative ideas of the war's consequences."[18] Poet Philip Freneau, for one, worried that "maimed and unrewarded" colonials had been thoroughly forgotten by the nation for which they sacrificed so much. In "The American Soldier, A Picture from Life" (1791), Freneau conjured a powerful image of noble suffering and national neglect:

> Deep in a vale, a stranger now to arms,
> Too poor to shine in courts, too proud to beg,
> He, who once warred on *Saratoga's* plains,
> Sits musing o'er his scars, and wooden leg.[19]

As a class, however, disabled veterans were not singled out for special recognition and remembrance. Although the federal government provided modest pensions for permanently injured soldiers and sailors, politicians tended to promote a "glorious, sanitized, and often sentimentalized" memory of the Revolutionary War, one that had little place for disabled vets.[20]

The "tentative character of memorialization" in the United States would end with the Civil War, a conflict that left some 620,000 dead and 1 million severely injured in its wake.[21] Well before the final shots were fired, the federal government and private activists—including many veterans themselves—began to reconstruct the war in popular memory. By the 1880s, participants on both sides had sponsored thousands of statues, monuments, and public displays of Civil War remembrance. Leading the charge was the newly formed Grand Army of the Republic (GAR), a group that was open to all Union veterans and was one of the most powerful political lobbies of the late nineteenth century. The GAR funded hundreds of veteran-themed holiday celebrations, memorial parades, and soldiers' reunions, and its legislative wing proved highly successful at mobilizing nostalgic memories of wartime sacrifice to carve out an expansive pension and medical system for veterans and their families.[22] However, when it came to building *permanent* memorials to the Civil War, even ex-soldiers tended to focus their energies on the dead rather than the living. The war dead occupied a prominent place in the newly reunited nation's memorial culture. Enshrined in national cemeteries, mausoleums, and political monuments, they served as symbols of the bravery and honor that both sides retroactively agreed had characterized the recent conflict.[23]

Calls to remember disabled Civil War veterans, by contrast, were typically reserved for one of three occasions: times of political and economic crisis, military holidays, or GAR lobbying campaigns. During the economic recessions of the late 1860s and early 1870s, artists, poets, and journalists routinely invoked the prolonged hardships of "empty sleeves" and one-legged veterans. Many disabled veterans promoted themselves as "living monuments" to war's violence, their maimed and shattered bodies tangible reminders of the "unresolved nature" of the Civil War. Whether taking part in left-handed writing contests or delivering political speeches, disabled veterans used their bodies to challenge postwar platitudes about the glories of battle and the triumph of military medicine. Unfortunately, as Brian Matthew Jordan has shown, within two decades of the end of the Civil War, disabled veterans had been largely erased from the nation's memorial landscape. Instead, Americans chose to cultivate a different memorial tradition, one that downplayed the war's legacy of disability in favor of "national healing" and the "romance of reunion."[24]

This pattern began to change in the aftermath of World War I. While Americans would continue to promote a thanatocentric (death-obsessed) memorial culture—epitomized by the cult of the "unknown soldier" that swept across Europe and the United States—in the 1920s and 1930s, mass campaigns emerged to commemorate the bodily sacrifices (and horrors) of the living.[25] The shift can be attributed to several factors, chief among them the ambiguous ending of the war, which precipitated two decades of skepticism toward U.S. military affairs. Convinced that the Great War had done little to "make the world safe for democracy," many former war supporters joined a burgeoning peace movement that by the 1930s was the largest in U.S. history. Eager to politicize Americans' anxieties about war-related disability, interwar peace groups such as American Peaceways and the Fellowship of Reconciliation embraced the disabled veteran as a symbol of war's cruelty and a powerful reason to abandon war as an instrument of U.S. foreign policy. In their posters, stage plays, photo albums, and memorial rituals, antiwar activists used representations of disabled soldiers to debunk romantic myths about the grandeur of war and showcase the lingering traumas of military conflict. To many peace groups, the bodies of disabled vets played a dual memorial function, serving as both monuments to the past war and omens of the next one.

In addition to peace groups, several newly formed veterans' organizations played a key role in promoting disability remembrance. The two most significant were the American Legion, an inclusive fraternity that was open to all Great War veterans, and the Disabled American Veterans of the World War (later shortened to the Disabled American Veterans), a group restricted to former soldiers and sailors who

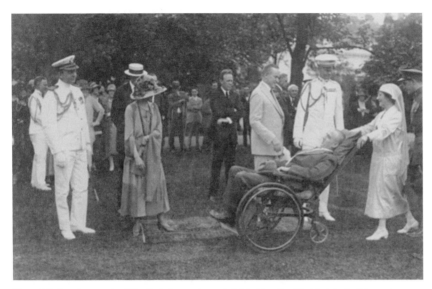

Figure 8.2. Carrying on a tradition from the previous administration, President Calvin Coolidge and his wife, Grace, host a garden party for disabled Great War veterans in 1925. Though portrayed as cozy get-togethers, such acts of political theater were meant to provide visual proof of the government's commitment to remembering disabled veterans. Library of Congress Prints & Photographs Division, LC-USZ62-131580.

had been "wounded, gassed, injured, or disabled by reason of service."[26] At the time the groups were formed (the American Legion in 1919, the DAV in 1920), government officials were sending mixed messages about the place of disabled veterans in public memory. On the one hand, politicians routinely went to great lengths to proclaim that they remembered disabled veterans. Throughout the 1920s, lawmakers on both sides of the aisle spoke at veterans' gatherings, issued remembrance proclamations on holidays, and reassured disabled veterans that they would never be forgotten (Figure 8.2).

On the other hand, federal and military planners sponsored a movement that would eliminate the need for remembrance altogether: rehabilitation.[27] Now the cornerstone of federal policy toward disabled vets, rehabilitation was first conceived as an integrated program of occupational therapy, psychological counseling, and vocational education. Its goal was to help disabled veterans avoid a life of state dependency by training them to become economically independent workers. If successful, the movement's supporters claimed, rehabilitation would not only lead to the "passing of the cripple" from modern life, it would also serve a distinctly *anti*-memorial function, allowing disabled veterans to "sink back into the mass of the people as though nothing ha[d] happened."[28] Skeptical of the "hero worship" that often accompanied veterans' homecomings, rehabilitationists saw excess remembrance as a kind of social pathology, a disease that doomed its victims to lives of delinquency, illness, and unhealthy nostalgia.[29] Until its decline in the late 1920s, the rehabilitation movement focused unprecedented public attention on the physical, mental, and socioeconomic problems of disabled veterans. But its advocates also elevated forgetting—or "moving on"—into a cultural and somatic ideal that would be achieved by government intervention and technical means.

While Great War veterans' groups embraced rehabilitation as a path toward economic reintegration, they remained steadfast in their commitment to "Keep the Spirit of the War Alive" in public memory. Throughout the 1920s and 1930s, the American Legion's Nation Memorials Committee took part in a wide range of memorial practices, from sponsoring Armistice Day parades to building playgrounds, parks, and other "practical memorials to victory and sacrifice."[30] The DAV organized similar remembrance projects, promoting veteran-themed holidays, orchestrating memorial fund drives, and selling photo albums that commemorated U.S. participation in World War I. For all their enthusiasm, Great War veterans did not promote remembrance for its own sake. Whenever possible, the American Legion and the DAV tied their memory work to their legislative campaigns, whose primary aims were to secure economic and health benefits from the state. At the same time, the two groups championed what American Legion chaplain Gill Robb Wilson called "remembrance as principle," the notion that collective memory could serve as a powerful force for political change.[31] Even as many Americans celebrated what Warren G. Harden dubbed a "return to normalcy," Legionnaires and DAV members sought to cultivate a nostalgic politics of remembrance of disabled veterans, a memorial tradition that would, as one veteran put it, "keep old and young alike impressed with the sacrifices in blood and tears made in war and in peace."[32] To that end, Great War veterans' remembrance practices tended to emphasize three themes: first, that the American public had a solemn duty to honor and protect those disabled by war; second, that veterans' disabilities were both medical and social in nature; and, finally, that as a class, disabled vets were "forgotten" men, shamefully ignored by the nation for which they had sacrificed so much.

Although World War I was soon overshadowed by other conflicts, the remembrance practices (e.g., posters, fund-raisers, disabled veteran–themed holidays, public rituals) and themes (e.g., horror, duty, sacrifice, neglect) Great War–era peace groups and veterans fostered remained firmly entrenched throughout the twentieth century. After World War II, the American Legion and the DAV were joined by new organizations such as the Paralyzed Veterans of America and the Blind Veterans of America that were eager to leverage remembrance of disabled veterans in order to win hearts and open pocketbooks. While disabled veterans continued to be underrepresented in the built memory of World War II—which tended to commemorate fatal casualties, scenes of heroic action, or both—they remained common sights in postwar literature and popular culture, much of it produced by veterans themselves. Blending sentimentality and social commentary, films such as *Pride of the Marines* (1945), *The Best Years of Their Lives* (1946), and *The Men* (1950) urged U.S. audiences to recognize the challenges disabled veterans faced when they came home. Even so, the memorial culture associated with disabled veterans of the "Greatest Generation" made few demands that American society change in any systematic way, particularly after the Cold War began to heat up.

Indeed, it would be another twenty years, during the Vietnam War era, before disabled veterans once again challenged accepted conventions about the nation's memory of military conflict. Even as the war still raged, disabled veterans led protest rallies, testified before Congress, and exhibited their bodies as evidence of war's destruction. Like Ron Kovic, author of the memoir *Born on the Fourth of July* (1976), Vietnam veterans played an important role in burgeoning disability rights movements. Working with military and civilian psychologists, they helped gain clinical recognition for PTSD, a form of psychological trauma that afflicted between 500,000 and 1,500,000 Vietnam vets.[33] Yet, as with the end of World War I, the aftermath of Vietnam brought neither consensus nor symbolic closure. Although early commentators frequently invoked the metaphor of the "healing wound" to describe Maya Lin's Vietnam Veterans' Memorial (1982) on the National Mall, postwar popular culture tended to cast disabled veterans in a different light: as lingering (and unhealable) threats to American society.[34] By the mid-1980s, disabled Vietnam veterans were relegated to the trash heap of memorial culture, their "broken" bodies and "damaged" minds testaments to a conflict most Americans would rather have forgotten.

Contemporary Memories

The latest wave of disability-themed memorial activism began in the early 1990s and continues to this day, thanks to the seemingly endless "Global War on Terror." Initially spurred by the U.S.-led victory over Iraq in 1991, the nation's increased attention to veterans' affairs reflected a broader cultural shift away from the perceived negativism of the Vietnam War era toward a renewed faith in all things military. Embracing what Andrew Bacevich calls the "New American Militarism," Americans of all political stripes came to adopt a "romanticized view of soldiers" and a "tendency to see military power as the truest measure of national greatness."[35] Their martial fantasies were fueled by Hollywood "militainment," the near-seamless merging of military propaganda and media spectacle that rose to prominence in popular culture in the quarter-century after the U.S. defeat in Vietnam. Big-screen blockbusters as diverse as *Top Gun* (1986), *Saving Private Ryan* (1998), and *Behind Enemy Lines* (2001) cast U.S. fighting men in a heroic light, simultaneously magnifying their individual acts of valor and reaffirming American faith in victory culture.[36]

Despite the increasingly pro-military climate, however, many in the veteran community worried that their disabled comrades could once again slip from public consciousness. "Super-crip" fables such as *Forrest Gump* (1994) notwithstanding, few militainment films dwelt on the long-term effects of war-produced disability. More important, the reorganization of the U.S. military into an all-volunteer force in the early 1970s guaranteed that only a small percentage of Americans would ever put on a uniform. While this development made it easier for the public to idealize the nation's wounded warriors—combat injury always seems more ennobling when viewed from afar—it also meant that disabled veterans could not rely upon numbers alone to ensure their remembrance. They would need new allies and new strategies for fighting public forgetfulness.

Over the past two decades, some of the loudest voices to call for the remembrance of disabled veterans have come from corporate America. Private-sector involvement in memorializing disabled veterans is hardly new. During World War I, Wrigley (the chewing gum manufacturer), Mabie Todd (the manufacturer of Swan fountain pens), and other companies regularly featured images of happily convalescing soldiers in their advertising campaigns. Similar images proliferated after World War II, when auto maker Oldsmobile made headlines by designing specially built steering systems for veteran amputees. However, since 9/11, the link between corporate branding and disabled veterans' remembrance has reached an unprecedented level of intimacy. Never one to miss an opportunity to "honor the troops," Major League Baseball has hosted scores of fund-raisers and memorial nights for recently disabled veterans and their families. Sears, Roebuck & Co. has raised millions of dollars to make disabled veterans' homes more accessible. Lesser-known businesses, such as Findmymattress.com and Liberty Cane, a walking stick manufacturer, have also jumped on the bandwagon, pledging to donate a portion of each sale to disabled veterans of the conflicts in Iraq and Afghanistan.

What is behind such efforts? We can never know for sure. Some companies are no doubt looking for an easy way to publicize their patriotism. Others appear to be genuinely grateful for disabled veterans' military service. The CEO of Findmymattress.com, for example, decided to fund the DAV in an effort to recognize the "scores of veterans who's [sic] sacrifices provide us with the freedom we cannot and should not take for granted."[37] Yet many corporate sponsors seem to view disabled veterans' remembrance as little more than a vehicle for serving their own pro-business ideologies. These include the promotion of neoliberalism, a capitalist economic-social order that champions the privatization of state functions, cuts in public welfare, and "free market" solutions to major social problems.[38]

This deliberate melding of neoliberalism and disabled veterans' remembrance is epitomized by soft drink giant PepsiCo's Dream Machine Recycling Challenge, perhaps the most widespread campaign of corporate memorialization to

Figure 8.3. PepsiCo automatic recycling machine at Oklahoma State University–Tulsa, September 2013. Promising to donate part of its proceeds to disabled veterans' relief, PepsiCo has placed recycling machines, recycling bins, and other corporate memorials at entertainment venues across the United States. As is the case with these machines, much of the memory work on behalf of disabled veterans today is articulated within a corporate model of "giving back," one that casts disabled veterans in the role of heroic yet helpless victims in need of public sympathy. Such public memorials also contribute to the notion that disabled veterans are the only population of disabled Americans deserving of public support. Photo by author.

date. Launched on Earth Day 2010, the program is (purportedly) designed with two goals in mind: to help disabled veterans transition to civilian life and to encourage Americans to recycle their empty beverage containers. To this end, PepsiCo has rolled out some 2,500 trademarked Dream Machine recycling bins and interactive kiosks in pharmacies, ballparks, and university buildings across the United States (Figure 8.3). According to PepsiCo press releases, the more Americans recycle, the more the company vows to donate to the Entrepreneurship Bootcamp for Veterans with Disabilities, a "national program offering free, experiential training in entrepreneurship and small business management to post-9/11 veterans with disabilities."[39] Beyond branding the soft drink maker as pro-veteran, the Dream Machines perform considerable ideological work on behalf of PepsiCo and its corporate affiliates. They memorialize the "sacrifice and service" of U.S. troops; promote a pro-consumption, business-friendly brand of environmentalism; and extol free-market capitalism and private enterprise (rather than state welfare programs) as the best way to make disabled veterans' dreams come true. Lest any potential recyclers miss the broader political import of the company's campaign, PepsiCo has supplemented its physical Dream

Machines with a website and Facebook page complete with inspirational videos, links to upbeat media coverage, and testimonials to the (neoliberal) virtues of veteran entrepreneurship.

PepsiCo is not the only organization to go online to promote disabled veterans' remembrance and relief. Following the commercialization of the Internet in the mid-1990s and the advent of Web 2.0 shortly thereafter, groups such as the American Legion, the DAV, the Healing Heroes Network, and the National Coalition for Homeless Veterans have transformed the Internet into a vital site of civic activism and communal remembrance. The Wounded Warrior Project (WWP), which was founded in 2003 with a vision of fostering "the most successful, well-adjusted generation" of disabled veterans in U.S. history, maintains an especially impressive cyberpresence. On its website and Facebook page, disabled veterans can find and share news, photographs, practical advice, and YouTube videos "related to wounded warriors and [the] nation's military community."[40] By linking its home page to other sites, the WWP serves as an online hub for disabled vets, stitching together a broad array of activists, charity organizations, message boards, and businesses. Far more than any stone monument, the WWP's online network is the ideal memorial for the digital age—instantly accessible, constantly updating, and infinite in its global reach.

However, the Wounded Warrior Project and other veterans groups have been reluctant to abandon traditional remembrance practices altogether. As part of its mission to "honor and empower wounded warriors," the group arranges disabled veteran meet-ups, hosts fund-raising bike rides, and sponsors WWP-themed credit cards (identified by a silhouette of a soldier carrying his wounded comrade over his shoulder). In fall 2007, the WWP announced the opening of its own educational memorial, the Sacrifice Center, in the group's Jacksonville, Florida headquarters. Organized around what the WWP considers to be the seven defining "character traits" of the nation's disabled veterans—duty, honor, courage, commitment, integrity, country, and service—the Sacrifice Center features interpretive displays of prosthetics and body armor, exhibits depicting patients undergoing rehabilitation, and video testimonials to WWP programs. According to WWP executive director and founder John Melia, the center was designed to provide disabled veterans with something they have never had before—a permanent shrine. "Now and in the future," he proclaimed, "a place exists to honor this generation's wounded soldiers, educate the public about their core values and personal successes, and forever immortalize their tremendous sacrifice."[41]

A similar desire has been the driving force behind the American Veterans Disabled for Life Memorial (AVDLM), which is scheduled to open in Washington, D.C., in October 2014. Touted as the United States' first national monument to disabled vets, the $86 million project is designed to "celebrate those men and women who may be broken in body—but never in spirit." When complete, the memorial will take the form of a small tree-lined park across from the United States Botanic Garden. Its focal point will be a "star-shaped reflecting pool, its surface broken only by a ceremonial flame," surrounded on three sides by walls of granite and laminated glass. The memorial will also include a collection of four bronze sculptures (each 3 inches thick and roughly 5 by 8 ½ feet in size) depicting soldiers in silhouette in various stages of injury.[42]

When asked why such a memorial is necessary, AVDLM supporters typically give two reasons: social obligation (the need to repay the symbolic "debt" owed to disabled veterans) and social recognition (the need to "bring the immense sacrifices of disabled veterans to a deeper level of public consciousness," as the DAV's official testimonial puts it).[43] Unlike other memorials, however, the AVDLM is not intended to provide disabled veterans or the nondisabled public with a sense of closure. Rather, as one AVDLM board member explains, the memorial is meant to serve as a "starting point," a place to both remember the past and contemplate disabled veterans' future struggles.[44]

It will take years, if not decades, to determine whether the American Veterans Disabled for Life Memorial lives up to its lofty promise. Ultimately, the most successful war memorials are living institutions whose meanings and social value are more a product of how they are used than how they are initially designed. That said, several elements of the AVDLM threaten to undermine its long-term viability as a national staging ground for remembrance of disabled veterans. To begin with, it appears to be wedded to a thoroughly uncritical view of American foreign policy and military conflict, a view that no doubt will alienate a number of veterans and civilian visitors. More surprisingly, it fails to acknowledge the diversity of disabled veterans' injuries and experiences, both during wartime and after. According to the AVDLM website, the four bronze statues are meant to tell the "*universal* story of the disabled veteran's pride of service, trauma, challenge of healing and discovery of purpose" (my italics).[45] In other words, it lends weight to the fiction that all veterans' political and somatic trajectories are the same. Moreover, the only part of the memorial meant to portray an actual disabled person, a bronze statue entitled "Reflecting and Recalling," relies on an outdated visual cliché: a one-legged amputee leaning on a crutch. Not only does the memorial fail to represent veterans with other kinds of impairments, but all of the figures depicted in the AVDLM (with one possible exception) are explicitly identified as male—a symbolic erasure of the growing number of women in the ranks of those disabled by war.[46] In short, while the AVDLM purports to honor the bodily sacrifices of all disabled veterans, it reaffirms stereotypical thinking about the politics, nature, and gender of war-produced disability in American history.

Conclusions

For scholars of disability, this brief history of disabled veterans' remembrance suggests a number of lessons. First, it offers yet another reminder of how disabled populations have struggled to win public recognition from the state and the non-disabled public. Borrowing memorial techniques from other veteran populations, civil rights groups, and peace activists, disabled veterans have sought to insert their collective memory into a national narrative that has in the past rendered them socially, politically, and materially invisible. Further, it suggests the need for more scholarship on how disabled people use cultural memory to give meaning to their lives. For many disabled veterans, remembrance is about more than fund-raising or building statues; it is about constructing a framework for making sense of their individual and collective impairments. In addition, I hope this history will spur other scholars to explore the relationship between disability and public "forgetfulness." To be memorialized (in any form) is to be assured that one exists—that one's history matters. Unfortunately, the FDR Memorial (1997) and the AVDLM notwithstanding, U.S. memorial culture remains a bastion of ableism, with disabled people collectively forgotten.

Above all else, this history demonstrates the willingness of disabled veterans, past and present, to distinguish themselves from other disabled populations. This point was reiterated for me during a discussion with ADVLM spokesman Dennis Joyner. At the age of twenty, Joyner was severely injured in a firefight in Vietnam, losing both legs and his left arm below the elbow. He joined the DAV while still in the hospital, eventually rising through the ranks to national commander in 1983–1984. Since that time, Joyner has dedicated much of his time to raising money for veterans' memorial projects, including the Vietnam Women's Memorial in Washington, D.C., and the AVDLM. He is especially proud of the confrontational attitude exhibited by disabled veterans of the Vietnam generation, whom he credits with helping to raise public awareness for all disabled people. When men like him returned home, Joyner explained, the mentality was: "We're not going to be a handicapped person, and be holed up . . . like someone born with a disability. We're coming out, and you're going to have to deal with us." At a time when, as Joyner put it, "everyone wanted to forget us . . . whether we were disabled or not," Vietnam vets refused to play the role of Cincinnatus and return to anonymity without a fight.[47]

Though doubtless meant as a sincere comment, Joyner's distinction between disabled veterans like himself and "someone born with a disability" is telling, for it underlies disabled veterans' central claim to remembrance. The Sacrifice Center, the ADVLM, and other sites of remembrance are meant to lend weight to the notion that disabled veterans *are* different—from other veterans (men and women who did not suffer physical or mental injury while fighting for their country) and from other disabled people (who by accident of birth or twist of fate must live their lives with permanent impairments). Implicit in disabled veterans' memorial activism, both in the past and in the present, is a hierarchical and nationalist politics of disability remembrance and social identity—a belief that by sacrificing their bodies and minds in service to their country, disabled veterans have earned a privileged place in the national memory, one that distinguishes them from the great mass of (presumed unworthy) "handicapped." As a result, there is little reason to believe that disabled veterans' remembrance projects will translate into greater rights and recognition for all disabled people—at least not in the short term. If anything, they will further segment the disabled population in the United States at a time when coalition building and mass action are more important than ever.

Notes

1. For newspaper accounts of the first Forget-Me-Not Day, see "Forget-Me-Not Day," *Frederick Daily News* (Frederick, Md.), December 16, 1921; "Plan U.S. Tag Day for Wounded Vets," *Appleton Post-Crescent* (Appleton, Wisc.), December 10, 1921; "Forget-Me-Not Day," *Iowa City Press-Citizen*, December 9, 1921; "Legion Post Plans to Help Disabled," *Oakland Tribune*, December 8, 1921.

2. The American Legion sold blood-red Flanders Field Remembrance Poppies, the Veterans of Foreign Wars sold trademarked Buddy Poppies, and the American Loyalty League sold No Man's Land Roses.

3. Robert S. Marx, "Forget-Me-Not Day Next," *Charleston Daily Mail*, December 22, 1921, Sunday magazine, 1.

4. Frances Montgomery, "Little Blue Flower Flourishes as City Shows Remembrance," *Oakland Tribune*, November 6, 1922; "Many Disabled Veterans Ask Aid of Public," *Oakland Tribune*, December 2, 1927.

5. See Marita Sturken, *Tangled Memories: The Vietnam War, the AIDS Epidemic, and the Politics of Remembering* (Berkeley: University of California Press, 1997); Edward T. Linenthal, *The Unfinished Bombing: Oklahoma City in American Memory* (New York: Oxford University Press, 2001); Jenny Edkins, *Trauma and the Memory of Politics* (Cambridge: Cambridge University Press, 2003); Jay Winter, *Remembering War: The Great War between Memory and History in the Twentieth Century* (New Haven, Conn.: Yale University Press, 2006).

6. Carol Gluck coined this term to describe fictive kinship groups united around shared experiences, memorial practices, and political goals; quoted in Winter, *Remembering War*, 136.

7. Andrew J. Bacevich uses the term "new American militarism" to describe America's recent "marriage of a militaristic cast of mind with utopian ends"; *The New American Militarism: How Americans Are Seduced by War* (New York: Oxford University Press, 2005), 3.

8. Sturken, *Tangled Memories*, 73.

9. Theo Farrell, *The Norms of War: Cultural Beliefs and Modern Conflict* (Boulder, Colo.: Lynne Rienner, 2005), 72.

10. Seth Koven, "Remembering and Dismemberment: Crippled Children, Wounded Soldiers, and the Great War in Great Britain," *American Historical Review* 99, no. 4 (1994): 1169.

11. On the link between war memorials and social processes of healing and mourning, see Jay Winter, *Sites of Memory, Sites of Mourning: The Great War in European Cultural History* (Cambridge: Cambridge University Press, 1995).

12. Jo Stanley, "Involuntary Commemorations: Post-Traumatic Stress Disorder and Its Relationship to War Commemoration," in *The Politics of War Memory and Commemoration*, edited by T.G. Ashplant, Graham Dawson, and Michal Roper (London: Routledge, 2000), 240.

13. Winter, *Remembering War*, 75.

14. Dennis Joyner, discussion with the author, November 2009.

15. On the link between soldiers' homes and disabled veterans' identity, see Patrick J. Kelly, *Creating a National Home: Building the Veterans' Welfare State, 1860–1900* (Cambridge, Mass.: Harvard University Press, 1997).

16. G. Kurt Piehler, "Honoring the Soldiers and Forgetting Their Cause: American Memories of the Civil War and the Second World War," *Rikkyo American Studies* 31 (March 2009): 116.

17. Sarah J. Purcell, *Sealed with Blood: War, Sacrifice, and Memory in Revolutionary America* (Philadelphia: University of Pennsylvania Press, 2002), 2.

18. Ibid., 113.

19. Philip Morin Freneau, "The American Soldier, a Picture from Life," in *A Freneau Sampler*, edited by Philip M. Marsh (New York: Scarecrow Press, 1963), 119.

20. Purcell, *Sealed with Blood*, 113. On federal pensioning schemes in the early republic, see Dixon Wecter, *When Johnny Comes Marching Home* (Cambridge, Mass.: The Riverside Press, 1944); John Resch, *Suffering Soldiers: Revolutionary War Veterans, Moral Sentiment, and Political Culture in the Early Republic* (Amherst, Mass.: University of Massachusetts Press, 1999).

21. G. Kurt Piehler, "The American Memory of War," in *The American Experience of War*, edited by Georg Schild (Paderborn: Federinand Schöningh, 2010), 224.

22. On the GAR's legislative and memorial campaigns, see Stuart McConnell, *Glorious Contentment: The Grand Army of the Republic, 1865–1900* (Chapel Hill: University of North Carolina Press, 1997).

23. Piehler, "The American Memory of War," 227–228; David W. Blight, *Race and Reunion: The Civil War in American Memory* (Cambridge, Mass: Belknap Press of Harvard University Press, 2001).

24. Brian Matthew Jordan, "'Living Monuments': Union Veteran Amputees and the Embodied Memory of the Civil War," *Civil War History* 57, no. 2 (2011): 121, 125, 152.

25. For example, G. Kurt Piehler points out that on Armistice Day, celebrated to mark the end of World War I: "The dead would be remembered, but the focus of this holiday would be on the distinctive sacrifice of the living veterans who paraded on main streets across the America." Piehler, "The American Memory of War," 234.

26. *Proceedings of the 11th National Convention Disabled American Veterans of the World War*, 72nd Cong., 1st Sess., 1931, H. Doc. 50, 119.

27. On the development of rehabilitation, see Beth Linker, *War's Waste: Rehabilitation in World War I America* (Chicago: University of Chicago Press, 2011).

28. "The Passing of the Cripple," *Outlook*, October 3, 1917, 166; Gertrude Atherton, "Beggars No More," *Carry On* 1, no. 4 (November 1918): 20.

29. On disabled veterans' perceived difficulties with overcoming the "army habit of mind" and the "lethargy" of hospital life, see T. B. Kidner, "Guiding the Disabled to a New Job," *Carry On* 1 (September 1918): 18; Douglas C. McMurtrie, "The High Road to Self-Support," *Carry On* 1 (July 1918): 17–21; Major John L. Todd, "The Meaning of Rehabilitation," *Annals of the American Academy of Political and Social Science* 80 (November 1918): 7; John Galsworthy, "The Gist of the Matter," *Carry On* 1 (January 1919): 22–28.

30. Richard Seelye Jones, *A History of the American Legion* (Indianapolis: Bobbs-Merrill, 1946), 242–243. Douglas I. McKay described memory preservation as "the fourth of the fundamental principles of the American Legion"; quoted in *Proceedings of the Tenth National Convention of the American Legion*, 70th Congress, 2nd Sess., H. Doc. 338, 61.

31. Speaking at the legion's tenth annual convention in 1929, Wilson declared, "Strong men remember and determine! The American Legion is founded not upon remembrance as human attribute, but upon remembrance as a vessel in the temple of history, which has been brewed in the soul of the nation." *Proceedings of the Tenth National Convention of the American Legion*, 19.

32. Louis Johnson quoted in William Gellermann, *The American Legion as Educator* (New York: Teacher's College, Columbia University, 1938), 72.

33. Richard A. Gabriel, *The Painful Field: The Psychiatric Dimension of Modern War* (New York: Greenwood Press, 1988), 29.

34. Sturken, *Tangled Memories*, 72.

35. Bacevich, *New American Militarism*, 2.

36. On the rise of "militainment" in American culture, see Roger Stahl, *Militainment, Inc.: War, Media, and Popular Culture* (New York: Routledge, 2009).

37. "Proud Supporter of Disabled Veterans," http://www.findmymattress.com/Content/DisabledVeteransOfAmerica.html, accessed June 20, 2011.

38. For a succinct introduction to neoliberalism, see David Harvey, *A Brief History of Neoliberalism* (New York: Oxford University Press, 2005).

39. PepsiCo Press Release, "Dream Machine Challenges Americans to Commit to Recycle Cans and Bottles from Summertime Cookouts to Support U.S. Veterans," June 28, 2010. Initiated by Syracuse University business professor Mike Haynie and currently held at a consortium of universities across the country, the Entrepreneurship Bootcamp for Veterans with Disabilities offers selected disabled veterans a one-week crash course in business and management education aimed at transforming "warriors into entrepreneurs."

40. The Wounded Warrior Project's primary online presence can be found at two locations, http://www.woundedwarriorproject.org and http://www.facebook.com/wwpinc.fans, although linked and related sites proliferate across the Internet.

41. "Wounded Warrior Project (WWP) Opens Sacrifice Center—New Center Tells Story of the Sacrifices and Triumphs of This Generation's Wounded Warriors," http://

www.woundedwarriorproject.org/content/view/378/921/#ixzz1ROVgxQW2, accessed June 15, 2011.

42. American Veterans' Disabled for Life Memorial website, http://www.avdlm.org, accessed June 5, 2011.

43. "To Construct a Monument to Commemorate the Sacrifices of America's Disabled Veterans," Disabled American Veterans Resolution No. 220, http://www.avdlm.org, accessed June 5, 2011.

44. Joyner, discussion with author.

45. American Veterans' Disabled for Life website.

46. As noted above, the figures represented in the bronze silhouettes are identified as masculine (e.g., servicemen, infantryman) in their official descriptions. The one possible exception is "Carrying the Wounded," a statue featuring the outline of a soldier carrying his "comrade" over his shoulder. The use of the gender-neutral "comrade" leaves open the possibility that the wounded soldier is a woman, although none of the AVDLM publicity materials suggests this is the case.

47. Joyner, discussion with author.

PART THREE

Bodies, Medicine, and Contested Knowledge

The study of definitions, practices, and experiences that have their roots in medical understandings of bodies and minds are the focus of this section. As you read the following essays, consider the tension points, the areas of collaboration, and the multiple meanings of disability that emerge.

1. How do histories of disability shape interpretations of medicine, authority, and the creation of knowledge?
2. What factors influence the meanings applied to bodies and minds? Who decides these meanings, and why does that matter?
3. In what ways are critical disability histories also histories of medicine (and vice versa)? In what ways do these histories depart from one another?
4. What theoretical frameworks shape each essay? How do these interpretive lenses influence the authors' key points?
5. How does historical context, including time and place, contribute to the meanings excavated from these studies?

CHAPTER 9

Smallpox, Disability, and Survival in Nineteenth-Century France

Rewriting Paradigms from a New Epidemic Script

CATHERINE KUDLICK

> Epidemics ordinarily exit with a whimper, not a bang. Susceptible individuals flee, die, or recover, and incidence of the disease gradually declines. It is a flat and ambiguous, yet inevitable sequence for a last act.
> —Charles Rosenberg, *Explaining Epidemics*

KEYWORDS: *Centuries*: eighteenth; nineteenth; *Geographical Areas*: Europe; *Sources*: Memoirs; Serials; *Themes*: bodies, medicine, and contested knowledge; family, daily life, and community; culture; theory

How would the eminent historian of medicine Charles Rosenberg's script read if we placed survivors at the center of the epidemic story? Too long framed by the acute phases of disease and subsequent mortality, outbreaks such as tuberculosis, typhoid, polio, syphilis, and AIDS offer an opportunity to explore our field's key questions and the analytic possibilities for the future of disability history. Such an approach helps reframe the complex relationship between medicine, disease, and disability that critical disability studies increasingly calls into question. It also opens up a greater conversation with historians of medicine and public health by providing new ways of understanding the social impact of epidemics in history. Put another way, perhaps Rosenberg's final act of the epidemic drama would be less anticlimactic if disabled actors were allowed on the stage.

Yet until recently disability historians have somehow failed to notice that the play was even in town. Examples of a full integration of disability into the epidemic script have been few and far between.[1] Even polio, which gave birth to a gifted generation of disability rights activists and scholars, has produced parallel histories: one that has focused on the acute, dramatic phases of the epidemics, which includes the race for a cure, and another that has concentrated on the stories of survivors.[2] A history that understood the feistiness of an Ed Roberts, the polio survivor who is widely considered the father of the early 1960s United States disability rights movement, and the drive of an Albert Sabin or a Jonas Salk, who competed to find a vaccine in the 1950s, as products of the same postwar era would offer new ways to write the narrative of polio. Thinking of these histories and the people involved as more alike than different invites us to expand the reach of disability history.

To demonstrate the rich possibilities that exploring the complex relationship between epidemics and disability offers, I examine smallpox, the epidemic disease that was most feared and widespread during the period when France was making its early nineteenth-century transition to modernity. If "history's greatest killer" affected as many as 1 in 10 of the country's 35 million people during the worst epidemics of the eighteenth century and the disease killed approximately 30 percent of its victims, as has been claimed, then the remaining 70 percent could have included as many as 3 million people (many of them children) who lived with permanent facial scarring, 300,000 of whom also suffered from the corneal ulceration that caused blindness.[3] Placing disability broadly defined at the center of the epidemic story rather than burying it within a list of consequences, I want to understand why the histories have remained separate. But more, I seek to demonstrate how reintegrating them will allow us to rethink the impact of smallpox and explore disability during a key period of sociocultural transformation.

When we assume that epidemics and disability inhabit the same conceptual cosmos, new opportunities open up for evaluating the life of someone such as Thérèse-Adèle Husson (1803–1831), the daughter of artisans from Nancy in eastern France. Blinded by smallpox at the age of nine months, Husson went on to become a prolific Parisian writer in the early nineteenth century.[4] She specialized in moralizing fiction for young adults, a highly emotional melodramatic genre that blended victimhood and survival. In one of the first memoirs written by a blind woman of the artisan class, Husson was quick to condemn social reactions and misunderstandings more than the disease, especially when it came to her disability:

> I have just reached my twenty-second year, and I still don't remember ever having formed a single regret concerning the loss of my eyes, a loss which seems to me to be of little importance, because people who see tell me: "You don't have the slightest understanding of treasures you have never known." I would like to believe in the justice of this reasoning, which, however, does nothing to persuade me that I am unhappy; if anything, it's the sad exclamations of people who see me that do that.[5]

Elsewhere, we have evidence that Husson suffered from at least one bout of depression (and perhaps more) brought on by frustration and isolation.[6] Though not a direct response to a specific epidemic moment, such reactions nevertheless invite us to think of the longer-term impacts of diseases. Just as demographers point to the impact of smallpox on subsequent birthrates and inheritance practices, historians of disability contribute to the broader perspective by underscoring how survivors faced courtship and marriage prospects. Here, appearances come to play an interesting role in defining the experience of disability; while "disfigurement" was not always understood to impede someone's functioning in the same way as blindness, its social import was appreciated both by contemporaries and people today. Thanks to humanities scholars' attention to "affect" in recent years, we might come to have a greater understanding of personal responses to epidemic diseases and to disabling conditions historically.[7] Unpacking the emotional responses to epidemic diseases would not only bring greater complexity to how historians understand an important phenomenon in the past, it would also raise questions about what is often taken for granted about reactions, be they individual or at the level of policy. At the very least, greater attention to affect allows us to understand expressions such as Husson's as more than one person's inner emotional turmoil. Instead, they must be approached as an equally important part of the aftermath of an epidemic, like the descriptions of empty houses and deaths in the streets.[8]

For too long, the historical study of epidemics emphasized the role of elites and biological factors such as causes, symptoms, modes of transmission, demography, and cures. With the exception of physicians, people remained surprisingly absent from these histories.[9] Only in the second half of the twentieth century, with the rise of the social history of medicine, did scholars turn their full attention to how epidemics simultaneously reflected and shaped broader social, political, economic, and cultural developments that had implications for the general public. Thanks to the pioneering studies of scholars as diverse as Charles Rosenberg and Michel Foucault, historians no longer approach epidemics either as timeless phenomena or as quaint reminders of how much progress has been made.[10] Tethered to specific cultures, governments, religions, and economies, epidemics now are seen to have significance in their own right, as events with far-reaching consequences beyond their biological-medical impact. That these once-radical ideas about epidemics have become standard thinking bodes well for the new views disability historians propose.

Such metaconnections between epidemics and disability are based on a concrete reality: along with war, diseases—especially those on a mass scale—are the primary producers of disabled people. Rubella, polio, syphilis, tuberculosis, and, most recently, AIDS have left behind a variety of physical and mental impairments that affect not just individual "victims" but also families, communities, and entire societies. During the eighteenth century, prior to the introduction of Jenner's vaccine, smallpox was a leading cause of blindness in Western Europe; it also produced severe facial scarring, deafness, mobility impairments, severe aching in the joints, permanent loss or alteration of the voice, and a host of chronic physical and mental illnesses.[11] And because of wide resistance to vaccination throughout the nineteenth century, France's lower classes continued to suffer from periodic epidemics and their disabling consequences.[12]

At the center of Enlightenment and revolutionary thinking from the 1790s to the 1840s, France became *the* place to study medicine and explore its broader relationship to social issues.[13] Influential figures such as Dr. Louis-René Villermé (1782–1863) and Louis-François Benoiston de Chateauneuf (1776–1856) marshaled quantitative data to prove definitively that social class and physical environment determined someone's predisposition to ill health and early mortality, using their findings to galvanize bourgeois outrage over the appalling circumstances of the poor. In fact, before Pasteur and others introduced microbiology, the most prestigious medical professionals devoted their energies to "public health," an emerging field that was heavily influenced by Enlightenment thinking that blended medicine and society. Its early raison d'être was to fight epidemics such as yellow fever, cholera, and a host of other diseases, and smallpox figured prominently in such efforts.[14]

This was part of a much larger approach to government intervention that incorporated medicine as a key ally. Understood as a blend between ideas and practices, the new notion was far-ranging enough to hold progressive and conservative ideas simultaneously. As one doctor explained in 1839,

> Public health concerns itself with the man in society, and considers him as a species. Religion, government, morals and customs, institutions, relations from man to man, and from people to people—all of this is its jurisdiction. In a word, [public health] touches upon every aspect of our social existence; it does even more, for . . . it tends to perfect human nature generally.[15]

This emerging field promised a better future by placing medicine in the service of an ever-improving society, although all of the implications of this shift were not yet clear. Anticipating the enthusiasm of France's leading physicians and administrators, the influential *philosophe* Condorcet (1743–1794) argued that public health was synonymous with civilization itself and believed that preventive medicine held the keys to health and expanded life expectancy because it would end epidemic diseases and illnesses and "fevers" caused by climate, diet, and occupation.[16] It is easy to imagine the place of disabled people in this scenario, even at a time before "disability" emerged as a separate category.

As many contemporary critics and subsequent scholars have pointed out, the synergy among medicine, health, and politics suggests that the story had a more problematic side that was linked to the efforts of the emerging French bourgeoisie defending its interests.[17] Seen in this way, public health offered the justifications and tools for extending government's penetration into private lives in order to manage individual behavior among the recently revolutionized lower classes of the rapidly expanding cities. The new public health movement also promoted the idea of standardized, productive bodies for factory work and the new modes of production fueled by urban and industrial growth. Originally launched in response to major epidemics, this collaboration between professionalizing doctors and government officials served capitalism by establishing medical criteria for defining and measuring the physical and moral parameters of human bodies and the spaces they occupied. Viewed from this critical perspective, it is not difficult to read sinister motives into the most optimistic pronouncements. For example, much as would be the case with disability in the following century, the movement's call to eliminate poverty could easily be understood by some as eliminating actual poor people. This belief inspired riots against doctors that resulted in grisly murders at the height of the 1832 cholera outbreak.[18] These were especially sensitive issues as France grappled with mounting social unrest in the aftermath of revolution and the choppy expansion of capitalism, both of which were affected by ongoing outbreaks of epidemic disease.

As with other aspects of the public health agenda, the campaigns against smallpox revealed the movement's Janus-like quality. In some ways Edward Jenner's 1796 intervention epitomized the new modern science, for it quickly proved effective against a terrifying disease that had ravaged Europe for centuries. The mild-mannered Englishman was building upon and perfecting the much more risky, if also more permanent, protection brought by inoculation. Also known as "variolisation," this early technique was popularized by Lady Wortley Montagu, the wife of the English ambassador to Turkey in the 1710s. Instead of stimulating the immune system by pricking the skin with live human pox, as had been the practice in many parts of India and China since ancient times, Jenner found it easier, cheaper, and safer to use cow pox.

By the first decade of the nineteenth century, Jenner's new procedure had demonstrated considerable success in France. Yearly reports from the Comité Central de Vaccine documented impressive correlations between those who had been vaccinated and declining numbers of victims. In just eight years, from 1803 to 1811, the number of cases had decreased to a tenth of what they had been in previous decades.[19] The government's extensive mobilization at every level introduced public health and preventive medicine as the grand coup Condorcet had predicted. This initial success greatly enhanced the movement's prestige. Writing in 1801, the secretary of the Comité Central de Vaccine, Dr. Henri-Marie Husson (1772–1853; no relation to Thérèse-Adèle), touted vaccination as "among medicine's greatest gifts to posterity." Even some religious authorities described it as "an act of Providence" and as "a precious gift that God, in his generosity, has offered to man."[20]

These far-reaching government responses to smallpox introduced unprecedented measures for intervening in the daily lives of citizens. Not surprisingly, given vaccination's newness and the counterintuitive requirement of knowingly injecting disease into a healthy body, many expressed misgivings about it. Both skeptical doctors and religious officials feared that humans were wrongly intervening in processes that should be left to God and nature. Seizing on popular anxieties, satirists even suggested that injecting the bovine-based vaccine could lead to monstrous crossovers between humans and cows. For example in the widely circulated 1802 caricature by the British illustrator James Gillray, "The Cow-Pock—or—the Wonderful Effects of the New Inoculation!," we find images of people predominantly from the working classes with parts of cows emerging from various orifices, severe facial swelling, and overall disfigurement. But more often clergy as well as physicians expressed legitimate concerns about impure vaccine, incompetent vaccinators, and even several highly publicized cases of children who were mistakenly injected with the virus for syphilis (the great pox).[21]

Along with fears of the actual vaccine, the greater visibility of government authority made it easy for contemporaries and, later, historians to raise the question of ulterior motives. With both professional credibility and the nation's health riding on vaccination's success, the nascent public health movement launched a systematic crusade to inject as many French citizens as possible. This required establishing an impressive bureaucratic structure to distribute, deploy, and document vaccine, from the hushed corridors of France's prestigious medical establishments down to the smallest attics and one-room shacks. Moreover, its success depended upon convincing and then engaging France's reinvigorated religious establishment to preach the gospel of vaccination from the pulpit of every parish.[22] In some respects, this might be considered one of the earliest, most systematic attempts to transform public opinion.

While the realities of this process revealed it to be far from totalitarian, the visible mobilization of so many resources nevertheless represented a new, obvious form of government intervention. Given resistance to vaccine and to authority itself, officials also had to use their influence to convince people from all social classes and walks of life—especially wary parents—to comply. Authorities used everything: positive and negative financial incentives, public vaccinations of royal children, threats, prison terms, and public shaming.[23] To a country reeling from a decade of revolutionary turmoil during which mandatory universal conscription, forced requisition of crops, and memories of sanctioned state violence known as The Terror epitomized government excess, vaccination against smallpox could be a tough sell.

Disability proved to be an expedient weapon for both sides in the raging debate over vaccination. As demonstrated above, for example, satire seized upon the horrors of disfigurement to malign Jenner's practice by depicting grotesque images of misshapen limbs and contorted faces as humans turned into cows. Some parents refused to allow their children to be vaccinated, arguing that they stood a greater chance of severe facial scarring from the vaccine than from the disease.[24] Meanwhile, pro-vaccination forces invoked "deformity and disfigurement" among the consequences that the vaccine would *prevent*, a particularly common tactic when health officials wished to enlist the support of local religious authorities.[25] In this formulation, disfigurement, blindness, infirmity, and other lingering visible signs extended the disease not simply into the future but also into the realm of the living dead. In one particularly egregious example, the prefect of Nancy (coincidentally, the original home of Thérèse-Adèle Husson) paraded a blind man through the streets wearing a sandwich board bearing the inscription: "Give alms to an unfortunate victim of smallpox."[26] That someone would come up with such an idea—and that his peers would decide to offer the brief account in their annual published report—reveals just how powerfully disability figured in the popular imagination. This use of a disabled person was potent, yet seemingly uncontroversial. How else might we explain why everyone on both sides of the debate appeared to accept that disability was a horror greater even than death? Certainly the zealous official who came up with this idea had other ways to make his point, such as parading corpses ravaged by smallpox through the streets. And what of the blind man himself? Was he outraged at being used so callously or did he derive satisfaction from being useful in a society that otherwise had no place for him? As examples such as this make clear, smallpox and disability were integral to efforts to fuse a solid relationship between medical and social pathologies.

The vaccination campaign of the early nineteenth-century public health movement also helped define disability and establish it as a concept. Interestingly, the desire to acquire this qualitative information came from an exploding enthusiasm for numbers that captured the imagination of French society, especially the medical community, not long before Jenner's discovery.[27] Unlike their counterparts across the English Channel, French doctors discovered "medical arithmetic" so late that they offered only minimal numerical analysis of vaccine's precursor, inoculation. Freed from the burden of the staid faculties of medicine after the French Revolution, the public health movement that formed within the Royal Society of Medicine in the late eighteenth century jumped at the opportunity to test the latest thinking and technology in its vaccination campaign. Among the new "technologies" at its disposal were numeric tables that required systematic data collection, careful planning about what data would be included, and close attention to how information would be tabulated, organized, and presented. The presence of disability in this context suggests that it carried real significance, either because of how officials were thinking about smallpox or because of something within their sociocultural milieu that made them single it out for scrutiny.

Whatever the reason, beginning in 1804, the Ecole de médecine de Paris sent out pre-printed forms to officials in every locality throughout France, which, among other things, solicited information about disability.[28] Divided into two parts, the fourteen-page questionnaire was heavily weighted toward the second part, which asked a series of nineteen detailed questions about how vaccinations were carried out: what time of year, by whom, under what circumstances, what the skin around the insertion point looked like, what sorts of physical symptoms people displayed, and so forth. Some items revealed the newness of survey-taking as a genre, such as the run-on question in Part II #4:

> At the moment of injecting the virus, after having noted the age, sex, individual constitution, diet, all manners of behavior, what did one observe in relation to the different phases of life, more or less dangerous, such as teeth, puberty, etc., relating to the diseases that the vaccinated person has had or been subjected to, either because of exposure or heredity, or through having acquired them, such as convulsions, rickets, scrofula, sores, scurvy, fever, whooping cough, diarrhea, bleeding, etc., etc.? Has the influence of artificial smallpox on these pre-existing conditions been irrelevant, beneficial or harmful?

We do not have the minutes of the Comité Central de Vaccine's meetings, so we have no way of knowing whether such questions came into being by consensus or by fiat. But the many "et ceteras" that served as synonyms for the great unknown and the awkwardly posed, breathless queries aimed at squeezing in every possible variable convey a certain urgency as top officials attempted to sort out what they needed to know and how best to find it out. It is as if public health officials, who occupied an awkward place between believing all to be knowable and sensing that they in fact knew almost nothing, believed that this survey offered but one chance each year to take the nation's pulse.

Preceding this barrage of questions, the relatively brief first part of the report solicited information to get at the big picture, which included disability. Here five short items asked about the number of smallpox cases since December 1789, what people remembered from earlier outbreaks, and whether any patterns could be discerned in relation to other diseases such as measles. Question 3 asked: "How many persons have remained infirm or horribly disfigured . . . as the result of smallpox," elaborating "such as the loss of one or two eyes, the loss of hearing, the loss of a limb, etc. Etc." Focused and direct compared to many of the other queries on the form, the brief questions gave the impression that measuring these aspects of smallpox was reasonably straightforward yet still essential for understanding responses to vaccination. Because they conceived the questionnaire to present disability in this way, officials clearly saw it as a central, if poorly understood, part of the epidemic reality.

But the reality depicted on the approximately 75 percent of forms that finally made their way back to the Comité Central de Vaccine was another matter. While "disfigurement and deformity" appeared prominently on the final tables published in the elegant, leather-bound annual reports, recorded numbers varied dramatically, often incongruously, from one community to another. For example, the data from Paris, where the streets teemed with nearly 1 million inhabitants of every description, indicated almost no deformities or infirmities at all between 1813 and 1816, compared with the yearly average of approximately 950 in Charente, a relatively sparsely populated administrative department. Such discrepancies of course said far more about people's uncertainty about what constituted a disability or about administrative priorities than they did about the behavior of the disease or even the prevalence of disabilities in the popular imagination. Or perhaps the qualifier "horribly" proved impossible to ascertain.

Even so, simply by engaging the question, officials compiling information about vaccinations throughout France were surely laying the groundwork for a greater awareness of disability and the need to frame it within the new doctrine of public health. Sitting in cramped, drafty quarters, desperately trying to meet the Comité Central de Vaccine's deadlines, harried medical practitioners, priests, and local officials with varying degrees of education and experience were forced, at least for a brief moment, to consider people they knew or had treated in terms of these criteria. What did this mean for Monsieur B——, who could no longer open his eyes due to scarring but could still tend his flock and get to mass on Sundays? Or for 7-year old Louisa de S——, now so marked by pox that she would likely never find a suitor? In a world that would lack defined criteria for gauging even something seemingly unequivocal such as blindness for another 150 years, let alone tools for measuring relationships between physical stigma and emotional scars, reporters had to make their own judgments.[29] To be sure, these determinations would likely have had no impact on a particular person, boiled down as they were to a number entered into a table. Given the circumstances under which data was compiled, it seems implausible to expect that the concerned party even knew of the label her local official had assigned to her. Yet folding an individual who was previously understood to have certain qualities into a quantitative aggregate of hitherto disparate characteristics constituted an important first step toward establishing a modern notion of the disabled person. Moreover, such connections placed different disabilities on the same conceptual plane, prompting contemporaries to understand something such as facial disfigurement as being on par with blindness. At the most basic level, officials had created a category and a label for disability at the center of the country's earliest, most important public health initiative. Such queries might well be the first systematic national survey of disability in Western history, a step that would be widely emulated by the scores of foreigners who came to study medicine in the capital so that they could return home with the latest ideas.[30]

The vaccination crusade cemented a growing association between disability and medicine, one that began defining and enumerating disability within the context of a particular set of social relations. Asking local officials, health practitioners, and even priests to record disabling conditions as part of a medical response to epidemic disease marked the beginning of an important transition from the community and pastoral realm to that of a secular national government. As the vaccination campaign made clear, local and religious relationships were key, with all the foibles, subjective judgments, and inefficiencies of human beings firmly intact, even as they served the public health movement's aspirations to improving civilization through objectivity, systematization, and rigor. When all was said and done, the data neatly compiled in the bound volumes that lined the walls of France's medical establishments represented a growing belief in medicine's ability to conquer a major scourge that had dogged civilization for centuries. While each report documented the trials and tribulations of introducing a new medical procedure to an entire—albeit wary—nation, the sheer magnitude of the effort also reflected the success of a new faith. Disability, like epidemic disease, provided an important opportunity to put these beliefs to the test, since both challenged humans' quest to have the universe on their terms.

Given the close associations among war, epidemics, and disability, it would be tempting to expect similar rhetorical and other links to those Susan Sontag highlighted in her classic 1978 exploration of tuberculosis and cancer in *Illness as Metaphor*.[31] Interestingly, however, these struggles against smallpox lacked the overt military associations that might be expected as France found itself embroiled in the Napoleonic Wars. Although the army would have been an ideal place to implement vaccination efforts, especially since Napoleon famously said that he could refuse nothing Jenner asked of him, vaccination never became central to the French army, as it would in other armies, especially those of the German lands.[32] In the absence of in-depth cultural histories of daily life, vocabulary, and medical practices during this undeniably military period, scholars can only speculate on the importance terms such as "campaign" in conjunction with "fight" and "struggle" must have had for how the average French citizen understood vaccination. An equally fruitful avenue of investigation would explore religious imagery—which had been inextricably intertwined with military imagery since the rise of Christianity—in the "crusades" against smallpox.[33]

However widespread such military or religious ideas may have been, it was clear that intervention was far from systematic. After the early, heady days of the vaccination campaign during the first years of the nineteenth century, promoters of the public health movement discovered the challenges to be far more complicated than they had thought. Vaccination, it turned out, suffered periodic setbacks, partly because of problems with manufacturing the serum, partly because people needed to be revaccinated a decade later to ensure immunity, and partly because the population and even officials had grown more complacent.[34] Even the optimism about being able to document progress seemed misplaced, or at least in need of refinement.

The responses to the query regarding "disfigurement and deformity" offer a particularly clear example of this disillusionment. In 1841, after nearly four decades of publishing wild disparities among administrative departments and even within the same department from one year to the next, the Comité de Vaccine finally conceded that "the number of deformities and lasting infirmities that follow smallpox is even more difficult to certify than that of actual cases of pox." It went on to explain that in addition to "unequivocal cases of grave infirmities, such as loss of sight, persistent ulcerations of the eyelids or deformity resulting from profound alteration of the face which all observers comment upon, there are more or less pronounced scars, the pockmarks that some note on their forms and that others do not take into account, any more than the affected subjects themselves."[35] The brief observation is remarkable for a number of reasons. First, it admitted that there was something wrong with the system of collecting data, that subjective reporters were not providing the objective information that was so important to the public health movement. At the same time, the paragraph implicitly called for better criteria for defining disability. While it did not propose any alternatives, it raised the question of how this might be done. Ironically, a public health movement dedicated to establishing definitive criteria for everything is what introduced uncertainty, fluidity, and complexity into the definition of disability, and a solution for these problems continues to elude us to the present day.

Finally, and most strikingly, the phrase "any more than the affected subjects themselves" acknowledged the values of the people actually living with the conditions. Here we have a report that was part of the professionalizing public health movement, one that increasingly touted medical expertise, calling for what today's scholars would call "patient-centered histories." Given that the doctor-patient relationship was still evolving into one where physicians prescribed rather than listened, such an approach could be a holdover from the past. But—to use today's terminology—it could also be recognition of the fact that disabled people did and should enjoy historical agency. It must also be noted that the report used the term "affected" rather than "afflicted" (*affecté* vs. *affligé*), the word modern historians might expect to flow from the pen of a nineteenth-century doctor who was unwittingly helping to invent a medical paradigm of disability.

Thanks to the critical perspective of disability history, we can imagine such a phrase opening a door into thinking differently—even radically—about smallpox and disability. Within this formation, "the affected subjects themselves" are historical actors who are not merely responding to a devastating disease but reshaping it to suit their needs. Once we shift the optic to actual survivors, we begin to ask different questions. What were their lives like once they had learned to live again? What was most difficult? Where did they find pleasure? Would they recognize themselves in the reports written about them? How did they look back on the epidemic experience and what narrative script would they produce? Literature and memoir of course offer abundant and rich accounts of people living with smallpox, especially aristocratic women who faced isolation because of their diminished marriage prospects.[36] But as I hope this essay has made clear, we need to use tools from disability history to analyze these descriptions, asking what forces shaped the people who produced them, whether they were playing to conventions, writing from their hearts at a particular moment, documenting a truth as they saw it, or some combination of these. By interrogating the structures that invested disabilities with a particular meaning in the time of smallpox, we can gain a much fuller sense of the reality of the epidemic for everyone.

Thérèse-Adèle Husson provides a fascinating contrast with aristocratic writings about smallpox and invites us to reimagine the epidemic script. Having lived with the effects of the disease for nearly all of her life, she mentioned it only in passing, at the same time that she understood its literary value by introducing it into her fiction. In her novel *The Three Sisters, or The Effects of Blind Motherhood* (1833), Husson's protagonist Laure was temporarily blinded but suffered from severe scarring from smallpox. Laure, a difficult, unpleasant little girl who watches (and attempts to sabotage) her unaffected sisters' romantic and marriage prospects, could have been created from Husson's own experiences.[37] Or not. Throughout her writing and indeed her life, we have evidence of a savvy woman who knew how to present what she believed people wanted to hear. Certainly the fiction does not reflect the story she recounts in her autobiographical notes, where we find a blatant contradiction between her adamant assertions that blind men and women should not marry and her marriage to a musician and inventor, Pierre-François Victor Foucault (1797–1871), himself a survivor of smallpox. While she never wrote about their time together, we do know that their lives were made extremely difficult by poverty—no doubt resulting from their blindness, but more because of their inability to find work than because they could not see. For a time they each managed to live from their creative labor, Thérèse-Adèle from her writing and Pierre-François as a horn player. The key point is that they survived much like the vast majority of other poor people living in Paris in the 1820s. Moreover, they did find one another, and they were part of a vibrant community of blind musicians, writers, and others who lived in the shadow of the Quinze-Vingts Hospital and the National Institute of Blind Youth. Since we know that smallpox was the leading cause of blindness for the early part of the nineteenth century, it is likely that this was in some respects a society of survivors, people drawn together into all the areas of community life, from courtship to infighting.

In the spirit of the 1841 report's "affected subjects themselves," I propose that we consider "survivors" as a synonym for and characteristic of "the disabled" rather than "victims" or "the afflicted." Survivor could apply to numerous other epidemics in history, such as leprosy, AIDS, rickets, rubella, measles, scarlet fever, polio. All left behind survivors who struggled with one form of disability or another and sometimes more than one. And as Husson revealed, many of these problems were linked as much to social marginalization as they were to physical symptoms. What does it mean for our understanding of disability to broaden the definition in this way? What theoretical work are we doing when we—like some contemporaries— equate such symptoms of disability not automatically with disaster and failure but possibly as omens of survival and good fortune? In other words, to gain a more nuanced understanding of the past, we need to refine our definition of disability so that it can hold a number of counterintuitive notions simultaneously. That such a radical move might provoke outcries from survivors of experiences not readily associated with disability brings us back to the complex relationship between the medical and social paradigms; if disability had a different sociocultural valence, the equation with survival would introduce new avenues for exploring what we take for granted about the human condition. Even if the analogy ultimately proves to be inappropriate, the conversation is worth having.

As the case of smallpox in France makes clear, epidemics have a hidden history that is deeply interwoven with disability and survival. Because of this, disability history has the potential to transform how we understand the impact of epidemic disease, not just at the level of individual reactions but also at the level of social and political responses. By focusing on survivors rather than on mortality, we can reimagine epidemic scripts as we take advantage of the copious documentation generated in times of anxiety and crisis. But epidemics do more than offer invaluable resources for unearthing experiences and responses to disability: they provide the all-important stage for re-presenting disability and disabled people in history.

Our field's challenge is to rewrite Charles Rosenberg's final act to make sure disabled actors are on the stage. Of course this will require a new approach to the entire play, one in which the social and medical paradigms are understood as dynamic and mutually constitutive. Using these same tools, we can and should go even further, to reimagine not just the stage but the very idea of theater itself.

Notes

1. For an excellent exception, see Leslie J. Reagan, *Dangerous Pregnancies: Mothers, Disabilities, and Abortion in Modern America* (Berkeley: University of California Press, 2010).

2. David M. Oshinsky, *Polio: An American Story* (New York: Oxford University Press, USA, 2006); Naomi Rogers, *Dirt and Disease: Polio before FDR* (New Brunswick: Rutgers University Press, 1992); Daniel J. Wilson, *Living with Polio: The Epidemic and Its Survivors* (Chicago: University of Chicago Press, 2007); Tony Gould, *A Summer Plague: Polio and Its Survivors* (New Haven, Conn.: Yale University Press, 1995).

3. Donald R. Hopkins, *The Greatest Killer: Smallpox in History* (Chicago: University of Chicago Press, 2002), 75; Pierre Darmon, *La longue traque de la variole : les pionniers de la médecine préventive* (Paris: Perrin, 1986), 56–62.

4. Thérèse-Adèle Husson, *Reflections: The Life and Writings of a Young Blind Woman in Post-Revolutionary France*, translated and with commentary by Catherine Kudlick and Zina Weygand (New York: New York University Press, 2001).

5. Ibid., 16–17.

6. Ibid., 68–69, 89–91.

7. David M. Halperin and Valerie Traub, *Gay Shame* (Chicago: University of Chicago Press, 2010); Melissa Gregg and Gregory J. Seigworth, *The Affect Theory Reader* (Durham, N.C.: Duke University Press Books, 2010).

8. Adding disabled actors to the epidemic drama has been made possible by the rise of critical disability studies and its influence on a growing number of historians. This approach to disability challenges the long-dominant view of what many refer to as the "medical" or "pathology model," i.e., seeing disability as a problem or deficit located in an individual who is perceived to be biologically damaged, a situation that can be fixed only through medical intervention or through an individual's striving to overcome a disability in order to be as much like a "normal" person as possible. Here, "cure" meant erasing disability without calling definitions of normality into question. While it does not deny that medicine can be useful, the newer paradigm, known as the "social" or "minority" model invites scholars to examine the social, cultural, economic, and political factors that structure the lives of disabled people and determine their status. The social model developed as a counterpoint to the medical one and critiques the earlier assumptions as narrow, elitist, and ignorant of the people most concerned. It proposes a broader, more democratic, pluralistic approach that grants disabled people agency and inserts disability, like race and gender, into a broad range of historical concerns. Simi Linton, *Claiming Disability* (New York: New York University Press, 1998); Harlan Hahn, "The Politics of Physical Differences: Disability and Discrimination," *Journal of Social Issues* 44, no. 1 (1988): 39–47; John Gliedman and William Roth, *The Unexpected Minority: Handicapped Children in America* (New York: Harcourt, 1980), chapter 1; Bill Hughes and Kevin Patterson, "The Social Model of Disability and the Disappearing Body: Towards a Sociology of Impairment," *Disability and Society* 12, no. 3 (1997): 325–340.

9. This is less true for early histories of epidemics, such as in the works of Thucydides, Hippocrates, Boccaccio, and Defoe.

10. Charles E. Rosenberg, *The Cholera Years: The United States in 1832, 1849, and 1866*, 2nd ed. (Chicago: University of Chicago Press, 1987); Michel Foucault, *Power/Knowledge: Selected Interviews and Other Writings, 1972–1977* (New York: Vintage, 1980), chapter 9; Michel Foucault, *The Birth of the Clinic: An Archaeology of Medical Perception* (New York: Vintage, 1994); For an excellent discussion of Foucault and epidemics, see E. Thacker, "The Shadows of Atheology: Epidemics, Power and Life after Foucault," *Theory, Culture & Society* 26, no. 6 (December 2009): 134–152.

11. Zina Weygand, *Les causes de la cécité et les soins oculaires en France au début du XIXe siècle: 1800–1815* (Paris: Diffusion PUF, 1989), 95–118; Darmon, *La longue traque de la variole*, 40–41.

12. Darmon, *La longue traque de la variole*, 298–303; Louis Chevalier, *Laboring Classes and Dangerous Classes in Paris during the First Half of the Nineteenth Century* (New York, N.Y.: H. Fertig, 2000), 332–337. A fascinating study remains to be written about the relationship between contagion and disability, especially in light of recent calls to reintegrate impairment and disability. Throughout his book *Stigma*, Goffman offers an intriguing point of departure in his exploration of stigma through notions of "spoiled identity" and "guilt by association." Erving Goffman, *Stigma: Notes on the Management of Spoiled Identity* (New York: Touchstone, 1986). See also Hughes and Patterson, "The Social Model of Disability and the Disappearing Body"; and Priscilla Wald, *Contagious: Cultures, Carriers, and the Outbreak Narrative* (Durham, N.C.: Duke University Press, 2008)

13. Erwin H. Ackerknecht, *Medicine at the Paris Hospital, 1794–1848* (Baltimore, Md.: Johns Hopkins University Press, 1967).

14. William Coleman, *Death Is a Social Disease: Public Health and Political Economy in Early Industrial France* (Madison: University of Wisconsin Press, 1982); Ann Elizabeth Fowler La Berge, *Mission and Method: The Early Nineteenth-Century French Public Health Movement* (Cambridge: Cambridge University Press, 2002); Erwin H. Ackerknecht, "Hygiene in France, 1815–1848," *Bulletin of the History of Medicine* 22, no. 5 (April 1948): 117–155; James C. Riley, *The Eighteenth-Century Campaign to Avoid Disease* (Hampshire, UK: Palgrave Macmillan, 1987); George Rosen, *From Medical Police to Social Medicine: Essays on the History of Health Care* (Cambridge, UK: Science History Publications, 1974).

15. Quoted in Catherine Kudlick, *Cholera in Post-Revolutionary Paris: A Cultural History* (Berkeley: University of California Press, 1996) 72.

16. La Berge, *Mission and Method*, 12.

17. Foucault led the charge in his essay "The Politics of Health in the Eighteenth Century" in *Power/Knowledge*, chapter. 9.

18. Chevalier, *Laboring Classes and Dangerous Classes*; Kudlick, *Cholera in Post-Revolutionary Paris*, 184–92.

19. Darmon, *La longue traque de la variole*, 199.

20. H. M. Husson, *Recherches historiques et médicales sur la vaccine* (Paris: Chez Gabon et Cie., Ecôle de Médecine,1801, 1; Darmon, *La longue traque de la variole*, 205–206.

21. Darmon, *La longue traque de la variole*, 219–262.

22. Yves-Marie Bercé, "La clergé et la diffusion de la vaccination," *Revue d'histoire de l'Église de France*. 69, no. 182 (1983): 87–106.

23. Darmon, *La longue traque de la variole*, 201–207.

24. Yves Marie Bercé, *Le chaudron et la lancette: Croyances populaires et médecine préventive, 1798–1830* (Paris: Presses de la Renaissance, 1984); Darmon, *La longue traque de la variole*, chapter 11.

25. The archives of the Académie Nationale de Médecine (ANM, Paris), Série V (Vaccination) contain numerous examples.

26. Comité central de vaccine (1824), "Rapport présenté par le Comité central de vaccine (puis par l'Académie de médecine) sur les vaccinations pratiquées en France, 1803–1937," n.d., 21, ANM.

27. Andrea A. Rusnock, *Vital Accounts: Quantifying Health and Population in Eighteenth-Century England and France* (Cambridge: Cambridge University Press, 2009).

28. "Instruction pour les rédaction des tableaux demandés par l'Ecole de Médecine de Paris," ANM V1 d1 n.8. The reports based on the pre-printed forms regarding vaccinations were issued under a variety of titles throughout the nineteenth century and into the twentieth century under the auspices of shifting government departments and agencies. See Darmon, *La longue traque de la variole*, 461. For purposes of this essay, I have opted to use the "Comité Central de Vaccine" and the "Report" that can be found in the Archives Nationales de Médecine V series.

29. For a discussion of the definitions of blindness in the French historical context, see Weygand, *Les causes de la cecite*, 7–10.

30. John Harley Warner, *Against the Spirit of System: The French Impulse in Nineteenth-Century American Medicine* (1998; repr., Baltimore, Md.: Johns Hopkins University Press, 2003); David McCullough, *The Greatest Journey: Americans in Paris* (New York: Simon & Schuster, 2011) chapter 4; Ackerknecht, *Medicine at the Paris Hospital*.

31. Susan Sontag, *Illness as Metaphor* (New York: Farrar, Straus and Giroux, 1978).

32. Peter Baldwin, *Contagion and the State in Europe, 1830–1930* (Cambridge: Cambridge University Press, 2005) chapter 4; Bercé, *Le Chaudron et la lancette*, 70–72.

33. Bercé, *Le Chaudron et la Lancette*, 121–150.

34. Darmon, *La longue traque de la variole*, pt. III.

35. Comité central de vaccine, "Rapport pour 1841," 133–134, ANM.

36. Catriona Seth, *Les rois aussi en mouraient: les lumières en lutte contre la petite vérole* (Paris: Editions Desjonquères, 2008), chapter 4; David E. Shuttleton, *Smallpox and the Literary Imagination, 1660–1820* (Cambridge: Cambridge University Press, 2007), chapter 5.

37. Husson, *Reflections*, 87–88.

CHAPTER 10

"Unfit for Ordinary Purposes"

Disability, Slaves, and Decision Making in the Antebellum American South

DEA H. BOSTER

KEYWORDS: *Centuries*: nineteenth; *Geographical Areas*: North America; *Sources*: legal documents; medical documents; manuscripts and archival materials; *Themes*: bodies, medicine, and contested knowledge; family, daily life, and community; citizenship and belonging; culture; labor; law and policy; slavery

In 1852, the Supreme Court of North Carolina heard the case of *Bell v. Jeffreys* on appeal from the Wake County Superior Court. The plaintiff, Bushrod W. Bell, had purchased an otherwise healthy female slave who was nearsighted—or, as Bell described her, "defective in her vision"—and successfully sued the seller, William B. Jeffreys, to recover damages for breach of warranty. The superior court originally had instructed the jury that the defect should be considered an "unsoundness" if "the slave was thereby rendered incapable to perform the common and ordinary business in the house and field, which slaves are taught and expected to perform." This rubric was rather broad; for an adult enslaved woman, "common and ordinary business" could include domestic service as well as hard agricultural labor, concubinage as well as childbearing. Upon appeal, Supreme Court Justice Thomas Ruffin took issue with the court's grounds for determining unsoundness. In Ruffin's view, assigning unsoundness to some arbitrary degree of imperfection was a slippery slope, particularly for a "defect" such as nearsightedness, for "it is known, that there are more myopic persons, among the educated and refined classes, than in others, and many more among the white than the black race. . . . I never knew a white person rendered unfit for the offices of life by this defect of vision." Nevertheless, the court upheld the jury's verdict, determining that while myopia was not a disabling condition for people in other walks of life, it did constitute a significant unsoundness in the enslaved African American woman. In his opinion for the Supreme Court's decision, Justice J. Pearson cited livestock law precedents to affirm that nearsightedness, which affected "an important organ," was indeed a significant defect in a slave. As Pearson pointed out, "A horse, that has had his eyes knocked out, and has got well, is healthy . . . but it does not import, that the structure of the body of the animal is perfect and free of defect. . . . If there be a defect in it, so as to make it unfit for ordinary purposes, the animal is unsound." Furthermore, nearsightedness seemed of particular concern in a female slave of childbearing age because "if it was hereditary . . . it was more likely to fall on the issue, as opposed to having been caused by accident."[1] In this case, the North Carolina court delivered a decision about slave "unsoundness" that seemed to equate human property with animals but was tailored specifically to the slave's race and gender.

The conversation between Pearson and Ruffin in *Bell v. Jeffreys* articulates an important but often overlooked discourse in antebellum slavery, the professional arbitration of "unsoundness" that rendered slaves "unfit for ordinary purposes." The many historical actors who debated about the fluid and contingent boundaries between human and property and about "sound" and "unsound," indicate that remarkably few solid conclusions about those boundaries were reached in the antebellum South. For instance, Judge Abraham Nott from South Carolina admitted in 1821 that there were no universal legal definitions of slave "vice" or unsoundness.[2] However, as this chapter seeks to demonstrate, a host of assumptions and expectations about race, gender, controllability, and even desirability were at play in this professional discourse and decision making.

Legal and medical writings on slave disability relied on many different perspectives and on widespread assumptions about race and gender to establish boundaries between able-bodiedness and disability in human chattel, but those boundaries were a constant source of conflict.[3] As South Carolinian James L. Petigru complained to fellow rice planter Robert F. W. Allston in an 1837 letter, juridical disagreements about definitions of defects in slaves

> [open] the door to the whole contest, as to what does or does not constitute unsoundness. As regards horseflesh there is a vast contrariety of opinions, some judges holding that every sickness or defect almost is ground to rescind a sale, others that nothing short of some constitutional, radical infirmity will answer the purpose. Then again if Judges would agree Juries cannot and the whole subject is one of the greatest uncertainty.[4]

Throughout the antebellum period, slaveholders, traders, lawyers, doctors, judges, and slaves alike participated in ongoing (and often thorny) negotiations about meanings of bondage versus freedom, "blackness" versus "whiteness," person versus property, and soundness and disability in African American slaves. This chapter uses state appellate court decisions, primarily from breach-of-warranty litigation suits in the lower South, to identify professional assessments of "sound" and "unsound" African American slaves.[5] Many legal and medical historians— including Walter Johnson, Ariela J. Gross, Jenny Bourne Wahl, Sharla Fett, Steven Stowe, and Todd L. Savitt—have noted the uncertainties evident in constructing and reconstructing meanings of race, bondage, and enslaved bodies in the antebellum South. However, few have discussed in detail the connections between those conversations and constructions of slave disability, or "unsoundness." Slaves with disabilities existed in a nebulous discursive space between "human" and "chattel" and were often held to unique standards for soundness that were influenced by their skin colors and genders. This in turn profoundly influenced southern legal and medical cultures and social discourse on disability.

Analyzing disability and slavery involves finding intersections and layers of meaning in two social constructs that were more fluid and contested than many antebellum observers would have admitted. I approach my study of disability in African American bondspeople from the perspective that disability, like race and slavery, is defined by interactions between bodies and their physical, social, cultural, and aesthetic environments. This relational view of disability rejects the notion that those who could be considered "disabled" have always been defined in contrast to a central and unproblematic, able-bodied norm. In this sense, the contrast between "able-bodied" and "disabled," "slave" and "master," or "black" and "white" cannot be expressed as a simple, fixed binary; as scholars such as Daniel Wickberg and Kenneth Greenberg have observed, we must instead seek out the language (both verbal and visual), the contexts, and the interactions that created and recreated those categories and power dynamics in history.[6] In many cases, any and all visible and invisible conditions that might affect a slave's "soundness"—including skin color, gender, character, vice, health, body, and emotional state—were brought to bear in southern courts and medical consultations. Like the judgment rendered in *Bell v. Jeffreys*, the professional decisions that resulted from these encounters ultimately assessed disability in ways that were specific to the slaves in question rather than generally applicable to the enslaved population as a whole.

In discussions of disability and slavery, many scholars use the nineteenth-century concept of "soundness," a term the slaveholding class used to indicate an individual slave's overall state of health and, by extension, his or her character and worth in the marketplace. As historian Sharla M. Fett has noted, the concept of soundness was rooted at the intersection of medicine and the southern political economy and provided slaveholders with a language to determine the physical condition of their human chattel in terms of market value and productivity.[7]

Sources of soundness or unsoundness were individual characteristics of a slave's body, mind, or character, and discussions of a slave's soundness emphasized that those characteristics were not necessarily mitigated by the slave's job or environment; a slave with unsound qualities could be judged unsound in any situation. Furthermore, as southern medico-legal expert Juriah Harriss noted in 1859, certain diagnoses, such as epilepsy or syphilis, could make otherwise healthy slaves unsound because there was no way to predict when symptoms would reappear, even in well-treated slaves; thus, the concept of soundness encompassed conditions that were apparent as well as those that were not.[8] Unlike Harriss, I argue that the calculus of soundness was never quite so codified and that soundness was assessed using a subjective and fluid system to determine the predictability and docility of a slave.

In most of these cases, assessments of "soundness" or disability seemed to hinge on the simple question of whether or not slaves were able to perform whatever labor was expected of them by their masters at the time of sale.[9] For many adult slaves in the nineteenth century, this often meant agricultural labor on a plantation, but slaves were purchased to perform a variety of duties for slaveholders and their families that would change over the lifetime of the slave.[10] However, all conditions that *might* affect a slave's soundness were admissible in court, particularly in cases of breach-of-warranty litigation. For such cases, expert medical witnesses were crucial in deliberations on the health and mental states of warranted slaves. In 1858, Juriah Harriss, then a professor at Savannah Medical College, noted the widespread demand for (and necessity of) medical opinions regarding the soundness of slaves:

> Physicians in the South are daily called upon to give medical evidence in court, in cases of prosecution for sale of an unsound negro, or by a citizen to pronounce upon the soundness of a negro slave, whom he proposes purchasing, or finally as a medical examiner for insurance companies, to determine the condition of negroes as regards health.[11]

In the first half of the nineteenth century, southern courts increasingly focused on aspects of slave soundness—including "character" and "vice"—as medicalized conditions and employed doctors as medico-legal authorities.[12] Many southern physicians argued it was necessary to apply different diagnoses and treatments to their black and white patients and believed that they alone possessed the specialized knowledge to judge the physical and mental conditions of African American slaves in the South.[13] One early example of this is the certificate of Louisiana physician Samuel Robinson, who deposed on July 6, 1809, that a "negro woman" belonging to a Mr. C. Stuart was "much diseas'd" and "intirely [*sic*] unfit for any kind of labour."[14] The terse conclusion in this document implies that this woman's physical condition rendered her completely valueless and possibly infertile or undesirable as a mother to more slaves. Such a broad conclusion indicates the extent of Robinson's authority on matters of slave soundness. Five decades later, in the Arkansas case of *Thompson v. Bertrand*, the court upheld the principle that only medical professionals had the authority to determine the causes and prognoses of "unsound" conditions in slaves.[15] The importance of physicians' judgments of slave soundness is also apparent in correspondence between South Carolina slave traders Z. B. Oakes and A. J. McElveen in 1853. McElveen, who was traveling to collect slaves to sell at Ryan's Mart in Charleston, describes several slaves with potentially disabling conditions and noted the necessity of having them "Examind by a Doctor you approve off [*sic*]."[16] In the case of a young man with a "Soar leg" that seemed like it might be curable, McElveen noted that "I had him Examined by Dr Ingram [and] he advises his owner Mr Mcleod to warrant him Sound."[17] Significantly, the doctors that McElveen hired had the authority to assess the marketability of slaves with potential physical problems and to vouch for the soundness of a slave who was known to have sore leg, which was widely accepted as an "unsound" condition. Reading into such depositions, we can infer that doctors took slaves' ages, genders, and overall physical or emotional states into account; for instance, the young man with a potentially "unsound" sore leg may not have been deemed a candidate for treatment if he had been older, or if he had been a woman, or if he had other "unsound" qualities such as a character flaw or mental instability. The fact that the physicians in these examples did not need to demonstrate or prove their conclusions indicate that physicians, even in a nontherapeutic situation, enjoyed considerable authority to judge slaves' soundness in a legal setting.

Legal institutions throughout the antebellum South were highly concerned about the potential trade of "defective" slaves in the open market and maintained considerable authority to intervene in cases of slave unsoundness. After the closing of the international slave trade in 1808, the internal slave trade, or "second middle passage," became the only legal avenue for masters to purchase new human chattel, and even without a fixed calculus of slave prices, slaves were expensive investments. Generally, young male field hands and healthy attractive young women were the most expensive slaves in the South, costing as much as several thousand dollars, whereas children and the disabled—those who were elderly, crippled, scarred, or otherwise impaired—sold for significantly lower prices.[18] As the institution of slavery spread westward with settlers and planters, slave sales—particularly in major centers such as New Orleans, Richmond, and Charleston—flourished, but Richard Tansey, in his study of New Orleans trader Bernard Kendig, claims that "the laws governing slaves offered customers little protection" and that it was difficult for plaintiffs to prove that slaves were unsound at the time of sale.[19] As more recent scholars have argued, however, the sheer number of breach-of-warranty cases in the early nineteenth-century South indicates that some slaveholders and traders knowingly sold overpriced "defective" slaves whom they claimed were sound, and while the burden of proof still fell to the purchaser, southern states had a number of different laws designed to protect buyers from fraudulent sales guarantees.[20] In Louisiana, where fraud cases involving slaves were particularly common, the transfer of slave property was highly regulated, and redhibition laws—which allowed for the cancellation of slave or livestock sales up to one year after purchase if hidden defects were discovered—provided a good deal of protection to buyers.[21] The state civil code specified a number of "relative" vices in slaves' characters, such as theft or a propensity to run away, and three "absolute vices" of their bodies—madness, leprosy, and epilepsy—that could provide legal ground to rescind a sale or demand a price reduction.[22]

While other southern states employed some regulations to protect purchasers, they relied more heavily on the principle of caveat emptor in soundness warranty cases. In South Carolina, for instance, a "sound price" rule—based on market calculations that took a slave's age, skin color, and gender into account—dictated that a purchaser who paid the full value for a slave with no obvious or observable defect at the time of the sale could presume to receive an "implied warranty" that the slave was physically sound; a buyer who paid less than full value needed to produce an express guarantee from the seller to make a claim of a fraudulent sale.[23] A similar practice existed in other states. For instance, in the Alabama case of *Clopton v. Martin* (1847), the seller of a boy with a long history of "spasms or fits" had disclosed the slave's condition and negotiated a discounted price but accidentally issued a warranty of soundness in the bill of sale, which was finalized three days after the transaction. The state Supreme Court decreed that the purchaser had no right to sue for breach of warranty because the seller had issued the guarantee by mistake and that the seller had been aware of the slave's unsoundness at the time of the transaction.[24] Similarly, in the Texas case of *Williams v. Ingram* (1858), the state Supreme Court affirmed that general soundness warranties did not cover slaves if buyers "traded with their eyes open" and were aware of "a particular unsoundness" at the time of sale.[25] Such rulings indicate that despite the authority of medicolegal experts, the ultimate responsibility to judge unsoundness in human chattel in sales transactions often fell on buyers themselves. Slaveholders' expectations and decisions therefore contributed to an ongoing, complicated discourse about the nature of slave disability.

In states where the rule of caveat emptor prevailed, courts took the precise language of warranties, as well as broader assumptions, into account in their determinations of slave soundness. In *Harrell v. Norvill* (1857), the North Carolina Supreme Court determined that Kennedy, a slave with impaired motor skill because the little fingers on both hands were permanently contracted, was not "sound" but that his observed "defect" was not covered under the warranty in his sale, which only guaranteed him to be "sound in mind and health." Citing *Bell v. Jeffreys*, Justice Battle observed that Kennedy was certainly healthy and of sound mind and ruled that because his physical state was otherwise unmentioned in the bill of sale, Kennedy's purchaser could not sue for breach of warranty.[26] In one Georgia case, *Nelson v. Biggers* (1849), the court ruled that a warrant for a woman named Betty containing the word "healthy," rather than "sound," extended only to the body of the slave. Although the jury originally found that "the said negro Betty, from imbecility of mind, was, as a slave, incapable of performing the ordinary work and labor," the state Supreme Court overturned the decision, noting that "we do not say a person has a healthy mind, when we wish to convey the idea of a sound intellect, nor do we say a person has an unhealthy mind, when we wish to convey the idea of a weak intellect."[27] These cases indicate important distinctions between health and able-bodiedness in the nineteenth century; the presence of "disease," which was often read as acute or curable, did not necessarily render the body "unsound." Conversely, the presence of a psychological condition such as insanity, or a developmental impairment such as "idiocy" or "imbecility," did not make a person "unhealthy." However, in most cases, the semantics of soundness guarantees were not definitive. In Betty's case, for example, her gender may have influenced the Georgia court's expectations of her intellect and its role in the work she had been purchased to perform. In this respect, courts drew on a complicated variety of factors, including gender, to determine whether or not slaves could be judged sound or unsound at the time of sale.

Many warranty cases focused on the observability of a slave's defect, which was an important consideration in breach of warranty cases. The principle of the "sound price" rule hinged on the idea that many sources of unsoundness were discernible, or at least should be apparent, to buyers and sellers. As the North Carolina Supreme Court noted in the appellate case of *Fulenwider v. Poston* (1856), "Where the seller of a slave refuses to insert a warranty of soundness in a bill of sale . . . [and] the negro is unsound, the symptoms being not hidden or hard to discover, the maxim of caveat emptor applies."[28] The apparentness of a slave's "defective" condition at the time of sale was not an absolute standard for determining their soundness, however, and there was a wide variety of less apparent sources of unsoundness that could influence the legal aftermath of transactions. In *The Bondsmen's Burden*, historian Jenny Bourne Wahl notes that if a court determined that a seller should have known about a slave's hidden defect, the seller was liable for not informing potential buyers.[29] However, it was often difficult to prove or disprove whether a seller knew of hidden disabilities prior to a sale.

Slaveholders brought warranty cases to court for a wide variety of latent "defects" they observed in their purchased slaves, including less obvious impairments, unexpected illnesses, and even "unruly" behavior.[30] For instance, in the Louisiana case of *Nelson v. Lillard* (1840), the plaintiff claimed that five slaves he had purchased for a total of $5,000 from the defendant were afflicted with different redhibitory defects. The plaintiff described his purchased slaves as Cynthia, a woman with an injured hip who died shortly after the transaction; Moses, a "consumptive" man; Willis, an "idiot"; Solomon, a "club-footed epileptic"; and Frank, a man who was simply listed as "diseased." The Supreme Court of Louisiana upheld the rescission of the sales of Cynthia and Moses but determined that Solomon had not been guaranteed at the time of sale and that there was no way to prove that Frank's condition had existed prior to the transaction.[31] In 1850, the Supreme Court of Arkansas heard a case involving the warranted sale of an eight-year-old "likely mulatto girl" named Hannah who seemed to be afflicted with paralysis in her arm and leg. Although several witnesses claimed they had observed the condition in the girl prior to her sale, a physician testified that "persons not in the habit of examining or not acquainted with the disease, might not notice it. . . . No one could see the negro without discovering the defect, but . . . persons not skilled could not tell what caused it."[32] The court agreed that Hannah's "unsoundness" constituted a breach of the seller's guarantee:

> A defect in property when sold, which is obvious to every observer, and required no skill to detect it is not covered by express warranty. But where a slave, warranted sound, is afflicted with a disease of such a nature as not to be observed by an unskilled eye, though the effects of the disease might be easily seen, such defect is covered by the warranty.[33]

Although Hannah was very young, the court's description of her as "likely" and "mulatto" is telling. The adjective "likely" was a vague, yet common market term for desirability, particularly for attractive female slaves. However, the term could also refer to the appearance of physical strength, compliance, affability, or the potential to produce more capital for a slaveholder.[34] Since a lighter skin color was often considered attractive for female slaves, the expectation that Hannah could be desired both as a sexual object (or a progenitor of future slaves) and as a source of labor probably influenced the court's assessment that her physical qualities were unsound.

Even "misbehavior"—including running away, laziness, or malingering—was a defect that could be considered a source of unsoundness in southern courts. Some southern physicians did medicalize "vicious" character traits observed in human chattel, such as Samuel A. Cartwright's notable definitions of *drapetomania Aethiopicus* (a disease that compelled slaves to run away repeatedly) or *dysaesthesia Ethiopica* (a more general laziness or insensibility), and applied such diagnoses to slaves alone.[35] Although it is difficult to ascertain how influential Cartwright's racialized disease categories were in daily southern medical practice, legal historian Ariela J. Gross has argued that many southerners discussed slave vice in terms of "negro diseases."[36] In Louisiana, the law determined that slaves who escaped thirty days prior to a sale or within sixty days after a sale could be considered "flawed" at the time of purchase, although a number of factors—including the slave's age and the way he or she had been treated—influenced how the law was applied. For example, in the case of *Fazende v. Hagan* (1844), the plaintiff successfully sued a trader because a ten-year-old boy he had purchased escaped back to his seller twenty days after the transaction. Two weeks after the slave was returned, he fled again, and drowned. The Louisiana Supreme Court overturned the original verdict for the plaintiff because, as Justice Martin noted in his opinion, there was no indication that the slave had attempted to flee prior to the sale, and "the habit of running away in a boy of ten years of age, is supposed to be extremely rare."[37] As Walter Johnson has noted, courts that defined "vicious" habits as "unsoundness" were likely concerned that those habits would spread like a contagion among other slaves.[38] Clearly, courts incorporated notions about the potential spread of disability—as congenital defects such as myopia, as in *Bell v. Jeffreys*, or as acquired habits such as a proclivity for escape or resistance—into determinations of slave soundness. In this case, however, the boy's age was a key factor in assessing the warrantability of his condition and its potential spread.

The paramount consideration in breach-of-warranty cases was whether or not an "unsound" slave would be able to perform their expected duties. In such instances, antebellum courts applied double standards of disability and attempted to create definitions of disability that were unique to individual slaves, particularly women. This is particularly evident in questions of slave madness or mental incompetence. As the Supreme Court of Louisiana opined in 1841, "It is very difficult if not nearly impossible to fix a standard of intellect by which slaves are to be judged."[39] In some cases, the litmus for slaves' mental soundness was based on what, in the eyes of the law, were reasonable expectations for their ability to perform their duties and observe their subordinate roles.[40] In *Simpson v. McKay* (1851), the North Carolina Supreme Court determined that guarantees of soundness necessarily extended to mental as well as physical conditions and that "the value of a slave depends as much, if not more, upon his having sense enough to do the work ordinarily done by slaves as upon the soundness of his body."[41] In the New Orleans case of *Chapuis v. Schmelger* (1851), which concerned the intellectual soundness of a 23-year-old woman named Nelly, one witness claimed "she had common sense enough for a field hand" and called into question the plaintiff's claim that the slave talked and sang to herself because "it appears . . . that white persons are more apt to speak to themselves than negroes."[42] These cases demonstrate that prevailing definitions of intelligence and mental defect—particularly those that courts might apply to free white individuals—had less bearing on cases of slave soundness than the question of whether or not slaves were competent to perform their expected duties. The North Carolina court's opinion in *Sloan v. Williford* (1843) claimed that assessments of slaves' mental soundness had to rest on whether or not they could understand their duties and perform their expected roles effectively. In other words,

> if the slave, though not actually an idiot, be so weak in understanding and possess so dim a reason, as to be unable to comprehend the ordinary labors of a slave, and perform them with the expertness that is common with that uneducated class of persons, his mind must be deemed unsound within the meaning of the warranty.[43]

The phrase "though not actually an idiot" is significant in this context. The court admitted that prevalent definitions of mental instability among the free (Anglo) population did not necessarily apply in cases of slave soundness. The Supreme Court of Alabama cited *Sloan v. Williford* in its decision in the case of *Athey v. Olive* (1859), which concerned the "common sense and mental capacity" of a slave named Matilda. In the court's opinion, "If a slave is neither insane, nor idiotic, nor subject to any mental derangement which interferes with the natural operations of the mind, the mere fact that he has less mental capacity than is usually found among slaves does not constitute a breach of warranty of sound mind" as long as he or she was still able to perform an expected role of servant.[44]

The intellectual capacity to perform agricultural labor was an adopted standard in courtroom decisions, since many men and women spent at least a portion of their adult lives working in plantation fields. However, as Alabama breach-of-warranty case *Stevenson v. Reaves* (1854) indicates, a female slave's soundness and, by extension, value could be defined by her obedience and breeding capacity as well as her ability to work; in this case, a female slave was deemed "unsound" at court because she was apparently barren and "deceitful in pretending to be sick frequently."[45] Judges based their conclusions about enslaved women's mental states not only on widespread assumptions about women's bodies and mental capacity but also on what they considered to be appropriate (gendered) responses to the unique circumstances of slave life. For instance, a slave mother who ranted or sobbed uncontrollably after being sold apart from her family could seem to be emotionally unsound, but perhaps less so than a mother who did *not* lose control on the auction block in similar circumstances.[46] In the Arkansas case of *Pyeatt v. Spencer* (1842), the court declared that a slave named Sophia, who allegedly talked to herself and ran away after being sold, was deranged and "unsound" at the time of her warranted sale. Testimony in the appellate case revealed she had been sold away from her young children, however, and that her new master had staked her naked in the yard, whipped her, and rubbed salt into her wounds. The Supreme Court reversed the original verdict, claiming that "whatever seeming wildness and aberration of mind might be perceived in the slave, it is but reasonable to suppose, was caused by grief and the excessive cruelty of her owner" rather than mental defect.[47] In *Buhler v. McHatton* (1854), the employer of a woman named Jane sought damages from her owner because she was supposedly insane and because her cooking was worse than he had expected. The Louisiana court ruled that lack of culinary skill did not constitute a redhibitory defect unless that was the express purpose for which she had been hired. It also found that the plaintiff's evidence for Jane's mental illness was flimsy. According to witnesses, she behaved "'oddly and strangely' [but] did not attract particular attention," and her peculiar habits—including refusing to eat on certain days of the week and once burning her clothes—were "ascribed to religious enthusiasm and grief at being separated from her children" rather than to insanity.[48] A mother's separation from her children seems to have been an important consideration in other kinds of soundness assessments as well. The North Carolina court hearing the case of *Spencer v. Hawkins* (1846) found it important to record that prior to exhibiting a defect in her ankles, Daphne had been sold away from her child,[49] as if the event had somehow triggered her impairment or perhaps to establish a motive for malingering. In either event, Daphne's gender, maternity, and the experience of being sold away from her child played a role in the court's determination of her soundness.

Emotional responses to the harrowing condition of sale were not just a factor in deliberations of soundness for female slaves. A similar verdict was delivered in the Tennessee case of *Farnsworth v. Earnest* (1846), which concerned a breach of warranty in the sale of a ten-year-old boy. At the time of the auction, the boy had been crying "and the purchaser could not judge his mental capacity." After five years, his master concluded that he "was weak of mind, if not altogether an idiot." The court determined that while it was apparent that the slave was less intelligent than most other slaves, "for the ordinary services of a field hand, it is probable he will be found equal to other slaves of his age." The state supreme court upheld the verdict for the seller.[50] This case indicates that the prepubescent boy's tears at the time of sale were deemed to be a normal response (even by the seller, who apparently did not view crying to be a definitive source of unsoundness at the time) and were not an indication of a weak mind in a fifteen-year-old.

One of the most important considerations in antebellum warranty cases was epilepsy, a latent, or unpredictable, source of unsoundness that seemed to be applied fairly equally to men and women. As mentioned earlier, the diagnosis of fits, even in seemingly healthy individuals,[51] was associated with dangerous uncontrollability. In Louisiana, epilepsy, as an "absolute vice," could allow a buyer to sue for breach of warranty just by its existence.[52] Furthermore, in the words of one medical witness, "the causes of fits are very numerous, and the cause is frequently so obscure that we can not [*sic*] detect it."[53] Frequently the diagnosis of epileptic fits was accompanied by observations of other defects, which in breach-of-warranty cases made slaves seem particularly unsound.[54] In the Louisiana Supreme Court case of *Bayon v. Vavasseur* (1821), for example, a buyer sued the defendant because a slave he had purchased began experiencing frequent epileptic episodes about two weeks after the transaction. The court overturned a jury's decision that the seller was not responsible for the soundness of the slave because the bill of sale did not include a guarantee of health. In the appeal, a witness claimed that the buyer was unconcerned with other ailments observed in the slave (including a sore on his leg) but felt that the presence of epilepsy nullified their sales agreement:

> She heard the plaintiff propose to the latter, to take the slave back, as he was epileptic, observing, that the defendant ought to recollect, that when he sold him to the plaintiff, the latter mentioned, he did not think any thing [*sic*] of the sore on his leg, but that if he had epileptic fits, or any other redhibitory disease, he would not take him on any consideration. When the defendant replied, the fellow had only a sore on one of his legs, and that he did not mention any other disorder in the bill of sale; but that this was only to avoid difficulties. He gave his word of honor, that the slave had no epileptic fits.[55]

Because epilepsy was easy to conceal (by a slave as well as a trader), it was considered a redhibitory disease in many parts of the antebellum South. The buyer in this case seems to have been more concerned with the unpredictable nature of his slave's fits and the possibility of having been duped during the sale than he was by the presence of an obvious and likely curable unsoundness in the man's leg.

In other cases, witnesses argued that the origins of "fits" influenced whether or not the condition should be deemed a genuine "unsoundness." In the New Orleans case *Metoyer v. Caretta* (1859), two physicians identified different origins of "fits" in a nineteen-year-old slave named Ellen Dorn. One doctor, who witnessed Ellen having a seizure and could not rouse her from the episode even after applying a hot coal to her leg, claimed that her condition was epilepsy; another physician, testifying for the defendant, noted that her convulsive episodes could have arisen from a number of "curable" conditions (the identification of which may have been influenced by the slave's gender), such as drunkenness, hysteria, or "excess of love."[56] The jury and the appellate court, however, found the plaintiff's physician more convincing, and the purchaser was able to recover his purchase price for the unsound slave.[57]

In the multitude of breach-of-warranty cases that arose in antebellum courtrooms, the uncertain task of defining slave disability was a central project. Judges relied on a variety of factors to determine whether or not a slave was guaranteed "sound" at the time of purchase. The language of warranties, the visibility or invisibility of disabling conditions, and the potential for the spread of those conditions could influence the outcome of the case. However, the most important consideration of "soundness" was whether or not a slave was able to perform the duties expected of him or her, and those expectations were often influenced by assumptions about other factors, including a slave's gender, age, or physical appearance. Participants in breach of warranty cases—plaintiffs, defendants, witnesses, and judges—read "soundness" in the bodies, actions, and reactions of slaves and contributed to constantly evolving ideas about disability that were closely intertwined with other expectations and factors. As the exchange of opinions between Justices Pearson and Ruffin in *Bell v. Jeffreys* indicates, definitions of disability or unsoundness in slaves were elusive and constantly under negotiation in southern courtrooms. Determining whether a slave ought to be considered "unfit for ordinary purposes" was a factor in a variety of cases, particularly those that involved a breach of a soundness warranty and assigned liability for damages to enslaved employees. A closer glimpse at local legal records, depositions, and the early hearings that led to state supreme court appeals would allow us to disentangle these perspectives and perhaps identify the roots of discourse on the concept of soundness. Nonetheless, from the rudimentary transcripts of state appellate cases examined in this chapter, it is apparent that southern courts often employed definitions of soundness and standards for liability that were, at least in part, tailored to African American slaves, who seemed to exist in a liminal social and racial category somewhere between "person" and "property" in the eyes of the law, and to individual slaves using a host of criteria, including expectations about labor and performance. At the same time, a close reading of these cases indicates telling conversations about the nature of disability more generally. Pearson and Ruffin, for instance, were divided not only on the issue of whether or not the woman in question suffered from an eye defect that rendered her "unsound" but also about whether there existed a "perfect" form of the eye at all. In Pearson's view, while there was no model for perfection in general body structure, the eye, as an organ, could be said to be perfect if it was free from defect; conversely, Ruffin argued that there could not be a model for a perfect eye, since so many individuals—particularly free whites—had different degrees of vision, "and I confess it never occurred to me to call such a person unsound."[58] These comments belied a deeper concern about deciding the nature of able-bodiedness and disability in general and suggest that southern courts discussing the unique fitness of slaves were also establishing a discourse about the "soundness" of all.

Notes

1. *Bell v. Jeffreys*, 35 N.C. 356, 1852 N.C. LEXIS 57, 13 Ired. Law 356. See also Jenny Bourne Wahl, *The Bondsman's Burden: An Economic Analysis of the Common Law of Southern Slavery* (Cambridge: Cambridge University Press, 1998), 30.

2. *Smith v. McCall*, 1 McCord 223–24, 12 S.C. LEXIS 91 (1821), cited in Andrew Fede, "Legal Protection for Slave Buyers in the U. S. South: A Caveat Concerning Caveat Emptor," *American Journal of Legal History* 31 (October 1987): 334.

3. See Judith K. Schafer, *Slavery, the Civil Law, and the Supreme Court of Louisiana* (Baton Rouge: Louisiana State University Press, 1994), 133.

4. James F. Petigru to Robert F. W. Allston, Charleston, April 15, 1837, quoted in J. H. Easterby, ed., *The South Carolina Rice Plantation as Revealed in the Papers of Robert F. W. Allston* (Columbia: University of South Carolina Press, 2004), 69.

5. Legal scholar Laura F. Edwards has demonstrated persuasively that state law was fundamentally incompatible with local law in the first half of the nineteenth century. Multiple sites of juridical authority and significant legal changes in local jurisdictions are not reflected in state court transcripts, which were created to give an illusion of a standardized, unified legal system. However, although state law was not the primary legal standard in many southern juridical cultures, transcripts of appellate decisions are a useful source for this study of slave disability because their language provides a glimpse into deeply held assumptions about impairment and the racial and social implications of "unsoundness." These transcripts also identify significant similarities across time, space, and locality in nineteenth-century law. See Laura F. Edwards, *The People and Their Peace: Legal Culture and the Transformation of Inequality in the Post-Revolutionary South* (Chapel Hill: University of North Carolina Press, 2009), 4–6.

6. Daniel Wickberg, "Heterosexual White Male: Some Recent Inversions in American Cultural History," *Journal of American History* 92, no. 1 (June 2005): 140, 156; Kenneth S. Greenberg, *Honor and Slavery: Lies, Duels, Noses, Masks, Dressing as a Woman, Gifts, Strangers, Death, Humanitarianism, Slave Rebellions, the Proslavery Argument, Baseball, Hunting and Gambling in the Old South* (Princeton, N.J.: Princeton University Press, 1996), xi.

7. Sharla M. Fett, *Working Cures: Healing, Health, and Power on Southern Slave Plantations* (Chapel Hill: University of North Carolina Press, 2002), 20.

8. Juriah Harriss, "What Constitutes Unsoundness in the Negro?," *Savannah Journal of Medicine* 1 (May 1859): 11.

9. For example, see *Pleasants v. Clements*, 29 Va. 474 1831, Va. LEXIS, 2 Leigh 474, quoted in Helen Tunnicliff Catterall, ed., *Judicial Cases Concerning American Slavery and the Negro*, vol. 1 (Washington, DC: Carnegie Institution of Washington, 1926), 163. Buyers suing sellers for breach of warranty after the purchase of "defective" or "unsound" human chattel made up the bulk of litigation in some southern jurisdictions; indeed, as legal historian Ariela J. Gross points out, "contests over whether a slave was 'sound in body and mind' at the time of sale or hire were the most common cases involving slaves . . . throughout the South, at the trial as well as the appellate level." Ariela J. Gross, *Double Character: Slavery and Mastery in the Antebellum Southern Courtroom* (Princeton, N.J.: Princeton University Press, 2000), 3, 122.

10. For a more in-depth analysis of disability and slave labor, see Dea H. Boster, "'Useless': Disability, Slave Labor, and Contradiction on Antebellum Southern Plantations," *Review of Disability Studies* 7 (December 2011): 26–33.

11. Harriss, "What Constitutes Unsoundness in the Negro?," 146.

12. See Gross, *Double Character*, 8–9, 123–24, 133–34; and Fett, *Working Cures*, 25.

13. See M. D. McLoud, "Hints on the Medical Treatment of Negroes" (MD thesis, Medical College of the State of South Carolina, 1850), 4, 17, Waring Historical Library, Medical University of South Carolina, Charleston.

14. Deposition of Samuel Robinson, July 6, 1809, Series 3, Box 2, Folder 6, Butler Family Papers 1663–1950, in Jean L. Cooper, ed., *Records of the Ante-Bellum Southern Plantations from the Revolution through the Civil War* (Jefferson, N.C.: McFarland & Co., 2009), Series I, Part 5, Reel 13.

15. *Thompson v. Bertrand*, 23 Ark. 730; 1861 Ark. LEXIS 192. See also *Brabo v. Martin*, 5 La. 275; 1833 La. LEXIS 44.

16. A. J. McElveen to Z. B. Oakes, Sumterville, South Carolina, October 27, 1853, quoted in Edmund L. Drago, ed., *Broke by the War: Letters of a Slave Trader* (Columbia: University of South Carolina Press, 1991), 59.

17. A. J. McElveen to Z. B. Oakes, Sumterville, South Carolina, November 7, 1853, quoted in Drago, *Broke by the War*, 61.

18. Walter Johnson, "Introduction: The Future Store," in *The Chattel Principle: Internal Slave Trades in the Americas*, edited by Walter Johnson (New Haven, Conn.: Yale University Press, 2004), 2, 6–7; John Hope Franklin and Loren Schweininger, *Runaway Slaves: Rebels on the Plantation* (New York: Oxford University Press, 1999), 282, 285. See also Dea Boster, *African American Slavery and Disability: Bodies, Property, and Power in the Antebellum South* (New York: Routledge, 2012).

19. Richard Tansey, "Bernard Kendig and the New Orleans Slave Trade," *Louisiana History* 23 (Spring 1982): 172–173.

20. Judith K. Schafer, "'Guaranteed against the Vices and Maladies Prescribed by Law': Consumer Protection, the Law of Slave Sales, and the Supreme Court in Antebellum Louisiana," *American Journal of Legal History* 31 (October 1987): 311; Wahl, *The Bondsman's Burden*, 6, 34–35.

21. Schafer, "'Guaranteed against the Vices and Maladies Prescribed by Law,'" 308; Walter Johnson, *Soul by Soul: Life inside the Antebellum Slave Market* (Cambridge, Mass.: Harvard University Press, 1999), 183.

22. Harriet Beecher Stowe, *A Key to Uncle Tom's Cabin: Presenting the Original Facts and Documents Upon Which the Story Is Founded* (London: T. Bosworth, 1853), 131; Gross, *Double Character*, 6, 34, 170n15; Schafer, *Slavery, the Civil Law, and the Supreme Court of Louisiana*, 128–130, 147–148; Wahl, *Bondsman's Burden*, 35; Thomas D. Morris, *Southern Slavery and the Law, 1619–1860* (Chapel Hill; London: University of North Carolina Press, 1996), 111.

23. Fett, *Working Cures*, 22; Fede, "Legal Protection," 327, 333, 338, 343; Wahl, *The Bondsman's Burden*, 5.

24. *Clopton v. Martin*, 11 Ala. 187, 1847 Ala. LEXIS 44.

25. *Williams v. Ingram*, 21 Tex. 300, 1858 Tex. LEXIS 82.

26. *Harrell v. Norvill*, 50 N.C. 29, 1857 N.C. LEXIS 11, 5 Jones Law 29.

27. *Nelson v. Biggers*, 6 Ga. 205, 1849 Ga. LEXIS 26. See also Wahl, *The Bondsman's Burden*, 31–32.

28. *Fulenwider v. Poston*, 48 N.C. 52, 1856 N.C. LEXIS 151, 3 Jones Law 528.

29. Wahl, *The Bondsman's Burden*, 40.

30. Fett, *Working Cures*, 22; Schafer, "'Guaranteed against the Vices and Maladies Prescribed by Law,'" 308; Schafer, *Slavery, the Civil Law, and the Supreme Court of Louisiana*, 129. For an example in which a slave was deemed unsound for being "dishonest, and of very bad character," see *Cozzins v. Whitaker*, 3 Stew. & P. 322, 1833 Ala. LEXIS 23.

31. *Nelson v. Lillard*, 16 La. 336, 1840 La. LEXIS 403; Schafer, *Slavery, the Civil Law, and the Supreme Court of Louisiana*, 162–63.

32. *Jordan v. Foster*, 11 Ark. 139, 1850 Ark. LEXIS 21.

33. Ibid. However, the court reversed judgment in the case because they concluded that the jury had been given misleading instructions for their consideration of the bill of sale.

34. Michael Tadman, *Speculators and Slaves: Masters, Traders, and Slaves in the Old South* (Madison: University of Wisconsin Press, 1989), 189.

35. Samuel A. Cartwright, "Philosophy of the Negro Constitution," *New Orleans Medical & Surgical Journal* 9 (1853): 204.

36. Ariela J. Gross, "Pandora's Box: Slave Character on Trial in the Antebellum Deep South," *Yale Journal of Law and the Humanities* 7, no. 2 (1995): 294.

37. *Fazende v. Hagan*, 9 Rob. 306, 1844 La. LEXIS 297; Wahl, *The Bondsman's Burden*, 35; Tansey, "Bernard Kendig and the New Orleans Slave Trade," 173.

38. See Johnson, *Soul by Soul*, 146–147.

39. *Briant v. Marsh*, 19 La. 391, 1841 La. LEXIS 438. See also Gross, "Pandora's Box," 274.

40. Gross, "Pandora's Box," 277.

41. *Simpson v. McKay*, 34 N.C. 141, 1851 N.C. LEXIS 38, 12 Ired. Law 141.

42. *Chapuis v. Schmelger*, Docket #2328 (New Orleans series) (December 1851), Louisiana and Special Collections Department, Earl K. Long Library, University of New Orleans, Louisiana.

43. *Sloan v. Williford*, 25 N.C. 307, 1843 N.C. LEXIS 7, 3 Ired. Law 307.

44. *Athey v. Olive*, 34 Ala. 711, 1859 Ala. LEXIS 317.

45. *Stevenson v. Reaves*, 24 Ala. 425, 1854 Ala. LEXIS 60. Ariela J. Gross has argued that cases having to do with slaves with "vicious" characters mostly concerned men; women who exhibited rebellious or disobedient behavior were more likely to be labeled idiotic or insane in legal proceedings. Gross, "Pandora's Box," 276, 295, 297–298; Gross, *Double Character*, 8, 148.

46. See Michael Tadman, *Speculators and Slaves: Masters, Traders, and Slaves in the Old South* (Madison: University of Wisconsin Press, 1989), 185; Conevery Bolton Valencius, *The Health of the Country: How American Settlers Understood Themselves and Their Land* (New York: Basic Books, 2002), 70; and Johnson, *Soul by Soul*, 127.

47. *Pyeatt v. Spencer*, 4 Ark. 563, 1842 Ark. LEXIS 128; see also Wahl, *The Bondsman's Burden*, 30–31.

48. *Buhler v. McHatton*, 9 La. Ann. 192, 1854 La. LEXIS 104.

49. *Spencer v. Hawkins*, 39 N.C. 288, 1848 N.C. LEXIS 98, 4 Ired. Eq. 288, quoted in Helen Tunnicliff Catterall, ed., *Judicial Cases Concerning American Slavery and the Negro*, vol. 2 (Washington, D.C.: Carnegie Institution of Washington, 1929), 118.

50. *Farnsworth v. Earnest*, 26 Tenn. 24, 1846 Tenn. LEXIS 40, 7 Hum. 24.

51. See *Ingraham and Baker v. Russell*, 4 Miss. 304, 1839 Miss. LEXIS 28, 3 Howard 304.

52. Schafer, *Slavery, the Civil Law, and the Supreme Court of Louisiana*, 130; Schafer, "'Guaranteed against the Vices and Maladies Prescribed by Law,'" 310. See also *DeWees v. Morgan*, 1 Mart. (o.s.) 1, 1809 La. LEXIS 1; *Nichols v. Alsop*, 10 La. 407, 1836 La. LEXIS 223; Tansey, "Bernard Kendig," 175–176.

53. *Hopkins v. Tilman*, 25 Ga. 212, 1858 Ga. LEXIS 48.

54. For instance, see *Orr v. Huff,* 27 Ga. 422, 1859 Ga. LEXIS 91. For an example of a white individual with epilepsy who was also considered an "idiot" and incapable of caring for himself, see *Segur v. Pellerin*, 16 La. 63, 1840 La. LEXIS 322.

55. Bayon v. *Vavasseur*, 10 Mart. (o.s.) 61, 1821 La. LEXIS 76.

56. *Metoyer v. Caretta* (Unreported Louisiana Supreme Court Case, Docket #5665, 1859), quoted in Schafer, "'Guaranteed against the Vices and Maladies Prescribed by Law,'" 313.

57. Ibid.

58. *Bell v. Jeffreys*, 35 N.C. at 358, 360, quote at 360.

CHAPTER 11

Rehabilitation Staged

How Soviet Doctors "Cured" Disability in the Second World War

FRANCES L. BERNSTEIN

KEYWORDS: *Centuries*: twentieth; *Geographical Areas*: Europe; Asia; *Sources*: plays; *Themes*: bodies, medicine, and contested knowledge; culture; labor; war

The Soviet Union emerged from the Great Patriotic War, as the Second World War was known, victorious though battered. With more than 34 million serving in the armed forces over the duration, hardly a family was left untouched, and each could personally measure the country's losses in a sorrowful accounting of loved ones who were missing or dead or who had returned from the front in some way impaired. It is next to impossible to calculate accurately the number of Soviet soldiers who were permanently disabled as a result of their war service. Because of the difficulties in establishing disability classifications and the reluctance of the state to do so, the actual figure was likely substantially higher than the official estimate of 2.75 million.[1]

Given the sheer numbers involved, one would expect to find that the presence of so many seriously impaired veterans resonated widely in Soviet society. Yet beyond the celebration of a few iconographic examples, the representation of disabled soldiers in popular culture was decidedly complicated. Newspaper articles and radio addresses hailed their bravery and sacrifices. They figured increasingly in fiction and, eventually, in film.[2] Yet visual portrayals were noticeably lacking.[3] In such media as posters and graphics, returning servicemen either appeared "intact" (perhaps slightly grazed, a modest bandage wrapped around a forehead) or they were wholly absent, marked by an empty helmet or an eternally waiting mother. As historian Denise Youngblood notes, for a country with no clear separation between home front and battlefront, "realistic depictions . . . were out of the question, for they would be far too demoralizing to an already demoralized population."[4] This invisibility was a notable departure from the practices of other dominant World War II combatants.[5]

With the exception of the military itself, the Soviet institution most intimately connected to the soldiers' experience of becoming disabled was the medical profession. Doctors treated injuries, supervised rehabilitation, and played a key role in determining benefits. Yet beyond the formulaic and ubiquitous pledges of devotion to the war effort offered by every segment of society, medical discussion about disability and in particular the depiction of those whose damaged bodies physicians treated was confined primarily to professional gatherings and publications.

This essay explores one of the few medical efforts to engage the public in an in-depth consideration of the subject of those disabled by war: three plays developed by physicians for popular consumption and performed widely throughout the country during and after the war. The works featured rare visual representations of Red Army men with impairments, all of whom were symbolically "healed" by the final curtain. The definition of disability projected by these plays was decidedly instrumentalist and Soviet. The plays also stressed that the solution to the disability "problem" was in the hands of three groups: the doctors who healed the disabled, the women who cared for the disabled, and the Red Army veterans themselves.

Ultimately the narratives decentered those who had been disabled in the Great Patriotic War even as they were about them. In none of the plays did the men call on their own resources to initiate their cure. By focusing instead on what others should do for impaired soldiers, the works always addressed them at several removes. Indeed, the only way these plays managed to make the Great Patriotic War invalids their subject matter was by presenting dramas about restoring their agency while simultaneously undermining it. Foregrounding doctors displaced and marginalized the disabled individuals.

Through these dramas of impairment and cure, the Soviet regime "safely" acknowledged and managed the anxieties posed by so many disabled bodies. Demonstrating the state's competence and commitment to caring for this population, the plays also served a broader therapeutic agenda. While expressing gratitude for those who had been wounded in the defense of their country, the productions were ultimately far less concerned with realistic portrayals of impairment and treatment than they were with articulating the civic and patriotic obligations to which the entire populace was held. Like the successfully "rehabilitated" on stage, the country's trauma and grievous injuries could be overcome with the proper motivation.

In light of the intended reach of their message, it is somewhat surprising that the plays' depiction of soldiers excluded women. As with representations of the

Red Army more generally, these veterans were all male, even though a substantial number of women fought during the war.[6] Because disability was coded as feminizing, rehabilitation necessitated a reassertion of the traditional gender roles and hierarchies on which the nation's recovery appeared to rely. Likewise, unless characters were specifically marked as otherwise, the characters were assumed to be ethnically Russian. State ideology promoted a supranational "Soviet" identity that was supposed to have erased the divisions and hierarchies that separated ethnic Russians from the country's more than 100 other nationalities. Russians remained the first among equals in this purported brotherhood of nations: even though millions of non-Russians had died for their homeland, their minority status was never fully erased.

The roles of those who had been wounded in the Great Patriotic War were played by "able-bodied" actors. Given the mass mobilizations and high incidence of severe injury on the battlefield, presumably it would not have been difficult to find performers who were living with the impairments depicted in the play. Using nondisabled actors made the symbolic cures achieved by the soldiers easier to envision: the actors' scars, limps, and stumps ultimately disappeared once the curtain fell. Perhaps the thinking was that audiences did not need graphic reminders of the consequences of war on their loved ones' bodies.

Based in Moscow, the Theater of Sanitary Culture was founded in 1925 to further the state's agenda of providing basic health information to the population, which was deemed a crucial task in light of the epidemics of the early revolutionary era.[7] In 1928 it was incorporated into the newly established Institute of Sanitary Culture, the body responsible for formulating and directing popular health education across the Soviet Union.[8] The theater was closed in 1938, but it was revived in 1941 to serve the wartime demand for mass propaganda on health-related matters.[9] Over the course of its short second life (it disbanded for good in 1947), the troupe performed for hundreds of thousands of spectators, soldiers and civilians alike. It traveled to collective farms, hospitals, garrisons, factories, and schools.[10] Selections from its repertoire were sent to regional health education theaters throughout Russia and the Soviet Union. The institute also encouraged the use of its materials by amateur collectives.[11]

While the theater employed professional actors and directors, all aspects of productions were firmly under medical supervision.[12] The institute commissioned works based on physicians' assessments of health needs, and authors who were not physicians were paired with medical consultants during the writing process. The ideal performance was introduced by a health educator who also answered audience questions at its conclusion; for occasions when this was not possible, recommendations about staging, set design, music, costumes, and character motivation were provided along with the scripts.[13]

The institute determined several programmatic areas for its repertoire when the theater was resurrected. In addition to what are perhaps the more obvious choices of topics (such as first aid on the battlefield, blood donation, and infectious disease prevention), "the heroic actions of the medical profession during the war" featured prominently among the themes.[14] One play in this category, *The Wife*, was also the company's first production to address those disabled by the Great Patriotic War directly. Based on a story by E. Kononenko and written by M. Levina, this brief sketch entered the repertoire in 1942.[15]

The Wife takes place just before Captain Grigorii Ivanov, a decorated pilot, is scheduled for discharge from a Moscow military hospital. Seriously wounded in combat, Ivanov has undergone eleven operations, including the amputation of an arm, and now walks with the aid of crutches, his face scarred and burned. Haunted by his "disfigurement," he experiences a "severe nervous condition," expressed through his pale, sad face and halting movements.[16] Sitting on his bed in his pilot's uniform, the empty left sleeve of his shirt tucked into his belt, Ivanov reads aloud from the letter he has just composed. Deeply in love with his wife, he has decided not to return to her for fear of rejection. Instead, he plans to follow the example of a former ward mate who has been abandoned by his fiancée and "lock[s] himself away" in a home for the disabled.

Nikolai Aleksandrovich Abramenko, the surgeon who saved Ivanov's life, then enters. The senior, experienced doctor looks Ivanov over, marveling at the pilot's recovery—and his own handiwork. For his part, Ivanov, while mindful of the doctor's skill and grateful for his efforts, is unconvinced that it was worth it:

IVANOV: Who needs me like this!

ABRAMENKO: You're crazy, Ivanov! . . . Get a grip on yourself . . . Shame on you! Who needs you? Dimwit. . . . Who needs you? Everyone. The whole country. The motherland, for whose sake you shed blood. Humanity.[17]

Ivanov confesses his fear of his wife's reaction: "How will I seem to her? A freak! A cripple!" Abramenko reproaches him lightly: "Children should take off their hats when they encounter you on the street. Your wife should be proud, walking arm in arm with you around the city."

According to the staging notes, Nikolai Abramenko is committed to curing Ivanov's physical and emotional wounds.[18] To this end the surgeon has secretly corresponded with Tania, Ivanov's wife, revealing the nature and extent of the pilot's injuries. On cue, Tania rushes out from her hiding place behind Ivanov's hospital room door. She reassures her husband that she loves him and prizes his sacrifice for her and country. His confidence restored, Ivanov appears to be instantly cured: he calls Abramenko a "miracle worker." The couple thanks him and departs, and the scene concludes with the surgeon's final declamation: "Life is good—damned good."

Following the well-worn conventions of revolutionary agitprop theater to which audience members would have been accustomed, the play depicted easily comprehensible characters, clear-cut dilemmas, codes of conduct, and resolutions.[19] Even as it referenced the universal debt of gratitude each citizen owed to the country's soldiers, *The Wife* also laid out the more specific duties of its three archetypal characters. Soldier, wife, and surgeon were exemplary. Ivanov is a decorated hero; Tania a devoted spouse. It could easily have been otherwise. Perhaps too painful to show, the play alluded to the consequences of an unhappy alternative. With no fiancée to care for him, Ivanov's jilted ward mate consigned himself to an institution, the typically unwelcome fate of disabled veterans who lacked a family that was willing or able to support them.[20] The "healing" of impairment was thus dependent on both the ex-soldiers themselves and on the women who were deemed responsible for them.

The Wife imparted the message that the love of a good woman was critical. But just as necessary for the patient's recovery was the love of a good doctor. Although the play depicted the positive and negative courses of action available to both wife and patient, it offered no parallel negative equivalent for the physician. Unfaithful women may have lurked in subplots, but unfaithful doctors never appeared. Like all the physicians who populated the company's productions, Abramenko demonstrated exceptional skills and utter devotion to his calling. Such displays of medical competence would reassure audiences that loved ones were in good hands.[21] The larger message was that the country itself could be mended, despite its own disfigurement and debility.

The faith invested in the authority of the physician was crucial to recovery: belief inaugurated cure. That a theater charged with propagandizing the cause of good health would emphasize the healer is not in and of itself surprising. But the demanding yet loving father figures who were central to these narratives served an additional wartime function. During the early part of the war, the fervent encomiums to the party and Stalin that had been so ubiquitous in the 1930s receded, a change that signaled the widespread mistrust and rancor with which many Soviets regarded them after the brutalities of that decade.[22] These were replaced by invocations to "homeland" and "people," a depoliticized patriotism. Here the physician substituted as an emblem of paternal devotion, a reminder of the state's commitment to its people but one who was untainted by overt, perhaps negative, political associations.

In certain respects this curative process corresponded to a more general pattern in postwar fiction. In her study of Soviet writers as "healers of wounded souls," Anna Krylova argued that literature performed a new therapeutic role in the early postwar years in its acknowledgment of the psychological component of soldiers' disabling injuries. This emphasis contrasted markedly with the Communist Party's insistence that the minds of returning veterans were healthy, no matter what damage had been done to their bodies.[23] With their ability to discursively treat and thus assuage the traumas of war, writers faced no competition from the medical personnel who appeared in their works. Notably, psychiatrists were absent from these postwar novels.[24] Doctors played a crucial although auxiliary function; although they tended to patients' bodies, the "ultimate" healing was beyond their realm of expertise.

In *The Wife*, in contrast, Abramenko performed both functions; he was a "miracle worker" precisely because he cured Ivanov's body and mind. In the postwar fiction Krylova studied, success was measured by disability overcome through the veterans' successful reintegration into society. This required that they leave the hospital. In contrast, the health dramas under consideration here were confined to a medical space where doctors' supremacy in the battle against impairment remained unchallenged, regardless of the fact that any actual doctoring that took place in the plays occurred offstage. Thus, in *The Wife*, the evidence of Abramenko's surgical skill was Ivanov's discharge. The hospital functioned as an intermediate space and a neutral territory that was halfway between battlefront and home front. Within that territory, the doctor had the autonomy he needed to put the rehabilitation plot in motion. Disability was conceptualized as a problem that was not just medical but was also psychosocial, and the final procedure the doctor performed on his patient was psychotherapeutic. Surgically emasculating Ivanov through amputation of his damaged limb, Abramenko could then rebuild his manhood in the place that "counted" more: the head.

That psychological treatment was the last step in the restorative process is evident in the thematic and structural parallels between *The Wife* and *The Near Relation*, by N. Shapovalenko, another offering in the company's repertoire that is set in blockaded Leningrad during the brutal winter of 1942. The devoted doctor at the center of the action is Dmitrii Mikhailovich Ivanov, world-renowned professor of psychiatry at a military hospital for nervous disorders. Ivanov is described as "selflessly devoted to his calling and to the motherland," language that is almost identical to the words used to describe Abramenko in *The Wife*. Because of his dedication, Ivanov has elected to remain in the city despite the risks and hardships, which are underlined by the sound of explosions in the background and the winter coats and boots the characters wear.[25]

The focus of his concern is 22-year old lieutenant and war hero Nikolai Petrovich Maksimenko. Maksimenko, a Ukrainian, suffers from severe depression and loneliness, convinced that everyone he left behind has been killed by the Germans. He receives neither visitors nor letters and is tormented by the happy voices of other patients' loved ones. Refusing his medicine, he lays in bed with his face turned to the wall and contemplates dying.[26]

224 · FRANCES L. BERNSTEIN

Ivanov tells Nadezhda Nikolaevna, a doctor assisting on the ward, "There's nothing you can do. Or me. . . . Medicine's not enough. . . . We need outside help. And it should be special, subtle, sensitive. . . . But where can it be found? Where?"[27] In answer to his prayers Olia Krasovskaia appears, an eighteen-year-old student who has also chosen to remain in the city, where she volunteers at the hospital. Ivanov tells Olia about the difficult case of Maksimenko but is unconvinced that even she can reach him. She asks to be allowed to try, and in the few minutes' walk from Ivanov's office to Maksimenko's room devises a plan: she will pretend to be his relative.

Ivanov tells the patient that he has a visitor and in walks Olia, who has been hiding behind the door in the hallway and who now speaks in the same heavily accented mix of Ukrainian and Russian as Maksimenko. He is quickly and easily convinced by her (somewhat dubious) explanation of their kinship: his father was her uncle, a second cousin of her mother, and also her father's grandmother's brother-in-law. With Ivanov's gestures of encouragement from his hiding place in the corridor Olia assures her countryman and granduncle that his loved ones "almost certainly" are still alive.[28]

By the time the bell signaling the end of visiting hours rings, only a few seconds after their meeting, Maksimenko is smiling and laughing. Olia promises to return, and the "relatives" share a heartfelt farewell. The scene ends with Ivanov at Maksimenko's bedside. In answer to the doctor's query Maksimenko declares that he is feeling much better. He readily gulps down his medicine and wonders when his relative will return. Ivanov smilingly promises him that she will be back.

Given the normative assumption that the characters are Russians in comparable works, the fact that Maksimenko is Ukrainian is noteworthy. His grief would have been understood and shared by many in the audience who lost loved ones to the brutal German occupation of the western part of the country, including, perhaps, the play's author, who had a Ukrainian surname. But the ease with which Maksimenko is fooled suggests a childlike gullibility that is more plausible in a non-Russian, at least, presumably, to a predominantly ethnically Russian audience and government.

Therapeutic success is achieved in both plays through two elements: the remarkable suggestibility both Maksimenko and Ivanov display and a collusion between a doctor and a wife (or wife surrogate). Only with the addition of a complicit woman was a cure attainable; in *The Wife* and *The Near Relation*, the women were so important to the plot's resolution that the works were named for them. Soviet practitioners of this time had a decidedly flexible attitude toward doctor-patient confidentiality,[29] but in these two plays medical deception—for the patients' own good—was elevated to a crucial plot point.

The plays avoid any reference to *kontuzhennye*, the Russian term for those suffering from what had been labeled "traumatic neurosis" (shell shock) by European psychiatrists some decades earlier.[30] Even Maksimenko, who is hospitalized in a psychiatric facility, is "nervous" rather than "shell-shocked." During the war, there was no clear consensus among Soviet psychiatrists about whether traumatic neuroses had an underlying somatic cause. Eventually (as did their European colleagues), they decided in favor of a psychogenic explanation because of the success of psychotherapy with patients with this illness.[31]

At pains to stress the absence of a somatic origin and the temporary nature of the characters' conditions, the plays use generic descriptors such as "depressed" and "nervous" to shield the soldier-patients from the stigma associated in Russia with mental illness.[32] Moreover, coupling these conditions with such visible markers as scars, stumps, and crutches serves to acknowledge the "authenticity" of the men's injuries (sidestepping the debate over an organic basis for war trauma) at the same time it locates the "true" source of disability and emasculation in the psyche.

In her study of the "unmaking of Soviet Man" in socialist realism,[33] literary scholar Lilya Kaganovsky has distinguished between two contradictory models of "exemplary masculinity." Juxtaposed with the "virile and productive male body" of the iconic revolutionary steel worker was the similarly pervasive image of "the wounded, long-suffering invalid."[34] Through the sacrifice of his "traitorous" body, the "heroic invalid" of Stalinist texts offered an easily recognizable symbol of ideological dedication to the state. At the same time, it recognized "real" men's distance from political power: because of their injuries, they posed no threat to Stalin's own (presumed) perfection. This was "the perverse logic of Stalinism: the desire to produce maimed, wounded, and disabled male bodies whose damaged forms would point to notions of sacrifice and submission."[35] With his limitations inscribed upon his body, the heroic "invalid" of socialist realism represented the "real goal of Stalinist masculinity." This was a unique departure from literary depictions of disabled men elsewhere.[36]

Postwar literature likewise required of women their own forms of sacrifice, on the levels of the body (to physically compensate for and care for the bodies of their husbands) and of memory (to erase their wartime experience). In this way the wartime disruptions of gender norms could be "corrected," the symbolic Soviet family reconstructed.[37] Women's activity was directed toward the reassertion of male dominance, even if only on the symbolic level, and hence a return to their own passivity. Paradoxically, reestablishing this passivity in the interests of the "heterosexual romance" necessitated active feminine deceit. In many ways, then, the Soviet "remasculinization" narrative followed the lines of much European and American twentieth-century fiction.[38] As historian David Gerber has observed, the trope of women aiding the recovery of disabled men through trickery was fairly common: "In such dramas, the responsible woman's role is to coax and to manipulate the man into becoming 'his old self' again."[39]

Here the Soviet rehabilitation romance parted company with its Western equivalents. These health productions complicated the formula by adding a new player to the equation: the older, authoritative, and necessarily male doctor.[40] Just as women in the plays intruded upon the doctor-patient relationship, doctors intrude upon the process of gender and sexual recovery. If the reestablishment of intimacy between husband and wife required feminine deception (itself a stereotypical female behavior), it also required a breaching of the confidentiality of the doctor's (intimate) relationship with his patients. In *The Wife*, the surgeon Abramenko instigated the deception, whereas in *The Near Relation* the initiative lay with Olia, with Professor Ivanov's enthusiastic encouragement. But all access to hospital patients was strictly regulated, authorized only with the explicit permission of the head physician. As in the classic Oedipal drama, the attainment of masculinity required the intervention of a woman as both infantilizing mother and lover.[41] Yet in a particularly Soviet twist, the doctor as powerful father need not be eliminated for man to be remade. Quite the opposite: only in the physician's presence could the woman begin to act to restore the ex-soldier's impaired manhood.

Moreover, a repaired Soviet masculinity was still a dependent masculinity. While in American or European representations, the physician was important primarily as a catalyst to the patient's recovery, in this context his authority lingered. The Soviet remasculinization narrative required the continued reassertion and recognition of the doctor's guidance and influence. The physicians, not the soldiers, were the center of these productions. However, they did not need to be trained experts in the study and treatment of psychic trauma to command these curative powers. The surgeon Abramenko employed the same therapeutic methods and enjoyed the same success as the psychiatrist Ivanov. What counted was age, competence, decades of experience (no unfit novices here), and confidence, represented by the white coat.

In the final stages of the war, with victory in sight, the agenda of the Institute of Sanitary Culture shifted to reflect the imperatives of demobilization and reconstruction.[42] The themes of love, fidelity, and gratitude for the soldiers' sacrifice that characterized the earlier productions were no longer sufficient. Instead, getting soldiers recuperated and working was the highest priority for those charged with their care. Reemployment of those who had been injured in the war, ideally in industry, was vital to rebuilding the country's devastated economy. Crucially, an employed soldier no longer needed financial support from the state.[43] *House in the Mountains*, a three-act drama that was approved for staging in 1945, underscored this agenda.[44]

While this play also took place in the hospital grounds, it explicitly addressed the circumstances and expectations of life after discharge. If economic and political motives dictated that veterans be "unmade" as a special-interest group as soon as possible,[45] this was doubly true for the disabled among them. Whatever their bodily sacrifices, those who had been disabled in the Great Patriotic War who were poised for reentry into the wider world could expect no special status. Nor were they exempted from the continued sacrifices required of the entire country, which likewise would need to shake off its collective trauma and rededicate itself to the postwar mission. Through their efforts and their successful reintegration into society, ex-servicemen with disabilities could reaffirm their own commitment to the nation.

As is befitting for a full-length drama, *House in the Mountains* was far more complex than the one-act sketches. Its characters include two deceptive-though-caring females, several injured men, and the skilled physician at the center of the action. Set in a military hospital for those wounded in the war in the Soviet Republic of Kirgizia (in Central Asia), the play follows another one-armed and decorated hero, Dmitrii Buinovskii. A talented and prize-winning painter before the war, Buinovskii has sustained extensive injuries that required that his (dominant) right hand be amputated.[46] The action opens in the courtyard of N—skii Hospital, with Ivan Konstantinovich Semigradskii, director and head surgeon, observing the embittered Buinovskii.[47]

Buinovskii's misery at his loss is impeding his recovery from a severe concussion, a point emphasized by the sudden appearance of pilot Sergei Shcheglov, a former patient who has lost both feet in battle. Now, with the aid of prosthetics, Shcheglov has returned to the skies to deliver medicine and blood to hospitals. Patients and staff rush out to greet him, overjoyed at his arrival and his success: "Serezhechka! He flew in on his own!" Semigradskii joyfully embraces his former charge, and after watching him "slowly but confidently" climb the stairs to the terrace, reproaches Buinovskii: "See for yourself! That is what a will to live means. And he had reasons to despair."[48]

Semigradskii's use of the plural ("reasons"), signaling the extent of Shcheglov's sacrifice, heightens the contrast with Buinovskii (who was "only" missing one hand). In the next scene, the former artist is with Il'in, a patient who leans heavily on a stick and whose head is wrapped in bandages. Noting Buinovskii's despondency, the equally embittered Il'in remarks: "You're a man, a decorated hero; you should bear your misfortune calmly. . . . Of course now you won't be an artist, but are paintings what life is all about? You can find something for one arm. I have arms and legs, but nowhere to return. My wife found herself a new friend."[49] Buinovskii and Il'in are thus both emasculated, although as he compares his emotional loss to Buinovskii's physical one, Il'in judges his own scars to be more severe and permanent. Moreover, his wife's departure echoes that of his mother, who died when Il'in was three.[50] In contrast, Buinovskii's fiancée Lidiia remains unfailingly loyal and accessible. While tirelessly searching for Dmitrii, Lidiia had also assumed the care and responsibility for his sickly mother. Although he has made no attempt to find them since departing for the front three years earlier, the long separation from his loved ones has deepened Buinovskii's depression.

Lidiia's sudden arrival sets in motion the drama's multiple conflicts and eventual resolutions. Lidiia has never stopped searching for news of Dmitrii and has finally located him with the help of Semigradskii's wife, Dar'ia Antonovna, whose appeal for information about Buinovskii's next of kin she heard over the radio and with whom she has been in secret contact. Explaining to Lidiia the reason for inviting her to the hospital, Dar'ia Antonovna says, "Thinking like a woman, I decided that your love could bring him back to life."[51] In a later scene Lidiia also acknowledges the special healing power "good" women possess: "When even the devil is helpless, send in a woman."[52] Dar'ia and Lidiia thus provide a positive model of wifely deception to counter the negative example of Il'in's wife.

Overjoyed at their reunion, and unaware of Dmitrii's loss (he is wrapped in a bulky robe) Lidiia announces that the pair will leave the hospital together to resume their creative work, as she, too, is an artist. Having allowed himself the briefest moment of happiness at her appearance, Dmitrii now coldly rejects her. A devastated Lidiia prepares to leave, convinced that Buinovskii no longer loves her, when Dr. Semigradskii issues her a challenge. The doctor gives her permission to stay on, ostensibly to conduct art therapy with the patients but with the ulterior motive of renewing Buinovskii's interest in art and with it a willingness to consider the idea of becoming a teacher. If successful, this strategy will help reconcile Buinovskii to the permanence of his disability and make him employable.[53]

Gradually Buinovskii warms to the idea of teaching art, if not yet to reconciliation with Lidiia. Again he encounters the misogynist Il'in, who accuses Lidiia of having an affair with Chumakov, the hospital political officer. Although he does not believe it, Buinovskii collapses from the shock of the charge—another blow to his already diminished masculinity—but not before again ordering Lidiia to leave the hospital.[54]

Once again Dr. Semigradskii prevents Lidiia from leaving, counseling her to find another way to reach Dmitrii. Sympathetically stroking her right (dominant) arm, he recounts the story of a patient he treated before the war, a young man with an ulcer and a damaged heart whom everyone, including the doctor, expected to die. The only exception was the man's wife. Never leaving her husband's side, she refused to believe the prognosis. She was adamant that he would live, and live he did. The force of her will was so strong, the doctor explained, that she was able to transmit this determination to her husband, who succeeded in conquering his illness.[55]

While Semigradskii relates the anecdote, Lidiia begins doodling on his notepad with her left hand. Despite her protestations that she is not up to the fight to win him back, Lidiia unconsciously sketches a shaky but unmistakable likeness of Buinovskii. A new plan of attack dawns on her. However, her resolve immediately falters when a nurse rushes in to alert the surgeon that Buinovskii has lost consciousness. "He is dying!," Lidiia cries. Semigradskii grabs her by the shoulders and stares deeply into her eyes. "He will live! He will live! Right?!" Lidiia responds enthusiastically, "He will live!"

Through the force of his hypnotic will, Semigradskii reanimates Lidiia just as he will revive Buinovskii. Eventually the patient recovers sufficiently to be permitted to walk in the garden, where he encounters Lidiia. Buinovskii begs her forgiveness for his earlier behavior but again insists that they part:

> BUINOVSKII: Lida, you always were strong, help me!
> LIDIIA: Help you with what? We're equals.
> BUINOVSKII (SADLY): Equals! (He takes out a cigarette and tries to light it with a lighter.)
> LIDIIA: Let me help you.
> BUINOVSKII: This is our equality! It will be the leitmotif of our lives: "Here, let me help you!" I don't want that![56]

Defeated, Lidiia prepares to leave. But before doing so she resolves to show Buinovskii what she has learned during his relapse and recuperation: she has taught herself to draw using her left hand. This secret is now revealed to Semigradskii, Buinovskii, and the other patients who come upon her sketching in the courtyard, with Turubai, a Kirgiz boy, serving as her model.

> LIDIIA (HAPPILY): Mitiusha! Look! (She continues to work.)
> BUINOVSKII (LAUGHING JOYFULLY): Lidiia! . . . The left hand!

As the others crowd around to view her work, Lidiia rubs her tired arm.[57]

> BUINOVSKII: Lidusha, try my technique. There, in the eyes.
> LIDIIA: Try it yourself.
> BUINOVSKII (tentatively twirling the pencil)
> LIDIIA (TAKES HIS HAND): Like this . . . (helps him)
> BUINOVSKII (MAKES A FEW STROKES): There.
> ROMANCHENKO (YELLS): He lives! (whistles)
> SEMIGRADSKII: Oh, stop it!!
> BUINOVSKII (YELLS): He lives![58]

It is no wonder that Lidiia's arm was so tired: in this highly suggestive passage, she literally stimulated Buinovskii's confidence and hence his manhood as she supported his hand taking its first strokes. In the previous scene, an impotent Buinovskii was unable to light his own cigarette and refused Lidiia's offer of assistance. Now, having passed artistic authority (together with the pencil) back to Buinovskii, Lidiia could resume the secondary, supporting role in their relationship. When Turubai complains that Buinovskii will ruin his picture, Lidiia tells him not to worry: Buinovskii draws better than she does.

With Buinovskii's cry of "he lives," his resurrection is complete. "Happy birthday!" the doctor exclaims.[59] Buinovskii is not the only one to be born anew by the end of the play. His comrade Romanchenko finds love with Niura, a nurse, who will accompany him when he returns to his native Kuban. Il'in is cured as well. Instead of a new woman to heal his trauma, however, he finds what will perhaps be a more steadfast alternative: employment. When he is chastised by political officer Chumakov and Romanchenko for his poor behavior, Il'in discloses that he is utterly alone and has nowhere to go.[60] The two men begin fighting over him, competing for the chance to find him a place to live and work: as an engineer, Il'in is a most attractive commodity. Romancheko invites him to his collective farm, promising rewarding labor, a beautiful landscape, and (in last place) women to help him forget the past. Chumakov insists that Il'in stay with his family in the Urals, where a friend can get him a position in a factory. Initially confused, Il'in is restored to himself by their concern. To highlight his transformation, he appears in the final scenes without the bandages that were wrapped around his head earlier.[61] The two jobs (and the two desiring men) compensate for his double abandonment by his mother and his wife. Only after he is "cured" through the promise of employment can he repent his injustice to Lidiia: he silently approaches her and kisses her hand.[62]

In Chumakov's contribution to Il'in's rebirth, *House in the Mountains* reflected the renewed emphasis on the leading role of the party in postwar life. However, the party's penetration of the hospital poses no threat to the authority of the surgeon or to the romance between Lidiia and Buinovskii. On the contrary: Chumakov is in on Lidiia's scheme and permits a breach of (military) hospital regulations in allowing Turubai to enter the facility. As political officer, Chumakov would have been responsible for the ideological education of the staff and patients, an aspect of his job that is entirely absent from the stage. Instead, the play emphasizes his concern for the physical and emotional well-being of his charges. As the personification of the party, Chumakov, like the other stock characters, was exemplary; he was solicitous, kind, and flexible, exhibiting qualities that were distinctly absent in many of his real-life counterparts.[63]

In this play, the party (which is not referred to in the previous works) appears as an institution that was not entirely identified with the figure of the Leader, Josef Stalin. In fact, Stalin is only mentioned once, in the second-to-last scene, when Lidiia invokes him to get Turubai to stand still while he is posing. She predicts that Turubai will become a famous shepherd who will one day be personally recognized by Stalin himself as "the best son of the motherland" for providing the army with such delicious meat and cheese.[64] Even here, the emphasis seemed to be less on Stalin's leadership than on his symbolic role as the nation's father. In this case, his approval of Turubai will show that the honor of "favorite son" is open to everyone, regardless of national background.

It is important to recognize the role of non-Russian nationalities—and the ability of the women in the play to draw on and manipulate those nationalities—in achieving therapeutic success. Turubai in this context performed a similar "prosthetic" function to that of Olia's faux Ukrainian in *The Near Relation*; he is a device Lidiia uses in her campaign for Buinovskii's recovery. Turubai's native, childish innocence underlines the servicemen's infantilized status. While many military treatment facilities were established in the safety of Central Asia during the war, N—skii Hospital appears to be an entirely Russian institution; Turubai is the only Kirgiz national represented. With Russians positioned at the top of the multinational pyramid, the setting nods ever so slightly to the trumpeted diversity of the Soviet people. Thus, in addition to the presence of Turubai, the Kuban Romanchenko's speech is peppered with Ukrainian pronunciations and expressions.

The geographic isolation of the hospital in the mountains serves a number of symbolic functions. The vastness of the distance over which Lidiia travels to reach Buinovskii emphasizes the literal lengths of her commitment. The hospital's remoteness likewise suggests the pronounced divide that separates the impaired selves of the former soldiers from the able-bodied world to which the rehabilitated men will return. Thus, Buinovskii and Lidiia will head to Moscow to resume his "important work."

If we measure the play's conclusion against its programmatic theme (readying those injured in the war for employment), *House in the Mountains* is a resounding success: Shcheglov will fly, Romanchenko will farm, Il'in will engineer, and Buinovskii will paint. Buinovskii is lucky enough to have regained both work and love. Even Turubai, according to Lidiia's prophecy, will one day labor on behalf of his country. But the message the play sent about disability was ambiguous at best. Not only did all the injured resume their previous occupations, their masculinity depended on it.

In their analysis of the narrative function of disability, literary scholars David T. Mitchell and Sharon L. Snyder have pointed to the "physiognomic" style of reasoning behind the anxiety such impairment produces: the assumption of correspondence between the external (visible body) and the internal (psyche). They have noted, "If form leads to content or 'embodies' meaning, then disability's disruption of acculturated bodily norms also suggests a corresponding misalignment of subjectivity itself."[65] Extending this physiognomic paradigm to the Soviet context underlines the social and political threat so many "invalids" posed; the slow pace of their rehabilitation raised questions about their commitment—or even their loyalty—to the state. But if a violated exterior signifies a potentially corrupted interior, then perhaps the reverse might also be true, and mending psychic damage will override and cancel out any damage inflicted upon the external body. Thus, at the end of the play Buinovskii's arm is still missing, but because he believes in his own potential and has the support of Lidiia and Semigradskii, his disability status has effectively been erased. The lesson for the country was clear. Once the profound psychological damage of the war was healed, the physical rehabilitation of the land would follow: like Il'in and Buinovskii, it too could be reborn.

Just as the earlier productions did, *House in the Mountains* ignored the realities of life awaiting soldiers with disabilities once their wounds had healed. The physical and emotional pain involved in the rehabilitation process or in accommodating to artificial limbs or, for that matter, the all-too-frequent discharge of patients from hospitals before their recovery was complete were obscured. The prostheticized pilot Shcheglov's efforts occurred offstage, as would the strenuous therapy that would be required before Buinovskii could return to his easel. In fact, the only character seen performing any sort of physical exertion and training was the able-bodied Lidiia. Missing from the stage were those whose injuries could not be so easily treated and who, moreover, would continue to need care and financial support. In returning to their former professions, veterans such as Buinovskii would most likely be denied a disability classification and hence entitlement to the benefits such a designation provided. Those capable of resuming their prewar occupations, regardless of the magnitude and nature of their injuries, would not be considered "officially" disabled.[66]

Whether they could find these jobs was another matter entirely. In actuality disabled veterans who sought to reenter the workforce faced substantial obstacles: employers were loath to hire them, despite laws that required them to do so, or they gave them lower-paying jobs that were far beneath their demonstrated level of competency, such as security guard or watchman.[67] Nor did these works acknowledge the other hardships facing them: the inhospitable landscape of the war-ravaged country and the material and financial barriers to their mobility and participation.

The men are presented as overcoming the obstacles imposed by their own bodies and especially by their psyches, arriving at consciousness by the final scene. All that remained was to give credit where credit was due. Buinovskii speaks for everyone: "Ivan Konstantinovich, you've helped us feel alive again. Thank you, thank you." Semigradskii, embarrassed, responds: "I love you all." Just then a nurse enters, holding a surgical gown: "Ivan Konstantinovich," she says, "wounded have arrived."[68] Quickly removing his jacket and donning the gown, he answers, "I'm coming," and exits as the curtain falls. Thus, the little victories achieved by disabled veterans were overshadowed by those of the principle positive hero: the physician. He is there when the injured arrive and will remain long after the rehabilitated have left, representing continuity and dependability. Buinovskii might be returning from the protected wilderness to the reality of Moscow, but it is Semigradskii—not Stalin—who will serve as his inspiration. With the benefit of hindsight, the emphasis given to the heroic efforts of individuals such as Semigradskii is poignant. The play was performed in 1945, just before Stalin's next and last big push for a more regimented and hierarchical mass culture.[69] It may well have been among the last heroic self-portraits of a profession that would be demonized just a few short years later.[70]

Notes

1. G. F. Krivosheev, *Soviet Casualties and Combat Losses in the Twentieth Century* (London: Greenhill Books, 1997), 92. See also Mark Edele, *Soviet Veterans of the Second World War: A Popular Movement in an Authoritarian Society, 1941–1991* (Oxford: Oxford University Press, 2008); Beate Fieseler, "The Bitter Legacy of the 'Great Patriotic War': Red Army Disabled Soldiers under Late Stalinism," in *Late Stalinist Russia: Society between Reconstruction and Reinvention*, edited by Juliane Furst (London: Routledge, 2006), 46–61.

2. Vera Dunham, "Images of the Disabled, Especially the War Wounded, in Soviet Literature," in *The Disabled in the Soviet Union: Past and Present, Theory and Practice*, edited by William O. McCagg and Lewis Siegelbaum (Pittsburgh: University of Pittsburgh Press, 1989), 151–164.

3. With one or two exceptions, cinema did not depict recognizably disabled soldiers until the late 1940s; notably, these parts were played by nondisabled actors. Liliya Kaganovsky, *How the Soviet Man Was Unmade: Cultural Fantasy and Male Subjectivity under Stalin* (Pittsburg: University of Pittsburg Press, 2008); and Denise J. Youngblood, *Russian War Films: On the Cinema Front, 1914–2005* (Lawrence: University Press of Kansas, 2007). In contrast, several American war-era films featured actors with disabilities. See Martin F. Norden, *The Cinema of Isolation: A History of Physical Disability in the Movies* (New Brunswick: Rutgers University Press, 1994), chapter 5; and David Gerber, "Heroes and Misfits: The Troubled Social Reintegration of Disabled Veterans in *The Best Years of Our Lives*," in *Disabled Veterans in History*, edited by David Gerber (Ann Arbor: University of Michigan Press, 2000), 70–95.

4. Youngblood, *Russian War Films*, 58.

5. Carol Poore, *Disability in Twentieth-Century German Culture* (Ann Arbor: University of Michigan Press, 2007), chapter 2; James M. Diehl, "Victors or Victims? Disabled Veterans in the Third Reich," *Journal of Modern History* 50 (December 1987): 705–736; David Serlin, *Replaceable You: Engineering the Body in Postwar America* (Chicago: University of Chicago Press, 2004), chapter 1; and George Roeder Jr., *The Censored War: American Visual Experience during World War Two* (New Haven, Conn.: Yale University Press, 1993).

6. Beginning in the summer of 1942, women were actively recruited into the armed forces. Catherine Merridale, *Ivan's War: Life and Death in the Red Army, 1939–1945* (New York: Metropolitan Books, 2006), 165–166; Svetlana Alexiyevich, *War's Unwomanly Face*

(Moscow: Progress, 1988); Anna Krylova, *Soviet Women in Combat: A History of Violence on the Eastern Front* (Cambridge and New York: Cambridge University Press, 2010). For a recent assessment of the scholarship on gender during the Stalinist era and the war, see Krylova's introduction.

7. John Hutchinson, *Politics and Public Health in Revolutionary Russia, 1890–1918* (Baltimore, Md.: Johns Hopkins University Press, 1990), 193.

8. Frances Bernstein, *The Dictatorship of Sex: Lifestyle Advice for the Soviet Masses* (DeKalb: Northern Illinois University Press, 2007), chapter 4.

9. State Archive of the Russian Federation, Moscow, Russia (hereafter GARF), Sanitary Enlightenment Institute 9636/5/7/1–13, 9636/5/19/1, 9636/5/302/27.

10. On other theatrical wartime mobilizations, see Harold B. Segel, "Drama of Struggle: The Wartime Stage Repertoire," in *Culture and Entertainment in Wartime Russia,* edited by Richard Stites (Bloomington: Indiana University Press, 1995), 108–125.

11. GARF, 9636/5/19/12; 9636/5/301/38.

12. GARF, 9636/5/19/2.

13. GARF, 9636/1/278/2 reverse side.

14. GARF 9636/5/19/1–1 reverse side, 3.

15. M. Levina, *Zhena* (The Wife), in *Sbornik sanitarno-prosvetitel'nykh p'es* (Anthology of Sanitary-Enlightenment Plays), edited by N. Shapovalenko (Moscow: Narkomzdrav SSSR Institut sanitarnogo prosveshcheniia, 1944), 14–17.

16. Ibid., 14.

17. Ibid., 15–16.

18. Ibid., 14.

19. Lynn Mally, *Revolutionary Acts: Amateur Theater and the Soviet State, 1917–1938* (Ithaca, N.Y.: Cornell University Press, 2000); Elizabeth A. Wood, *Performing Justice: Agitation Trials in Early Soviet Russia* (Ithaca, N.Y.: Cornell University Press, 2005).

20. Beate Fieseler, "La protection social totale: les hospices pour grandes mutiles de guerre dans l'Union sovietique des années 1940," *Cahiers du monde russe* 49, no. 2 (2008): 419–440.

21. Despite the truly heroic efforts and sacrifices made by countless physicians, there was grave dissatisfaction with the care provided to wounded soldiers both during and after the war. Amnon Sella, *The Value of Human Life in Soviet Warfare* (London and New York: Routledge, 1992), 67; Christopher Burton, "Soviet Medical Attestation and the Problem of Professionalisation under Late Stalinism, 1945–1953," *Europe-Asia Studies* 57, no. 8 (2005): 1214–1218; Elena Zubkova, *Russia after the War: Hopes, Illusions, and Disappointments, 1945–1957* (London: M. E. Sharpe, 1998), 24.

22. Jeffrey Brooks, *Thank You, Comrade Stalin! Soviet Public Culture from Revolution to Cold War* (Princeton, N.J.: Princeton University Press, 2000), 176–178; Catherine Merridale, "The Collective Mind: Trauma and Shell-Shock in Twentieth-Century Russia," *Journal of Contemporary History* 35, no. 1 (2000): 49.

23. Anna Krylova, "'Healers of Wounded Souls': The Crisis of Private Life in Soviet Literature, 1944–1946," *Journal of Modern History* 73 (June 2001): 307–331.

24. Ibid., 317.

25. N. Shapovalenko, *Blizkii rodstvennik* (The Near Relation), in *Sbornik sanitarno-prosvetitel'nykh p'es* (Anthology of Sanitary-Enlightenment Plays), 18.

26. Ibid., 22.

27. Ibid., 20.

28. Ibid., 24.

29. Frances Bernstein, "Behind the Closed Door: VD and Medical Secrecy in Early Soviet Medicine," in *Soviet Medicine: Culture, Practice, and Science*, edited by Frances L. Bernstein, Christopher Burton, and Dan Healey (DeKalb: Northern Illinois University Press, 2010), 92–110; Chris Burton, "Medical Welfare during Late Stalinism: A Study of Doctors and the Soviet Health System, 1945–53" (Ph.D. diss., University of Chicago, 2000), 253–254.

30. Ben Zajicek, "Hysteria and the Red Army Soldier: Soviet Psychiatrists and the Debate over War Trauma during the Second World War," paper presented at the annual meeting of the American Historical Association, Chicago, January 6, 2012, 8; Ben Zajicek, "Psychiatry and Mental Illness in the Soviet Union, 1941–1953" (Ph.D. diss., University of Chicago, 2009), 123–126.

31. Zajicek, "Hysteria and the Red Army Soldier," 13.

32. Merridale, "The Collective Mind," 51; Merridale, *Ivan's War*, 268–270; Edele, *Soviet Veterans*, 82.

33. Socialist realism is a style of realist art whose purpose was to advance the goals of communism and socialism. See Katerina Clark, *The Soviet Novel: History as Ritual* (Chicago: University of Chicago Press, 1981).

34. Kaganovsky, *How the Soviet Man Was Unmade*, 22.

35. Ibid., 146.

36. Ibid., 4, 120.

37. Krylova, "'Healers of Wounded Souls,'" 324–327.

38. Eliot Borenstein, *Men without Women: Masculinity and Revolution in Russian Fiction, 1917–1929* (Chapel Hill, N.C.: Duke University Press, 2001). The term "remasculinization" comes from Susan Jeffords, *The Remasculinization of America: Gender and the Vietnam War* (Bloomington: Indiana University Press, 1989).

39. Gerber, "Finding Disabled Veterans," 10–11.

40. Because of their mass prewar mobilization into the profession, women were a significant percentage of physicians by the time the war started. The posts of surgeon and head doctor would still mostly likely have been held by men. Kate Sara Schecter, "Professionals in Post-revolutionary Regimes: A Case Study of Soviet Doctors" (PhD diss., Columbia University, 1992).

41. Gerber, "Finding Disabled Veterans," 10.

42. Mark Harrison, *The Economics of World War II* (New York: Cambridge University Press, 1998), chapter 7; Jeffrey Jones, *Everyday Life and the Reconstruction of Soviet Russia* (Bloomington: Slavica, 2008).

43. Mark Edele argues that the provision of welfare services and pensions was intentionally inadequate (rather than accidentally or circumstantially so) to force the disabled back to work; see *Soviet Veterans*, 90.

44. GARF, 9636/1/278/6 reverse side.

45. Edele, *Soviet Veterans*, 11.

46. GARF, 9636/5/44/1–49 (A. Zalog and N. Karel'skaia, "Dom v gorakh" [House in the Mountains], 1–49).

47. Ibid., 4.

48. Ibid., 8.

49. Ibid., 4–5.

50. Ibid., 12.

51. Ibid., 29.

52. Ibid., 19.

53. Ibid., 11.

54. Ibid., 21.

55. Ibid., 32.

56. Ibid., 38.

57. Ibid., 47.

58. Ibid., 48.

59. Ibid.

60. Ibid., 30.

61. Ibid., 40.

62. Ibid., 49.

63. Merridale, *Ivan's War*.

64. Zalog and Karel'skaia, "Dom v gorakh," 46.

65. David T. Mitchell and Sharon L. Snyder, *Narrative Prosthesis: Disability and the Dependencies of Discourse* (Ann Arbor: University of Michigan, 2000), 58.

66. Edele, *Soviet Veterans*, 82; Bernice Madison, *Social Welfare in the Soviet Union* (Stanford, Calif.: Stanford University Press, 1968); Sally Ewing, "The Science and Politics of Soviet Insurance Medicine," in *Health and Science in Revolutionary Russia*, edited by Susan Gross Solomon and John Hutchinson (Bloomington: Indiana University Press, 1990), 69–96; and Ethel Dunn, "Disabled Russian War Veterans: Surviving the Collapse of the Soviet Union," in *Disabled Veterans in History*, edited by David Gerber (Ann Arbor: University of Michigan Press, 2000), 251–271.

67. GARF, Social Welfare Ministry 413/1/651/7–18.

68. Zalog and Karel'skaia, "Dom v gorakh," 49.

69. Clark, *The Soviet Novel*, chapter 9.

70. Yakov Rapoport, *The Doctors' Plot of 1953* (Cambridge: Harvard University Press, 1991).

CHAPTER 12

The Curious Case
of the "Professional Hemophiliac"

Medicine, Disability and the Contested Value
of Normality in the United States, 1940–2010

STEPHEN PEMBERTON

KEYWORDS: *Centuries*: twentieth; twenty-first; *Geographical Areas*: North America; *Sources*: memoirs; interviews; *Themes*: bodies, medicine, and contested knowledge; culture; family, daily life, and community; activism; theory

In 1991, historian Susan Resnik spoke to 29-year-old Harold H about his mother's earliest advice on how he should manage his hereditary bleeding disorder and negotiate the debility associated with it. "She was training to be a psychologist before I was born [in 1962]," said Harold, and she felt that most "teenagers and young men with hemophilia . . . were emotionally crippled."[1] Most were living at home, she maintained, not for economic reasons but for emotional ones. Harold then opined about his mother's therapeutic perspective on the majority of young men with hemophilia: "They didn't have the ability to cope with life's stresses. They had turned that over to their parents. She said, 'I think that kind of thing is worse than a physical disability.'"[2]

By Harold's account, his mom raised him to treat his hemophilia as a core part of his identity; she socialized him to be a perceptibly independent person in a supposedly progressive society that still was not particularly accepting of disability or other perceived differences from the mainstream. Harold had in mind one pivotal event from his childhood when relating his own path to independence. In the mid-1960s, the local preschool in his hometown of Portland, Oregon, would not admit him on account of his hemophilia. He recalled: "We weren't Jewish but the

Jewish community accepted me [into their preschool] because they really under-stood being different, discriminated against and excluded." The folks at the Jewish school acknowledged that there were "a lot of risks" in taking on a student with hemophilia, but they sought to minimize them to make Harold's "experience as normal as possible." School officials urged Harold "to tell my class members what hemophilia was about." Critically, his mother "encouraged that kind of talking about my illness and talking about what I did to take care of myself at an extremely early age." As Harold put it, her insistence that he "take an active role . . . [and] be really independent and involved in my care" allowed him to emerge as "a very smart little kid, very verbal, lots of manual dexterity and self-esteem and coping." "That's ter-rific," said Resnik, after hearing Harold. "In other words, there was an attempt to mainstream you and normalize life, your life. Right?" "Right," he said.[3]

These reflections by Harold H (1962–1996) and the views that he attributed to his mother belong to a culture of self-care that emerged within the U.S. bleeding-disorders community in the two decades after World War II. Americans in this emergent community of the 1950s and early 1960s began invoking the word *nor-mal*—and its linguistic kin *normality* and *normalcy*—when imagining the improving prospects of people with hemophilia. The American media followed suit. Such in-vocations that people with hemophilia were capable of relatively normal lives were unprecedented in their optimism.[4] Prior to the advent of mass blood transfusions (around 1938), hemophilic bleeding was largely intractable; physicians deemed it unusual for any male with a severe or moderate form of the bleeding disorder to live beyond his thirtieth birthday. As one journalist wrote in 1959, "Only one or two of every ten hemophiliacs lived to be twenty" before the 1940s, and those who did make it to adulthood before the present age "ended their lives in braces, in wheel chairs, or as bedridden bundles of tortured human geometry."[5]

For many hemophilic boys and men, the act of talking publicly about their condi-tion in the postwar decades became a critical aspect of "taking an active role in their care." Not surprisingly, the therapeutic world developed its own medicalized take on this self-care culture. As one 1981 manual on the psychological and behavioral aspects of physical disability put it, "It is common for hemophilic boys to give sci-ence reports to their classes about their genetic disorder and to be active educators of those whom they meet." An "extension" of this phenomenon, as the manual then described, is "the patient who becomes the 'professional hemophiliac.'"[6]

As an ontological category, the hemophiliac has almost always been gendered male in medical and popular discourse because physicians had long characterized hemophilia as a sex-linked inheritance that occurred predominantly in males. The few physicians who specialized in hemophilia care between the 1950s and early 1970s worked with an overwhelmingly male and pediatric population. Therefore, when experts and laypersons spoke of the person with hemophilia's opportunities to be normal in the second half of the twentieth century, they did so in both age-related and gendered terms. The self-care culture that first emerged in the American bleeding-disorders community in the 1950s reflected this social reality. The therapeutic focus on hemophilia, both among experts and lay advocates, was on transforming sickly boys into "normal," productive men. The hemophilia management strategies that postwar physicians advanced sought overwhelmingly to bring bleeding under control and to diminish—if not eradicate—the physical impairments (especially the pain and crippling) that repeated joint bleeds entailed. By the early 1970s, modern treatments—in the form of a new commercially produced clotting-factor concentrates—were being touted as the "hemophiliac's passport to freedom."[7] Medicine was delivering on its postwar promises; many boys and men with hemophilia were actually beginning to experience lives that approached those of "normal," "able-bodied" males.

This essay situates the curious idea of the professional hemophiliac alongside the strategies of self-care articulated by Harold H and his contemporaries. Both phenomena point to the critical role that medical and social means of normalization played in the lives of Americans with hemophilia in the second half of the twentieth century. Testimonials such as Harold's implicitly call on historians of medicine and public health to converse with critical disability scholars and invite disability historians to engage more readily with specialists of medical and health history. Critical disability historians adeptly explain how cultural values—including masculine heteronormativity, whiteness, middle classness, and perceived able-bodiness—are part of the social constellation that constitutes normal in modernizing societies. Historians of medicine and health thoughtfully narrate and analyze the evolving forms of medicine. This essay argues that the peculiar idea of the professional hemophiliac and the culture of self-care that emerged around hemophilia in the United States from the 1950s through the 1970s are two sides of the same historical phenomenon. They reflect a convergence of medical and nonmedical forms of care related to American hemophiliacs, a meeting of expert and lay experiences with chronic illness and debility that elevated normality into a preferred but contested means to improve the quality of life among people with hemophilia. This convergence gives testimony to the fact that normality is a pervasive ideological force in modernizing societies precisely because of its transformative power. Moreover, the fact that the outcomes of such transformation have proven—in the curious case of the professional hemophiliac—to be neither uniformly good nor even desirable exemplifies the rich historical and social understandings of chronic disease and debility that emerge when historians of medicine and disability historians treat the sociocultural histories of medicine and disability with equal weight.

The Goals of Hemophilia Therapy

Hemophilia is an exemplary disease for analyzing the relationships between medicine and disability precisely because physicians in the United States and other advanced industrialized nations had proven remarkably successful by 1980 at managing the severest forms of bleeding disorders. In both real and imagined ways, many Americans with hemophilia in the 1970s were experiencing what they themselves called increasingly normal lives. This changing experience was the direct result of medical and social advancements in the management of hereditary bleeding disorders (although it would be a radical mistake to reduce the change to a simplistic story about biotechnological progress). As traditionally told, a significant part of hemophilia's visibility in the age of transfusion medicine and mass blood donation is attributable to medicine's high profile since the 1940s and the fact that medicine had actually delivered on many of its promises about care of hemophilic bleeding by 1980. People with hemophilia—the presumed consumers of medicine—played critical roles in shaping both popular and professional impressions of bleeding disorders. As suggested by Harold H's recollections of his own path to self-care, people with hemophilia were critical agents in shaping their destiny. Integral to the self-conception of many boys and men with hemophilia in the United States were strategies for gaining visibility for both hemophilia (the "disease") and themselves (the "patients"). Such visibility often served the interests of boys and men with hemophilia by reducing stigmatization and promoting better medical care.

Hemophilia is among the oldest hereditary diseases on record, but it did not emerge as a subject of sustained medical attention until the nineteenth century. Physicians knew it as an invariably dismal disease in the mid- to late 1800s. Prince Leopold (1853–1884), Queen Victoria's youngest son and the world's most famous hemophiliac by the turn of the twentieth century, was unusual among hemophiliacs of his era for reaching adulthood, marrying, and fathering children. By the 1910s, clinicians had identified hemophilia's three cardinal characteristics: frequent and prolonged bleeding into joints and soft tissue, a family history of uncontrollable bleeding among male family members, and a laboratory test that indicates that the patient's blood is slow to clot. While many educated Americans and Europeans knew hemophilia as a disease of royalty by the 1920s, they were usually told very little about its characteristic features until the two decades following World War II. The change was prompted by the growing availability of plasma transfusions for hemophilia in the 1940s and 1950s, which required very public calls for fresh blood donors and public education about the disease. Postwar Americans learned that hemophilia affected ordinary families—predominantly boys and young men—when they learned that hemophiliacs required frequent transfusions of blood plasma to preserve their health. The National Hemophilia Foundation

(NHF; est. 1948) and other family-based hemophilia advocacy groups led these efforts.[8] In fact, hemophilia-related social events appeared in many cities and towns
as the need for blood donors prompted families and physicians to work together
to provide hemophilic children with the attention and resources they required to
treat their condition effectively. Blood drives and charity balls were the order of
the day. By all extant accounts, the rising visibility of hemophilia was welcomed,
as it allowed physicians and people with bleeding disorders to highlight both real
and imagined progress.

Expectations about hemophilia changed considerably within the American
bleeding-disorders community as physicians and scientists developed increasingly powerful hematological tools for diagnosing and treating bleeding disorders. In the 1950s, experts were not only working on and delivering better ways
to control bleeding but were also envisioning a life of medical management for
their pediatric hemophilia patients. At University Hospital in Cleveland, the median life expectancy at age one for more than 400 patients classified as severe
hemophiliacs had risen from 27 years in 1940 to nearly 40 years by 1960.[9] With
state-of-the-art transfusion therapies, boys diagnosed with severe to moderate
hemophilia were increasingly living beyond adolescence and into adulthood. The
semblance of normality for boys and men with hemophilia—including attending
college, pursuing a career, marrying, and raising children—was increasingly visible
in the malady's popular portraits. As *Reader's Digest* related to Americans in 1959,
transfusion therapy and orthopedic care had advanced to the point that leading
hemophilia therapists and advocates could say to parents of a hemophilic child
that they should only protect their hemophilic sons "up to a point" so that they
could also "lead a normal life—up to a point."[10] By the early 1960s, the National
Hemophilia Foundation was explicitly advocating the therapeutic goal of "normality within limits" in their widely disseminated handbook for parents, *Home Care of
the Hemophilic Child.*[11]

The pursuit of "normalcy" in the American hemophilia community was always
a joint production that involved medical professionals and individuals and families
affected by the disease. Advocacy and media portraits almost always stressed the
serious (if not lethal) nature of hemophilia, the need to get transfusion therapies
and other medical services to patients, and the related, indeed critical, need for
local communities to aid people with hemophilia through blood donation. Yet even
as popular representations of the hemophiliac stressed the vulnerable nature of
affected individuals, they also vehemently stressed how degrees of normality were
deliverable to patients. Moreover, as was suggested by the growing incidence of
affected boys who were maturing into "normal" men with prospects for "college,
careers, marriages, and families," the hemophiliac was overwhelmingly cast as a
mainstream individual: someone who was heteronormative, masculine, ethnically

white, and had "normal," middle-class aspirations.[12] Such imagery—while serving the general needs of the hemophilia community—did not represent the ethnic and class diversity of American boys and men with the condition. And most certainly it did not take into account the variety of less clinically severe bleeding disorders that occur as often among females as among males (and constitute the demographic majority of persons with bleeding disorders).[13] But this dominant image of the hemophiliac in America served the bleeding-disorders community well from the 1950s through the mid-1970s, as it helped marshal medical and social resources in ways that promoted greater health and autonomy for the most severely affected and visible of bleeders—the hemophiliacs.

As medical "progress" accelerated in the 1960s and 1970s with additional therapeutic advances, the popular portrait of the hemophiliac as someone capable of a "normal" life was further reified, which is to say that the long-sought-after portrait of the hemophiliac as a normal person increasingly represented a reality that affected boys and men actually experienced. The transition was undoubtedly precipitated by the introduction of increasingly potent ways of controlling hemophilic bleeding, first with the introduction of cryoprecipitate in 1965, soon followed by the first commercially-produced high-potency clotting-factor concentrate in 1968. Medical advances were central to the production of normality for people with hemophilia, but medicine alone was incapable of delivering "normal" lives for the boys and men with the severest forms of this bleeding disorder.

Novel, overtly political forms of hemophilia advocacy also proved critical to normalizing the lives of boys and men with hemophilia in the 1970s because very few of them could afford the new hemophilia treatments that existed by the late 1960s. In 1973, for example, when Louis Friedland, president of the NHF, testified before the U.S. Congress in favor of federal support for comprehensive hemophilia treatment centers, he brought with him a golf bag filled with orthopedic braces that his hemophilic son Eric had worn throughout his first seventeen years of life. Routine use of anti-hemophilic clotting-factor concentrates—the revolutionary hemophilia treatments that were first marketed widely in 1968—rendered those cumbersome leather and metal braces unnecessary. Senators Harrison Williams of New Jersey and Peter Dominick of Colorado were amazed to see that Eric's regular use of these commercial blood products allowed him to build up his physique to the point that his mobility and overall appearance were visibly fit, or "normal." Eric, in his own testimony, stressed that "no hemophiliac will ever have to be deprived of treatment." In dramatic fashion he infused himself with clotting-factor concentrate while speaking to Senator Williams's congressional committee about the transformative nature of these treatments. In less than three minutes, Eric's testimony exemplified what the two-day hearing on the proposed hemophilia bill was really about: Americans with hemophilia were capable of living "normal" lives if the federal government would help facilitate access to costly hemophilia treatments such as the one that allowed Eric to abandon his orthopedic braces and become independent.

These high-profile performances by Lou and Eric Friedland showcased many features of hemophilia's rise to visibility, including the systems of privilege that undergirded how the hemophiliac was portrayed (as white, male, upper-middle-class, and increasingly able-bodied). Lou Friedland, who was also president of MCA-TV in New York City, repeatedly stressed that Eric's transformation reflected the privileged lifestyle that a prominent television executive could deliver his son, and indeed, Lou's prior friendship with Senator Harrison was instrumental in getting the problem of hemophilia treatment some much-needed visibility on the national political stage. The 1973 hearing on behalf of a proposed Hemophilia Act eventually led Congress to fund comprehensive hemophilia treatment centers across the United States in 1975, which suggests how effectively hemophilia advocates had deployed the popular trope in the United States that modern medicine had the power to transform lives for the better when deserving Americans were given access to it. Above all, the Friedlands' testimonies reflected how the sophisticated strategies of normalization the hemophilia community had embraced were variously medical, social, cultural, and political by the 1970s.[14]

The normalizing self-care approach that Harold H and the Friedlands valorized was more than just political rhetoric; it was a commonly lived and widely embraced experience within the bleeding-disorders community. When people with hemophilia constituted a self-care culture around the problem of hereditary bleeding in the second half of the twentieth century, they usually did so by first embracing whatever form of "normalization" their physicians considered to be state of the art. Thus, with the growth of transfusion medicine in the 1940s and 1950s, people with hemophilia not only became vocal proponents of transfusion medicine but also vocal promoters of voluntary blood donation. Later, when more potent plasma-derived treatments became available after 1965, patients and their families argued with physicians for their right to self-administer these products at home, at work, and at school rather than having to find a physician at a clinic or hospital who was authorized to administer such treatments.[15] In short, while persons with hemophilia often embraced the normalizing strategies of their chosen therapists, they usually did so in ways that reflected their own sense of what was worthwhile.

People with hemophilia and their therapists imagined themselves as partners in a team effort not only to control hemophilia but also to create "normal" lives.[16] In fact, there was widespread consensus by 1980 that every person with hemophilia in America could expect a nearly normal lifespan given the current state of medical management. In a relatively short time, comprehensive care programs for hemophilia brought the median life expectancy of many Americans living with hemophilia (67.5 years) in line with that for all U.S. males (71.1 years).[17] Such results were widely appreciated in the hemophilia community as confirmation of the obviously different quality of life that people with bleeding disorders had experienced after embracing clotting-factor replacement therapies and comprehensive care. Not only were many boys with hemophilia avoiding or giving up orthopedic braces and crutches, they were also participating in activities—most notably, sports—that would have been unthinkable a few years earlier. People with hemophilia had fewer absences from school or work, and social workers as well as physicians were happy to report that measures of "productivity" among this group had increased.

For Americans who experienced the dramatic progress of the 1970s, the attainment of some normalcy for persons with hemophilia proved to be all too brief. At least 16,000 Americans were being treated for hemophilia in the early 1980s. Through the standard transfusions of clotting-factor concentrates (a commercially pooled plasma product often composed of plasma from thousands of donors), nearly 60 percent of patients with hemophilia in the United States contracted the human immunodeficiency virus (HIV) that causes acquired immunodeficiency syndrome (AIDS). The infection rate approached 90 percent among the persons classed as severe hemophiliacs, the nearly 10,000 Americans who used clotting-factor concentrates most frequently.[18] Post-transfusion hepatitis—both hepatitis B and hepatitis C—was also widespread in the U.S. hemophilia population. Most Americans treated for hemophilia in the 1980s had died by 2000 as a result of post-transfusion AIDS or (far less visibly) hepatitis C.[19]

Predictably, this turn of events brought the normalizing expectations of the bleeding-disorders community into question. The mid-1980s witnessed the resurgence of old stigmas and obstacles and the creation of new ones as people with hemophilia were widely reported to be carriers of AIDS and hepatitis. The increasing media attention to AIDS created a new cultural and social context for persons with hemophilia: the hemophiliac was now widely portrayed as a victim not only of disease but also of society. In particular, the well-publicized experience of Ryan White, from his exclusion from school attendance as a presumed AIDS carrier in 1986 to his death in 1990, pointed to the ways that transfusion-related AIDS exposed people with hemophilia, especially the children among them, to vicious stereotypes to which they had previously been thought immune.[20] Boys and men with hemophilia, who had long been cast as white, middle-class, and heteronormative, were suddenly brought into close identification with stereotyped portraits of three other high-risk groups for AIDS: homosexuals, Haitians, and intravenous drug users (so-called heroin addicts).[21] Collectively, these at-risk groups were widely called the "4-H Club."[22]

Americans with bleeding disorders had diverse views on subjects such as race, class, gender, and sexual orientation, but everyone affected by hemophilia had to adjust to the growing perception in the 1980s that anyone associated with AIDS was suspect. Many Americans believed or were told that people who acquired HIV-AIDS through transfusions were innocent victims. But the mere mention of innocence presumed a framework of culpability in which people with hemophilia became the unwitting victims of other people's imprudent, if not immoral, behaviors (sexual impropriety, drug abuse, etc.).[23] As AIDS activist Cindy Patton summarized in 1985, "The myths about hemophilia and taboo[s] about blood and bleeding make AIDS among hemophiliacs not quite 'clean' and best kept hidden." In fact, one anonymous person with hemophilia told Patton that shifting prospects for people with hemophilia in the 1980s amounted to a veritable epidemic of "hemophobia," fueled by a "growing fear that hemophiliacs are dangerous to employ or to have in schools." Not coincidentally, this man also spoke to her "wryly of coming out of the 'clot closet,'" which was a sentiment shared by many men with hemophilia.[24] Years later, Andrew Flagg similarly described his own experience of acquiring AIDS from his hemophilia treatments: "The big impact of HIV, aside from the concern about getting sick, was the feeling that I needed to go underground again."[25]

Both before and after AIDS, the acculturated preference for normal lives for hemophiliacs had profound implications for Americans with bleeding disorders. Medicine, science, and technology undoubtedly played critical roles in constituting the hemophiliac as the kind of individual whose "natural" disposition toward disability could be normalized in the late twentieth century. But it is also important to understand that by the 1970s, people with hemophilia were viewing themselves as normal people and being treated that way in many contexts. They embraced normality as an unproblematic goal of therapy until the therapeutic community's chosen management strategy turned out to create lives that no one could justifiably characterize as normal.

Even as hemophilia advocacy increasingly touted the potential for normalcy in the postwar decades, people with hemophilia and their therapists were far from aware of the diverse ways they deployed the word *normal*. The idea of normality had always been powerful precisely because its meanings were fungible. From the perspective of primary-care physicians, normal for the hemophilia patient was a relative measure of physical or mental fitness. For hematologists, normal entailed levels of clotting factor in the bloodstream that ensured prompt coagulation. For orthopedists and physical therapists, normal meant joints and muscles that allowed full, flexible, and pain-free movement. For psychiatrists and social workers, normal was a measure of how well adjusted the hemophilia patient was in light of his physical limitations: was he happy and productive? Of course, these medical registers of the word normal mattered to people with hemophilia and their families, but the people being treated as patients also had their own diverse measures of what normality entailed and how to pursue it. Medical experts were undoubtedly aware of the more popular meanings of normal, and it would be correct to say that the medical experts' views of normality usually coincided with what their patients or their families assumed to be normal. Ideas of normal among both doctors and patients were inflected with mainstream, typically hegemonic views of gender, class, and race. In fact, it undoubtedly served the interests of physicians to align their specialized grasp of "normal" (say, a clotting-factor level that produced promptly effective blood coagulation) with the presumed aspirations of patients to, say, attend college, have a career, or create meaningful social interactions.

As heterogeneous as the meanings of the word normal could be, there was a widespread presumption in the American bleeding-disorders community during the postwar decades that achieving some normalcy in one's life was tantamount to achieving an autonomous lifestyle that was relatively free of impairment or disease. The philosophy of self-care that situated normalcy as the path toward independence thus stood in productive tension with the medical goal of normalization that postwar medical specialists advanced. What usually went unsaid was how normality—as a surrogate for actual autonomy—was predicated on conformity to a vision of the hemophiliac as someone who was white and middle-class and who was approaching degrees of productivity that were typical of a nondisabled male. In short, the dominant cultural values surrounding hemophilia and its management were rooted in forms of patriarchy, white privilege, and capitalism, and this fact made it highly unusual for anyone in the United States to question the therapeutic or social value of normality.

While normality has not disappeared as a valuable goal for many people concerned with the problem of hemophilia today, it is not the dominant or pervasive ideal that it once was. Before the AIDS era, Americans interested in the problem of hemophilia saw the medical and social management of the disease as a benign enterprise. If things were not getting better, at least they were getting no worse. That illusion and the idealized notions of normality that undergirded it were dealt a serious blow by the iatrogenic catastrophes of transfusion-related HIV (in the 1980s) and hepatitis C (in the early 1990s). As told elsewhere, the American hemophilia community's views on ideals such as normality underwent drastic changes in the 1990s as the focus turned away from normal lives to the promotion of autonomy and social justice in the wake of tainted transfusions.[26] The fallout from post-transfusion HIV and hepatitis helped check enthusiasm for the ideology of normalization within the American bleeding-disorders community even as the enterprise of hemophilia management has continued to advance.

So what does this history of hemophilia reveal about the goals of a therapeutic perspective that valorizes normality? Normalizing ideas and practices have been ubiquitous in American medicine since the nineteenth century, but that does not mean that they have been transparently so. The degree to which medical therapists seek to normalize their patients and the extent to which health care professionals acknowledge their investments in normalization has varied considerably across time and space. Hemophilia is one of those somatic conditions whose treatment generated increasingly explicit talk of social as well as medical normalization in the second half of the twentieth century. This therapeutic focus has been less often strictly medical in its orientation than one might guess, precisely because persons with hemophilia have always had their own ideas of what their lives entailed.[27]

The Professional Hemophiliac and Self-Care

Harold H was particularly reflective about his life with hemophilia when he spoke to historian Susan Resnik in August 1991 because he was already sick from the transfusion-related HIV infection that would end his life in 1996. Harold stressed how his deeply ingrained coping skills grew out of a communal effort to help him normalize his life. In recounting his earliest memories, Harold reflected on the ways he had learned from his mother and his community to take charge of his care, how he had involved himself in blood drives at an early age, and how he became invested in hemophilia advocacy as an adolescent and adult.[28] Characterizing himself as independent was clearly very important to Harold, and he saw his sustained willingness over the years to speak openly with others about his hemophilia as a critical element in his broader effort of self-care. Harold's approach to his existential lot was what in an earlier era might have invited therapists to label him a professional hemophiliac.

The professional hemophiliac label was a term that physicians, psychologists, and social workers occasionally used in hemophilia management of the 1970s and 1980s to describe boys and men with hemophilia who actively portrayed themselves in public settings as someone whose experiences were representative of his kind. Ostensibly, the term allowed the therapist to give expression to the fact that the patient was psychologically compensating for his physical illness or debility in ways that might not necessarily be to his personal benefit. The therapist's goal was to help the patient achieve an appropriate balance in his self-presentation to the world, to maximize the social benefits of being outwardly sick or impaired and minimize its risks (e.g., unnecessary stigma). Like many therapeutic labels, this one had questionable utility. It was by no means clear from testimonies of people with hemophilia what problem this diagnosis was meant to address. Wherever testimonies by boys and men with hemophilia have been found, there has been little evidence that taking a publicly visible role in their own care has ever been problematic. In fact, where persons with hemophilia have deployed the phrase professional hemophiliac, they seemed to use it in a colloquial, descriptive sense that was unaware of and perhaps unrelated to the therapeutic label.

The therapeutic term professional hemophiliac is also of indeterminate origin, likely used informally in professional circles more often than in formal medical and professional writing. It appears that the first widely visible "professional hemophiliacs" emerged in the 1950s alongside popular efforts by hemophilia advocates and the media to publicize the experience and dilemmas facing Americans with a bleeding disorder. Some of these individuals were leading figures in the national and international hemophilia advocacy movements. Frank Schnabel (1926–1987), who founded both the Canadian Hemophilia Society (est. 1953) and the World Hemophilia Association (est. 1963), was among the earliest and most influential of these individuals. He once described his emergence as a very public hemophiliac:

> I wanted to be like everyone else. I didn't want to be different. So I never told anyone what was wrong with me. Then it occurred to me that if all hemophiliacs hid their problem, how could we ever expect to make any progress? I felt we had to educate people about hemophilia, and then push, and push hard, for better treatment and more career opportunities. So I went to the other extreme and just refused to stop talking about hemophilia.[29]

The common desire to fit in—to be judged as fit for life "like everyone else"—was what Schnabel and many other persons with hemophilia sought as the twentieth century progressed. They and their advocates promoted the idea that hemophiliacs were normal people who were capable of living normal lives, even if the means to that end were extraordinarily complex, burdensome, and ultimately risky.[30]

As the bleeding-disorders community came into being in the decades following World War II, there were struggles within that emergent community about whose perspectives should lead the broader effort to manage hemophilia. The earliest leaders of the National Hemophilia Foundation were white parents who wished to assert their authority on issues of treatment policy and social inclusion. And while the NHF had medical advisors from its earliest inception, the advocacy association was a federation of small family-based organizations that was mainly focused on serving the white male pediatric population living with hemophilia in the United States during the late 1940s and 1950s. NHF medical advisors were very interested in advancing medical research (especially in hematology), and they often preferred to deal with parent leaders who were willing to allocate resources away from direct aid and medical services in the hope of delivering advanced treatment (if not a cure) in the foreseeable future.[31] Understandably, parents tended to prefer direct aid for their hemophilic sons. Tensions within the hemophilia community became even more complicated as the boys and teenagers grew into adults who wished—like Harold H—to take an active role in their lives by occupying leadership positions in the advocacy movement.

As the majority of these adults with hemophilia reported to social worker Alfred Katz in the 1960s, men with hemophilia wanted parents with hemophilic sons to encourage normality above all else. For the most part, parents and sons agreed that some combination of self-care and communal involvement were necessary to achieve some semblance of normality. Yet there were times when tensions between parent leaders and adults with hemophilia occasionally manifested as outright hostility toward the parent-dominated hemophilia associations. As one man with hemophilia told Katz in the mid-1960s:

> Parents should be cautioned against telling everybody about a child's condition—he has a right to his privacy as a person even as a child. I doubt much good is really accomplished by the parent telling everyone about their child's disease—in reality it probably satisfies parental needs for recognition. Certainly it doesn't contribute to the child's integrity or health individuation. I would also warn parents away from the hemophilia assocs [*sic*]. It's jargon but to the point to say they are "sob sisters."

This man's response was prompted by Katz's question to adults with hemophilia about what advice they would recommend to parents of children with hemophilia. The strong opinion expressed here can be read as an attack on the kind of self-care regime the NHF promoted in the early 1960s. It is certainly quite critical of parents like Harold H's mother, who sought every opportunity to tell people in her local community about Harold's hemophilia. Harold, who was still a young boy at this point, certainly took it upon himself to speak to adults as well as to peers in his community about his hemophilia. Not every boy or man with hemophilia embraced the dominant, normalizing narrative the hemophilia associations advanced. However, many boys and men raised within this self-care regime took it upon themselves to speak out in their own ways. Sometimes they urged acceptance of hemophiliacs. Other times, they promoted better understanding of the disease experience (i.e., its medical or social aspects). But whatever explicit message they sought to emphasize, the underlying motive for speaking publically about their experiences with hemophilia was to empower themselves and others living with bleeding disorders.

It is difficult to say whether the professional hemophiliac label is actually a concept that originated in the grassroots social phenomenon that Frank Schnabel embodied and that Harold H described in 1991. If it did, then the use of the term in therapeutic circles suggests that at least some health care professionals resisted the emergence of an ethic of self-care among Americans with bleeding disorders. By questioning the motives of boys and men who were most open about their condition, these therapists seemed willing to pathologize what was a critical, and perhaps even necessary survival tactic among predominantly white American boys and men with hemophilia in the post–World War II decades. For instance, the experts were not apparently taking into account the considerable stress on patients and their families that community blood shortages put on them. Only by getting the word about hemophilia out in the community and normalizing the disease and people living with the disease was it possible to render people with hemophilia as something other than charity cases: fragile, dependent, disabled.

The social, cultural, and economic setting surrounding hemophilia in the post–World War II decades made an acculturated form of self-care a fitting response to the needs and pressures that people with hemophilia experienced from the 1940s through the 1970s. But conditions changed dramatically in the 1980s with the emergence of AIDS. Thus, the hemophilia-specific culture that prompted boys and men with hemophilia to be open and proactive about their medical and social condition in the post–World War II decades has continued to evolve through the 1990s and early 2000s.

Consider, for instance, the case of Shawn Decker (b. 1975). Decker has spent a good deal of time educating people about safe sex, HIV-AIDS, hepatitis, and bleeding disorders. He published a well-regarded memoir of his disease experiences in 2006, entitled *My Pet Virus: The True Story of a Rebel without a Cure.*[32] Like several thousand other boys living with hemophilia during the 1980s, Decker acquired HIV, hepatitis B, and hepatitis C through clotting-factor concentrates. However, unlike most memoirs about the post-AIDS hemophilia experience, this one opens with the theme "when bad names happen to good people."[33] Decker therefore highlights something that most people living with a chronic disease or impairment experience more or less regularly: namely, that many of the challenging problems people with a chronic condition face begin not with physical or mental debility per se but rather with medical diagnosis and treatment. In fact, as critiques of the biomedical model of disability have long emphasized, the disabling attitudes that are so endemic to modern medical understandings of bodily difference effectively ensure that patients with a chronic condition will experience social complications with their therapy. As Decker put it: "I can be laid back about my lot in life because I now realize I was destined for a life of medical drama from day one."[34]

My Pet Virus is a playful, consistently funny memoir, but no one should doubt that Decker was making some serious points about his cohabitation with hemophilia, HIV, and hepatitis.

> Maybe my life isn't so enviable, and yes, I've been given a lot to deal with in my first thirty years of living. But that's the circle jerk of life: everyone has obstacles and labels to overcome, mine just involve life-threatening medical conditions. And

instead of dying like I was supposed to, I became a thinblooded positoid with a sick sense of humor, merrily making my way in a thickblooded world.[35]

For Decker, what is really critical is the individual's cultivated sense of autonomy in the face of his or her particular challenges. On one level, his philosophy of self-care suggests that autonomy, contrary to popular opinion, is part and parcel of vulnerability and dependence; it is not their opposite but an affirmative adaptation to the universally difficult conditions of life.[36] On another level, Decker's language and "sick sense of humor" constitute a historically appropriate response to the ironic conditions of life created by the previous half-century of hemophilia management. These aspects of *My Pet Virus* suggest why historians of disability, health, and medicine will find something of value in this man's testimony.

Poet and writer Tom Andrews (1961–2001) has provided one of the most sustained reflections currently available on what the professional hemophiliac epithet entails. In writing his 1998 memoir *Codeine Diary*, Andrews sought to distance himself from the idea that he was the "kind of professional hemophiliac" who could be "recklessly confident" in speaking for "all bleeders." He even characterized his memoir as a kind of ambivalent illness narrative:

> To a certain extent then, I disagree with the idea behind personal accounts of illness such as this one. To put it another way: this book, by its very nature, flirts with a way of thinking about illness that I believe is dangerous and seductive to the ill. The battle is over identity. Every day the question arises: Am I a hemophiliac who happens to be a writer (or cashier or househusband or whatever), or am I a writer who happens to be a hemophiliac?[37]

The full significance of this ambivalence becomes very apparent in the life experiences Andrews shares in *Codeine Diary* and in the book's explicit raison d'être: "To me there is a central justification for such a book: to demythologize illness, for myself and (one hopes but cannot presume) others, revealing it not as a rarefied tragedy but as the commonplace event it is."[38] Andrews astutely acknowledges that "demythologizing illness requires the work of a great many people." Indeed, a central aspect of the broader enterprise of disease management involves just that: demythologizing illness in order to reduce stigma. Yet Andrews is very clear about what people living with the condition contribute:

> A hemophiliac's role in this project, I believe, is to be absolutely candid about what happens to him during a typical bleed. By "bleed" I mean the following series of events. A blood vessel (or vessels) breaks, releasing blood into a joint and the surrounding muscles. Clotting factor is given in an IV drip to retard the bleeding, but it takes time for the infusion to take effect. Meanwhile, blood fills the joint. The pain is staggering. The limb locks. The muscles atrophy. One is faced with weeks

of waiting for the body to absorb the blood, followed by weeks of physical therapy to straighten and regain the joints original range of motion.

This is where Andrews's demythologized account of hemophilia begins, with a thoroughly biological event and its medical treatment. His social and cultural interpretation of his own experience as a hemophiliac builds on this candid base, in which disease and debility are a ubiquitous aspect of the human experience.

In publically framing his hemophilia experience as a commonplace event, Tom Andrews gets at the heart of why boys and men with hemophilia had long sought to publicize their experience, but with a more contemporary twist than the older emphasis on normality and fitting in. In the wake of the transfusion-related AIDS catastrophe, Andrews had every reason to cast the circumstances of hemophiliacs as a rarefied tragedy. But for him, several real-life barriers stood in the way of this rendering. First of all, Tom Andrews did not acquire HIV-AIDS through his treatments, making him an "HIV-negative hemophiliac," a rarity among persons with hemophilia of his generation. But more importantly, Andrews' experience of hemophilia was also unusual because he was regarded as the healthiest child in his family. Tom's brother, who ultimately died from kidney failure, was the "sicker" child in the West Virginia home of the Andrews family. Because of this, Tom not only avoided thoughts of giving himself over to his illness (like his more fatalistic brother apparently did), but Tom experienced bodily difference (in the form of disease) as a thoroughly ubiquitous feature of the human condition. As he tells in *Codeine Diary*, there was nothing exceptional or extraordinary about his having an illness except for the way he dealt with it: by being self-consciously reckless, for instance. *Codeine Diary* highlights some of Tom's more dangerous activities, like his forays into off-road motorcycle racing and other ways of "being a bad insurance risk." The paperback edition of *Codeine Diary* has the revealing subtitle: "True Confessions of a Reckless Hemophiliac."[39]

In contrast to the "reckless" Tom Andrews and the "rebellious" Shawn Decker, men of Frank Schnabel's generation went to extraordinary lengths to fit in, to appear "normal," and (even) to follow doctors' orders. That performance of normality could be interpreted as unrealistic—especially before effective means for controlling bleeding episodes were widely available. The very existence of the professional hemophiliac label suggests as much because some therapists who treated boys and men with hemophilia in the 1960s and 1970s apparently saw the patients extraordinary efforts to normalize their illness as a problem that merited intervention. The fact that medicine itself had helped create and encourage this form of role-playing was apparently lost on those therapists who took the professional hemophiliac diagnosis seriously. In any case, Andrews' focus on making embodied difference commonplace separates him, Decker, and their fellow "thinbloods" from that earlier generation of publically visible men with hemophilia who sought, like Frank Schnabel, to be normal, "like everyone else."

Critical Historical Perspectives on Medicine and Disability

The curious case of the professional hemophiliac not only points to the fact that medical experts have long had difficulty dealing with patients on their own terms but also highlights that lifelong reliance on medicine is neither uniformly good nor consistently bad. Both features of the professional hemophiliac idea illustrate why historians of disability and historians of medicine have a common interest in critically assessing the relationship between medicine and disability.

Historians of medicine and health have often neglected the ubiquity of normalizing ideas and practices in medical endeavors even as they have long struggled to capture the experiences of patients in relationship to the social and medical developments that have been their primary focus. Critical disability history, by contrast, has given concerted attention to how cultural values—including masculine heteronormativity, whiteness, middle classness, and perceived able-bodiness—are part of the social constellation that constitute "normal" in modernizing societies. Precisely because first-hand experiences of embodied difference have been a focus in critical disability studies, historians of disability, including Paul Longmore, James Trent, and David Gerber (to name just a few), have exposed readers over the past decades to the wide variety of embodied difference in human societies. Others, such as Alice Domurat Dreger, David Serlin, Richard Scotch, and Lennard Davis, have shown how the flexible idea of normality has been used to manage such difference, ranging from forms of accommodation and integration to outright neglect or erasure of otherness.[40]

Historians of medicine and health thus would do well to turn to critical disability histories for models of how to interrogate the experiences of patients or better analyze medicine's normalizing aspects.[41] At the same time, historians of disability would benefit from sustained engagement with histories of medicine and health precisely because disability studies too often treat medical interventions—particularly in the form of biomedicine—as little more than sophisticated mechanisms for obliterating embodied difference. Denigrating people with perceived disabilities is seldom the intent of physicians and other medical experts. Yet there has been a tendency within disability studies to treat medical experts as unwitting agents of social control, an approach that often overlooks patients who have actively chosen medical interventions and found such interventions to be important if not unproblematic.[42] Sustained critique of biomedical models of disability is extremely valuable—both as challenge to the hegemony of biomedicine and as a hallmark of what critical disability histories are capable of delivering more generally to our historical understanding. But to realize fully the critical imperative of disability history, scholars will need to articulate more nuanced, contextualized understandings of medical enterprises and the people invested in them.[43]

As illustrated by the history of hemophilia management and the bleeding-disorders community, there is still much to learn about the varied meanings of disability and normalcy. Americans with hemophilia who lived during the second half of the twentieth century often embraced therapeutic perspectives and practices that endorsed normalization because these forms of medicine fit their own cultivated sense of what they needed to live more fulfilling, autonomous lives. And while the quest for normal lives did eventually receive the scrutiny it deserved after transfusion-related AIDS, the use value of biomedicine was barely called into question by the bleeding-disorders community when normalcy waned as a therapeutic and social ideal. In fact, most Americans with hemophilia are currently quite excited about the prospects of what biomedicine holds for them in the immediate future. Normalization could full well return to its former glory. After two decades of faulty but still tantalizing promises, the biomedical enterprise popularly known as gene therapy now appears to be tantalizingly close to eliminating bleeding episodes for some patients with hemophilia B (factor IX deficiency).[44] This development, along with others, is powerful testimony that the bleeding-disorders community continues to embrace what biomedicine is capable of offering—even if normalcy has been reduced to a weakened, if not dead, trope. So what does this case study entail for the practice of the history of medicine and the history of disability? The peculiar figure of the professional hemophiliac, like the social and cultural history of the bleeding-disorders community itself, is not only challenging historians to question our own assumptions about whose voices are valid and what events are deserving of a privileged hearing but also encouraging us to improve our handling of "unruly" experiences that do not conform to our current categories for managing knowledge.

Notes

1. Interview with Harold H of Portland, Oregon (1962–1996), telephone interview conducted by Susan Resnik, August 7, 1991, 25. Harold H is a pseudonym Resnik used at Harold's request. The original tape and transcript are archived at the Columbia Center for Oral History, Columbia University Libraries, New York. My thanks to Susan for sharing this interview and discussing Harold's life with me.

2. Ibid.

3. Ibid., 26–27.

4. See Stephen Pemberton, *The Bleeding Disease: Hemophilia and the Unintended Consequences of Medical Progress* (Baltimore, Md.: Johns Hopkins University Press, 2011), 11–13, 116–188, 138–151.

5. Robert Littell, "Bearer Is a Hemophiliac," Reader's Digest 74 (1959): 214–215.

6. James E. Lindemann, *Psychological and Behavioral Aspects of Physical Disability: A Manual for Health Practitioners* (New York: Plenum Press, 1981), 25.

7. Quote from "Passport to Freedom for the Hemophiliac," a four-page advertisement printed in February 1970 for the high-potency (human) AHF concentrate manufactured by Courtland Scientific Products, a division of Abbott Laboratories, based in North Chicago, Illinois. Kenneth M. Brinkhous Papers, Francis Owen Blood Research Laboratory, University of North Carolina at Chapel Hill.

8. Susan Resnik, *Blood Saga: Hemophilia, AIDS, and the Survival of a Community* (Berkeley: University of California Press, 1999).

9. Paul K. Jones and Oscar D. Ratnoff, "The Changing Prognosis of Classic Hemophilia (Factor VIII 'Deficiency')," *Annals of Internal Medicine* 114, no. 8 (1991): 644.

10. Littell, "Bearer Is a Hemophiliac," 214–215.

11. Dorothy White, *Home Care of the Hemophilic Child* (New York: National Hemophilia Foundation, 1958), 14 pages, quote on 1.

12. Pemberton, *The Bleeding Disease*, 138–151.

13. Ibid., 7–8, 81–84, 109–112.

14. *Hemophilia Act of 1973: Hearing before the Subcommittee on Health of the Committee on Labor and Public Welfare, United States Senate, Ninety-Third Congress, First Session, on S. 1326 to Amend the Public Health Service Act to Provide for Programs for the Diagnosis and Treatment of Hemophilia, November 15, 1973* (Washington, D.C.: U.S. Government Printing Office, 1974), especially 1–41. See also Pemberton, *The Bleeding Disease*, 217–227.

15. Pemberton, *The Bleeding Disease,* 209–217.

16. See ibid., 270–282.

17. Jones and Ratnoff, "The Changing Prognosis of Classic Hemophilia," 644.

18. Ronald Bayer, "Blood and AIDS in America: The Making of a Catastrophe," in *Blood Feuds: AIDS, Blood, and the Politics of Medical Disaster*, edited by Eric Feldman and Ronald Bayer (New York: Oxford University Press, 1999), 33–35.

19. For excellent overviews, see Resnik, *Blood Saga*; and Douglas Starr, *Blood: An Epic History of Medicine and Commerce* (New York: Alfred A. Knopf, 1998).

20. See Sander Gilman, *Disease and Representation: Images of Illness from Madness to AIDS* (Ithaca, N.Y.: Cornell University Press, 1988), 268; and Pemberton, *The Bleeding Disease*, 262–270.

21. See Pemberton, *The Bleeding Disease,* 258; and David Kirp, "The Politics of Blood: Hemophilia Activism in the AIDS Crisis," in *Blood Feuds: AIDS, Blood, and the Politics of Medical Disaster*, edited by Eric Feldman and Ronald Bayer (New York: Oxford University Press, 1999), 293–321.

22. Randy Shilts, *And the Band Played On: Politics, People, and the AIDS Epidemic* (New York: St. Martin's Press, 1987), 197.

23. Peter Brandon Bayer, "A Life in Limbo," *New York Times Magazine*, April 2, 1989, 44–55, especially 55. See also Pemberton, *The Bleeding Disease*, 269–270.

24. Cindy Patton, *Sex and Germs: The Politics of AIDS* (Boston: South End Press, 1985), 23.

25. Interview with Andrew Flagg, in Laura Gray and Christine Chamberlain, *The Gift of Experience: Conversations about Hemophilia* (Boston: Boston Hemophilia Center, 2007), 159–166, quote on 163.

26. Pemberton, *The Bleeding Disease*, 262–293. See also Corey Dubin, "Hemophilia: A Story of Success—Disaster and the Perseverance of the Human Spirit, Part I," *Journal of the Association of Nurses in AIDS Care* 10 (May/June 1999): 90–93; Corey Dubin, "Hemophilia: A Story of Success—Disaster and the Perseverance of the Human Spirit, Part II," *Journal of the Association of Nurses in AIDS Care* 10 (July/August 1999): 88–92; and Patricia Siplon, *AIDS and the Policy Struggle in the United States* (Washington, D.C.: Georgetown University Press, 2002), chapter 3.

27. This experience is not unique to hemophiliacs. See Daniel Wilson, *Living with Polio: The Epidemic and Its Survivors* (Chicago: University of Chicago Press, 2007), 71–2, 226–227.

28. "Interview with Harold H," 24–27.

29. David Page, "Remembering Frank Schnabel," *Hemophilia World* 10 (March 2003): 10.

30. See Pemberton, *The Bleeding Disease*, 151–156.

31. Ibid., 128–137.

32. Shawn Decker, *My Pet Virus: The True Story of a Rebel without a Cure* (New York: Tarcher/Penguin, 2006), 1.

33. Ibid., 1.

34. Ibid., 6.

35. Ibid.

36. See, for comparison, Nancy Mairs, *Waist High in the World: A Life among the Non-Disabled* (New York: Beacon Press, 1997).

37. Tom Andrews, *Codeine Diary: A Memoir* (Boston: Little, Brown, 1998), 28.

38. Ibid., 30.

39. Ibid., 62, 218–220. The paperback edition is Tom Andrews, *Codeine Diary: True Confessions of a Reckless Hemophiliac* (New York: Mariner Books, 1999).

40. See, for example, Paul K. Longmore, *Why I Burned My Book and Other Essays on Disability* (Philadelphia: Temple University Press, 2003), David Gerber, ed., *Disabled Veterans in History* (Ann Arbor: University of Michigan Press, 2000), James W. Trent Jr., *Inventing the Feeble Mind: A History of Mental Retardation in the United States* (Berkeley: University of California Press, 1994), Alice Domurat Dreger, *One of Us: Conjoined Twins and the Future of Normal* (Cambridge: Harvard University Press, 2004), David Serlin, *Replaceable You: Engineering the Body in Postwar America* (Chicago: University of Chicago Press, 2004), Richard K. Scotch, *From Good Will to Civil Rights: Transforming Federal Disability Policy* (Philadelphia: Temple University Press, 2001), and Lennard Davis, *Enforcing Normalcy: Disability, Deafness, and the Body* (London and New York: Verso, 1995).

41. See for example Wilson, *Living with Polio*; and Beth Linker, *War's Waste: Rehabilitation Medicine in World War I* (Chicago: University of Chicago Press, 2011).

42. For works that, while insightful, frame biomedicine and doctors in this fashion, see Harlan Lane, *The Mask of Benevolence: Disabling the Deaf Community* (San Diego: DawnSignPress, 1999); Joseph Shapiro, *No Pity: People with Disabilities Forging a New Civil Rights*

Movement (Boston: Three Rivers Press, 1994); and Steven Noll, *Feeble-Minded in Our Midst: Institutions for the Mentally Retarded in the South, 1900–1940* (Chapel Hill: University of North Carolina Press, 1995).

43. See Julie Livingston, *Debility and the Moral Imagination in Botswana* (Bloomington: Indiana University Press, 2005), a nuanced model.

44. Amit Nathwani et al., "Adenovirus-Associated Virus Vector—Mediated Gene Transfer in Hemophilia B," *New England Journal of Medicine* 365 (December 22, 2011): 2357–2365.

CHAPTER 13

Border Disorders

Mental Illness, Feminist Metaphor,
and the Disordered Female Psyche
in the Twentieth-Century United States

SUSAN K. CAHN

KEYWORDS: *Centuries*: twentieth; twenty-first; *Geographical Areas*: North America; *Sources*: memoirs; serials; medical documents; *Themes*: bodies, medicine, and contested knowledge; culture

Sin Fronteras—without borders.[1] Feminists have pushed us to look beyond the borders that divide us, to explore borderlands to understand the people situated between or near borders as having a certain wisdom, an ability to bridge differences, to teach us ultimately about both ourselves and others.[2] Queer theorists, too, have shaken off any notion of fixed, unified sexual identity and replaced it with fluid desires that gravitate toward particular identity narratives that are, in essence, *not of the essence* but culturally produced.[3] Disability studies scholars have also challenged us to explore the "liminal spaces" and put forward an idea of illness-based identities as socially constructed within social and medical discourses. Poststructuralism undertakes a related endeavor, breaking apart the unified "self" inherited from the Enlightenment and modernism. Identities are fictions. The self is contingent. As a result, we know that we are both less than and more than any simply articulated sense of "self."

There is a certain romance to fluidity; a wisdom of location attributed to borderlessness. Coincidentally (or not?), during the same decades when feminist and other theorists focused such energy on issues of the self and boundaries, psychologists and psychiatrists were busy trying to pin down another elusive relation of self to borders and boundaries: a pathological form of borderline existence that in 1980 was entered in the *DSM-III* (*Diagnostic and Statistical Manual of Mental Disorders*, third edition) as "borderline personality disorder," or BPD.[4] It has become a trendy, catchall diagnosis of the past few decades; by some estimates it has been applied to as many as 63 percent of all psychiatric inpatients with personality disorders.[5] It operates in multiple domains, from hospitals to court rooms and prisons, from low-cost mental health clinics to pricey residential treatment programs. Social workers, psychologists, and psychiatrists make ready use of the diagnosis. So do TV talk shows and filmmakers, who devote episodes to BPD or feature "borderline" characters in blockbuster movies such as *Girl, Interrupted*.

An estimated 70–77 percent of those diagnosed with BPD are women, most often late adolescents or women in their twenties and thirties.[6] The illness is racially unmarked in psychiatric literature, and in that sense it is culturally scripted as a "white" disorder. Popular movie characters associated with borderline traits have been cast as beautiful white women, including Glenn Close in *Fatal Attraction* and Jennifer Jason Leigh in *Single White Female*. However, the few studies that consider race as a variable have found BPD to be equally prevalent in populations that include high numbers of poor women and women of color.[7] Significantly, studies analyzing race and ethnicity in personality disorders have been conducted in prisons or public hospitals, suggesting that the likelihood of a BPD diagnosis may correlate less with race than with access to mental health services or, conversely, encounters with forced psychiatric examination. Women who end up in hospitals, intensive treatment programs, or, increasingly, in prisons—the psychiatric institutions of the twenty-first century—are apt to receive a diagnosis of BPD, a diagnosis that is no longer limited to young white women of means, if it ever was. While the seductive allure attributed to borderlines might, because of racist standards of beauty, lead to a cultural reading of BPD as "white," any woman who presents a set of specified emotional and behavioral traits to psychiatric professionals —and strikes them as very difficult to deal with—has a good chance of acquiring this diagnosis.

Borderline personality disorder has become a generic female malady resembling the early twentieth-century diagnosis of hysteria, which, according to historian Elizabeth Lunbeck, was used "less as a proxy for symptoms than as an epithet expressive of . . . [psychiatrists'] disdain for troubling aspects of womanhood."[8] In our own time, the troublesome behaviors identified by the *psy* professions— a term referring to psychiatry, clinical psychology, social work, and psychiatric nursing—contain a mixture of conventionally masculine and feminine traits. The "post-feminist" woman's (masculine) anger and sexual assertiveness added to the hysteric's (feminine) emotionalism, irrationality, and craving for attention create a new recipe for madness: Combine anger and sex, replace the hysteric's psycho-somatic bodily pains with the borderline tendency to inflict pain on her own body, and the Victorian "hysteric" emerges as the postmodern "borderline."[9]

This essay builds on insights from disability studies about the social construc-tion of illness and feminist critiques of BPD to explore questions of mental illness, the self, and suffering.[10] To do this I first analyze psychiatric literature to sketch out the evolving medical model of this disorder from a feminist historical perspective. I then put the academic literature about BPD in conversation with first-person narratives by women "living under the description of" BPD, a phrase Emily Martin used to call attention to the "social fact" that women have received a psychiatric diagnosis while reminding us that this is just one of many possible descriptors for such a person.[11] How can feminist disability history help us understand both the "biography" of an illness and the biographies of people said to suffer from it? And how are these narratives, in particular the pivotal redefinition of BPD in the 1970s and 1980s, evidence of gender conflicts in the broader culture?

I argue that an illness that is defined by its very indeterminacy has become reified in ways that simultaneously perform a useful service for psychiatric professions and do a great disservice to those living with the diagnosis. Standard psychiatric literature refers to a person with BPD as "the borderline," a metaphor that masks the significant cultural work that the "fact" of BPD does. The diagnosis creates a pathologically disor-dered "character" that cloaks the intellectual incoherence and implicit moral viewpoint of supposedly discrete *DSM* diagnoses, in the process affirming the power of today's biologically oriented psychiatry. In addition, the diagnosis covers up boundary confu-sion among therapists who treat "borderlines," redirecting responsibility for therapeutic failures or ethical violations back onto the client.[12] In all, the highly volatile "borderline" helps stabilize psychiatric knowledge, and thus authority, in the face of its own insta-bilities.

Autobiographical accounts of women diagnosed with BPD as early as the 1960s and as recently as the 1990s suggest, however, that we must move be-yond any simple critique of the medical model and take seriously the pain and problems experienced by people living with this diagnosis. If the preponder-ance of disability studies scholarship has focused critical attention on physical disabilities rather than mental illness, early feminist work on madness viewed mad women as staging a valiant protest against the impossible constraints of a patriarchal society.[13] Moving us away from a romance of resistance at the borders and a suspicion of medicalized mental illness, accounts of emotional pain by women with borderline diagnoses suggest that borders, boundaries, and thera-peutic treatment can be desirable and necessary to one's being, to having a self (however we might define it).

Firming Up the Borderline

The illness that became borderline personality disorder initially developed within the world of American psychoanalysis. In 1938, Adolph Stern first employed the term as an adjective to describe a "borderline state" between psychosis and neurosis.[14] In 1942, Helen Deutsch used the term differently to name a mental state bordering on schizophrenia, elucidating a character type she called the "as if" personality who functioned "as if" everything were normal but lived "a sham existence."[15] Deutsch described one woman who despite "good intelligence" and reality testing "was always just what was suggested to her by her environment."[16] In 1959, Melitta Schmideburg focused on the paradoxical nature of the borderline individual as "stable in his instability."[17] From the 1940s through the 1970s Freudians theorized multiple ways of conceptualizing the term borderline—as various states, traits, personality organizations, or disorders. Along with describing the border of some other recognized mental disorder, "borderline" also designated an in-between location: between sanity and insanity, neurosis and psychosis, or being well- or ill-suited to psychoanalysis.[18]

Among cultural critics and analytic psychiatrists of the mid-twentieth century the "new borderline personality" became part of a much broader discussion of a new type of patient who presented distinctly different symptoms than the Victorian neurotic of old. In contrast to men of sound character who struggled with the sexual repression requisite for a civilized society, this new "borderline patient" shared the characteristics of postwar society that cultural critics most disparaged. "He" exemplified the shallow, inauthentic search for immediate gratification that critics such as David Riesman and Christopher Lasch associated with a permissive, pleasure-oriented consumer culture.[19] As cultural critics and analytic popularizers attributed these qualities to a new "modal personality" consisting of a "false self," psychoanalysts created an image of these flaws in extreme: "the empty, grandiose narcissist and the histrionic, manipulative, impulsive, and self-destructive borderline."[20] Throughout this period, the varied meanings and applications of the term left a very loose clinical notion about the exact nature, or even existence, of borderline personalities and whether both the symptoms and etiology of the condition could fairly be categorized as a distinct mental illness.

Since psychiatrists treated symptoms and their causes rather than specific diagnoses, questions of definition and accuracy posed few problems initially. Then a confluence of events reshaped BPD as an "official" illness in the 1980 *DSM-III*. After Robert Spitzer assumed control of revising the *DSM-II* (1968) during the 1970s, the new edition took an entirely different, systematizing approach to psychiatric diagnoses and classification. This project coincided with and contributed to new trends—one within psychiatry and the other within the broader political economy of health care. Internally, psychiatry encountered challenges to its authority that the field struggled to overcome.[21] Spitzer and the task force he led sought to regain scientific credibility for psychiatry by creating clearly defined diagnostic categories that would pass the test of scientific reliability and validity. The revised *DSM* outlined new diagnostic criteria that clearly delineated one mental disorder from another. Theoretically at least, *psy* professionals in widely different settings and locations would arrive at the same diagnosis when they confronted the same symptoms.[22] Operating out of this more "scientific" paradigm, subsequent revisions of the *DSM* enumerate nearly 300 distinct mental illnesses, some tied to mood dysfunction and others rooted in a notion of a fundamentally disordered personality.

In the same decades when the "borderline personality" became the "new patient" of psychiatry, powerful pharmaceutical companies developed psychotropic drugs that were mass-marketed not only to the "mentally ill" but also to the anxious housewife or businessman suffering from "the blahs."[23] Treatment protocols transformed significantly, and doctors began prescribing pills to treat a malfunctioning "brain," supplementing or replacing therapists who were treating a disturbed "mind." By the 1980s biopsychiatry had become the dominant paradigm and psychoanalysts had largely faded from the stage. The greater legitimacy of biopsychiatry and pharmaceutical treatment went hand in glove with two other coinciding shifts. First, *psy* professions broadened their reach beyond the ranks of the "mentally ill" to treat problems of everyday living, offering "counseling" services that eventually reached millions of Americans who, if possible, used health insurance policies to subsidize treatment. In the new bureaucracy of third-party payers, health insurance or managed care companies were no longer satisfied by vague diagnoses and treatment plans. They sought clearly delineated mental illnesses that were responsive to medical treatment, especially newly developed drugs and, if necessary, short-term psychotherapy—renamed "talk therapy."[24] It was in this context that the diagnostic criteria for BPD established in 1980 transformed the earlier psychoanalytic concept of borderline personality into a disorder recognized as scientifically valid by doctors, hospitals, therapists, and insurance companies. None of these changes boded well for the women who, more than ever before, were labeled "borderlines."

From a "False Self" to "the Most Difficult Patient"

In the words of women diagnosed with BPD, borderline is "what they call people whose lifestyles bother them" or "is simply the illness of not being taken seriously."[25] The *psy* professions have taken BPD very seriously, however, because of the intellectual problems posed by the diagnosis and because of the therapeutic difficulties clinicians encounter when dealing with women diagnosed as "borderline." Psychiatry defines personality disorders as a set of deeply embedded traits deemed inflexible, maladaptive, and causing significant distress and/or impairment in the ability to function both practically and interpersonally; they are viewed as less remediable than mood disorders such as depression or anxiety.[26] Although there are numerous types of personality disorders—such as narcissistic, histrionic, or antisocial—the *psy* professions regard borderline personality as one of the most intractable. And since at least the 1970s, newer iterations of BPD have ceased to be gender neutral.

How did borderline personality become a decidedly female disorder? Some clues lay in the criteria for the diagnosis itself, others in the historical backdrop against which the diagnosis became "female." One qualifies for BPD by meeting at least five of nine *DSM* criteria, which fall into four types of psychic distress: unstable self-image, chaotic interpersonal relationships, emotional lability, and marked impulsivity.[27] As theorized, BPD describes a kind of "empty self" plagued by feelings of despair, loneliness, and a desperate fear of abandonment, problems that typically appear in early adulthood. The psyche defends against the resulting pain with a flood of unregulated, intense emotions, which include self-hatred, anguish, a fierce and clinging love, venomous anger, acute depression, and suicidal wishes. Desperate to gain a sense of control, the sufferer engages in impulsive, self-injurious behaviors ranging from suicide attempts or gestures to cutting and burning one's skin or high-risk behaviors such as binge eating or spending, reckless driving, and sexual impulsivity, defined (problematically) as sex with multiple partners, with relative strangers, and "without much forethought."[28]

Feminists have critiqued these criteria on the grounds that they isolate behaviors that occur more often in women than men, for instance self-injurious cutting and burning, compared to behaviors that are more common among men, such as self-medicating with alcohol. Or they are behaviors that may appear in either gender but are viewed as more problematic in women.[29] If self-injury is somehow feminine, explosive anger has historically been gendered masculine. A second gendered symptom is sexual impulsivity, typically referred to as "promiscuity." The same sexual behaviors that are deemed promiscuous in women might, in male behavior, signify masculine virility. Susana Kaysen, who was diagnosed with BPD when she was a teenager in the 1960s, wryly commented on the difference in terminology, asking, "How many girls do you think a seventeen-year-old boy would have to screw to earn the label 'compulsively promiscuous.' . . . Probably in the fifteen-to-twenty range, would be my guess—if they ever put that label on boys, which I don't recall their doing."[30]

BPD's "sex change" can also be understood through its broader historical context. The diagnosis radically transformed from its mid-twentieth-century connotation as a vague malaise and/or a flaw in the national character to a clearly delimited mental illness that is now the most popularly diagnosed personality disorder for women. This shift in meaning occurred largely in the 1970s and 1980s, decades when radical feminists fought to legitimate women's anger and sexual expression while simultaneously asserting a right to protection from physical or sexual abuse. In the same decades, right-wing "pro-family" activists sought to shore up "traditional" families and reverse the gains of feminism.[31] It was during this period that a new concept of BPD consolidated into a medical narrative, casting women's anger and morally questionable sexual behavior in the light of mental pathology.

I do not claim that the revised diagnosis reflects a conscious backlash against feminist anger and assertiveness. Neither do I assume that male clinicians dispense this diagnosis more than female *psy* professionals, although during the years BPD took on its current gendered connotation, male psychiatrists most actively theorized the disorder. Rather, within the broader U.S. culture these particular traits were unsettling and discomfiting, leading to a more critical view within psychiatry. Mary Ann Jimenez argues in her analysis of gendered mental disorders that "the concept of borderline personality disorder is rooted in a moral vision of what constitutes mentally healthy behavior," a vision that developed in a period of feminist activism and "growing flexibility in gender roles." Jimenez calls attention to a 1980 study, "Clinical Features of the Borderline Personality Disorder," that employs a series of judgmental adjectives to describe hospitalized borderline patients as angry, argumentative, irritable, sarcastic, demanding, manipulative, and inappropriately behaved.[32] The authors identify these attributes as "clinical features"—symptoms of illness. Qualities that may make any person unlikable are viewed, in the context of psychiatry, as both symptomatic and determinative when present in women experiencing mental "illness."

Particularly revealing are the hallmark characteristics that differentiate BPD from other typically female diagnoses: excessive anger, usually alternating with perceived seductiveness, and being notoriously difficult as a therapeutic patient. In their study of "difficult patients" Bauke Koekkoek and co-authors found that "psychiatrists mentioned the diagnosis borderline personality disorder *up to four times more often* than any other diagnosis when asked about characteristics of difficult patients."[33] The clinician's adverse response to the patient likely guides the choice of diagnosis, making BPD "at best a confusing concept, and at worst, a countertransference diagnosis, which robs the patient of the opportunity of much needed treatment."[34] In casual usage, "borderline" has come to describe a diverse group of "psychic bleeders," "reassurance addicts," skillful manipulators, and attention seekers who leave therapists angry and burned out.[35] The term "borderline," says feminist psychologist Judith Herman, functions as an epithet as much as a diagnosis, "little more than a sophisticated insult" aimed primarily at women.[36]

"This slippery mishap of a label"

Seeking to pin down its precise meaning, in 1984, Dr. Hagop Akiskal described "borderline" as an adjective in search of a noun.[37] But in fact, professionals use the word as a noun far more than an adjective. When one is diagnosed with BPD, one becomes simply "a borderline." Critics have offered "person with BPD" as a less stigmatizing term, but many experts continue to prefer the simpler noun, one that invariably invokes a female pronoun.[38] In a 1992 study by Janice Cauwels, a chapter titled "The Most 'Difficult' Psychiatric Patients" states that because women comprise at least two-thirds of borderline patients, "Borderlines are thus referred to throughout most of this book by feminine pronouns (and therapists by masculine ones because of male dominance in psychiatry.)"[39] Cauwels makes the move from adjective to noun to feminine pronoun in the blink of an eye, even though she astutely recognizes that unlike any other current *DSM* diagnoses, the term "borderline" does not describe a specific state or behavior, as depression or obsessive-compulsive disorder do. As such, the term borderline is "a slippery mishap of a label," functioning as a metaphor rather than a description.[40]

This reification turns a large range of symptoms that many critics argue do not form a meaningful classification into a stigmatized mental illness assigned primarily to women. Thus it uses an indeterminate descriptor to create systemic order where there is none. Indeed, most clinicians and theorists characterize BPD in part by its very indeterminacy and paradoxical nature. Researchers have remarked upon the borderline patient's peculiar quality of "mild amiability . . . readily converted to evil," a "disparity between good social behavior and poor intra psychic structure," a tendency to "vacillate between transient superficial relationships and intense dependent relationships."[41] Other odd couplings include being charming but angry; being a professional overachiever yet being unable to hold down a job; being overly rigid but highly adaptive; being extremely sensitive to interpersonal nuances yet unaware of one's effects on others; being primitive yet sophisticated; being severely dysfunctional yet apparently competent.[42] In *Girl in Need of a Tourniquet*, Merri Lisa Johnson points to the vexed nature of her diagnosis: "Unstable, mercurial, self-injurious, contradictory, seductive, clingy, the term BORDERLINE PERSONALITY has borderline personality. It is in crisis. It is poised to self-destruct."[43]

Yet it has persisted, despite experts' awareness of the many internal contradictions of the diagnosis. Lacking the skeptical wit of Johnson, the director of the Yale Psychiatric Institute concluded in all seriousness, "the most important thing about borderlines: they are more different than they are similar." What they do share, says Thomas McGlashan, is the ability to make "a clinician's hair stand on end" such that professionals "know when we have borderline patients in front of us even though we don't know exactly what the illness is."[44]

"I choose hell again and again"

What we also know is that people living with this diagnosis experience emotional pain so great that it often feels unbearable. Here I use a collection of seven memoirs, published between 1993 and 2011, by women who were diagnosed with BPD to explore the nature of psychic pain and methods of coping with it.[45] Six of the authors are white, one is African American; class backgrounds range from working class to upper-middle class. All at some point were designated "borderline," although always with other accompanying diagnoses. While I use these narratives to explore the experiences of women living with mental illness (and a BPD diagnosis), their experiences are not unmediated; they are shaped by the discursive frameworks through which they have come to understand their illness and by the demands and economics of the publishing world.

Although I use them as a counterpoint to my critical analysis of the medical model of BPD, the memoirs are not counternarratives to medical discourse. Each author entered therapeutic treatment (with different levels of willingness) and, in most cases, benefited from it. Thus, even as the seven women move beyond therapy in writing their own stories, their memoirs are best seen as in conversation with a powerful *psy* discourse that has shaped personal understandings of self and illness. The genre of illness memoirs traditionally emphasizes recovery and has a narrative arc that moves from symptoms to diagnosis to treatment and, finally, to "beating" the disease. Highlighting the valor of struggle "against" illness, recovery narratives typically begin with travail and end with triumph, testifying to the cumulative insights that illness and recovery can engender.[46] The selected authors follow that narrative path to varying degrees; a few see themselves as "recovered," others see themselves as still struggling with mental illness, and some challenge the very categories of mental illness. What they all share is an ability to decipher painful emotional states in ways that illuminate mental illness and suggest an underlying "sense" to the emotional and behavioral patterns that have long been a source of irritation and exasperation to psychiatrists.

The authors frequently use the image of being "skinless," feeling every emotional sensation as if through nerve endings "raw and vulnerable to even a feather's touch."[47] This intensity of feeling combined with variability of mood is at times pleasurable but mostly destabilizing, likened to living in a "world that can shift with a breeze."[48] At the same time, authors offer detailed accounts of feeling "nothing," or like "an empty shell." Rachel Reiland explained that despite her pain, "At my core, I'd feared being nobody."[49] Others envisioned the "nothingness" as a deep, dark hole, a "hole that can never be truly filled, simply due to the fact that everything you place within it disappears so quickly."[50]

Women writing about BPD often used strategies that they recognized, then or later, as counterproductive and contributing to their status as "difficult." Frequent rages allowed them to express anger at the injustices they felt, but for Stacy Pershall the rage was "so out of control that the bottom dropped out from under me like the world was a Gravitron and I was plastered to the wall."[51] Seeking a "savior" also tended to end badly. Memoirists described a limitless need for attentions of a loved one, whether from the men and women they dated or from their therapists. Naming "Men! My drug of choice," Njamile Zakiya writes, "When I get that attention . . . it validates that I'm ok at the basic core level—which is not set in stone in my own world."[52] Yet relationships based on desperate need and the fear of loss eventually proved impossible to sustain. When breakups occurred, the dreaded abandonment created even more "rage, isolation, and despair" as women pushed away the loved one they hoped to keep close.[53]

Constantly under siege, internally and externally, the authors describe a state of utter exhaustion, mental, physical, and emotional. But the struggle never ceased. Merri Lisa Johnson described the habitual nature of her torment, stating simply, "I choose hell again and again."[54] Plagued by recurring episodes that went from bad to worse, Njamile Zakiya recounts the frustrating expectation that "no matter how many times I go through this cycle . . . I'm supposed to have a never ending well of strength springing up inside me" so she can "pick the pieces back up and start again."[55] Delving deep inside themselves to find resources for sheer survival created a level of self-absorption that was maddening to themselves and others. Stacy Pershall recounts that in "the agony of sleepless, tortured hours watching the world get smaller and uglier," a severely depressed person "is selfish because her self, the very core of who she is, will not leave her alone, and she can no more stop thinking about this self and how to escape it" than a prisoner can stop thinking of her torturer.[56] In retrospect, Susanna Kaysen comments, "One of the great pleasures of mental health (whatever that is) is how much less time I have to spend thinking about myself."[57]

Prolonged agony combined with feelings of invisibility invited a testing of borders between inside and out, life and death. The authors all used various forms of self-injury, ranging from starving themselves to head banging; cutting, scraping, and burning skin; and the most risky of all choices, attempting suicide. Susanna Kaysen used wrist-banging, a cumulative injury, to validate her pain. "I was demonstrating externally and irrefutably, an inward condition," attempting to communicate to others her emotional pain, at the same time soothing it.[58] Pain, injury, and tempting fate eventually joined up with thoughts of suicide, both a product of inner terror and a source of pleasant relief. After her first aborted suicide attempt, Stacy Pershall "knew it was for me. It was the relief I sought; I dug my toes into suicide like cool wet sand after a walk on hot pavement."[59] For Njamile Zakiya, suicidal wishes stemmed from "a desperate desire to end the pain by any means necessary." Yet she, too, notes a dual quality, calling suicide "a desperate place . . . [but] also soothing—in a morbid way—to know that I have a way out."[60] Susanna Kaysen debated the question endlessly, until "the debate was wearing me out. Once you've posed that question, it won't go away. . . . Actually, there was only part of myself I wanted to kill: the part that wanted to kill herself." Ingesting fifty aspirin, she performed "a kind of self-abortion."[61]

Clear about the many varieties of suffering that attend their illness, women labeled "borderlines" show much greater ambivalence about the diagnosis. Many discovered their diagnosis years after it had been written into their charts—medicine's version of history. Often initially scribbled into the record by a *psy* professional they met only briefly during an "intake" interview, the diagnosis followed them in every encounter with the mental health system. The diagnostic surprise was uniformly upsetting and, at least initially, experienced as a kind of character assassination. "This bitingly clinical text literally ripped my character to shreds," remembered Rachel Reiland.[62] Some women then came to embrace the diagnosis because it gave them a name for long-standing psychic pain and abuse (by others or themselves). To Stacy Pershall, "The diagnostic criteria for the disorder were essentially an outline of my life." After receiving the diagnosis multiple times in hospital stays, she came to accept that "I was definitively borderline," but added "I hate that word, by the way."[63] In contrast, Kiera Van Gelder fully embraced the label and became a "poster child" for her illness, making BPD education her mission. Yet she was constantly aware of the tremendous discomfort even self-labeling as BPD caused others because of the powerful stigma attached to the diagnosis.[64] Njemile Zakiya may have discovered the stigma only upon publication of her memoir. Zakiya labels her own experience "depression," but the publisher of *A Peek inside the Goo* subtitled the narrative *Depression and the Borderline Personality* "to make this book as helpful as Njemile intended it to be," explaining that "there is more on the table here than just the issue of depression."[65] The publisher's decision—her ability to "set the table"—demonstrates that the nodes of power and authority that define encounters between "mentally ill" women and psychiatric professionals continue to operate beyond the clinic when women seek other venues of self-expression and narration.

Several authors found the diagnosis as much of a trap as the feelings and behaviors that elicited it. Describing the diagnosis as a self-fulfilling prophecy, Reiland writes that having never self-injured, "I began to imitate what I'd read, slapping myself in the face, digging my fingernails into my arms and scratching. . . . I was a borderline, and I was convinced that this was what a borderline would do." Even when authors embraced the diagnosis, publishing their books as BPD "recovery" narratives, they continued to express ambivalence about it and record their critical insights. Discovering her BPD diagnosis only twenty-five years after the fact, Susanna Kaysen remains the most skeptical. Of the "borderline" portrait she notes, "It's accurate but not profound," and asks whether instability in mood, self-image, relationships, and long-term plans isn't "a good description of adolescence" in general.[66] No matter what their level of acceptance or ambivalence, every author felt degraded by the cultural connotations of "being borderline." All seven also insightfully noted the overlap between their BPD diagnosis and the multiple other diagnoses ascribed to them and the proximity between "borderline behavior" and the emotions and activities of women who are deemed normal.

"Borderline" in this sense might be understood as a conceptual space women use to try to comprehend their own bewildering psychic agony. It also provides a designated set of behaviors that bring attention to the ways women try to communicate their pain and solve emotional conundrums. Asking whether this makes BPD a "real" illness misses the point. It is real in the sense that a wide and contradictory collection of behaviors and expressed emotions form enough of a pattern that *psy* professionals knit them together into some recognizable "it" that garners the label borderline. It is equally real in the sense that as a diagnostic entity, it operates powerfully to shape the self-understandings and treatment options of women labeled as borderline. But a collection of symptoms, even if they are recognizable, does not necessarily hold up under closer scrutiny, as it fails to delimit or successfully explain experiences of mental illness. Under the pretense of a distinct psychopathology, BPD implies expertise about extremely painful psychic experiences that in reality continue to baffle experts.

Since the 1990s, new developments in treatment have, according to both therapists and clients, offered those who experience this pattern of emotional and behavioral "traits" better success at relieving psychic pain and recovering aspects of daily life that are judged normal or unimpaired—lasting interpersonal relationships, adequate housing, and some financial stability. In particular, during the 1980s and 1990s psychologist Marsha Linehan developed a form of therapy named Dialectical Behavior Therapy (DBT), a derivation of cognitive therapy. Linehan, who was herself committed to a psychiatric hospital as a teenager, believes that women who self-injure and fit the criteria for BPD come from invalidating environments where abuse is common. Rather than viewing them as manipulative—attempting to influence "by indirect, insidious, or devious means"—she sees parasuicidal and "therapy-interfering" gestures as direct, often unartful attempts to communicate needs or feelings. Designed with a Zen-based dialectical emphasis on a woman's acceptance of herself and her situation balanced by trust in her "inherent capability to change," Linehan's theory adopts a "nonjudgmental and nonperjorative" tone rooted in compassion.[67]

Yet Linehan and the many DBT therapeutic programs she has spawned continue to purport the existence of an actual "borderline" person with a clearly definable and explainable "mental illness" that is treatable by measures tailored specially for women with BPD.[68] We can recognize—must recognize—the suffering conveyed in therapeutic settings and in published illness narratives. We can even appreciate that some symptom combinations correspond to noticeable patterns in behavior and affect. This does not, however, make the collection of "traits" any more coherent or explanatory.

BPD as a Stabilizing Instability

I suggest that the reified "borderline" female patient stands in for three different kinds of borderlands, areas of *psy* professional discourse and practice in which boundaries that appear to be well marked are in fact quite blurred. In this way, the "stable instability" attributed to "borderline" individuals functions to create an epistemological stability that masks instabilities in diagnostic criteria and treatment.[69] First, BPD reveals that the *DSM*'s promise of well-delineated, clinically distinct illnesses is a myth. Very few people who are labeled "borderline" are given a singular diagnosis. Memoirs, academic literature, and popularized self-help books all recount case after case of multiple diagnoses. "Comorbid factors," or other complicating illnesses, include depression, anxiety, bipolar disorder, posttraumatic stress disorder, attachment disorder, other personality disorders, and chemical dependency or substance abuse.[70] Therefore, far from an illness with explanatory value, BPD acts rather as a list of difficult-to-treat symptoms that overlap with many of the symptoms of other "mental illnesses" as currently defined. In particular, the concept of the borderline woman creates a veneer of clarity around the most current controversy among researchers–the relationship between BPD and posttraumatic stress disorder (PTSD) caused by childhood physical or sexual abuse.

Buried in the psychiatric literature on BPD is the noteworthy statistic—replicated in multiple studies—that the majority of women with the diagnosis have themselves been sexually or physically abused as a child.[71] Several studies estimate that two-thirds to three-fourths of women diagnosed with BPD experienced childhood abuse.[72] The complicated relationship between BPD and PTSD (called "identical cousins" by one researcher) is beyond the scope of this essay, except to note that a history of abuse appears nowhere in *DSM* criteria. Moreover, in cases of incest and other acts of sexual and physical abuse, it is the perpetrator who "lacks boundaries," committing criminal and harmful violations of the child's physical and psychic boundaries.[73] These acts cause severe childhood trauma that often persists in adulthood. But in the language of psychiatry, the reified depersonalized figure of the "borderline" buries both the doer and the deed.

In masking diagnostic imprecision, psychiatrists have been quick to see the borderline patient as herself wearing many masks. Robert P. Knight's originating 1953 essay on "Borderline States" explained that "the neurotic defenses and the relatively intact ego function may enable the borderline patient to present a deceptive, superficially conventional, although neurotic, front" by using "cover up" methods that deceive the analyst.[74] Decades later, John Gunderson and Margaret Singer's 1975 overview of BPD research warned clinicians "not [to] be deterred by the presence of a stable work history or superficial social adequacy" when encountering the borderline patient. In fact, a defining feature of BPD is "social adaptiveness" that can manifest itself as good work achievement, social awareness, and appropriate manners and appearance. Such ostensible strengths, they argue, "may reflect a disturbed identity *masked by mimicry*, a form of rapid and superficial identification with others."[75]

Both the personality traits attributed to BPD and the troubled relationships between so-called borderlines and their therapists resonate with earlier diagnostic trends in psychiatry. Over the last century, experts have regarded certain "mentally ill" women as tricksters whose ability to masquerade as "normal" disguised serious illness or defect and created havoc in society. In the early decades of the twentieth century the diagnoses of "hypersexual," "psychopath," and "borderline intelligence" shared some of the features of BPD. The seduction, impulsivity, and promiscuity psychiatrists in the 1910s and 1920s attributed to the hypersexual woman mirror the "borderline" patient's noted capacity to seduce, fool, and provoke troubling behavior in others, including their psychiatrists.[76] The hypersexual female fell under the broader gender-neutral umbrella of "psychopaths," who are also recognized for many of the qualities now attributed to BPD. Not only did psychopaths display emotional instability, poor impulse control, and self-centered vanity, but they also radiated a deceptive personal magnetism, delightfulness, and charm.[77] A third predecessor lies in psychology's assessments of mental capacity, especially with the advent of the Stanford-Binet IQ test in 1916. The apparent intelligence, competence, charm, and verbal abilities thought to mask deeper moral and psychic defects in women of "borderline intelligence" suggests the ability of another group of so-called "borderlines" to mask their fundamental dysfunction by "apparent competence."[78] These striking similarities suggest that in both the early and late twentieth century, *psy* professionals exhibited insecurity about their ability to "see" certain individuals accurately, revealing some chinks in their armor of expertise. Moreover, in both periods they projected discomfiting social changes occurring in the broader culture onto a group of pathologized persons with a diagnosis that attached itself with growing frequency to troubled and troubling women.

"People like this bring you close to murder"

The term "borderline" also works to rationalize, or mask, therapeutic failures by focusing on the supposed manipulative skills of female clients accused of breaching the therapeutic boundaries established to protect both client and therapist.[79] The literature on BPD and countertransference, however, suggests that it is clinicians who often find themselves crossing boundaries they routinely maintain with other clients. Thus, the second "borderland" created by BPD is a discursive space where *psy* professions can speak about—and evade blame for—relationships that blur standard professional boundaries between therapists and clients.

Michael Balint writes that while "not easy to admit," the borderline patient "somehow seems able to get under the analyst's skin. He begins to know much too much about his analyst . . . [not] from any outside source of information but apparently from an uncanny talent that enables the patient to 'understand' the analyst's motives and to 'interpret' his behavior."[80] Many therapists observe professional ethics and do effective, sometimes innovative, work with people diagnosed with BPD. Nevertheless, A. B. Dennis and R. Sansone maintain that therapists should always seek outside supervision, because "when you're treating borderlines. . . . I don't care how good you are—they force whatever part of you is chaotic and crazy to get mixed up in their problems."[81] These authors hint at a role reversal that generates significant self-doubt in the analyst. As Balint notes, the almost telepathic quality of these particular clients makes the analyst feel "as if the patient could see inside him."[82] Thus, the borderline patient, not the therapist, sees inside the person across the room, demonstrating intuitive ease and interpretive skill.

Some therapists have had additional reasons to doubt themselves. In a controversial 1989 article on BPD and patient-therapist sex, psychiatrist Thomas Gutheil claimed that borderline patients "possess the ability, as it were, to seduce, provoke, or invite therapists into boundary violations of their own in the countertransference."[83] Less inflammatory but on the same point, Harold F. Searles describes a dynamic in which the borderline woman reveals her symptoms "in a basically coquettish, seductive manner, while the enthralled therapist struggles to match the priceless material with brilliantly penetrating interpretations." Seduced and guilt-ridden, Searles writes, "one's ego functioning undergoes a pervasive de-differentiation: one loses the ability deeply to distinguish between one's self and the patient, between the whole realms of fantasy and reality."[84] Complaining of ego diffusion, depersonalization, and episodic breaks with reality, it is the therapist who displays classic symptoms of BPD![85]

By determining that it is in the nature of the illness to cause such problems for clinicians, the "fact" of BPD secures the boundary between a pathologized patient and expert professional, redirecting psychic weakness and moral judgment from the therapist back to the client. For example, in a 1982 article, Dr. David Hellerstein describes the borderline patient as able to "glitter and strike like a cobra," an image of attractive allure followed by deadly violence. But from which direction does the violence come? Hellerstein goes on to say that no matter how knowledgeable the therapist is about BPD, theories "give little protection; your knowledge entitles you to no mercy. People like this bring you close to murder."[86] Protective care has shifted from the clinician's duty toward a client to the clinician's need in the face of a dangerous client, while the therapist expresses his own retaliatory rage toward the woman in treatment. Who, in this scenario, is exhibiting the symptom of "inappropriate" anger?

"Was I crazy or right?"

The very contradictory character of BPD, its ability to "present" as normal and even alluring and its subsequent ability to blur boundaries between client and clinician, suggests a third "borderland," the gray area between what we might call mental health and illness, or between sane and "mad." Hospitalized at age 18 and held there until she was almost 20, Susanna Kaysen knew that she lived somewhere in between accurate perceptions of reality and "madness." Yet she also sees her state of "contrariety," her refusal to live according to the plans laid out for her, as a healthy response to the societal demands made on girls and women in 1967. During and after hospitalization, she wondered, "Was I crazy or right?" Given the pervasive sexism and cultural narrowness of her environment, Kaysen inquires, "What would have been an appropriate level of intensity for my anger at being shut out of life?"[87]

Acknowledging some degree of mental illness, Kaysen adds that her kernel of madness contained clarity about the world she inhabited, one in which despair and desolation made sense. In all seven memoirs, the narrator sees that in some way her "mental illness" overlapped with an acute reading of her immediate environment and the broader world. In a sardonic summary, Kaysen notes, "Every window on Alcatraz has a view of San Francisco."[88] Yet rather than reward patients for such positive "insights," in the hands of experts the slippery line between illness and health becomes a part of the illness itself.

In their 2004 guide to living with BPD called *Sometimes I Act Crazy*, Jerold Kreisman and Hal Straus explain that BPD is "as chameleon like as the people who inhabit it," imitating not only "other illnesses" but also health and wellness.[89] The authors forewarn unsuspecting readers that "the borderline's attractive qualities are typically evident, sometimes even striking," urging the fatally attracted to beware the underlying pathology. Kreisman and Straus call special attention to the anger of "borderlines," asserting that what makes it distinctly borderline "is its concealment and unpredictability."[90] By this definition, the signature "borderline rage" on the surface looks no different than the rage of every woman—often concealed, suppressed, turned inward, or episodic. BPD masquerading as health muddles the distinction between mental illness and health, between the freakish mad woman and the benign if somewhat irritable woman of good sense.

In *Siren's Dance: My Marriage to a Borderline*, psychiatrist Anthony Walker recounts a cautionary tale about this very confusion. As a fourth-year medical student he met a 22-year-old woman who was admitted to the ER for overdosing on antidepressants. Despite being only hours removed from possible death, Michelle dazzles him. "Her smile was her allure. I was instantly seduced by it," writes Walker. The hospital's chief of psychiatry warns Walker against his involvement with Michelle, not as a breach of medical ethics but because "borderlines can be charming and manipulative" and have an unquenchable need that "will suck you dry and destroy your spirit." The smitten Walker ignores the advice, thinking "Surely this was not the face of mental illness." But it was, and worse. Before long, "the face of mental illness" showed up in the doctor's own mirror. Walker proceeds to tell a story of a miserable two-year marriage in which Michelle's illness dragged them down so far that he wondered, finally, if it had come to "my being her, assuming her personality."[91]

Other self-help books and illness narratives echo this notion of contagion, hinting at the "borderline's" ability to infect healthy loved ones who try to help. This creates a messy picture, one that blurs relations of power as well as conditions of illness. Though *Siren's Dance* reads as a tale of woe, upon their final parting Walker romantically recalls "the day I met her, and how even with the tubes and intravenous lines, she had seduced me." By specializing in psychiatry and treating adolescent BPD patients, Walker regains the authority of medicine. He now writes as an expert, presenting his book as a teaching device (recommending the movie *Fatal Attraction* as well), which he hopes "can titillate even as it teaches."[92]

Conclusion

The wide range of emotional experience and behavioral patterns currently characterized as "borderline" point to the vague and dubious nature of the diagnosis as a distinct "disease entity."[93] The symptoms of BPD are real and serious. But these same symptoms also resemble the sometimes weak egos, angry unpredictable reactivity, chaotic lives, and difficulty maintaining intimate relationships that many individuals experience at times, regardless of where people fall on a spectrum of illness to health. By creating "the borderline" first as a thing, U.S. medical and popular culture turned a metaphor into a monstrous illness so repellent it only makes sense to wash our hands of it. Further, personifying an illness as an evil seductress disguised by charming allure and false normality turned the victims of illness into villains, all the while concealing murkiness in medical classification, in boundaries between client and therapist, and in the very understandings of medically determined mental illness, whether it is attributed to biochemical malfunction, inherited vulnerability, or a set of enumerated traits.

"Borderline" might better be reclaimed from its reified status as person or thing and used as a conscious metaphor of space. The medical entity called borderline personality disorder works at a number of cultural levels. It serves as a space of ambiguity that strengthens the myth of medically distinct mental illnesses that are recognizable by enumerated symptoms. It also mystifies the trouble therapists who cross ethical lines with clients encounter in the process of countertransference. Trained to maintain a professional distance, they shift responsibility for ethical missteps or violations to the "borderline" in the room. The discourse around borderline pathology also casts the line, if indeed there is a "line," between mental health and illness as hard and fast rather than as a hazy border between sanity and madness.

BPD works to create a false intelligibility around psychic experience and psy professional expertise, while women labeled with BPD struggle to make their own pain intelligible to the very people from whom they seek help. Trying to convey the extraordinary difficulty she has navigating her daily life, Njamile Zakiya states simply, "What a little thing is to you, isn't necessarily a little thing to me."[94] Thus the diagnosis raises far more questions than it answers. To pose just three: How do we understand the interplay between the corporeal body and social environment in producing mental suffering? How do we collectively work to prevent, ameliorate, or heal severe emotional pain, especially when it is disabling and persistent over time? How do we turn harmful gender bias into salutary gender insights?

The answer does not lie in a singular critique of disability—whether physical, cognitive, or emotional—as socially constructed within a medical paradigm. Anna Mollow and Elizabeth Donaldson's work on disability and mental illness constructively critiques the impairment-disability model that lies at the foundation of a politicized study of disability. The first generation of disability studies offers the critical insight that if impairments are physical losses of some kind, such as vision or mobility, disability is produced only when a society constructs barriers to movement, access, or services that turn impairment into a disabling condition. Mollow and Donaldson, through readings of memoir and fiction, respectively, argue for the need for attention to the "phenomenological aspects of impairment."[95] Donaldson writes that when we allow for the corporeality of mental illness, "the boundary between impairment and disability becomes harder to maintain."[96] Both also believe that the anti-psychiatry movement's view of mental illness as a "myth" must be qualified. Donaldson critiques feminist literary critics who romanticize madness as a form of resistance to gender subordination, contending instead that madness offers little possibility for effective rebellion.[97] Mollow argues against a view of mental illness as a form of social control, suggesting that for black women "lack of access to health care, rather than involuntary administration of it" may be the most potent political issue.[98]

In this vein, the narratives of women diagnosed with BPD call for attention to suffering as a condition of mental illness. Their lived experience also calls into question the uncritical use of metaphorical borders and boundaries by feminist scholars. The tendency to figure borderlines and boundaries as frontiers of opportunity where, released from confining spaces and identities, women are free to explore relationships unencumbered by constricting categories and conventions can be misleading and romanticized. One person's meaningful metaphor can indeed be another person's burden.

Narratives of women living under the sign of BPD persist in trying to convey an extreme anguish that is incomprehensible to people who have not experienced it. They describe an intensity of emotion, an inability to predict or control feelings, an intolerable terror, and a wish for death in the absence of healing relief. This is not a safely bounded existence. The inability to self-soothe, to find emotional equilibrium, to trust one's feelings or believe that anyone else's love or concern could be lasting and genuine speaks to a tortuous absence of an affirmative sense of self or identity. After critiquing psychiatric, academic, or popular discourses of identity and the authentic self, at the end of the day it is nice to feel like you have one—that something about you, or me, is whole and holds together.

Women diagnosed with BPD tell a story that is ultimately about desiring boundaries that create a feeling of safety, internal cohesion, and a trust in one's self that makes trust and interconnectedness with others possible. The historical record tells a story of highly suspect thinking and mistreatment in the face of those desires.

Notes

I would like to thank my colleagues David Herzberg and Michael Rembis for their helpful readings of earlier versions of this essay.

1. This essay was originally written for and presented at the 2005 Berkshire Conference on the History of Women. The conference theme was "Sin Fronteras/Without Borders."

2. For her groundbreaking discussions of "borderlands," see Gloria Anzaldua, *Borderlands/La Frontera: The New Mestiza* (San Francisco: Spinsters/Aunt Lute, 1987). For other work that explores the idea or ideal of borders, bridges, and interstices, see Cherrie Moraga and Gloria Anzaldua, eds., *This Bridge Called My Back: Writings by Radical Women of Color* (Watertown, Mass: Persephone Press, 1981); and other titles in the field of borderland studies in history and geography.

3. For a critique of this tendency, see Brad Epps, "The Fetish of Fluidity," in *Homosexuality and Psychoanalysis*, edited by Tim Dean and Christopher Lane (Chicago: University of Chicago Press, 2001), 412–431.

4. *Diagnostic and Statistical Manual of Mental Disorders III* (Washington, D.C.: American Psychiatric Association, 1980).

5. Marsha Linehan, *Cognitive-Behavioral Treatment of Borderline Personality Disorder* (New York: Guilford Press, 1993), 3; Janice M. Cauwels, *Imbroglio: Rising to the Challenges of Borderline Personality Disorder* (New York: W. W. Norton, 1992), 16.

6. Dana Becker, *Through the Looking Glass: Women and Borderline Personality Disorder* (Boulder, Colo.: Westview Press, 1997), xxii. Becker cites numerous studies of gendered diagnoses, finding that women make up 70 to 77 percent of those diagnosed with BPD.

7. Ricardo Castaneda and Hugo Franco, "Sex and Ethnic Distribution of Borderline Personality Disorder in an Inpatient Sample," *American Journal of Psychiatry* 142 (October 1985): 1202–1203; B. Kathleen Jordan, William E. Schlenger, Juesta M. Caddell, and John A. Fairbank, "Etiological Factors in a Sample of Convicted Women Felons in North Carolina," in *Role of Sexual Abuse in the Etiology of Borderline Personality Disorder*, edited by Mary C. Zanarini (Washington, D.C.: American Psychiatric Press, 1997), 45–69.

8. Elizabeth Lunbeck, *The Psychiatric Persuasion: Knowledge, Gender, and Power in Modern America* (Princeton, N.J.: Princeton University Press, 1994), 226.

9. On similarities between hysteria and BPD, see Mary Ann Jimenez, "Gender and Psychiatry: Psychiatric Conceptions of Mental Disorders in Women," *Affilia* 12 (July 1997): 163.

10. For a feminist critique of BPD, see Becker, *Through the Looking Glass*; and Janet Wirth-Cauchon, *Women and Borderline Personality Disorder: Symptoms and Stories* (New Brunswick, N.J.: Rutgers University Press, 2001). For a general feminist critique of mental illness, including BPD, see J. Ussher, *Women's Madness: Misogyny or Mental Illness?* (Amherst: University of Massachusetts Press, 1992). On gender bias in diagnosing BPD, see D. Becker and S. Lamb, "Sex Bias in the Diagnosis of Borderline Personality Disorder and Post-traumatic Stress Disorder," *Professional Psychology: Research Practice* 25, no. 1 (1994): 55–61.

11. Emily Martin, *Bipolar Expeditions: Mania and Depression in American Culture* (Princeton, N.J.: Princeton University Press, 2007), 10.

12. Janet Wirth-Cauchon sees the diagnosis as a "rhetorically accomplished" fictional coherence in the face of "incomprehensible stories or resistant actions in therapy." See Wirth-Cauchon, *Women and Borderline Personality Disorder*, 20.

13. See, for example, Phyllis Chesler, *Women and Madness* (New York: Doubleday, 1972); and Elaine Showalter, *The Female Malady: Women, Madness, and English Culture, 1890–1980* (New York: Penguin, 1887).

14. Adolph Stern, "Psychoanalytic Investigation of and Therapy in the Border Line Group of Neuroses," (1938) in *Essential Papers on Borderline Disorders: One Hundred Years at the Border*, edited by Michael H. Stone (New York: New York University Press, 1986), 54–73.

15. Schizophrenia has also been a long-standing catchall diagnosis. The science behind it, its interpretation, and its assigned demographic has changed significantly over the past century, especially in its shift from a "white" to a "black" disease. See Jonathan M. Metzl, *The Protest Psychosis: How Schizophrenia Became a Black Disease* (Boston: Beacon Press, 2009).

16. Helene Deutsch, "Some Forms of Emotional Disturbance and Their Relationship to Schizophrenia," (1942) in *Essential Papers on Borderline Disorders: One Hundred Years at the Border*, edited by Michael H. Stone (New York: New York University Press, 1986), 86.

17. Melitta Schmideburg quoted in Theodore Millon, *Disorders of Personality: DSM-III, Axis II* (New York: John Wiley and Sons, 1981), 341. See also Melitta Schmideburg, "The Treatment of Psychopaths and Borderline Patients," (1947) in *Essential Papers on Borderline Disorders: One Hundred Years at the Border*, edited by Michael H. Stone (New York: New York University Press, 1986), 92–118.

18. On the history of the borderline concept, see Reuben Fine, "Introduction" and W. W. Meissner, "Theoretical Perspectives," in *Current and Historical Perspectives on the Borderline Patient*, edited by Reuben Fine (New York: Brunnel/Mazel, 1989), 1–15 and 161–197, respectively; Theodore Millon, "The Borderline Construct: Introductory Notes on Its History, Theory, and Empirical Grounding," in *Borderline Personality Disorder: Clinical and Empirical Perspectives*, edited by John F. Clarkin, Elsa Marziali, and Heather Monroe-Blum (New York: Guilford Press, 1992), 3–23; Stone, introductions to Parts I–IV, in *Essential Papers*, 1–13, 45–53, 149–158, 411–432, respectively.

19. David Riesman, *The Lonely Crowd: A Study of Changing American Character* (New Haven, Conn.: Yale University Press, 1950); and Christopher Lasch, *The Culture of Narcissism: American Life in an Age of Diminishing Expectations* (New York: Norton, 1979). On the new modal personality, see Elizabeth Lunbeck, "Borderline Histories: Psychoanalysis Inside and Out," *Science and Text* 19, no. 1 (2006): 151–173.

20. Lunbeck, "Borderline Histories," 152. See also Elizabeth Lunbeck, "Identity and the Real Self in Postwar American Psychiatry," *Harvard Review of Psychiatry* 8, no. 6 (2000): 318–322.

21. See Ellen Herman, *The Romance of American Psychology: Political Culture in the Age of Experts* (Berkeley: University of California Press, 1995).

22. On the history of the DSM, see Herb Kutching and Stuart A. Kirk, *Making Us Crazy: DSM: The Psychiatric Bible and the Creation of Mental Disorders* (New York: Free Press, 1997); Rick Mayes and Allan V. Horwitz, "DSM-III and the Revolution in the Classification of Mental Illness," *Journal of the History of the Behavioral Sciences* 41 (Summer 2005): 249–267; and Alix Spiegel, "The Dictionary of Disorder: How One Man Revolutionized Psychiatry," *New Yorker*, January 3, 2005, 56–63.

23. David Herzberg, *Happy Pills* (Baltimore, Md.: Johns Hopkins University Press, 2009).

24. Mayes and Horwitz, "DSM-III and the Revolution in the Classification of Mental Illness," 254.

25. Susanna Kaysen, *Girl, Interrupted* (New York: Vintage Books, 1993), 159; and Cauwels, *Imbroglio*, 114.

26. Becker, *Through the Looking Glass*, 39.

27. Michael H. Stone, *Abnormalities of Personality: Within and Beyond the Realm of Treatment* (New York: W. W. Norton, 1993), 215–257.

28. Randy A. Sansone and Michael W. Widerman, "Borderline Personality Symptomology, Casual Sexual Relationships, and Promiscuity," *Psychiatry* 6, no. 3 (2009): 36. For a critique of BPD as a diagnosis of sexual norm violations, see Maire Kushner, "Sexuality in Borderline Personality Disorder: Gender and Culture Uncovered," 2011, unpublished paper in author's possession. See also Jimenez, "Gender and Psychiatry," 154–175.

29. Jimenez, "Gender and Psychiatry," 162–164.

30. Kaysen, *Girl, Interrupted*, 158.

31. Mary Jo Buhle, *Feminism and Its Discontents: A Century of Struggle with Psychoanalysis* (Cambridge: Harvard University Press, 1998), 280–317.

32. Jimenez, "Gender and Psychiatry," 163–164.

33. B. Koekkoek, B. Van Meijel, and G. Hutschemaekers, "'Difficult Patients' in Mental Health Care: A Review," *Psychiatric Services* 57 (June 2006): 797, my italics.

34. Hagop Akiskal, "Demystifying Borderline Personality: Critique of the Concept and Unorthodox Reflections on Its Natural Kinship with Bipolar Spectrum," *Acta Psychiatrica Scandinavica* 110 (December 2004): 401–407.

35. Stern, "Psychoanalytic Investigation of and Therapy in the Border Line Group of Neuroses," 57; and Cauwels, *Imbroglio*, 197.

36. Judith Herman, *Trauma and Recovery* (New York: Basic Books, 1992), 123.

37. H. S. Akiskal, S. E. Chen, G. C. Davis, V. R. Puzantian, M. Kashgarian, and J. M. Bolinger, "Borderline: An Adjective in Search of a Noun," in *Essential Papers on Borderline Disorders: One Hundred Years at the Border*, edited by Michael H. Stone (New York: New York University Press, 1986), 549–568.

38. Paul T. Mason and Randi Kreger agree "that the term 'person with BPD' is less stigmatizing" but decide that to avoid being "overly verbose, we will use 'borderline' or 'BP' instead." Mason and Kreger, *Stop Walking on Eggshells: Taking Your Life Back When Someone You Care about Has Borderline Personality Disorder* (Oakland, CA: New Harbinger Publications, 1998), 23.

39. Cauwels, *Imbroglio*, 16.

40. Merri Lisa Johnson, *Girl In Need of a Tourniquet: Memoir of a Borderline Personality* (Berkeley: Seal Press, 2010), 138.

41. Deutsch, "Some Forms of Emotional Disturbance and Their Relationship to Schizophrenia," 77; and John G. Gunderson and Margaret T. Singer, "Defining Borderline Patients: An Overview," in *Essential Papers on Borderline Disorders: One Hundred Years at the Border*, edited by Michael H. Stone (New York: New York University Press, 1986), 460, 471.

42. On "apparent competence" in adulthood, see Linehan, *Cognitive-Behavioral Treatment of Borderline Personality Disorder*, 80–84.

43. Johnson, *Girl In Need of a Tourniquet*, 197.

44. Interview with Thomas McGlashan, in Cauwels, *Imbroglio*, 30–31.

45. Kaysen, *Girl Interrupted*; Johnson, *Girl in Need of a Tourniquet*; Stacy Pershall, *Loud in the House of Myself: Memoir of a Strange Girl* (New York: W. W. Norton, 2011); Meri R. Kennedy, *My Enemy, Myself: Personal Journey through Healing Childhood Sexual Abuse and Borderline Personality Disorder* (Baltimore, Md.: Publish America, 2006); Rachel Reiland, *Get Me Out of Here: My Recovery from Borderline Personality Disorder* (Center City, Minn.: Hazelden, 2004); Kiera Van Gelder, *The Buddha and the Borderline: My Recovery from Borderline Personality Disorder through Dialectical Behavior Therapy, Buddhism and Online Dating* (Oakland, Calif.: New Harbinger Publications, 2010); Njemile Zakiya, *A Peek inside the Goo: Depression and the Borderline Personality* (New York: Asabi Publishing, 2006).

46. On illness narratives, see Arthur Kleinman, *The Illness Narratives: Suffering, Healing, and the Human Condition* (Boston: Basic Books, 1988); and Arthur W. Frank, *The Wounded Storyteller: Body, Illness, and Ethics* (Chicago: University of Chicago Press, 1995).

47. Van Gelder, *The Buddha and the Borderline*, 50.

48. Kennedy, *My Enemy, Myself,* 59.

49. Reiland, *Get Me Out of Here,* 351, 286.

50. Kennedy, *My Enemy, Myself,* 72.

51. Pershall, *Loud in the House of Myself,* 81.

52. Zakiya, *A Peek inside the Goo,* 38.

53. Reiland, *Get Me Out of Here,* 237.

54. Johnson, *Girl in Need of a Tourniquet,* 123.

55. Zakiya, *A Peek inside the Goo,* 33.

56. Pershall, *Loud in the House of Myself,* 135.

57. Kaysen, *Girl, Interrupted,* 157.

58. Ibid., 153.

59. Pershall, *Loud in the House of Myself,* 78.

60. Zakiya, *A Peek inside the Goo,* 55.

61. Kaysen, *Girl, Interrupted,* 36–38.

62. Reiland, *Get Me Out of Here,* 54.

63. Pershall, *Loud in the House of Myself,* 8, 83.

64. Van Gelder, *The Buddha and the Borderline,* 150–178.

65. Tressa Sanders, "A Note from the Publisher," in Zakiya, *A Peek inside the Goo,* n.p.

66. Reiland, *Get Me Out of Here,* 185; Kaysen, *Girl, Interrupted,* 150, 152.

67. Linehan, *Cognitive-Behavioral Treatment of Borderline Personality Disorder,* 16–18, 20.

68. For information about DPT, see Linehan, *Skills Training Manual for Treating Borderline Personality Disorder* (New York: The Guilford Press, 1993). Every worksheet from the standard DBT workbook has "From Skills Training Manual for Treating Borderline Personality Disorder" printed on the bottom of the page. However, any reading of the "skills" for regulating emotion, tolerating distress, improving personal relationships, and being "mindful" would seem to offer good practices for any person who encounters any degree of emotional difficulty.

69. I am indebted to Elizabeth Lunbeck's insight that the category "borderline" can be most usefully conceived as "a conceptual space in which both novel and enduring symptoms and behaviors have been subjected to examination." Lunbeck, "Borderline Histories," 164. See also Wirth-Cauchon, *Women and Borderline Personality Disorder,* 1–36.

70. A recent report to Congress on borderline personality disorder offered a remarkable list of comorbid diagnoses that are commonly assigned to individuals with BPD: "bipolar disorder (10–20 percent), major depressive disorder (41–83 percent), substance misuse (64–66 percent), panic disorders (31–48 percent), obsessive-compulsive disorder (16–25 percent), social phobia (23–47 percent), and eating disorders (29–53 percent)." Co-occurring personality disorders were also common with BPD, including "avoidant (43–47 percent), dependent (16–51 percent), and paranoid personality disorders (14–30 percent)." U.S. Department of Health and Human Services, Substance Abuse and Mental Health Services Administration, *Report to Congress on Borderline Personality Disorder,* HHS Publication SMA-11-4644 (Washington, D.C.: U.S. Department of Health and Human Services, 2011), 16–17.

71. See Mary C. Zanirini et al., "Severity of Reported Childhood Sexual Abuse and Its Relationship to Severity of Borderline Psychopathology and Psychosocial Impair-

ment among Borderline Inpatients," *Journal of Nervous and Mental Disease* 100 (June 2002): 381–383.

72. Judith Herman and Bessel van der Kolk, "Traumatic Antecedents of Borderline Personality Disorder," in *Psychological Trauma*, edited by Bessel van der Kolk (Washington, D.C.: American Psychiatric Press, 1987), 118.

73. Cauwels, *Imbroglio*, 85. On the relationship between BPD and PTSD, see J. L. Herman, J. C. Perry, and B. A. van der Kolk, "Childhood Trauma in Borderline Personality Disorder," *American Journal of Psychiatry* 146 (April 1989): 490–495; and Becker, *Through the Looking Glass*, 70–77. The relationship between BPD and sexual history and behavior is deserving of its own full-length feminist analysis.

74. Robert P. Knight, "Borderline States," in *Essential Papers on Borderline Disorders: One Hundred Years at the Border*, edited by Michael H. Stone (New York: New York University Press, 1986), 159–173, quote on 165.

75. Gunderson and Singer, "Defining Borderline Patients," 469–470, my italics.

76. Elizabeth Lunbeck, *The Psychiatric Persuasion: Knowledge, Gender, and Power in Modern America* (Princeton, N.J.: Princeton University Press, 1994), 185–208.

77. Lunbeck, "Borderline Histories," 168.

78. On the social danger of borderline intelligence, see Susan K. Cahn, *Sexual Reckonings: Southern Girls in a Troubling Age* (Cambridge: Harvard University Press, 2007), 166–168.

79. See Becker, *Through the Looking Glass*, 152, and Akiskal et al., "Borderline," 566, on the misuse of the term to cover diagnostic imprecision.

80. Michael Balint, "The Basic Fault," in *Essential Papers on Borderline Disorders: One Hundred Years at the Border*, edited by Michael H. Stone (New York: New York University Press, 1986), 385–409, quote on 392.

81. Cauwels, *Imbroglio*, 282.

82. Balint, "The Basic Fault," 392.

83. Thomas Gutheil, "Borderline Personality Disorder, Boundary Violations, and Patient-Therapist Sex: Medicolegal Pitfalls," *American Journal of Psychiatry*, 146 (May 1989), 597–602. For a scathing critique of Gutheil, see Herb Kutchins and Stuart A. Kirk, *Making Us Crazy: DSM: The Psychiatric Bible and the Creation of Mental Disorders* (New York: Free Press, 1997), 176–199.

84. Harold F. Searles, "The Countertransference with the Borderline Patient," in Stone, *Essential Papers on Borderline Disorders: One Hundred Years at the Border*, edited by Michael H. Stone (New York: New York University Press, 1986), 498–526, quotes on 512, 521.

85. Therapists report seeing colleagues with borderline patients respond with their own "disorganization, chronic fatigue, franticness, guilt, chronic eating, or increased drug and alcohol use," all classic symptoms of BPD. Amy Baker Dennis and Randy A. Sansone, "The Clinical Stages of Treatment for the Eating Disorder Patient with Borderline Personality Disorder," in *Psychodynamic Treatment of Anorexia Nervosa and Bulimia*, edited by Craig Johnson (New York: The Guilford Press, 1991), 142.

86. David Hellerstein, "Border Lines," *Esquire*, November 1982, 128, quoted in Cauwels, *Imbroglio*, 17.

87. Kaysen, *Girl Interrupted*, 132, 156.

88. Ibid., 6.

89. Jerold J. Kreisman and Hal Straus, *Sometimes I Act Crazy: Living with Borderline Personality Disorder* (Hoboken, N.J.: John Wiley and Sons, 2004), 10, 131.

90. Ibid., 51, 158.

91. Anthony Walker, *Siren's Dance: My Marriage to a Borderline–A Case Study* (Emmaus, Pa.: Rodale Press, 2003), 6, 13, 16, 109.

92. Ibid., 166, vii. In this ending, Anthony Walker regains not only narrative and medical control but sexual control; he has the power to titillate now, no longer the helpless victim of a sick seductress.

93. Akiskal and colleagues argue that the current BPD diagnosis maps "a large universe of chronically and seriously ill 'difficult' patients' who don't fit into existing categories of mood or personality disorders." "Borderline," 566.

94. Zakiya, *A Peek inside the Goo*, 38.

95. Anna Mollow, "'When *Black* Women Start Going on Prozac. . . .': The Politics of Race, Gender, and Emotional Distress in Meri Nana-Ama Danquah's *Willow Weep for Me*," in *The Disability Studies Reader*, 3rd ed., edited by Lennard J. Davis (New York: Routledge, 1997), 486.

96. Elizabeth J. Donaldson, "Revisiting the Corpus of the Madwoman: Further Notes toward a Feminist Disability Studies Theory of Mental Illness," in *Feminist Disability Studies*, edited by Kim Q. Hall (Bloomington: Indiana University Press, 2011), 105.

97. Donaldson, "Revisiting the Corpus of the Madwoman," 92–93.

98. Mollow, "'When *Black* Women Start Going on Prozac," 486.

PART FOUR

Citizenship and Belonging

What does it mean to be a disabled citizen? The essays in this section offer interdisciplinary examinations of status, power, and relationships among individuals, groups and broader societies.

1. How does the study of disability contribute to your understanding of citizenship and belonging?
2. How do these authors conceive of authority and power? How does this shape their interpretations of disability, citizenship, and belonging?
3. How have disabled people fought and struggled for their citizenship rights and for integration into the larger community? What lessons can you draw from this?
4. How does thinking about disability in connection with race, class, and gender change our understanding of citizenship and belonging, and of disability history? What new connections, insights, and questions does this raise for historians of disability?
5. Upon which theories and sources do these authors primarily draw? How has this influenced their work?

CHAPTER 14

The Paradox of Social Progress

The Deaf Cultural Community in France
and the Ideals of the Third Republic
at the Turn of the Twentieth Century

ANNE QUARTARARO

KEYWORDS: *Centuries*: nineteenth; *Geographical Areas*: Europe; *Sources*: manuscripts and archival materials; speeches; *Themes*: citizenship and belonging; culture; activism, law and policy

Although social activism within the French deaf cultural community increased during the last decades of the nineteenth century, it is paradoxical that the policies and values of the Third Republic, which focused on economic liberty and social progress, did not seem to transform the lives of deaf people in the way that deaf cultural leaders had hoped. Just as the French republic exhibited cultural and racial prejudice toward its colonial subjects[1] and denied civil liberties to women,[2] it often relegated deaf people to the margins of French society.

In this essay, I will investigate the historical context of the turn-of-the-twentieth-century impasse between liberal republicans and French deaf cultural activists who sought more economic and social progress for their community. First, I will consider why the Third Republic did not respond in significant ways to the social and economic concerns that emerged in the deaf cultural community. It is important to take a closer look at the political ideology of solidarism that many liberal republicans embraced in the late nineteenth century as a way to merge capitalist principles with social welfare activism.[3] The leadership of the Third Republic did not want significant social change, but they realized that they should accommodate requests for modest social improvements. Many deaf cultural leaders embraced solidarism as a reasonable expression of the opportunity the republic was offering to even its marginalized populations.

Liberal republicans equated economic opportunity with oralism,[4] the method of instructing deaf youth through the use of articulated speech. Oral language for deaf people under the Third Republic was supposed to represent the most effective way to "integrate" deaf people into a larger hearing society. However, the use of oral language and its connection to economic opportunity became a source of disagreement between the leaders of the Third Republic and the leaders of the deaf cultural community. Deaf leaders generally concluded that an exclusively oral education only made it more difficult for deaf people to secure good jobs in France's rapidly changing economy at the turn of the twentieth century.[5]

In the second part of the essay, I will turn to the strategies of deaf cultural activists who understood that social and economic gains for many deaf people were limited because of insufficient education and placement in low-paying jobs. Many deaf cultural leaders readily embraced the liberal economic ideas of self-reliance and individual responsibility the leaders of the Third Republic promoted. At the same time, they also recognized that the deaf population was not receiving a fair chance at employment that would allow them to move up the economic ladder. By 1900, these concerns were coming to a head; deaf cultural leaders felt that economic marginalization was keeping deaf people poorer and more uneducated than the rest of the French populace. The idea of solidarism seemed more futile to deaf cultural activists who wanted more change than the government was willing to deliver. They began to examine labor movement ideas such as syndicalism as a way to advance their own plan for economic development within the deaf community.[6]

This essay attempts to bridge the different but complementary fields of deaf history, French history, and disability history. As a rule, historians choose one area of study, perhaps because our areas of expertise are well defined and we are reluctant to go too far afield. In French history, the study of the deaf cultural community and other marginalized groups has grown over the last decade and has focused more directly on how disabled populations have developed their own cultural identity despite many political and socioeconomic obstacles.[7] In this essay, I argue that that despite the social initiatives that were directed at the poor and marginalized populations of France, the Third Republic was unable and sometimes unwilling to promote economic and social progress for its deaf minority population.

The Third Republic's Social and Economic Plans for the Lower Class

The French Third Republic was created in the wake of the Franco-Prussian War of 1870–1871 as the model of government that divided the French the least.[8] By the late 1870s, a moderate group of republican leaders had emerged with a social and political agenda for France that they felt would set the country on a path toward social improvement and greater national integration.[9] Republicans consciously sought to mold citizens to adopt the civic values of dedication to the nation, decency, discipline, and self-improvement, and they initiated a variety of social programs to shape this new cultural outlook for France in a modern, industrial age.

One of the prominent examples of this social and cultural program was the educational reforms spearheaded by the republican leader Jules Ferry. During the 1880s, Ferry firmly established the state's role in universal, free, secular education for the nation's youth (boys and girls). Although Ferry did not equalize opportunity among different classes (there were specific educational tracks),[10] he offered the promise of more educational advancement to lower-class children, who were able to attend state-supported public elementary schools for free under the new policies.

In 1880, during the same period when republican leaders debated and then finally enacted education reforms, they also officially endorsed a teaching pedagogy known as oralism for the education of deaf youth. Oralism, which was based on the concept that articulated speech was superior to the signed language of deaf people, was not a new approach to deaf schooling. Throughout the nineteenth century it had slowly gained supporters, especially among medical doctors, government officials, and hearing educators of deaf youth.[11] French republicans embraced oralism because of the cultural effect it might produce; they believed that if spoken language could be used in the education of deaf children, then the larger problems of the social and economic integration of deaf people into French society might diminish. Oralism dovetailed with the overall plans of Third Republic leaders to "modernize" lower-class education.[12]

In addition to their interest in education, moderate republicans had long associated their political values with the idea of national assistance for vulnerable and poor populations. Beginning in the 1830s and 1840s, they supported the concept of mutualism, especially for the lower classes.[13] Mutualism—a variety of insurance funds against illness or unemployment—became one way for both republicans and royalists to encourage the idea of self-help among the lower class. These voluntary mutual benefit associations were supposed to provide a cushion for poor and marginalized people against catastrophic life events, and political leaders saw them as vehicles for teaching members of the lower classes prudence and self-discipline.[14] Members of the deaf community willingly participated in the mutualist movement during the 1840s and 1850s and were dedicated to helping those who had fallen on hard times.[15] As the concept mutualism began to take root, the idea of solidarism also developed in the mid-nineteenth century, influenced by the example of Masonic lodges. In its earliest form, solidarism focused on "human solidarity" to emphasize that each person was responsible for other members of French society.[16] The concepts of mutualism and solidarism became key elements of how republican leaders in the late nineteenth century viewed their mission to improve French society.

During the 1890s, the radical republicans, a group of left-leaning politicians, became more interested in social programs that would benefit the working classes and the poor. Their goal was to enact a national system of public assistance for the lower classes, as had been the agenda of the first revolution of 1789. Many radical republicans wanted to find a way to use the power of the state to improve the condition of the most vulnerable in French society. In 1893, they secured the necessary votes in the French Parliament to pass a health care plan that required all towns in France to establish a formal association with a nearby urban hospital. Local leaders would identify indigent sick men and women who could receive free hospital care. The national government subsidized up to 80 percent of the cost of treating indigent people in local hospitals.[17] A few years later, in 1898, the republican government passed a workplace accident insurance law, and in 1910, it adopted a provision for a national pension plan.[18]

Radical republicans became more active in social issues in the last decade of the nineteenth century for a number of reasons. They saw themselves in an ongoing contest with the Catholic Church over who would perform the humanitarian actions that would improve French society. Up to the turn of the twentieth century, the preponderance of aid to poor people had very little to do with national government. The Catholic Church had long stressed charitable acts to benefit indigent people, especially in the countryside. But the radical republicans wanted to change this perception and win support among the French public for a secular and state-directed plan to reduce poverty.[19] One of the serious concerns for republican leaders in the last decades of the nineteenth century was the growing problem of homeless persons, known at the time as "vagabonds." Discussion about this group was a significant part of the national discourse; practically every year, officials convened national meetings on vagrants and beggars to try to find a solution for the problem.[20] To address the problems of homelessness and want, the republic's leaders in 1905 restructured the nation's public assistance offices. In the new structure, financial support flowed only to those who were physically unable to work each day.[21] Homelessness that was attributable to an economic crisis (such as crop failure or the loss of a job) was not enough to qualify for assistance from the *bureaux de bienfaisance*. However, even though hearing society generally viewed deaf people as part of the "deserving poor," deaf cultural leaders in the late nineteenth century insisted that their community should be seen as productive and self-sufficient.[22]

The Meaning of Solidarism for Social Progress

In this social climate, radical republicans such as Léon Bourgeois[23] who believed in solidarist ideals attempted to address important social problems with a new vision of economic progress that would smooth the harsher edges of a capitalist society. During the 1890s, radical republicans were seen as a moderate-to-left-leaning group that favored measured social change and anti-clericalism. Their main supporters had come from the lower class; they were small businessmen, craftsmen, and small farmers. But the political landscape in France was changing, and radical republicans were concerned about the rise of socialists on the political left who were building their power base from the growing industrial working class.

The social theory of solidarism was best explained by Léon Bourgeois at the turn of the twentieth century through his writings and public lectures. It encouraged French citizens to show profound respect for human liberty and the value of that liberty for the well-being of the entire nation. Bourgeois wrote, "Any social or political arrangement that will try to determine the limits of men's liberties will be contrary to the natural evolution of society. But these liberties are not independent forces from each other; men are not isolated beings, but rather associated ones."[24] Here we find the heart of Bourgeois' solidarist philosophy: while inherently free, men and women could not escape their essential ties with each other in a political and social community. The effect of solidarism was to make citizens more decent and moral and consequently to develop the morality of the nation itself.[25] Thus, by its nature, solidarism was socially inclusive and acknowledged that French society needed to provide assistance, when necessary, to its more vulnerable citizens.

Solidarists did not favor abrupt social change and saw mutualism as the best way forward. Mutualism depended on the choices of individual citizens in voluntary groups to make rational decisions about their lives. As a form of solidarist action, it became very popular at the turn of the twentieth century. In 1898, the French republic gave mutualist societies the same rights under the law as it had established for trade unions in 1884. They had the freedom to defend their economic interests but were not allowed to participate in overtly political activity. In a court of law, mutualist societies and trade unions both had the right to litigate their economic interests, but French law did not permit them to "own land or buildings beyond what was strictly necessary for their meetings, libraries and professional courses."[26] Through public forums such as national congresses and mutualist newspapers, participation in the movement became an accepted public activity for men and women, a way to demonstrate a kind of "public service" for the good of the republic. By one estimate, there were over 15,000 societies in France with about 3 million active mutualist members by 1910.[27] Mutualism definitely had a "feel-good" quality for wealthier French citizens who made donations to their favorite societies. But in reality, mutual aid societies paid out only small sums for pensions or insurance benefits to the average working person.[28]

Radical republicans did not count exclusively on the actions of these voluntary mutual societies. They introduced a national pension law in the Chamber of Deputies, which they called "an act of solidarity" with 10 million workers. However, it took nearly ten years for the law to pass both houses of Parliament (1910). Employers and workers entered a strange alliance in which each side fought the concept of a state-sponsored pension plan because it required mandatory contributions from both sides (unlike mutualist organizations, which were voluntary). Neither side had enough confidence it would produce a workable insurance program for old age.[29] The limits of solidarism were all too apparent.

Solidarism, Oralism, and the Institut départemental Baguer à Asnières

Like many political leaders before him, Léon Bourgeois viewed education as the most obvious route to economic and social progress for all social classes at the turn of the twentieth century. Bourgeois openly criticized those who "coldly" viewed impoverished children as someone else's problem.[30] When Bourgeois attended the dedication of new buildings at the Institut départemental Baguer à Asnières (in the Paris suburbs) in 1907, he connected the social opportunity available to deaf children to the ideals of a solidarist society.

The Asnières institute was a unique establishment that was created by the department of the Seine in 1894 for deaf youth (both boys and girls) and was placed under the jurisdiction of the Ministry of Public Instruction.[31] Other schools for deaf children run by the national government or other local schools (both lay and religious) had been under the supervision of the Interior Ministry since the late eighteenth century and had remained so even after the republican education reforms of the 1880s. The Asnières institute was directed by Gustave Baguer, who was determined to use the oral method that the national government had enthusiastically approved a decade earlier, after the Congress of Milan.[32] Educators and government officials alike saw the Asnières institute as a living laboratory that would confirm the benefits of speech and lip-reading for deaf children. Bourgeois' attendance at the dedication of the new buildings at Asnières was significant because he was a well-known supporter of public instruction as conceived by the republic. In addition, by attending the Asnières ceremony, he was endorsing the republic's standard of oral education for deaf children.

In his speech, Bourgeois associated the Asnières institute with the kind of social progress that solidarists had always embraced. He referred to the school's director, Gustave Baguer, as an innovator in deaf education because he connected the instruction of deaf children to the duty of the republic's public school teachers to carry out the mandate of universal education. Because Baguer had persisted with his goal of using oral speech as the cornerstone of the school's pedagogy, Bourgeois acclaimed him as "ingenious" and "admirably persistent."[33] Bourgeois pointed out that deaf children were not voluntarily isolated from the rest of society but had been intentionally kept apart from French society (presumably by hearing people) through no fault of their own. Bourgeois and other republican leaders viewed the Asnières institute as a key instrument in righting this social wrong because it sought to integrate deaf youth into a larger society.[34]

Bourgeois emphasized the moral values that students were absorbing at the institute in much the same way that a government minister of the early twentieth century would have stressed the moral lessons taught at a typical primary school.[35] He used the stories of two children from the Asnières institute who had performed individual acts of courage to illustrate how these "isolated" deaf children were just as morally capable of exceptional deeds as any other young person. One boy had saved a girl from accidental drowning in the Seine River and another young man had put out a fire at the school at some risk to his own life.[36] For Bourgeois, both anecdotes illustrated that the school's moral training program was achieving its desired goal. He asked the audience, "Isn't it true that they have learned social duty?"[37]

In his concluding remarks, Bourgeois reasoned why "backward" deaf children should be properly educated in French society, peppering his observations with the language of solidarism. The inferiority of deaf children was "involuntary," and the larger French community had a debt to pay that would finally end this inferiority. Deaf youth should not be kept in isolation from other people but instead should be given the opportunity to have an education just like any other French child. Bourgeois called for "assimilation" of deaf students in other schools in the republic so they would experience the same school discipline and pedagogical methods (oral instruction) as other children.[38] In sum, Bourgeois placed solidarism on the political side of mainstreaming deaf children into the public schools of the Third Republic.

The French Deaf Cultural Community and Solidarism

The discourse of solidarism gave the French deaf cultural community reason to believe that the radical republicans would come to their aid and create more economic opportunity for deaf individuals at the turn of the twentieth century. They did not, however, have much clout in numbers. The actual deaf community was small: some 25,000 to 30,000 people out of a total national population of 38 million in 1900.[39] Some of their early community activities had revolved around mutualism and the creation of the Société Centrale in the 1830s. The Société Centrale grew from the banquet movement begun in 1834 when three deaf teachers—Ferdinand Berthier, Alphonse Lenoir, and Claudius Forestier—organized a fraternal gathering of fifty-four deaf men in Paris to celebrate the birthday of Abbé de l'Epée, a beloved teacher of deaf youth in the late eighteenth century. This became an annual event, and the annual banquets became the basis of the Société Centrale. Eventually, Berthier requested permission from the Interior Ministry to formalize this group into a mutual aid society in 1838.[40] Those who joined the Société Centrale came from many walks of life; they were teachers, printers, graphic designers, artists, and day laborers. They were not always unified and even had a falling out in the 1840s, when some of them formed a competing mutual society. But despite the ups and downs of mutualist activity, there was a general consensus among the better-off in the deaf community that vulnerable deaf individuals deserved more economic help.[41]

The official focus on oral language after the 1880 Congress of Milan in schools for deaf youth was supposed to generate new economic opportunities, but by the turn of the century, certain deaf cultural leaders did not see the often-promised results. Unlike the solidarists who were enthusiastic about oralism, most French deaf cultural leaders looked on this pedagogy with caution and even with hostility. Deaf teachers had been excluded from teaching at schools for deaf youth after the 1880s (since they were deemed incapable of practicing the oralist pedagogy effectively), which further soured the cultural climate between radical republicans and deaf cultural activists.[42] In 1902, during the annual distribution of prizes at the Institut National de Jeunes Sourds de Paris, Professor Danjou, a hearing person, warned the students to "above all avoid socializing with older deaf individuals who would . . . engage you [in conversation] with sign language." Danjou thought that this kind of association would undo all the hard work of teaching them oral language. They might revert back to sign language and would no longer be able to speak or write properly.[43]

This professor's concern about deaf students' natural propensity to use signed language when they gathered socially with other deaf people does not seem exaggerated. Henri Gaillard (1866–1939), a deaf cultural activist in Paris at the turn of the century, had observed that although the pure oral method of instruction was used exclusively in 59 of 69 schools for deaf children, the reality was actually very different. He pointed out that all these schools actually relied on signed language *and* oral language (as per the official regulations). Offering up his own brand of criticism of the oral method, Gaillard argued that a minority of "oralists" had originally changed the law and that they were responsible for "subjugating the majority of teachers."[44] Gaillard contended that teachers of deaf children wanted to use sign language in the classroom but that the state had arbitrarily taken that regular option away from them. It is difficult to interpret Gaillard's reading of the history of the French deaf population as anything but indignant. In one direct jab at the republican state, he claimed that only 4,000 of 7,000 deaf children were receiving any primary schooling, a situation he called "humiliating for France."[45] There is no easy way to verify the numbers Gaillard cited, but his indictment of the Third Republic for social neglect of deaf children and hostility toward sign language—the natural language of deaf people—was all he really needed to convey to his readers.

Ever committed to the debate on educational quality and pedagogy, Gaillard wrote an extended commentary on the "failure of the oral method" that was eventually published in the American deaf community's paper, *The Silent Worker*, in 1910. He focused on a report written in 1907 by psychologist Alfred Binet and a medical doctor, Théodore Simon, who had collected information on the success of the oral method from graduates of deaf schools. Gaillard pointed out that it was difficult to track down these deaf former students, for "all the individuals of the working population lose themselves in the eddies of the Great City."[46] The two researchers concluded that "backward" and congenitally deaf children (especially those who had lost hearing before the age of one) should be spared "the fatigue and loss of time" of an educational method that "fails completely more than four-fifths of the time."[47] Gaillard used the example of the graduation exercises at the Asnières institute to illustrate the inherent problems with oralism. Students at the ceremony were asked specific questions, very slowly, but "usually the pupils [did] not comprehend. . . . After much effort and lost time, the method [was] often given up, seeing that the pupil [did] not understand[,] and the question [was] put in writing."[48] Gaillard, a former member of the Commission of Improvement at the Asnières institute, claimed that he had been "ousted" from his position because he wanted an independent examination of the pupils to determine whether or not they could benefit from the oral method.[49] Maybe Gaillard had been too assertive, or perhaps the director had not wanted to be reminded that the oral method was not as successful as authorities had always claimed.

Gaillard also concluded that the oral method was not very useful once the young person entered the workplace. The speech of institute graduates was often difficult for others to understand, and Gaillard pointed out that a deaf man would be reluctant to use spoken language "until after a considerable time in his new surroundings."[50] Gaillard completed his series in *The Silent Worker* with the predicable view that only the truly gifted students had a chance to succeed using the oral method. For the rest of deaf children, he wrote, "unhappily it is too well know that the mirage is deceitful and that we must come down from these ideal heights . . . to a more practicable ground of combination of methods."[51] It seems clear that Gaillard was attempting to convince the education ministry to come to terms with a pedagogy that over a span of thirty years had worked at best imperfectly. A generation of deaf students had been the subject of a failed experiment.

Economic Opportunity
and the French Deaf Population

The question of economic opportunity was invariably connected to the difficult debates over the quality and availability of schooling for deaf children at the turn of the twentieth century. If solidarists believed that education was the pathway to economic and social well-being, then deaf people had cause for concern with the solidarist program. No one in the French deaf cultural community thought the republic had done enough to provide deaf people with the same chance at advancement in the workplace as the hearing community. The combination of cultural stereotypes and a lack of schooling made it more difficult for deaf people to secure good jobs. For instance, Gaillard, who was a typesetter, a novelist, and a journalist, was forced to argue in the 1890s that deaf people were not lazy by nature; like other French people, they wanted to earn enough money to enjoy life.[52] That Gaillard had to defend the work ethic of deaf people suggests that certain negative views had been well ingrained for a period of time.

Just like all workers in the Third Republic at the end of the nineteenth century, deaf people were trying to make their way in a marketplace that did not always offer them security. The job market was full of uncertainty partly because of a series of recessions that affected workers from the late 1870s to 1908. Larger structural changes in the economy were also occurring in the late nineteenth century that affected some types of employment. As a whole, specialized craft work was declining in importance, and the French economy was shifting toward more white-collar trades and petit bourgeois service jobs.[53] For example, the growth of the number of employees in banks, insurance companies, and railroad services was a different direction in employment from the 1850s. In this shifting environment, unskilled and skilled workers, those engaged in manual labor or office work, were generally fearful about the loss of work or a reduction in their hours that could mean the difference between self-sufficiency and hardship. Even when the head of the household was fully employed, 35 percent of male-headed households were considered poor.[54] In 1907, a government study determined that unskilled or service workers "probably spent more than 80% of their yearly earnings on food and rent."[55] Workers who needed such a high percentage of their income for basic necessities knew that if the primary breadwinner became ill or lost his job the situation could quickly become dire for the entire family.

Changes in the structure of the labor market in the late nineteenth century affected deaf people perhaps in a more serious way than they did the general population. Deaf children had more problems attaining basic skills in reading, writing, and calculating even when they were enrolled in primary school. Gaillard referred to the situation many lower-class deaf people faced as "intellectual poverty."[56] Through no fault of their own, many deaf children had not received the kind of education that would be useful in the new job market.[57] Gaillard also believed that lower-class deaf people suffered from social discrimination, arguing that they were kept in "scornful isolation" in French society.[58] Although these handicaps made life more difficult for lower-class deaf people, Gaillard believed that many deaf people were successfully earning a modest livelihood. He reserved his greatest criticism for the so-called wealthy deaf who were not gainfully employed, who were supposedly "below average" in intelligence, and who lacked the right kind of social conscience about poorer deaf individuals who might need some help.[59] Gaillard was most sympathetic to the struggles of the lower class, and he wanted the affluent deaf to become more responsible about promoting the interests of the deaf community.[60]

At the turn of the century, Gaillard felt that two career paths were open to deaf people: manual labor and the so-called intellectual life. He saw the workplace for deaf people as divided into these two broad categories. For Gaillard, some men labored in workshops and others managed businesses and the intellectual life was inherently different from these other two pursuits. This view was likely derived from his own life experiences. As a young man, Gaillard began working as a typesetter/printer after he left the Institut National de Jeunes Sourds de Paris in the early 1880s and then became more of an independent businessman-printer when he took over the *Journal des Sourds-Muets* in 1894.[61] When he was not working in printing, he participated in the cultural life of the Parisian deaf community and helped organize a number of special conferences (for example, the International Congress on Education of the Deaf of 1900). The written word was an important part of Gaillard's adult life; he considered himself a writer of poetry, short stories, and even novels. Gaillard occupied a unique position in the French deaf cultural community; he could understand the life of the average working man but he was also captivated by the life of the mind. Perhaps he was reflecting on his personal experience when he wrote, "It is rare that those who have too much cerebral activity are good workers."[62]

Economic Discussions at the Paris International Congress of 1900

In 1900, Gaillard served as the general secretary of the International Congress on Education of the Deaf, which was held in Paris on the grounds of the Exposition Universelle. For many deaf cultural leaders, this congress was a frustrating experience because it confirmed the separation between two societies: the hearing and the deaf. Deaf cultural leaders were not allowed to participate fully in the development of the congress's agenda. At every turn, their proposals were rejected by hearing educators and medical doctors who already had their own ideas about what they wanted to discuss about deaf people's educational and social conditions without them present.[63] In the end, two congresses were convened simultaneously in August, one for hearing people and the other led by deaf people. The segregation between the two groups was a sad indication of the rift that had grown since the introduction of oralism in schools for deaf youth in the 1880s.[64]

If we consider the most important issues discussed at the conference, education and employment were by far the most debated and troublesome for members of the deaf cultural community. Many of the presenters revisited the debate about oral language versus a "mixed method" (signs and writing, with only a little spoken language). Others made a plea that schools for deaf children be placed under the jurisdiction of the Ministry of Public Instruction. These were very predicable views that deaf cultural leaders had been advocating for quite some time. Other discussions at the congress, however, demonstrated how deeply concerned members of the French deaf community were about the kinds of economic opportunities available to deaf people at the turn of the twentieth century.[65] French deaf cultural leaders delivered presentations about a variety of social and economic issues that were important to the community in 1900, including Henri Genis's discussion of a concept of a retirement home for elderly deaf individuals, Eugène Graff's paper on deaf artisans in workshops, and Gaillard's presentation about the kinds of careers and professions available to deaf people.

Henri Genis (1835–?), one of the older participants at the conference, was a Belgian by birth who had moved to Paris around 1860 to find better job prospects than were available in his native country. Although he had been an engraver in Brussels, Genis became a clerk at a law office in Paris, the kind of lower-class service job that became more prevalent by the end of the century.[66] At the 1900 congress, Genis used the ideals of solidarism to point out that it was the "obligation" of both young and old deaf people to discuss the "fate" of aged or ill deaf people who were marginalized in French society.[67] He painted a picture of elderly deaf men and women who had worked at poorly paid jobs their entire lives and were living in miserable conditions in old age, abandoned by society. Their disability had made them "pariahs" who went from one public health office (*bureau de bienfaisance*) to another looking for a place to find shelter and food. In his comment about disability, Genis referred to deafness as a "natural disability" that complicated the vulnerability of marginalized populations. In this "fight for life," Genis was certain that deaf people were more miserable than other destitute individuals because they could not easily make themselves understood among hearing people.

Invoking the ideals of the radical republicans, Genis declared, "We are all Solidarists . . . by the duties that mark our humanitarian feelings, and by the concern for the future, because none of us is certain about tomorrow."[68] He argued that it was the primary responsibility of the French republic to fund a retirement home that might accommodate some 500 deaf men and women, but he also argued that deaf mutual aid societies should collect money to support the institution.[69] Apparently even the relatively well-funded deaf association in Champagne had been unable to finance this kind of project, though it had been on the agenda for a number of years.[70]

Another deaf cultural activist, Eugène Graff (1862–1935), a skilled wood turner by trade, was looking to the French government to provide economic opportunities for young deaf people. Graff had become a skilled sculptor upon leaving the deaf school in Nancy in 1879. When he arrived in Paris in 1882, he joined the workshops of the firm Joveneau.[71] Graff regretted that so many deaf workers who wanted jobs in skilled crafts seemed to be locked out of the workshops. Either the employer was reluctant to hire a deaf person because of communication problems (it was necessary to use paper and pencil to really understand each other) or the workshop's master craftsman recruited deaf workers simply to exploit them. Graff claimed that many deaf craftsmen were forced to work for unscrupulous employers because the "better" enterprises would not hire them. Ironically, deaf workers would then be criticized for lowering all the wage rates in the workshop, much as female (hearing) workers were accused of lowering wages in factory jobs and jobs in printing companies.[72] Graff, a devoted republican, believed that the way to end this cycle of hardship and unethical working conditions was to turn to the power of the national government. He wanted the International Congress on Education of the Deaf, held in Paris in 1900, to back his proposal that officials set aside a certain number of jobs for deaf people in the Post Office and other state-run workshops.[73] For Graff, the republican state was the place of refuge from deception and bad luck. But if deaf people were to be employed by the state, they would most likely occupy lower-level white-collar jobs than positions in workshops, and these new jobs required skills in mathematics, penmanship, and spelling, all part of a solid primary education.[74] Members of the International Congress on Education of the Deaf remained skeptical that primary schooling for deaf youth was preparing them for even modest employment in the service sector.[75]

This skeptical tone at the congress sometimes became more strident as presenters such as Gaillard wondered why so many years had passed without any measurable improvement in the economic lives of deaf men and women. He reminded other deaf cultural leaders that "it is necessary that deaf people energetically battle for the right to take charge of deaf people themselves; it is necessary that the deaf impose on the public authorities the obligation of listening to their demands."[76]

Like other French deaf cultural leaders, he used the language of solidarism to establish his claim to deaf rights in the Third Republic:

> [During] this era of open discussion, of open inquiry, of free adoption or rejection
> [of ideas], in this time of active solidarity, it would be criminal to shut out the deaf
> from their rights and their duties as citizens who are interested in their own [com-
> munity] affairs. It would be anti-human, monstrous, to deny them the power to
> know what they need to do.[77]

There was a consensus among deaf leaders that notwithstanding the ideals of solidarism, deaf people felt excluded in the French republic. Gaillard argued that the
government should "open the doors of its workshops and factories" to deaf laborers (as Eugène Graff had proposed). He gave the example of the National Printing
Office in Paris, where only three deaf men were employed in 1900.[78]

As a rule, deaf men had generally worked as farmers, gardeners, cobblers, typesetters, joiners, statuary artists, and sheet metal workers. Deaf women tended to
find regular employment as seamstresses, laundrywomen, pieceworkers, and typesetters.[79] Deaf people did many other kinds of jobs in the late nineteenth century,
but mostly they seemed destined to occupy lower-paying and, in many instances,
unskilled jobs. However, deaf cultural leaders wanted to look forward. The marketplace was changing, and the future of deaf employment would be in book-
keeping and secretarial work. Only 0.2 percent of all deaf people were employed
in accounting positions at the end of the nineteenth century, and they would need
special training if they were to have any hope of moving into this kind of white-
collar office job. There was a concern that educated and capable deaf people would
be mostly relegated to manual labor because hearing people assumed that they had
no other skills.[80]

One of the principal ideas Gaillard floated at the international congress in Paris
was a Bureau des sourds-muets (Office for Deaf People) inside the Bourse du travail (Labor Exchange). The *bourses*, which were originally intended as local trade
unions in the 1840s, grew in number during the 1880s when the national government became more tolerant of workers' unions (it permitted unions to organize
in 1884, but strike actions were still punished severely).[81] Parisian city officials
were the first municipal authorities to encourage the growth of *bourses du travail*
in the Third Republic. In any town, the Bourse du travail functioned as a kind of
employment exchange. During the 1890s, the cultural importance of these centers
grew for the French working class. The *bourses* encouraged leisure activities among
workers, offered job training, set up lending libraries, and generally became the
central focus for any sort of job action against employers.[82] They became an umbrella organization for a variety of workers' groups that represented different kinds
of skilled labor. Solidarists generally approved of the concept of the *bourses* because

they were another productive way to reform society through solidarity of action. When Léon Bourgeois served as prime minister in 1895–1896, he promised more support for the Paris Bourse du travail and claimed he would pay more attention to the grievances of workers.[83] By the 1890s, the number of *bourses du travail* had begun to increase, and by 1908, there were at least 157 *bourses* throughout France. They were popular with workers because the offered them a way to have some control over their lives in the workplace.[84] In this context, Gaillard felt that the *bourses* would be a good place for an "office for deaf people."[85] Deaf workers could use their bureau as a placement office and a center of information about all kinds of employment notices. The key concept was to group deaf workers into associations that would advance their skills and offer them a sense of solidarity.

Deaf People and Popular Organization before World War I

Although the ideals of solidarism permeated the writings of deaf leaders to a certain extent during the turn of the century era, it is also apparent that in political action, members of the French deaf cultural community were beginning to endorse the rising socialist movement and syndicalism in order to pressure the national government for more economic benefits. The growing socialist and syndicalist movements appeared to offer more leverage to deaf working people against a comfortable republican elite. In the late 1890s, syndicalism had distinguished itself from the socialist party in France in two distinct ways. First, it tried to organize unskilled as well as skilled workers in France; and second, syndicalism adopted a form of anarchism that was dedicated to radically redefining the relationships between workers, employers, and the state. As a leader in the *bourse de travail* movement, Fernand Pelloutier (1868–1901) was also a known anarchist who believed that "laws are useless because the industrial oligarchy controls the state."[86] Pelloutier, who had a skeptical view of bourgeois ideals and economic goals (as championed by the solidarists), encouraged workers in the *bourses du travail* and *syndicats* to place more emphasis on direct action. Economic change depended on the workers themselves, whose self-emancipation was an important principle of syndicalist ideology. Syndicalists promoted strike actions, but they wanted practical results from their public demonstrations.[87]

In the first decade of the twentieth century, many deaf workers debated the merits of syndicalism and tried to decide if they should join the movement. Gaillard had already embraced the *bourses du travail* at the International Congress on Education of the Deaf in 1900. Membership in the *bourses du travail* and *syndicats* often overlapped at the end of the nineteenth century. The *bourses du travail* were "societies of trade unions grouped on a local basis." They benefited from municipal funds especially for meeting spaces. Frequently, the more radical union members led the *bourses* and associated freely with the growing syndicalist movement.[88] Deaf cultural leaders learned about some of these syndicalist activities through their own press. In his journal *Revue des sourds-muets*, Gaillard followed the news in Paris quite closely. For instance, Joseph Weber was described as a "socialist" friend of the deaf cultural community in his position as a member of the Paris City Council. Weber often tried to find ways to help deaf mutual aid associations, channeled city funds to help deaf people attend three deaf congresses, and was responsible for placing deaf workers in jobs at municipal workshops. He had also supported the creation of the deaf school at Asnières, and he had been partially responsible for the appointment of Henri Gaillard and another deaf leader, Joseph Cochefer, to a supervisory board at the Asnières institute.[89] The deaf-run press made sure that the deaf cultural community was aware that certain politicians were their advocates and deserved their continued support.

To the extent that deaf workers became involved in syndicalist activity, they also were participants in different strike actions that grew in number in the first decade of the twentieth century as workers began to demand better wages and working conditions. For example, typesetters struck in the capital in April 1906. The workers gathered at the *Bourse du travail* to discuss their demands for higher salaries and a nine-hour day. *Le Petit Parisien*, which covered the strike, noted that there had been no salary increase for the typesetters since 1878, suggesting that workers' demands were within reason. The newspaper portrayed this strike action as part of a larger nationwide strike against the publishing industry, in which printer-owners were trying to deny workers better wages.[90] The socialist newspaper *L'Humanité* also covered the typesetters' strike, placing the story on page one.[91] *L'Humanité* was more interested in the action in Paris than in the provinces, and stated that some 8,000 workers were participating in syndicalist group meetings throughout the Paris region. They sought an increase in daily wages from 6fr.50 to 7fr.20, but only 50 percent of employers had agreed to this demand. The nine-hour workday was also a key demand.

While neither of these articles mentioned deaf typesetters, we know from the *Revue des sourds-muets* that deaf workers were members of the syndicalist groups who were agitating for changes in pay and work rules. The *Revue* noted that deaf workers participated in the Federation of Book Workers strike in April 1906 and in the larger General Confederation of Labor, which was demanding an eight-hour day (a radical proposal for the time period). A large number of deaf workers were involved in the protest, whether or not they had joined the *syndicat* (*la fédération nationale des travailleurs du Livre*). Even deaf women workers had apparently joined in the strike. Deaf women who were fortunate enough to be employed as typesetters (surely a small number) could be mobilized more easily than women in unskilled occupations, who worked in greater isolation. The *Revue* reported that "the deaf [workers] have understood the duty of worker solidarity."[92] These strike actions generally peaked in 1906–1907, when the government began to use police and paid informers to break up strike actions by syndicalist unions.[93] Although syndicalists were always a minority among workers, their philosophy helped mold worker identity in significant ways. As one deaf syndicalist worker pointed out, "The *syndicat* today is everywhere; it has branches, it is in all trades, in all professions. . . . If the associations of mutual aid take care of the moral and material conditions of the deaf, the *syndicat* comes to the workshop to usefully complete the project. . . . At the workshop, the *syndicat* is already the natural-born defender of the "salary." . . . It establishes professional classes where the results are amazing. . . . [The *syndicat*] decreases unemployment."[94] This was no doubt an optimistic view of what the syndicalist movement could accomplish. However, for deaf workers, syndicalism offered a way to organize around social and economic issues that were important to them. Henri Gaillard recognized that syndicalist unions could give deaf workers a measure of protection in a society where they were often abused and "sacrificed to the egoism of cunning people."[95] That some deaf cultural leaders began to support more radical ways of organizing deaf workers indicates that they had grown impatient with the incremental reforms of the radical republicans.

Conclusion

The idea of social progress that the French solidarists developed in the late nineteenth century was a complex proposition that both enticed and frustrated many leaders in the deaf cultural community. Although radical republicans supported social change, they preferred that it come at a gradual pace. The solidarists believed that they had ready answers to the difficult social questions that most affected deaf people at the turn of the twentieth century—the quality of schools for deaf children and inequality of opportunity in the workplace. For radical republicans such as Léon Bourgeois, the position on oralism seemed reasonable enough because spoken language was considered a skill that deaf people needed in order to function like a more normal (hearing) member of French society. Republicans saw oralism as a pathway to modernity and social improvement. They assumed that deaf youth could succeed in their oral school environment through hard work and self-discipline. But deaf cultural leaders such as Henri Gaillard exposed the fallacies of this view. Deaf children who could not use oral language did not get enough benefit from primary schooling. In addition, the republic largely left them under the supervision of religious teaching orders, although it condemned this practice for hearing children.[96] By 1900, deaf cultural leaders understood that the oral method had stunted the educational development of many deaf children over several decades. The republican state was obstructing the very social progress it proposed as the ideal standard for its citizens.

   Deaf cultural leaders were also focused on the issue of economic opportunity at the turn of the twentieth century. Although deaf people had embraced mutualism as a way to build networks of assistance inside their community, the larger issues of obtaining meaningful work and good benefits on the job seemed far from settled. Perhaps to their detriment, deaf cultural leaders often sought solutions exclusively from the national government; an example is their call for more jobs in government workshops for deaf workers. The numerous economic downturns in France since the 1870s had left deaf *and* hearing workers in the vulnerable position of having almost nothing to protect them from homelessness. Radical republicans had tried to respond with subsidized health care for the poor, accident insurance, and a national pension plan. These policies, which were enacted incrementally over twenty years, completed their reformist plans for French society. But two of these policies were based on employment, which many deaf workers struggled to find. By 1900, the finer craft work that some deaf workers had apprenticed in, such as lithography, industrial design or wood and marble sculpture in the mid-nineteenth century was now less important when compared to white-collar office work or even industrial labor. While some deaf cultural activists became involved in municipal and parliamentary elections to try to draw support from more politicians, deaf workers began to embrace syndicalism as a way to achieve greater protection in the workplace.[97] For French deaf people at the turn of the twentieth century, the paradox of social progress meant that they wanted to enjoy life like other citizens, but their pathways to social opportunity, whether through improved schooling or better jobs, were far more restricted than the leaders of the Third Republic would ever have admitted.

Notes

   1. Alice Conklin, "Colonialism and Human Rights, a Contradiction in Terms? The Case of France and West Africa, 1895–1914," *American Historical Review* 103, no. 2 (1998): 419–442.
   2. Joan Scott, *Only Paradoxes to Offer: French Feminists and the Rights of Man* (Cambridge: Harvard University Press, 1996), 98–99.
   3. Judith Stone, "The Republican Brotherhood: Gender and Ideology," in *Gender and the Politics of Social Reform in France, 1870–1914*, edited by Elinor Accampo, Rachel G. Fuchs, and Mary Lynn Stewart (Baltimore, Md.: Johns Hopkins University Press, 1995), 49.
   4. Oralism, or articulated speech, had long been a competing pedagogy with signed language in the education of deaf children. In the late eighteenth century, deaf bookbinder Pierre Desloges noted that priest Abbé Deschamps used spoken language as his main technique in class, whereas Abbé de l'Epée in Paris had developed his own version of

signed language (known as "methodical" signs) to teach his pupils. Desloges believed that signed language was a more effective and natural way to teach deaf youth. See Pierre Desloges, *Observations d'un sourd et muet sur un cours élémentaire des sourds et muets publié en 1779 M. l'Abbé Deschamps, chapelain de l'Eglise d'Orléans* (Paris: B. Morin, 1779).

5. Robert Buchanan, *Illusions of Equality: Deaf Americans in School and Factory, 1850–1950* (Washington, D.C.: Gallaudet University Press, 1999), xiv. Buchanan points out that the suppression of sign language in American schools hampered the "vocational and intellectual progress" of many deaf students. This predicament would also prove to be the case in France.

6. Syndicalism spread in France during the late nineteenth and early twentieth centuries. It was a movement based on workers' "bread and butter" demands at the workplace and relied on the general strike to achieve gains for its membership. See Roger Magraw, *France, 1815–1914: The Bourgeois Century* (New York: Oxford University Press, 1983), 301–304.

7. Some of the current literature on deaf history and disability history for modern France includes Yves Delaporte, *Les Sourds, C'est comme ça* (Paris: Editions de la Maison des sciences de l'homme, 2002); André Gueslin and Henri-Jacques Stiker, eds., *Handicaps, pauvreté et exclusion dans la France du XIXe siècle* (Paris: Editions de l'Atelier, 2003); Zina Weygand, *The Blind in French Society from the Middle Ages to the Century of Louis Braille*, translated by Emily-Jane Cohen (Stanford, Calif.: Stanford University Press, 2009); François Buton, *L'administration des faveurs: L'Etat, les sourds et les aveugles* (Rennes: Presses Universitaires de Rennes, 2009); Nicholas Mirzoeff, *Silent Poetry: Deafness, Sign and Visual Cultural in Modern France* (Princeton, N.J.: Princeton University Press, 1995); and Anne T. Quartararo, *Deaf Identity and Social Images in Nineteenth-Century France* (Washington, D.C.: Gallaudet University Press, 2008).

8. Charles Sowerwine, *France since 1870: Culture, Politics and Society* (New York: Palgrave, 2001), 27. The comment of "dividing France the least" came from Adolphe Thiers, who acted as the republic's first executive during the transition from the Second Empire to the provisional republic after its capitulation to the Prussians.

9. The "integration" involved the creation of a national market economy where different social classes could participate in the growing wealth of the French state. Republicans needed the political support of small farmers, small businessmen, and larger investors. Their economic policies of protectionism and slow growth reflected an effort to balance conflicting interests as the republican government tried to move the economy forward. See Magraw, *France, 1815–1914*, 225–234.

10. Throughout the nineteenth century, France had a two-tiered educational system: one for the lower class and the peasantry and another for the middle and upper classes. At the end of the nineteenth century, most children from the lower classes did not attend school beyond the age of 13. Upper-class students, especially boys, were groomed for secondary schooling, known as the *lycée*, and a small percentage went on to university education. See Robert Gildea, *Education in Provincial France, 1800–1914: A Study of Three Departments* (Oxford: Clarendon Press, 1983), 179–208, passim. For other material on French social policy and education, see Sowerwine, *France since 1870*, 36–38; Linda L. Clark, *Schooling the Daughters of Marianne* (Albany: State University of New York Press,

1984); Elinor Accampo, Rachel Fuchs, and Mary Lynn Stewart, *Gender and the Politics of Social Reform in France, 1870–1914* (Baltimore, Md.: Johns Hopkins University Press, 1995); and Anne Quartararo, *Women Teachers and Popular Education in Nineteenth-Century France* (Newark: University of Delaware Press, 1995).

11. Quartararo, *Deaf Identity*, 86–91.

12. Ibid., 91–93. The French national government regulated the curriculum and pedagogy used at the National Institutes of the Deaf in Paris, Bordeaux, and Chambéry, but it did not effectively control deaf schooling at the local level. Deaf education at the end of the nineteenth century remained largely an effort of localities, which often used religious orders to teach deaf youth.

13. Philip Nord, "The Welfare State in France, 1870–1914," *French Historical Studies* 18 (Spring 1994): 837.

14. Theodore Zeldin, *France, 1848–1945*, vol. 1 (Oxford: Clarendon Press, 1973), 660–661.

15. Quartararo, *Deaf Identity*, 127–128.

16. Nord, "The Welfare State in France," 827. The Masonic lodges probably drew their idea of solidarity from the social contract philosophy of the Enlightenment era.

17. Timothy B. Smith, *Creating the Welfare State in France, 1880–1940* (Montreal: McGill-Queen's University Press, 2003), 42–43.

18. Nord, "The Welfare State in France," 821.

19. Smith, *Creating the Welfare State in France*, 18, 24.

20. Timothy B. Smith, "Assistance and Repression: Rural Exodus, Vagabondage, and Social Crisis in France, 1880–1914," *Journal of Social History* 32 (Summer 1999): 824–825. No one is exactly sure how many people in France were homeless at the end of the nineteenth century, but one common perception among republicans and the popular press was that some 400,000 French people (or 1 percent of the population) could be potentially classified as "vagabonds." Historians generally place the number at closer to 200,000 to 300,000 who were in economic distress during the 1890s.

21. Nord, "The Welfare State in France," 826.

22. The creation of Abbé de l'Epée's school in Paris in the 1750s solidified the idea that deaf people were deserving of education and could be molded into useful members of society.

23. For background information on Léon Bourgeois' life, see Marc Sorot, *Léon Bourgeois (1851–1925), un moraliste en politique* (Paris: Bruno Leprince, 2005).

24. Léon Bourgeois, *Solidarité*, 3rd ed. (Paris: Librarie Armand Colin, 1902), 99–100.

25. Ibid., 28–29.

26. Zeldin, *France, 1848–1945*, 206–207, 661.

27. Ibid.

28. Ibid., 663.

29. Ibid., 666–667.

30. Léon Bourgeois, *La Politique de la prévoyance sociale*, vol. 2 (Paris: Bibliothèque-Charpentier, 1919), 22.

31. Departement de la Seine, *Etat des communes à la fin du XIXe siècle: Asnières; notice historique et renseignements administratifs* (Montévrain: Imprimerie typographique de l'école d'Alembert, 1902), 45–46.

32. "A Flourishing School for the Deaf in France," *The Silent Worker* 14, no. 9 (1902): 144.

33. Bourgeois, *La Politique de la prévoyance sociale*, 25.

34. Ibid., 26.

35. One good example is Ferdinand Buisson, *Leçons de morale à l'usage de l'enseignement primaire* (Paris: Hachette, 1926). Buisson was a radical republican who fervently supported public education and solidarism.

36. Bourgeois, *La Politique de la prévoyance sociale*, 27. Lion, the young man who extinguished the school fire, had to spend a week in the hospital.

37. Ibid., 28.

38. Ibid., 31.

39. E. Castelot, "Stationary Population in France," *The Economic Journal* 14, no. 54 (1904): 250; and Adolphe Bélanger, *L'Enseignement des sourds muets en France* (Paris: Atelier typographique de l'Institution nationale des sourds-muets, 1908), 11. Bélanger estimated that there were 25,000 deaf persons in France in 1908, but another author gives that same number for the 1880s. The culturally active deaf community perhaps numbered 10–20 percent of the total deaf population.

40. Anne T. Quartararo, "The Life and Times of the French Deaf Leader, Ferdinand Berthier: An Analysis of His Early Career," *Sign Language Studies* 2 (Winter 2002): 190–192.

41. Quartararo, *Deaf Identity*, 115–118.

42. One of the best examples of an excellent deaf teacher who lost his teaching position at the Institut National de Jeunes Sourds de Paris after 1880 was Ernest Dusuzeau, who devoted the rest of his life to deaf community affairs. See Quartararo, *Deaf Identity*, 156–158.

43. "Distribution des prix à l'Institution nationale des sourds-muets; discourse de Mr. Danjou, Professeur," *Revue générale de l'enseignement des sourds-muets* 4 (octobre 1902): 56.

44. Henri Gaillard, *La Situation des sourds-muets en France au début du XXe siècle* (Paris: Bureaux de l'Echo des sourds-muets, 1904), 32–33.

45. Ibid., 30.

46. Henri Gaillard, "The Failure of the Oral Method," translated by F. R. Gray, *The Silent Worker* 22, no. 5 (February 1910): 96. *The Silent Worker* was a New Jersey publication run by deaf people.

47. Ibid., 96.

48. Henri Gaillard, "The Failure of the Oral Method," *The Silent Worker* 22, no. 6 (March 1910): 115.

49. Henri Gaillard, "The Failure of the Oral Method," *The Silent Worker* 22, no. 8 (May 1910): 145. Joseph Cochefer (1849–1923), who also sat on the commission, was a highly respected member of the French deaf community who created a mutual aid society in the 1880s. See Quartararo, *Deaf Identity*, 140–143.

50. Gaillard, "The Failure of the Oral Method," *The Silent Worker* 22, no. 6 (March 1910): 115. In *Illusions of Equality*, Robert Buchanan points out that the majority of employers in the United States preferred to use "a combination of writing, sign language and fingerspelling for communicating with their deaf workers" rather than lip-reading (33).

51. Henri Gaillard, "The Failure of the Oral Method," *The Silent Worker* 23, no. 6 (March 1911): 115.

52. Henri Gaillard, *Le Sourd-Muet à l'ouvrage en France, carrières et professions* (Paris: Chez l'auteur, 1894), 6.

53. Lenard R. Berlanstein, *The Working People of Paris, 1871–1914* (Baltimore, Md.: Johns Hopkins University Press, 1984), 6–7, 41–43. The periods of economic downturn included 1878, 1883–1887, 1889, 1892, 1900, 1902, and 1908.

54. Ibid., 43.

55. Ibid., 46.

56. Gaillard, *La Situation des sourds-muets en France*, 3.

57. Buchanan, *Illusions of Equality*, xv and 72. Buchanan points out that vocational training for deaf workers lacked consistency in the late nineteenth century and that "deaf leaders and adults were typically cautious, even differential, regarding their status and rights as workers."

58. Gaillard, *La Situation des sourds-muets en France*, 3.

59. Ibid., 4–5.

60. One of the wealthier deaf leaders from the region of Champagne, Emile Mercier, was a close friend of Henri Gaillard. See Quartararo, *Deaf Identity*, 143–145.

61. Ibid., 160.

62. Gaillard, *La Situation des sourds-muets en France*, 4.

63. Quartararo, *Deaf Identity*, 183.

64. Ibid., 183–184.

65. Henri Gaillard and Henri Jeanvoine, eds., *Congrès international pour l'étude des questions d'éducation et d'assistance des sourds-muets. Compte rendu des débats et relations diverses* (Paris: Imprimerie d'ouvriers sourds-muets, 1900).

66. Quartararo, *Deaf Identity*, 151.

67. Henri Genis, "Maison de retraite pour sourds-muets," in *Congrès international pour l'étude des questions d'éducation et d'assistance des sourds-muets. Compte rendu des débats et relations diverses*, edited by Henri Gaillard and Henri Jeanvoine (Paris: Imprimerie d'ouvriers sourds-muets, 1900), 173. Genis was a well-respected member of the deaf cultural leadership.

68. Ibid., 174.

69. Ibid., 175.

70. Ibid., 177. Genis calculated that it would cost 250,000 francs per year to maintain a retirement home for deaf people, after procuring land and buildings. This was so expensive that it was unlikely to be adopted by the radical republicans.

71. Quartararo, *Deaf Identity*, 148.

72. Eugène Graff, "Le Sourd-Muet à l'atelier," in *Congrès international pour l'étude des questions d'éducation et d'assistance des sourds-muets. Compte rendu des débats et relations diverses*, edited by Henri Gaillard and Henri Jeanvoine (Paris: Imprimerie d'ouvriers sourds-muets, 1900), 178–179. See also Magraw, *France, 1815–1914*, 288.

73. Graff, "Le Sourd-Muet à l'atelier," 179.

74. Berlanstein, *The Working People of Paris*, 18, 31.

75. Albert Vendrevert, "Création d'Ateliers dans les Institutions," in *Congrès international pour l'étude des questions d'éducation et d'assistance des sourds-muets. Compte rendu des débats et rela-*

tions diverses, edited by Henri Gaillard and Henri Jeanvoine (Paris: Imprimerie d'ouvriers sourds-muets, 1900), 27–28.

76. Henri Gaillard, "Carrières et professions de sourds-muets; assistance part le travail," in *Congrès international pour l'étude des questions d'éducation et d'assistance des sourds-muets. Compte rendu des débats et relations diverses*, edited by Henri Gaillard and Henri Jeanvoine (Paris: Imprimerie d'ouvriers sourds-muets, 1900), 180–181.

77. Ibid., 181.

78. Ibid., 191.

79. Ibid., 183–184, 187.

80. Ibid. The congress had spent considerable time discussing the need to train deaf teachers for the classroom. The obvious impediment was the oralist curriculum that mandated spoken language as the instructional method in all schools for deaf children.

81. Magraw, *France, 1815–1914*, 293; and Zeldin, *France, 1848–1945*, 243.

82. Magraw, *France, 1815–1914*, 306.

83. Judith F. Stone, *Sons of Revolution: Radical Democrats in France, 1862–1914* (Baton Rouge: Louisiana State University Press, 1996), 155. Zeldin points out that Léon Bourgeois drew the anger of workers because he instituted new rules that forced the Bourses to share control of their organization with municipal authorities. See Zeldin, *France, 1848–1945*, 245.

84. Zeldin, *France, 1848–1945*, 244.

85. Gaillard, "Carrières," 194.

86. Fernand Pelloutier quoted in Magraw, *France, 1815–1914*, 306. For background on Pelloutier, who was a hearing leader of the syndicalist and *bourses du travail* movement, see Zeldin, *France, 1848–1945*, 248–249; and Jacques Julliard, *Fernand Pelloutier et les origines du syndicalisme d'action directe* (Paris: Editions du Seuil, 1971).

87. Zeldin, *France, 1848–1945*, 248–249.

88. Ibid., 244–245.

89. "Joseph Weber," *Revue des sourds-muets* 1, no. 3 (juillet 1906): 33–34. Gaillard began this journal in 1900 after leaving the *Journal des sourds-muets*.

90. "Les Travailleurs du Livre," *Le Petit Parisien*, 19 avril 1906, 3–4.

91. "La grève de l'imprimerie: pour les neuf heures," *L'Humanité*, 19 avril 1906, 1.

92. *Revue des sourds-muets* 1, no. 2 (juin 1906): 23.

93. Magraw, *France, 1815–1914*, 310.

94. "Réponse à Mr. Guillaume Geffroy, par un sourd-muet syndiqué," *Revue des sourds-muets* 2, no. 4 (août 1907): 53.

95. Henri Gaillard, *Du Placement des sourds-muets* (Paris: n.p., 1913), 4.

96. Gaillard, *La Situation des sourds-muets en France*, 27.

97. "Informations," *Revue des sourds-muets* 1, no. 2 (juin 1906): 21–22.

CHAPTER 15

Property, Disability, and the Making of the Incompetent Citizen in the United States, 1860s–1940s

KIM E. NIELSEN

KEYWORDS: *Centuries*: nineteenth; twentieth; *Geographical Areas*: North America; *Sources*: legal documents; manuscripts and archival materials; *Themes*: citizenship and belonging; bodies, medicine, and contested knowledge; family, daily life, and community; law and policy

When James Otis made his famous pre–Revolutionary War speech against the British writs of assistance in 1761, he proclaimed that "the fundamental principles of law" guaranteed the basic rights of human beings. He even acknowledged, according to his astonished friend and future U.S. president John Adams, "the rights of Negroes" (but didn't mention women or those of indigenous nations). Otis explained that control of one's own property, the "freedom of one's house," was "one of the most essential branches of English liberty." The only group of people whose rights could be "surrendered or alienated," Otis insisted, was "idiots or madmen."[1] Ten years after James Otis exempted "idiots or madmen" from his rights claims, his family ironically had him declared non compos mentis.[2] He then lost his property rights. Otis was by no means the first colonialist to be declared incompetent. Indeed, from 1773 to 1776 Boston selectmen investigated sixteen men and ten women for incompetence: all 26 were found non compos mentis and were assigned legal guardians.[3]

The U.S. political democracy is built on the premise that people have rights. Citizens are assumed to be fit to debate, vote, own property, and exercise supervision of self and to exercise those rights. Who those citizens are, however, has changed over time. Taking note of race, class, and gender, scholars of several intellectual generations have examined the historical expansion of democracy's legal frameworks and definitions of civic fitness. The U.S. electorate, for example, has expanded from one of landholding white males to one with no property, racial, or sex qualifications. However, election laws continue to maintain requirements regarding age and criminal indictments.

"Idiots or madmen," as Otis succinctly phrased it, have been another story. When adults are determined non compos mentis—to be "idiots or madmen"—and are placed under guardianship, they lose some of their rights. In nearly all U.S. states, if a legal determination is made that an adult is "incompetent to have the charge and management of one's property," he or she is assigned a legal guardian.[4] In the past, some states used county probate courts and others, mirroring English legal tradition, used lunacy commissions. The guardian manages and controls all property, whether it be land, goods, or the physical and economic results of labor. The incompetent person cannot make legally standing decisions or sign legal documents. The majority of those who were considered non compos mentis were not institutionalized (at least, in my study), though the percentage who were varies from county to county and, in some places, from decade to decade. Historically, incompetency hearings reinforced the linkage between citizenship rights and competence by quite literally taking away the right to own and manage property from citizens who were deemed inadequate.

An examination of the cases of individuals who were determined legally unfit for property ownership and supervision of self allows us to examine changing historical standards of civic fitness.[5] Incompetency hearings, not surprisingly, reflected a society's already-existing power structures of gender, race, age, marital status, and bodily ability. They also illustrate how definitions of unfit have changed over time. Standards of civic fitness, which are grounded in understandings of disability and ableness, have shaped democratic rights from the early years of the nation, and using disability as an analytical tool can teach us much about the development of democracy in the United States.

This chapter examines the cases of Wisconsin citizens who were determined incompetent to fulfill the task of property ownership by county probate courts from the 1860s until approximately World War II.[6] During this time period, Wisconsin law left the definition of non compos mentis remarkably vague. Unlike the process required to commit someone to an institution, the non compos mentis hearing required no medical or psychological determination. The term served as a catchall category with no set criteria, allowing county judges to set their own community standards and to seek the opinions of family members, neighbors, and the occasional medical or asylum personnel about whether or not the individual in question was "competent" to manage his or her property. The reasons for declaring someone legally incompetent, thus restricting his or her citizenship rights, varied tremendously. Successful charges included "excessive old age," "feeble mindedness," "excessive use of intoxicating liquors," deafness, blindness, and "mental imbecility and idiocy." But most often, the charge was simply "incompetence." Additionally complicating the records is the fact that the courts and those who testified in them frequently used the terms "insane" and "incompetent" interchangeably. Thus, in the courts, insanity was characterized as anything from deafness to mental "retardation" to attempted suicide.

Unfit for Property Rights

In April 1890, Frank Wilson petitioned the Dane County, Wisconsin, probate court to declare his unmarried stepson, 23-year-old Andrew Wilson, legally incompetent. According to the petition, Andrew was "subject to fits" and a wagon accident in his early childhood had left his right leg and arm partially paralyzed. Frank Wilson claimed that Andrew was "in the habit of spending foolishly what little money he would get—buying little trinkets and things like that." The county court agreed with Frank and determined Andrew incompetent. Stepfather Frank then became Andrew's legal guardian with control of all his property and finances. For a 23-year-old, the financial assets were significant. As a result of his dead father's estate, Andrew shared with his mother Wilma (Frank's current wife) an interest in the "family" farm valued at $4,700.[7]

About two years later, Andrew moved to Iowa to live with a brother. Perhaps he no longer wanted to live with his stepfather and mother. Perhaps he chafed at the restrictions placed upon him. Perhaps his brother needed his help. All we know is that he removed himself from contact with his legal guardian in order to live and work on his brother's farm. In 1897, however, Andrew, who by then was 33, returned to Wisconsin for a three-week visit. He had the opportunity to purchase a farm near his brother's farm in Iowa and wanted the legal right to control his money.[8]

Andrew apparently convinced his stepfather of the rightness of his actions. Frank again filed a court petition, this time to have the guardianship and incompetency status overturned. "There was a marked change in him," Frank testified about Andrew. "He seemed all right, except for his crippled condition. . . . a different man from what he had been before. There was no disposition to spend money, or to squander his means. On the contrary he seemed to be saving and frugal in his habits." The county court again agreed with Frank and released Andrew from his guardianship. The young man presumably resolved the financial entanglement with his mother that remained from his father's will, bought the Iowa farm, and lived happily ever after.[9] In this case, a physical disability may have made easier the initial judgment of Andrew's incompetency, but it was not the dominant factor.

What made Andrew Wilson incompetent? No one ever alleged that he was insane. In his first hearing in 1890, petitioners highlighted his partial paralysis and "fits"—a physical disability. Examining the 1897 hearing that overturned Andrew's incompetency status, however, reveals a far more complicated story. As stepfather Frank testified in 1897, Andrew's "crippled condition" had not changed. Nor did it leave him unable to earn an income. Indeed, Andrew wanted to buy and manage a farm. What had changed since the original hearing, what rendered Andrew competent at his second hearing, was the development of frugal financial habits. He now behaved in a fiscal manner his parents considered appropriate for a responsible young white man.

The story of Andrew Wilson reveals that legal incompetency involves complex cases of public and familial politics that are difficult to untangle. Unstated but obvious in the court records of Andrew Wilson is the economic interest of his guardian Frank Wilson and his mother Wilma in maintaining the economic value of Wilma's inheritance and dower rights. The couple did not want Andrew to squander his money away. Indeed, because he held joint interest in the farm with his mother, his poor economic decisions could hurt them. If Andrew really did foolishly waste money, it was to their economic advantage to have him declared incompetent in order to stop such behaviors.

While Wilson's case is not stereotypical, his story reveals both the fluidity and complexity of disability. What was his disability? How did his "fits" and paralysis matter? What made him incompetent and then competent? For the young white man, it appears that the achievement of appropriate manliness as expressed by successful financial management overrode the stigma of a nonnormative body. In Andrew's case, civic fitness was defined as the ability to earn and properly manage—as determined by the court and his parents—those earnings.

Wisconsin adults who were placed under legal guardianship in this period fall into four primary categories: institutionalized individuals, alcoholics, elderly women, and those who embodied multiple and intersecting vulnerabilities. The largest group was adults who either were or had been institutionalized. Approximately one-third to one-half (depending on the county) of men and women determined incompetent were institutionalized in asylums prior to their hearings.[10] (In my research, counties that either housed or were close to institutions had higher institutionalization rates than those that were farther away from institutions.) When individuals were institutionalized, theoretically nothing could be done with their property. If the property was in land, it could not be rented, sold, or improved upon. If the property was a pension, it could not be received or spent. If an institutionalized person had an interest in but not complete ownership of family property, the other owners could not act. Family members thus often accused institutionalized individuals of incompetency in order that property actions could be taken.

For example, after Dane County courts committed Peter Baird to the regional insane asylum in 1868, his wife Molly Baird and his five minor children had no means of support. Though Peter Baird owned personal property and mortgages valued at $4,400, he had rented the land on which his family lived. Without access to her husband's personal property, Molly Baird had no cash to pay rent. Her son-in-law John Finn, the husband of the couple's oldest child, petitioned that Peter Baird be declared incompetent and Finn be declared guardian. Finn promised to use "said moneys" in order to provide "a home and support" for his mother-in-law and her minor children. The court agreed and gave Finn guardianship.[11] In a similar case, in 1880 Katrina Abel asked the court to declare her husband John Abel, then a resident of the Wisconsin State Hospital for the Insane, incompetent. John Abel owned no property, but he received a monthly pension for his service in "the war of the Rebellion." The court appointed a local banker as his guardian, and the banker then dispersed the money to Katrina so she could support herself. (However, he had the legal right to control her spending.)[12] In these cases, like many others, the institutionalization of husbands exacerbated women's economic vulnerability. They and others used competency hearings to gain access to property in order to protect themselves from economic crisis.

In 1870, Matthew Murdock charged that his institutionalized sister, Emma Murdock Greenlow, was incompetent. Though she was at the State Lunatic Asylum, she owned a one-quarter interest in their parents' estate. Matthew wanted to sell the property and could not do so without her legal permission. The court declared a neighbor her guardian; and the neighbor subsequently gave Matthew permission to sell the property. Matthew initiated charges so that he could do what he wanted with the jointly owned estate.[13]

Alcohol usage and alcohol-related behaviors considered excessive were the reasons a significantly large group of people were determined to be non compos mentis. Approximately 20 percent of incompetency charges included problematic alcohol consumption—which was phrased as "excessive drinking" or "spendthriftiness"—and over 99 percent of people in this group were men.[14] Immediate family members or county officials usually initiated these petitions with the clear purpose of securing the economic support of other family members. These accusations charged that the man's drinking diminished his estate, endangered the support of his family, and left the county vulnerable to the possibility that it would have to provide economic support for the family. An 1885 accusation against Elijah Runn by his wife charged that alcohol "induce[d]" him by "gaming, idleness, and debauchery" to waste his money, "endangering his own as well as his family's support."[15] In 1893, Calumet County officials charged David Alberts with incompetency, but only after he had inherited land valued at $2,000. His "excessive drinking and debauchery in frequent drinking saloons," the petition complained, "expose[d] the town . . . to charge" for the support of his family.[16]

Nearly all incompetency petitions that were dropped before the scheduled legal hearing involved drinking men, likely indicating that family members used such petitions as attempts to coerce alcoholic men into curtailing their drinking. Christian Jones, Billy Boyle, and Edmund Miller, for example, all had wives and minor children who relied on them for economic support. Boyle's family, like the others listed here, charged that his "use of intoxicating drinks" meant that "his estate is likely to be and is being seriously injured and impaired." In each of these cases a family member—a wife, a brother, a son-in-law—initiated the petition but later asked that it be dismissed.[17]

Incompetency accusations including alcohol are drenched in concerns about failed masculinity. Twenty-eight percent of the incompetency accusations against men included charges of excessive alcohol consumption. Alcohol in and of itself was not the problem. The "problem" was that alcohol rendered these men incapable of economically providing for their households. They not only failed to fulfill the basic tasks that were expected of white men but also created the possibility that the community would be required to shoulder the economic responsibilities considered to be those of a male head of household.

Gender was a factor in incompetency accusations of "excessive old age." Women were more than twice as likely as men to be thus accused; women, all of whom were widowed, accounted for 34 percent of such petitions, while men, all of whom were single, accounted for 15 percent. The historical records in these cases are skimpy. Because women tended to be accused of old age by their adult sons (a hard-to-deny accusation that was made against women who were from 60 to 90 years old) and because this happened much less often to older men, it's easy to speculate about monetary motivations. There seems to have been a lot of men who didn't want to wait until their mothers died to gain control of their mother's resources. Conversely, the evidence could suggest that a lot of men wanted to help their mothers by handling the woman's finances. Inadequate social welfare legislation, limited access to economic resources throughout their lifetime, patriarchal households, and the growing physical frailty of old age worked together to set elderly women up to be considered disabled and incompetent, even in their own families. When family members accused older men of incompetency, the accusations tended to include multiple additional factors (such as blindness, paralysis, or drunkenness and age). Widowed women were most vulnerable during the five years after the death of their husband.

A few women fought against the vulnerability created by age, gender, and widowhood. In 1897, for example, 61-year-old Eliza Dorca, a widow with three adult children, was living alone. She owned property and goods worth approximately $10,000, a considerable sum. Presumably to secure her financial wherewithal as a widow, she entered into a contract with a neighbor whereby the neighbor would buy her property for less than its value in exchange for giving her "support and maintenance during her lifetime." For reasons unknown, she chose not to depend on her children to help her manage her finances. Her son, Moses, and her two married daughters, Melinda Keller and Annabel Little, however, petitioned the courts in January 1897 to have her declared mentally incompetent and asked that her son-in-law William Keller (Melinda's husband) be appointed her guardian.[18]

Three months later, the county court agreed that Eliza was "incompetent to have the care and management of her property" and gave her son Moses (not the son-in-law, as requested) guardianship of his mother and her nearly $10,000 in assets. Eliza hired an attorney and nineteen days later filed an appeal. In an extensive trial, in which she apparently did not testify, the court overturned its original decision and declared Eliza competent to manage her own labor and goods.[19]

What happened between 1897 and 1905 is unclear. In 1905, Eliza was living with her daughter Melinda and son-in-law William Keller. Once again, her family members filed a petition asking that she be declared incompetent and that her son-in-law be declared her guardian. The adult children this time took care to get the testimony of two doctors who declared her incompetent, presumably because they believed that medical determinations would carry greater weight in court. Melinda also testified to her mother's incompetency. Although Eliza didn't testify, she left evidence of her anger in her actions; she again hired her own attorney. Court records indicated that even though Eliza lived with her daughter Melinda and son-in-law William Keller, she hadn't spoken to William since the court case eight years earlier, when he had asked to be appointed her legal guardian. Despite this, when Melinda was pressed by her mother's attorney, she insisted that she did not know whether her mother was angry about the request that her son-in-law be appointed as her legal guardian. Once again the courts determined Eliza to be incompetent. This time Eliza didn't appeal. In addition, this time her son-in-law, with whom she lived but did not speak, became her guardian.

Eliza Dorca's case reflects the slowly growing authority of medical practitioners to assess competency throughout the late nineteenth and early twentieth centuries. Her family considered doctors to be the ultimate authorities on incompetency and assumed that their judgment would carry greater weight in court, but the family turned to them only in the second hearing.

The last major group of those accused of incompetency involved men and women who embodied multiple and intersecting vulnerabilities. Emma Killian's case provides one example. In 1911 the single, blind, 44-year-old woman lived with her brother Jacob and her father William on William's farm. She managed the house. Emma, who had been blind since birth, owned property valued at approximately $3,000 that she had recently inherited from her mother. In December, while Emma was temporarily hospitalized, a cousin from the same county filed a petition asking that she be declared incompetent due to her "blindness, sickness, and infirmity of body and mind." Though the cousin proposed that he be declared guardian, in January 1912 the judge appointed a local attorney as guardian instead. In the fall of 1913, Emma and her brother Jacob contested the ruling that Emma was legally incompetent.[20]

When Emma testified, she insisted that she could transact her own business affairs and would seek assistance if she needed it. The opposing attorney made much of her blindness and kidney troubles (she had been diagnosed with dropsy, which today is known as edema). One doctor testified that she was incompetent but not insane, and another thought she was "mentally competent." The opposing attorney attempted to discredit Emma's brother Jacob by drawing attention to the fact that he read Shakespeare, perhaps an innuendo about his sexuality. When lawyers and the judge questioned Emma about her competency, they focused on gender. The criteria by which they judged her competency—her ability to clean the house, do laundry, prepare meals, sew clothes, milk cows, and gather eggs—suggest that the ability to adhere to heteronormative definitions of femininity played a role in determining her legal status.

Emma, several neighbors, several housekeepers, several doctors, and her brother Jacob presented opposing evidence regarding Emma's competence to manage the farm household. However, the county judge still found her incompetent, and she, her property, and all the economic results of her labor remained under guardianship until at least 1926. During that time, she continued to manage the household where she lived with her brother and father. Emma's daily activities of physical, economic, and mental labor continued unchanged despite the fact that she had been determined incompetent to manage her own labor. Emma's blindness, gender, and perhaps her unmarried status, trumped the realities of her daily labor in the court's definition of disability.

Being a single, 44-year-old woman likely rendered Emma Killian suspect. Marriage and conformity to heteronormative masculinity and femininity mattered enormously in incompetency hearings. In the hearings examined in this study, 60 percent of the men and 91 percent of the women accused of incompetency were not married at the time of the accusation. Unmarried people were far more vulnerable to incompetency charges, and unmarried women were far more vulnerable than unmarried men. In a historical irony, the lingering remnants of married women's feme covert legal status perversely protected them from incompetency accusations. Married women owned little property in their own name; unmarried women had property and thus became vulnerable to incompetency accusations. In some ways the findings of this project echo Carol Karlsen's analysis of the economic motivations for witchcraft trials: whether they had been institutionalized or not, the women who were most likely to be charged with incompetency were single or widowed (without male legal protection) and had control of property.[21] Gender alone, however, is not enough of an explanation, considering that the majority of men accused were also single. Even for men, being married offered protection from attempts by others to place them and their property under legal guardianship. Heterosexual marriage, or at least the assumption of it, protected individuals from charges of incompetency.

Though being married diminished the likelihood of incompetency accusations, the presence of family played out in multiple ways. Overwhelmingly, family members initiated legal accusations of incompetency. Ninety percent of the women accused of incompetency were accused by family members; for men, the statistic was 82 percent. An optimistic analysis might suggest that family members were more likely than those outside the family to know when someone needed guardianship and that kindness was the motivation for their desire to protect that individual and their resources. However, the reality is that family members often had concrete economic interests of their own. Incompetency hearings became one strategy to ensure that economic resources stay inside the family or simply that they be taken over by one individual. When courts determined women incompetent, eldest sons benefited economically most often, and if not eldest sons, then some other male relative.

Being female increased one's chances of being accused of incompetency. Women constitute approximately 40 percent of the defendants—a large percentage considering that women certainly owned less than 40 percent of the property in U.S. society at this time. When women lost control of their money, it almost always went to a male family member. As the once-institutionalized Elizabeth Packard charged in the late nineteenth century, women's subordinate position in patriarchal societies left them vulnerable to accusations of insanity based on spurious reasons.[22]

Using Incompetency, or Strategic Non Compos Mentis

Just as historian Johanna Schoen has shown that a small number of women attempted to use the coercive legal strictures of sterilization to their own advantage,[23] in a very small number of cases individual women and their families manipulated the legal status of incompetency in unexpected ways. The case of Blanche Hilliard provides one example. With her support, Hilliard's brother had her declared incompetent in 1886, less than a year after her divorce. As her guardian, he controlled her property for two years, during which time the then legally incompetent Blanche remained in the former marital home, where she parented her two small children; taught at a county school; and managed her own household affairs. Once her ex-husband left town, the brother asked the county to reverse its earlier decision, and it did so. It may be that Blanche Hilliard and her brother used the legal status of incompetency in order to protect her property from the claims of the ex-husband. If this was the case, then county officials collaborated in this effort when they hired her to teach in one of the county's public schools.[24]

Abigail Salles also attempted to use the legal status of incompetency to protect herself, but in a much more profoundly sad circumstance. In 1873, the 77-year-old widow herself asked that she be declared incompetent and that one of her neighbors be declared her guardian. She and eight of her neighbors signed the petition. Her son Peter had "moved into her house very much against her wishes." Because of "his indolent habits and bad associates," he was failing to support his "very large family of children" and the formerly successful farm was "despoil[ed]."[25] The petition detailed the sorry state of the fields and house. In addition, he gave his mother little to eat and squandered her money. Mrs. Salles clearly felt herself either personally or legally unable to insist that her son and his family leave her house. The court agreed with her and her neighbors and declared a local man her guardian. Presumably Peter and his family then moved out. Though his mother got her wish, he left her with a house "spoiled by a family of badly taught children."[26]

Husbands had even greater potential than sons to wreak havoc. The court testimony I examined did not detail physical abuse connected to excessive alcohol consumption, but it is likely that women who endured such abuse sought not only to protect themselves and their children economically but also to protect themselves from physical violence.[27] Since such women had few economic resources in their own control, counties had an economic self-interest in supporting charges that alcoholic husbands were incompetent so county resources would not be needed to support such families. Immediate family members or county officials primarily initiated these petitions with the clear purpose of ensuring that other family members would support the family. Whether or not wives formally initiated the charges, their support for the guardianship requests and their displeasure about their husbands' alcohol consumption weaves throughout the court cases.

The vast majority of those who apparently tried to use incompetency hearings to their own advantage were female. Women had fewer economic and legal resources to draw on in order to protect themselves and their property. They requested that they be declared incompetent from positions of legal and social weakness. Because of their vulnerability, they had less to lose by being declared non compos mentis.

African American and Native American families in Wisconsin never used incompetency hearings for family members. Certainly they had fewer property resources for a guardian to control, and families tended to need income from the labor of as many family members as possible. They also had far fewer reasons to trust or willingly involve themselves in the legal system. Forced or coerced removal to boarding schools left many Indigenous communities highly resistant to or fearful of institutionalization. African American and Native American peoples who were determined to be insane tended to experience the very worst abuses of institutionalization or imprisonment. The few African Americans who were accused of incompetency in the probate records were so accused by people who were not family members, and the voices of family members do not appear in the probate records. Those who were determined to be incompetent remained at home, but the family lost direct access to their limited economic resources.[28]

Disability and the Democratic State

The courtrooms that heard competency cases in the records I have examined became a site where families, attorneys, local officials, and medical authorities (increasingly, but unevenly, in the twentieth century) debated what was required for a person to participate in a democracy. What it meant to be a competent American, someone who was entitled to own and manage property by him- or herself, someone who was capable of participating in a democratic nation-state, was fought out in the guardianship hearings of those accused of incompetency.

Competency hearings and the determinations of non compos mentis also suggest that the ability to earn a living and manage a living contributed to changing historical definitions of disability. A "good" citizen was one who owned and managed property in an economically successful fashion. "Bad" citizens were believed to be so incapable of managing property that their property rights were taken away. Management of property, however, was not ideologically neutral ground. Race, age, gender, and marital status became interwoven and became part of ableist ideologies that defined productive potential. Despite the daily productive farm and household labor of blind and single Emma Killian, for example, she was defined as incompetent for productive labor. My examination of incompetency hearings strongly suggests that more historical work needs to be done to unpack the relationships between capitalism, citizenship, and disability.

Incompetency hearings illustrate that competence is an ever-changing historically bound construct that is built upon and amidst a society's already-existing power structures. In his study of two sisters in Ilasco, Missouri, who were charged with incompetency in the early twentieth century when a powerful company desired their land, Greg Andrews argued that "gender, class, and law shaped the history of property and labor relations." In this (perhaps extreme) case, county authorities and economic leaders used "the instruments of guardianship and insanity confinement" to transfer the property in the ways they desired.[29] My study of incompetency hearings makes clear that courts' implementation of competency criteria reflected the changing power structures of communities and families.

Likewise, these hearings illustrate that disability is also a historically bound construct. Competency hearings marked specific individuals as inherently deficient, inherently disabled citizens. In these cases, the ever-changing, ever-slippery spectrum of what has constituted disability is almost overwhelming. Gender, age, race, marital status, behavior, family politics, the power of capital, and embodiments contribute to definitions of disability. The use of disability as an analytic tool matters in the story of the United States because it forces us to analyze the strengths, weaknesses, and contradictions of American ideals.

Notes

1. James Otis, "Against the Writs of Assistance," 1761, National Humanities Institute website, http://www.nhinet.org/ccs/docs/writs.htm, accessed June 23, 2011.

2. Nancy Rubin Stewart, *The Muse of the Revolution: The Secret Pen of Mercy Otis Warren and the Founding of a Nation* (Boston: Beacon Press, 2008), 43.

3. Mary Ann Jimenez, *Changing Faces of Madness: Early American Attitudes and Treatment of the Insane* (Hanover, N.H.: University Press of New England, 1987), 59. According to Jimenez, shortly after the court declared Otis incompetent, he successfully challenged that legal status.

4. Historians have not written much about incompetence proceedings. For some examples, see Gregg Andrews, *Insane Sisters: Or, the Price Paid for Challenging a Company Town* (Columbia: University of Missouri Press, 1999); John Starrett Hughes, *Alabama's Families and Involuntary Commitment of the Insane, 1861–1900: New Solutions to Old Problems* (Madison: Institute of Legal Studies, University of Wisconsin Law School, 1987); John Starrett Hughes, "Commitment Law, Family Stress, and Legal Culture: The Case of Victorian Alabama," in *Constitution, Law, and American Life*, edited by Donald G. Nieman (University of Georgia Press, 1992). Being declared non compos mentis is not the same as being determined incompetent to stand trial; that is a different legal process with different legal implications.

5. For an analysis of civic fitness debates, see Kim E. Nielsen, "Helen Keller and the Politics of Civic Fitness," in *The New Disability History: American Perspectives*, edited by Paul Longmore and Lauri Umansky (New York: New York University Press, 2001), 268–290.

6. My database includes the complete records of Calumet County, a rural county in north-central Wisconsin, which provided 150 cases from 1870 to 1968; and Dane County (in which Madison is located), which provided 165 cases from 1864 to 1891. All of the personal names have been changed in the cases I discuss to ensure confidentiality.

7. Case of Andrew Wilson, Dane County Guardianship and Insanity Files, Box 1037 (Box 7, Folder 3), Dane County Probate Court Collection #121. (The Wisconsin Historical Society has renumbered the boxes in this collection but has retained both numbering systems to identify each box.)

8. Ibid.

9. Ibid.

10. Institutionalization in an insane asylum did not necessarily imply what is today understood to be insanity. As historian Gerald Grob explains, the "eclectic" admission policies of nineteenth-century institutions meant that they "accepted the very young, the

aged, the infirm, and the mentally ill, among others." Gerald N. Grob, *Mental Institutions in America: Social Policy to 1875* (New York: Free Press, 1973), 13.

11. Case of Peter Baird, Dane County Guardianship and Insanity Files, Box 1011–1014 (Box 2, Folder 2), Dane County Probate Court Collection #121.

12. Case of John Abel, Dane County Guardianship and Insanity Files, Box 1024 (Box 4, Folder 2), Dane County Probate Court Collection #121.

13. Case of Emma Murdock Greenlow, Dane County Guardianship and Insanity Files, Box 1015–1016 (Box 2, Folder 3), Dane County Probate Court Collection #121.

14. Almost 30 percent of the accusations against men included charges of excessive use of alcohol.

15. Case of Elijah Runn, Calumet County Guardianship Files, Calumet County Probate Court Collection.

16. Case of David Alberts, Calumet County Guardianship Files, Calumet County Probate Court Collection.

17. Case of Christian Jones, Dane County Guardianship and Insanity Files, Box 1023 (Box 3, Folder 5); case of Billy Boyle, Dane County Guardianship and Insanity Files, Box 1024 (Box 4, Folder 1); case of Edmund Miller, Dane County Guardianship and Insanity Files, Box 1030 (Box 5, Folder 1); all in Dane County Probate Court Collection #121.

18. Case of Eliza Dorca, Calumet County Guardianship Files, Calumet County Probate Court Collection.

19. Ibid. This is one of the few cases I found in which a woman appealed the decision.

20. Case of Emma Killian, Calumet County Guardianship Files, Calumet County Probate Court Collection.

21. Carol Karlsen, *The Devil in the Shape of a Woman: Witchcraft in Colonial New England* (New York, Vintage Books, 1987).

22. Elizabeth Packard, *Modern Persecution, or Insane Asylums Unveiled* (1875; repr., New York, Arno Press, 1973); Barbara Sapinsley, *The Private War of Mrs. Packard* (New York, Paragon House, 1991).

23. Johanna Schoen, *Choice and Coercion: Birth Control, Sterilization, and Abortion in Public Health and Welfare* (Chapel Hill: University of North Carolina Press, 2005).

24. Case of Blanche Hilliard, Dane County Guardianship and Insanity Files, Box 1032 (Box 5, Folder 4), Dane County Probate Court Collection #121.

25. Case of Abigail Salles, Dane County Guardianship and Insanity Files, Box 1019 (Box 2, Folder 7), Dane County Probate Court Collection #121.

26. Ibid.

27. Linda Gordon, *Heroes of Their Own Lives: The Politics and History of Family Violence— Boston, 1880–1960* (Chicago: University of Illinois Press, 2002).

28. For examples, see the Dane County probate cases of Charles Abraham Washington and Boston Williams.

29. Andrews, *Insane Sisters*, 13.

CHAPTER 16

"Salvaging the Negro"

Race, Rehabilitation, and the Body Politic
in World War I America, 1917–1924

PAUL R. D. LAWRIE

> It is extremely difficult for the opposite race to see the colored soldier in
> a fair and impartial light. The fact is that we are invariably received and
> treated as a colored man and not as a disabled soldier.
>
> —Pvt. James Sanford to Dr. J. R. Crossland,
> Veterans Bureau Negro Advisor, 1921

KEYWORDS: *Centuries*: twentieth; *Geographical Areas*: North America; *Sources*: government documents; serials; *Themes*: family, daily life, community; citizenship and belonging; bodies, medicine, and contested knowledge; labor; war

In August 1922, Buster Sunter, an African American veteran of World War I, informed the Veterans Bureau of alleged mistreatment at his local veterans' training center. Sunter, who had been diagnosed with tuberculosis, wrote "I want to let you know that I have not been treated right here, when I take this training I was suppost to have four years here but they have cut my time down to two years. . . . They bully me and have me work like I aint sick so I want you to look into the matter for me for I am not able to work like that." The experience of Private Sunter—of having officials refuse to treat or even acknowledge his condition—reveals how ideas of race and disability shaped the policies and practices of rehabilitation in early twentieth-century America. Postwar models of disability were both medical discourses and social constructs that were developed by physicians, legislators, administrators, and veterans who operated within the broader constructs of labor, gender, citizenship, and race. The cultural politics of remaking men for work in the "great industrial army" fused the health of ex-servicemen with that of the republican body politic in explicitly racial terms, readily evincing the writer Randolph Bourne's dictum that "war is the health of the state."[1]

Modern war brutalized bodies in shockingly new and gruesome ways. The human cost of World War I was staggering: 8.5 million dead, 20 million wounded, and more than 8 million permanently disabled. Despite being a latecomer to the conflict, the United States lost 116,708 men, and an additional 210,000 were classified as wounded or disabled. The disabilities came in many forms: mental illness (victims of shell shock), tuberculosis, syphilis, blindness, loss of hearing, and amputations.[2] The mechanized murder of the trenches irrevocably shattered Victorian ideals of heroism and war as a rejuvenating social force. To many observers, the war had done little to restore vigor to a seemingly overcivilized and effete West. For Lothrop Stoddard—author of the bestselling works *The Rising Tide of Color against White World Supremacy* and the Revolt Against Civilization the war was "a catastrophe" because its "racial losses were certainly as grave as the material loses."[3] For Stoddard and many of his racialist peers—those who saw race as the prime engine of historical change—the carnage of war and its ensuing economic and physical "waste" did not occur in an ideological vacuum. Historian Joanna Bourke notes that all soldiering bodies "were endowed with signs and declarations of age, generation, class, ethnicity and race and that within these social frameworks, bodies lived, died, and were broken."[4] Moreover as David Gerber reminds us, "only in making victims can war achieve its political ends," the human consequences of which are evinced in the broken bodies of disabled veterans.[5]

Rehabilitation was a deeply political process that fundamentally rested on the question of the state's obligation to its veterans. Either the state would secure the employment of tens of thousands of injured men or it would abandon them to an unpredictable marketplace and the pitying attitudes of their fellow citizens. After World War I, science displaced sentimentalism as the core principle of veterans' care. Joanna Bourke notes that throughout the West the question of rehabilitation was "a theoretical, an economic, and finally a moral one, but its consequences for veterans were eminently practical." Veterans' groups argued that "if the state had the power to draft men, it also had the responsibility to prevent the war from ruining the lives of those it conscripted." Loath to encourage an emasculating and enfeebled culture of dependency, officials pledged that "the government is resolved to do its best to restore [veterans] to health, strength, and self-supporting activity."[6] Heretofore the soldiering body had been viewed as a source of social contagion and vice. Immediately after the armistice, officials at the Federal Board of Vocational Education (FBVE) reconfigured the crippled soldier's body into a source of national and racial regeneration. However, rehabilitationists' visions of social uplift through physical perfectionism were constrained by America's unique racial dynamics and historical distrust of an activist federal state.

This chapter examines how federal efforts to rehabilitate disabled African American veterans produced new forms of racial knowledge in postwar America. Positing war as work, I chart how racial models of the "fit" and "unfit" body colored policies about veterans, African American proletarianization, and the postwar labor economy. Though the war did not create the impetus for the state's surveillance and discipline of working bodies, it intensified and encouraged the proliferation of new regulatory institutions and practices such as the draft and vocational rehabilitation, which in turn produced new figurative and literal bodies of racial knowledge. One such institution, the Federal Board of Vocational Education, was charged with rehabilitating the productive citizen-soldier into the efficient citizen-worker. FBVE officials linked scientific management and evolutionary theory to both reinforce and produce catalogues of racial labor taxonomies that delineated which bodies could do which kinds of work. Rehabilitationists, fearful of increasing labor radicalism and racial unrest, sought to mend the social fabric one individual at a time. Yet throughout the stages of diagnosis, job training, and hospitalization, rehabilitationists struggled to determine whether they could, or even should, mend broken black bodies, which were often understood as defective by definition.[7] FBVE policies devalued, deskilled, and institutionalized disabled African American veterans and dismissed their claims to rehabilitation as spurious attempts to unjustly profit from their "natural inferiority." African American ex-servicemen resisted these processes and contested their right to rehabilitation as soldiers, citizens, workers, and men.[8]

FBVE officials drew on social scientific theories of what historian Daniel Bender has termed "industrial evolution" an ideology that linked racial development with labor fitness to separate the deserving from the undeserving disabled. When the story of races was paired with the narrative and standardized structures of Frederick W. Taylor's theories of industrial management, it became one of development and decline, efficiency and inefficiency, and the constant tension between civilization and savagery.[9] Analysis of the FBVE's policies towards African American veterans provides key insights into the production of interwar racial labor hierarchies, the rise of racial expertise, and the drive to shape social policy along biological lines. These trends culminated in 1924, with passage of the Immigration Restriction Act and Virginia's Racial Integrity Act (which banned interracial marriage and authorized involuntary sterilization of the mentally and physically "unfit"). Historian Matt Price describes rehabilitation as a utopian exercise in which "many broken threads, representing physical, mental, and social factors, must be unraveled and rewoven to make a consistent pattern" of national health.[10] Rehabilitation was fundamentally an exercise in individual and social perfectionism that was premised on contemporary ideologies of gender, work, and race. In the summer of 1919, reformer Elizabeth Upham argued that "the wide prevalence of defects found through the physical examinations of the draft justifies a careful consideration of physical and mental racial health when developing programs of reconstruction."[11] Elites conceded that while rehabilitation could remake the "near-white" immigrants of eastern and southern Europe into dutiful, efficient Americans, nonwhite peoples such as Asian Americans, Native Americans, and African Americans required social and occupational segregation to protect them from themselves and society at large.

"To Make the World Safe for the Negro": African Americans in World War I

On April, 2, 1917, President Woodrow Wilson thrust the United States into World War I to make the "world safe for democracy." African American responses to the war effort were initially mixed. Intellectuals such as W. E. B. Du Bois argued that military service would confer full citizenship rights on blacks. In his infamous July 1918 editorial "Close Ranks" in the NAACP's *The Crisis*, he wrote, "Let us while the war lasts . . . close our ranks shoulder to shoulder with our own white fellow citizens and the allied nations that are fighting for democracy."[12] Many African Americans connected the fight against foreign aggression abroad to the struggle against racial segregation at home. Labor leader A. Philip Randolph stated that rather than volunteer to make the world safe for democracy, he would fight to make "Georgia safe for the Negro."[13] Communist Party activist Hubert Harrison wrote that black support for the war was a "surrender of life, liberty, and manhood."[14] Yet despite the radical antiwar sentiments of some blacks, the majority of African Americans wholeheartedly supported the war effort. By the end of the war, federal draft boards had registered approximately 2.3 million African Americans, comprising just over 9.6 percent of the total registration. Despite the fact that they faced widespread segregation and discrimination at home, approximately 370,000 African-Americans were eventually conscripted into the nation's armed forces.[15]

Anxieties about blacks' lack of martial fitness denied most a combat role. Colonel E. D. Anderson, chairman of the Operations Branch, noted that "the poorer class of backwoods Negro has not the mental stamina and moral sturdiness to put him in the line against opposing German troops who consist of men of high average education and thoroughly trained."[16] Ultimately only 38,000 blacks served in overseas combat units, constituting only 3 percent of the army's combat forces.[17] The vast majority of African American recruits were relegated to segregated service battalions in which they performed the inglorious work of war as stevedores, cooks, and menial laborers. White officers assigned to these battalions often treated their charges as little more than beasts of burden "noting that all niggers are made to work."[18] After the war, tens of thousands of African American troops were charged with the gruesome task of exhuming the American dead for reinterment in France or the United States. African Americans' physical absence from the battlefield led to their figurative absence from postwar debates over the rights and responsibilities of rehabilitation.[19]

On the domestic front, World War I transformed the African American worker into an industrial worker on the national stage. Wartime labor shortages in the industrial north, shifts in the world cotton economy, and the daily indignities of Jim Crow pushed hundreds of thousands of African Americans into the industrial north. From the spring of 1917 to the fall of 1929, African Americans left the South at an average rate of 500 per day, or more than 15,000 per month.[20] What had once been the nation's most rural population was rapidly becoming its most urban. Yet tensions over jobs, housing, and federal repression of labor radicalism enflamed race relations nationwide. Whites seeking to maintain the racial status quo increasingly turned to brutal extralegal violence against black persons and their property. At the center of this conflagration stood the figure of the African American soldier, the living embodiment of the assertive New Negro. In the Red Summer of 1919, more than seventy African Americans—ten of whom were still in uniform—were lynched by white mobs enraged by blacks' sartorial pretensions to martial manhood.[21] Given the postwar rise of nationwide de facto and de jure segregation and increasing racial violence, the federal resolve to remake ex-servicemen inevitably varied across the racial divide.

The Roots of American Vocational Rehabilitation

Rehabilitation was a transnational project that united reformers and elites from London, Paris, and New York. Beginning in 1915, throughout the various belligerent nations, a coalition of social, medical, and scientific reformers founded a new science called "rehabilitation." Joanna Bourke notes that "the military requirements of modern warfare and industry provided governments with a powerful incentive to intervene in new areas of the economy including the construction of men's bodies."[22] Recent advances in medical and surgical care in fields such as orthopedics meant that more men could be "salvaged" than in previous conflicts. Throughout the Western world, aggressive normalization through vocational education was conceived as a balm to the dysgenic effects of modern warfare.[23] A piece in the spring 1923 issue of the FBVE's official organ, *The Vocational Summary*, remarked: "Conservation of our natural resources has been one of the most important developments of the twentieth century. We have reclaimed our arid lands; we have plowed our burned forests into fertile fields; we have taken our discarded metals from the scrap heap and remolded them to other uses. By a natural evolution, crystallized by the casualties of war, we have come to the problem of salvaging our men."[24] Lieutenant Henry Mock of the Army Sanitary Corps agreed, citing "scientific human conservation" as one of the "greatest byproducts of the war."[25] By war's end, the drive to sustain the best in nature coincided with a desire to conserve the best of humanity.

Vocational rehabilitation was written into law with the passage of the Smith-Hughes Act in February 1917. The act called for federal support to "train people who have entered upon, or are preparing to enter upon, the work of the farm."[26] Administration of the act at the state level was facilitated through the Federal Board of Vocational Education.[27] Developing provisions for the rehabilitation of disabled soldiers and sailors was originally only one of the FBVE's duties, but it soon became its primary function. Beth Linker notes that "unlike Europe and Canada, where rehabilitation was largely a voluntary component of a disabled veteran's benefits package, the United States compelled disabled servicemen to undergo long-term medical treatment."[28] In January 1918, a bill was presented to Congress that recommended that rehabilitation work be administrated by a commission of five persons who represented the Office of the Surgeon General, the Department of War, the Department of Labor, the Bureau of War Risk Insurance, and the FBVE. On June 27, 1918, the Vocational Rehabilitation Act was passed with a federal appropriation of approximately $2 million. The act provided for "the vocational training, after their discharge from the service, of persons disabled in the military or naval forces of the United States, and for their assistance in obtaining gainful employment." Although the FBVE initially focused on restoring veterans' disabled bodies, it soon extended its work to the general conservation of "national energies" by providing services to civilian victims of industrial accidents."[29]

Postwar rehabilitation policy was a direct response to previous veterans' programs that had seemed to be characterized by inefficiency, waste, and corruption. At the turn of the century over 1 million Americans were receiving pensions totaling $150 million a year, approximately 38 percent of the entire federal budget. By 1917, the federal government had spent $5 billion on military pensions since 1776, the bulk of which went to Union veterans of the Civil War. Progressive reformers who were wedded to the cult of efficiency believed that the aging veterans of the Grand Army of the Republic were a drain on federal resources and the national work ethic. To prevent increasing the size of this "dependent army of cripples," the Vocational Rehabilitation Act stated that only "severely disabled" soldiers who qualified for compensation under the War Risk Insurance Act were entitled to retraining.[30] One FBVE official bluntly defined the bureau's policy as "one of conservation[;] in the treatment and placing of disabled men back into industry, there is no room for the spectacular."[31] Dr. W. S. Bainbridge of the FBVE used loftier rhetoric: "The rehabilitation of the soldier is a heroic and redemptive act for the nation—it demonstrates a nation's moral fiber and authorizes that nation's economic success."[32]

FBVE models of rehabilitation vacillated between the pragmatic and the utopian. Many of the bureau's personnel saw vocational rehabilitation as a means to transform the "lucky handicap" into a more productive version of his former self. Harry Mock, a professor of industrial medicine who had also served in the army medical corps during the war, noted that "practically every man, no matter how handicapped he may be, can come back. In fact a handicap puts more fight into a man, makes him strive harder than ever before, and results quite often in his making good to a greater extent than if he had never been disabled."[33] Willpower was essential for escaping the dreaded state of deformed dependence. Mock triumphantly cited the case of a double amputee who remarked, "'Watch me! I am going to make good with both feet.' And he has. This is the spirit! Determination and grit—stick-to-itiveness—are the qualities which every disabled man must have or must acquire to crawl out or jump out of that hated class—The Disabled."[34]

Rehabilitationists focused as much attention on conserving the physical output of bodies—the natural kinetic power crucial to economic success—as they did on efforts to restore battered male psyches. The FBVE "Creed of the Disabled Man" pledged veterans to become "a MAN among MEN in spite of their physical handicap."[35] Historians have noted that throughout the West, social scientists conflated the male body with maleness, believing that "an incomplete version of the former could, without careful training and rehabilitation, destroy one's sense of the latter."[36] Harry Mock claimed that the apparent unsuitability of "the unassimilable Chinese, East Indians and Negroes" as sources of additional labor, meant that the nation's greatest source of labor lay "in making that which we have (i.e. white workers) doubly efficient."[37] Rehabilitationists were convinced that "manpower," a gendered and racial vision of natural energies that linked masculinity to physical exertion, needed to be replenished at all costs for the good of the nation.

Diagnosing and Monetizing Disability at the Bureau of War Risk Insurance

For FBVE officials, the diagnosis of disability coincided with its monetization. Veterans' various disabilities were rendered invisible outside the system of monetary compensation established by the FBVE. According to the Vocational Rehabilitation Act of 1918, "persons who had been disabled through their service in the military or naval forces of the United States—whether caused by injury, disease, or aggregation of a previous medical condition—were afforded vocational training and assistance in obtaining gainful employment."[38] Individuals could not enter training until awarded compensation by the Bureau of War Risk Insurance (BWRI). The services and facilities of the Public Health Service were used to provide examination, medical care, treatment, and hospitalization for beneficiaries of the War Risk Insurance Act. Initially the Vocational Rehabilitation Act was intended "to divorce compensation from patriotic sacrifice or physical or mental suffering and instead link it to the reimbursement of potential lost future income due to disability and the general disadvantages it caused the veteran in the labor market."[39] Vocational rehabilitation as defined by the FBVE produced a disabled identity rooted in the imperatives of contemporary political economy, reducing physical impairment to an expression of value or lack thereof.

Because few African Americans suffered combat wounds, their experience of vocational rehabilitation differed from that of their white peers. African Americans' initial diagnosis of disability did not occur during convalescence in domestic or overseas field hospitals but when they submitted disability claims through the BWRI. In the five years following the end of the war, approximately 930,000 veterans applied for disability benefits. Though applicants were required to indicate their race on their appraisal forms, the FBVE and its successors at the Veterans Bureau did not compile statistics on which claims were filed or rejected based on race. Walter Hickel notes that "racial segregation was integral to the social networks within which disability was diagnosed."[40] One bureau official observed that "southern representatives who are of course always white, will not, as a matter of principle, forward us all the necessary evidence to complete the Negroes' claim. As a rule, the fact that the claimant is a Negro in their eyes is sufficient evidence that he is not in need of disability assistance."[41] FBVE doctors contended that the majority of African American veterans were disproportionately afflicted with the ostensibly hidden wounds of "colored diseases" such as venereal disease and tuberculosis. Local officials—such as the FBVE manager of District Five (which included the Carolinas, Georgia, Florida, and Tennessee)—were suspicious of black veterans' claims, suggesting that "the majority of the disabilities of the southern Negro are traceable to TB and VD which in the majority of cases were judged to have existed in the race as a whole before enlistment."[42]

In contrast with traditional military pensions, the model the BWRI developed was not calculated in relation to a veteran's prewar or current occupation. Instead, it measured the average reduction in earning capacity a veteran with a specific disability was likely to incur in any skilled or unskilled occupation. Since reduction in earning capacity varied with the type and severity of the impairment, disability was expressed as a percentage, representing the deviation between the estimated production of an "average" working body and the capacity of a disabled veteran. To help in the calculation of this percentage for "specific injuries of a permanent nature," the BWRI developed a disability rating schedule that included a comprehensive index of amputations, injuries, diseases, and mental disorders. This schedule assigned percentages for each impairment based on its purported effect on the veteran's ability to work. While rates of compensation varied according to marital status and dependents, veterans who were given a 10 percent rating or more for a temporary disability were entitled to approximately $80 to $120 a month. Those who were judged to be suffering from total disability, including blindness, multiple amputations, and the "helpless and permanently bedridden," were assessed at a flat rate of $100 a month.[43]

Veteran's benefits were dispensed as inducements for the disabled to redirect their productive energies in unprecedented and profitable ways in both the public and private sector. Westinghouse's medical director, Charles Lauffer, insisted that "in this age of specialization and diversified industry, arms and legs are really incidental, for with mechanical devices, such handicaps are virtually overcome."[44] For ex-servicemen with serious physical impairments, officials stressed the mental acuity needed to perform skilled industrial labor: "While from his neck down a man is worth about $1.50 a day; from his neck up, he may well be worth $100,000 a year."[45] Conversely, appeals to veterans experiencing mental disorder emphasized the need for physical vigor and the resistance to fatigue that was required for modern industrial work. One army official noted, "A man is crippled only to that extent to which he allows his physical handicap to put him down and out. If he ceases to be an economic factor in society—an earning, serving unit—he is a cripple."[46] For a postwar managerial elite steeped in industrial management and evolutionary theory, disability was both an identity and a commodity: a corporeal index of labor capital or lack thereof.

FBVE officials believed that their disability rating schedule democratized veteran entitlements by defining disability in relative terms—as a declension from a productive or "normal" body. Early twentieth-century models of republican manhood dictated that the ideal or normative working body was that of a white man. Economic and social dependency and noncitizenship were associated with women, children and people of color such as African Americans.[47] FBVE officials and African American veterans both understood disability as a social construction with distinct racial and gender dynamics. Hickel contends that in defining disability, both groups "emphasized the structure of local labor markets, racial segregation, and social norms, which assigned men their roles as workers, providers, and citizens."[48] For all veterans, disability denoted more than an individual medical condition or a purely legal entitlement to benefits. African American veterans saw their injuries as marks of patriotic sacrifice that entitled them to veterans' benefits, while rehabilitationists saw them as indelible proofs of blacks' pathological inferiority.

Notwithstanding the race-neutral posture they took, many FBVE officials recognized that benefits paid to black veterans could potentially undermine white dominance rooted in income distribution, regional labor markets, and citizenship rights. Compensation could amount to several times more than the $30 a month black agricultural laborers earned on average in the South, and it could more than equal the $500 to $600 annual income of most rural black families. Though modest, these benefits would enable black veterans to temporarily forego poorly paid menial "colored" jobs, and gain a small measure of financial independence.[49] The financial and educational opportunities black veterans received could also work to undermine many of the dubious property and literacy requirements that restricted black voting rights in the south. The FBVE's characterizations of blacks as congenital racial cripples effectively rationalized the economic and social imperatives of southern and national white supremacy.

"The right peoples for the right work": Race and Vocational Training at the FBVE

The difficulties African American veterans experienced with drawing compensation—with its pernicious subtext of black dependency—invariably circumscribed their access to job training. Sympathetic observers linked war to work when they argued that black veterans had a right to rehabilitation: "The Negro soldier left a civil occupation to take up his gun. These recruits were not loiterers, but laborers in the larger sense. They were contributing to the nation and the world's work in various ways both skilled and otherwise."[50] In the initial stage of physical reconstruction—which was conducted by the Office of the Army Surgeon General—disability was perceived as a source of entitlement to re-training. When the process shifted to vocational rehabilitation, disability was redefined as a chance to remake oneself. For FBVE officials, this represented an unprecedented opportunity for the "crippled Negro race" to work its way to civilized respectability. Vocational rehabilitation reinforced the masculine character of racial uplift through its efforts to "not only make the Negro a better workman, but also teach him to build a better home and live a more ideal life."[51] FBVE policy was motivated by "the idea to elevate the economic status of these (black) men sufficiently to enable their children to attend school and their women to give more time to the moral and hygienic development of the home."[52] On both sides of the color line, the ethic of rehabilitation equated fit bodies with healthy homes.

African American veterans' wounds were a form of social currency that supposedly entitled them to vocational rehabilitation. Initially, the state appeared willing to forego racial bias to let them receive this service in the name of national efficiency. FBVE official Callie Hull noted that "if the Negro is coming into our lives to stay—and we need him—we should recognize the fact that he is perfectly capable of profiting under vocational instruction and becoming a worker worthy of the name."[53] However most FBVE officials were not so accommodating. Frederic

Keough felt that "the fact that a man is a disabled soldier or sailor is not enough to place him in any systematic manufacturing plant. He must be productive." Most importantly, Keough concluded, vocational rehabilitation "must terminate in an economic advantage to the *community*."[54] Yet amid what historian Matt Guterl describes as a "southernization" of postwar national race relations, appeals that focused on the advantages to the community of rehabilitation significantly limited the kinds of work African Americans could do and where they could do it in light of these spatial racial divisions.[55]

In the summer of 1918, the FBVE established the Rehabilitation Division to undertake the vocational education and placement of veterans. This division had three types of offices: the Central Office at Washington D.C., fourteen district offices that covered two or more states, and 100 or more local offices. Each district office was headed by a district vocational officer, who supervised two or more assistant district vocational officers. One of these officers was responsible for training supervisors in the local offices and another for industrial relations and employment aid. Dr. J. R. Crossland, an African American and a self-described "fearless defender of the claims of the Negro," was appointed by the FBVE as a "special expert on Negro affairs."[56] Though some in the black community saw Crossland's post as little more than ceremonial, he was a key mediator between black ex-servicemen and the often Byzantine workings of the FBVE.[57]

Fears that disabled veterans and the disabled in general would become burdens on society led to repeated calls that integration, not segregation, was essential for any truly effective program of rehabilitation. FBVE officials drew on a transnational network of rehabilitation policies and practices to craft effective programs of rehabilitation stateside and avoid the specter of the "burdensome cripple." Foreign officials such as Major John L. Todd of the Canadian pension board believed that "there is a danger inherent in the reservation of specific employment for disabled men. It makes a special class of cripples; employments reserved for them cannot fail to become characterized as subnormal occupations."[58] Long segregated into menial "subnormal occupations" African American veterans now found themselves trapped in a double bind of race and disability.

The FBVE's "one size fits all" policy of reintegrating veterans into the general work force collapsed in the summer of 1921. Amid mounting allegations of corruption and inefficiency, the FBVE was absorbed into the Veterans Bureau in August 1921. All federal officers of the FBVE were eliminated, and complete authority for determining the eligibility of ex-servicemen for training was delegated to the district offices. The decentralization of the FBVE allowed local mores regarding race, labor, and disability to emerge as the dominant model in the bureau's day-to-day operations. Given that four out of five black veterans lived south of the Mason-Dixon line, southerners exercised a tremendous influence over FBVE policy. During the mass exodus of blacks to the North, East Coast elites increasingly deferred to southern "racial expertise" to deal with the sudden "Negro problem" in their midst. Medical models of rehabilitation allowed southern FBVE officials to couch their traditional animus toward African Americans in the more palatable rhetoric of scientific racism. Noting tubercular blacks' apparent inability to undertake "strenuous vocational rehabilitation," officials in the FBVE's central office in Washington, D.C., concurred with their southern counterparts that "tuberculosis is in the colored race as a whole."[59] In light of these apparent biological facts, any attempts to retrain tubercular African Americans for industrial labor were dismissed as foolish and contrary to the laws of science and nature.

Vocational rehabilitation in the south was a key mechanism for segmenting labor along racial lines. Biological rationales for African American inferiority bolstered the socioeconomic imperatives of Jim Crow laws. And while these rationalizations were undeniably racist, they were not irrational in the context of contemporary political economy. African Americans *were* indispensable to the southern rural economy. Blacks comprised 48 percent of all southerners engaged in agriculture, they cultivated two-thirds of the region's land, they owned or rented 41,000,000 acres of farmland worth approximately $1 billion, and they tilled some 60,000,000 more as laborers. Southern elites prevailed upon the FBVE to provide the "Negro with the kind of education that he needs and demands, namely, vocational agricultural education."[60] From November 1917 to November 1918, federal funds subsidized the creation of thirty-nine vocational education schools for African American veterans and workers. FBVE agent H. O. Sargent proudly noted that "in these schools little attention is given to preparing students for college" and that "classes were directed solely to the productive field of farming."[61] Violence—real and imagined—sustained Jim Crow laws and invariably colored African Americans' experiences of rehabilitation. When FBVE officials assigned Oscar Woods to undertake tailoring training in Georgia despite his extensive background in auto mechanics, he protested to special Negro Advisor J. R. Crossland: "I would prefer to pass through Alabama in an aeroplane, driving fast at that, of course . . . on account I hers they have the KKK in Georgia and Alabama and Ises know how they hates working niggers." Woods fearfully insisted that if he was sent to Alabama, "when yous bring me back ise won't need no meal ticket. My flag draped casket will be enough."[62] This combination of regional racialized labor practices and hierarchies and the constant threat of violence forced many African American veterans to confront the brutal and practical limits of vocational rehabilitation.

Theories of African Americans as racial cripples were not confined to the South. Northern FBVE officials also maintained a circumscribed list of semiskilled and unskilled trades for the minority of African American veterans who qualified for vocational rehabilitation. Throughout the nation, African American veterans were disproportionately placed in training for shoemaking and tailoring, with auto mechanics—the sole mechanical occupation—ranking a distant third. If blacks selected trades that did not appear on the approved list, bureau officials were instructed to keep them out of training indefinitely. When Mack Hudson of Philadelphia, who had an undisclosed injury, reported to his local FBVE office upon being certified for training, he requested auto mechanics but was offered shoe repair. When Hudson refused, he was told that the board "could do nothing more for him."[63] J. R. Crossland protested, "It appears from the complaints which constantly pour into my office that several districts believe there are certain occupations in which they cannot afford colored men. And it is not always true that the necessary facilities are not present and readily available. The whole thing is working a great injustice upon the men of my racial group."[64]

Notwithstanding these various challenges, the majority of disabled African American veterans—emboldened by their wartime service and accustomed to the occupational segregation of Jim Crow—complied with their vocational placements. One official observed that most men went "into training at the trades they are given not with the view to being rehabilitated, or even ever working at the particular trade, but simply to draw the training pay for the allotted time." Like all veterans, African Americans placed more importance on their financial benefits than they did on the actual practices of physical rehabilitation. Bureau officials constantly complained that African American ex-servicemen were "lazy" in not taking up vocational training and should therefore be denied compensation. Similar charges of negligence were leveled against veterans of all backgrounds, but only African Americans were continually and disproportionally denied compensation and job training by the War Risk Insurance Act and the FBVE.[65]

To Make the Negro Anew?: Race and Health Care at Tuskegee Veterans Hospital

Debates surrounding the racial dynamics of policies for veterans culminated in the development and operation of Federal Veterans Hospital 91 at Tuskegee, Alabama. From its founding in 1923, institutionalization rather than rehabilitation was the hospital's guiding principle. Hospital staff were less concerned with making the Negro anew than with managing their patients' disabilities. Palliative rather than curative care was the norm, and segregation—occupational, residential, and social—became the rule of the day. Despite these attitudes, African American veterans believed that residence at Veterans Hospital No. 91 endowed their injuries with the stamp of federal authority that entitled them to the compensation needed for vocational rehabilitation.

In contrast to the army's rigorous enforcement of Jim Crow policies, racial segregation did not officially extend to rehabilitation hospitals. The commitment
of rehabilitationists to efficiency and standardization and the real and imagined
absence of blacks from the ranks of the "deserving disabled" accounted for this
seemingly integrationist policy. The surgeon general's office repeatedly claimed
that it had "no intention . . . to settle the so-called Race Question."[66] However, the
absence of de facto segregation did not preclude the practice of de jure racial segregation. Authorities throughout the nation often refused to hospitalize black veterans in integrated institutions for fear that their mere presence would undermine
(white) patient morale and enflame the local community. Especially troubling was
the specter of race mixing, in which white female nurses or physiotherapists could
find themselves in proximity to the crippled, diseased, and half-clothed bodies of
African American veterans.[67] For those blacks who were "fortunate" enough to be
admitted to Public Health Service hospitals, treatment was typically administered
in inferior segregated facilities. One veteran, Issac Webb, described his experience
in a letter to *The Crisis*:

> I am also one of the boys who volunteered in 1917 for services "over there" and I have
> spent six months in hospitals for the disabled. . . . At Mobile, I was handed my food
> out of a window, forbidden to use the front of the hospital to enter my ward, given
> no medical attention and forced to use the same toilet facilities fellows in advanced
> stages of syphilis and gonorrhea used.[68]

Because of such treatment, many African American veterans refused to seek treatment at Public Health Service facilities, and black hospitalization rates were almost
50 to 80 percent below those of whites.[69]

Tuskegee Veterans Hospital grew from the efforts of the Consultations on Hospitalization—or the aptly named White Committee—that were convened in spring
1921 by Secretary of the Treasury Andrew Mellon. Secretary Mellon enlisted a committee of medical experts who labored for two years to create a veterans hospital
system that was "not only national, but rational" in scope. Dr. John Farris, head of
the Red Cross Institute for the Blind and Disabled echoed this commitment to pragmatism when he argued that rehabilitation hospitals, "should be the nursery of new
hopes and ambitions, and not a Bridge of Sighs."[70] These new facilities would be
organized and financed by the federal government and would initially be restricted
to veterans with diseases and injuries related to combat service. The committee
was assisted by an advisory group that included representatives from the Public
Health Service, the National Committee for Mental Hygiene, the National Home
for Disabled Volunteer Soldiers, and the National Tuberculosis Association. The
committee's final report recommended that a separate national hospital for black
veterans be established at Tuskegee, Alabama, the mecca of black vocational edu-

cation. Although the original legislation that established the hospital system did not mention separate facilities for black veterans, the committee noted early in its deliberations that "one of the great American problems—that of race—obtruded itself more and more."[71]

Debates over whether to employ a white, black, or integrated staff spoke to the broader issues of professional expertise, racial segregation, and the right to define disability. The African American National Medical Association and the NAACP aggressively lobbied the federal government to employ black staff at Tuskegee to maintain the school's long-standing "commitment to race betterment." It was felt that in addition to providing much-needed jobs for African American physicians and nurses, blacks would provide better care to patients due to their supposed "racial affinity." Dr. J. F. Lane of Lane College remarked, "If we cannot serve our own people, where shall we work and whom are we to serve?"[72] The White Committee rejected Lane's petition because of a shortage of black orthopedic surgeons and a general aversion to recognizing any form of African American professional expertise. Instead, it chose to staff the hospital with white personnel.[73]

Demands for an all-black staff increased after the hospital's official dedication in spring 1923. General Frank T. Hines, newly appointed head of the veterans bureau in Washington, D.C., asked Tuskegee's Dr. Robert R. Moton whether he thought it advisable to staff the hospital with black doctors. Moton replied that "inasmuch as all the patients will be Negroes and since Negro physicians are not allowed at present to practice in any large hospitals it would be fair to give them this opportunity."[74] Tuskegee whites were infuriated at the prospect of "colored doctors," and the local Ku Klux Klan staged a number of dramatic and violent protests on the hospital grounds in the summer of 1923. The Klan denounced the presence of "carpet-bagging negro professionals" and demanded that the hospital maintain an all-white staff, even though this contravened a state law prohibiting white medical personnel—specifically female nurses—from treating blacks. Klansmen took the remarkable step of privileging white medical expertise over the alleged protection of white womanhood, stating that "we are not going to have any niggers in this state who we cannot control."[75]

While many in Washington were more than sympathetic to the Klan, most officials simply could not countenance attacks on federal property. Consequently the Republican administrations of Warren Harding and Calvin Coolidge reluctantly agreed to turn the hospital administration over to African Americans in order to curry favor with the growing bloc of urban black voters in the North. Tuskegee Hospital's white administrator, Dr. Robert Stanley, was quickly replaced with Dr. John Ward, a leading figure in black medical circles who had served in France.[76] Ward arrived at Tuskegee in July 1924 and directed his staff to maintain their focus on providing patients with "sympathetic aid and comfort," as opposed to occupational therapy, for which "our veterans would have little use given the social strictures placed on their advancement."[77]

At the Veterans Bureau's peak in 1923, it and the FBVE were active in rehabilitating approximately 2,500 African American ex-servicemen, and an additional 1,500 were rehabilitated in hospitals, the majority at Tuskegee. Yet in keeping with the era's racial paternalism, hospital officials on both sides of the color line defined broken black bodies as symptomatic of broken black homes. Reviewing the patient files of Mr. Tuttle Duke—a "rather foppish fellow" who was divorced—a Red Cross official remarked that his "enfeebled physical state as a tubercular" was matched "only by his predilection for vice so characteristic for a Negro of his type."[78] In their monthly reports, hospital officials routinely derided "deformed and malformed" patients as "unfit guardians" and "absentee fathers and husbands."[79] The diseased and deformed bodies of black veterans were read as evidence of their debased familial values and as a threat to the broader social fabric. One staff member noted that patients should be denied the opportunity to return to their families even if "many feel that they can take the treatment as well at home and worry needlessly about their families, for if the truth were known, many of the families are far better off when the patient is away."[80] In early 1924, the new Red Cross director, E. M. Murray, cited the increasing "tendency of patients bringing their families to Tuskegee as something which we are endeavoring to prevent as much as possible."[81] Hospital officials traded on prevailing theories of African American degeneracy as social contagion to rationalize the restrictive forms of care they insisted on. Tuskegee hospital's emphasis on palliative care reduced its patients to little more than wards of the state.

Tuskegee's paternalist ethos also exposed intraracial class tensions. Medical professionals drawn from the African American elite—those W. E. B. Du Bois deemed the "talented tenth"—who had been weaned on models of social Darwinism worried that the mental and physical injuries of their predominately working-class patients could, if left unattended, impede the race's progress to respectability. Therefore it followed that only black medical professionals could be entrusted to guide their patients back to a manly respectability.[82] From 1923 to 1925, Red Cross workers placed close to 200 ex-servicemen in local financial institutions such as the Bank of Tuskegee.[83] Hospital workers also took steps to confine some of the severely mentally and physically disabled in jails and insane asylums, effectively criminalizing perceived racial disabilities. An especially egregious example occurred when the Red Cross and the Veterans Bureau sent thirty tubercular African American veterans to the Central State Hospital for the Criminal Insane in Nashville, on the spurious pretext that "their condition could be attributed to a uniquely racial mental affliction."[84] Tuskegee officials, both black and white, eschewed vocational rehabilitation in favor of the various disciplinary institutions of the emerging postwar prison industrial complex.

Conclusion: Race and Rehabilitation in Interwar America

World War I–era policies and practices of rehabilitation reinforced long-standing models of white supremacy that sanctioned the discipline of black bodies under state and federal auspices. Beth Linker notes that rehabilitation "was born as a progressive era ideal, took shape as a military medical specialty, and eventually became a societal norm in the civilian sector."[85] The efforts of rehabilitationists to delineate the "deserving" from the "undeserving" disabled framed citizenship in decidedly corporeal terms. This focus on the body significantly limited opportunities for injured African American veterans, whose very physiognomy had historically marked them as defective. Whereas white veterans could draw on the seemingly latent superiority of their racial constitution to remake themselves into fit, efficient workers, black veterans were seen to be prisoners of their irredeemably primitive bodies. Historian Natalia Molina has shown how cultural mores and legislative imperatives have coalesced around issues such as immigration "to write race on the body so indelibly that they are almost indistinguishable from biological inscription."[86] FBVE officials conflated blackness, disability, and dependence—the antithesis of republican citizenship—as they consigned African American veterans to the margins of the interwar labor economy.

Henri-Jacques Stiker reminds us that models of rehabilitation that emerged from the Great War reconfigured disability from a curative condition tied to notions of "removal and individual health" to a "lack to be overcome" or a "deficiency to be remedied" through various legislative and institutional channels.[87] Through these new forms of rehabilitation, race became a key marker of difference in the real and symbolic postwar economy of disease and disability. Yet given rehabilitationists' oft-cited beliefs in the inferiority of African Americans, even seemingly limited forms of rehabilitation appeared to run counter to the core tenet of modern veterans' care: autonomy before charity. Elites in both the public and private spheres worried whether the state should actively enable "the worst dependent traits of the colored race" in a misguided and costly attempt to salvage the unsalvageable. Many proposed that the state should simply "cut the colored man loose" and let the dysgenic natures of war and industry finally do away with "the burdensome Negro problem."[88]

While FBVE policies were profoundly racialist, they were not driven by explicit racial prejudice. In fact, race hatred was quite beside the point. Michael Adas argues that "the successful management of the war effort emboldened social scientists to rationalize human systems and improve social morality (i.e. the work ethic) through the application of theories informed by analogies to the natural sciences and technology."[89] Rehabilitationists saw themselves as self-appointed guardians of evolution, weeding the fit from the unfit, and pruning society of its most undesirable elements. These practices were rationalized as the imperatives of efficiency rather than the mere capriciousness of racial animus. Rehabilitationists believed that limiting African American veterans' compensation, consigning them to menial occupations, and isolating them in segregated health care facilities were all necessary interventions in the processes of social evolution.[90]

Implicit in the policy and practice of rehabilitation—the drive for "aggressive normalization"—was a regulatory impulse to contain bodily and social difference, so readily embodied in the figure of "the Negro." Through these processes, evolutionary science combined with scientific management to reconcile racial form with labor function. These new forms of racial knowledge linked race and labor fitness to color and the body: the healthy, normative, white working body was juxtaposed against the degenerate, abnormal, black working body. Consequently, the wounds of black veterans were seen not as badges of patriotic honor but as the stigmata of atavistic agents that threatened to poison society from within. Even for the most liberal-minded rehabilitationists, the goal was never "to make the Negro anew" but to contain, or at best diminish, the far-reaching and dangerous socioeconomic effects of what they believed would be blacks' inevitable slide into degeneracy.

Vocational rehabilitation was a discursive and legislative tool postwar managerial elites deployed to come to terms with an emerging African American proletariat. New methods of labor division along racial lines were required as the Negro moved from the farm to the city. Rehabilitation fused biology with social policy to distinguish the practices and entitlements of "colored man's work" from those of "white man's work" in stark physiological terms. FBVE models of vocational rehabilitation perpetuated and institutionalized prevailing notions of the Negro as diseased, deviant, and congenitally unfit for modern industrial life. For the ideological and institutional architects of postwar white supremacy, the crippled and deformed body of the disabled Negro veteran was a harbinger of America's prospective racial decline, the canary in the nation's evolutionary mineshaft.[91] However these new bodies of racial knowledge produced by wartime testing and rehabilitation did not remain constant over time. Rather, they were repeatedly challenged by the exigencies of war, migration, and urbanization and by African Americans themselves in ways that eventually helped sever race from biology while still confining the average African American veteran and black workers as a whole to the margins of the postwar labor economy.

Notes

1. Harry Mock, "Reclamation of the Disabled from the Industrial Army," *Annals of the American Academy of Political and Social Science* 80 (November 1918): 30; Howard Zinn and Anthony Arnove, *Voices of a People's History of the United States* (New York: Seven Stories, 2004), 299.

2. Despite the public's fascination with amputees, fewer than 5,000 returning veterans needed prosthetics; see Michael Lansing, "Salvaging the Manpower: Conservation, Manhood and Disabled Veterans during World War One," *Environmental History* 14, no. 1 (2009): 2. Before the war, the United States was one of the world's largest producers of artificial limbs; see Beth Linker, *War's Waste: Rehabilitation in World War One America* (Chicago: University of Chicago Press, 2011), 98–99.

3. Lothrop Stoddard, *The Revolt against Civilization: The Menace of the Under Man* (New York: Charles Scribner's Sons, 1922), 120. See also Lothrop Stoddard, *The Rising Tide of Color against White World Wide Supremacy* (New York: Charles Scribner's Sons, 1920).

4. Joanna Bourke, *Dismembering the Male: Men's Bodies, Britain, and the Great War* (Chicago: University of Chicago Press, 1996), 11; "Caring for the Soldiers Health: Reducing the Loss from Sickness and Wounds, Businesslike Humanity—Burying 140 Men an Hour," *World's Work* 28 (October 1914): 119; David Gerber, "Introduction: Finding Disabled Veterans in History," in *Disabled Veterans in History*, ed. David Gerber (Ann Arbor: University of Michigan Press, 2000), 4.

5. Gerber, "Introduction," 4.

6. Bourke, *Dismembering the Male*, 1–3.

7. Early twentieth-century racial thought held deeply contradictory views of the black body. Whereas blacks were generally assumed to be physically superior to whites—because of the former's supposed innate savagery—this advantage was seemingly compromised by blacks' apparent mental and moral deficiencies; the savage strength of the black body was canceled out by the savage depravity of the black mind. For insight into how modern American racial thought saw a divide between the black mind and body, see Lee Baker, *From Savage to Negro: Anthropology and the Construction of Race, 1896–1954* (Berkley: University of California Press, 1998); Daryl Michael Scott, *Contempt and Pity: Social Policy and the Image of the Black Psyche, 1880–1996* (Chapel Hill: University of North Carolina Press, 1997).

8. Gerber, "Introduction," 4; and Bourke, *Dismembering the Male*. For insights into rehabilitation as a mechanism of colonial and transnational control of racial labor, see Elizabeth West, "Divine Fragments: Even India has Begun to Salvage Its Man Power," *Carry On* 1, no. 3 (1918): 22–25; Laura Frader, "From Muscles to Nerves: Gender, 'Race,' and the Body at Work in France, 1919–1939," *International Review of Social History* 44, supplement S7 (1999): 123–147; and Jennifer Keene, "Protest and Disability: A New Look at African American Soldiers during the First World War," in *Warfare and Belligerence: Perspectives in First World War Studies*, edited by Pierre Purseigle (Boston: Brill, 2005), 216–241.

9. Daniel Bender, *American Abyss: Savagery and Civilization in the Age of Industry* (Ithaca, N.Y.: Cornell University Press, 2009), 3. Literary critic Martha Banta has argued that Taylorism was an extended narrative structure and discourse system that extended far

beyond the factory floor to encompass every aspect of cultural existence; Martha Banta, *Taylored Lives: Narrative Productions in the Age of Taylor, Veblen, and Ford* (Chicago: University of Chicago Press, 1993), 4.

10. Matt Price, "Lives and Limbs: Rehabilitation of Wounded Soldiers in the Aftermath of the Great War," in "Cultural and Technological Incubations of Fascism," edited by Marcel Lieberman and Laura Kerr, special issue, *Stanford Electronic Humanities Review* 5 (December 1996): 5; Beth Linker, "Feet for Fighting: Locating Disability and Social Medicine in First World War America," *Social History of Medicine* 20, no. 1 (2007): 91–109; Bender, *American Abyss*, 243–245.

11. Elizabeth Upham, "Selective Placement of the Disabled," *The Vocational Summary* 2 (June 1919): 35.

12. W. E. B. Du Bois, "Close Ranks," *Crisis* 16 (July 1918): 111.

13. Richard Slotkin, *Lost Battalions: The Great War and the Crisis of American Nationality* (New York: Henry Holt, 2005), 238.

14. Ibid., 238–239.

15. Chad Williams, *Torchbearers of Democracy: African American Soldiers in the World War I Era* (Chapel Hill: University of North Carolina Press, 2010), 6.

16. Ibid., 108. See also Walter Shenk, *"Work or Fight!" Race, Gender and the Draft in World War One* (New York: Palgrave-MacMillan, 2005), 4–10.

17. Williams, *Torchbearers of Democracy*, 111.

18. Ibid. The most famous black combat regiment was the 369th Harlem Hell Fighters, who were attached to the French Fourth Army and became one of the most highly decorated Allied units of the war. John Hope Franklin, *From Slavery to Freedom: A History of American Negroes*, 3rd ed. (New York: Vintage Books, 1969), 455, 462–463; Gail Buckley, *American Patriots: The Story of Blacks in the Military from the Revolution to Desert Storm* (New York: Random House, 2001), 165; Keene, "Protest and Disability," 218–219.

19. Williams, *Torchbearers of Democracy*, 108–113.

20. By 1930, half a million blacks had left the region of their birth. At mid-century, 96 percent of black northerners and 90 percent of black westerners lived in urban areas; see Ira Berlin, *The Making of African America: The Four Great Migrations* (New York: Viking, 2010), 154. For analysis of African Americans' subsequent cultural and sonic engagement with urban modernity and industrial work, see Joel Dinerstein, *Swinging the Machine: Modernity, Technology, and African American Culture between the World Wars* (Amherst: University of Massachusetts Press, 2003).

21. Kevin Gains, *Uplifting the Race: Black Leadership, Politics, and Culture in the Twentieth Century* (Chapel Hill: University of North Carolina Press, 1996), 236; Franklin, *From Slavery to Freedom*, 480–481; Kennedy, *Over Here*, 214–225; "Returned Negro Soldiers," *The Survey* 42, no. 5 (May 3, 1919): 207. For insights on African American soldiers as vanguards of the postwar New Negro consciousness, see Williams, *Torchbearers of Democracy*.

22. Bourke, *Dismembering the Male*, 171. Alan Peacock and Jack Wiseman have referred to this process as the "inspection effect" of wartime economies; ibid.

23. One of the first progressives to cite the racially dysgenic effects of war was David Starr Jordan, president of Stanford University. See Starr's seminal work on the subject, *War and Waste*, which was published in 1913 and republished in 1914. Bender, *American*

Abyss, 233–234; Gerber, "Introduction," 8; W. M. Hussie, "How Forestry and Tree Culture Concern the Disabled Soldier," *American Forestry* 24 (December 1918): 725–726.

24. "War Disabled Negroes in Training," *The Vocational Summary* (Spring 1923): 33.

25. Mock, "Reclamation of the Disabled from the Industrial Army," 30.

26. William S. Holt, *The Federal Board of Vocational Education: Its History, Activities and Organization* (BiblioBazaar, 2000), 45.

27. Ibid.

28. Linker, *War's Waste*, 33.

29. Evangaline Thurber, *Preliminary Checklist of the General Administrative Files of the Rehabilitation Division Created under the Federal Board for Vocational Education (1918–21) and the United States Veterans' Bureau (1921–28), and Received from the Veterans' Administration* ([Washington, D.C.]: National Archives, 1944), 6. The FBVE administered this work until it was subsumed by the Veterans Bureau in 1921.

30. Black Civil War veterans, whose health had been historically read through the prism of morality, hypersexuality, and inferiority, were especially vulnerable to charges of "dependency" and subsequently were denied pensions at nearly double the rate of their white peers. For insight into late nineteenth-century discourses of race, health, and citizenship, see Jim Downs, *Sick from Freedom: African American Illness and Suffering during the Civil War and Reconstruction* (Oxford: Oxford University Press, 2012), 156–158. See also Robert Hughes, "The Lucky Handicap," *Carry On* 1, no. 3 (September 1918): 11–12; James Munroe, "The War's Crippled: How They May Be Made Assets Both to Themselves and to Society," *Survey* 60 (May 18, 1918): 179; and Scott Gelber, "'A Hard Boiled Order': The Reeducation of Disabled WW1 Veterans in New York City," *Journal of Social History* 3, no. 1 (2005): 167.

31. Douglas McMurtrie, "Your Duty to the War Cripple," *American Journal of Care for Cripples* 7, no. 1 (September 1918): 82.

32. W. S. Bainbridge, "Social Responsibilities in the Rehabilitation of Disabled Soldiers and Sailors," *American Journal of Care for Cripples* 7, no. 2 (December 1918): 126–132. See also "The High Road to Self-Support," *Carry On* 1, no. 1 (June 1918): 4–9; George M. Price, "Rehabilitation Problems," *The Survey* 41, no. 26 (March 29, 1919), 921–922; Kennedy, *Over Here*, 188; and Frederic W. Keough, "The Employment of Disabled Servicemen," *Annals of the American Academy of Political and Social Science* 80 (November 1918): 84.

33. Harry Edgar Mock, *Industrial Medicine and Surgery* (Philadelphia: W. B. Saunders, 1919), 777.

34. Mock, "Reclamation of the Disabled from the Industrial Army," 30.

35. "American Legion Notes," *National Service* 9, no. 6 (June 1921): 337.

36. Bourke, *Dismembering the Male*, 178.

37. Ibid.

38. Thurber, *Preliminary Checklist of the General Administrative Files of the Rehabilitation Division*, 6–7.

39. Ibid. 7.

40. K. Walter Hickel, "Medicine, Bureaucracy, and Social Welfare," in *The New Disability History: American Perspectives*, edited by Paul K. Longmore and Laurie Umansky (New York: New York University Press, 2001), 239.

41. Ibid., 239.

42. Ibid., 240.

43. Ana Carden-Coyne, "Ungrateful Bodies: Rehabilitation, Resistance and Disabled American Veterans of the First World War," *European Review of History* 14 (December 2007): 548.

44. Charles Lauffer, "The Injured in Industry," *Carry On* 1 (June 1919): 11.

45. "From His Neck up a Man May Be Worth $100,000 a Year," *Carry On* 1, no. 1 (June 1918): 23.

46. Mock, "Reclamation of the Disabled from the Industrial Army," 30. For early twentieth-century theories of labor power as a metric of social efficiency, see Anson Rabinbach, *The Human Motor: Energy, Fatigue, and the Origins of Modernity* (Berkeley: University of California Press, 1990), 242–244; Luther Gulick, "The Effect of Fatigue on Character," *World's Work* 10 (August 1907): 270–271; and Alice Hamilton, "Fatigue, Efficiency and Insurance Discussed by the American Public Health Association," *The Survey* 37, no. 6 (November 1916): 135–138.

47. Sociologist Robert Park famously characterized the Negro as the "lady of the races" because of a perceived love of finery and lack of vitality. See Davarian Baldwin, *Chicago's New Negroes: Modernity, The Great Migration, and Black Urban Life* (Chapel Hill: University of North Carolina Press, 2007), 26–27.

48. Hickel, "Medicine, Bureaucracy, and Social Welfare," 257.

49. Ibid.

50. Callie Hull, "Reopening Industry's Doors to the Returning Negro Soldiers," *The Vocational Summary* 2, no. 5 (September 1919): 88.

51. "James Sanford to Dr. J. R. A. Crossland, November 10, 1921, Entry 50, Box 2, General Correspondence File Folder, Record Group 15.5.2, Records of the Office of Veterans Affairs, Central Office Records, National Archives and Records Administration, Washington, D.C. (hereafter NARA). See also W. E. B. Du Bois, "Returning Soldiers," *The Crisis* XVIII (May 1919), 19; Nancy Bristol, *Making Men Moral: Civil Liberties and Public Morality* (Oxford: Clarendon Press, 1993), 176–177; and Sergeant Greenleaf B. Johnson, "The Negro's Part in the War in Democracy," *The Washington Bee*, January, 18, 1919.

52. Thomas Jesse Jones, *Negro Education: A Study of the Private and Higher Schools for the Colored People of the United States*, vol. 1 (Washington, D.C.: Government Printing Office, 1917), 10.

53. Hull, "Reopening Industry's Doors to the Returned Colored Soldiers," 88.

54. Keough, "The Employment of Disabled Servicemen," 93, Keough's italics.

55. Matthew Pratt Guterl, *The Color of Race in America, 1900–1940* (Cambridge: Harvard University Press, 2001), 12.

56. For Release: Biography of J. R. Crossland, Entry 50, Box 1, Misc. Correspondence File 1920–1925, Record Group 15.5.2, Records of the Office of Veterans Affairs, Central Office Records, National Archives and Records Administration, NARA.

57. Ibid.

58. John L. Todd, "The Meaning of Rehabilitation," *Annals of the American Academy of Political and Social Science* 80 (November 1918): 8.

59. Hickel, "Medicine, Bureaucracy, and Social Welfare," 256.

60. Callie Hull, "Reopening Industry's Doors to the Returned Colored Soldiers," *Vocational Summary* 2, no. 5 (September 1919): 88.

61. H. O. Sargent, "Vocational Agricultural Education for Negroes in the Southern Region," *The Vocational Summary* 1, no. 7 (November 1918): 12.

62. Quoted in J. R. Crossland to Acting Asst. Director Rehabilitation Division, U.S. Veterans Bureau, April 3, 1923, RG 15, Entry 50, Crossland Correspondence File, 1920–1925, Box 1, NARA.

63. Ibid.

64. Ibid.

65. Hickel, "Medicine, Bureaucracy, and Social Welfare," 258.

66. Charles M. Griffith to C. R. Forbes, Director, U.S. Veterans Bureau, April 29, 1922, RG 15.3, Entry 55, NARA.

67. See Ernest Luce to I. Fisher, "Disabled Negro Soldiers in Training," Veterans Administration, Ernest Luce, Office Files on Supervisor of Advisement and Training, October 1920, RG 15, Entry 20, Box 1, NARA.

68. Vanessa Gamble, *Making a Place for Ourselves: The Black Hospital Movement, 1920–1945* (New York: Oxford University Press, 1995), 73.

69. J. R. Crossland to Smith, Division of Vocational Rehabilitation, U.S. Veterans Bureau, January 3, 1922, RG 15.2, Records of the Bureau of Pensions and Its Predecessors, Entry 50, Box 2, General Correspondence File Folder, NARA.

70. Quoted in Ana Carden-Coyne, "Rehabilitation, Resistance and Disabled American Veterans of the First World War," *European Review of History* 4, no. 7 (2007): 547. See also Wiley Hill to J. R. Crossland, January 23, 1922, U.S. Veterans Bureau Division of Vocational rehabilitation for Disabled Soldiers, Sailors and Marines, RG 15, Entry 50, Box 4, General Correspondence File Folder, NARA.

71. Quoted in Vanessa Gamble, *Making a Place for Ourselves*, 73–74; see also "War-Disabled Negroes in Training," *The Vocational Summary* 4, no. 2 (June 1923): 33–34.

72. Quoted in William J. Schieffelin, "The Most Unforgettable Character I've Met: Robert Russa Moton," *Reader's Digest*, November 1950, 25.

73. Gamble, *Making a Place for Ourselves*, 73–74.

74. Schieffelin, "The Most Unforgettable Character I've Met," 25.

75. Mark Schneider, *We Return Fighting: Civil Rights in the Jazz Age* (Boston: Northeastern University Press, 2002), 236.

76. Gamble, *Making a Place for Ourselves*, 100–101. For an analysis of the rise of interwar forms of racial nationalism and the Ku Klux Klan's infiltration of 1920s government offices, see also Gary Gerstle, *American Crucible: Race and Nation in the Twentieth Century* (Princeton, N.J.: Princeton University Press, 2001), 120–126.

77. Thomas Ruth, Director War Service, to Directors of War Service re "Service Connection on Tuberculosis and Neuropsychiatric Diseases in Relation to Vocational Training," November 2, 1922, American Red Cross Records 1917–34, RG 200, Box 600. Hospitals and Training Correspondence, NARA, Washington, D.C.

78. Clifton Dummett and Eugene Dibble, "Historical Notes on the Tuskegee Veterans Hospitals," *Journal of the National Medical Association* 54, no. 2 (March 1962): 134–135.

79. Dummett and Dibble, "Historical Notes on the Tuskegee Veterans Hospitals," 135; Thomas Ruth, Director War Service, to Directors of War Service, regarding "Service Connection on Tuberculosis and Neuropsychiatric Diseases in Relation to Vocational Training," November, 2, 1922, American Red Cross Records 1917–34, RG 200, Box 600, NARA;· Evelyn Phelps to Helen Ryan, "Monthly Report of the American Red Cross, Tuskegee, Alabama," June–August, 1923, RG 200, NARA.

80. Evelyn Phelps to Helen Ryan, "Monthly Report of the American Red Cross, Tuskegee, Alabama," June–August 1923, RG 200, NARA. Ana Carden-Coyne notes that the idea of placing grown men in nurseries indicated the ambiguous attitudes of military medical authorities toward disabled soldiers. However, the attitude toward African American veterans was somewhat less ambiguous, given the prevailing social scientific and anthropological notions of blacks as members of a backward, childlike race in need of constant supervision. See Carden-Coyne, "Rehabilitation, Resistance and Disabled American Veterans of the First World War," *European Review of History* 4, no. 7 (2007): 546–547.

81. E. M. Murray to Helen Ryan, "The American Red Cross, U.S. Veterans Hospital No. 91," Tuskegee, Alabama, May 1, 1924, Red Cross Files, RG 200, Misc. Correspondence, NARA, Washington, D.C.

82. Gamble, *Making a Place for Ourselves*, 71. On early twentieth-century ideologies of black masculinity and racial uplift, see also Gains, *Uplifting the Race*; and Martin Summers, *Manliness and Its Discontents: The Black Middle Class and the Transformation of Masculinity, 1900–1930* (Chapel Hill: University of North Carolina Press, 2004). For works on black eugenic ideology and the ensuing interracial class tensions, see also Greg Dorr, *Segregation's Science: Eugenics and Society in Virginia* (Charlottesville: University of Virginia Press, 2008).

83. E. M. Murray to Pauline Radford, "The American Red Cross, U.S. Veterans Hospital No. 91," January, 1925, Red Cross Records, RG 200, Misc. Correspondence File, NARA, Washington D.C.

84. Ibid.

85. Linker, *War's Waste*, 9.

86. Natalia Molina, "Medicalizing the Mexican: Immigration, Race and Disability in the Early Twentieth Century U.S.," *Radical History Review* 94 (Winter 2006): 23.

87. Henri-Jacques Stiker, *A History of Disability* (Ann Arbor: University of Michigan Press, 1997), 123–125.

88. "War-Disabled Negroes in Training," *The Vocational Summary* (Spring 1923): 33.

89. Michael Adas, *Dominance by Design: Technological Imperatives and America's Civilizing Mission* (Cambridge: Belknap Press, 2006), 203.

90. See Dan Bender, "Perils of Degeneration: Reform, the Savage Immigrant, and the Survival of the Unfit," *Journal of Social History* 42, no. 1 (2008): 7.

91. For an analysis of race and racial hierarchies as "the changing same" in American political economy, see Sundiata Keita Cha-Jua, "The Changing Same: Black Racial Formation and Transformation as a Theory of the African American Experience," in *Race Struggles*, edited by Theodore Koditschek, Sundiata Keita Cha-Jua, and Helen A. Nevill (Urbana: University of Illinois Press, 2009), 9–47.

CHAPTER 17

Engendering and Regendering Disability

Gender and Disability Activism in Postwar America

AUDRA JENNINGS

KEYWORDS: *Centuries*: twentieth; *Geographical Areas*: North America; *Sources*: organizational reports; government documents; manuscripts and archival materials; *Themes*: family, daily life, and community; citizenship and belonging; labor; law and policy; activism

In 1953, Mary E. Switzer, director of the U.S. Office of Vocational Rehabilitation, and Howard A. Rusk, chair of the Department of Rehabilitation and Physical Medicine at New York University College of Medicine, argued that "disablement of the wife and mother" was a leading cause of "broken homes and the disintegration of healthy family life." They warned that disability, especially of a wife and mother, had the power to "destroy a home, cast children adrift, exhaust the husband's earnings, and produce public costs which are so large, and so prolonged, as to be almost immeasurable."[1] While Switzer and Rusk penned their predictions of devastation as a consequence of the disablement of women, they did so because they assumed their readers already understood the disruptive potential of the disablement of a husband and father.

This chapter explores how gendered ideals worked to stigmatize disabled Americans and, conversely, how disability activists, both men and women, marshaled gendered language and ideals to normalize disability in the United States in the 1940s and 1950s. In her formative article on gender as a category of analysis, Joan W. Scott defines gender as "a constitutive element of social relationships based on perceived differences between the sexes." Moreover, she argues that gender represents "a primary way of signifying relationships of power."[2] More recently, historian Jeanne Boydston has criticized the notion that gender should be thought of as a category of analysis and that it always represents a *primary* signifier of power. Instead, Boydston calls on historians to consider gender a "cultural process, various and altering over time." The task of gender historians, she argues, should be to question the processes and "primary-ness" of gender and view it "as nested in, mingled with and inseparable from the cluster of other factors socially relevant in a given culture."[3] While these clarion calls to women's and gender historians might seem to be at odds, both have particular relevance for understanding the position of physically disabled Americans in the 1940s and 1950s. Disability discrimination often hinged on the perception that disability had the power to fracture normative social structures and distort the gender hierarchy. Ideas about disability and gender, not gender *or* disability *alone*, shaped the social and economic lives of people with disabilities and informed their relationship to the state.

American society viewed disabled citizens' capacity to serve as wives and mothers or fathers and breadwinners with skepticism. Instead, society often viewed disabled Americans as dependents—an identity that had both an emasculating and a defeminizing effect. Being cast outside heteronormative gender roles around which both society and the economy turned had particular weight in the United States during the 1940s and 1950s—the moment when the state began to explicitly regulate homosexuality and when links between marriage, reproduction, and citizenship were cemented.[4] Thus, the social exclusion of people with disabilities could and often did shape their exclusion from the benefits of full citizenship.

Scholars of disability have long argued that disability, like gender, race, class, and sexuality, can serve as an important tool for understanding power, politics, and society. More recently, scholars have begun to examine the intersections between disability, gender, race, and class.[5] However, historians have more work to do to uncover the ways that disability informed discrimination based on gender, race, class, and sexuality and the ways that disability discrimination hinged on ideas about these socially constructed categories. Finally, there is much to be done to understand how disabled people positioned themselves relative to these constructs.

By examining the work of the American Federation of the Physically Handicapped (AFPH), an activist organization that was chartered in 1942, this chapter analyzes how gender shaped the marginalization of disabled citizens and how activists used gendered arguments to demand inclusion. AFPH activists and leaders channeled their shared experiences of discrimination and disappointment with federal programs into a powerful critique of notions of being "fit" for employment and of the authority of rehabilitation, charity, and medical professionals.

The federated structure of the AFPH gave rise to communities where activists created significant social spaces and where their experiences were both normalized and politicized. The AFPH opened "participating" membership to people with a broad range of physical disabilities, regardless of the cause of those disabilities, and offered an "associate" membership to able-bodied individuals.[6] The organization's chapters, which were spread across the country, were heavily concentrated in urban and industrial areas. Given this geography and the organization's strong connections to organized labor at both the local and national levels, it is likely that many of the group's members were working class. Without membership records, it is difficult to determine with certainty the composition of the AFPH's many lodges. Most likely, however, diversity at the national level in terms of class, race, and experience of disability grew out of the combination of numerous relatively homogeneous local groups. For example, the AFPH's governing council welcomed African Americans but lodges were segregated in the South.[7] Local lodges—the places where members built communities—seemed far more vulnerable to prevailing prejudices and more likely to draw on connections beyond disability. This tendency undercut the national organization's claims that the experience of disability connected Americans in all walks of life. Still, this structure allowed members at the local level to focus on issues that were most reflective of their own experiences and communities.

At the national level, AFPH members pushed for federal intervention in the hiring process, demanding what amounted to an affirmative action program for people with disabilities, and federal responsibility for the health and education of the country's disabled citizens. National records and reports from local lodges reveal that particularly on the local level, men and women participated and held leadership roles in the AFPH in roughly equal numbers.[8] With thousands of members and numerous lodges across the country, the AFPH was a significant voice of disabled Americans in postwar America.[9]

Gender Disruptions

After years of hardship and amid growing Cold War fears, home and family occupied a central place in postwar society and politics. As Carolyn Herbst Lewis argues, "The American home, populated by a heterosexual couple and their children, became, symbolically and literally, a fortress against the anxieties provoked by the Cold War." Further, she contends that both marriage and family became "patriotic duties." Healthy marriages and families produced stable citizens and communities that would be able to resist Cold War threats.[10] With marriage and family increasingly linked to national security, both women and men felt growing pressure to conform to the "traditional" roles of wife and mother, father and breadwinner. These pressures and renewed prescriptions, according to historian Elaine Tyler May, encouraged American couples to marry early and produce large families.[11] While family and medical experts often assumed whiteness and middle-class status when articulating the role of marriage and family and discrimination and wage disparities certainly shaped the ability of men and women to follow these prescriptions, the ideal and the pressure to conform called to Americans across race and class boundaries.[12]

While various opinion leaders championed traditional family life as a bulwark against Soviet communism, significant numbers of women were, in fact, behaving differently. Trends of increased employment outside the home and organization among women persisted. Indeed, more women worked outside the home in 1955 than they had during World War II. Significantly, the number of working married women with children—across the spectrum of racial and ethnic identities—increased by 400 percent between 1940 and 1960. At the same time, these years gave rise to significant development in women's organizations and proved foundational for the political evolution of feminist agendas. Still, the ideals that fueled renewed emphasis on home and family contributed to continued discrimination against women, who could expect to be paid less for equal work and to have full responsibility for the upkeep of the home and the care of the children, whether they were employed or not.[13]

The records of activists in the AFPH suggest that disabled women sought inclusion in both of the contradictory trends of the postwar era: marriage and family and growing employment opportunities. But the situation was far more complex for women and men with disabilities. Limited by physical barriers and outright discrimination, disabled men and women faced obstacles to employment. Like their able-bodied peers, they felt the pressure to conform to normative gender roles. Yet disabled men and women heard repeatedly from parents, physicians, and other experts that for them, these expectations would not be met.

Parents often trained their disabled daughters to defy traditional roles. Historians Paul K. Longmore and David Goldberger argue that "physically disabled women have often been stigmatized as unsuited for the traditional wife-and-mother role." Parents, instead, pushed disabled young women "to establish alternative valid identities through school and career."[14] This phenomenon was not unique to the 1940s. One disability activist in the 1930s reported that her mother encouraged her to earn a professional degree and to become self-supporting in preparation for the likelihood that she would never marry. "Defined as both unmarriageable and unemployable," Longmore and Goldberger find, women joined activist organizations such as the League of the Physically Handicapped in the 1930s to demand greater opportunities.[15] But, as marriage, family, and the home assumed greater political significance in the 1940s, defying traditional gender roles took on greater social meaning.

The belief that women with disabilities might not be fit for the roles of wife and mother filtered into scientific studies of sexuality. In 1942, psychologists Carney Landis and M. Marjorie Bolles conducted a study of women with disabilities in New York. Focusing on personality and sexuality, Landis and Bolles probed into their subjects' childhoods and their dating, sexual, and marital histories. They interviewed 100 women between the ages of 17 and 30 with disabilities ranging from chronic cardiac conditions to orthopedic disabilities. Landis and Bolles concluded that "the fact of being handicapped (without regard to what that handicap might be) was associated with hyposexuality." They also noted that many of their subjects were "psychosexually immature." Their evidence showed that of the 100 women that they interviewed, only 17 were married. Further, over half of the women had experienced either only limited kissing or no physical intimacy with men whatsoever (one-third of the women fell into the latter category). All of the able-bodied women in the same age group interviewed by Landis and Bolles reported having had physical contact with men.[16] These interviews reveal that social attitudes had shaped the respondents' lives in concrete ways.

Oral histories demonstrate that women with disabilities struggled along with (and sometimes against) their families as they sought to plot their course in life in a society that set them outside the normative expectation of marriage and family. They received constant reminders that they could not expect to "fit in," be attractive to male partners, or experience the same (healthy) life course of marriage and children as able-bodied women. One interviewee, who received her PhD in biochemistry in 1965, remembered her mother's extremely negative attitude toward her orthopedic disabilities. Her mother once told her, "Well, of course you'll go to college. I wish that you could be a schoolteacher; that would be a good profession for you. But of course you can't because no one would hire you." Her mother worried that she would not be able to earn a living or marry.[17] Another interviewee, who had undiagnosed muscular dystrophy, reported that when she had difficulty climbing the steps of the church to her wedding in 1958, an aunt asked, "How is that child ever going to be [able to be] pregnant?"[18]

The power of disability to upset households and impair an individual's ability to uphold the prevailing gendered norms shaped how rehabilitation counselors judged, interacted with, and spoke about clients. In 1950, J. Hank Smith, president of the States Vocational Rehabilitation Council, presented a series of rehabilitation cases to a Senate subcommittee. Smith told the committee about a woman who "had a very bad harelip and a cleft palate with considerable disfiguration." The local factory refused to hire her "because she was not pretty to look at," and the woman was forced to support herself by chopping cotton. The woman's rehabilitation counselor arranged for her to receive plastic surgery. Smith commented that "the greatest thing in this case is what it did to the kids at home." The woman's children now had "a lot prettier mother to look at."[19] Smith presented another case of a young man who had been badly burned as a child, again arguing that the young man could not get a job because his arm was "not very pretty to look at." The rehabilitation office got the young man plastic surgery, and Smith showed the committee a photograph, remarking, "Look at the smile on that face. He knows he is not the horrible looking individual that he was a few years ago." Moreover, Smith reported, after his surgery the young man had married and became "an accepted citizen."[20] Physical difference and visual appearance had, in the eyes of the community and counselors, prevented both the woman and young man from appropriately fulfilling their gendered roles of wife and mother and husband and provider. On the surface, the woman from these case studies adhered to these roles—she was a mother and was likely married. But Smith questioned the competence of her performance in these roles because of her disabled appearance. Thus, even if disabled men and women married and had children, they might still be seen as failing to meet gendered expectations.[21]

Rehabilitation had historically been centered on "restoring" disabled workers to employment, a focus that worked to return men, mostly white, to their positions as productive breadwinners, but in the 1940s and 1950s federal policy reflected new concerns about disabled women and their capacity to be good mothers.[22] In 1945, the Office of Vocational Rehabilitation (OVR) began to see the need to train disabled women to be housewives. That year the rehabilitation service trained only 156 homemakers. This group was a tiny fraction of the 41,925 people who received rehabilitation services in 1945, but the program grew throughout the postwar era. By 1958, homemakers made up 13 percent of the year's rehabilitation recipients.[23] In addition, from 1951 to 1955, the OVR funded a project in the University of Connecticut's School of Home Economics that sought to use the principles of home economics and work simplification to increase "the competence of physically handicapped mothers of pre-school children."[24]

Dr. Elizabeth Eckhardt May, head of the University of Connecticut project, argued that the work of training disabled mothers was necessary to "build her morale, promote more normal family relationships and release other members of the household for productive work."[25] Professionals involved in the "Handicapped Homemakers" project conducted a study of disabled mothers in Connecticut to determine common problems in childcare and family relations. Members of the research team applied home economics theories to the problems their study participants reported. The end result of the project was a series of resource materials that aimed to use the science of home economics to address the childcare problems of women with disabilities.[26]

The OVR's attention to homemakers largely applied to women who had become disabled after they were already wives and mothers. While the program certainly implied that policymakers had serious questions about the ability of women with disabilities to care for their children and homes, changing notions of dependency in the postwar era further associated disability with unsuccessful mothering. As Jennifer Mittelstadt has demonstrated, liberals, conservatives, and welfare professionals reconceptualized notions of dependency in the postwar era as they sought to overhaul the federal Aid to Dependent Children program. Progressive-era reformers had tended to view the dependency of wives and mothers as natural and acceptable, but this view of dependency eventually gave way to new understandings of work and welfare that pathologized the dependency of some mothers in the 1950s, particularly women of color and single and divorced mothers. Public welfare officials began to view dependency less as a result of broad social and economic forces and more as a result of the individual failings of welfare clients. Welfare professionals, in this new language of dependency, diagnosed welfare mothers as having "social disabilities" or "handicaps" and saw them as in need of "rehabilitation." These changes in notions of dependency certainly would have informed how women with disabilities perceived their own situations as well as how public officials interpreted their behavior. This new language of dependency and "social disabilities" highlighted the ways that disability represented the antithesis of the normative gender roles of wife and mother.[27]

This is not to suggest that disabled women did not marry or have children. They did, though perhaps not as frequently as their able-bodied counterparts. Instead, I want to suggest that there was a social assumption, an expectation, that they probably would not marry and that they would likely not be successful wives and mothers. Further, disability was believed to threaten men's place within this order. Disability, through discrimination and physical barriers, tended to undercut a person's earning potential, which would, in turn, limit one's potential to support a wife and children. The idea that disability limited earning potential shaped social interactions and federal policy. For example, the War Risk Insurance Act of 1917, which served as a model for future legislation, aimed to provide financial security for disabled veterans by measuring and compensating for disabled veterans' lost work and earning potential.[28]

Even though society, public officials, and medical experts questioned the place of disabled Americans in the gendered hierarchy, disability remained connected to several important gender tropes, including the feminized worlds of care and the masculine worlds of war and heavy industry. Disability activists and advocates sought to reinforce these connections and used them to "normalize" the experience of disability.

Disability and the Feminine Worlds of Care

In October 1949, Representative Augustine B. Kelley (D-PA) placed a tribute to Mildred Scott, national secretary of the AFPH, in the *Congressional Record* along with a speech she had delivered earlier in the month. While many of his colleagues knew of Paul Strachan, founder and president of the AFPH, Kelley argued that behind Strachan stood a "fine woman" who had "conquered a personal handicap to devote her life to the physically handicapped." Kelley made much of Scott's role in supporting Strachan, a deaf man. He emphasized that it was "through Mildred Scott's ears that the woes of the handicapped . . . pour." For him, it was not only Scott's physical ability to hear but also, it seems, her emotional ability as a woman to "hear" and respond to the "woes" of people with disabilities that made Strachan's public activism possible. Kelley also pointed out the great sacrifice Scott had made to take on her public "crusading" role for people with disabilities; she had left a "good job" and a presumably quiet and normal life behind. He focused on the ways that Scott conformed to social expectations of women. She freely gave of her time and set aside her own desires to help those who, in Kelley's judgment, needed and were worthy of such assistance. Moreover, for Kelley, Scott was the good woman behind the great man, supporting and facilitating Strachan's activism.[29] Kelley's speech highlighted the ways that disability and disability activism concerned women and required their work. He feminized Scott's work in the organization, drawing on gendered ideals of care, concern, and feminine sacrifice. Many women in the AFPH adopted these same tropes as they talked about their lives and their activism.

For her part, Mildred Scott viewed disability as firmly within the woman's realm. In the speech Kelley entered into the *Congressional Record*, Scott told an organization of professional women that all women needed to be concerned with the "problem" of disability because in their role as mothers and "homemakers, they are closer to disaster, when it strikes." It would be women, she argued, who would have to find out where and how to receive appropriate services and budget for these services if a child or family member became ill or disabled. She encouraged her audience to examine their assets to see if a disability within the family would force them to take "a pauper's oath" to make ends meet. Finally, she concluded, she had pledged her life to work for a better federal program for people with disabilities so that "mothers, wives, daughters, sisters, and others who have assumed family responsibilities have things a bit easier than my own mother had."[30] In this analysis, Scott emphasized that women's roles as mothers and caregivers not only gave them special cause to be concerned about disability but also a right to have a say in disability policy.

Scott also hinted at the ways her personal experience of disability had prevented her from following a traditional path. She told her audience that she "had been encouraged and led to believe that" she could become a teacher, "the most popular profession for a woman."[31] But in her home state of Pennsylvania, and in several other states, people with visible disabilities were banned from teaching in public schools. She used the disappointment of finding out that she could not fulfill her life's goal to explain her path to activism. Omitted in her assessment was that this exclusion from teaching was one of many ways that women with disabilities encountered discrimination that prevented them from fulfilling traditional gender roles and entering gendered professions.[32]

Like Scott, many women in the AFPH attributed their turn to activism to a concern for their families. In 1952, Virginia A. Pearson described the "burden" that would be lifted from families if people with disabilities could attend college and find work.[33] Later, Mary Krasnogor explained that it had taken her twelve years to find suitable long-term employment, which she ultimately gained through self-employment. Her success came only after "undue sacrifice, physically and financially" by her parents.[34] Scott, Pearson, and Krasnogor argued that disability rights were a family concern. Ending discrimination, improving policies, and providing resources to disabled individuals would improve the lives of disabled individuals *and* their parents and siblings.

These activists and advocates explained disability activism in the context of traditional roles. They were "fine women" who were supporting public men and working for the greater good. They were dutiful daughters attempting to ease the burdens placed on their parents. And, finally, they were concerned women who were educating other women about the importance of disability politics to family life and stability. In a real sense, society had blocked many women of the AFPH from fulfilling traditional gender roles, yet their activism drew on these same expectations to justify expanded aid and employment programs for people with disabilities. Their work hinged on the centrality of families—not their own, but those of their parents. In many ways, their emphasis on their parents and siblings showed how women of the AFPH remained excluded from sexual citizenship. They made demands as daughters because they could not make them as wives or mothers. Still, in an era of heightened concern about "healthy" family life, anchoring disability to the home linked the work of the AFPH to the central unit of citizenship and national stability.

Wounded Warriors and Workers

While women in the AFPH positioned disability as a woman's concern, the national organization made major efforts to connect disability to war service and industrial labor. On the surface, these efforts might be read as savvy political maneuvering— veterans and organized labor wielded significant political power in the postwar era. On a deeper level, however, courting veterans and organized labor gave the AFPH an opportunity to counter popular beliefs about disabled men as emasculated while offering a new construction of masculine disability. In the realm of disability, wounded soldiers and injured workers had developed their disabilities in masculine pursuits, while they were protecting the nation and earning a living through honorable, productive labor. These disabled individuals stood apart from the "victims" of diseases and disorders. Placing an emphasis on disabled soldiers and workers allowed activists to highlight a masculine disability, one that sacrificed for the nation. It is important to note that this image often did not match the experience of AFPH members, many of whose disabilities stemmed from diseases, disorders, and injuries sustained in other arenas than the battlefield or the factory floor. The disconnection between members' actual experiences and the public image they promoted suggests both the rhetorical power and the masculine power of soldiers and workers.

AFPH leaders worked consistently to win the membership and support of disabled veterans. For example, the AFPH recruited Milliard W. Rice, national service director of the Disabled American Veterans (DAV), to serve as one of its vice-presidents.[35] The *A.F.P.H. Tribune* ran a veterans' column entitled "Uncle G. I. Joe Speaks" that lambasted the Veterans Administration's rehabilitation program for poor administration and organization. The author called on the agency to offer a more "efficient, effective" program, arguing, "Only in this way can we look our returning disabled service man in the eye and say, 'Welcome home, my boy!'"[36]

The AFPH went to great lengths to associate the organization with veterans; it publicized veterans' issues, incorporated veterans' concerns in their national agenda, and included veterans in their public programs. For example, when Paul Strachan learned in 1946 that Atlantic City civic leaders had succeeded in closing the Thomas M. England General Hospital, which served as an amputation center for injured soldiers, because the "amputees on the boardwalk at Atlantic City depress visitors," he took immediate action to remind numerous officials that people with disabilities voted and that AFPH members would learn about their actions.[37] While his fiery letters did not yield results, his swift and firm response characterized the organization's attention to soldiers and veterans.[38] Further, the AFPH recruited veterans to take an active role in their meetings and events. Harold Russell, the disabled veteran who had starred in *The Best Years of Our Lives*, spoke at a 1948 AFPH meeting.[39] Omar B. Ketchum, national legislative director of Veterans of Foreign Wars, participated in an AFPH-sponsored panel discussion, at which a DAV Honor Guard presented the flag.[40] These efforts went beyond recruiting new members; they shaped public perceptions of the organization and its affiliations.

The AFPH approached organized labor in a similar fashion, seeking support and drawing connections between labor and disability. AFPH leaders articulated a view of disability that emphasized the relationships between work, class, and disability. For example, in 1946, Paul Strachan contacted American Federation of Labor (AFL) president William Green to ask for assistance with AFPH legislation. He argued that Green personally knew of "affliction, in the shape of Physical Disability," maintaining that this "affliction" plagued workers more so than others.[41] Using this kind of language, Strachan continued to cultivate the organization's relationship with the AFL and successfully appealed to the Congress of Industrial Organizations (CIO), the United Mine Workers of America (UMWA), the International Association of Machinists (IAM), and many other unions for financial and legislative support.[42]

The AFPH's class-based arguments about disability appealed to labor unions, whose representatives emphasized the link between industrial accidents and disability in congressional hearings. For example, CIO representative William J. Pachler testified that between 1930 and 1948 about two million workers had suffered injuries at work each year and that about 100,000 of these injuries had resulted in permanent disabilities.[43] Thomas Kennedy, vice-president of the UMWA, asserted that his union's interest in disability grew out of experience. In any six-year period, every miner could expect to be either injured or killed on the job.[44] Similarly, George R. Nelson of the IAM argued that high accident rates among the union's members had brought IAM leaders "face to face with the real problems confronting the handicapped."[45]

AFPH members used similar language at their meetings. During a 1945 mass meeting, J. Cooke Howard, AFPH member and director of the Division of the Deaf and Deafened in the Michigan Department of Labor, asserted, "While we unstintingly honor the sons of Mars who faced the horrors of war, we must not forget the sons of Vulcan who forged the implements of war, and did their full part in the glorious victory."[46] Howard implied separate lineages for disabled veterans and disabled workers but argued that both had earned honor and respect. Interestingly, many AFPH members could not claim either lineage. Still, AFPH leaders and their chosen allies continuously asserted the connections between disability, work, and war service. These connections allowed the AFPH to leverage the political power of two particularly influential groups. But they also highlighted "masculinized" disability—disability developed through sacrifice to the nation—and established links between the AFPH and disabilities closely associated with the performance of masculine duties. In a sense, by linking themselves to the sons of Mars and Vulcan, the AFPH drew on "culturally available symbols" that in this case evoked proper masculinity.[47] Further, veterans and organized labor occupied a central place within the American welfare state. They had "earned" through their service and work the very benefits AFPH members sought.

Resexing Disability

Beyond the hypermasculine and the purely feminine, AFPH activists also positioned themselves as "normal" Americans. Gender and social interaction remained central to these claims. In remarks to the House of Representatives, Roger Arnett, a national vice-president of the AFPH, proudly proclaimed that he was not only married and father to three adopted children but was also a homeowner and a taxpayer. Arnett, who became paralyzed from the waist down after an accident in the early 1930s, emphasized his ability to provide for his family by running a gladiolus farm. Without that work, he suggested, his life would have been "completely useless," with "years of idleness and burden . . . stretched out until death."[48] In a real sense, Arnett served as proof that people with disabilities could and did become model fathers and breadwinners. Moreover, he likened dependency to a kind of social (and real) death. While many disability activists, Arnett included, had experienced dependency at some point in their lives, most attempted to distance disability from dependency. They did so by emphasizing the ways they followed gendered citizenship prescriptions.

In local lodges, members played sports, celebrated holidays together, organized social events, and courted and married fellow members. On the surface, AFPH members engaged in the same sort of social activities that able-bodied people at the time enjoyed, but in creating a separate space for disabled people to enjoy these activities, people with disabilities both staked a claim for their right to participate in society and rejected the cultural belief that people with disabilities were physically and socially handicapped. In 1945, Bill Uren of Detroit Lodge 27 proudly announced the victory of the lodge's baseball team over the team of the Flint Association of the Deaf.[49] That same year, the Detroit lodge hosted a "Grand Dance-Floor Show."[50] Members of one of the New York City lodges hosted a ball celebrating National Employ the Physically Handicapped Week in 1946.[51] In a short space of time in 1950, the Saginaw, Michigan, lodge held a meeting, a card party, a banquet, a dinner, and a Halloween party.[52] Members of Lodge 94 in Washington, D.C., hosted Christmas, Halloween, and Valentine's Day parties.[53] The frequency of these social events speaks to the importance of the AFPH in members' social and recreational lives.

In 1951, *Valor*, the AFPH's magazine, reported, "Wedding bells will ring for Eileen Crumley and John Shackelton on August 17." Both Crumley and Shackelton were active members and officers in Pittsburgh Lodge 113.[54] In 1952, *Valor* reporters wrote, "CUPID HAS JOINED AFPH! Proof is—from many Lodges we receive word that couples are pairing off, getting ready for the BIG LEAP YEAR. . . . It seems that AFPH is turning into a sort of matrimonial bureau."[55] Pat DeSoo and Beatrice Heise, both members of the Rochester lodge, announced their engagement to *Valor* readers in July 1953.[56] Florence Foerster, a national vice-president, had been engaged to marry AFPH member A. Robert Cox until his death. She later married Harry Leiner of Saginaw, also an active AFPH member.[57]

Few other experiences would have been as normative, and perhaps as meaningful, for members of the AFPH as marriage. Young men and women of the postwar era, Elaine Tyler May notes, formed "the most marrying generation on record."[58] Additionally, the institution carried political weight for people with disabilities. As historian Nancy F. Cott has demonstrated, marriage has been "bound up with civil rights," defining distinctions between citizens and legitimizing some families while stigmatizing others.[59] Thus, when AFPH members married one another, they asserted their rights to join their able-bodied peers in taking on the adult citizenship roles of husband and wife.

As with Arnett's testimony, much of the activity in this social space aligned with broader, gendered social expectations for able-bodied citizens. Men played sports and women organized dances and parties. On the local level, the organization facilitated the growth of a separate community in which members performed the very roles from which society often excluded them. Often their activities emphasized the physical—sports, dances, outdoor picnics—giving members opportunities to enact "healthy" lives and demonstrate masculinity and femininity. In their congressional testimony, activists emphasized how their lives adhered to traditional gender expectations, thus positioning themselves as normative citizens.

Alternate Identities

Despite the efforts of leaders and members to emphasize gender conformity, AFPH members continued to live in a world that doubted their ability to embody normative gender roles. Women, as much as men, took seriously the organization's mission to end discrimination in employment and education. Women in the AFPH fought alongside their male counterparts for anti-discrimination legislation and improvements in the administration of federal disability policy. For men, pushing for the right to earn a living constituted acceptable behavior, but for women, this same activist impulse placed them at odds with prevailing gender ideals. Still, as Longmore and Goldberger suggest, parents and community members had sent a clear message that disabled women could not expect to conform; instead, they should find ways to be self-supporting.[60] Through the AFPH, women did just that. They demanded employment and spoke out about the amplified discrimination they experienced as disabled women.

In 1948, Iride Valmassy, an officer in Detroit, told the press about the difficulties she faced as a disabled woman. She made the papers because she had landed a meeting with disabled actress Susan Peters. While the press was concerned about the novelty of two lovely girls in wheelchairs, the women discussed weighty matters, including disability discrimination. Valmassy had a less-than-optimistic view of the employment opportunities available for people with disabilities, especially women. She had worked during the war but had lost her job at the end of the war. It took Valmassy three years after the war to get a "tryout" position as a typist. She complained, "It's still so much harder for a woman to get a chance. You can't even get in to see the employment managers."[61]

While Valmassy focused on employment, Cynthia May Lurie of Arlington, Virginia, sought independence and self-sufficiency through education and then eventually through employment. She experienced difficulties similar to the ones that Valmassy described—disability discrimination amplified by gender discrimination. Lurie tried for more than a year to attend college, applying for admission to several schools. She complained, "Not one of these colleges would accept me because of spastic paralysis." At least one of the schools was direct about rejecting Lurie because of her disability. The dean, she reported, thought that the school would be too crowded for her and "feared that I would not fit into the college due to the fact that all of my classmates would be physically fit and I would be the only one handicapped." After failing to gain admission to a college or university, Lurie tried to find a job, a task that proved difficult at first. During the war, she landed a job with the War Production Board, but in October 1945 Lurie again joined the ranks of the unemployed because of postwar work force reductions.[62] She found that although employers might have sympathy for her, few wanted to give her an opportunity to work. "Some of those who interviewed me," she noted, "asked me if I had a warm home and plenty to eat. After telling them I did, they couldn't understand why I wanted to work." Still other employers, she argued, "treated me as though I was out of my mind and would rush me out of their office at the beginning of the interview."[63] Lurie's experience is suggestive. She sought numerous paths to developing a self-supporting, alternate identity, but she encountered resistance to that identity. Educators saw no place for her in the college community, and employers saw no place for her in the work force.

It is difficult to unravel the tangle of disability and gender discrimination these women experienced. Contradictory forces surrounded women's participation in the labor market (more women working, greater insistence that they shouldn't). For disabled women a more focused contradiction was present—the contradiction of being unable to fulfill domestic ideals but being encouraged to do so. In a real sense, they lived in a contradiction within a contradiction. Increasing numbers of women, including married mothers, entered the work force, yet society clung tightly to traditional domestic ideals. As disabled women, they received messages that they could not fulfill these domestic ideals, yet educators and employers often insisted their place should be in the home. What is certain is that women joined the AFPH in large numbers. While they took full advantage of the AFPH to create a social space, they also worked alongside their male counterparts to demand greater access to employment.

Conclusion

When AFPH activists justified their work, they often did so in explicitly gendered terms. Disability discrimination made it difficult for people with disabilities to live up to gendered expectations. Yet AFPH members and leaders used a variety of gendered notions to minimize their differences from their able-bodied peers. Women and men in the organization sought to highlight disability as either a feminine concern or a masculine problem. Further, the organization provided a space that members used to engage in the heterosocial activities from which the broader society excluded them. Leaders highlighted the gender normality of members before Congress. By emphasizing the ways that members adhered to prevailing gender prescriptions, the AFPH used gender to "normalize" the experience of disability and validate their demands. Still, the social exclusion members, particularly women, experienced pushed many individuals to use the organization to develop alternate identities that were anchored in activism and work. Most of the women and men who participated actively in the AFPH did not set out to change gender ideals. Instead, they used those ideals to demand inclusion in social and civic life.

Intertwined notions of disability and gender both shaped the lives of people with disabilities and informed changing ideas of dependency and fitness for citizenship. Much work remains to be done to draw meaning from the tangle of disability and gender and similar tangles of disability with class, race, and sexuality. Disability discrimination and activism is one avenue, but if, as numerous scholars have suggested, access to full citizenship in the United States in the postwar era hinged on marriage and the performance of heteronormative gender roles, scholars need to think critically about how ideas about disability and ability shaped these discourses. Feminist analysis has trained us to shift our critical focus beyond physical realities in order to uncover social constructions. But attention to the interconnectedness of gender and disability might well refocus our attention on the ways that differing physical bodies strained and stretched the prescriptive bounds of gender.

Notes

1. Mary E. Switzer and Howard A. Rusk, "Doing Something for the Disabled," Public Affairs Pamphlet no. 197, Public Affairs Committee, New York, June 1953.

2. Joan W. Scott, "Gender: A Useful Category of Historical Analysis," *American Historical Review* 91 (December 1986): 1067.

3. Jeanne Boydston, "Gender as a Question of Historical Analysis," *Gender & History* 20 (November 2008): 576.

4. Margot Canaday, *The Straight State: Sexuality and Citizenship in Twentieth-Century America* (Princeton, N.J.: Princeton University Press, 2009); Carolyn Herbst Lewis, *Prescriptions for Heterosexuality: Sexual Citizenship in the Cold War Era* (Chapel Hill: University of North Carolina Press, 2010). See also Robyn Muncy, "Coal-Fired Reforms: Social Citizenship, Dissident Miners, and the Great Society," *Journal of American History* 96 (June 2009): 72–98; Alice Kessler-Harris, *In Pursuit of Equity: Women, Men, and the Quest for Economic Citizenship in 20th-Century America* (Oxford: Oxford University Press, 2001); Rickie Solinger, *Wake Up Little Susie: Single Pregnancy and Race before Roe v. Wade* (New York: Routledge, 2000); Suzanne

Mettler, *Dividing Citizens: Gender and Federalism in New Deal Public Policy* (Ithaca, N.Y.: Cornell University Press, 1998); Linda Gordon, *Pitied But Not Entitled: Single Mothers and the History of Welfare, 1890–1935* (New York: Free Press, 1994); Linda Gordon, ed., *Women, the State, and Welfare* (Madison: University of Wisconsin Press, 1990); and Elaine Tyler May, *Homeward Bound: American Families in the Cold War Era* (New York: Basic Books, 1988, 1999).

5. See Kim E. Nielsen, "Historical Thinking and Disability History," *Disability Studies Quarterly* 28 (Summer 2008), http://dsq-sds.org/article/view/107/107; Michael Rembis, "'I ain't had much schooling'": The Ritual of the Examination and the Social Construction of Impairment," *Disability Studies Quarterly* 28 (Summer 2008), http://dsq-sds.org/article/view/121/121; John Williams-Searle, "Risk, Disability, and Citizenship: U.S. Railroaders and the Federal Employers' Liability Act," *Disability Studies Quarterly* 28 (Summer 2008), http://dsq-sds.org/article/view/113/113; Susan Burch and Hannah Joyner, *Unspeakable: The Story of Junius Wilson* (Chapel Hill: University of North Carolina Press, 2007); Audra Jennings, "'The greatest numbers . . . will be wage earners': Organized Labor and Disability Activism, 1945–1953," *Labor* 4 (Winter 2007): 55–82; Sarah F. Rose, "'Crippled' Hands: Disability in Labor and Working-Class History," *Labor* 2 (Spring 2005): 27–54; Kim E. Nielsen, *The Radical Lives of Helen Keller* (New York: New York University Press, 2004); Catherine J. Kudlick, "Disability History: Why We Need Another 'Other,'" *American Historical Review* 108 (June 2003): 763–793; Rosemarie Garland-Thomson, "Integrating Disability, Transforming Feminist Theory," *NWSA Journal* 14 (Fall 2002); Douglas C. Baynton, "Disability and the Justification of Inequality in American History," in *The New Disability History: American Perspectives*, edited by Paul K. Longmore and Lauri Umansky (New York: New York University Press, 2001), 33–57; and John Williams-Searle, "Cold Charity: Manhood, Brotherhood, and the Transformation of Disability, 1870–1900," in *The New Disability History: American Perspectives*, edited by Paul K. Longmore and Lauri Umansky (New York: New York University Press, 2001), 157–186.

6. AFPH activists used the term "physically handicapped" to describe people with certain physical conditions and diseases. See "Send in Your Memberships Now!," *A.F.P.H. Tribune*, August 1946, 17. On an individual level, this chapter uses this framework, but when appropriate, I use the terms "physical disability" or "disability." Beyond this relatively narrow frame, this chapter examines the social construction of disability and the ways ideas about disability informed and shaped power relationships.

7. "Who's Who and How Come, in AFPH," *Valor*, July 1952, 22.

8. Women's representation at the national level did not reflect their level of participation and leadership at the local level. This disparity grew out of the nature of the AFPH national council, where representatives of prominent labor and civic organizations joined members' representatives on the council.

9. AFPH papers are scattered throughout many archives. Without access to membership files, the size of the organization is difficult to measure, but in 1947, the organization's membership numbered 17,000. See Fred J. Zusy, "Fights for Jobs for Physically Handicapped," *The Marion Star* (Marion, Ohio), September 26, 1947, 6.

10. Lewis, *Prescriptions for Heterosexuality*, 4–6.

11. May, *Homeward Bound*, ix–x.

12. Lewis, *Prescriptions for Heterosexuality*, 43–44; May, *Homeward Bound*, 18–19.

13. Figures drawn from Ruth Rosen, *The World Split Open: How the Modern Women's Movement Changed America* (New York: Penguin Books, 2006), 19. The postwar era, women's historians have demonstrated, engendered considerable feminist action and organization among women. But the period was still marked by considerable discrimination and a tightening of gender roles compared to the war years. See Dorothy Sue Cobble, *The Other Women's Movement: Workplace Justice and Social Rights in Modern America* (Princeton, N.J.: Princeton University Press, 2004); Kessler-Harris, *In Pursuit of Equity*; Ruth Rosen, *The World Split Open*; Susan M. Hartmann, *The Other Feminists: Activists in the Liberal Establishment* (New Haven, Conn.: Yale University Press, 1998); Joanne Meyerowitz, ed., *Not June Cleaver: Women and Gender in Postwar America, 1945–1960* (Philadelphia: Temple University Press, 1994); Dorothy Sue Cobble, *Dishing It Out: Waitresses and Their Unions in the Twentieth Century* (Urbana: University of Illinois Press, 1991); May, *Homeward Bound*; Leila Rupp and Verta Taylor, *Survival in the Doldrums: The American Women's Rights Movement, 1945 to the 1960s* (New York: Oxford University Press, 1987); Susan M. Hartmann, *The Home Front and Beyond: American Women in the 1940s* (Boston: Twayne Publishers, 1982); Alice Kessler-Harris, *Out to Work: A History of Wage-Earning Women in the United States* (Oxford: Oxford University Press, 1982).

14. Paul K. Longmore and David Goldberger, "The League of the Physically Handicapped and the Great Depression: A Case Study in the New Disability History," *Journal of American History* 87 (December 2000): 915.

15. Ibid.

16. Carney Landis and M. Marjorie Bolles, *Personality and Sexuality of the Physically Handicapped Woman* (New York: Paul B. Hoeber, 1942), 1–19, 110–144, quote on 110.

17. Mary Grimley Mason, *Working against Odds: Stories of Disabled Women's Work Lives* (Boston: Northeastern University Press, 2004), 78–84.

18. Ibid., 43.

19. U.S. Congress, Senate, Subcommittee of the Committee on Labor and Public Welfare, *Hearings: Vocational Rehabilitation of the Physically Handicapped*, 81st Cong., 2nd sess. (Washington, D.C.: GPO, 1950), 423–426.

20. Ibid.

21. For a discussion of the use of plastic surgery to reconstruct bodies in the postwar United States, see David Serlin, *Replaceable You: Engineering the Body in Postwar America* (Chicago: University of Chicago Press, 2004), 57–110.

22. Edward D. Berkowitz, *Rehabilitation: The Federal Government's Response to Disability, 1935–1954* (New York: Arno Press, 1980), 85–86; U.S. Congress, House, Special Subcommittee of the Committee on Education and Labor, *Hearings: Assistance and Rehabilitation of the Physically Handicapped*, 83rd Cong., 1st sess. (Washington, D.C.: GPO, 1953), 108–111, 113–114. For more information about racial discrimination in the administration of federal programs more generally, see Ira Katznelson, *When Affirmative Action Was White: An Untold History of Racial Inequality in Twentieth-Century America* (New York: W. W. Norton, 2005).

23. United States, Bureau of the Census, *Statistical Abstract of the United States, Colonial Times to 1957* (Washington, D.C.: GPO, 1960), 295.

24. Handicapped Homemaker Project, Box 1, Folder 1, Elizabeth Eckhardt May Papers, Dodd Center, University of Connecticut, Storrs, Connecticut.

25. Ibid.

26. Ibid.

27. Jennifer Mittelstadt, "'Dependency as a Problem to Be Solved': Rehabilitation and the American Liberal Consensus on Welfare in the 1950s," *Social Politics* 8 (Summer 2001): 228–257; and Jennifer Mittelstadt, *From Welfare to Workfare: The Unintended Consequences of Liberal Reform, 1945–1965* (Chapel Hill: University of North Carolina Press, 2005). See also Nancy Fraser and Linda Gordon, "A Genealogy of Dependency: Tracing a Keyword of the U.S. Welfare State," *Signs* 19 (Winter 1994), 309–336.

28. K. Walter Hickel, "Medicine, Bureaucracy, and Social Welfare: The Politics of Disability Compensation for American Veterans of World War I," in *The New Disability History: American Perspectives*, edited by Paul K. Longmore and Lauri Umansky (New York: New York University Press, 2001), 236–237, 239–240.

29. 81st Cong., 1st sess., *Congressional Record* 95, pt. 16, October 11, 1949, A6220–A6222 (Representative Kelley of Pennsylvania paying tribute to Mildred Scott).

30. Ibid.

31. Ibid.

32. Ibid.

33. Virginia A. Pearson, "Mind over Matter," *Valor*, July 1952, 6, 19, 21, Box 8, UAW Veterans Collection, Archives of Labor and Urban Affairs, Reuther Library, Wayne State University, Detroit, Michigan.

34. U.S. Congress, House, Special Subcommittee of the Committee on Education and Labor, *Hearings: Assistance and Rehabilitation of the Physically Handicapped*, 83rd Congress, 1st Session (Washington, D.C.: Government Printing Office, 1953), 190–195.

35. "Lodge Notes," *A.F.P.H. Tribune*, November 1945, 12.

36. "Uncle G. I. Joe Speaks—The Veteran Problem," *A.F.P.H. Tribune*, October 1945, 22. See also "Uncle GI Joe Speaks," *A.F.P.H. Tribune*, November 1945, 1–2; and "Uncle G. I. Joe Speaks," *A.F.P.H. Tribune*, March 1946, 11.

37. Paul Strachan to David K. Niles, January 12, 1946; Paul Strachan to Robert Patterson, January 12, 1946; Paul Strachan to Joseph Altman, January 12, 1946; all in Box 1289, Official File 443, The Physically Handicapped (1945–47), Harry S. Truman Papers, Harry S. Truman Library, Independence, Missouri (hereafter Truman Papers).

38. Ibid.

39. N. S. Haseltine, "13,250 D.C. Disabled Have an Inning," *Washington Post*, October 3, 1948, B6.

40. "Neely to Speak: Handicapped Unit to Hold Mass Meeting," *Washington Post*, February 26, 1950, M10.

41. Paul Strachan to William Green, March 14, 1946, #23/11, RG 21–001, George Meany Memorial Archives, National Labor College, Silver Spring, Maryland.

42. For more on the relationship between the AFPH and organized labor, see Jennings, "'The greatest numbers . . . will be wage earners,'" 55–82.

43. U.S. Congress, House, Committee on Education and Labor, *Hearings: Federal Commission for Physically Handicapped*, 81st Cong., 1st sess. (Washington, D.C.: Government Printing Office, 1949), 8.

44. U.S. Congress, Senate, Subcommittee of the Committee on Labor and Public Welfare, *Hearings: Vocational Rehabilitation of the Physically Handicapped*, 379.

45. Ibid., 354.

46. J. Cooke Howard, "Military Casualties Less Than Those on the Home Front," *A.F.P.H. Tribune* (November 1945), 5.

47. Scott, "Gender: A Useful Category of Historical Analysis," 1067.

48. U.S. Congress, House, Committee on Education and Labor, *Hearings: Federal Commission for Physically Handicapped*, 97–98.

49. "Lodge Notes," *A.F.P.H. Tribune*, October 1945, 20.

50. "Lodge Notes," *A.F.P.H. Tribune*, June 1946, 17.

51. "Deaf, Blind Attend Ball," *New York Times*, October 13, 1946, 9.

52. "Who's Who and How Come, in AFPH," *Valor*, December 1950, 19.

53. Ibid.; "Handicapped Group Plans Yule Party," *Washington Post*, December 6, 1949, 9; "Handicapped to Hold Valentine Party," *Washington Post*, February 13, 1952, 17.

54. Ibid., 18.

55. "Who's Who and How Come, in AFPH," *Valor*, July 1952, 6, 19, 21, Box 8, UAW Veterans' Department Records, Archives of Labor and Urban Affairs, Walter P. Reuther Library, Wayne State University, Detroit, Michigan.

56. "Who's Who and How Come, in AFPH," *Valor*, July 1953, 11.

57. Ibid.; "A. Robert Cox," *Washington Post*, July 5, 1949, B2.

58. May, *Homeward Bound*, 14.

59. Nancy F. Cott, *Public Vows: A History of Marriage and the Nation* (Cambridge: Harvard University Press, 2000), 4.

60. Longmore and Goldberger, "The League of the Physically Handicapped and the Great Depression," 915.

61. "Susan Peters Cooks Up Plot with Crippled Detroit Girl," *Detroit Times*, reprinted in the American Federation of the Physically Handicapped newsletter, December 1948, Official File, Box 1289, Folder 443 (1948–March 1949), Truman Papers.

62. For more on work force reductions and reconversion, see James T. Patterson, *Grand Expectations: The Unites States, 1945–1974* (Oxford: Oxford University Press, 1996), 42–43; and Nelson Lichtenstein, *Labor's War at Home: The CIO in World War II* (Cambridge: Cambridge University Press, 1982), 203–232.

63. U.S. Congress, House, Committee on Labor, Subcommittee to Investigate Aid to the Physically Handicapped, *Hearings*, Part 20, Spastics, 79th Congress, First Session (Washington, D.C.: Government Printing Office, 1945), 2060–2061.

CHAPTER 18

Self-Advocacy and Blind Activists

The Origins of the Disability Rights Movement
in Twentieth-Century India

JAGDISH CHANDER

KEYWORDS: *Centuries*: twentieth; *Geographical Areas*: South Asia; *Sources*: government documents; interviews; organizational reports; *Themes*: activism; law and policy; citizenship and belonging

Blind activists were among the pioneers in the disability rights movement in India. Blind graduates of residential schools proved particularly important in shaping the nature of the movement. From the earliest days of their growth, residential schools evolved into seedbeds of advocacy in the 1970s. To date, however, most scholarship in disability history has focused on the global North. This chapter offers a different location and historical experience. It analyzes the origins of the disability rights movement in India by situating it within its social and historical context and analyzing crucial issues that shaped its nature during the initial years of its growth. After briefly detailing the approach to disability during the colonial period, this chapter considers key events in the field of education of the blind after Indians gained independence from British colonial rule in 1947. It then examines the rise and accomplishments of organized activism in the late twentieth century, culminating with the passage of India's first comprehensive disability rights law in 1995.

Residential Schools during the Colonial Period

Internal religious reform movements of the nineteenth century altered Indian society, changing social views on various issues, including the practice of sati (a heinous practice of burning widows along with the body of their deceased husband), widow remarriage, and child marriage. Views on disability, however, continued to be guided largely by the religious practices of ancient and medieval times. This was because even during the period of reform during the nineteenth century, very few Indians questioned the theory of karma. According to this theory, people became disabled because of sins they committed in their past lives.[1] Hindu philosophy also provided no mandate for the care and support of disabled people, which contributed to the marginalized experiences of disabled people. General society primarily identified disabled people by their physical or mental impairments during this period. Ideas about disability and disabled people and the material conditions of some disabled Indians' lives began to change with the arrival of Christian missionaries. During the latter part of the colonial era (1880s–1940s), these evangelists played a crucial role in initiating services that promoted educational and employment opportunities for people with disabilities.[2] In this way, Christians transplanted their charity-based approach to disability in India.

Educational institutions were a critical space for missionary work and, eventually, for blind people's activism. Annie Sharp, a Christian missionary from Ireland, established the first school for the blind in India in Amritsar, Punjab, in 1887.[3] Within a span of two decades, almost a dozen schools were opened in leading cities of the country, including Mumbai, Kolkata, Palayamkottai, and Tamilnadu.[4] All of these schools were considered "special schools" for the blind that also provided boarding and lodging. (Today they are generally called "residential schools for the blind"). Missions emphasized the value of charity as they sought support for their educational efforts, which reinforced the idea that blind people were dependent on the kindness of others. In broader Indian society, a mix of karma theory and the Christian charity model primarily shaped attitudes toward issues of disability and disabled people. Consequently, the task of providing work for the disabled was left mostly to associations, trusts, and charities that were largely guided by religious considerations.

This began to change as Indians gained independence from British colonial rule on August 15, 1947.[5] Following independence, although charitable institutions continued to play a dominant role in promoting educational and employment opportunities for people with disabilities, the state also gradually began to assume responsibility. New government initiatives, for example, promoted the professionalization of rehabilitation services for disabled people. The newborn Indian State gradually expanded educational and employment opportunities for disabled people. However, these efforts emerged within a welfare-oriented approach that coincided with and complemented the older "charity model" of Christian missionary work. Significantly, the new Indian state maintained the residential school model for educating blind students. Thus, education of the blind remained anchored to residential schools during the post-independence era in both charitable and state-based facilities.

Some of the residential schools that emerged in the immediate post-independence period played a crucial role in shaping activists who came of age in the late 1960s and later. The fact that blind people were concentrated in the segregated spaces of residential schools facilitated their organization. In essence, the schools served as training grounds for young activists and functioned as bases for carrying out the movement of the organized blind in Delhi and other parts of the country.[6] Resentment against school management, particularly the quality of the food, galvanized many students. They became increasingly politicized as they collectively sought ways to express their frustrations and expectations. Protests erupted within schools, for example, and became a strategy subsequent generations of student activists used. Santosh Kumar Rungta, who has been a prominent leader of the advocacy movement of the blind in India since the late 1970s, reflected on his early years in a residential school environment. As he explained, students practiced activist work and prepared for future leadership:

> I think that was when I was in the third class. There were lots of problems as one usually faces in residential school. This incident took place in 1964. I was nine years old. There were problems of food and hygiene. One evening, there was a sudden cause for our reacting sharply, and it finally resulted in the first ever strike in the history of school. I was mainly instrumental for the strike. What exactly happened was that I had caught a cook red-handed when he was taking away prepared food as well as uncooked material. When students went to report to the principal and he refused to take any action, I locked the cook in the kitchen itself. We maintained that unless a district administration's officer comes and registers a case, he would not be set free.[7]

The efforts of the young activists had an immediate impact. As Rungta described it:

> Ultimately, this incident led to the constitution of a committee which would look into the entire affairs of the school. We had a hot discussion on the matter because somehow the committee wanted to protect the employees and was favoring the administration. We did not allow it to happen. Ultimately, it was decided that the mess committee [the dining management committee] of students would be constituted to decide the menu, control and regulate the functioning of the kitchen. That was the first change that we could bring in.[8]

During the 1960s and 1970s, three schools were especially influential in determining the nature of the movement of the organized blind in India. Two of these schools were in the capital city of Delhi; Andh Maha Vidyalaya, located at Punchkuian Road (about one mile from downtown Delhi) was near the national headquarters of the National Federation of the Blind (NFB; founded in 1970), while the Government Senior Secondary School for Blind Boys, located in Guru Teg Bahadur Nagar, was fairly close to the University of Delhi campus. The third school, the Model School for the Visually Handicapped, was established in the Dehra Dun district in the state of Uttra Khand (which was formerly part of the state of Uttar Pradesh). Andh Maha Vidyalaya is the oldest residential school for the blind in Delhi. It was originally established in Lahore, which is now part of Pakistan, and was relocated to Delhi in 1947, when the country was partitioned. While a charitable trust initially ran the Andh Maha Vidyalaya, the Indian state began to partially fund it in the early 1980s; the other two schools are fully state funded.[9]

These schools fostered a close-knit community where students and blind employees found others who understood their experiences and shared their activist goals. For example, Bharat Prasad Yadav, who helped found the National Blind Youth Association in 1974, attended the Andh Maha Vidyalaya school. The school's location near the headquarters of the National Federation of the Blind and India's Parliament and the prime minister's home drew generations of activists to use the campus as a hub for advocacy work.[10] Location and affiliation similarly enhanced the political value of the Government Senior Secondary School for Blind Boys. This institution housed a hostel for blind college students attending the nearby University of Delhi. A core of blind college student activists developed here, and they shared their ideas and strategies with the younger residential school students. Vinay Kumar Mishra, another prominent leader in the National Blind Youth Association, attended both the government school and the University of Delhi.[11]

The Model School for the Visually Handicapped offered somewhat different advantages. As part of the National Institute of Visually Handicapped, this residential school had direct links to units that centered on rehabilitation and training, key issues for many blind people in India. Some of the participants in the institute's Training Center for the Adult Blind joined the blind rights movement, serving as role models to the younger students on the campus.[12] Additionally, because the central government oversaw the model school, students and graduates had greater opportunities to interact with political leaders and more direct access to government channels.[13]

Several other schools in the state of Uttar Pradesh, located in Kanpur, Varanasi, and Lucknow, also deserve special mention. These institutions produced many of the second-generation leaders among blind activists. Santosh Rungta, for example was an alumnus of both the Kanpur School for the Blind and the Model School for the Visually Handicapped. The Netraheen Hitkari Sangthan, the predecessor of the Uttar Pradesh branch of the National Federation of the Blind, was founded in the late 1960s.[14] Most of its members were blind employees or students of the residential school for the blind in Kanpur.[15] The Varanasi School for the Blind, located in the small religious city of Varanasi, was situated in close proximity to the school at Kanpur and educated children from grades 1 through 8. Most of the alumni of this school went on to attend the schools located at Lucknow, Dehra Dun, or Delhi; many of these individuals, including Sat Kumar Singh, directly contributed to the strength of the movement of the organized blind in the post-1978 movement.[16]

The Lucknow School for the Blind, established in the capital city of Uttar Pradesh in the later part of the 1960s, expanded the network of blind activists and became a hub for meetings of NFB activists.[17] Many former members of the Netraheen Hitkari Sangthan moved to Lucknow in the 1970s, and quite a few of them attended this school.[18] Most of the blind staff members, teachers, and students at the Lucknow School for the Blind had some connection with the NFB in the 1970s. In 1972, the headquarters of Uttar Pradesh branch of the NFB transferred to Lucknow. Second-generation blind activists who had attended schools in Uttar Pradesh initiated the first major split within the NFB (which I will discuss later) and pressed for changes within the movement. Particularly after 1978, many second-generation blind activists came from Delhi and Uttar Pradesh and, to a lesser degree, from two other neighboring states, Haryana and Rajasthan. In this new activist era, Lucknow became the preparing ground for emerging leaders within the NFB.

Between independence and the late 1970s, the schools in Delhi and in the neighboring state of Uttar Pradesh in north India established themselves as seedbeds of national-level advocacy. As in many other nations, residential schools offered unique resources to burgeoning blind activists: a concentration of a large population of blind people and a sense of community; encouragement from some blind teachers and other blind adults about engaging in political action; and geographical proximity to political resources, such as Parliament. The strong political culture of socialist movements in northern India during the late 1960s and 1970s, however, and India's history of colonial rule, distinguish the experiences of these blind activists from those in many Western and global North locations.

In the later 1960s, India witnessed the growth of the Naxalite movement, a radical communist movement based on Leninist and Maoist ideology. In addition, a strong socialist movement emerged in certain parts of northern India during the 1960s and early 1970s that was led by Jai Prakash Narayan and Ram Manohar Lohia.[19] This created an environment in which advocacy became a legitimate activity in India. The Indian state never accepted the Naxalite movement, and the movement had a limited social and political base across the country in its initial stage of growth. But the socialist movement led by Narayan and Lohia acquired a broad social and political base. University students in various parts of northern India were actively involved in this socialist movement during the late 1970s. The vibrant atmosphere of the universities in northern India helped foster and sustain prospective activists. While disabled people rarely were included in the mainstream political discourse in Indian politics, the emphasis on socialist philosophy in the political culture of the 1960s and 1970s influenced the thinking and ideology of educated blind people. In particular, it encouraged a strong interest among elite blind people in equity and rights.

The Uniform Braille Code

The introduction of a uniform Braille code in India provided a vital tool for blind people's political activism. It contributed significantly to the promotion of education for the blind in India, which in turn led to the emergence of an educated group of blind citizens who organized to fight for their rights by the early 1970s. Sharing information through Braille materials helped galvanize the community and introduced new political ideas to motivate blind people to take action.

In the early twentieth century and before independence, there were eight Braille codes in various parts of India.[20] Having unique Braille codes in different parts of the country was akin to having different languages in different places across the nation, and blind people from different parts of India were unable to communicate with each other in Braille. Braille readers from one part of the country could not access the reading material produced in Braille in other places. The absence of a uniform Braille code also was an obstacle to the production of Braille books on a large scale for circulation at the national level. In order to address these barriers, advocates and educators sought to develop a uniform Braille code in India.

In the early 1900s, several Christian missionaries had developed "oriental" Braille in India.[21] They applauded its supposed universal applicability across Asia, but the code was never used by many blind readers. By the 1920s participants at various conferences had begun to call for the creation of a common Braille code for Indian languages. Nearly two decades later, in 1941, the Union Ministry of Education appointed a committee to design a uniform Indian Braille code.[22] This committee's 1943 report generated considerable controversy. Many blind people complained because they wanted the code to correspond phonetically with Standard English Braille. Their demands helped shape the uniform Braille code in India. In 1945, Lal Advani, a blind Braille instructor at St. Dunstan's Hostel for the War Blinded, designed standard Indian Braille.[23] This code received a more favorable response, but no consensus could be reached regarding a uniform Braille code before the end of British colonial rule in 1947.

As a result of encouragement by Humayun Kabir, the joint educational adviser in the Ministry of Education, in April 1949 the ministry asked the United Nations Educational, Scientific and Cultural Organization (UNESCO) to take up this issue on a worldwide basis. The first international conference on Braille uniformity was held in Paris in 1950.[24] Lal Advani, who was a civil servant in 1950, and S. K. Chatterjee, a noted linguist, represented India at this conference. Advani and Chatterjee developed a uniform Braille code, which they called Bharati Braille, after participating in a conference in Beirut in 1951. An expert Indian committee approved it in April 1951. Bharati (Indian) Braille replaced all other codes in India.[25] Soon after that, the Central Braille Press, the first centralized Braille press in India, was established, facilitating the implementation of the uniform Braille code.[26]

The development of a uniform Braille code contributed to a base for a movement of the organized blind in two significant ways. First, a sizable group of educated blind people emerged as a result of the availability of books in vernacular languages. After the development of the uniform Braille code, books produced in one location could be read everywhere in the country in Hindi and other regional languages. Most blind people did not have access to education in English, as it has always been the language of the elite in India, and the English Braille code the English had introduced did not serve the blind population well.[27] A majority of blind people would have been deprived of education through Braille literature in their vernacular languages had a uniform Braille code not been introduced. The circulation of books produced by the Central Braille Press also ultimately promoted educational activities for the blind in different parts of the country, particularly in the Hindi-speaking areas of northern India. The uniform Braille code for Indian languages fostered a sense of affinity and unity among blind Indians across the nation.

The Central Braille Press at Dehra Dun, Uttar Pradesh, also produced Braille magazines in Hindi, including *Nayan Rashmi*, which began publication in the 1960s.[28] This and a few other similar Braille magazines that were published elsewhere in India and circulated throughout the nation enabled blind people to learn about what was going on in other places. Interaction through letters written in Braille and information accessed through Braille magazines helped the educated blind in different parts of the country establish and maintain connections with each other. They exchanged ideas and learned about the conditions their counterparts faced. This facilitated their mobilization as a consolidated group by the late 1960s and early 1970s. Increasingly conscious of their rights, elite blind people began to organize a unified movement to obtain them.

Education Scholarships and First-Generation Activists

In the same period when attention focused on a unified Braille code, education scholarships for blind people gained prominence. Unified Braille and funding for education provided both a vehicle for empowerment—education—and one of the key concepts of blind advocacy work: access.

Because malnutrition had been one of the primary causes of blindness histori-cally in India, most blind people came from the poor sections of society.[29] Their lack of access to material resources proved to be a great obstacle in gaining ac-cess to higher education. In order to fill this gap, the central government initi-ated a scholarship scheme 1952 with the intention of enabling deaf, blind, and physically impaired students to pursue higher education.[30] This support enabled blind students who were pursuing higher education to hire assistants to read the printed literature and scribes to write their exams. The financial support that was available through the scholarship scheme enabled most blind students to pursue higher education.

As a founding member of India's National Federation of the Blind, Akhil Kumar Mittal, has noted, support for access to higher education led directly to the creation of a group of educated blind graduates: "I am very sure that the scheme for scholar-ship grant for enabling blind students to pursue higher education was a significant contributory factor in creating a group of educated blind," Mittal claimed. "Even I got the scholarship under that scheme from class 9th onwards, which was a great help."[31] By the end of the 1960s, the first generation of blind activists in India had emerged.

Access to higher education sharpened blind activists' understanding of civil rights, but continued barriers to employment fueled their organizing efforts. For example, in 1970, they founded the National Federation of the Blind Graduates. Claiming to be a "movement of the organized blind," leaders subsequently renamed the organization the National Federation of the Blind, borrowing the name from blind activists in the United States, who had formed their own organization in 1940.[32]

International Influences

The decision to name their national organization after the North American as-sociation reflects the powerful role international forces played in India's history. Self-advocacy, a key concept and strategy in twentieth-century disability civil rights work in the United States, particularly appealed to many blind communities in other parts of the world. As the early leaders of the U.S. National Federation of the Blind, Jacobus ten Broek and Kenneth Jernigan, have pointed out, nearly every country had some type of service agency for the blind, but organizations of the blind that were committed to work based on the of philosophy of self-advocacy existed only in Europe, the United States, Australia, and New Zealand in the 1950s.[33] Discussion of the influence of the self-advocacy philosophy the leaders of NFB in the United States promoted inspired blind activists in India to launch their own self-advocacy movement.[34]

Helen Keller, the deaf-blind American icon, also played a role in the emerging Indian movement for blind people's civil rights. For about six weeks in the spring of 1956, Keller visited India as a guest of the state.[35] Pandit Nehru, the first prime minister of India, held a special reception in the president's house in New Delhi in Keller's honor. Keller's statement that she could understand the sound of the music of the national anthem by feeling the vibrations on the sofa impressed Nehru.[36] She was well received by high-level officials and leaders of the country, and she used the opportunity to bring issues relating to the education of blind Indians to their attention.

Following Keller's departure from India, Lal Advani, the only blind civil servant in India in the second half of the twentieth century and the liaison officer for Keller during her trip to India, pushed the government to implement plans that had been made—at least in principle—during her visit.[37] As Advani later recalled, Keller's time in India provided an impetus that enabled him to push for these changes:

> The first seminar [conference] on the education of the blind was held in Mussoorie [Uttar Pradesh] in April 1956. It was inaugurated by Dr. Helen Keller. One important recommendation of this seminar was that for rapid expansion of educational programs for the blind, integrated education should be tried out. It took me nearly two decades to get the idea accepted nationally.[38]

Advani's efforts to initiate and promote services for the blind in India and his commitment impressed Keller. She wrote a testimonial for him in the form of a letter to his boss, K. Saidden, a secretary in the Ministry of Education. She wrote:

> Lal Advani, who has worked so faithfully to establish the seminar, may remain long in the service of the Ministry of Education. . . . He brings to his many tasks not only true devotion but also the knowledge of all that is to be known about the blind of India. If a person with his energy, intelligence and willingness to accept suggestions from others is only given a chance, he will climb to the summit of his Mount Everest and show what man can do in the dark by the light of courage and perseverance.[39]

Advani considered this letter to be one of the greatest honors bestowed upon him and was very proud of it throughout his life.[40]

Keller's visit highlighted the need to create opportunities for empowerment for the blind in India, but the self-advocacy philosophy advocated by the leaders of the U.S. movement is what primarily motivated most blind activists in India. By the mid-1960s, the leaders of the NFB in the United States had decided to spread the self-advocacy philosophy in other parts of the world, and for this purpose, they founded the International Federation of the Blind (IFB), which came into existence on July 30, 1964, when its charter was signed in New York City.[41] It was established with the mission of connecting blind activists around the world in order to strengthen the global self-advocacy movement. In a meeting of delegates and prospective members, Dr. Jacobus ten Broek was unanimously elected president, Rienzi Alagiyawanna of Sri Lanka became the group's first vice-president, and Dr. Fatima Shah of Pakistan was named second vice-president.[42]

The IFB promoted its self-advocacy philosophy around the world through its monthly magazine, *The Braille Monitor*, which was available free of charge. Some of the members of the newly emerging group of the educated blind in India could read and write English and corresponded with their activist counterparts in the United States. They also had access to writings by prominent blind activists in the United States such as ten Broek and Jernigan. These leaders challenged the social construction of blindness and called for unity among blind people so they could advocate collectively for their rights. These writings inspired many early leaders of the NFB in India and motivated their own activist work.

Transnational connections also developed through collaborations on the ground. For example, in the late 1960s and 1970s, Isabelle Grant volunteered as an ambassador for the U.S. NFB and encouraged Indian activists to acknowledge Grant's influence on the early movement of the organized blind in India. Jawahar Lal Kaul, the founding member of the National Federation of the Blind in India and a prominent leader during the initial stage of its existence, described the impact of her work:

> During that period, Ms. Grant had travelled [to] 30 to 40 countries and this was her aim to spread the movement of "self-help." There were many countries where such [a] movement was totally missing. She used to share with us her experiences in those countries and educate us about the activists in different parts of the world. We used to interact with each other often through correspondence. The process of learning through correspondence was such a good way, which enlightened us tremendously.[43]

Grant's interaction with blind activists in India initially began when she visited that country to participate in the World Council for the Welfare of the Blind (WCWB) in October 1969. Fifty-one delegates, including representatives of the IFB, registered to participate.[44] Media reports stated that the conference's purpose was to address "various aspects relating to the blind like communication skill[s], adjustment problems, job placement and reservation needs [a quota system]."[45]

One outcome of the WCWB conference was the founding of the National Federation of Blind Graduates (NFBG) in India. The conference provided an opportunity for young, educated, and frustrated blind activists to establish connections with people working in the field of blindness services from different parts of the world and learn about what was going on in other countries. It also provided a platform for the emerging leaders of the movement of the organized blind in India to organize a protest in front of the conference venue, the Vigyan Bhawan, in Delhi to demand jobs for the educated blind.[46] The activists picketing in front of the Vigyan Bhawan also met with Grant during the conference. From that formative moment, Grant remained in communication with the emerging leaders of the organized blind in India, acting as a bridge between them and the activists of the NFB in the United States. In the wake of the picketing, two of the blind activists were immediately offered jobs on the basis of their qualifications: Jawahar Lal Kaul was appointed as a typist in the Delhi administration and Sant Lal Thareja was appointed as an assistant professor in Shraddhanand College of Delhi University.[47] Along with Akhil Kumar Mittal, Kaul and Thareja played key roles in the founding of the movement of the organized blind in India.

Transnational exchanges also developed as Indian activists visited the United States. For example, Akhil Kumar Mittal, Daljeet Gulati, V. B. Reddi and Gopinath Das trained at the Perkins School for the Blind in Watertown, Massachusetts, during the academic year 1969–1970. This had long been one of the leading schools for the blind in the United States and had offered education and training since the early 1800s. Helen Keller was educated at Perkins, for example.[48] Her teacher, Annie Sullivan, was also an alumna of Perkins. By the late nineteenth century, the Perkins School for the Blind had a reputation around the world as a champion in training teachers of blind children. While training at Perkins, Mittal, Gulati, Reddi, and Das contemplated the idea of establishing a self-advocacy organization of the blind based on the ideology of the U.S. NFB.[49] As Mittal later explained:

> We said to each other that after going to India we must form an organization in order to implement the philosophy of Kenneth Jernigan. There is nothing like this in India. National Association for the Blind [the largest service agency in the field of blindness] has just established its monopoly in the blindness field [in India] and younger group of blind people like us hardly get any participation in its running and decision-making process.[50]

The philosophy of self-advocacy inspired Mittal. He credited Kenneth Jernigan and his 1963 article, "Blindness: Handicap or Characteristic," with shaping his own ideas about a blind self-advocacy organization in India.[51]

When he returned to Delhi from the Perkins School for the Blind in the summer of 1970, Mittal found a job in a leading residential school for blind children in Delhi and began to explore the idea of setting up an organization in India similar to the U.S. NFB. He discussed this idea with Jawahar Lal Kaul, one of the organizers of the 1969 demonstration in Delhi. After the successful demonstration and an inspiring interaction with Grant, Kaul had also been contemplating ways to foster a self-advocacy movement of young blind activists.[52] During that meeting, Mittal shared his conversations at the Perkins School with his Indian classmates about establishing an organization similar to the U.S. NFB.[53] Drawing on the philosophy of self-advocacy and related literature produced by the NFB in the United States, Mittal expressed concern that the service agencies working in the area of blindness in India, which were led by sighted philanthropists and a few elite blind people, were not fully addressing the needs and interests of young educated blind people. Kaul and Mittal agreed to focus on this constituency and their specific needs. Modeling self-advocacy, this organization would seek ways to empower members and offer an alternative to service agencies such as the National Association for the Blind and the Blind Men's Association.

Formal Organization and Internal Divisions

While Kaul and Mittal quickly reached consensus about the goals of a national organization of the blind based on the philosophy of self-advocacy, they did not agree about its composition. Kaul believed that the organization should be broad based and represent the interests of blind people from all class backgrounds.[54] Mittal disagreed. He asserted that the "United States has [the] NFB and its membership is open to all, but we should not blindly follow the example of [the] USA. On the contrary, in India educated blind should take the lead."[55] Most of the other elite blind people, including Professor Ved Prakash Varma (who was the first blind professor in the University of Delhi), supported Mittal's position.[56] The self-advocacy movement of the organized blind was launched in India with the 1970 founding of the National Federation of Blind Graduates.

Clashes over the initial policy of limiting membership to college graduates revealed important differences in current and aspiring members' political, economic, and social values. International forces also played a role in the debates and the outcome. As Kaul, who led the organization during the initial stage of the movement, later remarked, "We continued for two years and seeing its success and the rising pressure, it was thought to be important to make it open to all." Kaul added, "It was a pressure from Isabelle Grant and also the popular demand to include the non-graduates in the organization."[57] The debate came to a head at the 1972 convention of the NFBG in Ahmedabad, Gujarat. By that time a majority of the members strongly favored broadening the membership base so that all blind activists who wanted to could join. Some elites within the leadership resisted this, but ultimately the more inclusive policy won out. However, the educated middle-class blind elite actively sought to maintain control of the organization.

By the mid-1970s, a second generation of activists who would challenge this hierarchy had begun to emerge. They expressed growing frustration with the mild methods of advocacy first-generation leaders had adopted. It likely also concerned second-generation activists that the older leaders had not come into power through a democratic process and that their primary base of support came from the educated blind elite. The reluctance of this first generation to share power with younger and newer activists exacerbated tensions. Partly in response to this, some second-generation activists formed smaller advocacy organizations in Delhi and sought connections with members of the younger generation of activists.[58] This resulted in power struggles within the National Federation of the Blind and, ultimately, to the first major split in the federation in 1978.

Evolving Activist Strategies and Community Achievements: 1978–2000

This fracturing had far-reaching implications for the movement, which underwent a significant change in methods and agenda. First-generation leaders eventually shifted their attitudes toward advocacy, the composition of the federation changed, and the decision-making process for general members was transformed. By the early 1980s, the federation had grown in size and shape and the movement had become more radical. Occasionally a demand for the enactment of legislation figured as an important demand, but the predominant agenda of the struggle at the national and state levels until the late 1980s was the demand for the right to employment. Once a sizable number of qualified blind people had been hired in jobs with the central and state governments, the federation began to broaden its agenda. Since the late 1980s, leaders have primarily called for disability laws that address multiple issues, including education, housing, and employment.

This focus on legislation resulted in new, formal protections for disabled persons' rights. In the mid-1980s and 1990s, disability activists claimed several victories: the passage of the Mental Health Act (1987) and the Rehabilitation Council of India Act (1992), and the National Trust for Welfare of Persons with Autism, Cerebral Palsy, Mental Retardation and Multiple Disabilities Act (1999).[59] For many blind and disability activists in the country, the enactment of a sweeping civil rights law, the Persons with Disabilities Act (1995), popularly known as the PWD Act, is the most significant achievement.[60] This law requires equal opportunity, equal protection of rights, and access to full participation in civic life.[61] In many ways it resembles the Americans with Disabilities Act (ADA) in the United States. The PWD Act is the most widely recognized development in providing protection for the rights of disabled people in India. In the years since the PWD Act was passed, disability activists in India, including blind members, have pursued different paths toward full inclusion and equity. Disability organizations include blind members, and more nongovernmental organizations have been engaged in the field of disability rights. The rights-based perspective is now widely embraced by the current generation of disability and blind rights activists, but diverse experiences, needs, and identities continue to characterize blind and other disability communities in India.

Conclusion

During the pre-independence period, religious outlooks and activities primarily shaped the approach to disability and disabled people, reinforcing a framework of charity and, for many, stigma. After the emergence of the Indian state as a "democratic-socialist" government, the central government assumed more responsibility for rehabilitating blind citizens, but its welfare programs shared many characteristics of the older activities of charitable organizations.

Within this complicated context of support and enforced dependency, important institutions for change emerged. Residential schools for the blind became seedbeds for activists, and government-supported scholarship programs and the development of a uniform Braille code had empowered a small but engaged community of blind people in India by the end of the 1960s. These early blind activists became highly conscious of their rights and had helped lay the foundation for a strong self-advocacy movement by the beginning of the 1970s. They and others led a sustained reform effort during subsequent decades. Blind activists in India were also inspired by the prevailing international atmosphere of blind people's activism, particularly the radical philosophy of self-advocacy that was propagated by blind activists in the United States. Shifting policies and strategies within blind organizations in India reveal some of the diversity of experiences in the twentieth century. While this essay has sought to expand understandings of blind and disability activist histories by detailing grassroots work in India, much work on this topic remains to be done. It is hoped that scholarly engagement with this history—like its activist counterpart—will continue to reflect critically and expansively on the people and the forces that shape human conditions in and beyond India.

Notes

1. Usha Bhatt, *The Physically Handicapped in India* (Bombay: Shivlaxmi Bhuvan Publication, 1963), 96; James I. Charlton, *Nothing about Us without Us: Disability, Oppression and Empowerment* (Berkeley: University of California Press, 1998), 110.

2. R. S. Pandey and Lal Advani, *Perspectives on Disability and Rehabilitation* (Delhi: Vikas Publishing House, 1995), 167.

3. T. N. Kitchlu, ed., *A Century of Blind Welfare in India* (Delhi: Penman, 1991), iv; Pandey and Advani, *Perspectives on Disability and Rehabilitation*, 70.

4. Sandhya C. Sanyal and P. K. Giri, *Education and Employment of the Blind* (Narendrapur, India: South Asian Publishers/UNESCO, 1984), 22.

5. Lloyd I. Rudolph and Susan H. Rudolph, *In Pursuit of Lakshmi: The Political Economy of the Indian State* (Chicago: University of Chicago Press, 1987), 66.

6. Jagdish Chander, "The Role of Residential Schools in Shaping the Nature of the Advocacy Movement of the Blind in India," in *Disability & the Politics of Education: An*

International Reader, edited by Susan Lynn Gabel and Scot Danforth (New York: Peter Lang Publishing, 2008), 207–208.

7. S. K. Rungta, interview with the author, April 4, 2005 quoted in Chander, "The Role of Residential Schools in Shaping the Nature of the Advocacy Movement of the Blind in India," 205–206.

8. S. K. Rungta, interview with the author, quoted in ibid., 206.

9. For a detailed discussion of the contributions of the students and alumni of these three schools to the movement of the organized blind in India, see ibid.

10. Jagdish Chander, "Movement of the Organized Blind in India: From Passive Recipients of Services to Active Advocates of Their Rights" (PhD diss., Syracuse University, 2011), 205; Chander, "The Role of Residential Schools in Shaping the Nature of the Advocacy Movement of the Blind in India," 207–208.

11. Chander, "Movement of the Organized Blind in India," 374.

12. Ibid., 107–108.

13. Ibid.

14. A. K. Sharma, interview with the author, Lucknow, June 6, 2005.

15. Ibid.

16. B. P. Yadav, interview with the author, Delhi, March 25, 2005, and April 17, 2005.

17. Sharma interview.

18. Ibid.

19. Madhu Limaye, "Socialist Movement in the Early Years of Independence," in *Fifty Years of Socialist Movement in India: Retrospect and Prospects*, edited by G. K. C. Reddy (New Delhi: Samata Era Publication, 1984), 38–53; Sirinder Mohan, "The Turbulent Years: 1952–55," in *Fifty Years of Socialist Movement in India: Retrospect and Prospects*, edited by G. K. C. Reddy (New Delhi: Samata Era Publication, 1984), 54–60.

20. L. Advani, interview with the author, Delhi, December 27, 2004.

21. R. S. Pandey and Lal Advani, *Perspectives on Disability and Rehabilitation* (Delhi: Vikas Publishing House, 1995), 71.

22. Pandey and Advani, *Perspectives on Disability and Rehabilitation*.

23. Ibid., 72.

24. Ibid.; Kitchlu, *A Century of Blind Welfare in India*, 2.

25. Pandey and Advani, *Perspectives on Disability and Rehabilitation*.

26. Advani interview, December 27, 2004.

27. Rudolph and Rudolph, *In Pursuit of Lakshmi*, 39–41; Achin Vanaik, *The Painful Transition: Bourgeois Democracy in India* (New York: Verso, 1990), 90.

28. R. K. Sarin, interview with the author, January 30, 2005.

29. Pandey and Advani, *Perspectives on Disability and Rehabilitation*, 42.

30. Bhatt, *The Physically Handicapped in India*, 31; D. Rama Mani, *The Physically Handicapped in India: Policy and Programmes* (New Delhi: Ashish Publishing House, 1988), 74.

31. A. K. Mittal, interview with author, May 16, 2005.

32. Floyd Matson, *Walking Alone and Marching Together* (Baltimore, Md.: National Federation of the Blind, 1990).

33. Ibid., 732.

34. See, for example, Margaret Davidson, *Helen Keller* (New York: New York, 1969); and Gare Thompson, *Who Was Helen Keller?* (New York: Grosset & Dunlap, 2003).

35. L. Advani, interview with the author, January 12, 2005.

36. Ibid.

37. Ibid.

38. L. Advani, interview with the author, January 20, 2005.

39. Helen Keller to Dr. K. Saidden, secretary, Ministry of Education, April 26, 1956, quoted in Jagdish Chander and Ali Baquer, *Lal Advani: The Torch Bearer (1923–2005)* (New Delhi: Indian Association for Special Education and Rehabilitation, 2005), 11.

40. Chander and Baquer, *Lal Advani: The Torch Bearer (1923–2005)*, 11.

41. Matson, *Walking Alone and Marching Together*, 732.

42. Ibid.

43. J. L. Kaul, interview with the author, February 14, 2005.

44. J. L. Kaul, personal communication.

45. Ibid.

46. Kaul interview.

47. Ibid.

48. Davidson, *Helen Keller*, 62–72; Thompson, *Who Was Helen Keller?*, 67–73.

49. Mittal interview; V. B. Reddi, interview with the author, July 31, 2005.

50. Mittal interview.

51. Ibid. See also Kenneth Jernigan, "Blindness—Handicap or Characteristic?" (1963), cited in Matson, *Walking Alone and Marching Together*, 176–186. This article, which articulated the social construction of blindness, is still one of the most widely cited of Jernigan's works.

52. Mittal interview; Kaul interview, 2005.

53. Mittal interview.

54. Kaul interview; Mittal interview.

55. Mittal interview.

56. V. P. Varma, interview with author, May 29, 2005; Kaul interview; Mittal interview.

57. Kaul interview; Mittal interview; H. Shah, interview with the author, March 24, 2005.

58. Chander, "Movement of the Organized Blind in India," 150–170.

59. National Human Rights Commission of India, *Disability Manual* (New Delhi: National Human Rights Commission, 2005), 27–39.

60. Government of India, *The Persons with Disabilities (Equal Opportunities, Protection of Rights and Full Participation) Act, 1995* (New Delhi: Government of India, 1996).

61. "India Ratifies U.N.C.R.P.D. and Then Just Forgets!" *Disability News and Information Service* 6, no. 8 (October 1, 2009), http://www.dnis.org/news.php?issue_id=8&volume_id=6&news_id=914&i=0, accessed September 7, 2011.

About the Contributors

FRANCES L. BERNSTEIN is associate professor of Russian history at Drew University. She is the author of *The Dictatorship of Sex: Lifestyle Advice for the Soviet Masses* and co-editor and contributor to *Soviet Medicine: Culture, Practice, and Science*. She is currently writing a book on Soviet disabled veterans after World War II.

DANIEL BLACKIE, PhD, is a Research Fellow at the Department of History and Classics, Swansea University. He is currently working on a project that examines disability in British coal mining for the period 1780–1880.

PAMELA BLOCK, PhD, has an autistic older sister and grew up within the cultural realms of disability advocacy movements and educational and service systems. She is Associate Dean for Research in the Stony Brook University School of Health Technology and Management, Associate Professor in the Occupational Therapy Program, and Director of the Disability Studies Concentration for the PhD Program in Health and Rehabilitation Sciences.

ELSBETH BÖSL, PhD, is a Research Fellow at the Centre for the History of Technology at Munich Technical University. She is the author of *Politiken der Normalisierung. Zur Geschichte der Behindertenpolitik in der Bundesrepublik Deutschland* (The Politics of Normalization: On the History of Disability Politics in the Federal Republic of Germany) (Bielefeld, 2009) and co-editor (with Anne Waldschmidt and Anne Klein) of *Disability History: Konstruktionen von Behinderung in der Geschichte: Eine Einführung* (Constructions of Disability: An Introduction) (Bielefeld, 2010)

DEA H. BOSTER received her PhD in history at the University of Michigan and is currently on the humanities faculty at Columbus State Community College. Her research interests include health, illness, medicine, the body, and disability in the United States in the nineteenth and early twentieth centuries.

SUSAN BURCH, PhD, is associate professor of American studies at Middlebury College. Her various works in deaf and disability histories include *Unspeakable: The Story of Junius Wilson* (with Hannah Joyner), *The Encyclopedia of American Disability History* (editor in chief), and *Signs of Resistance: Deaf Cultural History from 1900 to World War II*.

SUSAN K. CAHN is a professor of history at the University at Buffalo, specializing in U.S. women's history. She has written on women's sports, adolescent sexuality in the U.S. South, lesbian history, and chronic illness. Her current research is on the gendered history of mental illness.

ALLISON C. CAREY is associate professor of sociology and director of the Interdisciplinary Minor in Disability Studies at Shippensburg University. She is author of *On the Margins of Citizenship: Intellectual Disability and Civil Rights in 20th Century America* (Temple University Press, 2009), and co-editor of *Disability and Community* (Emerald Press, 2011) and *Disability Incarcerated: Disability and Imprisonment in the United States and Canada* (Palgrave MacMillan, 2014).

FÁTIMA GONÇALVES CAVALCANTE, PhD, is a professor in the Masters and Doctoral Programs in Psychoanalyses, Health and Society and of the Psychology Course at Veiga de Almeida University Rede Ilumno (Ilumno Network) and associate researcher at the Latin American Center on the Studies of Violence and Health, National School of Public Health, Oswaldo Cruz Foundation, Brazil.

JAGDISH CHANDER earned his PhD in disability studies from Syracuse University and is currently working as an associate professor of political science at Hindu College, University of Delhi. His areas of interests include disability narratives, disability rights, inclusive education, and policies and legislations relating to disability.

AUDRA JENNINGS earned a PhD at Ohio State University in 2008. Her current book project, *Out of the Horrors of War: The Politics of (Dis)Ability in the Postwar United States*, is being published by University of Pennsylvania Press. She is the recipient of the 2013 Disability History Association Outstanding Article Award.

JOHN M. KINDER is assistant professor of American studies and history at Oklahoma State University. His book, *Paying with Their Bodies: American War and the Problem of* *the Disabled Soldier*, will be published in 2015 by the University of Chicago Press. He is currently writing a transnational history of zoos and modern war.

CATHERINE KUDLICK is professor of history and director of the Paul K. Longmore Institute on Disability at San Francisco State University. She has published widely in disability history but is best known for her *American Historical Review* essay "Disability History: Why We Need Another 'Other,'" published in June 2003.

PAUL R. D. LAWRIE is an assistant professor in the Department of History at the University of Winnipeg. His research focuses on African American sociocultural history and the intersections of race, labor, and disability in modern American political economy. He currently is completing *Forging a Laboring Race: The African American Worker in the Progressive Imagination* (with New York University Press).

HERBERT MUYINDA is a social anthropologist and a Senior Lecturer at the College of Health Sciences at Makerere University in Uganda. He has done research among disabled children and among vulnerable populations that include people with disabilities in conflict situations. He is currently examining mental illness and disability in postconflict northern Uganda.

Historian **KIM E. NIELSEN** is professor of disability studies at the University of Toledo (United States). She is the author of many books and articles, most recently including *A Disability History of the United States* (Beacon Press, 2012).

KATHERINE OTT is a curator at the Smithsonian's National Museum of American History, where she works on and writes about disability, medicine, the body, and sexuality. She teaches an introduction to material culture class at The George Washington University and tweets @amhistcurator.

STEPHEN PEMBERTON is associate professor in the Federated Department of History at New Jersey Institute of Technology and Rutgers University, Newark, New Jersey. He is the author of *The Bleeding Disease: Hemophilia and the Unintended Consequences of Medical Progress* (2011), and co-author of *The Troubled Dream of Genetic Medicine* (2006).

JEREMY PRATT contributed the cover art for the paperback edition of this book. Currently, he is working on drawing pictures using overlapping shapes with shading in all kinds of colors within the shapes, sides, corners, tops, and bottoms of the drawing. He also enjoys painting with watercolors. More information about Jeremy can be found on the website for Starlight Studio and Art Gallery, http://starlightstudio.org/.

ANNE QUARTARARO, a historian of modern European history, specializes in nine-teenth- and twentieth-century France and deaf cultural history. She is the author of *Deaf Identity and Social Images in Nineteenth-Century France* (Gallaudet University Press, 2008) and has contributed articles to *Sign Language Studies* and the *Journal of Social History*.

MICHAEL REMBIS is director of the Center for Disability Studies and an assistant professor in the Department of History at the University at Buffalo (SUNY). He is the author of *Defining Deviance: Sex, Science, and Delinquent Girls, 1890–1960*. Rembis and Kim Nielsen are co-editors of the Disability Histories book series with the University of Illinois Press.

PENNY L. RICHARDS, PhD, holds a Research Scholar affiliation with UCLA's Center for the Study of Women. She has served as president of the Disability History Association and as co-editor of the H-Disability listserv.

Index

Gerber, David, 101, 225, 253, 322
Germany, Federal Republic of: collective
memory in, 137, 141, 144; disability rates
in, 148, 161n74; perceptions of disability
in, 140, 141, 145–149; postwar reconstruction in, 137, 141; as welfare state, 7, 137,
140–141, 149, 151
Global War on Terror, 165, 173–174
Great Britain, 18, 58, 364, 365, 369
Greenfeld, Josh: advocacy of fathers of children with disabilities, 65; ambivalence
toward medical intervention, 62, 69, 70,
71, 76n56; and challenges of caregiving,
67, 71; negative and positive feelings toward son, 71
Greenfeld, Noah, 62, 67, 69–71
Grünenthal AG, 136, 138, 139. See also Contergan (thalidomide)
Gulu Landmine Survivors' Association
(GULMSA; Uganda), 98, 108–113

heads of household, 20–23, 25–26, 30, 51,
104
healthscape, 27–29, 34n50
hematology, 245
hemophiliacs (people with hemophilia) and
hemophilia: activism among, 240–243,
248–249; associated impairments, 239;
and the bleeding disorder community,
238, 243, 248; blood transfusions and
donation, 238, 241, 243; and heteronormativity, 239, 244, 253; and Jewish communities, 3, 237–238; life expectancy of,
238, 240–241, 243–244; management
strategies, 239; as memoirists, 250–252;
"professional," 8, 247–250, 251; relation
to HIV and AIDS, 244–246, 250, 252, 254;
self-care culture, 238, 239, 243, 249–250;
social construction of, 238–239, 240–242,
246, 248, 249; U.S. federal support for,
242–243
heredity, 60, 202, 238. See also genetics
heteronormativity: and citizenship, 346, 359;
and privilege, 120, 140, 315–316, 346–348,
359; of rehabilitation services, 140, 349–
351; and representations of hemophiliacs, 3, 239, 244, 253. See also sexism and
heterosexism
HIV and AIDS, 8, 130–131, 244–245

hospitals. See institutions and institutional-
ization
Hunt, Douglas, 64, 65, 69, 75n21
Hunt, Nigel, 64, 65, 69, 75n21
Husson, Thérèse-Adèle, 186–187, 196, 197
hysterics and hysteria, 212, 259–260

identity and identity categories: and authenticity, 217, 276; collective, 165–169, 179,
286, 301; formation of, 137, 237, 286, 301;
and intersectionality, 3, 12n9, 77–79; narratives of, 258, 346, 358; and objects, 119,
120; and political economy, 328; relation
to disability, 2–3, 8, 108, 329; and stigma,
141, 358; and theory, 122
ideology, 2, 5, 132, 278–290, 300–302
idiots and idiocy. See people with intellectual
disabilities and intellectual disability
impairments: effects of, 22, 29–30; and eugenics, 9, 60, 126, 132, 147; and memorial
practices, 168, 177; and predictability, 61,
64, 204, 211, 273–274; relation to disability, 2, 95n29, 96n30, 199n12; relation
to productivity, 2, 3, 140, 244; as result of
war, 99, 111, 165–166; and sexuality, 259–
261, 263–264, 271; as ubiquitous, 27–29.
See also soundness and unsoundness, of
slaves; and individual impairments
inclusion and integration: advocacy of, 62–
66, 70, 71; in community setting, 63–66,
81, 83, 87–88, 111, 331; costs of, 70–71; of
deaf people through oralism, 287, 291; in
educational setting, 81, 87, 291; in family
setting, 28, 36, 50, 63–66; proposals for,
297; relation to disability, 120; in social
structure, 38, 51, 285. See also activism and
advocacy; normalization
incompetence. See competence and competency hearings
independence: in daily life, 44, 85, 87, 237–
238, 357–358; economic, 171, 330, 357–
358; as ideal, 108, 126, 237–238, 246; and
independent living, 91; and interdependence, 21, 36, 50, 108; and philosophies of
self-care, 238, 246; in public discourse, 51,
243, 247; relation to dependence, 44, 51,
126, 251; and vulnerability, 47. See also dependence; stereotypes of disabled people
and disability

The University of Illinois Press
is a founding member of the
Association of American University Presses.

Composed in 10.5/13 Marat Pro
by Lisa Connery
at the University of Illinois Press
Manufactured by Cushing-Malloy, Inc.

University of Illinois Press
1325 South Oak Street
Champaign, IL 61820-6903
www.press.uillinois.edu